TOTAL WARS AND THE MAKING OF MODERN UKRAINE, 1914–1954

D1526656

Between 1914 and 1954, the Ukrainian-speaking territories in East Central Europe suffered almost 15 million "excess deaths" as well as numerous large-scale evacuations and forced population transfers. These losses were the devastating consequences of the two world wars, revolutions, famines, genocidal campaigns, and purges that wracked Europe in the first half of the twentieth century and spread new ideas, created new political and economic systems, and crafted new identities.

In *Total Wars and the Making of Modern Ukraine, 1914–1954*, George O. Liber argues that the continuous violence of the world wars and interwar years transformed the Ukrainian-speaking population of East Central Europe into self-conscious Ukrainians. Wars, mass killings, and forced modernization drives made and re-made Ukraine's boundaries, institutionalized its national identities, and pruned its population according to various state-sponsored political, racial, and social ideologies. In short, the two world wars, the Holodomor, and the Holocaust played critical roles in forming today's Ukraine.

A landmark study of the terrifying scope and paradoxical consequences of mass violence in Europe's bloodlands, this book will transform our understanding of the entangled histories of Ukraine, the USSR, Germany, and East Central Europe in the twentieth century.

GEORGE O. LIBER is a professor in the Department of History at the University of Alabama at Birmingham.

Total Wars and the Making of Modern Ukraine, 1914–1954

GEORGE O. LIBER

UNIVERSITY OF TORONTO PRESS
Toronto Buffalo London

© University of Toronto Press 2016
Toronto Buffalo London
www.utppublishing.com
Printed in the U.S.A.

ISBN 978-1-4426-4977-4 (cloth)
ISBN 978-1-4426-2708-6 (paper)

Library and Archives Canada Cataloguing in Publication

Liber, George, author
Total wars and the making of modern Ukraine, 1914–1954 / George O. Liber.

Includes bibliographical references and index.
ISBN 978-1-4426-4977-4 (bound). – ISBN 978-1-4426-2708-6 (paperback)
1. Ukraine – History – 1917–.   I. Title.

DK508.812.L52 2016   947.708'4   C2015-906533-X

This publication was made possible by the financial support of
the Shevchenko Scientific Society, USA, from the Ivan and Elisabeth
Chlopecky Fund.

University of Toronto Press acknowledges the financial assistance
to its publishing program of the Canada Council for the Arts and the
Ontario Arts Council, an agency of the Government of Ontario.

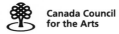

For Deborah, always

War is just the continuation of politics by other means.

Carl von Clausewitz

Wars and revolutions ... have thus far determined the physiognomy of the twentieth century ... the interrelationship of war and revolution, their reciprocation and mutual dependence, has steadily grown, and ... the emphasis in the relationship has shifted more and more from war to revolution.

Hannah Arendt

We have made Italy, now we have to make Italians.

Massimo d'Azeglio

Contents

Contents

Acknowledgments

This project started over ten years ago, when Alexander J. Motyl and I taught classes at Harvard's Summer School. At the end of that semester, he suggested that I write a brief history of modern Ukraine, the topic of my course. I conceived the outline of this "short course" on the eve of Ukraine's 2004 Orange Revolution, and after it unfolded that November and December, I took several long and meandering detours. My planned concise history became a long and convoluted one. I am grateful to several friends, especially Liah Greenfeld, who showed me the error of my initial approach.

I am most indebted to Jacqueline Olich, former associate director of the Center for Slavic, Eurasian, and European Studies at the University of North Carolina, who invited me to a conference on the Holodomor at Chapel Hill in September 2008. Preparing a paper for her conference forced me to re-view the flow of the history of Ukraine in the twentieth century through the lens of its creation and development in the framework of the conflicts within the European state system.

Holly Brasher, Guido Hausmann, Jeff Jones, Nazar Kholod, Matt Payne, Lisa Sharlach, and Sergei Zhuk read earlier versions of various chapters and made perceptive comments on them. My colleague Andrew Demshuk evaluated one draft and commented on revised versions of two chapters. His assessments helped me shorten the scope of my project and, simultaneously, to better focus it. Hiroaki Kuromiya, Bill Risch, and Bohdan Vitvitsky critically assessed later drafts. Olga Bertelsen read the 2013 versions of chapters 6 and 7; Alex Motyl commented on chapters 8 and 9. Both provided sharp and profound insights. Paweł Machcewicz read chapters 4 and 8 and supplied me with excellent advice on how to improve them. Oleh Wolowyna always promptly replied to my emailed questions concerning Soviet statistical data and their interpretation. Bruce McComiskey, Francesca Mereu, Jenñy Wilson, David Cairns, and Elise Kimerling Wirtschafter also furnished wise counsel at critical points in the evolution of this book.

My graduate and undergraduate assistants, Kathy J. Hakim, Kaye Nail, Jennifer Philips, Lonnie Goldberg, John-Mark Phillips, Maya Orr, and Mike Barrett, proofread various drafts, suggested improvements, and found information relevant to my argument. They challenged me to explain my ideas in simple, not simplistic, ways to an audience that knew little about the history of East Central Europe, Russia, or Ukraine.

The University of Alabama at Birmingham's Mervyn H. Sterne Library is small and underfunded, but its friendly and professional staff is without peer. Brooke Becker, Sterne's extraordinary social and behavioural sciences librarian, and Eddie Luster, its superb interlibrary loan administrator, have helped me accumulate the books and articles necessary to create this book. In the process of writing this book, I also used the library resources at the University of Alabama and at the University of Chicago. I am grateful to their staffs as well as to Hugh K. Truslow, the Librarian of Harvard's Davis Center for Russian and Eurasian Studies, who digitally provided me with a rare copy of Sylvia Gilliam's 1954 monograph on the nationality problem in the Soviet Union.

I spent the summers of 2002, 2009, 2012, and 2013 in Washington, DC, thanks to grants from the Kennan Institute and from UAB's College of Arts and Sciences (2012). Blair Ruble, Will Pomeranz, and Liz Malinkin helped make my stay in DC intellectually productive. At the Library of Congress, I am grateful to Jurij Dobchanskyj for his bibliographic prowess and for many enriching luncheon conversations. Like Jurij, the professionals at the Library's European Reading Room are indispensible.

In Washington, DC, I held fruitful conversations with Nick Eberstadt, Paweł Machcewicz, and Sarah Cameron, who generously shared her dissertation on the famine in Kazakhstan with me. Martha Bohachevsky Chomiak and Rostyslaw Chomiak always provided enthusiastic encouragement.

Without the support of Paul Bushkovitch, Jeff Brooks, Liah Greenfeld, and Hiroaki Kuromiya, who wrote letters and recommendations on my behalf, this book would not have been written.

I received a fellowship in the spring of 2004 from the Harvard Ukrainian Research Institute, where the idea for this book first germinated, despite the fact that I won the fellowship for another project. I hope that Michael Flier, the director at the time, and Roman Szporluk, who initiated many insightful conversations about the history of Ukraine, Europe, and Eurasia, will forgive me. I also received short-term funding from the Kennan Institute, the International Research and Exchanges Board (IREX), and UAB's College of Arts and Sciences. Thanks to this funding, I received financial support from the Shevchenko Scientific Society USA's Ivan and Elisabeth Chlopecky Fund, which made this publication possible.

Richard Ratzlaff is the best editor I have ever had. I am grateful to Brigid O'Keeffe for singing his praises. I am also grateful to Leah Connor, Stephen Shapiro, and James Leahy, my production team at the University of Toronto Press, for their professionalism and speed. They are the *komanda* of all *komandas*!

My maps were expertly prepared by Kelly Koenig of the University of Alabama's Cartographic Research Library under the supervision of Craig Remington. The majority of them were inspired by Paul Robert Magocsi's *Historical Atlas of Central Europe* (Seattle: University of Washington Press, 2002); *Historical Atlas of East Central Europe* (Seattle: University of Washington Press, 1993); *A History of Ukraine* (Seattle: University of Washington Press, 1996); and *Ukraine: A Historical Atlas* (Toronto: University of Toronto Press, 1985).

I based map 7 on a map produced by the MAPA Digital Atlas of Ukraine Project at the Harvard Ukrainian Research Institute, reproduced in *Uriadovyi kur"er* on 22 November 2013, and on the information on population losses in 1932–4 provided by Oleh Wolowyna and his colleagues at the Institute of Demography at the National Academy of Sciences of Ukraine. Map 9 is based on the map produced in *Wysiedlenia, wypędzenia i ucieczki 1939–1959: Atlas ziem polskich, Polacy, Żydzi, Niemcy, Ukraińcy*, ed. Witold Syenkiewicz and Grzegorz Hryciuk (Warsaw: Demart, 2008).

The transliteration of geographic terms throughout the text and in the maps comes from Paul Robert Magocsi's *Historical Atlas of Central Europe* and Volodymyr Kubijovič's *Encyclopedia of Ukraine: Map and Gazetteer* (Toronto: University of Toronto Press, 1984). Steven Seegel, Andrew Demshuk, Oleh Wolowyna, and Serhii Plokhy reviewed several versions of my maps.

In the penultimate draft, Zenon Kohut generously read the Introduction and chapter 1 and corrected errors in table I.1. Roman Senkus reviewed chapters 4 and 8; and John Micgiel, chapter 4.

I am grateful to all who helped me, but I alone take responsibility for my interpretations and for the facts presented.

In the course of my life and this project many wonderful people offered me help and encouragement, but did not live to see its completion. I would like to remember my mother, Maria Liber; my aunt, Xenia Antypiw; my mother-in-law, Mary Bemis; my Dovzhenko mentor, Roman Korohodsky; my colleagues, Andrea R. Brown, Raymond A. Mohl, and Glenn Feldman; my northwest Indiana neighbours, Erna Hnatyk and Vasyl Shuya; my Texas in-laws, Barbara and Rocky Veiera; and my Bluff Park neighbours, Sarah Branch, and Eloise and Cyrus Hughen.

I am most grateful to my mentors at Indiana University, Fedor Cicak and William B. Cohen, who passed away just as this book started to form. Without their encouragement and generosity, I would not have chosen this "less traveled" road. At Harvard, Karl W. Deutsch, Ned Kennan, and Omeljan Pritsak taught me to view the world from a global and trans-national perspective. At Columbia, Marc Raeff and Leopold Haimson inspired me to look for the "big picture." During my New York days, Dr Jaroslaw Padoch befriended me and helped me in countless ways. As I edited these acknowledgments in late April 2015, I learned that Catharine Theimer Nepomnyashchy passed away. We both started our graduate studies and our careers at the same time at Columbia. Her friendship, energy, and enthusiasm will forever be missed. This book would not have appeared without her help decades ago.

May all of my late family members, friends, and neighbours rest in peace.

30 April 2015

Note to Readers

Mark LaGory, one of my now-retired colleagues at the University of Alabama at Birmingham, often responded to the convoluted state of the world with a pithy phrase: "It's all so complex!" How true this statement remains, especially after the completion of this interpretative essay and the host of special challenges it presented.

In envisioning this political and social history, I sought to write an easily comprehensible narrative that described and analysed the impact of the twentieth century's total wars on the formation and development of modern Ukraine and its evolution as a geopolitical pivot and as a divided state. I strove to make my story understandable to a broader audience without oversimplifying it.

Russian and Ukrainian are normally transcribed in the Cyrillic alphabet, and there is no standard system of transliterating these languages into English. I tried to give the English-language reader a reasonably accurate rendition of the original, while avoiding diacritical marks and other subtleties which linguists may consider necessary. In this book I used a slightly modified Library of Congress version for Russian and Ukrainian, as adopted by the *Journal of Ukrainian Studies*, published by the Canadian Institute of Ukrainian Studies, Edmonton, Alberta.

To make this text as readable as possible, I adopted common English-language renderings of personal and place names wherever possible: for example, Kiev, Moscow, Warsaw, Bukovina, Alexander II, Leon Trotsky (not Lev Trotskii), Mykhailo Hrushevsky, Grigory Grinko (not Hryhory Hrynko). In the endnotes, I left personal names in the language in which they appear in the original text and added soft signs.

In light of the complex impact of imperial and state policies on the evolution of national identities, I employed geographic names less familiar to the American reader in the official language of the state that ruled over diverse sets of people at the time: thus, Lemberg until 1918, Lwów from 1918 to 1939, then Lviv after 1939. For towns and cities in the Russian Empire through 1917, I transliterated from the Russian; from 1918, from the dominant languages of the region. In conforming to this organizational system, I hope to remind the reader of the fluidity, malleability, and contingency of the development and institutionalization of the Ukrainian national project within the framework of the twentieth-century competition among Europe's Great Powers, multinational empires, multinational states, powerful nationalist movements, and religious communities.

In my description of the region under study, I relied primarily on territorial (such as "Right Bank") and administrative (such as "Galicia") terms. To distinguish between the old and new ways of looking at the world, I applied the terms (1) "Little Russian," "Ruthenian," or "Rusyn" to those who viewed local traditions compatible with imperial rule; and (2) "Ukrainian" to activists who questioned the unity of the East Slavs and the legitimacy of the Austrian and Russian empires. This inquiry traces how this small second group defined, attracted, expanded, and helped secure this national project within the cauldron of conflicting multilingual, multi-confessional, and multi-political worlds in East Central Europe in the first half of the twentieth century.

"Narodna" may be translated either as "national" or "people's." In dealing with the revolutionary period in chapter 3, I will employ the term "Ukrainian National Republic" (not "Ukrainian People's Republic") for *Ukrains'ka Narodna Respublika*.

To designate areas with large potentially Ukrainian populations in my text and maps, I utilized the term "majority Ukrainian-speaking territories (or provinces)," which does not necessarily presuppose a developed national consciousness on the part of the majority Ukrainian-speaking population. Nor does it imply an "ethnically pure" Ukrainian population within the multiple administrative borders and subdivisions the Russian, Austrian, Austro-Hungarian, Polish, Czechoslovak, Romanian, or Soviet states created. It merely affirms the obvious: that within these official bureaucratic constructions, the majority of the population spoke a common, non-standardized language and vaguely identified themselves (or could be mobilized to think of themselves) as different from other groups within their midst. "Majority Ukrainian-speaking provinces" included towns and cities with large Polish-speaking and sizeable Yiddish-speaking urban areas (such as Lemberg/Lwów before 1939) in Austria-Hungary and Poland as well as large Russian-speaking cities (such as Odessa and Kiev in the Russian Empire) before and after 1917.

Just as empires differ from states and states from nations, in this text I distinguished between "ethnicity" and "nation." By ethnic or ethnographical, I mean groups which recognize their differences with other groups in terms of their language, religion, and/or culture, but which cannot precisely define the borders of these dissimilarities with all groups. When pressed, members of ethnic groups hesitantly describe themselves as part of small, compact, local, or regional communities.

When individuals or groups identify their cohort in more sophisticated terms, I characterized these persons or groups as possessing a "national consciousness," an awareness that one or one's people belongs to a larger imagined community with a common vision of the past, present, and future. The emergence of a national consciousness does not necessarily make one a nationalist, someone who aspires to create an autonomous political arena for one's group or an independent nation-state. But it remains a necessary precondition for the emergence of mass nationalism.

National identities are not primordial, acquired at birth, or permanently fixed after their development. The process of acquiring a national identity is neither preordained nor inevitable; nor does it emerge or develop in a social or political vacuum. Although Joseph Stalin defined the key elements of a nation in such supposedly objective terms as "a historically constituted, stable community of people, formed on the basis of a common language, territory, economic life, and psychological make-up manifested in a common culture," nations and national consciousness are not divorced from subjective and situational environments. They thrive in fluid and contentious social and political systems, responding to external stimuli and to various perceived incentives, sanctions, humiliations, and indignities. Although it is difficult to formulate a nuanced assessment of the evolution of national identity formation, national consciousness, national movements, nation building, and nationalism, it is not impossible.

I have gleaned many valuable bits of information from Imperial Russian and Soviet censuses and statistical handbooks and included them in these pages. Despite my reliance on them, I agree with Gwendolyn Sasse, who asserted that "Soviet statistical data is problematic and can, at best, indicate trends" (*The Crimea Question: Identity, Transition, and Conflict* [Cambridge, MA: Harvard Ukrainian Research Institute, 2007], 122).

For the sake of convenience, all dates follow the Julian calendar until 1 January 1918. Soviet Russia adopted the new (Gregorian) calendar on 14 February 1918; the Ukrainian Central Rada embraced the modern chronological framework on 1 March 1918.

Soviet Ukraine's Administrative-Territorial Structure

Even for the informed reader, the many administrative and territorial changes that took place on the lands that became a united Ukraine in the twentieth century are confusing. Before the outbreak of the First World War in August 1914, the Russian and the Austro-Hungarian empires held all of the Ukrainian-speaking territories in East Central Europe. The war, the subsequent revolutions, and the Second World War accelerated the evolution of Ukraine's administrative divisions. The creation of these political demarcations reflects power and control, and most of the modifications came about in periods of conflict and enormous demographic losses.

In 1914, Russia's Ukrainian-speaking provinces were split into nine gubernias (provinces), and subdivided into 102 povits (counties) and 1,989 volosts (rural districts). From the February Revolution in early 1917 until the mid-1950s, the political organization of Soviet Russia and the Union of Soviet Socialist Republics (USSR) experienced constant fluctuations, as did Ukraine's political architecture.

Despite the efforts of the Ukrainian Central Rada to create a new administrative framework for the Ukrainian-speaking provinces in March 1918, this reform was never implemented. At the end of the revolutionary period in 1920, the newly installed Soviet authorities restored the Russian imperial model with gubernias, volosts, and povits, increasing the number of gubernias to twelve.

With the creation of the Union of Soviet Socialist Republics (USSR) on 30 December 1922, the leaders of this new political entity recognized the national-territorial principle and divided the vast territories they controlled into national republics and autonomous republics, autonomous oblasts (provinces), krais (lands), okrugs (regions), raions (districts), and village soviets (councils). In the Ukrainian SSR, on 12 April 1923, 53 okrugs (regions) replaced the existing 102 povits. With border rectifications and the transfer of territories to the Russian SFSR, Ukraine retained 41 okrugs.

In October 1924, the Soviet authorities created the Moldavian Autonomous Soviet Socialist Republic (ASSR) along the Ukrainian republic's southwestern boundaries with Romania. In 1925, the authorities dissolved the gubernias, retaining only the okrugs and raions, as reflected in the first Soviet census of 17 December 1926. In August 1930 the Soviet Ukrainian government then abolished the okrugs. From September 1930 to February 1932 only raions remained as the principal administrative component of the Ukrainian SSR. At that time, this republic possessed nearly 600 raions, twenty-five of which were designated as raions for Ukraine's national and ethnic minorities. In 1932, the authorities introduced a new political framework with oblasts, raions, and rural soviets. In that year, the Ukrainian SSR created seven oblasts (Chernihiv, Dniepropetrovsk, Donetsk, Kharkiv, Kiev, Odessa, and Vinnytsia) and retained the Moldovan ASSR, as manifested in the "defective" second Soviet census of 6 January 1937. Two years later, there were fifteen oblasts and the Moldovan ASSR, as documented in the "official" second Soviet census of 17 January 1939. This oblast-raion arrangement remained a permanent feature of the USSR's administrative-territorial structure until its collapse in 1991.

With the Molotov-Ribbentropf Pact of 1939, the USSR acquired the Belarusan- and Ukrainian-speaking areas from Poland, and Bessarabia and Bukovina from Romania. In August 1940, the Soviet authorities separated the Moldovan ASSR from Ukraine and formed the new Moldovan SSR by incorporating the central section of Bessarabia, recently annexed from Romania. Encompassing an area of 33,843 square kilometres (13,067 square miles), it emerged as and remained the smallest republic in the USSR.

· Shortly after the Munich Agreement, Hungary acquired Transcarpathia (now Carpatho-Ukraine) from a truncated Czechoslovakia in April 1939. After the invasion of the USSR on 22 June 1941, Germany and Romania divided the Ukrainian SSR. The Germans created Reichskommissariat Ukraine from most of Eastern Ukraine and Western Volhynia, but added the oblasts of Drohobych, Lviv, and Stanislaviv, and Ternopil to the General Government. Germany annexed Poland's Podlachia, and Poland reacquired it after the war. Romania received Southern Bessarabia, Northern Bukovina, and parts of Odessa, Vinnytsia, and Mykolaiv Oblasts. These eastern areas, between the Buh and Dniester Rivers, became Romanian-controlled Transnistria.

At the start of the twentieth century, the Ukrainian-speaking territories of the Austro-Hungarian Empire were divided into two crown lands,

Galicia and Bukovina, which the Austrians administered. Transcarpathia belonged to Hungary. With the collapse of the Dual Monarchy in 1918, Galicia became a part of Poland, Bukovina a part of Romania, and Transcarpathia a part of Czechoslovakia.

In addition to Galicia, independent Poland acquired a part of the Russian Empire's Volhynia and created a system of voivodeships (provinces) which encompassed the Ukrainian-speaking territories. Poland governed these territories until the Soviet invasion of that nation-state on 17 September 1939. Shortly afterwards, the USSR annexed the majority Ukrainian-speaking voievodeships of Drohobycz, Lwów, Stanislawów, Tarnopol, and Western Wołyń to the Ukrainian SSR. In the summer of 1940 the USSR acquired the Ukrainian-speaking provinces of Bukovina and Izmail from Romania, and in 1945 Transcarpathia from Czechoslovakia, which reacquired it from Hungary. The territories incorporated to the Ukrainian SSR during and after the Second World War were organized into eight new oblasts. On 21 May 1959, the Drohobych Oblast was merged into the Lviv Oblast.

Crimea – a peninsula with a territory of 27,000 square kilometres (10,425 square miles) – had been a part of the Russian Soviet Federated Socialist Republic (RSFSR) as an Autonomous Soviet Socialist Republic shortly after the Soviet Union came into existence in late 1922. With the Soviet expulsion of the Crimean Tatars in early 1944, the Crimean ASSR became an ordinary oblast of the RSFSR on 30 June 1945. The Presidium of the Supreme Soviet of the USSR transferred the Crimean Oblast from the Russian Federation (RSFSR) to the Ukrainian SSR on 19 February 1954.

When Ukraine became independent in 1991, it inherited all of the territories the Ukrainian SSR possessed after February 1954. Most of the countries of the world, including the Russian Federation, recognized its independence and territorial sovereignty.

In response to Ukraine's Euromaidan Revolution of 2013–14, the Russian Federation invaded the Crimea and annexed it on 18 March 2014. At the same time, it started to support the pro-Russian separatists in Eastern Ukraine.

Sources: V. Kubijovič, "Administrative Territorial Division," *Encyclopedia of Ukraine* (Toronto: University of Toronto Press, 1984), 1:11–14; V. Kubijovyč, M. Miller, O. Ohloblyn, and A. Zhukovsky, "Crimea," in Volodymyr Kubijovyč, *Encyclopedia of Ukraine*, 1:611–17; Vasyl Danylenko, *Ukrains'ka intelligentsia i vlada. Zvedennia sekretnoho viddilu DPU USRR 1927–1929 rr.* (Kiev: Tempora,

2012), 22; *Historical Dictionary of Ukraine*, 2nd ed., ed. Ivan Katchanovski, Zenon E. Kohut, Bohdan Y. Nebesio, and Myroslav Yurkevych (Lanham, MD: Scarecrow Press, 2013), 14–17; R.W. Davies and Stephen G. Wheatcroft, *The Years of Hunger: Soviet Agriculture, 1931–1933* (New York: Palgrave Macmillan, 2004), xvi; Steven Fischer-Galati, "Moldova and the Moldavians," in *Handbook of Major Soviet Nationalities*, ed. Zev Katz, Rosemarie Rogers, and Frederic Harned (New York: Free Press, 1975), 415, 418; http://www.adm.dp.gov.ua (accessed 7 July 2014); and Matthew D. Pauly, *Breaking the Tongue: Language, Education, and Power in Soviet Ukraine, 1923–1934* (Toronto: University of Toronto Press, 2014), xix–xx.

Russian, Soviet, and Ukrainian Measurements

1 centner = 100 kilograms
1 centner = 0.1 metric tons
1 desiatin = 2.7 acres
1 hectare (10,000 square metres) = 2.47 acres
1 kilogram = 2.2046 pounds
1 kilometre = 0.6214 miles
1 metric ton = 10 centners
1 mile = 1.6093 kilometres
1 pood = 16.38 kilograms (36.11 pounds)
1 square kilometre = 0.3861 square miles
1 square mile = 2.5899 square kilometres
1 ton = 1,000 kilograms

Maps

Map 1: Contemporary Ukraine in Europe, 1 June 2014

Map 2: Majority Ukrainian-Speaking Provinces in the Russian Empire,
1 June 1914

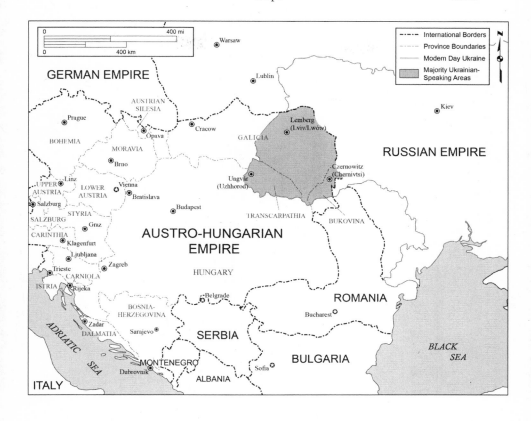

Map 3: Majority Ukrainian-Speaking Areas in the Austro-Hungarian Empire,
1 June 1914

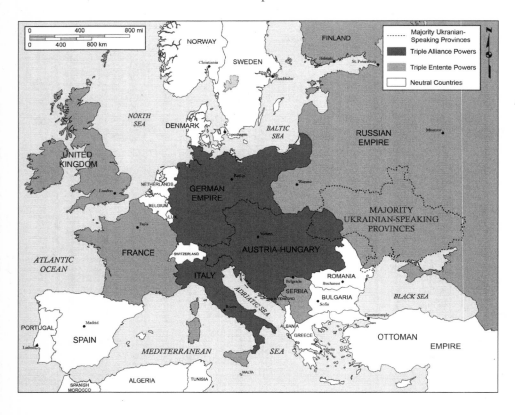

Map 4: Majority Ukrainian-Speaking Areas and European Alliances
on the Eve of the First World War, 1 June 1914

Note: When war breaks out in August 1914, Italy claims neutrality,
then joins the Triple Entente in May 1915. The Ottoman Empire unites
with the Triple Alliance in November 1914.

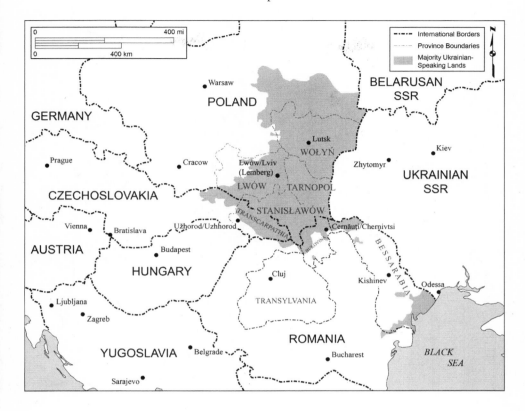

Map 5: Majority Ukrainian-Speaking Lands outside the Ukrainian SSR, 1930

Maps

Map 6: National Composition of the Ukrainian SSR's Rural Areas, 1926

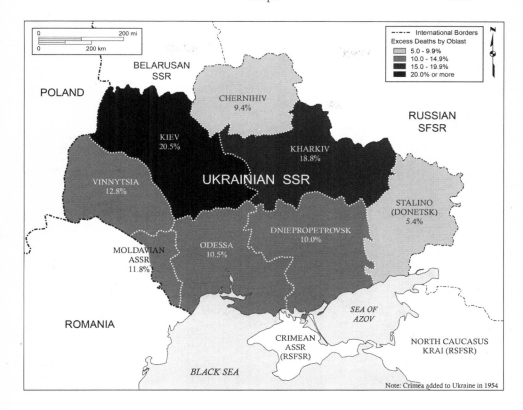

Map 7: Excess Deaths as Percentage of the Total Population
of the Ukrainian SSR by Oblast, 1932–1934

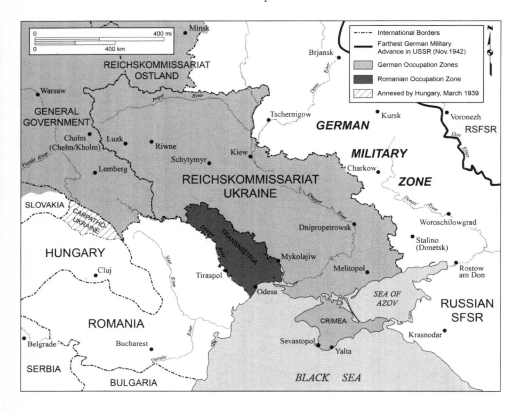

Map 8: Borders Imposed or Recognized by Nazi Germany after 22 June 1941

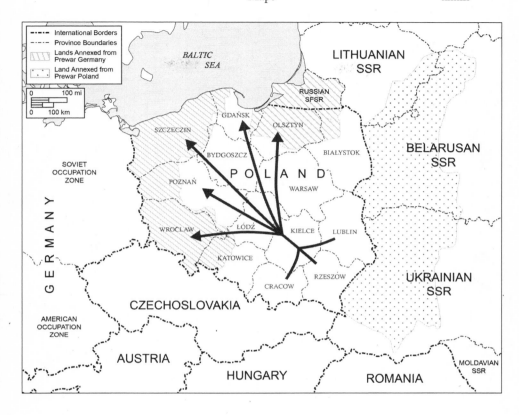

Map 9: Post-War Poland and the Ukrainian Population Transfer during Operation Vistula, April–July 1947

Map 10: Post-War Ukraine, 1945 to the Present

INTRODUCTION

Introduction

Wars, revolutions, occupations, forced deportations, voluntary evacuations, ethnic cleansings, and genocides in the first half of the twentieth century killed tens of millions of Europeans, displaced even more physically and psychologically, and profoundly altered the international political order for both the victors and the vanquished. The leading actors in these upheavals drew a grim lesson from past conflicts and radically escalated the pattern of mass violence to unprecedented levels.[1] As a consequence, each military contest and revolution built on the preceding one, produced more casualties and victims, and strengthened the power of each state over its populations.

Since the nineteenth century's demographic surge, industrial advances, and Europe's "political awakening," armies had become larger and more mechanized and military operations more intensive and extensive. The French revolutionary and Napoleonic wars, the American Civil War, and the 1870 Franco-Prussian War had activated civilian populations and homefront economies, no longer exempting them from enemy attack. All in all, the division between combatants and non-combatants slowly started to disappear.[2]

With the outbreak of the Great War in 1914, European leaders concluded that in an era of mass communications, mass politics, and mass production, "wars [would be] waged between whole populations, soldier and civilian alike."[3] The age of total war had arrived.[4]

Between 1914 and 1950, these total wars and state-sponsored interventions constituted the most destructive clashes in human history, "killing more people in aggregate absolute terms as well as per war."[5] In the First World War, more than ten million died and more than twenty million were gravely wounded. In the war's wake, the world also experienced a highly contagious influenza outbreak in the winter of 1918–19, killing up to fifty million. In the Second World War, nearly sixty million died.[6] Due to the widespread introduction of more destructive weapons of war, a communications revolution, and unbounded ideological enthusiasms, human losses rose dramatically between the first and second set of hostilities. Whereas only 5 per cent of the European deaths in the First World War included civilians, well over half of the victims in the Second World War did not wear a uniform.[7] More women and children died than ever before.[8] In addition to this human annihilation, these wars created large numbers of refugees: four to five million in 1918–22 and between 30 and 40.5 million between 1945 and 1950.[9]

By constantly vilifying their enemies, including non-combatants, the warring elites raised modern-day brutality and dehumanization to an unprecedented standard.[10] Mass hatred generated more mass hatred. Enormous battlefield casualties, depopulations, and extensive population transfers during these two total wars destabilized the majority of the home fronts of the belligerents, eroded the war efforts of the weaker powers, and mobilized national and social identities throughout the world. By activating enormous social and psychological dislocations, these total wars and revolutions not only accelerated previously existing trends, they also ignited powerful political movements and social contradictions.

These total wars encompassed not only wars *between* empires and states (external wars), but also violent political disorders *within* states. Those who sought to overturn a state's political and social order launched internal wars, which combined aspects of different types of violence, such as civil, national, and anti-colonial wars, revolts, rebellions, uprisings, guerilla wars, mutinies, jacqueries, coups d'état, terrorism, and insurrections.[11]

Total wars became a major driver of social developments, producing diverse sets of changes in different states and societies.[12] In various ways they recast the world's economies, political systems, social institutions, and cultures. By altering customs and behaviour, artistic and intellectual ideas and practices, the status of women, and the role of the family, each of these violent outbreaks shattered the level of social cohesiveness within each empire or state.[13] Not all of these developments proved cataclysmic. Some evolved in small, very subtle ways, maturing decades later.

These conflicts disrupted the international social, economic, and political status quo and undermined the hegemony of long-standing multinational empires. Not only did these major bloodlettings shape and realign the European state system, they also accelerated the processes of state building and nation building among groups that did not possess their own sovereign states. By creating a strong sense of "us against them," modern wars forced people to take sides and to "confirm their loyalty and identity" in public.[14] These mass disturbances transformed the Ukrainian-speaking populations of East Central Europe into actors, not just objects, of their own history. Unlike historians with the luxury of perspective decades after events, these men and women had to make choices within a confusing and very fluid environment (the "fog of war") and had "to consider their moves in almost complete ignorance of their opponents' intentions, resources, and will."[15] Their responses to this violence and their post-war representations helped delineate the imagined boundaries of the Ukrainian community.[16] These wars, in short, facilitated the making, remaking, and unmaking of modern Ukraine, currently the second-largest European state (after the Russian Federation) in terms of size (603,700 square kilometres/ 233,090 square miles) and sixth in terms of population (44,400,000).[17] The physical and psychological dislocations they generated also helped create self-conscious Ukrainians.

Over a forty-year period, the people living in the contiguous areas that became Ukraine bore the brunt of constant mobilizations and demobilizations and a long continuum of mass violence, which decimated entire generations of young men and killed enormous numbers of civilians. From 1914 to 1948, the territories encompassing Ukraine in its present form suffered approximately fifteen million "excess deaths": 1.3 million during the First World War; 2.3 million during the post-1917 civil and national wars (and during the brief Polish-Soviet War of 1920); 4 million during the state-induced famine of 1932–3, now called the Holodomor (murder by starvation); 300,000 during the Great Terror and the annexation of Poland's and Romania's eastern borderlands; 6.5 to 7.4 million during the Second World War; and 400,000 during the post-war famine and Stalin's campaign against Ukrainian anti-Soviet partisans in Western Ukraine.[18] In addition to these losses, the people of Ukraine also endured massive evacuations and forced population transfers to Central Asia and to the Far East. Many, not necessarily the majority, never returned.

Each of these armed contests changed international borders, fostered the creation of sovereign and quasi-sovereign states which sought to define their citizens, and sparked national and civil wars. Each of these catastrophes expanded on the previous ones and institutionalized the idea that the Ukrainian-speaking population differed from the Poles and Russians. These social earthquakes became the primary locomotives of the history of modern Ukraine and helped it emerge as what scholars have classified as both a pivotal and cleft state in the second half of the century, especially after independence in 1991.

The former US National Security Advisor Zbigniew Brzezinski once observed that the most important countries in the world are either geostrategic players or geopolitical pivots. Active geostrategic players possess "the capacity and the national will to exercise power or influence beyond their borders in order to alter ... the existing geopolitical state of affairs." They are, in his words, "geopolitically volatile." France, Germany, Russia, China, and India belong to this Eurasian club of geostrategic players.[19] In contrast to this group, geopolitical pivots are "states whose importance is derived not from their own power and motivation but rather from their sensitive location and from the consequences of their potentially vulnerable condition for the behavior of geostrategic players. Most often, geopolitical pivots are determined by their geography, which in some cases gives them a special role in either defining access to important areas or in denying resources to a significant player."[20]

In Brzezinski's view of the world, Ukraine, Azerbaijan, South Korea, Turkey, and Iran constitute important geopolitical pivots.[21] Throughout the twentieth century, the majority Ukrainian-speaking territories played a key role in shaping the competition between the great powers (active geopolitical players) of Central and East Central Europe, especially Poland, Germany, and Russia (later the USSR). In this period, the intensity of the political allegiances and the national identities of the peoples living on these territories helped decide the success of Moscow's efforts to assert its influence along its western flank. Ukraine's emergence as an independent state after 1991 both enhanced Poland's security and challenged Russia's hegemony over the post-Soviet region.[22] (See map 1.)

In addition to being a pivotal state, Ukraine is to some extent what the late Harvard political scientist Samuel P. Huntington called a cleft country. As defined by Huntington, a cleft country is one whose population includes large groups belonging to different civilizations. China, India, Indonesia, the Phillipines, Sri Lanka, Malaysia and Singapore, the Sudan, Nigeria, Tanzania, Kenya, and Ethiopia are all examples.[23] Internal conflicts develop in cleft countries "when a majority group belonging to one civilization attempts to define the state as its political instrument and to make its language, religion, and symbols those of the state."[24] The prevailing view becomes "we are different peoples and belong in different places."[25]

In his controversial book *The Clash of Civilizations and the Remaking of World Order*, Huntington problematically described Ukraine as "a cleft country with two distinct cultures. The civilizational fault line between the West and Orthodoxy runs through its heart and has done so for centuries."[26] Ukraine's political and cultural identity is both more complex and less fragile than he allows. But he raises a serious point. Ukraine's internal divisions often appear (especially after 1991) to overshadow the factors that unite it.

Ukraine's cleftness did not emerge in a political vacuum. External geopolitical contexts, the overall balance of power, and foreign interventions often helped shape its internal developments. Each of the past century's brutal wars, revolutions, and subsequent social cataclysms opened new doors and opportunities while closing others, producing a new set of menus, options, contingencies, and unintended consequences for the people living in the Ukrainian-speaking provinces. As the status quo crumbled with each catastrophe, chaos brought novel challenges as well as opportunities. Men and women had to adapt to a different world, one containing heretofore unimagined political and social possibilities. People had to reassess their embedded perceptions and assumptions of the world, create new mental maps, make serious political decisions, and even choose sides. Although the masses did not determine the political list of options from which to choose, they could select from various alternatives, however limited in number.[27] As mass politics dragged almost everyone into its volatile undercurrents, the possibility of neutrality disappeared. Ukraine's geographic location and turbulent political environment helped determine these outcomes.

Geographic Factors

Situated in the southwestern portion of the East European plain, Ukraine is slightly smaller in area than Alaska, Texas, or most of the Canadian provinces and territories. Poland, Slovakia, Hungary, and Moldova border it to the west; Belarus to the north; and the Russian Federation to the northeast and east. To the south are the Black Sea and the Sea of Azov. Richly endowed with natural resources, including iron ore, coal, timber, natural gas, and a limited amount of oil, Ukraine is also one of the most bountiful agricultural regions in the world. Its fertile plains offer a spacious passageway to Asia.

Ukraine (*Ukraina*, meaning borderland), as its name suggests, makes up one of Europe's eastern boundaries, the transitional zone between Roman Catholic and Orthodox Europe, between Christian Europe and the non-Christian Eurasia, and between the Slavic and the non-Slavic linguistic zones. Most importantly, this area's overwhelmingly flat natural terrain made it an intermediate region between different worlds. Approximately 40 per cent of Ukraine consists of a vast semi-arid, grass-covered plain (the so-called steppe), divided by the Dnieper (Dnipro) River, which flows into the Black Sea. With the exception of the Carpathian Mountains in the west and the Black Sea to the south, the Ukrainian territories lack natural boundaries.

As with most frontier regions throughout world history, the Eurasian steppe played an important role in the development of pre-modern and modern Ukraine. This land, which stretches for nearly 8,000 kilometres (5,000 miles) from Hungary in the west to Manchuria in the east, attracted the Mongols and other nomads who moved easily on horseback from one end of Eurasia to the other across an endless ocean of grasslands.[28] These horse-powered pirates rallied large, mobile cavalry forces, which quickly overwhelmed their opponents. They sought to control the steppe by organizing trade or by engaging in pastoralism, plunder, and slave hunting. To block nomadic incursions, agricultural settlers sought to stabilize the steppe and to regulate the human traffic passing through it. The Ukrainian territories soon became one of Eurasia's epicentres of the confrontation between the nomadic and settled worlds.

The steppe's vast, uninhabited distances highlighted the awesome power of nature and the powerlessness of man. The steppe presaged freedom, rebirth, and enormous opportunities for those who dared to endure its many threats. Oftentimes, it failed to deliver on its promises. Just as the flat uniformity of its landscape could easily lead the inexperienced astray and to death, the tall grasslands also camouflaged marauding nomads on slave-hunting expeditions. Despite these dangers over centuries, men and women braved the steppe in successive waves and put down roots.

In order to survive, these Slavic and Orthodox pioneers accommodated themselves to the wilderness's harsh conditions and adopted aspects of the nomadic lifestyle. These trailblazers slowly tamed the wild, organized a deep-rooted sedentary society, and later experienced absorption into neighbouring states and empires.[29]

Political Environment

The Ukrainian frontier nurtured various cultural and political breakthroughs, such as the emergence of Kiev Rus, the first powerful East Slavic and political/commercial entity on Eurasia's western steppe. Founded by the Vikings in the ninth century A.D., it stretched from the Baltic to the Black Seas. Its ruler, Grand Prince Volodimer the Great, accepted the Christian faith headquartered in Constantinople in 988 A.D. In the thirteenth century, with the withering of Eurasian trade routes passing through Kiev and with the Mongol conquest, Kiev Rus collapsed.

After its fall, Mongols, Ottoman Turks, Crimean Tatars, Lithuanians, and Poles competed to dominate the territories of present-day Ukraine. The Roman Catholic–led Polish-Lithuanian Commonwealth gained control of most present-day Ukrainian territories between 1569 and 1795, providing its Orthodox elites with a political model to follow. But the Commonwealth failed to maintain its initial tolerance of the Orthodox Christian faith or to protect adequately all of the Polish king's subjects from the Turks and Tatars.

If the Polish kings could not provide security on the steppe, the Cossacks – fierce frontiersmen – could. These Slavs and Orthodox believers escaped the serfdom of their Polish landlords, penetrated the steppe, created communities independent of Polish control, and learned to defend themselves from the Turks and Tatars by mastering the fighting methods of their enemies. In time, many came under the Commonwealth's jurisdiction. Although the Cossacks served as its frontier militia and safeguarded its southern borders, their interests and those of the Polish nobles often clashed. Cossack rebellions against the Commonwealth culminated in the bloody Khmelnytsky Revolution, which started in 1648 when the Cossack elite sought equality with Polish Catholic nobles and the masses struggled to end serfdom. Both groups failed to achieve their goals. This uprising established the Hetmanate, an autonomous polity that transferred its allegiance from Poland to Muscovy (Russia) by the Treaty of Pereiaslav in 1654. Subsequently, the Hetmanate was split into two: the Right Bank reverted to Polish rule while the Left Bank remained under Moscow's authority. By the early eighteenth century the Polish Lithuanian Commonwealth abolished the Right Bank Hetmante. Over the long run, this revolution and the subsequent Polish-Muscovite wars fatally undermined this autonomous Cossack entity and, a century later, the Commonwealth itself.

Until the Russian Empire secured the steppe in the second half of the eighteenth century, the inhabitants on these territories experienced constant onslaughts from the Ottoman Turks and their allies, the Crimean Tatars. With the conquest of the steppe and the partitions of the Polish-Lithuanian Commonwealth in the second half of the eighteenth century, the Russian and Austrian Empires acquired most of the Ukrainian-speaking territories and retained the institution of serfdom until the mid-nineteenth century (see table I.1).

As these various territories fell at different times under the domination of the Polish-Lithuanian Commonwealth, the Russian Empire, the Habsburg Monarchy, the Ottoman Empire, Poland, Czechoslovakia, Romania, and the Soviet Union, its people became subjects of these

Table I.1 Austrian, Muscovite, and Russian Imperial Acquisitions (1526–1917) of Territories That Became Part of the Ukrainian SSR, 1918–1954

Date Acquired	Territory to Muscovy and to Russian Empire	Territory to Habsburg Monarchy
1654	Left Bank/*Malorossiia*/Little Russia (Treaty of Pereiaslav) Right Bank (under Muscovite control, 1654–1667; with the Treaty of Andrusovo (1667), a part of the Polish-Lithuanian Commonwealth until 1793)	
1699		Transcarpathia (a part of the medieval Kingdom of Hungary since the eleventh century A.D.; a part of the Hapsburg Monarchy since 1699)
1772		Galicia (First Partition of Poland)
1774		Bukovina (area incorporated from the Principality of Moldavia after the Russo-Turkish War of 1768–74)
1793	Right Bank (Second partition of Poland)	
1739–1806	Southern Ukraine (*Novorossiia*) (area incorporated at the end of the Russo-Turkish Wars of 1735–9, 1768–74, 1787–92, and 1806–12)	
1783	Crimea (acquired from the Ottoman Empire)	

empires and states and experienced different political systems and political cultures, diverse institutional arrangements and socio-economic environments, and dissimilar religious and secular organizations, factors which nourished Ukraine's present-day religious, cultural, national, regional, and economic fault lines.[30]

The Orthodox political elites and intelligentsia (churchmen and lay) frequently expressed the idea that the Ukrainian-speaking population differed significantly from Poles and Lithuanians in the sixteenth and seventeenth centuries; the peasantry quickly absorbed this notion.[31] But the view that the Muscovites and Ukrainian speakers stood apart spread glacially to the peasant masses in the eighteenth and nineteenth centuries. In the course of the eighteenth century the concept of Little Russia with a specific historical consciousness and the idea of loyalty to a Ukrainian political entity within the framework of an Imperial Russia took hold.[32] The wars and revolutions of the twentieth century rapidly undermined this ambiguous, multilayered paradigm and institutionalized the dissimilarities between the two groups. By killing tens of millions and by displacing many more physically and psychologically, these wars and revolutions overturned the international status quo, undermined the hegemony of long-standing empires, and provided the native populations with hereto-fore unimagined political and social options.

By exploring how Ukraine became a geopolitical pivotal and cleft state, this history of the first half of the twentieth century recognizes that un-spoken assumptions about national identity and political engagement in the past do not necessarily coincide with those of the present. The peoples of Ukraine did not follow a linear, inevitable, or irreversible road to the present. Their history contains many contingencies, discontinuities, and complex turning points.

Unlike the excellent surveys produced by Orest Subtelny, Paul Robert Magocsi, Andrew Wilson, and Sergei Yekelchyk, this book concentrates on the formation and evolution of modern Ukraine as an interactive re-sponse to the total wars and mass violence of the last century.[33] My study affirms Timothy Snyder's assessment of East Central Europe as Europe's *bloodlands*, but challenges his claim that these mass murders started in 1932.[34] (The Great Powers inaugurated this long-term bloodshed in 1914.) By highlighting the famine of 1932–3 as Ukraine's second total war, an integral part of the continuum of the mass violence the First and Second World Wars unleashed, this account extends the arguments in Norman Naimark's *Stalin's Genocides* and builds on those in Terry Martin's *The Affirmative Action Empire*.[35]

This book seeks to provide a context to the unspoken assumptions, so-cial options, and individual choices of Ukraine's modern period, which begins with the late nineteenth century, building on the collective memo-ries of the past. The twentieth century's total wars, revolutions, and mod-ernization projects brought mass literacy and education, industrialization, urban growth and urbanization, increased secularism, and enhanced roles for women to the Ukrainian-speaking masses. By undermining their local and parochial loyalties, these wars and revolutions introduced the people of Ukraine to new ideas, which led to a renewed search for self-definition. These ferocious conflicts reinforced the region's role as a geopolitical piv-ot. At the same time, they helped transform it into a divided state.

In short, the twentieth century's wars, revolutions, and mass social en-gineering projects overturned the age-old status quo and generated a new environment conducive to the introduction of new identities and new po-litical systems in East Central Europe. But these breakthroughs came at great human cost – and with unintended consequences.

1

The Ukrainian-Speaking Provinces before the Great War

Small peoples. The concept is not quantitative: it points to a condition; a fate; small peoples do not have that felicitous sense of an eternal past and future; at a given moment in their history, they all passed through the antechambers of death; in constant confrontation with the arrogant ignorance of the mighty, they see their existence as perpetually threatened or with a question mark hovering over it; for their very existence is the question.

Milan Kundera[1]

In his notebooks from the 1950s, the Soviet Ukrainian film director Alexander Dovzhenko, a native of the Russian Empire's Chernigov (Chernihiv) Province, recorded a conversation he had with his father in his childhood:

> My father ... did not know to which nation he belonged, nor did his friends and co-workers before the [1917] revolution.
> But the Russian people, in his view, represented a different nation (than ours). Rafts from the Orlov Province floated down the Desna River. "Those are Russians," he said. "And who are we?" we small children asked. My father ... did not know how to reply ... "we are peasants, tillers of the soil, simple people, only peasants" ... We kept quiet for a while. My father held his tongue ... We were the only people in Europe who did not know who we were. And I belonged to these people.[2]

Written by a man who formulated his view of the world in the cauldron of the wars and revolutions of the twentieth century, Dovzhenko's passage highlights the ambivalence over identity that prevailed in the densely populated and majority Ukrainian-speaking provinces of the Russian Empire and the Austro-Hungarian Monarchy at the end of the nineteenth century and the beginning of the twentieth.

Before the outbreak of the First World War in 1914, the Ukrainian-speaking population of East Central Europe formed one of the largest groups in Europe without a state of its own. Of the approximately twenty-five million Ukrainian speakers in 1900, 84 per cent of the total lived in the Russian Empire and 16 per cent in the Austro-Hungarian Empire.[3] They represented the second-largest language group in the Russian Empire (constituting approximately 18 per cent of the 125.6 million total population) in 1897 and the sixth-largest in the Austro-Hungarian Empire (comprising 8 per cent of the fifty-one million of the Dual Monarchy's residents) in 1910.[4]

Peasant World

As subjects of two large, contiguous, and multicultural empires, most Ukrainian speakers worked the land, lived in poverty, and did not possess a clear sense of national identity. The elites promoting modernization lived in the towns and cities, and most identified themselves as Russians or Poles or Jews. But the peasants, a socially conservative group, could not imagine themselves as anything other than men and women working plots of land. They embraced this challenge. Bound closely to the soil, they remained unable or reluctant to move into the neighbouring cities long after their emancipation from serfdom in Austria (1848) or in Russia (1861). Instead, when given the opportunity to improve their economic situation, many preferred to travel long distances, even across continents and oceans, in order to gain larger and better plots.

Between 1871 and 1916, nearly 1.5 million peasants left the Right Bank and the Left Bank and settled in southern Siberia, today's Kazakhstan, and the Far East.[5] Their brethren in the Austro-Hungarian Empire responded in the same way. Although small numbers found work in Eastern Galicia's oil fields, large numbers took advantage of opportunities to go to the United States or Canada.[6] Between 400,000 and 700,000 Ukrainian speakers emigrated from Austria-Hungary and the tsarist provinces of Volhynia, Grodno, Siedlce, and Lublin to North America before 1914.[7] This complete commitment to the peasant way of life excluded urban and industrial possibilities.

In the Russian Empire, Ukrainian-speaking peasants defined themselves as members of the Orthodox faith who possessed a language different from others (officially: *Malorossiiskii*, or Little Russian) and whose origins belonged in the distant past. If pressed to identify himself, the peasant – much like Dovzhenko's father – would most likely reply: "tuteshnyi" (from here) or "pravoslavnyi" (Orthodox).[8]

As a pre-modern group, peasants retained a solidarity with their own kind. They defined themselves "not by reference to their own characteristics, but by exclusion, that is, by comparison with 'strangers.'"[9] Very few could clearly assert their group identity; most knew who they were not. They recognized that they were not Jews or Poles. But were they Russians? Although Russians spoke a different (but related East Slavic) language, they remained brothers and sisters in the Orthodox faith.

In the Austrian Empire, Ukrainian-speaking peasants in Galicia, Bukovina, and Transcarpathia also identified themselves through the prism of their religion until the late nineteenth century, when the Ukrainian national movement made inroads into the countryside.[10] In these areas, it was easier for the Ukrainian-speaking Greek Catholic peasant in Austria-Hungary to differentiate himself from Poles, Germans, and Jews than it was for the Ukrainian-speaking Orthodox peasant in the Russian Empire to distinguish himself from Russian speakers.

The confusion regarding the peasant self, the "other," and the criteria for distinguishing between the two emerged at the end of the nineteenth and beginning of the twentieth centuries, when the agrarian Ukrainian provinces within the Russian and Austro-Hungarian empires embraced industrialization, urbanization, and modernization. This ordeal – psychologically and economically – disoriented the peasants.

Reconceptualizations

In the pre-modern period, a person's social position and religious adherence defined his or her identity. A hierarchically based society helped determine what individuals recognized as important to themselves and within their environments.[11] With the spread of the romantic ideal of authenticity in the nineteenth century, a small number of men and women began to perceive the need to discover their "own original way of being," their identity, and their relationship to the wider world.[12]

An individual, however, does not define one's own identity in isolation. After asking "Who am I?" "Who are you?" "Who are we?" and "Who are they?" – the primal questions of identity – one negotiates the answers with others, especially those closest to oneself.[13] In the Russian Empire, these questions possessed profound long-term cultural and political implications. They emerged in the shadows of the ruling elite's disagreements over whether or not Russia belonged to the European cultural zone and over whether individuals or groups should identify themselves with the Russian national (russkii) or the Russian civic (rossiskii) idea.[14]

Engaged in the world of ideas, members of the East European intelligentsia initiated various cultural and political projects in order to uplift the masses. They started to reassess their own pasts in the context of the "lessons" they had learned from the French Revolution, the Napoleonic invasion, the Decembrist revolt of 1825, the Polish uprisings of 1830 and 1863, the European revolutions of 1848, the Industrial Revolution, the unification of Italy and Germany, and the political convulsions of the early twentieth century. Each of these events challenged the prevailing view of the world, helped reconfigure the political identities of members of the intelligentsia, and provided new – if not radical – alternatives, especially the idea of popular sovereignty.

Alienated by their inferior socio-economic, political, and cultural position, members of the small Ukrainian-speaking intelligentsia increasingly began to emphasize their differences with their imperial identities and their neighbours. By highlighting a nation of their own, they attempted to define their need for an emotional sense of belonging in rational, i.e., national, terms. They codified the shared memories and stories from the past and cast them into a framework of a shared language, culture, tradition, geographic origin, and, most importantly, distinctiveness from others.[15]

These components of identity did not emerge from a primordial consciousness, but from the models and practices that Johann Gottfried von Herder (1744–1803), a prominent German philosopher and literary critic, and the French Revolution developed at the end of the late eighteenth century.[16] The French Revolution and the subsequent Napoleonic Wars transformed the idea of "'the people' from an [non]-ethnic agglomeration of autonomous individuals into a national community" of brothers and sisters and introduced the prospect of mass politics into the Central and East Central European environment.[17]

The newly formed "national" intelligentsia then challenged the unspoken assumptions of the traditional world and created a modern political consciousness in their societies. Unlike the nobilities of nations with long-term states (such as the Poles and Hungarians), the intelligentsia in Central and East Central Europe looked to the future rather than to bygone eras. They stressed the need to "establish a new social order" rather than to "return to a golden age in the past," emphasizing innovation rather than renovation.[18] Most importantly, they redefined the core of their political nations by including the masses, especially the peasants, and integrated them into their vision of the future as equal political partners. The people and "the rabble" no longer remained synonymous terms. In the intelligentsia's view of the world, the people (not the nobility) represented the nation. Each was equal to other members and each possessed dignity, regardless of social class or wealth.

Once the intelligentsia defined their group identities, they hoped to spread their ideas to those they considered their countrymen and countrywomen. This initiative remained difficult to implement. Most of the non-German, non-Hungarian, and non-Russian intelligentsia did not control the educational or religious institutions in their homelands and could not diffuse their ideas easily. They needed governmental tolerance, if not support, and required authorities to recognize their new identities in the public sphere. Most of the leaders of the dominant religious and governmental institutions in East Central Europe understood such efforts as a secular challenge to the status quo and responded negatively. As a consequence, the mass acceptance of these new identities became not just a cultural choice, but also a political one, especially when governments sought to manipulate or to control them.[19]

Ukrainian Speakers in the Russian Empire

In the Russian Empire, the Ukrainian-speaking population lived primarily in the provinces of Poltava, Chernigov, and Kharkov (on the eastern bank of the Dnieper River; also called Little Russia [*Malorossiia*] or the Left Bank); Kiev, Podolia, and Volhynia (on the western bank of the Dnieper River, sometimes called the Southwest Region [*Iugozapadnyi krai*] or the Right Bank); and northern Tavrida, Kherson, and Ekaterinoslav (also called New Russia [*Novorossia*]) (see map 2). According to the 1897 Russian imperial census, the Ukrainian-speaking population also constituted a plurality of the Kuban Oblast, and a substantial minority in the Stavropol, Voronezh, Don Cossack, Grodno, Kursk, and Bessarabian provinces.[20] In light of the prevailing Russian imperial ideology, the authorities designated this Ukrainian-speaking population as Little Russians (*malorossy*), who spoke a dialect of Russian and who adhered to the Orthodox faith.

Ukrainian speakers comprised nearly three-fourths of the population in the above-mentioned majority Ukrainian-speaking provinces, which possessed a multi-ethnic, multinational, and multi-confessional character. In 1897, these territories contained not only seventeen million Ukrainian speakers, but also 2.7 million Russian speakers, 510,000 German speakers, 389,000 Polish speakers, and 1.9 million Yiddish speakers.[21]

Jews played a significant role in the history of the Ukrainian-speaking provinces in both the Russian Empire and in the Austro-Hungarian Monarchy. With the partitions of Poland in the late eighteenth century, the

Russian Empire acquired the world's largest concentration of Jews and restricted them to the so-called Pale of Settlement, which covered an area from the Baltic Sea to the Black Sea (see map 2). In 1897, this region (more than twice the size of France today) encompassed 4.9 million Jews (94 per cent of the entire Jewish population of the empire). In addition to this restriction, the tsarist government forbade them to own land, to join the civil service, to serve as officers in the army, or to enter the higher schools and universities. Over 1,400 different laws and regulations bound them to an inferior status. These anti-Jewish measures represented "a tsarist version of the Hindu caste system, with the Jews in the role of the Untouchables."[22]

Jews who lived in the densely populated Ukrainian-speaking provinces of the Pale comprised nearly 40 per cent of all Jews in the Pale. The Hasidic movement, centred in Beltz, Bratslav, Uman, Chortkiv, Chernobyl, and Ruzhin, and after the late eighteenth century, the Haskalah (Jewish enlightenment), enjoyed enormous popularity in this region.

The overwhelming majority of Jews lived in towns and hamlets (*shtetls*). In the first half of the nineteenth century, the tsarist authorities banned Jews from living in some of the major cities in the Pale, including Kiev, Nikolaev, Sevastopol, Yalta, and Taganrog, as well as in the countryside. Nevertheless, by 1897, Jews made up 30 per cent of the urban population of the nine Ukrainian-speaking provinces. Only Jews who were merchants of the first guild, persons with a higher education, those who completed their long-term military service, and artisans had the right to leave the Pale and to reside permanently in any part of Russia.[23]

In addition to members of the Jewish faith, large numbers of Roman Catholics and Lutherans also lived in the Ukrainian-speaking areas. Approximately 186,000 Turkic-speaking Crimean Tatars, adherents of Islam, inhabited the southern part of the Taurida Province.

Ukrainian Speakers in the Austro-Hungarian Empire

A similar mosaic developed across the border in the Habsburg Monarchy. According to the Austrian and Hungarian censuses of 1910, 3.4 million Ukrainian speakers lived in Galicia, 300,000 in Bukovina, and 470,000 in the seven northeastern counties of the Hungarian Kingdom[24] (see map 3). Ukrainian speakers constituted 40.2 per cent of the entire Galician crown land, a plurality (38.4 per cent) in Bukovina, and approximately 28.7 per cent of the total Hungarian seven-county population (in 1900).[25] In addition to large numbers of Polish speakers, German speakers, and Magyar speakers, Jews also played an important role in these Ukrainian-speaking

areas. In 1910, members of this last community formed nearly 11 per cent
of the total Galician population, nearly 13 per cent in Bukovina, and
11.4 per cent in Transcarpathia.[26]

As the Ukrainian national movement emerged in the Austro-Hungarian
Empire in the early twentieth century, its leaders demanded a redrawing of
the borders of the crown lands and the establishment of an autonomous
Ukrainian-speaking region, where the majority of their compatriots lived.
If only the most Ukrainian-speaking compact territories were considered,
Ukrainian speakers would have constituted a majority in Austria's eastern
Galicia (65 per cent), Transcarpathia (60.4 per cent), and northern Bukovina
(56.5 per cent).[27] But Habsburg bureaucrats opposed such changes. Once
one national group received a concession from the central authorities, they
reasoned, other national groups would demand as much, if not more.

Roman Catholicism prevailed in Austria-Hungary, but the Ukrainian-
speaking population of Galicia, Bukovina, and Transcarpathia identified
themselves, for the most part, as Greek Catholics. Formed in 1596, this religious group tore apart the unity of the Polish-Lithuanian Commonwealth's
Orthodox believers. At first, Polish authorities and the Roman Catholic
Church enthusiastically supported this hybrid faith (which recognized the
primacy of the Pope of Rome, but retained the eastern rite, the Slavonic li-
turgical language, administrative autonomy, and married clergy), primarily
as a means to convert the Orthodox to Roman Catholicism. After the brutal Cossack uprising of 1648–54, the Poles dismantled Orthodox institutions in the areas they recovered and favoured the Greek Catholic Church.
The local population, which initially reacted with intense hostility to this
religious metamorphosis, grew to accept this faith, but did not embrace
Roman Catholicism. Disappointed with this outcome, the Polish authorities discriminated against the Greek Catholics and considered them second-
class Christians. After the partitions of Poland, the Austrian monarchy
supported the Ukrainian-speaking Greek Catholics and raised their status
to equality with the Roman Catholics.

In addition to religious differences, linguistic divisions in the Romanov
and Habsburg empires complicated the emergence of a modern Ukraine.
The languages groups spoke corresponded closely with class divisions and
with urban and rural ways of life. The Ukrainian speakers dwarfed other
language and cultural communities, especially in the countryside. In the
Right Bank, for example, the overwhelming majority of peasants in 1897
listed Little Russian as their native language; the landlords, Polish
or Russian (although one-third of the landlords did list Little Russian);
and many of the townspeople, Russian or Yiddish.[28] In the Left Bank and

Novorossiia, the number of Ukrainian speakers surpassed the members of other language and cultural communities, especially in the countryside. Most of the urban residents identified themselves as Russian speakers. In the Ukrainian-speaking areas of Austria-Hungary, the majority of landlords and townspeople were Polish speakers, German speakers, Romanian speakers, or Hungarian speakers. A high percentage of those who identified themselves as Jews also lived in urban environments. Although these non-Ukrainian-speaking groups remained small, they played critical roles in the socio-economic development of the Austrian and Russian Ukrainian-speaking provinces in the late nineteenth and early twentieth centuries. In these provinces, the majority of members of the most powerful political, social, and economic elites in the towns and rural areas spoke languages other than those spoken in the Ukrainian-speaking countryside.

The Ukrainian National Movement

At the end of the eighteenth century and during the nineteenth, small clusters of urban intellectuals developed a modern Ukrainian national identity, first in the lands of the Cossacks in Left Bank Ukraine (Novgorod-Siversk and Kharkov), then in the Right Bank (Kiev), then finally in the Habsburg lands (Galicia).[29] As they defined this new identity and differentiated it from the Polish, Hungarian, Romanian, All-Russian, and Russian identities, they formed informal groups and networks of like-minded people, seeking to propagate their ideas to the peasants.

This modern Ukrainian national movement did not develop in a single or coherent direction. Instead, it evolved along the lines of the three-stage model pioneered by the Czech historian Miroslav Hroch in his study of the "small nations" of northern and central Europe.[30] In the *academic* stage, a small number of scholars and amateurs begin to discover the language, the culture, and the history of their ancestors and emphasize its uniqueness. In the *cultural* stage, "the fermentation-process of national consciousness," a large number of patriotic propagandists spread the national idea to the masses. Finally, during the *political* stage, the broad masses join the national movement and start to make demands on their respective governments. Only during the last stage, when national groups demand extensive political concessions from the authorities (especially autonomy or independence), does this stage enter a *nationalist* phase.

Although many historians of Ukraine identify the Left Bank primarily with the academic stage, the Right Bank with the cultural stage, and the Galicia with the political stage, each of these regions experienced all three stages, although for differing lengths of time and with varying success.[31] As with any historical framework, the dividing line between these periods remains fluid and overlaps in terms of chronology. These phases did not necessarily start with the academic stage and end with the political stage. They often started and continued in random order. Nevertheless, Hroch's model provides a useful framework for understanding the emergence of the modern Ukrainian national movement, which mobilized many, but not a majority, in the Ukrainian-speaking territories ruled by the Austrian and Russian empires before 1914.

The intelligentsia in the Ukrainian-speaking provinces emerged in the Left Bank during the first half of the nineteenth century. At first, the sons of the minor gentry, such as Mykola Hohol (better known as Nikolai Gogol), sought positions as bureaucrats, junior military officers, or educators.[32] With the emancipation of the peasantry in 1861 and the expansion of the educational system, the size of the intelligentsia increased. By the 1870s, the better-off peasants (such as Dovzhenko's father) began to encourage their children to acquire an education. The industrial revolution in the Donbass and in the Ukrainian-speaking eastern provinces demanded literate workers.[33]

As the educational system represented elitist values and operated with Russian as the primary language of communication, the intelligentsia in the Ukrainian provinces remained a small group. Those who identified themselves as Ukrainians constituted a minority within this minority. According to the Russian imperial census of 1897, approximately 235,000 men and women out of a total population of 23.4 million (around 1 per cent) in the nine Ukrainian provinces possessed some form of secondary or higher education. Only twenty-four thousand individuals completed some form of higher education, and only seventeen thousand some sort of specialized secondary training. The vast majority of the intelligentsia identified themselves as Russians, Jews, or Poles – not Little Russians. Of those with secondary or university training, 56 per cent declared themselves Russian and 19 per cent Little Russian.[34] For a variety of reasons, including socioeconomic and political pressures and the attraction of the prestigious imperial culture, many members of the intelligentsia with Little Russian backgrounds affiliated themselves with Russians, not with those who began to identify themselves as Ukrainians. In 1897, less than 25 per cent of all teachers, 16 per cent of all jurists, and 10 per cent of all writers and artists living in the Ukrainian-speaking provinces spoke Ukrainian.[35]

Inspired by the reaction to the Normanist and Anti-Normanist controversy in the eighteenth century and the Slavophile-Westernizer debates concerning Russia's uniqueness in the 1830s and 1840s, the small intelligentsia in the Ukrainian provinces became interested in the future of Russia and, concomitantly, in the future of the Ukrainian people. They began to clarify their place within the Russian and Austrian empires as they encountered complex, complementary, and sometimes antagonistic visions of "Polishness" and Russianness" in other intellectual circles.[36] In competition with other national and imperial visions, the "Ukrainian project" became a never-ending work-in-progress, nurtured in the uneven soil of vastly different regions and empires.

The proponents of these new Ukrainian perspectives recognized that they could easily have accepted their ultimate disappearance within the Russian or Polish nations, but they chose to resist this process. By creating the framework of a new culture for a small, impoverished, illiterate, and powerless people, they wagered that they and their Ukrainian-speaking compatriots would prevail.[37]

These thinkers came from the very institutions, such as the University of Kharkov (established in 1805), the University of Kiev (1834), and the Kiev Archeographic Commission (1843), that the tsarist government had created in order to integrate the Western borderlands into the Russian Empire. Each of these organizations attracted a small number of professors, professionals, and students dedicated to collecting, researching, and critically assessing materials concerning the Left Bank and the Right Bank. The University of Kharkov's professors (most of whom initially came from the German lands) introduced Western ideas and – influenced by Herder's interpretations – acknowledged Ukrainian folklore as worthy of study.[38]

Whereas some of the nobles sought to restore their ancient rights and privileges and to retain a hierarchical order, the intelligentsia embraced a more democratic vision of the Ukrainian identity. By accepting Herder's idea that all men and women – not just the nobles – belong to the nation, the intelligentsia started the process of undermining the multiple loyalties within the Russian Empire.

In all political systems, individuals possess a network of loyalties (political scientists call these multiple allegiances or "cross-cutting cleavages"), such as those to one's village, region, province, state, or empire, which remain compatible. In multinational states, in addition to the imperial identity, individuals may share one or more "national" loyalties or identities. In the Russian Empire, many Ukrainian-speaking people labelled themselves Little Russian and Russian at the same time. They did not think they contradicted themselves in doing so.[39] In contrast, members of the Ukrainian national movement, inspired by the poet Taras Shevchenko (1814–1861) and the historian Mykhailo Hrushevsky (1866–1934), introduced a new framework of mutually exclusive identities, setting the Ukrainian identity at centre stage and completely separating it from the Russian and Polish communities. Shevchenko played the same role in the history of Ukraine as did Alexander Pushkin and Adam Mickiewicz for their own nations. The Ukrainian poet emerged as the "Bard and Prophet, the inspired voice of the people, and the spiritual leader of the reborn nation."[40] Hrushevsky, in turn, provided a coherent nationalist model for framing the narrative of the Ukrainian past, present, and future.

If Shevchenko recognized the worthiness of the common peasant language, Hrushevsky validated the uniqueness of Ukraine's history. Employing a scholarly apparatus of historical texts, bibliographies, and footnotes, Hrushevsky scientifically proved that it existed.[41] Both gave the illiterate and powerless Ukrainian-speaking masses a national voice and a sense of dignity in an environment that had denied both.[42]

Integration and Russification

As the Russian state expanded its territorial holdings steadily from the sixteenth century to the eve of the First World War, "the addition of its separate parts never constituted a well-integrated whole."[43] Instead of a unitary state, the Russian government established an unwieldy empire containing different regions, religions, traditions and cultures, social groups, and proto-national bodies.

By the end of the nineteenth century, the Romanov dynasty – which hitherto had not identified itself completely with the Russian nation – now played the "Russian card." Haunted by the failure to integrate the Poles into its empire and following the example of Bismarck's 1871 unification of Germany (which unleashed a major campaign against its Catholic and Polish minorities), the Russian Empire became a nationalizing state. Under its last three tsars (Alexander II, Alexander III, and Nicholas II), Russia's political and cultural elites identified Russia as the ethnocultural core of the empire and claimed that the Russians occupied a weak cultural, economic, and demographic position within the state and within Eurasia. In order to overcome these handicaps, they gradually advocated policies favouring the language, culture, and political hegemony of the Russians over the non-Russians, especially in the empire's borderlands.[44]

The Russian Empire never pursued a policy of totally assimilating its entire non-Russian population into the Russian nation, but it benefited from long-term natural and voluntary Russification. Building on this natural

Russification, administrative Russification followed a different blueprint. In creating its empire, Russian leaders followed a pattern of conquest and acquisition, incorporation and assimilation.[45] Once an internationally undisputed territory came under effective Russian control, administrators soon introduced and extended the social and administrative system prevalent in Russian provinces. Muscovy and the territories it acquired did not possess a strong feudal tradition and Russian administrators did not respect political autonomy, juridical separateness, or regionalism.[46] Cultural and social integration soon followed.[47] With the conquest of non-Christian, nomadic societies, those that possessed people socially and economically less complex than contemporary Russians, imperial administrators sought to settle the nomads and to make them into peasants.

The conquest and incorporation of the Baltic provinces, Finland, and the Congress Kingdom of Poland (established by the Congress of Vienna in 1815), however, followed a different playbook. Because "the original acquisition had been accomplished through military conquest ratified by international treaty, the imperial government began by guaranteeing a special status to the newly conquered lands and by promising to respect the autonomy and privileges of the local ruling classes."[48]

These "special status" regions created a complex problem for the imperial authorities at the end of the nineteenth century. Their very existence "undermined the concept of the unitary nature of the Russian state and raised questions about the sovereign, who was the constitutional Grand Duke of Finland and the King of Poland, while remaining the autocratic Emperor of all Russia."[49] After suppressing the Polish revolt of 1863, the tsarist authorities sought to solve this political contradiction by introducing Russian institutions, laws, and the Russian language into schools and the local bureaucracy in order to bind the Congress Kingdom, the Baltic provinces, and Finland tighter into the empire. Despite enormous resistance, the distinctive features of the "special status" regions eroded. Under Alexander III, Russian authorities introduced similar policies among the Armenians, the Volga Tatars, the Georgians, and other groups.

Advocates of cultural Russification aspired to move beyond social and administrative uniformity – to assimilation. In their opinion, Russia "could only become a modern national state if her borderland minorities accepted the language and cultural and religious values of the Russian people."[50] They endorsed an accelerated form of natural Russification, especially among peoples closest culturally to the Russians. In the second half of the nineteenth century, the authorities emphasized administrative Russification for most of its non-Russian population. But with respect to the Ukrainians, Belarusans, and the peoples of the North, they promoted cultural Russification.

Although the Russian authorities tolerated the Ukrainophile movement in the Ukrainian provinces in 1845–6, 1859–62, and 1869–75, the tsarist government systematized its efforts against those who identified themselves as Ukrainians, not Little Russians (the official designation of the second-largest East Slavic group in the empire). In June 1847, after the arrests of the members of the Cyryllo-Methodius Society (which included Taras Shevchenko), A.F. Orlov, Tsar Nicholas I's chief of police, ordered his subordinates "to prevent teachers and writers on both sides of the Dnieper River from putting *rodina* (the motherland, region of birth) ahead of *otechestvo* (the fatherland, the state as a whole)."[51] In July 1863, Petr Valuev, the minister of internal affairs, banned all scholarly, religious, and pedagogical publications in the Ukrainian language. Only poetry and fiction could appear in the "Little Russian dialect." Valuev declared that the Ukrainian language "never existed, does not exist, and shall never exist." With the Ems Decree of 1876, Tsar Alexander II officially forbade the publication and importation of Ukrainian books and prohibited the use of Ukrainian on stage and in the elementary schools.[52] This ban lasted until early 1905, when the Council of Ministers accepted the Russian Academy of Sciences' recommendation to eliminate these restrictions.[53]

The tsarist government prohibited Ukrainian works "not because of their contents (the same books could have appeared in another language), but because of their language."[54] (Although conservative tsarist censors allowed the publication of *The Communist Manifesto* in Russian, they prohibited the Bible from appearing in Ukrainian). Tsarist policy towards Ukrainians, moreover, diverged from those directed at other national groups. Although the government oppressed the Poles, Finns, and Georgians, it did not challenge their claim to be distinct and separate nations. Ukrainians, however, were treated differently.

According to official tsarist imperial interpretations, Ukrainians formed the Little Russian part of the all-Russian, Orthodox nation, which possessed three branches (the Russian, Little Russian, and Belarusan lines). The Little Russians and Belarusans spoke mutually comprehensible East Slavic dialects and shared the Orthodox Christian faith (even the Ukrainian-speaking Greek Catholics in the Habsburg Monarchy had a similar liturgy).[55] Because the cultural differences among the East Slavs appeared to them to be small, authorities claimed that the Russians constituted approximately 66 per cent of the total population.[56] In reality, the Russians comprised only approximately 43.3 per cent of the total population of the empire in 1897 (the Ukrainians

17.1, and the Belarusans 4.6).[57] The discrepancy between the official understanding of these statistics and the numbers themselves represented the elites' national security concerns in an age of international competition.

Russian authorities did not discriminate against men and women of Little Russian origin who did not attempt to politicize their identity and who recognized their role within the "all-Russian" political landscape. Russian officials, historians, and public commentators interpreted the history of "Little-Russia" as an integral part of mainstream Russian history; they perceived the "Little Russians" as "nashi" (ours). In contrast, the government repressed all individuals who demonstrated a distinct Ukrainian identity "in the political or cultural sphere."[58] The authorities considered the act of identifying oneself as a Ukrainian instead of a Little Russian as a political and anti-governmental act.

The tsars, according to David Saunders, feared the subversion of the empire's Ukrainian community by outside powers and sought "to stamp out the proto-nationalist activities" of a small number of nationally conscious Ukrainian intellectuals.[59] In light of the constant competition among the European powers in the nineteenth century and Russia's seemingly permanent internal insecurity, the empire's political elite aspired to keep the Great Russians, the Little Russians, and the Belarusans together, by force if necessary.

As Saunders pointed out, Ukraine's geographic location in the empire and its population explosion influenced these Russian anxieties. Located at the Western borderlands, Little Russians constituted the second-largest East Slavic group and the second-largest Orthodox population within the empire. Most importantly, they participated in a hereditary land tenure system, not a repartitional communal one as did most Russian peasants.[60] Primarily a peasant group, they possessed nearly half of the total non-Russian peasants in the empire. Most importantly, from the perspective of those always concerned about the prospect of a peasant uprising, the empire's Ukrainian-speaking provinces experienced disturbing demographic changes in the second half of the nineteenth century.

Shortly after the emancipation in 1861, the peasants experienced small improvements in the availability and quality of rural health care, which made them embrace new ideas about their economic future. Although the size of the average household (between five and six members) did not decrease, the number of households did increase dramatically. This growth in population, combined with the gentry's ability to retain their lands, sharply reduced the average peasant's landholdings. In 1861 the amount of land per peasant averaged 2.9 *desiatiny*; by 1906, it had declined to 1.4.

Peasant holdings in Kiev, Podolia, and Volhynia comprised the smallest in the Russian Empire.[61] The peasants in the Ukrainian-speaking provinces, like those throughout the empire, ascribed their land hunger to the vastness of the landlord holdings.[62]

Although the emancipation of the serfs did not lead to a complete capitalist transformation of the Russian and Little Russian rural areas, by 1905 the Ukrainian-speaking provinces had become the breadbasket of Europe. "Ninety percent of its arable land was devoted to winter and summer grains which were exported in massive quantities along Russia's quickly expanding railroad network and through the thriving port cities on the Black Sea."[63] The steppe provinces of Kherson and Ekaterinoslav produced most of this trade. Chernigov, Poltava, and Kharkov on the Left Bank also sent grain abroad. The overpopulated Right Bank provinces, however, did not raise grain for an external market to the degree that the other Ukrainian-speaking provinces did.[64]

Following the same post-1861 trends within the empire, which produced one of the highest rates of growth in the world, the population in the Ukrainian-speaking provinces nearly doubled between 1870 and 1914. By 1897 the provinces possessed the highest population density (at 55 per square kilometre) in European Russia.[65] The Little Russians steadily increased their share of the total population in the nine provinces. By 1897, most Ukrainian speakers were under twenty years of age, and this cohort represented nearly 40 per cent of the *entire* population. At the turn of the century, this youth bulge grew rapidly, strengthening the Ukrainian-speaking majority in Russia's southwestern provinces.[66] Most precariously, almost all of these men and women engaged in agricultural pursuits. If these trends continued, the Ukrainian-speaking provinces would become a very crowded social and political tinderbox.

In light of this population explosion, the authorities "feared any effort to mobilize [this group] along national or social grounds" and introduced repressive measures to restrict the potential lines of communication between the small Ukrainophile intelligentsia living in the towns and cities and the overwhelming majority of Little Russians in the countryside.[67] These edicts hampered the intelligentsia's efforts to establish and institutionalize contact with the peasants and to overcome their illiteracy in their own language. By banning Ukrainian-language schools and publications, these decrees prevented the emergence of alternative communications networks linking the cities with the countryside. The Ukrainophiles wanted to empower the peasants, but this mission challenged "the political philosophy of the tsarist regime."[68]

As the Ukrainian-speaking provinces industrialized in the late nineteenth century, they attracted literate men from Central Russia to the new industrial centres but only a small number of Ukrainian-speaking peasants. This migration of Russian workers reinforced Russian as the language of work and of the cities. Industrialization, in effect, promoted an overwhelmingly Russian urban environment. The countryside remained a universe of spoken, but illiterate, Ukrainian.

The end of serfdom and the beginning of industrialization intensified the competition between Russian and Ukrainian. As the officially sanctioned language and as the language of modernization, Russian experienced an upsurge; Ukrainian, a decline. According to Ronald Wardhaugh, a language in decline is "likely to have a rural base only and to lack strength in towns and cities" and is "likely to have stronger associations with older, uneducated, and rural speakers and lack those of progress and modernity."[69] Industrialization and Russification, then, tilted the urban language competition towards Russian. Migration and Russification reoriented the migrants' "culturally defined need to read and write."[70] Migration into the cities made literacy a necessity and literacy in Russian essential. Learning to read and write in Russian made this national identity and culture attractive to those who already possessed the predisposition to change their social status. The mass illiteracy of the peasants who spoke Ukrainian and the governmental bans on Ukrainian-language schools and books hampered the Ukrainophile intelligentsia's efforts in primary "nation-building," which Ivan L. Rudnytsky defined as "the penetration of all strata of the population by the national idea, the transformation of an ethnic mass into a culturally and politically self-conscious national community."[71]

In order to establish an imagined community of Ukrainians, members of this group had to agree on a common set of characteristics that constituted their identity and its boundaries.[72] According to nationalists, not only did the Ukrainian speakers need to clarify their own identity, they also had to define the "other," especially the Russians, who remained culturally close to them. But in a hostile political environment and without Ukrainian-language schools, a mass-based literacy in Ukrainian, or Ukrainian publications, a mass dialogue on these critical issues could not develop. Without this vital discussion, the Ukrainian national movement could not attract the masses necessary to move from Hroch's academic stage to the cultural and nationalist stages. Without this exchange, members of the Ukrainian national movement could not form a consensus defining themselves and their compatriots.

Within the Habsburg Empire

The Austrian Empire, especially the Austro-Hungarian Empire after 1867, differed radically from the Russian and German empires. Although it had accumulated diverse territories over the centuries, it had never formed a strong centralized government or a nationalizing state in the nineteenth and early twentieth centuries. Despite occasional attempts to move in this political direction, the Empress Maria Teresa (ruled: 1740–80) and her Habsburg successors granted more freedoms to their subjects than did the Romanovs or the Hohenzollerns, especially in the cultural sphere.

In official documents and censuses, the Austrian government classified these Ukrainian speakers as "Ruthenen" (Ruthenians), which came from the term Rusyn, which many members of the local population called themselves. By categorizing themselves as *Rusyny* they identified themselves with the Kiev Rus state. Although these peasants understood that their ethnic and religious backgrounds separated them from their Polish neighbours, their distinctiveness did not constitute a clear national consciousness.[73] Only at the end of the nineteenth century, as the Ukrainian national movement expanded its influence, did they begin to adopt the modern term "Ukrainian" to better describe themselves and to separate themselves from their non-Ukrainian neighbours.[74]

By the end of the eighteenth century, the Austrian Empire controlled three Ukrainian-speaking territories: Transcarpathia, Galicia, and Bukovina. Despite the preponderance of Ruthenians in these provinces, all three possessed ethnically mixed populations and non-indigenous noble elites. With the incorporation of these territories into the empire, the Austrian authorities retained the Polish nobility (*szlachta*) in Galicia, the Romanian boyars in Bukovina, and the Hungarian nobles in Transcarpathia to rule over the peasants. At the same time, they introduced a new set of political actors, the Austrian bureaucracy, to implement imperial policies.

Although the Ukrainian speakers constituted the majority of the population in Eastern Galicia (62 per cent of the population in 1910), they did not possess political control of this region. Social divisions reflected national divisions: Poles formed the majority of the great landowning class, and of the 1,500 great landowners who owned 40 per cent of the land in Eastern Galicia, only 47 identified themselves as Ruthenians. Over 90 per cent of the Ruthenians worked as peasants; few – if any – belonged to the middle class.[75] Most of those who lived in the Galician towns and cities classified themselves as Poles or Jews.[76]

Unlike their compatriots in Eastern Galicia, the Ruthenians in Bukovina composed a plurality of the population (38.4 per cent of the province, according to the Austrian census of 1910). This province was a distinct administrative entity from 1775 to 1786, when the authorities united it with Galicia. After 1849 it formed a separate political unit. A Ukrainian-oriented intelligentsia emerged in this predominantly Orthodox crownland only at the end of the nineteenth century, after the expansion of its elementary school system and after the establishment of the University of Chernowitz in 1875. This Ukrainian Orthodox intelligentsia worked very closely with its Galician Greek-Catholic counterpart, its role model, in developing the Ukrainian identity in this region.

As the largest Slavic group in Bukovina, the Ruthenians competed with the Romanians (who represented 34 per cent of the province), who also sought to gain control of it.[77] Ruthenian efforts to divide Bukovina into a northern part (which contained the Ukrainian-speaking majority) from the southern part (which contained the Romanian-speaking majority) failed prior to the outbreak of the First World War.[78]

Transcarpathia constituted the most illiterate, the most impoverished, and the most isolated area within the entire empire. Here, the Hungarian nobles closely allied themselves with parish priests (mostly from the Greek Catholic Church) and politically and economically controlled the Ruthenians (who called themselves "Rusyns") living south of the Carpathian Mountains. After the Compromise of 1867, the Hungarian authorities introduced measures favouring the Hungarian (Magyar) language in the church, the bureaucracy, and educational institutions.

This official Magyarization limited the size and the impact of local Ukrainian intelligentsia, thwarting its efforts to mobilize the Ukrainian-speaking masses. By 1910, fewer than 1 per cent of the teachers, notaries, lawyers, priests, or journalists identified themselves as Ukrainian speakers.[79] In this region, the Hungarian, Russian, and local Rusyn identities competed with the Ukrainian identity and attracted many (if not the majority) of the small educated population.

Although the Rusyns in Hungarian-controlled Transcarpathia did not enjoy the same official support as did their compatriots in Austrian-controlled Galicia and Bukovina, all of the empire's Ukrainian speakers lived in a state that tolerated the slow emergence of a civil society, however weak its implementation on both sides of the realm.[80] Not only did the Habsburgs allow religious and cultural diversity, they also permitted broad civic and economic initiatives on the part of their subjects.

By allowing the peasants legal remedies in their struggles against their landlords, even granting them the right to sue the nobles in court, Maria Theresa and Joseph II (ruled: 1780–90) hoped to strengthen the peasants as a social class, not to set them against their lords. Although the peasants did not always win their lawsuits, this initiative transformed the Ruthenian masses in Galicia into loyal supporters of the Habsburg dynasty until the end of the monarchy in 1918. Austria, for the most part, operated as a Rechstaat, a state based on laws, however imperfectly implemented.

In addition to protecting peasants within the institution of serfdom, Austrian policies also helped create the Ukrainian intelligentsia, which emerged from within the ranks of the Greek Catholic Church. Like other European monarchs, Maria Theresa and Joseph II sought to subordinate the church hierarchy to Austria and to transform clergymen into state officials who would represent the secular authority of the state. By introducing policies that promoted equal rights for all Christian faiths within their kingdom, they strengthened the Ruthenian clergy, who had lived in poverty and ignorance. Maria Theresa, moreover, decreed that Austrian authorities employ the term "Greek Catholic" (instead of "Uniate") in order to promote the equality between the Greek and Roman rites.[81]

In order to transform these clergymen and clergywomen into efficient emissaries of the state, the Austrian authorities created a number of institutions to educate them properly. Maria Theresa and Joseph II established Greek Catholic theological seminaries in Vienna, Lemberg, Ungvár, and Czernowitz in the 1770s and 1780s. In 1784 the Austrian government founded the University of Lemberg and allowed members of the theological faculty to give lectures in Old Church Slavonic, the Ruthenian church language. In 1808 the authorities elevated the Greek Catholic Lemberg bishopric to the rank of Metropolitan See of Galicia.[82]

But even with the Austrian control of Galicia, the Ruthenian clergy and hierarchy continued to adopt Polish as their working language. Church leaders believed that the vernacular represented a vulgar, common language and prohibited their clergy from employing their native language in official correspondence. They found only Polish and Old Church Slavonic acceptable languages.

Under these circumstances, many Greek Catholic priests did not know how to read or write Ruthenian, the language of their parishioners. Many candidates for the priesthood, moreover, did not even know their prayers in that language. Instead, the clergy used Polish, which the Ruthenian peasants in Galicia generally understood. As a result, the Polish language and culture dominated the Ruthenian intelligentsia until the 1830s. A subsequent Polish-Ruthenian struggle over religion, schooling, and language sought to redress this actual and perceptual inequality.

As Austria emerged as a liberal autocracy, the Habsburg Monarchy became a haven for Poles, Ruthenians, and other non-German groups. After the great Austro-Hungarian Compromise of 1867, Austria's new constitution proclaimed that "all nationalities in the state enjoy equal rights, and each one has an inalienable right to the preservation and cultivation of its nationality and language" not only in private life, but also in schools, the civil service, and public life.[83] The leaders of these emergent non-German national movements then employed their limited constitutional freedoms and sought not only to enhance the quality of life of their national groups within the empire, but also to connect their movements with those of their compatriots within Romania, Serbia, and the German, Ottoman, and Russian empires.

Austria, although a liberal monarchy, did not constitute a democratic society. Elected deputies held the right to initiate legislation, supervise the activities of the government, and impeach its ministers, but the emperor, not the majority party or coalition of parties in the house of deputies, chose the Austrian government's ministers.

Despite these limitations, the Austrian political system after 1848 evolved in a semi-democratic direction. It allowed elected representatives; held free, generally fair and frequent elections; tolerated freedom of expression and voluntary associations; established an independent judiciary and an impartial and reasonably neutral civil service. This political environment differed radically from that prevailing in Russia, which never approximated the civil society Austria had created.[84]

Living under a system of constitutional law, the Ukrainian movement in Austria-Hungary became a mass movement by the eve of the First World War.[85] Concentrated in Eastern Galicia, with its capital of Lemberg (Lwów/ Lviv), it inspired the creation of thousands of Ruthenian civic organizations – clubs, banks, schools, bookstores, credit unions, and cooperatives that promoted the Ukrainian idea in the region. The mass diffusion of this imagined community occurred within an area of high population density, intense rural poverty, and clear ethnic diversity, which generated antagonisms with the Polish authorities, who controlled Galicia on behalf of the Austrians. The tensions between the Poles and the Ruthenians embittered both groups, forging a permanent state of mutual mistrust and enmity.[86] These political and socio-economic conflicts, in turn, made the Ukrainian idea very attractive to the Ukrainian-speaking masses.[87]

Most importantly, by the mid-nineteenth century the leadership of the Ukrainian movement in Galicia considered itself an integral part of the

Ukrainian homeland controlled by St Petersburg. During the revolutions of 1848, Austria's Supreme Ruthenian Council (Holovna Rus'ka Rada) declared that Ruthenians did not constitute a part of the Polish or Russian nations nor did they reside solely in the Austrian Empire. It asserted that Austria's Ruthenians constituted a part of a larger nation numbering fifteen million.[88] By identifying the Greek-Catholic Ukrainians in Austria with their Orthodox compatriots in Russia, this organization started the process of empowering the Ruthenians in Austria both psychologically and politically.

By establishing various civic, educational, and economic associations (not possible in the Russian Empire), the Galician Ukrainian populists penetrated the countryside. By the end of the nineteenth century they created three political parties, the Radical Party (est. 1891), the moderate National Democratic Party (est. 1899), and the Marxist Social Democratic Party (est. 1900). Each competed for votes among Ukrainians but cooperated with each other after the elections.[89]

The Austro-Hungarian government introduced another major electoral breakthrough at the imperial level in 1907.[90] It abolished the curial system of elections and instituted the general, equal, direct, and secret ballot, but only for men. This measure gave Ukrainian men their first opportunity to exert influence throughout the Austro-Hungarian Empire by parliamentary means, even though they received only half of the mandates due them based on proportional representation. Each Ukrainian deputy generally represented 102,000 Ukrainians, whereas one Pole legislated on behalf of 52,000.[91] Despite extensive gerrymandering and election fraud, the Ukrainians in Galicia elected twenty-seven deputies (seventeen National Democrats, three Radicals, two Social Democrats, and five Russophiles) in 1907. Together with the five Ukrainian deputies from Bukovina, they formed a small group in the 516-member Reichsrat, Austria's parliament, but not enough "to overcome the Polish dominance of Galician politics."[92]

In the 1890s the Ukrainian national movement in Galicia shifted from the cultural stage to the political stage. Nationally conscious Ukrainians in the Habsburg Monarchy started to abandon calling themselves "Ruthenians" (their traditional name) and assumed the name "Ukrainians," a national designation that the Ukrainian intelligentsia within the Russian Empire adopted by the early twentieth century.[93] In 1895 the Radical Party's Julian Bachynsky published *Ukraina irredenta*, which espoused the political independence of Ukraine five years before the Revolutionary Ukrainian Party in Kharkov adopted a similar slogan. Bachynsky defined Ukraine as the contiguous territory from the Sian River in the Habsburg Monarchy to the

Caucasus, including the nine Ukrainian-speaking tsarist provinces.[94] Soon all three Ukrainian parties in Galicia accepted the idea of Ukrainian independence as their ultimate goal.

New Opportunities and Options

In the last decade of the nineteenth century, a new generation of Ukrainian activists emerged within the Russian Empire. In the summer of 1891, a group of Ukrainian university students formed the secret Brotherhood of Taras (*Bratstvo tarasivtsiv*), which condemned the Ukrainophile movement for engaging only in cultural, not political, matters. As the first group of modern Ukrainian political activists in the Russian Empire, these men and women belonged to the Generation of 1917, as Olga Andriewsky coined the term. This cohort, mostly born between 1875 and 1886, became politically active around the turn of the century and started to support radical political solutions to Ukraine's problems and played a leading role in the Ukrainian Revolution of 1917–20. The powerful demographic wave at the end of the nineteenth century and the expansion of higher education, especially women's higher education, roused this generation to re-envision their political choices.[95]

Unlike the young men and women who entered the universities in the 1870s and 1880s and who enthusiastically joined the all-Russian student movement, this new generation formulated their Ukrainian identity and formed their own secret groups. When student protests escalated throughout the Russian Empire in 1899 and politicized most students, they created the Union of Ukrainian Students (Students'ka hromada). In 1900, a branch of this student group in Kharkov established the Revolutionary Ukrainian Party (RUP). In the same year, RUP published Mykola Mikhnovsky's pamphlet *Samostiina Ukraina* (Independent Ukraine), which presented a program for "a single, united, indivisible, free and independent Ukraine from the Carpathian to the Caucasian mountains."[96] Although Mikhnovsky did not precisely define this territory, he vehemently declared "Ukraine for Ukrainians." He asserted that even "if one foreign enemy remained in this territory, we do not have the right to lay down our weapons."[97] Although this pamphlet represented a minority view among the small number of nationally conscious Ukrainians, the issue of Ukrainian independence emerged. However far-fetched an idea at the beginning of the twentieth century, the tsarist authorities could not stamp out this radical political option. Their worst nightmare finally appeared on the horizon.

The idea of Ukrainian independence had developed slowly. Due to the overwhelming concentration of Ukrainian speakers in the countryside, the high level of rural illiteracy, the Orthodox religious faith, and the government's prohibitions against publishing in Ukrainian, the Ukrainian movement within Russia remained locked in the academic and cultural stages for nearly fifty years. Patriotic agitators, mostly intellectuals from the cities, could not establish a mass national movement in the countryside, the location of its largest potential base of support.

Only as a result of the massive unrest unleashed by the Russian Revolution of 1905 did the tsarist government stop enforcing the discriminatory measures against the Ukrainian language. That year the Imperial Academy of Sciences identified Ukrainian as a language separate from Russian. Spurred by the revolution and official tolerance, activists established many Ukrainian-language newspapers and journals, although readership remained small due to the illiteracy and poverty of the majority of the population. Nevertheless, the Ukrainian national movement slowly gained the sympathy and adherence of the rural intelligentsia, the so-called "Third Element," in the cooperative movement. They, in turn, attracted some of the peasants. Although the government's repressions after 1907 circumscribed the Ukrainian movement's gains, the rapid expansion of the cooperative movement in the urban and rural areas before the outbreak of the First World War helped the Ukrainian-speaking peasants to identify with the Ukrainian national movement.[98]

In March 1914, on the centenary of Shevchenko's birth, popular demonstrations with thousands of participants took place in Kiev and Kharkov. These demonstrations – however impressive in light of the Ukrainian movement's recent history – did not yet represent a socially integrated mass movement.

Conclusion

Despite their large numbers spanning the borderlands of two major empires, the Ukrainian-speaking population of East Central Europe on the eve of the twentieth century represented an ethnographic mass, not a single national community. According to the Austrian historian Andreas Kappeler, this group had three serious political, social, and cultural handicaps.[99] First of all, this large body of people did not possess an upper class representing their own group. Inasmuch as the Polish-Lithuanian Commonwealth destroyed the Cossack elite and the Russian Empire co-opted it, the Ukrainian-speaking population (with the exception of those on the Left Bank) had an "incomplete" social structure.[100] Although most of the ambitious Ukrainian speakers joined the Russian world, they did not necessarily become Russians. Some "retained a double loyalty, a Little Russian as well as a Russian identity," which could shift in emphasis depending on the social or political situation.[101] Some of these Left Bank nobles preserved the autonomist traditions of the Hetmanate, celebrated a Little Russian regional patriotism, and provided most of the Ukrainian national movement's activists and sponsors. But they never approximated the unity (much less the power) of the Polish nobility within the empire.

Second, the Ukrainian speakers in both empires formed "an ethnic unity, but not an independent political unit."[102] At the end of the nineteenth century, Ukrainian speakers were politically divided, living in three different administrative jurisdictions: the "Little Russians" in the Russian Empire, the "Ruthenians" in Austria, and the "Rusyns" in Hungary. The "Ukrainian homeland" also served as the homeland for many other groups.

Third, this large mass of Ukrainian speakers did not possess a standardized language common in both empires. According to George Y. Shevelov, a prominent linguist, a certain norm of usage existed, but "it was not codified, nor even exhaustively described, and there was no authority to prescribe it."[103] Despite regional dialectical differences, the leaders of the two Ukrainian national movements in Austria and Russia agreed that "all Ukrainians should have the same standard literary language and that that standard should be based on the Central Ukrainian (Kiev-Poltava region) dialects upon which the language of the most influential classical writers, Taras Shevchenko and Marko Vovchok (1834–1907), was built."[104] This goal was easier proclaimed than implemented.

According to the Russian imperial census of 1897, 81 per cent of Ukrainian speakers over the age of ten could not read or write, which constituted the second-highest illiteracy rate among the peoples of the western Russian Empire (only the Moldovans were more illiterate).[105] The situation was only slightly better in Austria-Hungary's Ukrainian-speaking territories. In 1900, 74 per cent of the adult population of Galicia, Bukovina, and Transcarpathia could not read or write.[106] This illiteracy undermined the diffusion of the Ukrainian idea, as did the 1863 and 1876 tsarist bans on the public use of the Ukrainian language. In an age without electronic mass media, Ukrainian activists could not spread their message very effectively without a literate population and without Ukrainian-language publications. They, moreover, had a difficult message to propagate.

In the second half of the nineteenth century, Ukrainophiles in Austria-Hungary sought to persuade Ukrainian-speaking peasants that they formed part of a larger Ukrainian world, not a local isolated identity (the Old Ruthenian movement) or a branch of the Russian people (the Russophile movement). Despite the social and economic handicaps they encountered, especially in Transcarpathia (a small geographically isolated area), the Ukrainophiles in the Austro-Hungarian Empire possessed an easier challenge than did their compatriots in Russia.

Ukrainian activists in the Habsburg Empire presented a vision of a "larger Ukraine" to their compatriots. But those in the Romanov Empire manifested a "smaller Ukraine."

In contrast to the Greek-Catholic Ukrainians in Galicia, who clearly perceived their differences with the Roman Catholic Poles, the overwhelming majority of Ukrainian-speaking peasants in the Russian Empire saw themselves as part of the overall Orthodox religious majority within their imperial domain. Ukrainophile agitators in the Russian Empire possessed the unenviable task of convincing Ukrainian-speaking peasants that they "belonged" to a different, but smaller world (the Ukrainian one) rather than to the larger peasant, Orthodox or Russian worlds. They had to persuade their intended brethren that their homeland encompassed only the nine Ukrainian-speaking provinces (not the entire Russian Empire) and the Austrian Ukrainian-speaking areas of Bukovina, Transcarpathia, and Galicia. In an environment of poverty, illiteracy, and political powerlessness, it proved difficult, but not impossible, to attract the masses to this new vision of their homeland.

PART ONE

The First Total War and Its Aftershocks

2

The First World War and
Imperial Convulsions

As much as anything, World War I turned on the fate of Ukraine ... Without Ukraine's population, industry, and agriculture, early twentieth-century Russia would have ceased to be a great power. If Russia ceased to be a great power, then there was every possibility that Germany would dominate Europe.

Dominic Lieven[1]

In all history, there is no instance of a country having benefited from prolonged warfare. Only one who knows the disastrous effects of a long war can realize the supreme importance of rapidity in bringing it to a close.

Sun Tzu[2]

The nineteenth century's industrial revolution, Europe's population explosion, and the emergence of mass politics helped unify Germany and Italy and hastened the Ottoman Empire's decay. The building of mass armies and their support systems spurred the creation of two rival military coalitions, the Triple Alliance (Germany, Austria-Hungary, and Italy) and the Triple Entente (Great Britain, France, and the Russian Empire) by the turn of the twentieth century (see map 4). The subsequent naval race between Germany and Great Britain, and conflicts in the Balkans among Austria-Hungary, the Ottoman Empire, Russia, and Serbia aggravated tensions among the major powers and set the stage for the world's first total war. The assassination of Austria's Archduke Franz Ferdinand and his wife, Archduchess Sophie, on 28 June 1914 ignited the conflict.

In response to these political murders, the Habsburg Monarchy declared war against Serbia on 28 July. This act transformed the Austrian-Serbian conflict from a local war to a European one, ultimately involving all of the world's major powers. Serbia's ally, Imperial Russia, mobilized its armed forces on 30 July, reaffirming its role as the defender of all Slavs. Germany then marshalled troops on 1 August and implemented the von Schlieffen plan, a highly intricate blueprint to defeat France (Russia's primary ally) and then smash the Russian Empire – all to prevent a two-front war. But this game plan failed. Both France and Russia survived Germany's initial blows and isolated the Central Powers. Although the Allies boxed in the Central Powers, they could not penetrate the box. Due to this stalemate, the First World War became "the first calamity of the twentieth century, the calamity from which all other calamities sprang."[3]

All of the belligerents fought to protect, if not enhance, their own national and imperial interests, but simultaneously they sincerely believed that "they were waging war because it would bring a new and radiant world into the future." This armageddon would redeem humanity and create "a purified world rid of a central flaw: war." Europe's political and military elites adopted this vision long before the popularization of President Woodrow Wilson's 1917 declaration that the conflict represented "a war to end all wars."[4]

By November 1914, just as the Ottoman Empire joined the Central Powers, troops on the western front became entrenched in a brutal ground war. Generals and politicians on both sides introduced unprecedented forms of violence to break the stalemate. Universal conscription generated "ever more apocalyptic confrontations, as the increased ease with which soldiers could be replaced led to ever bloodier fighting."[5]

The "messianic intensity of the war" produced hundreds of thousands, even millions, of casualties in a single battle without any significant breakthrough.[6] The first battle of the Marne (September 1914), the Gallipoli campaign (April 1915–January 1916), the battle of Verdun (February–December 1916), the Brusilov offensive (June–September 1916), the battle of the Somme (July–November 1916), the third battle of Ypres (July–November 1917), and the German spring offensive of 1918 *each* killed or wounded at least 500,000 soldiers.[7] The armed conflict between the two military alliances became a mechanized mass killing machine that lasted more than four years. Europe's industrialization in the nineteenth century led to industrialized warfare and to the institutionalization of the culture of mass violence in the twentieth.

Austria's short-lived thrust into Russian Poland on 19 September 1914 induced the Russian army to counter-attack, advancing nearly 300 kilometres into Austria-Hungary and occupying Eastern Galicia and part of Western Galicia.[8] Within six months of the war's beginning, the Austro-Hungarian army had lost over 1,250,000 men. and by March 1915 another

800,000.[9] But the Dual Monarchy's offensive in the spring of 1915 succeeded, and Austro-Hungarian troops expelled the tsarist army from Galicia.

As the Russian army withdrew, its generals initiated a "scorched earth" policy and forcibly removed several hundred thousand Austro-Hungarian civilians, including women and children, back behind their own lines. By the end of 1915, the Russian army had lost about four million men (killed, wounded, missing, and taken prisoner).[10] In June 1916, the Russian army redirected its attacks on the southwestern front in the direction of Galicia and reoccupied this territory a second time and for nearly a year.

By the end of the winter of 1916–17, the Russian army's morale had plunged to an all-time low; the generals no longer trusted the conscripts they commanded. Food shortages in the major industrial cities aggravated the situation. With an early spring thaw in late February 1917, hungry men and women participated in mass demonstrations in Petrograd against their own government. With the outbreak of street violence, instigated by the local police and military command, rank-and-file soldiers refused to shoot at the protesters and joined them. Facing a complete breakdown of the Russian political order during a major war, members of Russia's last parliament, the Fourth Duma, persuaded Nicholas II to abdicate.[11]

Immediately after the February Revolution in Petrograd, the new Provisional Government pledged to continue the war "solely for the defense of the Russian homeland," but the majority of the troops did not share this outlook. Most rank-and-file soldiers who came from the empire's rural areas lost faith in their officers and never gave the new Provisional Government a chance. Men defending the larger cities in the rear did not want to fight the Austrians, much less the Germans. Non-Russian soldiers and officers on the front lines insisted on creating separate military units solely composed of their compatriots.

Despite this breakdown within its military ranks, Russia's Provisional Government initiated another offensive on the southwestern front in late June 1917; a swift German counter-attack stopped this effort. After a loss of 200,000 troops in one week, the Russian army melted away. Soldiers "voted with their feet," taking weapons with them. They rushed back to their villages in order to claim a "fair share" of the land for themselves and their families.

The Russian and Austrian empires constituted the weakest links within the two competing military alliances. As large, multinational dynastic empires, they did not adjust well to the ever-increasing demands of the war. Russia's geographic isolation from its allies, bureaucratic mismanagement, and political backwardness brought defeat. Nicholas II and his subordinates could not imagine, much less implement, policies which would unify the military and home fronts. He and his inner circle never established a government of national unity, as did Britain, France, and Germany. The tsar considered any compromise of his political authority as an erosion of his autocratic power. In his narrow view of the world, reinforcing the autocracy remained the only strategy for Russian victory.[12]

At the start of hostilities, Nicholas's military entourage demonstrated a reckless level of incompetence by failing to equip recruits with enough rifles, ammunition, or boots. Russia's political leadership ignored public opinion, while Austria feared "imposing any strain on the doubtful loyalty of its population" and "barely attempted to plan a siege economy or to administer a rationing system."[13] Both empires introduced policies that alienated the very people whose support they needed to win the war. In the new era of total war, both empires collapsed.

Hearts and Minds

At the outbreak of hostilities, most citizens and subjects of the belligerent powers – including the Ukrainian speakers in both empires – enthusiastically embraced the war and their respective governments. With the major exception of the Bolsheviks (the radical wing of the Russian Social Democratic Workers Party), most Europeans saluted their own country's flags and sang national anthems with booming voices. But the front lines shifted often, conscripting, killing, and displacing not only millions of soldiers, but also millions of civilians. Enormous battlefield losses and the widespread destruction of villages and towns on the ever-shifting front disillusioned millions of soldiers, refugees, and civilians, even those far from the zones of engagement. By mobilizing "official" mass national identities and by forcibly evicting hundreds of thousands from their homes, these governments undermined the old pre-war imperial and dynastic loyalties. Radical, anti-imperial, and nationalist allegiances replaced them.[14]

On 1 January 1914, the Russian Empire possessed a population of 167.7 million; approximately 120 million lived in European Russia's fifty provinces. From 1 August 1914 until 1 April 1917, the authorities called up 13.7 million men, who joined the ranks of its peacetime army that numbered 1,423,000 at the start of the war. Approximately 90 per cent of the total number of men conscripted in European Russia came from its overpopulated rural areas, a disproportionate share of the empire's peasant population.[15] From 1914 to 1 September 1917, the military drafted approximately

2,885,000 men from the nine Ukrainian-speaking provinces, a total that did not include recruits from Bessarabia, Kursk, and Orel, which also possessed large Ukrainian-speaking populations. Of these men, nearly two million may have identified themselves as "Little Russians," but we may never know for certain.[16]

The tsarist authorities did not properly coordinate their inflow of peasants into the military. In the course of the war, the military recruited up to 40 per cent of the empire's able-bodied male population and requisitioned horses necessary to work the farms.[17] Peasant families in Novorossiia and the southwest provinces close to the front experienced extensive military and labour conscription. By 1917, nearly 40 per cent of all peasant households in some provinces, such as Kharkov, did not possess adult males to work the fields.[18] Although women stepped into the breach, the delicate inter-regional balance of grain production and railway transport encountered intense pressures and broke down.[19]

Approximately two million soldiers serving in the Russian army (nearly 10.5 per cent of those mobilized during the war) died on the battlefield or from wounds or diseases experienced there.[20] Although it is difficult to ascertain the national identities of those who died, one American scholar estimated in the 1960s that within the Russian army nearly 450,000 men from the Ukrainian-speaking provinces perished, as did nearly 120,000 from Austria-Hungary's Ukrainian provinces.[21] Recently, scholars at the Ukrainian Institute of Demography in Kiev asserted that in the Ukrainian-speaking provinces of Russia and Austria-Hungary some 1.3 million men, women, and children died prematurely during the First World War. Another 2.3 million "excess deaths" occurred during the post-1917 civil and national wars, the brief Polish-Soviet War of 1920, the famine of 1921–2, and the subsequent cholera, diphtheria, dysentery, and typhoid epidemics which followed wartime conditions and shortages.[22]

These statistics may not include birth deficits or emigration, but even without those, the losses are staggering. Most importantly, this long continuum of mass violence decimated an entire generation of young men from the Ukrainian-speaking provinces and even killed large numbers of civilians.

The survivors became disillusioned with the authorities and with the status quo. High attrition rates, the duration of the conflict, and the uncertainty of a speedy victory created an irreconcilable breach between (1) the soldiers, non-commissioned officers, and recently promoted junior officers and (2) their senior officers and generals. The frustrations in the lower ranks inspired them to find salvation in various radical national and social causes after the February Revolution.[23]

Even prisoners were not immune. The armies on the eastern front captured unprecedented numbers of prisoners of war and relocated them in isolated places far behind military lines. In addition to feeding their own men, European militaries spent scarce resources to guard and provide food for millions of their adversaries. By employing propagandists in the camps, the captors hoped to turn them against their former imperial masters. In summary, the war caused enormous social and economic upheavals, especially for those living in the Ukrainian-speaking provinces closest to the shifting front. It radicalized the masses and encouraged many Ukrainian speakers to imagine themselves as Ukrainians and to explore a new political concept, national independence.

Vincent Shandor, an important official in Transcarpathia in the interwar period, remembered his family's first encounter with Ukrainian speakers from the Russian Empire. During Shandor's childhood in the Great War, Iulian Bebeshko, a prisoner of war from the Russian army, lived with and worked for his family. According to an account recorded by Raymond Smith, Shandor's editor,

> The family soon discovered that they understood the language spoken by Bebeshko and the other prisoners from Eastern Ukraine far better than the language spoken by those from Moscow and other Russian regions. As Shandor relates the story, it was these prisoners who enabled the local Ruthenians to "perceive their linguistic and historical closeness to those who were from Ukraine. The prisoners were the first to talk openly about Ukraine, its history, traditions, and culture." The Ukrainian songs they learned "from the captured Russian Army soldiers of Ukrainian origin gave a strong impulse to the self-identification of Ruthenians from Transcarpathia, spurring national revival and development." After World War I, Shandor's father became politicized as a Ukrainian nationalist. In January 1919, the elder Shandor took part in a Congress in Khust that endorsed the unification of [Transcarpathia] with the rest of Ukraine, one of several political acts which provoked an angry response from local Hungarian officials.[24]

To the consternation of the imperial powers on the eastern front, the war accelerated the transmission and diffusion of the Ukrainian idea, even in the most backward regions.

Galicia's Occupations

According to Machiavelli, "a prince should make himself feared in such a way that, though he does not gain love, he escapes hatred, for being feared but not hated go readily together." In order to prevent hatred, Machiavelli advocated that a prince should not touch the property of his citizens and subjects or insult their sense of honour or dignity.[25] Russia's political and military leaders did not heed his advice. The Russian Empire's three conquests of Austrian territories during the First World War estranged not only the Germans, Jews, and Poles, but also the Ukrainians of Galicia and Bukovina, who had never lived under Russian imperial rule. Adhering to the prevailing imperial ideology, Russian officials imagined that the East Slavs in the Habsburg Monarchy were fellow Russians and acted accordingly.

Shortly after the Russian army captured Galicia and Bukovina for the first time in late September 1914 (and held the provinces until 22 June 1915), officials annexed these territories into the Russian Empire. They made plans to integrate the occupied territories into the empire's legal and administrative framework and to build "new Russian-gauge railroads tying Galicia to the Russian heartland."[26] They extended the tsarist imperial model of provincial administration to "the old Russian land" of Austria's Lemberg, Tarnopol, Czernowitz, and later Przemyśl. These newly acquired territories (which had been part of Kiev Rus, but not Muscovy or the Russian Empire) were subordinated to the headquarters of the southwest front in Kiev, which became "the defacto wartime capital of the newly united Ukrainian lands."[27]

The Russian occupational regime operated in a highly arbitrary manner and quickly became unpopular. The commander of the southwestern front, General Nikolai Ivanov, ordered the expulsion of large numbers of Jews and German peasants who had settled in Galicia several generations earlier, accusing them of espionage, subversion, and sabotage. The first deportations started in November 1914 as the authorities dispatched "unreliable" Jews, Germans, and Ukrainians to Siberia's Tomsk province.[28]

Ivanov, moreover, tolerated hostage taking and did not punish his troops who engaged in brutal pogroms against Jews, Germans, and other civilians in the front military zones.[29] The new regime viewed the Jews of Galicia, who had long enjoyed legal equality in the Austro-Hungarian Empire, as subversive elements, spies, and traitors and condoned the military's anti-Jewish violence throughout the winter of 1914–15.[30] Count Georgii Bobrinskii, the second military governor general during Russia's first occupation of Galicia, perceived the province as an integral part of the Russian Empire and replaced the Austrian officials with Russian bureaucrats from Kiev, Podolia, Volhynia, or Warsaw, or with the few remaining local Russophiles. Persecuted by the Austrian government before 1914, these Russophiles enthusiastically served the Russian administration in Galicia.[31]

Despite claims to adhere to international agreements concerning the occupation of foreign territories in wartime, the new rulers in Galicia quickly introduced Russian as the only language of instruction in the schools and government offices, and closed long-standing Ukrainian organizations, clubs, bookstores, and newspapers. They prohibited the sale as well as the private possession of all books in the "Little Russian dialect" and barred the use of this language in all private and public organizations, courts, and bureaucracy.[32] They also arrested thousands of prominent civic, cultural, political, and religious leaders, such as the Greek Catholic Metropolitan Andrei Sheptytsky, and deported them deep into the Russian interior. They also persecuted the members of the Greek Catholic Church and attempted to convert these believers to Russian Orthodoxy by force.[33] These brutal anti-Ukrainian measures far surpassed those the Polish nobility introduced under Austrian rule.[34] Just as most Ukrainians in Galicia and Bukovina realized that they had lived far better under Habsburg rule than their compatriots in Russia, Emperor Nicholas II travelled to his Lvov on 9 April 1915 in order to meet his "Russian" subjects and to reaffirm Galicia's long-standing "historic ties" with his realm.[35]

A few months later the Austrians and Germans counter-attacked. The Russian army suffered heavy casualties – over one million men killed or wounded and the surrender of another million – which forced them to withdraw from Austrian Galicia, all of Russian Poland, and a large part of the Polish-Russian borderlands.[36] During the retreat, the Russian military commander ordered the destruction of crops, livestock, and farm equipment. By coercive means this retreat removed several hundred thousand Ukrainian, Polish, and Jewish civilians from the region.[37] Up to 50 per cent of all Jewish settlements and the majority of all Jewish physical structures experienced damage or destruction.[38] Millions now lived under martial-law regimes in the neighbouring front-line provinces that the Russian Empire controlled.[39]

In June 1916, Russia's military regained the territories on the eastern front and reoccupied much of Bukovina and one-third of eastern Galicia for the next few months.[40] Its troops controlled the area around Tarnopol (now Ternopol), a large eastern Galician city near the Austro-Russian border, from September 1914 to the end of 1917.

The new civilian and military authorities then launched a vicious anti-Semitic campaign and persecuted Germans but modified the anti-Ukrainian policies of 1914–15. Continuing their Great Russian project (reuniting Russians, Little Russians, and Belarusans into one state led by Russia), they did not ban the Ukrainian language or shut down all Ukrainian-language publications and institutions.

The Russian language still served as the official language. Although the new governor general allowed the use of some of the local languages (Polish and Ukrainian, but not German or Yiddish) in the schools, the tsar's ministers in Petrograd objected. The authorities abandoned efforts to convert Greek Catholic believers to Russian Orthodoxy, but fought all manifestations of "Ukrainophilism," a very broad pejorative term.[41] Having suffered through the first Russian occupation and its scorched-earth policy the year before, the local population remained hostile to the Russians and sympathetic to the Austrians. They, after all, had been among the most loyal subjects of the Habsburg Monarchy since the late eighteenth century.

Shortly after Nicholas II's forced abdication in February 1917, the Provisional Government appointed Dmytro Doroshenko, a prominent Ukrainian activist from the Russian Empire, as the regional commissar (with powers of governor general) for occupied Galicia and Bukovina.[42] This decision reflected the plans of Pavel Miliukov, the Provisional Government's first foreign minister (from February to May 1917), to merge Austria-Hungary's Ukrainian districts with Russian Ukraine.[43] Doroshenko persuaded the Provisional Government to appoint three more Ukrainian activists as commissars for Volhynia, Czernowitz (now Chernovtsy), and Ternopol. This group of governors started to promote local Ukrainians into regional bureaucracies just before Alexander Kerensky, the new head of the Provisional Government, launched his late June 1917 offensive against the Germans and Austrians. The Central Powers counter-attacked and temporarily reclaimed most of Eastern Galicia in August, but the Russian army retook some of the territories it had lost.[44] Because of the breakdown of military discipline in the months before Russia withdrew from the war in December, this last Russian conquest became even worse than the first two.[45] Despite Doroshenko's efforts to alleviate the consequences of the devastation the people of Galicia had experienced over three years of the war and two Russian occupations, he could not. He had no authority over the military. The demands of the Russian front-line army in his province took precedence over the needs of the civilian population he governed.

Overall, governments on both sides adopted measures which "either privileged or disadvantaged one ethnic group over another in matters of language and schooling, religious practice, military service obligations, property rights, and other economic welfare measures."[46] Such actions activated national and even nationalist counter-responses from the local populations.

If, on the eve of the 1914 invasion, "strong pro-Russian sympathies [existed] among Galicia's Ukrainians, with a quarter of them voting for Russophile candidates to the Austrian parliament," these feelings quickly evaporated.[47] Russia's occupation of Galicia and Bukovina, its retreat, and the creation of a major refugee crisis ignited the Austro-Ukrainian hatred against Russia and Russians. By the end of 1915, the Russian military created approximately 400,000 refugees, most of them Ukrainians from Galicia, shepherding them eastward to Kiev and to the larger towns and cities in the Ukrainian-speaking provinces. By mid-1916, for example, they comprised 25 per cent of the population in Ekaterinoslav and other cities.[48]

Settling these refugees behind Russian lines undermined the political order by introducing large numbers of diverse groups with alien ideas to the local Orthodox Christian population. In hopes of preventing fraud by various relief organizations, the Russian authorities gave each refugee a green book recording his or her name, place of origin, and ethnic affiliation.[49] These registration books (a precursor to the Soviet internal passport system introduced in 1932) set the refugees apart from the local population.

The refugees from Galicia encountered new, foreign environments and often compared – consciously and unconsciously – their old and new surroundings. Displaced hundreds of kilometres from home, they were forced to interact with other refugees and local populations and experienced feelings of otherness, estrangement, and, at times, solidarity. The predominantly Greek Catholic Ukrainians from the Austrian Empire had the opportunity to assess their similarities with fellow Ukrainian speakers of the Orthodox faith and to see how they differed from the Russians. In the struggle for food and shelter, these evacuees also thought about how – and in what language – to educate their children. Inadvertently, they – as a group – took on the role of missionaries for the Ukrainian cause.

In turn, many locals who encountered these refugees had to reassess their own identities. For the first time, many Ukrainian speakers in the Left Bank, Right Bank, and Novorossiia met a nationally conscious Ukrainian population, which highlighted the idea that the Ukrainian-speaking territories of Austria and Russia constituted a single whole. This enormous group of involuntary migrants and their encounters with the host populations disrupted the old, often acquiescent patterns of behaviour, forcing the refugees, the local population, and the local and dislodged intelligentsia "to forms of action and ways of thinking that had been impossible to conceive" before the war.[50]

All of the refugees experienced a common trauma. Both the educated intelligentsia and ordinary men and women had suffered the same exposure "to the dehumanizing and debilitating consequences of refugeedom."[51] Sharing memories of their expulsion from their homelands, the elites and masses identified themselves with each other, as never before. This assessment rang as true for the Ukrainian refugees as it did for the Poles, Jews, and Germans, also forcibly removed from Galicia. The war's violence and dispersions made each group see the world through national (not just local or imperial) lenses. The majority of uprooted Ukrainian speakers from Galicia and Bukovina, along with many of their compatriots in the Russian Empire, recognized that the rulers and the ruled "should hail from the same people." In the wake of this mass removal and psychological rupture, their identities became nationalized. This new politicized national identity became not only "a perceptual framework through which they (could) define their interests and identify their (potential) alliance partners," but also the "organizational means through which individuals struggle to gain power."[52] They started to interpret Russian rule (whether tsarist, democratic, or Bolshevik) emanating from Petrograd or Moscow as "alien" rule.

Internationalization of Intra-Imperial Conflicts

In the course of the war, the Ukrainian provinces within Austria-Hungary and the Russian Empire became the object of broader geopolitical projects envisioned by the warring powers to weaken, if not revise, each others' territories. The Romanovs wanted to annex Austria's Galicia and Bukovina to the Russian Empire and floated plans to recognize an autonomous, re-united Poland under its auspices after the war. The exact borders of this re-envisioned Poland remained unclear but did not include Right Bank Ukraine or Galicia. At the same time, the Germans and, to a lesser extent, the Austrians sought to divorce Russia's western borderlands in order to reinforce the geopolitical security of the Central Powers. In the first two weeks of the war, some German officials advocated the liberation of Poland, Finland, Ukraine, and the Caucasus from Russia. Although Germany's war aims evolved in the course of the European conflagration, its leaders succeeded in realizing their ambitious annexationist policies in the east at Brest-Litovsk four years later.[53]

In the course of this brutal conflict, the leaders of all warring parties defined their enemies in national as well as state and imperial terms, stereotyping their opponents as completely evil and untrustworthy. Propagandists constantly highlighted the differences among the various national groups, always disparaging their enemies, including civilians among them. Even on the home front, the German authorities did not consider all of their compatriots loyal sons and daughters of the fatherland, especially the socialists.

The Russian government abolished the Pale of Settlement on 4 August 1915 and allowed Jews who had fled during the chaotic retreat from Poland

and Galicia that spring to settle outside the former Pale. But at the same time, the military command denounced Jews, Poles, and Germans living within the boundaries of the empire as disloyal elements and sought to expropriate their landholdings.[54] In 1915, the Russian army deported over 200,000 German settlers from the provinces of Volhynia, Kiev, and Podolia to Siberia and Central Asia.[55] Even though these German settlers had lived on their homesteads for several generations, Russian generals could not imagine that they would ever become loyal members of the Russian political community. In their eyes, once a German, always a German.

Tsarist officials also suspected Ukrainians of treason. Despite the Ukrainian national movement's declarations of loyalty and overall support for the Russian war effort, the government closed down all Ukrainian cultural and educational institutions shortly after the empire's declaration of war.[56] The authorities arrested a number of the movement's most prominent leaders, including Mykhailo Hrushevsky, who shortly after the war broke out had returned to Kiev to prove his loyalty and that of the Ukrainian national movement. (Although he had lived in Austria since 1894, teaching at the University of Lemberg, he still retained his Russian citizenship.)

Russia's authorities did not recognize the separate existence of the Belarusans and Ukrainians from the Russian people. Due to the hysteria ignited by the war, they remained suspicious of anyone who identified himself as a Ukrainian, not as a "Little Russian." But by 1914 most Ukrainian speakers from Galicia or Bukovina identified themselves as Ukrainians, not Ruthenians or Little Russians. This conflict between assumptions of what should constitute the political norm for Ukrainians/Ruthenians/Little Russians/Rusyns made many Russian nationalists uneasy about the Austro-Ukrainian refugees and about the local relief organizations created to help them.[57]

Russian leaders' concern about Ukrainians and the Ukrainian national movement were not completely misplaced. In Austria, on 3 August 1914, representatives of the three main Ukrainian political parties in Austria formed the Supreme Ukrainian Council (*Holovna Ukrains'ka Rada*, or HUR), which issued an appeal to the Ukrainian people calling for unity against the autocratic tsarist empire, "the greatest enemy of Ukraine."[58] For leaders of these political parties and for Ukrainian political émigrés from Russia, the Russian Empire represented not only an existential threat, but also a danger to the constitutional rights and freedoms they enjoyed in Austria. They understood that these Austrian liberties allowed their activists to build a "dense network of voluntary associations" and other components of civil society in order to institutionalize the Ukrainian national project. Without constitutional protections, the mechanisms "that gave the Ukrainian peasants in Galicia political weight and voice, and allowed them to defend their interests" would disappear.[59]

In order to prevent this, HUR created a Ukrainian Military Command, which would oversee the organization of the Sich Riflemen (*Ukrains'ki sichovi striltsi*), a group of Ukrainian volunteers that would fight on behalf of the Dual Monarchy.[60] Consisting primarily of nationally conscious students, peasants, and workers, they sought to protect Ukrainians within the Austro-Hungarian Empire during the war. In 1915, the General Ukrainian Council (*Heneral'na Ukrains'ka Rada*), HUR's successor, published a declaration, envisioning a free, independent Ukrainian state carved out of Russia and territorial national autonomy for the Ukrainian people within the borders of Austria.[61] In September 1916, the General Council asserted that this whole territory encompassed 850,000 square kilometres and contained thirty-five million people, a highly contested claim in a nationally mixed East Central Europe.[62]

On 4 August 1914, a group of Ukrainian political émigrés from the Russian Empire living in Austria organized the Union for the Liberation of Ukraine (*Soiuz vyzvolennia Ukrainy* – SVU), which espoused the victory of the Central Powers and the creation of an independent Ukrainian state on the ruins of the Russian Empire. SVU's inaugural platform advocated that this state possess a constitutional monarch, a democratic political system, a single legislative branch, and civil, linguistic, and religious rights for all national groups and faiths, with an independent Ukrainian Orthodox Church.[63] HUR and the General Ukrainian Council cooperated closely with the SVU. Under the sponsorship of the SVU, many intellectuals from Galicia and Bukovina worked in the Austrian prisoner-of-war camps and spread the Ukrainian idea to the "Little Russians" in them.

As rational political actors, the leaders of the Ukrainian national movement in Galicia understood that a full-scale war between two major European military alliances could bring them new political opportunities. The victors would rearrange the continent's boundaries, especially in the disputed terrain of East Central Europe. HUR and SVU leaders grasped that an autonomous Ukraine, much less an independent one, would not emerge ex nihilo without the approval and support of the war's victors. They calculated that Russia (due to ideological reasons and national security concerns) would not tolerate such an outcome and that if Russia and its allies won the war, the Romanovs would destroy the Ukrainian national movement as it had within its own borders. Austro-Hungary and Germany would not. HUR and SVU leaders perceived, in short, that the war would determine the very survival of the Ukrainian national movement and all Ukrainians (as opposed to Little Russians).

Emperor Franz Joseph's long reign since 1848 made him a beloved father figure, if not an institution, among Ukrainians, who placed their political bet on the ultimate triumph of the Central Powers. Even their non-Galician colleagues, the members of the SVU, agreed with their assessment of the overall political situation and future possibilities. Their common support for the Central Powers presupposed important concessions from Austria-Hungary.

HUR and the Main Ukrainian Rada repeatedly urged the Austrian government to create a separate administrative unit for Ukrainians in Eastern Galicia. In late 1915 and early 1916 Austria's prime minister promised the General Council that Galicia's Ukrainian-speaking area would become a separate province. Emperor Franz Joseph nullified this pledge just before his death on 21 November 1916. He had just agreed to establish the Polish Kingdom and to initiate the autonomy of Galicia, which would be controlled by Polish nobles without Vienna's supervision. In practical terms, this meant that the Ukrainian national movement's political progress in Galicia since 1848, gains which Vienna guaranteed, would be overturned. The General Ukrainian Council and the Austrian parliament's Ukrainian deputies expressed their outrage, demanding Galicia's division into Polish and Ukrainian parts and the creation of a separate provincial parliament for Ukrainian Galicia.[64] Franz Josef's successor, Karl I, assured Ukrainian representatives that after the war, everything – including the question of a separate Ukrainian Galician province – would be settled fairly on behalf of the Ukrainians. In this spirit, the new emperor decreed in the fall of 1917 that all Greek Catholics in Galicia were now to be categorized as Ukrainians (not Ruthenians) in all official documents and registries.[65]

The Ukrainian movement acquired official approval of its own self-definition as a people and also won vague assurances concerning regional autonomy for its people. These official vows and their reversals demonstrated how Galicia and plans for a resurrected Poland became a political football during the war. Not only did Austria and Germany espouse the creation of an independent Poland when Russia occupied this territory, Russia did the same when the Central Powers conquered Polish areas. Inasmuch as almost all Polish political leaders imagined that Galicia and Right-Bank Ukraine belonged to Poland, Poland's future determined Ukraine's fate. And Ukraine's overall political destiny, not just in Galicia, influenced Poland's.

Despite the Austrian political leadership's efforts to appease the empire's non-German and non-Hungarian peoples, its military command suspected large numbers of Czechs, Serbs, Romanians, and Ukrainians in their ranks of disloyalty. The war unleashed a torrent of hysterical lies, misrepresentations, and defamations, not always expressed in public. Since the Ukrainians in Eastern Galicia possessed compatriots across the border in the Russian Empire and because the Austrian generals exaggerated the influence of the Russophile orientation among them, these military leaders assumed at the outbreak of the war that the Ukrainians sympathized with or would actively collaborate with the Russians. Acting on these false assumptions, they sent thousands of Ukrainians far from the front. The Hungarian government also suspected their Romanian, Serbian, and Ruthenian/Rusyn/Ukrainian populations, especially those who lived in or near the war zones.[66]

Conclusion

The Great War's carnage on the eastern front shattered the Austro-Hungarian, German, Russian, and Ottoman Turkish empires.[67] The long and brutal conflict unleashed a political and social tsunami, which undermined these dynastic, multinational empires, ignited revolutions and created new states, and set the stage for an even more devastating war. In its wake, the twentieth century's first total war created the political and social environment which diffused the idea of national self-determination and fertilized the ideologies of communism and fascism.

The war internationalized, militarized, and radicalized "national questions" within the empires of East Central Europe, transforming ethnic communities into national communities. Austria-Hungary and the Russian Empire sought to intertwine their highly diverse components around a single unifying identity within their own realms. As the war continued, seemingly without end, its belligerents created categories, dividing the world into loyal allies and diabolic foes, seeking out subversive "enemy aliens" in their midst.[68] Entire communities now bore collective responsibility for the actions of a few of their compatriots. In an environment of mass violence, shifting boundaries, and decaying authority, Austria-Hungary and the Russian Empire applied these categories to their own loyal subjects, needlessly undermining their own imperial unity.

In the case of Austria-Hungary, the military command had created regiments of Serb, Czech, Romanian, and Ruthenian soldiers mixed with "reliable" German and Magyar troops as "an extra check upon suspect nationalities."[69] Although these suspicions surfaced long before Franz Joseph's death in November 1916, most rank-and-file soldiers from these problematic nationalities placed the blame on Karl I. Governmental suspicions became a self-fulfilling prophecy. Many of the non-German and non-Hungarian soldiers suspected of disloyalty resented this intense scrutiny and "began to question their role, the purpose of the war, and looked forward to a speedy peace."[70]

The resentments and frustrations of the Ruthenians in the Habsburg armies and the Little Russians in the tsarist armies prompted many to think of themselves as Ukrainians and to question their loyalty to their respective imperial structures. In an age of popular sovereignty and national self-determination, why not demand home rule or autonomy, even independence for the downtrodden Ukrainian masses? In these uncertain times, why not learn from and reproduce the Irish and Polish models of the struggle for national independence?

3

Political Collapse, Revolutions, and Social Upheavals, 1917–1923

Turning and turning in the widening gyre
The falcon cannot hear the falconer;
Things fall apart; the centre cannot hold;
Mere anarchy is loosed upon the world,
The blood-dimmed tide is loosed, and everywhere
The ceremony of innocence is drowned;
The best lack all conviction, while the worst
Are full of passionate intensity.

W.B. Yeats[1]

The February 1917 Revolution swept away the Romanov dynasty, brought the Provisional Government to power, and generated waves of mass expectations and political demands throughout Russia. But the new government could not simultaneously end the Great War, increase food supplies, improve working conditions in the cities, introduce a more equal distribution of the land in the countryside, or authorize non-Russian autonomy. Its members, moreover, viewed themselves as temporary stewards of Russia's fragile democracy, preparing the way for the elections to the Constituent Assembly, which they believed would tackle society's conflicting demands.

In response to the Provisional Government's slow, legalistic procedures, popular dissatisfactions multiplied and spread across the country. As a consequence, by the end of that summer, the Provisional Government lost power to the Petrograd Soviet, which also arose after Nicholas II's abdication and attracted Russia's leftist parties. By summer's end, the enthusiastic and ever-growing support for radical Bolsheviks within this body destroyed the authority of the moderate Menshevik and Socialist Revolutionary parties.

The Bolshevik seizure of power in Petrograd in October 1917 with the support of workers and under the cloak of the Second All-Russian Congress of Soviets did not necessarily foreshadow their ultimate victory. After October 1917 this political party (overwhelmingly urban, working class, and largely Russian) took another three and a half years to win power in a predominantly rural, peasant, and non-Russian society encompassing approximately 22 million square kilometres (8.5 million square miles). Taking full advantage of the social volatility and confusion within Russia and of the West's moral and physical exhaustion with the First World War, they stumbled to victory. The overall chaos and violence "drove Russia towards Bolshevism, sometimes despite the Bolsheviks."[2]

Three different, but interdependent mass revolutions – in the cities, in the countryside, and in the non-Russian areas – tore Russia apart. Between 1917 and 1921 each of these spontaneous revolutions evolved independently, but converged in a number of ways. Each attacked different remnants of the old political order, challenged the institutionalized inequalities of the past, and introduced unique alternatives. Building on the old imperial identity and on official designations of identity during the war, various groups promoted new national and social identities that expressed distinct interpretations of individual dignity and group interests and envisioned a broader sense of equality and democracy.

Conflicts over these identities and their parameters fuelled the urban, rural, and non-Russian revolutions. Although these national and social identities competed with each other, their contest also mutually reinforced each other.[3] Inasmuch as the "national question" in the new democratic Russia reflected the enormous social inequalities among national groups, all non-Russian national movements combined the national and the social struggles to become a single, "almost unstoppable democratic force."[4] "Social democracy" in its broadest sense and the "right of national self-determination" became the most repeated revolutionary slogans of the day. The men and women who assembled under their different banners sought to institutionalize these political catchwords. These efforts provoked a bitter conflict in the Ukrainian provinces, where revolutionary euphoria inspired efforts to create a new political order. What did this newly introduced democracy mean in practice, specifically for the Ukrainian-speaking population? Would popular sovereignty coincide with national sovereignty? Or class sovereignty? Most importantly, what were the contours of these sovereignties and where were the boundaries between them?

The Central Rada and Its Successors

On 7 March 1917 (Old Style), barely a week after Tsar Nicholas II's abdication and the emergence of the Provisional Government in Petrograd, a small party of Ukrainian intellectuals with moderate political views established the Ukrainian Central Rada (*Ukrains'ka Tsentral'na Rada*) in Kiev. This organization became the coordinating body for all Ukrainian groups attempting to win wide-scale political, social, and cultural rights for Ukrainians from the Provisional Government. In employing the term "Ukraine," the Rada claimed authority over all Ukrainian activities in approximately a 450,000-square-kilometre area. This region contained the provinces of Kiev, Podolia, Volhynia, Kharkov, Poltava, Chernigov, Ekaterinoslav, Kherson, and Taurida, but excluded the Crimea, Galicia, Bukovina, and Transcarpathia. Because of the deteriorating military situation on the eastern front, this large tract coincided with the Ukrainian territory actually under the control of the Provisional Government.

As these provinces contained a nationally heterogeneous population, the Ukrainian movement sought to come to terms with the non-Ukrainians. The newly elected head of the Rada, historian Mykhailo Hrushevsky, asserted that the new body respected "all the civil and political rights of the national minorities which inhabit the Ukraine and recognize the Ukrainian people as the masters of the Ukrainian territory and [those] who desire to join them as equals."[5] Hrushevsky referred to the numerical superiority of the Ukrainian-speaking population in the nine provinces. In the new era of revolutionary democracy, he declared, non-Ukrainians now had to take Ukrainians into account. In a new democratic order, these men and women now sat at the newly expanded political table and constituted the majority of the population.

When the Rada claimed the right to represent all Ukrainian-speaking majority-populated territories, its leaders included the non-Ukrainian-speaking urban areas within their jurisdiction. Although Hrushevsky admitted that the Ukrainian speakers constituted a minority in the urban centres on the territory proposed by the Rada, he asserted that "the cities must follow the majority of the surrounding population."[6] Although cities such as Kiev and Kharkov played a critical role in the formation of the leadership of the Ukrainian national movement in the nineteenth and early twentieth centuries, only one – Poltava – possessed a majority Ukrainian population in the second decade of the twentieth.[7] Between the 1897 Russian imperial census and the outbreak of the war in 1914, Ukrainian

speakers comprised between 32.5 and 46.1 per cent of the towns and cities.[8] Most of those living in the urban areas (including Jews) identified
themselves with the Russian language and culture. This sharp rural-urban
variation threatened to cripple the revolution in the Ukrainian provinces.

The Rada needed to address this issue, but only after mobilizing its peasant base. In order to confirm its self-appointed mandate in the spring and
summer of 1917, the Rada called on all Ukrainian organizations to meet to
discuss the present and future political status of the nine Ukrainian-speaking
provinces. With the inclusion of delegates from various cooperative, peasant, pedagogical, military, and political organizations, the Rada's membership increased to 600 by the end of July. At that point in time, the Rada
included only Ukrainians and defined itself as "the representative body of
the entire organized Ukrainian population" in the nine provinces.[9]

Members of the Ukrainian Party of Socialist Revolutionaries (UPSR)
emerged as the largest, most representative, and most enthusiastic supporters of the Central Rada's efforts to secure political autonomy from the
Provisional Government. This pro-peasant political party espoused land
reform and political decentralization. Although related to Russia's Socialist
Revolutionary Party (PSR), the UPSR had different agrarian goals than
the Russian party's. As the overwhelming majority of Ukrainian-speaking
peasants possessed their allotments in hereditary household tenure (unlike
Russian peasants, who held their land under communal tenure), they
feared the introduction of communal land reforms, which they identified
with the PSR. In response, the UPSR advocated individual farming and
attracted the majority of peasants in the nine provinces.[10]

The UPSR, like the other Ukrainian political parties, advocated promotion of the Ukrainian language within the educational and bureaucratic
systems of the nine provinces, an issue of enormous importance to the
peasants. According to Orlando Figes,

> The nationalist struggle for language rights was also a liberation movement
> for the peasants. Unless the peasants could understand the language of the
> government and the courts, they had no direct access to political or civil
> rights. Unless they could learn to read in their own tongue, they had no hope
> of social betterment. And unless they could understand their priests, they had
> reason to fear for their souls. The public use of their native language was not
> just a matter of necessity, however. It became the issue of personal pride and
> dignity for the Ukrainian peasant, and this gave the nationalists a profound
> base of emotional support.[11]

In this revolutionary situation, the Ukrainian national movement promised the peasant the political, social, economic, and cultural means to
achieve the dignity he desired, if the Provisional Government would agree.

In order to reach an agreement with Russia's Provisional Government,
the Rada sent a delegation of ten members to Petrograd at the end of May.
These envoys petitioned the Provisional Government to recognize the autonomy of Ukraine and the authority of the Rada, to allow the formation
of separate Ukrainian units within the military, and to permit the
Ukrainization of the educational system and the civil and ecclesiastical
administration. The Ukrainian demands did not include national-personal
autonomy, an issue that representatives of Jewish communities and cultural institutions raised for the first time on 23 May 1917.[12]

Shortly after the delegation's arrival, the Provisional Government rejected the Ukrainian petition, claiming that it expressed "the will of an organization which, because of the manner of its establishment, cannot claim the
right to represent the entire population of Ukraine."[13] Here, Russia's new
government opposed the idea of the Rada solely representing Ukrainian
national interests. In the eyes of many of the Provisional Government's
ministers, the Rada and its supporters expressed dangerous separatist intentions, which jeopardized the overall revolution as well as Russia's territorial
integrity.

In response to this criticism, on 10 June 1917, the Rada issued its First
Universal, a declaration modelled on the charters of the seventeenth-
century Cossack hetmans, whom the leaders of the Ukrainian national
movement claimed to be the founders of the early modern Ukrainian nation.[14] The proclamation defined the Ukrainian people as a "nation of
peasants, workers, and toilers" and affirmed its political allegiance to the
revolutionary Russian state. At the same time, the organization asserted
that the Ukrainians possessed the right of national self-determination and
that it would work with non-Ukrainians and the All-Russian Constituent
Assembly to create an autonomous Ukraine.

Despite this promise, many non-Ukrainians expressed anxiety about the
Rada's concept of autonomy and feared that important political decisions
would be made without their participation. The Southern Bureau of the
General Jewish Labor Bund of Lithuania, Poland and Russia (the most
prominent secular Jewish socialist party), for example, conveyed the fear
that the Universal "places the Ukrainian national movement on the road to
a break with revolutionary democracy and establishes the conditions for
the intensification of the internal friction among the population of the

Ukraine."[15] The Bureau's resolution asserted that the Central Rada could not become the sole political authority in the Ukrainian provinces, as it relied exclusively on the Ukrainian people. The Bund recommended that the Provisional Government call an all-Ukrainian territorial conference, with the participation of the Rada and other non-Ukrainian revolutionary organizations. This meeting would establish the territorial autonomy of Ukraine, guaranteeing minorities the right to national-cultural autonomy.

Until 24 June 1917, the Central Rada, the Small Rada (the Central Rada's executive committee), and the General Secretariat (the Rada's Council of Ministers) acted only on behalf of the Ukrainian people. Then, in reaction to the objections from the Provisional Government and the Bund, the General Secretariat began to reconstitute the Rada into a provisional, multinational territorial parliament that would represent the entire revolutionary democracy in the Ukrainian provinces. The leaders of the Secretariat envisaged the inclusion of delegates from the national minorities, proportionate to their population, into the Rada and not the incorporation of the Rada into a non-Ukrainian territorial organization, as the Bund proposed. The Rada's General Secretariat also appointed a commission of Ukrainians and non-Ukrainians to draft a constitution for the new political entity.

Preoccupied with a barrage of pressing issues, the Provisional Government ignored the Rada's requests. But with the proclamation of the First Universal, Russia's revolutionary leaders realized that they needed to reach an understanding with the Ukrainians, who occupied the territories bordering the shifting military front. After negotiations, the Provisional Government agreed to recognize Ukraine's autonomy and the competency of the Rada and the Secretariat. In turn, the Secretariat would create a more representative government by giving non-Ukrainians eighteen seats in the Small Rada (out of fifty-eight members), 30 per cent of the seats in the Great Rada, and four ministries (trade, food, justice, and posts and telegraph). On 3 July, the Second Universal acknowledged this new accord, which promised that the General Secretariat would represent the interests of the entire population, not just the Ukrainians.[16]

Despite this settlement, the leaders of the Provisional Government soon changed their minds. Strengthened by their victory over the Bolshevik grassroots uprising in Petrograd in July, they rejected the Rada's draft of the proposed Ukrainian constitution one month later.[17] The Provisional Government recognized the competency of the Secretariat in only five provinces (Kiev, Volhynia, Podolia, Poltava, and Chernigov) and restricted the composition of this body to nine members, four of whom non-Ukrainians would select.

In order to avoid further conflict with the Provisional Government, the Rada reluctantly accepted the Provisional Government's limitation of its authority and enthusiastically integrated the minorities into the structure of the Rada, the Small Rada, and the Secretariat. By early November the Central Rada included 848 members: 636 Ukrainians and 212 non-Ukrainians.[18] Minorities constituted one-quarter of the membership of the Rada, a figure almost proportionate to their population in the Ukrainian provinces.

The Provisional Government and the Central Rada represented moderate political organizations, which cooperated closely during 1917. But their goals did not coincide.

In an unstable revolutionary situation, the Rada sought to channel the diverse, often-conflicting aspirations of the Ukrainian population towards autonomy within the evolving post-tsarist Russian political structure. At the same time, the Provisional Government aimed to recover the lands the Russian imperial state lost (if not to expand them) and to restore the authority of the central government. The Rada often served as the Provisional Government's agent in Ukraine until September and October 1917, when chaos, radicalization, and the upsurge in support for the Bolsheviks and non-Russian nationalists throughout Russia fatally undermined the authority of the Provisional Government. Most members of the Rada did not mourn its passing.

The Bolshevik victory in Petrograd in late October 1917 and the disappearance of the Provisional Government's authority in the borderlands encouraged non-Russian secessionists. Lenin's new Council of People's Ministers (*Sovnarkom*) issued a flurry of decrees: the Decree on Peace, which demanded an immediate peace among the war's belligerents, a truce without annexations or indemnities, an end to secret diplomacy, and the publication of all secret treaties; the Decree on Land, which confiscated state and church lands without compensation and placed them in the hands of "workers who cultivate them"; and the Declaration of the Rights of the Nations of Russia, granting the non-Russian peoples the right of national self-determination, including the freedom to separate from Soviet Russia and to form independent states.[19]

These decrees reflected the rapid erosion of Russia's cohesion in 1917. At the insistence of the non-Ukrainian minorities, who believed that the Bolsheviks betrayed the February Revolution, the Small Rada issued the Third Universal on 7 November 1917, two weeks after the Bolshevik takeover. The document established a Ukrainian National Republic tenuously federated with the Russian Republic, but in reality independent of it. With the disappearance of the Provisional Government, the political future of the Ukrainian provinces became an open question.

The first two Universals issued by the Central Rada did not define the borders of Ukraine. Only with the Third Universal did the Rada assert that the nine provinces with Ukrainian majorities belonged to the Ukrainian National Republic (*Ukrains'ka Narodna Respublika*, or UNR). The Third Universal, moreover, claimed that the final demarcation of the borders of the UNR as well as the annexation of parts of the Kursk, Kholm/Chełm, and Voronezh provinces, where the Ukrainians constituted the majority of the population, "will be determined in agreement with the organized will of the people."[20] The Rada pledged to defend the free national development of all national groups living in Ukraine and promised a law on national-personal autonomy for the Russian, Jewish, Polish, and other peoples.[21]

Shortly after the Third Universal, the UNR established diplomatic relations with France, Great Britain, Germany, Austria-Hungary, Bulgaria, and the Ottoman Empire. (Even the United States, which sought to maintain a "Russia, one and indivisible" after the Bolsheviks assumed power in late October, opened a consulate in Kiev in December 1917.) The French and British emissaries sought to persuade the UNR to join their alliance against the Central Powers. But the UNR leaders refused. They sought to adhere to their position of peace without annexations and indemnities; a just peace with all the belligerents; and a determination to stay neutral.[22]

On 30 November 1917 the Soviet Russian Republic recognized the UNR, but shortly afterwards Petrograd's *Sovnarkom* accused the Rada of undermining Ukraine's soviets, disrupting the common front against the Germans and Austrians by recalling Ukrainian soldiers (until March 1918, both Russia and Ukraine were in a state of war with the Central Powers), and by aiding the Don Cossack "counterrevolutionaries" in South Russia. Shortly after the Central Rada rebutted these charges, the Petrograd government declared war on the Rada. Joseph Stalin, *Sovnarkom*'s Commissar of Nationalities, claimed that the Bolsheviks supported the universal right of national self-determination, but that the Rada's policies opposed the interests of Soviet Russia and represented a counter-revolutionary orientation. As such, these measures delegitimized this Ukrainian institution.[23] *Sovnarkom* then shifted its support to the newly established Soviet Ukrainian government, the People's Secretariat, headquartered in Kharkov.

With the Bolshevik army's invasion of Ukraine from the north and east, the Rada passed its Fourth Universal, on 25 January 1918 (New Style),

proclaiming the independence of the UNR within the boundaries delineated by the Third Universal. The post–February 1917 mobilization of
Ukrainians now became a war of nationalist secession, justified as the best
way to defend the political and cultural rights of all Ukrainian speakers in
the nine southwestern provinces. The Rada's declaration of independence,
however, alienated the non-Ukrainian minorities, who aspired to participate in a federated Russian state. With the exception of the Poles, all of the
non-Ukrainian parties within the Rada abstained or voted against the
Fourth Universal.[24] Despite this setback, the Ukrainians within the Rada
promised that all nations residing in the Ukrainian National Republic
would enjoy the right of national-personal autonomy, promulgated by the
law of 24 January 1918.[25] Nonetheless, many Ukrainian supporters of the
Rada felt betrayed by their non-Ukrainian compatriots.

The leaders of the Ukrainian movement possessed not only theoretical
and moral reasons for supporting the law on national-personal autonomy,
but pragmatic ones as well. By supporting the rights of the non-Ukrainian
minorities, they hoped to overcome the national differences between the
cities and the countryside. Realizing that they could not immediately reconcile these two groups, they aspired to mitigate their weaknesses and the
antagonism, if not the outright hostility, of the minorities towards the
Ukrainian demand for national-territorial autonomy. The revolutionary
events in the Ukrainian-speaking provinces, however, only exacerbated
these divisions.

The results of the various elections (with direct, equal, and secret ballots)
held in the nine Ukrainian-speaking provinces in late 1917 and early 1918
supported the Rada's Universals and actions. According to one source,
Ukrainian political parties led by the pro-peasant Ukrainian Party of
Socialist Revolutionaries (UPSR) won 80 per cent of the vote in the elections to the provincial and county assemblies.[26] In elections to the All-
Russian Constituent Assembly on 12 November 1917, they garnered
(largely separately, but also on joint lists with other parties) 5.5 million
votes, or 67.3 per cent, of the total vote in the eight Ukrainian provinces
excluding Taurida (see table 3.1).[27] In the elections to the Ukrainian
Constituent Assembly on 9 January 1918 – held in areas not controlled by
the Bolsheviks – voters selected 171 of the 301 designated representatives.[28]

The urban populations, however, did not recognize the authority of
the Rada or the Secretariat. The results of the elections to the city councils
in the summer of 1917 and to the All-Russian Constituent Assembly
in November demonstrated the political impotence of the Ukrainian movement in the urban areas. In Kiev, Ukrainian parties received approximately

Table 3.1. Votes Won by Ukrainian Political Parties to the All-Russian Constituent Assembly, 1917

Province	Votes won by Ukr. parties	Total votes cast	Percentage of total
Kiev	1,161,033	1,502,725	77
Volhynia	569,044	804,208	71
Podolia	656,116	830,360	79
Chernigov	497,106	973,646	51
Poltava	760,022	1,149,256	66
Kharkov	(800,328)*	1,093,321	73
Ekaterinoslav	556,012	1,193,049	47
Kherson	(332,118)*	620,720	53

*Joint list of Ukrainian and non-Ukrainian political parties.
Source: Oliver H. Radkey, *Russia Goes to the Polls: The Election to the All-Russian Constitutent Assembly, 1917* (Ithaca, NY: Cornell University Press, 1989), table 1, 148–51.

21.4 per cent of the vote in the summer of 1917 and in the elections to the Constituent Assembly in November 1917 – approximately 26 per cent.[29]

Although these results do not necessarily provide evidence of the hostility of the non-Ukrainians to the Ukrainian movement, they do demonstrate that, in this period, nationally and politically conscious urban Ukrainians and non-Ukrainians could not agree on a common political platform. The socialist programs of the majority of the Ukrainian political parties must also have aggravated the small urban Ukrainian middle class. Thus, the countryside provided the bulk of the vote for the Ukrainian parties to the Constituent Assembly, but even here not all the peasants voted along national lines.[30]

Non-Ukrainian opposition to the Ukrainian national movement's goals exemplified the most important problem in the struggle for majority rule in multi-ethnic societies, especially in societies where the minorities possess a disproportionate share of the country's political and socio-economic resources.[31] According to one scholar, "Majority rule works only when the minority has such confidence in the ultimate reasonableness of the majority and minority interests that it can afford to respect the right of the majority to rule without undo obstruction."[32] But trust and a common pool of interests between the Ukrainians and the non-Ukrainians in this revolutionary environment barely existed.

During the revolutionary fervour of early 1917, the leaders of the Ukrainian movement naively believed that they would attract the necessary administrators from the assimilated Ukrainian intelligentsia. "Our Russified intelligentsia will join us," Volodymyr Vynnychenko, the head of the General Secretariat, predicted. "We will rouse them, shame them, sensitize them, inspire them and draw them to work with us."[33] But in the course of 1917 and 1918, this expectation did not bear fruit. As a result, the Rada's bureaucracy attracted politically inexperienced journalists, teachers, and lawyers, and a small group of political émigrés from Galicia.[34] The Ukrainian movement engaged in two different courses of action at once – nation building and state building – and could not master both simultaneously.

The Ukrainian movement's nation-building project had to complete the transition from Hroch's mass cultural phase to the mass political phase, in order to create a single imagined community of Ukrainians from a group of people who possessed the same language and culture, but experienced diverse histories, religions, and levels of Russification. At the same time, the movement's state-building project had to expand the capacity and effectiveness of the Provisional Government's institutions and consolidate the Ukrainian-speaking territories. The first process developed in an environment of constant flux, especially within an uncertain revolutionary situation. The second's success ultimately depended on persuasion, on the establishment of a monopoly of violence, or a combination of the two. Since it attracted only a small number of individuals qualified for both activities, the Ukrainian movement sought to emphasize only one – nation building – and to draw non-Ukrainians into the state apparatus.

Polarization and Collapse

Although the overwhelming majority of those living in the countryside supported Ukrainian political parties, the elections of 1917 and early 1918 did not inaugurate a new era of political stability. These votes represented snapshots of single moments in a very turbulent and fast-moving sequence of chaotic and contentious events. Once they took place, the picture changed, sometimes even before the tabulation of results. Those who cast their ballots for one political party often switched sides, responding to current frustrations, changed circumstances, or increasing economic hardships. Ukrainian-speaking peasants and peasant soldiers represented the Rada's most powerful, but also most volatile, supporters.

The first group craved land, and they wanted it immediately. Peasant demands for agrarian reforms and the Rada's appeal for political autonomy converged in the spring and summer of 1917, but frayed in the fall and in the winter-spring of 1918. The peasants sought an agrarian revolution in the countryside and assessed all governments, even the Ukrainian ones, by that standard.[35] If a government did not satisfy these pleas, then the peasants retreated into a state of economic self-sufficiency, abandoning any effort to feed the cities or the various armies advancing into the steppe.

Despite the Rada's best efforts to meet peasant claims, it encountered other issues competing for attention.[36] In any case, to solve the contentious land question in the most densely populated region of the Russian Empire by providing each homestead with enough land to survive would be a daunting task. The peasants expressed clearly what they required, and they did not want to hear about difficulties or demographic constraints. Expropriate the land of the nobles and the bloated holdings of the Orthodox Church and redistribute the properties of the wealthy peasants (the so-called "kurkuls," also known as "kulaks" in Russian), they demanded. These actions would solve the agricultural and demographic crises, they imagined. Not surprisingly, the peasants gravitated towards any political party that gave them what they wanted, regardless of the complex realities of the situation.

The support of Ukrainian soldiers also became problematic. The army, as mentioned earlier, came predominantly from the countryside. Its members also wanted land and an end to the war. Approximately one-third of the troops on the southwestern and Romanian fronts, those camped out on Ukrainian-speaking territories, voted for Ukrainian socialist parties.[37] But this backing remained volatile. Within the context of a very divided society, the interests of the senior officers, junior officers, and rank-and-file soldiers came into conflict, and not just over the future of the war. Many Ukrainian-speaking junior officers (oftentimes teachers from the villages) and soldiers hoped to create units composed of their compatriots. These national military formations would introduce the Ukrainian language as the language of command and as a means of communication with central headquarters. (Most senior officers opposed this demand, claiming correctly that it undermined the effectiveness of an already overstrained Russian army). Perhaps intoxicated by their possession of weapons and their knowledge of how to use them, these Ukrainian-speaking warriors pressured the Rada to embrace more radical positions when dealing with Petrograd.[38]

According to one scholar, as "long as the Ukrainian formations remained at the front, they were loyal to the Rada; but the longer the Rada delayed with concrete social and political measures that addressed the needs of the peasants and soldiers, the more that soldier support melted away."[39] Soldiers began to desert in large numbers after the Provisional Government's disastrous June 1917 campaign, emasculated the national military formations they had clamoured to create earlier, and radicalized the entire political environment by destabilizing the authority of both the Provisional Government and the Central Rada.[40] Revolvers and rifles brought them heretofore unimaginable power in the countryside as they joined their friends and neighbours in seizing land across the Ukrainian-speaking provinces. The Rada now lost all potential military support.

By December 1917, nearly all of the soldiers in garrisons on the territory the Rada claimed would not fight either on the Bolshevik or the anti-Bolshevik side. Millions of soldiers who had earlier enthusiastically embraced the Ukrainian cause "neutralized" themselves.[41] They chose the reality of land over the abstraction of political autonomy. When the Bolsheviks began their 1917–18 winter drive, the Rada did not enjoy widespread popular support among the peasants nor did it command an adequate military force to resist them.[42]

Urban residents generally endorsed the Russian political parties; the workers increasingly rallied around the Bolsheviks, who won only 10 per cent of the vote in the elections to the All-Russian Constituent Assembly in the nine Ukrainian provinces. Since most Bolsheviks did not believe that peasant enthusiasm for the Ukrainian political parties represented true revolutionary democracy, they did not respect the vote's outcome. In early December 1917, the Bolsheviks in Ukraine sought to undermine the Central Rada by creating a separate, Soviet Ukrainian government in Kharkov and by enthusiastically greeting Bolshevik military units from Soviet Russia to bolster it.

In response to these events, the Central Rada negotiated a separate peace with the Central Powers on 9 February 1918. At the first Treaty of Brest-Litovsk, Germany, Austria-Hungary, Bulgaria, and the Ottoman Empire recognized the UNR within the borders proclaimed by the Fourth Universal and "the frontiers which existed between the Austro-Hungarian Monarchy and Russia, prior to the outbreak of the war."[43] The Austro-Hungarian authorities transferred the disputed Polish-Ukrainian district of Kholm/Chełm to Ukraine and promised in a secret agreement to create a separate province out of Eastern Galicia and Bukovina in the near future.[44]

At the second Treaty of Brest-Litovsk, the agreement signed between Soviet Russia and the Central Powers one month later, the Central Powers forced Russia to recognize its loss of Ukraine.[45] The first Treaty of Brest-Litovsk defined Ukraine's western borders with Austria-Hungary, the second one determined Ukraine's boundaries with Soviet Russia. Although the Entente powers did not participate in these settlements, both agreements placed Ukraine and the Ukrainian Revolution on the modern international stage for the first time and in the camp of the Central Powers.

These two treaties recognized the UNR and the Central Powers as the new state's patrons and protectors. By March 1918 the German and Austrian military forces quickly pushed into the Ukrainian provinces and eliminated the Bolshevik threat to the Central Rada. They divided Ukraine into two occupational zones, one German, the second Austrian, making the new country a "political ward of the Central [Powers]."[46]

The German and Austrian governments supported the Ukrainian national cause primarily due to their desperate need for grain to feed their starving populations. Imperial Germany had already rationed bread as early as January 1915.[47] Over the course of the war, Germany's and Austria's agricultural production had decreased by at least 40 per cent, food rations became smaller, and nearly 500,000 civilians in both countries died as a result of the British naval blockade. Discontent grew; anti-governmental demonstrations broke out.[48] The availability and affordability of food on the home front became a pressing national security issue.

From the perspective of the German and Austrian political and military leaders, this peace treaty constituted a "bread peace," a necessary alliance with, if not actual occupation of, Europe's most important granary. The two allies quickly lost their patience with their Ukrainian clients, who could not deliver the promised grain. In their eyes, food security at home justified their violations of Ukrainian sovereignty, culminating in the dispersal of the Central Rada and their sponsorship of a new government (the Hetmanate) under General Pavlo Skoropadsky, one of Ukraine's richest landowners, on 29 April 1918. Shortly afterwards, Skoropadsky introduced new agricultural policies, which sought to dismantle the Rada's limited land reforms, undo peasant expropriations, and re-empower the wealthy landlords in the countryside. Although the German and Austrian authorities imagined that these measures would bring them more grain, they soon radicalized the Ukrainian population, which led to extensive peasant uprisings and anti-Skoropadsky guerilla actions.[49]

German and Austrian forces intervened to end the uprisings but could not secure the situation in the country or accumulate the grain they needed at home. Shortly after the armistice with the Entente in November 1918, they withdrew their nearly one-million-man occupational force, plunging Ukraine into total chaos. A new Ukrainian nationalist organization, the Directory of the Ukrainian National Republic, swept Skoropadsky's regime aside in December 1918 and sought to restabilize the situation in Ukraine. But the Bolsheviks in Ukraine as well as the Soviet Russian government also hoped to retake political control of the Ukrainian provinces.

After the Ukrainian nationalists lost the protection of Austria and Germany, the international situation turned against the UNR.[50]

On 22 January 1919 the Directory and the government of the West Ukrainian National Republic proclaimed the unification of all Ukrainian territories in East Central Europe (with the exception of Transcarpathia). But this coalition fell apart shortly afterwards, as both sides sought to anchor their political future in their own territories and ally themselves with the enemies of their fellow compatriots. Symon Petliura, the Directory's minister for military affairs, joined the Poles against the Bolsheviks, and the Galicians united themselves with White Russian General Anton Denikin, however temporarily.

In the course of 1919, the post-revolutionary chaos in the Ukrainian provinces reached its peak. Nine different governments with nine different sets of armies competed to gain control of the region's population and resources.

Although the Directory of the Ukrainian National Republic claimed control in early January, advancing Bolshevik armies swept them away by February. By the summer of 1919, large areas of the countryside came under the control of anarchist bands led by Nestor Makhno and others, prior to General Anton Denikin's capture of Ukraine in August. Denikin's anti-Bolshevik forces pushed out the Bolsheviks, but not for long. His advocacy of a "Russia, Great, United, and Indivisible" and restoration of properties to large landowners alienated the nationally conscious Ukrainians and the peasants. The Soviet army regained Ukraine in December, then lost it for a short period when the Poles invaded in April 1920. By June 1920, the Red Army swept the Poles out of this area and marched on Warsaw, where the Poles stopped the Soviet advance on Western Europe in August. This "miracle on the Vistula River" led to the Treaty of Riga (18 March 1921), which divided most of the Ukrainian territories in East Central Europe between Poland and Soviet Russia over the next twenty years.

In this period, Ukrainian nationalists lost public support and became politically powerless. They competed not only with the local agencies of the Provisional Government, local soviets, and Soviet Russia, but also with a more competent enemy – anarchy. Perceiving the breakdown of all authority, the peasants, demobilized soldiers, and those "considered to be a part of Ukrainian, Red, or White armies" sought to alleviate their anxieties, frustrations, and rage over their perceived socio-economic inferiority by expropriating the land and participating in pogroms against local Jews.[51] In

1918–19, according to one source, 1,236 pogroms took place in the Ukrainian provinces.[52] In this chaotic period, approximately 40 per cent of the recorded pogroms – more than in any other area – took place on the territories nominally controlled by the Directory.[53] Here, unorganized drunken mobs and anti-Semitic marauders carried out the majority of this anti-Jewish violence, which spread like an epidemic from village to village, from region to region.[54] Despite Vynnychenko's and Petliura's condemnation of these pogroms, little could be done in the chaos to curb these horrific crimes.[55] The UNR lacked authority. This whirlpool of anti-Jewish violence tarnished the international reputation of the Ukrainian National Republic and its commander-in-chief, Petliura.

Estimates of the number of those massacred during the pogroms of 1917–21 run in the tens and even hundreds of thousands. In 1920 Jewish organizations in Soviet Russia issued a report estimating the total number of victims from all pogroms throughout the former Russian Empire committed by Whites, Ukrainian nationalists, anarchists, invading Polish forces, and Bolsheviks at approximately 150,000.[56] This, most likely, undercounts the number of victims. In Ukraine, according to one leading American scholar, fifty to sixty thousand Jews were killed in this period, although – as he admits – these calculations may be "very conservative."[57] The high number of Jews killed in the Ukrainian-speaking provinces reflects not only the inter-communal tensions aggravated by the post-revolutionary chaos and the breakdown of law and order, but also the fact that these overcrowded provinces served as the epicentre of the Russian Empire's Pale of Settlement until 1915. This institutionalized inequality created a highly dysfunctional relationship between the Jews and their Christian neighbours, which exploded after 1917.

Bolshevik Response

Between 1917 and 1920, the Central Rada, Skoropadsky's regime, the Directory, and the Central Powers created and recreated their own versions of "Ukraine" from Russia's nine southwestern provinces. In order to win power in this area, Bolshevik leaders had to acknowledge these provinces as a single political unit, potentially alienating their own supporters.

The views of the Bolsheviks on the national question during the Russian Revolution remained contradictory, and the party did not speak with a single unified voice on this issue. Two trends emerged within the party. The first, represented by Vladimir Lenin and Joseph Stalin, acknowledged that the Bolsheviks had to recognize the power of non-Russian nationalisms and to incorporate them into their overall political strategy. The second, advocated by Nikolai Bukharin and Georgi Piatakov, viewed any concession to these nationalisms as a compromise with the party's ideological purity. Both trends, however, subordinated non-Russian aspirations for political autonomy to the demands of the worldwide class struggle.[58]

Prior to October 1917, the Bolsheviks aggravated the tensions between the Provisional Government and the non-Russian nationalities.[59] After they took power in Petrograd, they sought to extend their influence and gain control over the non-Russian borderlands, especially Ukraine, which they considered an integral part of Russia. Piatakov, the chairman of the Kiev Bolshevik committee and a fierce opponent of Lenin's concept of national self-determination, best expressed this pro-Russian class perspective in June of that year:

> Generally we should not support the Ukrainians, for this movement is not advantageous to the proletariat. Russia cannot exist without the Ukrainian sugar industry, the same can be said for coal (the Donets Basin), grain (the Black Earth belt), etc. The branches of [Ukrainian] industry are closely connected with all the rest of Russia's industry. Moreover, the Ukraine does not form a distinct economic region, for it does not possess banking centers, as Finland does.[60]

According to Piatakov's logic, the economic needs of the proletariat transcended the aspirations of the Ukrainian-speaking peasant majority. Although this statement may have violated democratic principles, social democracy, in his mind, meant that the interests of the "most progressive class in history" possessed special privileges. To any nationally conscious Ukrainian, Piatakov's statement represented Red imperialism.[61]

After the collapse of the tsarist order in 1917, Bolsheviks in the Ukrainian provinces organized themselves into two separate groups: the Southwestern Organization, headquartered in Kiev; and the Donets-Krivoi Rog organization, centred in Kharkov. The former possessed about 7,800 members, the latter 15,800. Bolsheviks appealed to the working classes that had grown dramatically during the war but emerged tired, underemployed (if not unemployed), and hungry in the post-revolutionary period. Unlike the peasants who were tied to the land, the workers had time on their hands. Because most identified themselves as Russians or as Russian speakers, Ukrainians constituted a small minority in the Bolshevik ranks. In 1918, only 3.2 per cent of the total members of the newly created Communist Party of Ukraine (Bolshevik) identified themselves as Ukrainians.[62] In the

Donets-Krivoi Rog organization, where Russians comprised an absolute majority, Bolsheviks stood for the complete integration of the Ukrainian-speaking provinces with Russia. Although the leaders of the Southwestern Organization did not want to compromise with the Ukrainian national movement, its Ukrainian members called for an alliance with the peasant masses.[63]

Each of these groups and factions, in addition to those generated within the Bolshevik party's Central Committee, played an important role in helping to define the borders of the Ukrainian homeland and the sovereignty of the future Soviet Ukrainian Republic. With the overthrow of the Provisional Government in 1917, the Bolsheviks actively competed with the Central Rada in spreading their influence over the Ukrainian provinces with their vision of class-based sovereignty.

Although Lenin's Council of People's Commissars recognized the Ukrainian National Republic and its right to secede from the Russian Republic, the Bolshevik organization opposed the Rada's "non-recognition of the Soviets and Soviet power in Ukraine." The Rada's efforts to implement a national sovereignty based on the majority of the population identifying itself as Ukrainian provoked the Council of People's Commissars to disavow it as "the plenipotentiary representative of the working and exploited classes of the Ukrainian republic," even though the overwhelming majority of Ukraine's "exploited classes" were Ukrainian-speaking peasants.[64] At the First All-Ukrainian Congress of Soviets in Kiev on 25 December 1917, local Bolsheviks rhetorically deposed the Central Rada and announced the creation of the first Soviet Ukrainian government – the People's Secretariat of the Ukrainian National Republic – in Kharkov five days later.[65]

Fearing that the Rada's delegation at Brest-Litovsk would strike a separate deal with the Central Powers, Lenin sent Red Guard units from Petrograd, Moscow, and other northern industrial centres into Ukraine. These groups quickly brought pro-Bolshevik Soviet power to Ekaterinoslav, Odessa, Poltava, Mariupol, Kherson, and other cities.[66]

With this external intervention, the Bolshevik-led People's Secretariat won Kiev in late January 1918. After this new government moved its capital from Kharkov to Kiev on 12 February 1918, the Bolsheviks in Kharkov announced the secession of the Donets-Krivoi Rog (DKR) Soviet Republic from Ukraine, following Soviet Odessa's declaration of independence on 30 January 1918. Dissident Bolshevik factions within the DKR organization sought to divorce the industrial areas of the Ukrainian provinces from their agricultural counterparts. For a short period, three Soviet republics existed simultaneously in this region: (1) the People's Secretariat representing the Right Bank, but claiming all nine Ukrainian provinces; (2) the Donets-Krivoi Rih Soviet Republic, representing Ukraine's industrial centres in eastern and southern Ukraine; and (3) the Soviet Odessa Republic.[67]

After the successful German advance into Ukraine, the People's Secretariat split into factions, and on 24 February 1918, most of its members resigned. Mykola Skrypnyk, a Ukrainian Bolshevik, chaired a new cabinet. In early March 1918, his government unilaterally proclaimed the reintegration of the Donets-Krivoi Rog, Odessa, and Don republics into Soviet Ukraine within the boundaries established by the Third and Fourth Universals of the Central Rada.[68]

The Second All-Ukrainian Congress of Soviets, held in Ekaterinoslav in March 1918, approved the merger of these republics into a single Soviet Ukrainian Republic, which would remain independent of Soviet Russia.[69] Purely tactical considerations motivated this action. The party's left faction, which dominated the Congress, opposed Soviet Russia's Brest-Litovsk treaty and "hoped that by proclaiming Ukrainian independence from Soviet Russia, it could continue to fight against the German invaders, without involving Russia in a war with the Central Powers."[70] The Soviet Russian government immediately recognized the independence of Soviet Ukraine, but – of course – the Austrians and Germans did not.

Despite their expectations, the Bolsheviks – who proclaimed peasants should seize the land without compensating the landlords – did not win the loyalty of the Ukrainian peasantry.[71] Instead, the Borotbists, the former left wing of the Ukrainian Party of Socialist Revolutionaries, became the most influential political party in the countryside.[72]

When the war in Europe came to an end on 11 November 1918, the Germans and Austrians rapidly withdrew from Ukraine. Two days later, the Bolsheviks revoked the Treaty of Brest-Litovsk, moved military forces into Ukraine, and formed a provisional Workers' and Peasants' Government of Ukraine, under Piatakov's chairmanship. On 5 February 1919 the Bolsheviks re-took Kiev, and by the end of March they occupied nearly all of the Ukrainian provinces.[73]

Shortly before the defeat of the forces of the Ukrainian National Republic that winter, the provisional Soviet Ukrainian government proclaimed the formation of the Ukrainian Socialist Soviet Republic (later the Ukrainian Soviet Socialist Republic). This political entity included the Ukrainian lands which earlier had been part of the Russian Empire: the provinces of Kiev, Poltava, Podolia, Kharkov, Kherson, Ekaterinoslav, Chernigov (without its four northern counties), Volhynia (without its western part which Poland annexed), Taurida (without the Crimean peninsula), and part of the region of the Don Cossack Host.

But not all Ukrainian-speaking territories became part of the Ukrainian SSR. The Soviet-Polish Treaty of Riga of 1921 established Ukraine's western borders with Poland, leaving Eastern Galicia and Western Volhynia under Polish rule. The 1919 Treaty of Saint Germain and the 1920 Treaty of Paris united Bukovina and Bessarabia, respectively, to Romania. At the Paris Peace Conference, the victorious Allies assigned Transcarpathia to Czechoslovakia. Some of the Ukrainian-speaking territories came under the control of the Belarusian SSR and the Russian SFSR. In 1924 and 1925, Soviet authorities transferred the Shakhty region and three-quarters of the Taganrog okrug from the Ukrainian SSR to the Russian Soviet Federated Socialist Republic (RSFSR) and parts of three RSFSR provinces (Briansk, Kursk, and Voronezh) to the UkrSSR.

Only in 1926 did the Soviet authorities finally delineate the southern and eastern borders between the Ukrainian SSR and the RSFSR. But even with this final demarcation, approximately 1.5 million Ukrainian speakers still lived in Russian areas directly bordering Ukraine, not to mention the nearly 1.5 million living in the Kuban region of the North Caucasus, which belonged to the RSFSR.[74]

Yet, despite its hostility to all manifestations of nationalism, the Russian Communist Party – reacting to an adverse situation in Ukraine – inadvertently recognized the territorial and national integrity of the nine provinces and, in effect, agreed with the position espoused by the Ukrainian nationalists. Not only did Lenin's tactical choices lead to the formation of the Soviet Union several years later, but they also reinforced the Ukrainian and other non-Russian national identities in the USSR for decades afterwards. These critical events would not have happened without the war, the collapse of the Russian Empire, and – in the chaos that ensued – the emergence of the Central Rada and the Ukrainian National Republic. Millions of Ukrainian-speaking peasants supported, however inconsistently, these institutions and Europe's major powers recognized the UNR, at least for a short period.

In addition to the establishment of the Ukrainian SSR, the creation of an "autonomous" regional Communist Party in Ukraine also built on the legacy of the Central Rada and the Ukrainian Revolution of 1917–20. Founded in April 1918, shortly after the Germans occupied the area, the Communist Party (Bolshevik) of Ukraine [CP(b)U] retained an "independent relationship" with the Russian Communist Party.[75] But the CP(b)U's small membership hampered its effectiveness. Although the party grew from 22,500 in August 1917 to nearly 36,000 by May 1919, the majority of communists in Ukraine lived in the industrialized Left Bank. The party's influence faded in the western agricultural regions. Because non-Ukrainians constituted the overwhelming majority of the CP(b)U's members, they remained indifferent, if not hostile, to Ukrainian aspirations. Despite claims to the contrary, the CP(b)U remained a regional unit of the Russian Communist Party.[76]

The Bolsheviks launched three military campaigns over the course of two years (January–February 1918, December 1918–March 1919, December 1919–January 1920) to win the Ukrainian cities and the countryside. Unlike the Ukrainian nationalists, the Bolsheviks concentrated on the large cities (such as Nikolaev, Kremenchug, Kharkov, Ekaterinoslav, and Odessa) and on the Donbass. In August 1917, only 16 per cent of all Bolsheviks in the Ukrainian provinces lived and worked in the countryside.[77] Although local support for the Bolsheviks varied, these new recruits from the cities remained far more disciplined and ready to fight for their cause than the Ukrainian peasants, who rarely left their districts (they, after all, had to work their lands and defend them). Building on this urban alliance as well as the one with the Borotbists, the Bolsheviks finally succeeded.[78]

Cities emerged as the "strategic keys" to victory over the Ukrainian countryside. Bolshevik control of the urban rail centres, seaports, warehouses, factories, and natural resources strengthened their hand in the struggle against the countryside. Possessing the wealth of the cities, "the Bolshevik party could woo the peasant masses, who would probably give their loyalty to the power that held the reins firmly and distributed manufactured goods cheaply."[79] The cities also contained large numbers of hungry and unemployed men, ready to be mobilized.

Only after the final military victory over Denikin and Petliura in December 1919 and early 1920 did the Bolsheviks re-evaluate their nationality policy in Ukraine. Having won on the battlefield, they now reviewed their recent political mistakes.

Bolshevik Reassessments

Even before the final victory in 1920, a number of prominent party leaders recognized that they had alienated the Ukrainian peasantry. M. Ravich-Cherkasskii, the first official historian of the Bolshevik Party in Ukraine, admitted that the party had succeeded in mastering the cities, but had failed in the countryside:

Soviet power in Ukraine during its second campaign learned unsatisfactorily the peculiarities of the Ukrainian village. It was time to realize that Ukraine, oppressed by tsarism, did not lose its national identity. As a result of centuries-old Russification of the ... bureaucracy, the cities had been completely deprived of a national context, but the village remained Ukrainian.[80]

Although Lenin and the Bolsheviks created the Ukrainian Socialist Soviet Republic, modelled on the structure of the RSFSR, this political entity did not enjoy complete sovereignty within its borders. Many of the Soviet Ukrainian commissariats were subordinated to similar Soviet Russian commissariats in Moscow. The Soviet Russian government enhanced the sovereignty of the government of the Ukrainian SSR on 11 December 1919. But two weeks later, Lenin openly questioned whether Ukraine would remain a separate Soviet Republic in a federation with Russia or whether it would cease to exist and become an integral part of Russia. The next Ukrainian Congress of Soviets would decide this issue, he asserted.[81] In light of these stark choices, the various Ukrainian communist political forces (such as the Ukrainian Bolsheviks, the Borotbists, and members of the Ukrainian Communist Party, the Ukapists) sought to preserve, if not enhance, the Soviet Ukrainian Republic's sovereignty.[82]

On 19 February 1920, when the All-Ukrainian Revolutionary Committee reorganized itself into the regular government of the Ukrainian SSR (this time headed by Christian Rakovsky), the authorities possessed only seven People's Commissariats (internal affairs, agriculture, education, food, labour and social welfare, health, and justice).[83] The most important commissariats, such as those concerning military, economic, and foreign affairs, remained in Moscow.

Two months later, on 20 May 1920, the Fourth Congress of the Soviets of Ukraine reasserted Soviet Ukraine's sovereignty. Although the Congress repeated the Ukrainian adherence to the defence treaty of 1 June 1919, it claimed that the agreement dealt only with military matters. In addition, it demanded that all the commissariats dealing with defence issues become joint agencies of all the Soviet republics rather than solely agencies of the RSFSR.[84]

Conflicts over this resolution led to a new accord between the Russian SFSR and the Ukrainian SSR on 28 December 1920. The treaty proclaimed that both partners represented separate and entirely sovereign states, forming a partial federation for purposes of mutual defence and peaceful economic development. The RSFSR yielded to many of the major demands proposed by the Fourth Ukrainian Congress of Soviets. It increased the number of People's Commissariats in the government of the Ukrainian

SSR to sixteen, including: foreign affairs, internal affairs, justice, social welfare, education, agriculture, food, state control, health, army and navy, labour, post and telegraph, finance, transport, trade, and the Supreme Council of the National Economy. The first nine remained independent Ukrainian commissariats, while the last seven joined the corresponding commissariats of the RSFSR.[85]

Despite the retention of its own Commissariat of Foreign Affairs, the sovereignty of the Ukrainian SSR remained incomplete. Although the Ukrainian SSR proclaimed itself a sovereign and independent state and remained actively engaged in foreign affairs (concluding forty-eight bilateral and multilateral international treaties and agreements with other countries between 1920 and 1923), it did not control its own internal affairs.[86] Soviet Russian violations of the December 1920 concord increased over the next few years.

By 1922, the RSFSR's Commissariat of Foreign Affairs claimed to represent the interests of the four independent Soviet republics (the RSFSR, the Ukrainian SSR, the Belarusan SSR, and the Transcaucasian Federal Soviet Republic, which encompassed Georgia, Armenia, and Azerbaijan) to the outside world. As a result of the conflicts erupting between the RSFSR and the other Soviet republics, the Politburo of the Russian Communist Party [RKP(b)] in August 1922 formed a special commission to discuss the future relationship of the four Soviet republics. Stalin chaired the commission, and Dmytro Manuilsky, Mikhail Frunze, and Mykola Skrypnyk represented the CP(b)U.[87] On 23–4 September 1922, the commission heard Stalin's presentation to merge all of the republics into the RSFSR with the maintenance of cultural autonomy of the non-Russian nationalities within the RSFSR. Shortly afterwards, Lenin sent the Politburo members a letter sharply critical of Stalin's plan and suggested the establishment of a "union of equals."[88]

Lenin's proposal possessed an important geopolitical subtext. Inasmuch as the Bolsheviks anticipated a revolution in Germany in the near future, a Soviet Germany would most likely prefer to enter a Union of Soviet Socialist Republics of Europe and Asia than the Russian Federation.[89] On 6 October 1922, the Central Committee of the RKP(b) discussed Lenin's proposal and agreed with his idea of creating a new superstate – the Union of Soviet Socialist Republics (USSR), which would consolidate the four Soviet republics. Inasmuch as all of these non-Russian republics enjoyed brief periods of independence between 1917 and 1921, the new Soviet state reflected a compromise between proletarian internationalism and non-Russian nationalism. Although Russians would comprise the majority of the USSR's residents, the new state's political engineers envisioned the new body as "an internationalist state raised in the spirit of friendship of peoples."[90] Unlike the new European countries created as national states after 1918, the first socialist state would represent the interests of all national groups within its borders, not just the Russians. Of course, not all party members (the majority of whom identified themselves as Russians or Russified) understood or supported this distinction.

Nevertheless, the RKP(b)'s Central Committee bound all regional communist parties to champion this new political structure. In the second half of October 1922 the Central Executive Committee of the Ukrainian SSR and the All-Ukrainian Seventh Congress of Soviets agreed to form the Soviet Union.[91]

The First Congress of Soviets of the USSR convened in Moscow on 30 December 1922 and established the Union of Soviet Socialist Republics. After the Ukrainian SSR agreed to join the USSR, this geopolitically important republic retained only six independent People's Commissariats (agriculture, internal affairs, justice, education, health, and social welfare) and five joint ones, those subordinated to the corresponding Moscow agencies (finance, food supply, labour, workers' and peasants' inspection, and the Higher Council of National Economy). The new Soviet government completely took over five commissariats – foreign affairs, army and navy, transport, foreign trade, and communications.[92]

Although Ukraine entered the union as a "sovereign" state, the new Soviet authorities soon whittled away almost all of its sovereignty.[93] Nevertheless, the Communist Party created the Soviet Union, federal in form, centralized in content, as reflected in the political architecture of the Soviet constitutions of 1924, 1936, and 1977. As Richard Pipes first suggested in 1954, the design of the first socialist state represented a "subversive institution" within the heart of the Soviet political system.[94] The federal structure of the Soviet Union constructed in the early 1920s produced waves of unintended consequences over the next 100 years.

Conclusion

The cumulative repercussions of the First World War, Russia's February Revolution, the Bolshevik Revolution, German occupation, the disintegration of the Russian, Ottoman, German, and Austro-Hungarian empires, and the emergence of new nation-states from this political debris "radically dislocated existing social organization(s), strengthening old antagonisms between groups and inaugurating new ones."[95] Each of these convulsive events comprised a small, but integral part of the Great War and its post-war consequences.[96]

Ten years of mass violence destroyed the old social order and launched an unprecedented era of revolutionary upheaval. In the course of the war, revolutions, and social upheavals, Ukraine evolved from an imprecise territorial designation to an officially recognized Ukrainian homeland with distinct boundaries. In response to the fierce resistance the Bolsheviks encountered in the Ukrainian provinces, the Russian Communist Party's leadership approved the establishment of the Soviet Ukrainian state, possessing clear borders (separating it from the Russian and Belarusian republics) and claiming control over a well-defined, contiguous territory. This new political entity included the nine (not five, as the Provisional Government claimed in August 1917) former tsarist provinces where Ukrainians constituted the majority of the population. The Ukrainian SSR emerged as an interactive compromise on the shoals of social antagonisms, nationalist aspirations, Bolshevik visions, and political realities. It included both the overwhelming populous agricultural regions as well as the less-populous, smaller industrial regions, including the breakaway Krivoi Rog-Donetsk and Soviet Odessa Republics.

In addition to its importance as a granary, a region with natural resources, and a major industrial area, Ukraine occupied a pivotal geographical location in East Central Europe. Situated at its eastern end, a pro-Bolshevik Ukraine could help ignite the much-anticipated international civil war against Western imperialism. The collapse of the Austro-Hungarian Empire and the unexpected birth of the Hungarian Soviet Republic (March–August 1919), the Red Army's drive against Poland in 1920, and the Soviet-directed stirrings of "international revolution" in Germany in the early 1920s only reinforced Ukraine's geopolitical importance to Lenin's party.[97]

Bolshevik leaders in effect created the Ukrainian SSR within the parameters declared by the UNR's Third Universal. They reluctantly recognized this territory with its agricultural and industrial regions as the homeland of the Ukrainians and implicitly acknowledged the leading role of Ukrainians in it. At the same time, they also granted the equality of all nations within the borders of Soviet Ukraine. This equality coincided with the views of Hrushevsky and the other leaders of the Central Rada, as exemplified by the law on national-personal autonomy.

Despite the outward appearance of a state, the Ukrainian SSR (like the other republics) remained more of a quasi-state rather than a true "sovereign" one. Soviet Ukraine's communist party and government did not completely control those who lived within the newly delineated entity, which possessed one primary and unspoken mission: to win over the Ukrainian peasants to the Bolshevik cause. Lenin's ideas prevailed; the communist leadership recognized the legitimacy of a separate Ukrainian identity (which the tsarist government had never done) and institutionalized it within the framework of a Soviet Republic, a constituent member of the federated Union of Soviet Socialist Republics. In spite of "the suspicious attitude of the significant majority ... the working class and, at the beginning, even of part of the peasantry," the Ukrainian SSR emerged, but with many political, national, and social contradictions.[98] These shortcomings would haunt the Ukrainian Soviet Socialist Republic (and independent Ukraine) over the next century.

4

The Ukrainian Movements in Poland, Romania, and Czechoslovakia, 1918–1939

Everyone knows and feels that this peace is merely an inadequate blanket thrown over unappeased ambitions, hatreds that are more indestructible than ever, and fierce, unextinguished national resentments.

Captain Charles de Gaulle, 1918[1]

Much like the Ukrainian speakers in the Russian Empire, Ukrainians in Austro-Hungary also experienced a revolution at the end of the Great War and embraced it enthusiastically. Like their compatriots in Russia's south-west provinces, their fervour did not succeed in winning them power. Despite the failure to establish an independent Ukrainian state on the ruins of the Austro-Hungarian and Russian empires, the Ukrainian national movement enlarged the base of those who identified themselves as Ukrainians. The period between the end of the First World War and the start of the Second mobilized Ukrainian-speaking populations throughout Europe, especially in the USSR, Poland, Romania, and Czechoslovakia.

By late 1918, the Central Powers had no hope of winning the war "to end all wars." On 31 October 1918, a group of Ukrainian officers and Sich Riflemen seized control of Lemberg (Lviv/Lwów), Galicia's capital. On 1 November, the Ukrainian National Council (Ukrains'ka Narodna Rada), a newly constituted body representing the Ukrainians of Austria-Hungary, proclaimed the creation of the West Ukrainian National Republic (ZUNR), two weeks before the establishment of the Polish Republic.[2] According to these political leaders, ZUNR would unite Eastern Galicia with Northern Bukovina and Transcarpathia in a densely populated area of about 70,000 square kilometres (27,027 square miles), containing a total population of approximately six million. Ukrainians constituted nearly two-thirds of its population, Poles 17 per cent, Jews 13 per cent, Hungarians 2 per cent, and Romanians 1 per cent.[3]

The leaders of the new Polish Republic demanded the restoration of "historic Poland" (in its pre-1772 borders, which included not only Galicia but also Right-Bank Ukraine) and disputed the ZUNR's claims. In light of this irreconcilable conflict, Eastern Galicia became one of the most contested areas of the former Habsburg Empire as both the Poles and Ukrainians took up arms to defend their cause. Lviv/Lwów and the Drohobych (Drohobycz)-Boryslav oil district emerged as the most important centres of the Polish-Ukrainian War. By successfully exploiting this oilfield, Austria-Hungary had become the third-largest oil-producing state in the world by 1909, accounting for 5 per cent of the world's total production, just behind the United States (61 per cent) and Russia (22 per cent).[4] Without this oilfield, both the Polish Republic and the ZUNR would remain backward, impoverished states, if they survived at all.

At the end of November 1918, Polish troops took Lviv/Lwów, but failed to gain control of the oilfield from the Ukrainians until May 1919. ZUNR's government fled to Ternopil/Tarnopol, then Stanyslaviv/Stanisławów, but managed to merge, however temporarily, with the Ukrainian National Republic on 22 January 1919. In the chaos of the overall Eurasian civil and national wars, this alliance soon collapsed.

In early 1919 the Western Ukrainians on their small territory possessed a numerically greater military capacity (with approximately 100,000 men) than the new Polish state, with its much larger territory and greater population. But as reinforcements from France arrived, the Polish army grew quickly and numbered 300,000 by the end of the summer.[5] By mid-July 1919, Poles occupied all of Eastern Galicia, at the cost of approximately fifteen thousand Ukrainian and ten thousand Polish lives.[6] Senior ZUNR officials, headed by Evhen Petrushevych, fled to Vienna, where they created a government-in-exile.[7]

Polish victory on the battlefield, however, did not guarantee permanent control of Eastern Galicia. Fearing Soviet Russia's revolutionary appeal throughout the world, the victorious Allied Powers became concerned about the Polish-Ukrainian War and resolved, however reluctantly, to implement Woodrow Wilson's (not Lenin's) vision of national self-determination in East Central Europe. To negotiate the borders of the new states established in this area, Allied diplomats had to make sense of the frenzy of claims, counterclaims, and half-promises they received after January 1919. Throughout the negotiations, most of the American delegates at the Versailles Peace Conference remained confused about the complexities of the nationally mixed areas of East Central Europe. While the British criticized the creation of a "Greater Poland," the French strongly supported a resurrected Poland containing Eastern Galicia, claiming that "Poland would suffer more than Ukrainians from losing East Galicia."[8]

This position prevailed at Versailles. Western ignorance of Eastern Galicia and Poland's military victory over the ZUNR helped the Polish delegation's propaganda campaign succeed. Although Polish diplomats admitted that Ukrainians constituted 58.6 per cent of the population of Eastern Galicia, socio-economic factors nullified their "right" to national self-determination. Over 60 per cent of its population, they claimed, remained illiterate and poor, making Ukrainians incapable of managing their own affairs. They, in short, remained politically immature and potential supporters of the Bolsheviks.[9]

These claims fell on fertile ground. Infected with an exaggerated fear of Bolshevism, the victorious Allies strengthened the newly created states of Poland, Czechoslovakia, and Yugoslavia, and enlarged the size of Romania. According to the calculations of the negotiators, these four states would protect Europe's eastern flank against a resurgent Germany and the "Bolshevik plague."[10]

The Allies desired to create a new bulwark against Soviet Russia and Germany in East Central Europe. They favoured the Polish cause, and France emerged as one of new Poland's most enthusiastic supporters. France, which owned majority shares of Poland's petroleum industry, fused its economic and political interests, and planned to surround Germany with strong states allied to the home of "liberty, equality, and fraternity."[11]

Despite the total mobilization of the Ukrainian population against the Poles, the ZUNR soon disintegrated. Shortly after the leaders of the Polish Republic won the public relations war in Paris, the Allies supplied military forces which secured Eastern Galicia, Volhynia, and Belarusan territories for the new state.

Other majority Ukrainian-speaking territories met the same fate. With the mobilization of national identities during the war, the post-war political settlements did not bring peace. In light of the hostile international situation after 1918 and the Great Depression after 1928, the Ukrainian question within the USSR, Poland, Romania, and Czechoslovakia represented not just four separate domestic issues, but a single transborder issue involving all the major European states, even those without significant Ukrainian minorities. Many Ukrainians who participated in the struggle for independence viewed their defeat as a personal and collective humiliation. They fought to reshape the ruins of collapsed imperial structures in the name of national, political, social, and economic equality. Their failure forced them to live in a world shaped by others.[12] Very few accepted the structural reality of the time: that international conjunctures were not yet in place for an independent Ukraine to emerge. For most, it was easier to believe the first interpretation than the second.

Despite the best of intentions, the Treaty of Versailles did not bring a just peace after the Great War. In appeasing the winners and humiliating the losers, the Allies unintentionally bolstered the emergence of Europe's authoritarian and totalitarian regimes and their experiments with state violence in the 1920s and 1930s. They set the stage for the outbreak of an even more brutal Second World War. The culture of war "did not die with the armistice" or with the subsequent peace treaties.[13]

Nationalizing States

After the collapse of the Austro-Hungarian, German, and Russian empires, newly independent states, such as Estonia, Latvia, Lithuania, Austria, Hungary, Finland, Poland, Czechoslovakia, and Yugoslavia, emerged in East Central Europe. They joined Greece, Romania, Bulgaria, and Albania, states that had already gained their independence from the Ottoman Empire in the nineteenth century. Not only did these new countries incorporate territories with populations sharing the same national identities, they also absorbed large areas with peoples who did not.

Taking advantage of the chaos generated by the First World War and the post-war revolutionary situation, Poland, Romania, Czechoslovakia, and Soviet Russia partitioned territories the Central Rada proclaimed as those constituting Ukraine. Poland won control of Eastern Galicia from Austria-Hungary and Western Volhynia and Kholm gubernia from Russia. Romania gained Bukovina from Austria-Hungary and Bessarabia from Russia. Czechoslovakia acquired Austria-Hungary's Transcarpathia (see map 5). The overwhelming majority of the Ukrainian-speaking territories in East Central Europe, those that had belonged to the Russian Empire, were now incorporated into the Soviet Union, the world's first self-proclaimed "proletarian state."

The enormous chasm between the ideal of national self-determination propagated during the war and the post-war reality embittered many of the thirty-one million Ukrainians, who remained the largest national group in Europe that failed to create an independent state after the First World War.[14] Despite their substantial numbers, its national movements could not overcome serious handicaps: its reliance on the peasants, the weak Ukrainian presence in the towns and cities, or the hostile international environment. To add insult to injury, the 3.8 million Ukrainians living under Polish control in 1921 possessed a population larger than that of the newly formed states of Estonia, Latvia, Lithuania, and Finland, states which possessed powerful international patrons.[15]

In Czechoslovakia, Poland, and Romania, as in the other new East Central European states, the ruling elites sought to integrate different pre-war regions with different political histories and different bureaucracies into a single, coherent, and efficient unit. In addition, these elites needed to reconcile the national minorities within the new borders to new post-war political realities. Although each of these states contained a core nation which comprised the majority of its population, each also possessed a large number of minorities (constituting up to one-third of their populations).[16]

Although most of the Ruthenian (also known as the Rusyn) population living in the northeastern counties of Hungary and Eastern Slovakia welcomed incorporation into Czechoslovakia, the overwhelming majority of Ukrainians who lived in the four eastern Polish voivodeships, Bukovina, and Bessarabia did not want to become citizens of Poland or Romania. Ukrainian aspirations for national independence came into conflict with the efforts of post-war states in East Central Europe to transform themselves into nationalizing states or to expand their territories.

Recognizing the possibility of conflicts between national majorities and national minorities in the newly created states of East Central Europe, the negotiators at Versailles also crafted and imposed special treaties dealing with national minorities on Czechoslovakia, Poland, Romania, and other countries in the region.[17] These Allied arbitrators anticipated that the newly created League of Nations would guarantee the rights of minorities, but they did not encourage national-personal autonomy (which only Estonia introduced in the 1919–39 period).[18]

This noble Allied effort to protect national minorities collided with the anxieties of the ruling elites in Poland and Romania, which constructed their respective new states as nationalizing states, countries that introduced policies favouring their respective core nation. In the view of the leading political and cultural elites within each state, independence did not overturn the consequences of nationally discriminatory policies or trends from the past.[19] They, in short, conceived their core nation as the legitimate "owner" of the state, one that should promote the language, culture, demographic position, economic development, and political hegemony of the majority population.[20]

In adopting these policies, Poland and Romania became nationalizing states that alienated their large minorities and aspired to assimilate their Ukrainian minorities. Both interwar governments overturned Austro-Hungary's liberal approach regarding the Ukrainians, repealing many of the laws that had protected Ukrainian rights in education and in the state bureaucracy. The Polish and Romanian regimes introduced discriminatory measures against the Ukrainian language and culture in the former Russian territories they acquired after 1918. The Polish government, moreover, attempted to isolate physically the former Russian territories of Volhynia (Polish: Wołyń) and the Kholm (Polish: Chełm) region from those of former Austrian-ruled Galicia.[21]

To better integrate Ukrainian-speaking territories into their new states, both Poland and Romania redrew their internal boundaries. The Polish authorities eliminated Galicia as an administrative unit and renamed its eastern region, where the majority of Ukrainians lived, as Eastern Little Poland (Małopolska Wschodnia), dividing it into three voivodeships (Lwów, Stanisławów, and Tarnopol) and packing in as many non-Ukrainians as possible. In the 1920s the Romanian rulers abolished all of their provinces, including the province of Bukovina, and redrew their counties, diluting some large Ukrainian areas with Romanians and other national groups.[22]

The Polish and Romanian post-Versailles regimes also sought to weaken the Ukrainian national orientation of both the Orthodox and Greek Catholic churches on their territories. In the 1930s, Polish authorities supported the forcible conversion of Orthodox churches to Roman Catholicism and physically destroyed hundreds of their churches in Chełm voivodeship, Western Wołyń, and Polesie (Ukrainian: Polissia).[23]

The Soviet Union reacted in a more complex manner. In the 1920s, the USSR favoured its large non-Russian populations and supported a quasi-sovereign Soviet Ukrainian political entity (see chapter 5). By the early 1930s, Stalinists altered its political landscape and remade the first socialist state into a hybrid socialist-Russo-nationalizing state (see chapters 6 and 7).[24]

Poland

In the interwar period, the Polish Republic possessed the largest territory and population (27,177,000 in 1921; 31,915,800 in 1931) in East Central Europe and contained most of the Ukrainians living outside the USSR.[25] Restored and located between a castrated Germany and the new Soviet state, Poland remained one of the most strategically important countries in the region. Due to the Entente delineation of the Polish-German and Polish-Czech borders and to its own successful efforts against the Bolsheviks in the east, Poland acquired large numbers of Lithuanians, Belarusans, Jews, and Ukrainians and approximately four million Orthodox believers. Adherents of Orthodox Christianity lived primarily in the Belarusan-speaking and Ukrainian-speaking territories (which now became Wołyń, Polesie, and

Chełm voivodeships), areas of the former Russian Empire where the Russian Orthodox Church predominated after 1875.[26]

Although the Treaty of Versailles (28 June 1919) blessed Poland's creation, the Allied Council of Ambassadors postponed making a decision on the future status of the Ukrainians in Eastern Galicia. In 1923, the Allied Council allowed Poland to keep this region. The Allies, especially the French, chose to bolster Poland as a *cordon sanitaire* (a quarantine line) against Germany and the Soviet Union rather than provide national self-determination for the Ukrainians.[27] According to the above-mentioned treaties as well as the new Polish constitution (adopted on 17 March 1921), Ukrainians and Poland's other minorities were guaranteed equality before the law, the right to maintain their own schools, and the right to employ their own languages in the public sphere.[28] But Poland's fragile geopolitical position convinced many of its leaders that national security concerns were more important than compromises with its large non-Polish populations, especially the Ukrainians.

Despite Poland's possession of several important industrial centres, the new state remained one of Europe's poorest regions. According to the 1931 census, 60 per cent of the total population remained dependent on agriculture.[29] Despite the pressing issue of rural overpopulation and extensive land hunger, alleviating poverty and transforming the agriculturally based economy into an industrially based one did not emerge as the new Polish elite's first priority.[30] Instead, the new political establishment hoped to overcome the legacy of the partitions and fuse the Austrian, German, and Russian institutions and political cultures into a coherent whole. Poland's elites conflated plans for political consolidation with national integration, especially of its large Lithuanian, Belarusan, and Ukrainian populations.

The different political cultures the Polish state inherited and the new proportional representational system it inaugurated produced political gridlock. Between November 1918 and Marshal Joseph Piłsudski's coup in May 1926, fourteen different governments and political coalitions ruled Poland.[31] These constant electoral swings highlighted the country's conflicting aspirations and popular expectations, long unexpressed under the partitioning powers, and paralysed the new state. Many Polish observers proclaimed that Poland needed someone to maintain its national unity in order to avoid foreign intervention and a new set of partitions.

Joseph Piłsudski, the war hero, fit the bill. Although he never held the presidency or the prime ministership, he established a regime that combined "a personal military dictatorship" with a "centralized authoritarian oligarchy" and dominated the new republic from 1926 to 1935.[32] He centralized power in the executive branch, watered down the parliament's checks and balances of the government, and arrested the leaders of the leading opposition parties, thereby thwarting the emergence of a centrist movement. Although a staunch opponent of the National Democratic Party, he accepted some of their assumptions.

Haunted by Poland's past and influenced by the radical right-wing National Democratic Party, the new Polish ruling elite rejected for the most part the Polish-Lithuanian Commonwealth's tolerance of its large multinational and multi-religious populations prior to the Counter-Reformation. The National Democrats, Poland's largest political party in the interwar period, claimed that its non-Polish and non-Catholic populations "stabbed Poland in the back" in the seventeenth and eighteenth centuries and undermined the commonwealth's independence. Its spokesmen asserted that the newly restored Polish state would not repeat the commonwealth's "mistakes." Only the Poles would be masters of the new Poland, and the core nation would assimilate most of its minority groups, except for the Germans and Jews. The new rulers believed that the Jews remained unabsorbable and would be expelled or expatriated.[33]

Unlike the Ukrainians, Belarusans, and Germans, Polish Jews did not constitute "a compactly settled national group with a territorial claim against the Polish state or with the government of a neighboring state prepared to intervene on its behalf." Of all of Poland's national minorities, the Jews "represented the least tangible threat to Polish national security."[34] Nevertheless, the Polish authorities considered the Jews as the minority "whose assimilation was least desirable, and whose presence was most destabilizing."[35]

Although members of the PPS, the Democratic Party, and the Communist Party of Poland consistently opposed anti-Semitism, most could not accept the idea of Jewish cultural distinctiveness. They fervently believed that "full Polonization of the Jewish masses would eventually occur in a democratic and tolerant Poland."[36] But for most Poles, a democratic and tolerant state would have to wait. Poland's resurrection in the twentieth century after its partitions in the eighteenth century demanded internal security, political consolidation, and national integration. Most importantly, the new country needed a firm hand.

The National Democratic Party consistently advocated such a position. It attracted support throughout Poland and influenced all Polish governments in the interwar period, including Joseph Piłsudski's authoritarian regime.[37] During the leadership crisis after his death on 12 May 1935, the Polish public recognized Poland's vulnerability in regard to Nazi Germany and the Soviet Union. In this environment, the views of Roman Dmowski, the founder of the National Democratic Party, gained even more adherents. Most Poles interpreted all efforts by the non-Polish minorities to differentiate themselves in public from the majority Polish population as treasonable activities which the state had to suppress. Not surprisingly, these ideas and actions promoting a nationally pure Poland provoked a hostile reaction, especially from Ukrainians, who constituted approximately 15 per cent of the total population and whose number grew from 3.8 million in 1921 to approximately 5.3–5.5 million by 1939.[38]

Poland's Ukrainian speakers lived in areas far poorer, less industrialized, and more agriculturally backward than western or central Poland. About two-thirds of Poland's Ukrainian speakers lived in the eastern Galician voivodeships of Lwów, Stanisławów, and Tarnopol; the remainder resided mainly in the voivodeships of Wołyń and Polesie. Smaller groups lived near Chełm in Lublin voivodeship and in the Lemko region of the Western Carpathians (Cracow voivodeship).[39] In these eastern domains, Ukrainians constituted almost 66 per cent of the population, and the Poles 25 per cent. As in the Ukrainian-speaking provinces of the former Russian Empire, Ukrainians inhabited the rural areas and Poles and Jews dominated in the towns and cities. A Polish population, moreover, dominated Lwów, the largest city in Małopolska Wschodnia (Eastern Galicia).[40]

Although not all Ukrainian speakers in Poland hated the Poles, Polish policies often needlessly inflamed them.[41] The highly centralized Polish administration, based on the French political system, provided few opportunities for self-government to territorially concentrated Ukrainians, Belarusans, and Lithuanians, who remained embittered by the government's failure to introduce any land reforms benefiting them.[42] As the Ukrainian population exploded from 1921 to 1939, they became even more impoverished. The Great Depression plunged the economy into a downward spiral.

The Polish government reached a short-lived agreement after 1935 with the Ukrainian National Democratic Alliance (UNDO), the largest and most moderate Ukrainian political party in Poland in the interwar period.[43] Founded in 1925 as a fusion of various Ukrainian political and social groups and led by Greek Catholic clergy and the intelligentsia, UNDO aspired to create an independent state with a democratically elected parliamentary system. But the Polish government's efforts to colonize Ukrainian lands and dispossess Ukrainian Greek Catholic and Orthodox churches destroyed this political cooperation in 1938. Although UNDO declared its loyalty to the Polish state at the outbreak of the Second World War on 1 September 1939, many (if not most) Ukrainians hoped that the Germans would completely overturn the status quo and did not mourn Poland's collapse.[44]

Whether led by Roman Dmowski's National Democrats on the right or by Piłsudski and the Polish socialists on the left, interwar Polish governments often violated treaties that proclaimed the equality of Ukrainians under the law. Long before the government abrogated the Polish Minority Treaty in September 1934, it sought to blur (if not destroy) the Ukrainians as a group distinct from the Poles by restricting the use of their East Slavic language in public, by limiting Ukrainian organizations, and even by banning the term "Ukrainian."[45]

Local Polish officials tore down road and street signs written in Ukrainian. They reprimanded and persecuted individuals for publicly expressing themselves in their native language, for subscribing to Ukrainian newspapers, for sending their children to Ukrainian schools, and for belonging to Ukrainian organizations. Not only did the Polish authorities arbitrarily engage in these indignities and public humiliations against nationally conscious Ukrainians, they also sought to dismantle Ukrainian civil society and to subordinate the Ukrainians in Małopolska Wschodnia and Western Wołyń.

In 1924, the Polish government passed laws that prohibited the use of the Ukrainian language in the state bureaucracy and converted the majority of Ukrainian-language public schools into bilingual (Polish-Ukrainian) ones, and ultimately into Polish schools.[46] If 3,600 Ukrainian-language elementary schools operated in Poland in 1919, 650 remained during the 1930–1 academic year, and only 139 in 1938–9, even with the large increase of the Ukrainian-speaking population in the interwar period.[47] At the beginning of 1919, thirty Ukrainian-language high schools operated in Galicia and Western Wołyń.[48] By 1938–9, only twenty-four remained to serve a Ukrainian population of 5.5 million.[49]

Polish authorities also reconstructed the University of Lemberg, a Polish-Ukrainian institution in the Austrian Empire, into a Polish-language university. They abolished the Ukrainian history and literature chairs, dismissed Ukrainian professors, and denied admission to students who had not served in the Polish army during the Polish-Ukrainian War (which excluded all Ukrainian males of university age). The government also closed a majority of the reading rooms belonging to Prosvita, the mass-based enlightenment society, and harassed the Ukrainian cooperative movement, which sought to improve farming methods and the peasant's standard of living. The political elite, moreover, heavily censored the Ukrainian press and banned many publications. In the 1930s the government dissolved the Ukrainian scouting organization (Plast) and the Union of Ukrainian Women (Soiuz ukrainok), the most influential women's organization in Poland's eastern domains.[50]

Between 1920 and 1925, the Polish government provided financial incentives for the migration of 300,000 Poles from central Poland to Małopolska Wschodnia and Wołyń, areas that already possessed a high population density and possessed less productive soil than central Poland's.[51] This colonization effort as well as Poland's discriminatory policies angered Ukrainians and undermined the few opportunities left to reconcile the two antagonistic communities after the short, bitter war of 1918–19. The land reform process administered by the authorities favoured the Polish migrants, not the impoverished local Ukrainian population. Approximately 79 per cent of peasants in the three voivodeships of Lwów, Stanisławów, and Tarnopol owned on average five hectares (twelve acres) or less, a size generally incapable of providing for a family of four to six members.[52] Despite the emergence of a highly successful Ukrainian agricultural cooperative movement in the interwar period, most Ukrainians remained poor, becoming even poorer during the Great Depression.[53] Their low incomes, Poland's slow economic growth, and the collapse of the international agricultural market created not just a permanent state of poverty, but total demoralization, especially among the young.

To most Ukrainians coming of age in the 1920s and 1930s, the social, economic, and political situation in Poland's eastern domains appeared hopeless. In light of the officially sanctioned discriminatory measures they encountered, Ukrainians recognized that their parents and grandparents had enjoyed more opportunities to better themselves in the Austrian Empire (where imperial officials had considered them equal with the Poles) than they would in independent Poland. Due to the crushing population pressures in the countryside, most young people wanted to leave for towns and cities, or to migrate to North America. But few, if any, found educational or employment opportunities in the urban areas or could leave for the new world. In the 1920s the United States introduced racist legislation restricting the immigration of Southern and East Central Europeans as well as Asians, but Canada did not. Despite this opportunity, only sixty-five to seventy thousand Ukrainians from Poland migrated to Canada.[54] As the Polish economy collapsed during the Great Depression, young men and women could find no means of gainful employment. Profoundly angry and frustrated with their situation, many Ukrainian-speaking young people embraced extremist solutions, such as communism and integral nationalism, a form of nationalism less tolerant than the liberal nationalism espoused by UNDO and the Greek Catholic Church.

Founded in 1919, the Communist Party of Western Ukraine (CPWU), an autonomous part of the Communist Party of Poland, gained some support in the 1920s. In demanding the redistribution of land to Ukrainian peasants without compensation to the landowners and the annexation of Poland's southeastern region to the Soviet Union, the CPWU represented a major national security threat to Poland. Warsaw feared that Moscow could exploit the social unrest in its eastern borderlands and intervene militarily. (The Soviet Union, in turn, dreaded another Polish invasion of its territories.)[55] Not surprisingly, many Ukrainians, especially in densely populated Wołyń, enthusiastically supported the CPWU.[56] During the last reasonably free elections in Poland in 1928, Communist front parties in Wołyń won 48 per cent of the vote; in Małopolska Wschodnia, they won only 13 per cent.[57]

The CPWU remained less popular in Małopolska Wschodnia than in Wołyń for several reasons. Most Ukrainians in Małopolska Wschodnia remembered the brutal Russian occupations during the war and very few favoured Eastern Galicia's and Western Volhynia's incorporation into Soviet Ukraine. When Ukrainians learned of the forced Soviet collectivization drive and the Holodomor of 1932–3, support for the CPWU and sympathy for the Soviet Union completely vanished.[58] Despite retaining their scepticism towards the Soviet regime, the majority – even staunch anti-communists, nonetheless approved of the Soviet policy of Ukrainization and imagined Soviet Ukraine as a stage in the evolution of an independent Ukrainian state.[59]

As communism's appeal declined, another ideology, integral nationalism, won the allegiance of most Ukrainians who came of age in the interwar period. Members of this radical right-wing movement acquired certain ideological principles from the traditional conservatives, but sought to create a mass movement based on new principles.[60] Its ideology embraced a different tone and view of the world than the liberal Ukrainian nationalism practised in Eastern Galicia before the Great War. Unlike the leaders of the Ukrainian national movement in the Austro-Hungarian Monarchy, post-war radical nationalists refused to compromise with the political status quo or recognize the Polish state's existence. These men and women raised the struggle to create an independent Ukrainian state above all other values, including humanitarian ones. By glorifying action, war, and violence, this small group – organized in a single party and led by a charismatic leader – unflaggingly engaged in illegal (if not immoral) activities in order to spark a radical political realignment in Europe and to pave the way for an independent Ukraine.

The Organization of Ukrainian Nationalists (OUN) embodied this proactive stance.[61] Founded in 1929 as a merger of various nationalist student organizations and groups of Ukrainian war veterans (who encountered official Polish hostility throughout the interwar period), this organization vowed to form an independent, united, national state in the territories where Ukrainians lived. The group built upon the Ukrainian Military Organization (UVO), established in 1920 in Prague to continue the armed struggle against the Polish occupation of Eastern Galicia. UVO had provided a haven for many Sich Riflemen and veterans of the Polish-Ukrainian War of 1918–19, men who initiated a series of assassinations, bombings, and other acts of terror against the Polish authorities and Ukrainian "collaborators" in the interwar period.[62] Even after the Allied Council of Ambassadors finally recognized Polish sovereignty over Eastern Galicia on 15 March 1923, which "raised doubts among many Ukrainians about the sense of continuing armed resistance," UVO continued its actions.[63]

Like UVO, the OUN accepted violence as a political tool against external and internal enemies. Inspired primarily by Mussolini's Fascist Party, by the success (not the ideology) of the Nazi Party in Germany, and by the writings of Dmytro Dontsov (1883–1973), the OUN sought to overturn the political status quo created at Versailles and establish an independent Ukrainian state in East Central Europe.[64] Despite widespread sympathy for the fascist and national-socialist movements in Italy and Germany, which promised to overturn the European political order and confront the USSR, the OUN leaders did not identify their organization as a fascist one. They claimed that their group represented the "revolutionary integral nationalism of a stateless nation" aspiring to establish an independent state, not take over an existing one.[65] In their pronouncements, Ukrainian state creation remained the ultimate goal of their struggle for national liberation. Colonel Evhen Konovalets, an officer in the Sich Riflemen during the First World War and the head of UVO, assumed the leadership of OUN and held it until his assassination by a Soviet agent in Rotterdam in 1938.

The OUN's founding represented a declaration of war on Poland. During this internal war, the OUN engaged in terror, which T.P. Thornton defined as "a symbolic act designed to influence political behavior by extranormal means, entailing the use or threat of violence."[66] This group employed this rationally calculated violent tool to terrify the agents of the Polish state to end their occupation of Eastern Galicia and Western Volhynia. Members of this group organized boycotts of Polish tobacco and liquor monopolies, torched the estates of Polish landlords, led armed attacks on police stations, post offices and governmental buildings (physical symbols of the hated Polish state), and assassinated nearly sixty Polish officials and uncounted numbers of Ukrainian "traitors" in the eastern voivodeships. An "epidemic" of sabotage and terror swept Galicia in 1930–1, the first great wave since 1922–3, when the Allied Council of Ambassadors acknowledged Poland's right to incorporate Eastern Galicia.[67]

As a prelude to the November 1930 parliamentary elections, the Polish authorities introduced repressive countermeasures, such as the "Pacification" campaign from September to November 1930, which sought not only to stop "terrorists," but also punish the Ukrainian population as a whole. In the course of this brutal implementation of the principle of collective guilt to the OUN's terror campaign, the authorities arrested, imprisoned, and tortured hundreds of leading Ukrainian activists, including women. These large-scale anti-Ukrainian campaigns did not pacify the Ukrainians.[68] Just the opposite. The OUN responded with a more intense level of violence, which culminated in the organization's 15 June 1934 assassination of Bronisław Pieracki, the minister of the interior and the architect of the Pacification campaign. The Polish government cancelled its minority treaty three months later.

Although the OUN may have attracted somewhere between eight thousand and twenty thousand members by 1939, its influence far outweighed its small numbers.[69] The spirit of selfless, even fanatical, dedication to the Ukrainian cause appealed to young people, especially those who had no place in interwar Polish society and who were attracted to extreme black-white ideologies and "to holistic black-and-white solutions."[70] They imagined that their parents' generation failed to create an independent Ukraine. One OUN courier, recruited at the age of fourteen in 1940, shortly after the Soviet annexation of Eastern Galicia, recounted her ideological training in her memoirs:

> My contemporaries and I searched for an answer to the baffling and painful question: "Why was Ukraine not an independent nation?" It was difficult to understand why, after so many revolutions and uprisings, Ukrainians had been unable to establish a sovereign state. Where did the fault lie? What was missing? We discussed these questions over and over again at our weekly meetings. This self-evaluation coupled with our patriotism made us painfully aware of our second-class status, *which we had inherited from our fathers, our grandfathers, and our great-grandfathers.* We talked about the unsuccessful attempts to create an independent Ukraine during World War One, *and we could not forgive our parents for letting that opportunity slip through their hands.* We learned in the OUN's Youth Section that it was our duty to fight for our land, our customs, and our proud heritage.[71]

This young woman eloquently expressed her own frustrations and that of her generation growing up in interwar Poland. Who was at fault for Ukraine's defeat? For them, individuals, groups, nations, even those within one's own nation – not structural factors, not the First World

War's alliance system and its collapse – prevented the emergence of an independent Ukraine. Like many in her generation, she absorbed the OUN's "maximalist" orientation, especially the organization's emphasis on single-party rule and uncompromising hostility towards its enemies and wayward allies.[72] Although a majority of Ukrainians did not embrace the OUN's ideology, most agreed that they should respond to each Polish indignity and provocation with "an eye for an eye, a tooth for a tooth."

In comparison to the mass arrests of traitors, "wreckers," and "saboteurs" a few years later in Hitler's Germany and in Stalin's USSR, the number of arrests, trials, and convictions in Poland were very small.[73] But the overall brutality of the Pacification campaign in the context of the past Austrian environment alienated the Ukrainian population from the Polish regime and, for many, justified the actions of the OUN. Each act of brutal force provoked a violent reaction. The cycle of violence and counter-violence became self-perpetuating and more intense, undermining moderates among both Poles and Ukrainians.

The radicalization of the Polish and Ukrainian communities also spawned divisions within the Ukrainian community. In this hostile environment, the leadership of UNDO, an older generation educated in the nuanced pre-war cosmopolitan culture of Vienna that sought to represent Ukrainian interests by legal means, could not reach an accommodation with the Poles or compete with the radicalized OUN members. These young radicals presented themselves as harbingers of the future and would not subordinate themselves to their elders or to the wisdom of elected Ukrainian parliamentary officials. This generational conflict intensified in the 1930s as many rank-and-file OUN members embraced fascist practices, although not necessarily the entire ideology's mindset.[74] Despite the radicalization of many young people, UNDO (with the Ukrainian Socialist-Radical Party, a member of the Labour and Socialist International, as its junior ally) remained the dominant political coalition among Galician Ukrainians throughout the 1920s and 1930s.[75]

In addition to UNDO, the Ukrainian Greek Catholic bishops, especially Metropolitan Andrei Sheptytsky, publicly opposed the activities of the OUN.[76] As an individual who enjoyed the highest respect in the Ukrainian community, he hoped to restrain OUN's violence. He asserted that OUN's actions catalysed new repressions against its compatriots and would not destroy the power of the Polish state. His call for an end to the violence did not persuade either the Poles or the OUN.[77]

Although the overwhelming majority of Ukrainians despised Polish rule, they came to different conclusions about what they could accomplish within this adverse environment. UNDO's leaders aspired to work within the Polish system in a non-violent manner, but often found themselves thwarted by Polish rulers and colonists, who increasingly embraced intolerant political positions and blocked intercommunal reconciliation. The Polish power elite needlessly marginalized UNDO and undermined its authority among Ukrainians.

By engaging in terrorist activities against the Polish state and its representatives, the OUN sought to publicize its cause and deliberately provoke government reactions that would alienate the Ukrainian population, increase support for its agenda, and create an opening for expanded subversive activities.[78] By waging a violent struggle against the Poles, the OUN hoped to win over the "uncommitted fence-sitters" among Ukrainians.[79] But, in effect, these actions only helped the authorities cripple UNDO's already limited political influence within the Polish political system.

Extremism also emerged in Wołyń, which differed from Małopolska Wschodnia. In Wołyń, the overwhelming majority of Ukrainians belonged to the Orthodox Church, not to the Greek Catholic Church. Before 1914, when the Russian Empire had controlled the area, the Ukrainian-speaking population did not possess a national consciousness as intense as that of their compatriots in Austria's Galicia.[80]

After Wołyń became a part of Poland, the situation changed. The new Polish government started to favour the small Polish population. According to a local 1937 census, it recorded 348,079 who identified themselves as Poles (16.7 per cent of the total population), 205,615 as Jews (9.9 per cent), and 1,420,094 as Ukrainians (68.1 per cent).[81] The authorities introduced land reforms that benefited only the Poles, supported and subsidized the arrival of several hundred thousand Polish colonists (often demobilized soldiers and their families), and transferred a large number of Polish administrators and bureaucrats from central Poland.

The Polish state also introduced other measures that further aggravated the Ukrainian population. In the 1920s, for example, authorities inaugurated compulsory Polish-language education in the province, but this skill did not lead to employment during the Great Depression. Instead, the educated became an under- or unemployed intellectual vanguard that incited the disaffected Ukrainian majority against the Polish state.

Henryk Józewski (1892–1981), the new governor of Wołyń (1928–38), hoped to create an attractive environment for Ukrainians and blunt the attraction of Soviet Ukraine (located next door) and the Ukrainian nationalists' vision of an independent Ukraine. A Pole born in Kiev, he had served for a short period as the deputy minister of the interior in the Ukrainian

National Republic in 1920 and as Poland's minister of the interior from December 1929 to June 1930. As Wołyń's governor, he introduced extensive cultural concessions to the Ukrainians, including Ukrainian-language courses in all state schools, while establishing a base for espionage operations against the Soviet Union. He even supported the Ukrainizing efforts of the Polish Orthodox Autocephalous Church, established in 1924, in his province.[82] But he could do little about land reform or about the 300,000 Polish colonists Warsaw sent.[83] Józewski succeeded "in fostering a Ukrainian patriotism in Wołyń, but failed to connect this new trend to Polish statehood."[84] After 1935, the governor lost the confidence of the Ukrainian majority and control over his own province. The Polish army intervened, destroying Orthodox churches and expropriating Ukrainian properties, which embittered the local population even more.

The Promethean Movement

Józewski also played a key role in the Polish Promethean movement, an ambitious project Marshal Piłsudski initiated to undermine the integrity of the USSR. Piłsudski, the self-appointed guardian of Polish independence, hoped to re-establish a strong homeland, to "shatter Russia into a series of nation-states," and to create a federation of these newly liberated lands under Poland's sphere of influence.[85] By including Belarus, Lithuania, and Ukraine, this Polish-led alliance would replace Russia as the great power in East Central Europe. Named after the mythical god Prometheus, who brought fire (a symbol of the struggle for freedom) to humankind, this group would serve both Polish and non-Polish long-term interests.

The Promethean project possessed a number of closely intertwined invisible and visible threads. The first encompassed covert Polish intelligence operations against the Soviet Union, such as those Józewski and his colleagues initiated. The second embraced the public sphere, with large-scale efforts to organize anti-Soviet propaganda or to engage in concrete actions, such as the unsuccessful campaign to prevent the USSR from taking a seat at the League of Nations.[86] Each of these strands remained tightly interwoven and, in the case of the Promethean League of Nations Subjugated by Moscow (better known as the Promethean League), difficult to disentangle. In 1925, Piłsudski's trusted men formed this anti-Communist international, which brought together representatives of various anti-Soviet governments-in-exile scattered across Europe and Turkey and headquartered the League in Warsaw. Over the next fifteen years, the Polish military, foreign ministry, and their allied intelligence services covertly supported this and other similar organizations diplomatically and financially. This anti-Soviet operation achieved its most notable successes between 1926 and 1932.

The complex relationship between Piłsudski and Petliura, the head of the Ukrainian National Republic (UNR) during the revolutionary period, profoundly influenced the Promethean project of the 1920s and 1930s. Piłsudski, who had always considered Russia to be Poland's primary enemy, had dreamed of reducing the empire's size even before the outbreak of the First World War. The February and October Revolutions and subsequent civil and national wars gave him the opportunity to do so. After many preliminary negotiations, he and Petliura signed the Treaty of Warsaw on 21 April 1920 as a prelude to their joint military operations against the Soviet Ukrainian and Soviet Russian governments. The Polish side recognized the right of Ukraine to an independent political existence and Petliura's Directory as the "supreme government" of the UNR, which would encompass Central Ukraine, the territory between the Zbruch and Dnieper Rivers (far less than the territory the UNR claimed). Although the new Polish government surrendered all claims to Right-Bank Ukraine, which the Polish-Lithuanian Commonwealth controlled until the First Partition of Poland in 1772, it insisted on keeping Eastern Galicia.[87]

This Polish-Ukrainian treaty annulled the Act of Unity of 22 January 1919 that had united the UNR with the West Ukrainian National Republic (ZUNR). The leadership of the two Ukrainian republics disagreed over which state represented the greatest danger to Ukrainian national interests. For the heads of the ZUNR, Poland remained the foremost enemy; their counterparts in the UNR perceived Russia (whether Bolshevik or White) as the primary threat. Bowing to the reality of its fragile existence and to Polish pressures, the UNR reluctantly recognized that Eastern Galicia and Western Wołyń would remain under Polish control. Without Polish help, Petliura understood that he could not win against the Bolsheviks, who had already occupied most of the territory he claimed. If he could not wrest some area for the UNR and successfully defend it, the Ukrainian nationalist cause would fail. Petliura recognized that he did not possess any viable alternatives and that he was forced to take the opportunities presented to him and not hold out for political miracles.

Everything hinged on the ultimate victory of the combined Polish-Ukrainian forces against the Communist/Bolshevik regime in Ukraine, which commenced several days after the signing of the Warsaw Treaty. The first weeks of the invasion succeeded beyond all expectations, and the joint forces entered Kiev in early May 1920. The Bolsheviks launched a successful counter-offensive in June, which led them to the gates of Warsaw in August. Piłsudski's counter-thrust expelled the Red Army from Poland, but he permanently lost most of the central Ukrainian territories he and Petliura had captured.

The Treaty of Riga, signed on 18 March 1921, marked the end of formal hostilities between Poland and the Soviet republics. The new Polish government gained only about one-third of the territories that the Polish-Lithuania Commonwealth possessed before the First Partition, while Soviet Russia kept the rest.[88] These two newly created countries divided the Ukrainian and Belarusan territories between them and established the western boundaries of Soviet Ukraine and Soviet Belarus. Although the treaty weakened Poland's influence in East Central Europe, Piłsudski did not abandon his dreams of destabilizing the USSR or of creating a federation in this region. In his mind, the Polish-Soviet agreement represented a temporary setback for Poland's rebirth on the international stage. Aspects of the earlier Polish-Ukrainian agreement, especially its hostility to the USSR, remained intact. Hence, the Promethean League.

Although a number of prominent Ukrainians participated in the Promethean League, most of its Ukrainian members came from Central and Eastern Ukraine, not Małopolska Wschodnia.[89] They took advantage of the many think tanks (such as the Oriental Institute, the Polish Institute of Nationalities Research, and the Ukrainian Scientific Institute in Warsaw) and publications (*Wschód/L'Orient, Biuletyń Polsko-Ukraiński,* and *Prométhée*) sponsored by the Polish government. Although the Piłsudski regime subsidized the UNR government-in-exile after the debacle of 1920, the Polish leader's authoritarianism increasingly intensified in the late 1920s and early 1930s and he became identified with Polonization, the Pacification campaign, and the administration's anti-Ukrainian policies in the Lwów, Stanisławów, Tarnopol, and Wołyń voivodeships.

Although many of Piłsudski's followers outwardly showed respect to Poland's Belarusan and Ukrainian minorities, many also adhered to a sense of Polish cultural superiority, persuaded that they could raise the level of the "less developed" Eastern Slavs and eventually transform them into Poles. They differed, for the most part, from Dmowski's supporters in terms of tactics, not necessarily in the overall strategy of creating a homogeneous Polish nation-state.

In response to these hostile policies and views, the Ukrainians in Poland's eastern regions rejected Prometheism. Inasmuch as the Promethean movement engaged in a semi-covert set of activities promoting the creation of an independent Ukrainian state, it operated on a *state-to-state level*. A large number of Prometheans, like Józewski, may have sincerely defended Ukrainian culture, but the Polish government and its agents – following the National Democratic vision of the world – actively oppressed and harassed Ukrainians *as a people*. Most Ukrainians viewed their antagonistic relationship with the hostile bureaucracy as official Polish policy and did not whole-heartedly condemn the OUN's assassination of Tadeusz Hołówko (1889–1931), the overall coordinator of the Promethean movement. Although Hołówko promoted the Polish government's close cooperation with the UNR and the Promethean movement, the OUN accused him of "spiritually disarming" Ukrainian society.[90]

Many (if not the majority of) Ukrainians in these Polish borderlands, moreover, did not possess a high opinion of Petliura's exiled UNR, which – in their assessment – had abandoned them. After Petliura's 1926 murder in Paris, the exiled UNR ceased to play a significant role in their lives.

As Ukrainians reassessed their position in interwar Poland, the Polish political leadership also reappraised its relationship with the USSR and with its own Ukrainian population. Stalinist repressions in Ukraine, such as the public trial of the Union for the Liberation of Ukraine in early 1930, the forced collectivization drive, and subsequent Holodomor, killed millions and dispirited survivors, inducing mass social despair. The Soviet state's success in implementing large-scale, brutal measures convinced Piłsudski's inner circle that the possibility of mass anti-Soviet rebellions in Ukraine had passed.[91] Many now started to argue that Poland's international projects, such as the Promethean movement, should not take priority over Poland's own internal concerns. Aggravated by its restive national minorities, the rise of Hitler's Nazi Party and the possibility of a German invasion, widespread communist activities in Wołyń, and the Great Depression, Poland's ruling elite embraced the issue of strengthening its internal security over efforts to destabilize the USSR. The government expanded its repressive measures against Poland's largest national minority and then signed a non-aggression pact with the Soviet Union on 25 July 1932.

For Ukrainians in the Polish voivodeships, a cruel reality emerged after the First World War. The end of the brutal conflict destroyed all promise of union with their brothers and sisters across the Zbruch River (the international border dividing Poland from the USSR), or of political autonomy or independence. By mobilizing large numbers of Polish and Ukrainian speakers along national lines, the First World War and the Polish-Ukrainian War of 1918–19 seriously undermined the possibility of a political reconciliation or compromise with the Poles. The actions of the Polish military, police, and bureaucracy in the majority Ukrainian-speaking territories generated painful reminders of "hopes deferred and fears fulfilled" on a regular, almost daily, basis.[92] The OUN responded in kind, which only infuriated the Poles and accelerated the cycle of violence.

Two non-negotiable views of the world set the stage for the conflict between Ukrainians and Poles. Ukrainians did not want to recognize Polish control of the borderlands or to integrate into Poland. They understood that integration meant assimilation and national marginalization, if not extinction. Ukrainians considered the areas where they resided as the majority population as their homeland. They wanted the Polish state's public acknowledgment of their national dignity.

The majority of Poles, in turn, wanted to dominate these regions, which they regarded as their historical homeland. Despite Polish conquest of these areas, the potentially explosive anti-Polish hostility remained a threat. Active and passive Ukrainian resistance to Polish rule raised national security concerns to a feverish pitch for the Polish elite and for Poles living in Małopolska Wschodnia and Wołyń. By the end of the 1930s, these Poles considered Ukrainians disloyal citizens of Poland and active fifth columnists. With the exception of Józewski (and to some extent Piłsudski), the majority of the Polish ruling elite did not want to validate the Ukrainians as a group with equal national rights or provide them with full citizenship rights. These conflicting perspectives led to an unending spiral of violence and inter-communal hatred, preparing the ground for the horrid Polish and Ukrainian ethnic cleansing campaigns during the Second World War.

Romania

After the First World War, Romania emerged as the second most populous state in East Central Europe (17,793,250 in 1930).[93] During the 1919–20 peace settlements, Romania acquired Bessarabia from Russia, southern Dobruja from Bulgaria, and Transylvania, Bukovina, and the Banat from Austria-Hungary, doubling its pre-war territory.[94] Like Poland, this state possessed a poor economy with 72 per cent of its population dependent on agriculture.[95] After annexing these territories, Romania acquired 500,000 to 900,000 Ukrainians, or approximately 3 per cent of its total population.[96] Romania's post-war government gained Allied recognition of its control of Bukovina at the Treaty of Saint-Germain in September 1919 and of Bessarabia at the Treaty of Paris in October 1920. But the Soviet Union never recognized Romania's right to Bessarabia.

The new Romanian state was not a nationally homogeneous one. According to its census of 1930, Romanians comprised 70.8 per cent of the total population and included sizeable minorities, such as Hungarians and Germans.[97]

Of the three provinces Romania incorporated in 1918 (Bessarabia, Bukovina, and Transylvania), Bukovina possessed the smallest number of Romanians. Ukrainians resided in compact areas in the northern half of the region, where they barely outnumbered the area's Romanians. The relationship between Ukrainians and Romanians in Bukovina paralleled in many ways the antagonism between Ukrainians and Poles in Galicia.[98]

Much as the voivodeships of Lwów, Stanisławów, and Tarnopol differed from Wołyń, Bukovina differed from adjacent Bessarabia. As part o the Austro-Hungarian Empire, Bukovina received a greater degree of self-government than any other Ukrainian region and nurtured a well-developed Ukrainian civil society before the First World War. But Bessarabia – a part of the Russian Empire since the early nineteenth century – was one of the most economically and politically underdeveloped areas with a Ukrainian-speaking population. Not surprisingly, Ukrainian national consciousness existed at a weaker level here than in Bukovina. Whereas the Ukrainian population in the northern half of Bukovina constituted 65 per cent of the population of the province in 1930, in Bessarabia Ukrainians constituted only 11 per cent of the total population.[99] The Ukrainian national movement in both regions experienced intense Romanian hostility during the interwar period.

The new Romanian government dismantled Ukrainian achievements from the Austrian period. Officials prohibited the use of the Ukrainian language in public administration, in the courts, and in the schools and replaced it with Romanian. Post-war Romania acquired 216 Ukrainian-language schools from the Austrian period; within a decade the authorities converted all of them into bilingual Romanian-Ukrainian schools, then Romanian-language schools.[100] They abolished Ukrainian-language professorships at the University of Czernowitz (Romanian: Cernăuţi; Ukrainian: Chernivtsi) and banned the Ukrainian press and political parties. Although the government eased this state of siege in the Ukrainian areas in the late 1920s, they reimposed it a decade later, prohibiting all Ukrainian organizations and closing all Ukrainian-language schools. Its ministers and legislators sought to disfranchise its Ukrainian population linguistically and politically.[101] In 1924, the Romanian parliament enacted a law that described Ukrainians "as Romanians who have lost the native tongue of their ancestors."[102] This official definition of Ukrainians set the tone for Romanian-Ukrainian relations during the interwar period. Within a few years after their incorporation into Romania, Ukrainians lost their status as a recognized national minority and were forced into the melting pot of Romanianization.

Yet, despite the enforcement of discriminatory measures against Ukrainians, the twenty-year Romanian control of Bukovina and Bessarabia did not succeed in denationalizing this group. Instead, the government needlessly antagonized its Ukrainian population and unintentionally provoked an irreconcilable hatred of the Romanians.

Czechoslovakia

In the nineteenth century, the Czech lands of Bohemia and Moravia emerged as one of Austria-Hungary's major industrial centres. After 1918, Czechoslovakia became the most developed economy in East Central Europe, among the ten largest in the world. In 1930, for example, only 33 per cent of its overall population remained dependent on agriculture.[103] Czechoslovakia's economic success strengthened its overall liberal political orientation, although it did not win over all of its national minorities.

In February 1921, the newly established state possessed almost 13.4 million inhabitants, and by December 1930, 14.7 million, making it the fourth most populous country in East Central Europe (Yugoslavia being the third).[104] The country's 7.2 million Czechs constituted over half the population; its nearly two million Slovaks represented almost 14 per cent.

The country's 3.3 million Germans, who lived primarily in the Sudetenland, comprised 23 per cent of Czechoslovakia's population.[105] The overwhelming majority of them did not want to belong to this new state, which the Czechs had centralized, "denying German opponents refuge in federalist structures."[106] Czech authorities favoured their fellow compatriots in the public sector job market and Czech-owned businesses in the private sector.[107] As the Great Depression impoverished Czechoslovakia's German population, Hitler – who had campaigned on a platform of creating a "Greater Germany" – came to power and introduced reforms that improved the Third Reich's economy. Germany's economic and political resurrection in the 1930s emboldened Czechoslovakia's Germans to destabilize their new state. The antagonistic relationship between the Germans and Czechs helped undermine Czech rapport with the Slovaks and Rusyns/Ukrainians.

Czechs and Slovaks had much in common, but the two leading nations in Czechoslovakia possessed more differences than the state's founders imagined. Although Czechs and Slovaks spoke similar West Slavic languages, their experiences within the Austro-Hungarian Empire differed completely. The Slovaks were almost overwhelmingly agricultural. They, who had lived under Hungarian rule for nearly one thousand years and experienced pressures to assimilate into the dominant group, grew to fear the Czechs, "their numerically and economically stronger partner."[108] Although Czechs constituted a majority of the total population and held themselves superior to the other national groups within this hybrid state, they had never introduced nationalizing policies, unlike the Poles and the Romanians.[109]

Although the Czechoslovak government experienced serious difficulties with its German and Slovak minorities, which threatened the integrity of the new state, its difficulties with the Ukrainian-speaking population in Transcarpathia remained less problematic. In 1930, 446,916 East Slavs lived in Transcarpathia, Czechoslovakia's most economically and politically underdeveloped region, and another 200,000 in the adjacent Prešov region of Slovakia.[110] Although the government employed the designation "Ruski" to refer to these East Slavs (which the Austro-Hungarian government defined as Ruthenians) in their 1921 and 1930 censuses, "Ruski" did not represent the Russians, Ukrainians, or Carpatho-Rusyns in the modern sense of these terms.[111] These East Slavic speakers spoke a series of dialects "closely related to the Ukrainian dialects of Galicia."[112] But language and dialectical similarities did not necessarily predispose these speakers to accept a modern-Ukrainian identity or to identify with the Ukrainian political project. Altogether, the Ukrainian speakers constituted 4 per cent of the new state's total population.[113]

As the Habsburg Empire began to dissolve in the last months of 1918 and the early months of 1919, the Ruthenians formed numerous national councils, which discussed the political future of this region. The options included complete independence, autonomy within Hungary, or union with Russia, Ukraine, or the new state of Czechoslovakia. In light of their small numbers, their animosity towards the Hungarians, and Bolshevik victory in Russia and Ukraine, the Ruthenians chose the last option. The victorious allies then approved this decision at the Treaty of Trianon (4 June 1920), one of the many treaties that ended the First World War and defined the borders of the post-war world. In recognizing Czechoslovak sovereignty over the region, the negotiators asserted that these East Slavs should receive "the widest measure of self-government compatible with the unity of the Czechoslovak Republic."[114]

Contrary to the provisions of the treaty, however, the Czechoslovak constitution (promulgated earlier on 29 February 1920) and its subsequent amendments did not establish an autonomous Transcarpathia until October–November 1938, although it did create a distinct province, known officially as Subcarpathian Rus (Podkarpatská Rus). Although officials claimed that the Ruthenians remained too politically immature to govern themselves within the framework of an autonomous province, national security concerns outweighed all others. The Czechoslovak government feared not the Ruthenians, but the province's large Hungarian population, which in conjunction with the Hungarian government across the border, hoped to destabilize the region and annex it to Hungary.[115] Giving Subcarpathian Rus political autonomy would provide opportunities for Hungarian irredentists to legitimize their cause.

Despite these anxieties, the Czechoslovak authorities did manage to raise Transcarpathia's living standards and cultural and educational conditions in the 1920s. During the 1913–14 school year, this area possessed only thirty-four elementary schools with some form of Ukrainian (or Russian or local Slavic dialect) as the language of instruction. By 1931 the Czechoslovak authorities had established 425 schools with some variant of the local language in this region and approximately another one hundred in the Prešov region.[116] The Czechoslovak government also invested in adult education programs, which helped to raise the literacy rate in this region from 22 per cent in 1910 to 60 per cent in 1930.[117] On the negative side and despite the introduction of large public-works projects, the Czechoslovak government failed to alleviate peasant poverty. The world's Great Depression swept away the government's economic accomplishments in the region, and chronic mass unemployment, seasonal labour migration, and poverty followed.

The legacy of poverty hampered the process of consolidating a single East Slavic identity in this area. The Rusyn/Ukrainian-speaking population's small landholdings, conservatism, weak political awareness, high illiteracy rate, and small number of educated persons enfeebled the region's political and economic development. These factors, in turn, restrained the emergence of a consensus regarding the national identity of the local population.

As in Galicia fifty years before, the struggle over language divided the small number of members of the intelligentsia, which consisted of clerics, teachers, and lawyers. Although some of them still embraced a pro-Hungarian orientation, Hungary's appeal declined in the interwar period. Pro-Ukrainian and Russophile sympathies slowly replaced it, as did the Rusynophile response, a local patriotism which distinguished itself from the Ukrainian, Russian, Slovak, and Hungarian nations.[118] In the interwar period, the Czechoslovak government supported the pro-Ukrainian, pro-Russian, and pro-Rusyn identifications at different times.[119] Subsequently, many families in Transcarpathia possessed "a 'Russian' child, a 'Ukrainian' child, and a 'Rusyn' child."[120] By the 1930s, the Czechoslovak government favoured the

Rusynophile orientation, which retained a pro-Czechoslovak position. By the end of the interwar period, however, the Ukrainian national orientation made greater headway than its Russian or Rusyn competitors.[121]

Although the Czechoslovak government failed to satisfy the Ruthenian minority's hopes and expectations, it never introduced the assimilatory policies of Poland or Romania. The Ukrainian speakers of Czechoslovakia participated in fair and free elections at the village, county, provincial, and national levels throughout the interwar period, unlike their compatriots in Poland, Romania, or the USSR. Of all the Ukrainian speakers in the territories of East Central Europe (including the USSR) in the interwar period, those living in Subcarpathian Rus experienced the most generous political opportunities. Only poverty, illiteracy, and an adherence to the peasant way of life hampered their efforts to take full advantage of them.

Conclusion

In the period between the twentieth century's two world wars, Ukrainians comprised the second-largest national group within the Soviet Union (despite declining from 21 to 16 per cent of its total population) and Poland (15 per cent) and a small minority within Czechoslovakia (4 per cent) and Romania (3 per cent).[122] Although outside observers often viewed these people as a demographic minority within each of these newly formed and/or reformed states, Ukrainian speakers (with the exception of those who adhered to the Rusyn orientation in Czechoslovakia) did not think of themselves in this way.

Because Ukrainians remained "compact local majorities in the regions of their settlement," not "dispersed minorities," and because they resided on territories their fathers and forefathers had farmed for generations, they did not consider themselves minorities within their own homelands.[123] Indeed, in the Ukrainian-speaking territories controlled by Poland, Czechoslovakia, and Romania after 1918, those who identified themselves as Ukrainians constituted 63.4 per cent, 61.6 per cent, and 43.4 per cent, respectively, of each region's total population.[124] They envisaged themselves as the majority in their own contiguous areas and sought recognition as such.

In East Central Europe, two of the three states with substantial Ukrainian populations – Poland and Romania – tried to suppress these efforts. Due in large measure to the success of the Ukrainian nation-building efforts in the Austro-Hungarian period, these two post-war governments failed to do so. Although Poland and Romania often employed their state institutions against the Ukrainians and other national groups, neither government won complete power within their own societies or created the political efficiency of Nazi Germany or the Soviet Union in the 1930s. Polish and Romanian authoritarian practices could cripple, but they did not decisively eradicate Ukrainian resistance. Various legal loopholes remained for Ukrainian nationalists, even in these authoritarian states. Moreover, until the mid-1930s, both the Polish and Romanian governments recognized the need to placate world opinion, especially the League of Nations, which monitored the implementation of minority rights throughout East Central Europe.

Polish and Romanian efforts to crush the Ukrainian national movement in the interwar period failed. Instead of breaking resistance, the Polish authorities – more so than the Romanian – raised the level of the Ukrainian national consciousness to a fever pitch. Inadvertently, the Polish and Romanian interwar governments helped mobilize their Ukrainian populations, but could not demobilize them. Just as the Polish and Romanian governments could not destroy the Ukrainian national movements within their own borders, the Ukrainian movement could not destroy the Polish and Romanian states. A seething resentment on both sides produced a violent stalemate.

In the standoff in Poland, Ukrainians began to perceive themselves politically as members of a constantly besieged community and psychologically as "orphans of the universe," not unlike the Kurds, the largest national group in the Middle East not to have gained a state after the Great War.[125] Isolated and marginalized, Ukrainians generally discounted the USSR's periodic condemnation of the post-Versailles order and understood that they did not have any external protectors or patrons.

Despite the noble ideals espoused by the League of Nations, the overwhelming majority of Ukrainians in East Central Europe believed that the international community had abandoned them. Democracy and the reconfiguration of European borders in conformity with Woodrow Wilson's vision of national self-determination did not bring them justice. With the Great Depression, most European states abandoned the democratic order and embraced authoritarian solutions to the complex political and economic crises they encountered. With the selective introduction of Woodrow Wilson's vision of national self-determination and with the unenforceable "rights of minorities" within the framework of nationalizing states, post-Versailles Europe failed to establish a peaceful and just post-war political order. Despite the OUN's contacts with German military intelligence before the outbreak of the Second World War, this group failed to persuade the German government to support an independent Carpatho-Ukrainian state after Czechoslovakia's post-Munich dissolution in 1938–9. Nazi racial theories, proclaiming the inferiority of Slavs, trumped German military and strategic concerns, as they would in the course of the war on the eastern front.

In order to attain their own version of national self-determination, most Ukrainians realized that they could not rely on outside forces, not even Nazi Germany, Europe's most powerful revisionist power, but only on themselves. Born in despair, this interpretation of reality helped prepare them for the Second World War.

PART TWO

The Second Total War: Social Engineering

5

Soviet Ukraine in the 1920s: Managed Diversity

While recognizing the right of national self-determination, we take care to explain to the masses its limited historic significance and we never put it above the interests of the proletarian revolution.

Leon Trotsky, 1922[1]

The theory of the merging of all nations of, say, the USSR, into one common Great Russian language is a national-chauvinist, anti-Leninist theory, which contradicts the basic tenets of Leninism that national differences cannot disappear in the near future, that they are bound to remain for a long time even after the victory of the proletarian revolution on a world scale.

Joseph Stalin, 2 July 1930[2]

Between 1917 and 1921, the Bolsheviks (renamed the Russian Communist Party in 1919) toppled the Provisional Government and dismantled most of the vestiges of the old tsarist order. In the process of doing so, they fervently believed that they would spark a worldwide revolution and establish a classless society. But by 1921, this possibility faded. The revolutionary party now had to secure its power within its own borders and build the world's first Marxist state without Western help or a clear blueprint. Despite their military setbacks and ideological compromises, party leaders still aspired to create a new Soviet man in the image and likeness of their revolutionary enthusiasms. Starting in the early 1920s, under Lenin's leadership they introduced the New Economic Policy (NEP) and innovative policies to accommodate their large non-Russian populations. In the late 1920s, Stalin ignited rapid industrialization and mass collectivization drives as well as mass purges of the party and society. The First World War, the revolutionary period, and the subsequent civil and national wars helped consolidate a powerful one-party state, which launched these ambitious social engineering projects.

After October 1917, during the long, brutal struggle which claimed nearly ten million lives, the Bolsheviks radically expanded the power of the revolutionary Soviet Russian state over society and the economy.[3] By 1921, Lenin and his inner circle "created a centralized, one ideology dictatorship of a single party which permitted no challenge to its power."[4] The leadership of the Bolshevik Party, which experienced a radical spurt in growth from 24,000 members in February 1917 to 732,000 by 1921, reshaped the organization along more centralized and hierarchical lines. The secret police (best known by the evolution of its acronyms – the Cheka, the OGPU, the GPU, NKVD, MGB, and finally the KGB) gained unprecedented powers to persecute all real and imagined enemies. Although the Soviet Russian constitution of 1919 guaranteed civil rights to all of its citizens, the ruling party refused to implement them when dealing with its political enemies. The new regime also repudiated the tsarist debt, expropriated important sectors of the economy, such as large industries, banking, transport, and foreign trade, and subordinated agriculture and domestic trade to heavy state regulation.[5]

Fuelled by revolutionary impatience and mass violence, these policies brought catastrophic results. The transportation system and agricultural production broke down, increasing food shortages and widespread rationing in the cities. The Soviet government then sent detachments of workers to confiscate "surplus" grain and to ignite class war in the countryside. The peasants, in turn, deployed one of the most damaging weapons in their limited arsenals: they reduced their sowings.

Agricultural production fell even further and major social cataclysms loomed on the horizon. Soviet Russia and its allied republics "faced almost total economic collapse: gross industrial output had fallen to less than one-fifth of the level before the First World War ... Matters were hardly less catastrophic in agriculture: when the 1921 harvest produced significantly less than one half the pre-war average, famine and epidemics ensued, claiming millions of lives."[6] Wide-scale peasant revolts broke out in Tambov province, the Volga region, Siberia, the North Caucasus, and Ukraine, not to mention the revolt of the workers and sailors at Kronstadt, one of Petrograd's most prominent strongholds of support. By banning private manufacturing and private trade, nationalizing most industries, seizing peasant grain, and by eliminating money as a means of exchange, radical Bolshevik policies (dubbed "war communism" between June 1918 and March 1921) became unsustainable.[7] If the Bolsheviks continued these policies under these circumstances, the Soviet experiment would soon collapse.

The Tenth Party Congress

The Russian Communist Party's Tenth Congress in March 1921 marked the end of this radical political utopianism. Here, the party's leaders – if not the rank and file – understood that they had narrowly won power by violent means. Now they had to learn not only to govern a totally exhausted country, but to do so effectively while transforming it into a communist society. But how – in light of contradictory pressures – were they to overcome this economic catastrophe?

Bolshevik leaders reluctantly embraced a three-pronged approach. In the political sphere, they outlawed oppositional political parties, even on the left (they had already banned moderate and right-wing political parties shortly after October 1917). Instead of embracing greater internal democracy within the party as many delegates demanded, its leaders prohibited factions, such as the so-called Workers' Opposition.[8] The Bolsheviks adopted the theory of "democratic centralism," in which "the dominant faction in any debate could define any minority opinion as a deviation, and force any minority to submit to the will of the majority" as the party's internal operating system.[9] The Soviet state officially became a one-party state; even within the Communist Party itself, the inner circle barred all challengers.

In the economic domain, Lenin introduced the New Economic Policy (NEP), which replaced the disastrous fever of "war communism" and which sought to transform, through evolutionary means, the remnants of the old economic order into a semi-socialist system. Under this policy, the Soviet state retained control of the "commanding heights" of the economy, such as the major industries, railways, banks, and foreign trade. Individuals could now own land in the countryside, small industries, and the retail trade. The Soviet state abolished grain requisitioning and introduced taxes in kind, which allowed the peasants to sell their surplus on the open market. In Ukraine peasants created cooperatives and private farming grew rapidly. NEP reinvigorated the agricultural sector and helped revive the entire Soviet economy. By 1926, both the USSR and the Ukrainian SSR finally reached the level of their pre-war outputs.[10]

In the sphere of the relationship between the Russians and non-Russians, the Tenth Party Congress announced the complete equality of all non-Russian languages and cultures with the Russian language and culture, but did not address the tsarist legacy of Russification or how to overcome it. Two years later, at the Twelfth Congress in 1923, the party leadership introduced the policy of indigenization (*korenizatsiia*), a radical preferential policy to win over the non-Russians. The emergence of a moderate nationalities policy became closely intertwined with its moderate policy towards the peasants. In the view of most Bolsheviks, the USSR's peasant question and the national question represented the primary components of the new Soviet state's backwardness.

Much like the second Treaty of Brest-Litovsk, the Tenth Party Congress represented an important turning point in the history of the recently founded worker's state. This meeting established political and economic controls at the top, proscribed all non-communist political parties, and limited political discussions within the Communist Party itself. At the same time, it abandoned war communism's extreme controls over the peasantry.

Although the Bolsheviks, a working-class party, managed to pacify the peasants, its leaders recognized that this victory remained a temporary revolutionary respite. The New Economic Policy, in effect, recognized the importance of the interests of the twenty-five million peasant households in the political economy of Soviet Russia and its allied republics. Concomitantly within this economic policy, Bolshevik leaders acknowledged the cultural and national diversity of the Soviet republics by including the policy of indigenization. Both policies became closely intertwined in the 1920s.

National Diversity and the Tsarist Legacy

Of the 140 million people living under Bolshevik control in 1921, 75 million identified themselves as Russians and 65 million as non-Russians. Of the latter, nearly 30 million designated themselves as Ukrainians and 30 million as those with a Turkic heritage.[11] If the Russians constituted 44.3 per cent of the total population of the Russian Empire in 1897, they comprised 53 per cent of the Soviet Union's total population thirty years later – due primarily to the war, revolutions, Civil War, famine, disease, and the independence of Poland, Estonia, Latvia, Lithuania, and Finland. According to the first Soviet census of 1926, Ukrainians also boosted their proportion within the new political entity, constituting 21.3 per cent of the total population.[12]

Although many of the non-Russian territories possessed rich natural resources, most remained economically underdeveloped. Capitalism barely penetrated most of these areas prior to the outbreak of the First World War. As a result, the majority of the non-Russian groups did not possess a native middle class or even their own working class. In terms of cultural development, they varied widely. Some national groups – such as the Poles, Finns, and Latvians remaining in the Soviet state – possessed highly developed languages, cultures, and literatures. Others, such as the Belarusans and Tatars, started the process of developing their own distinct languages and literatures in the late nineteenth century. The Ukrainians stood between these two groups. Finally, a last group – which included the Mordvinians, the majority of the mountain tribes of the Caucasus, and the Votiaks – did not even have their own alphabets.[13] Literacy rates differed enormously across the Soviet Union.

In recognizing these problems, the communist leadership concluded that the social, economic, and cultural legacy of the tsarist order generated a greater hostility between the cities and the countryside in the non-Russian areas than in the central Russian provinces. These non-Russian areas possessed predominantly peasant populations and sometimes even semi-nomadic or semi-tribal groups, as in Central Asia. Russian and Russian-speaking settlers often outnumbered non-Russians in the towns and cities, especially in areas that Russian settlers had founded and industry predominated. The Russians maintained their own culture and rarely interacted with the native populations. Most of the members and supporters of the Communist Party throughout the former Russian Empire – those who possessed an ideological preference for industrial workers over peasants and nomads – came from urban and industrial centres.[14] Most identified themselves as Russians.

This should not be surprising. Although Russians constituted only 53 per cent of the total Soviet population in 1926, they represented 72 per cent of the total membership of the Russian Communist Party (RKP[b]) in 1922.[15] Ukrainians, Belarusans, minority peoples of the RSFSR, and Central Asians remained under-represented in the party's ranks. In contrast, party members who identified themselves as Poles, Estonians, Latvians, Lithuanians, Jews, Armenians, and Georgians were over-represented.[16] After experiencing tsarist discrimination of one form or another, they felt more comfortable in an internationalist political party than in their own national parties.[17]

Local Russian or Russified Bolshevik cadres often alienated the indigenous populations and destabilized the political environment. Bolshevik leaders realized that the high percentage of Russians in the party organizations in non-Russian areas often transformed the class struggle into a national conflict and hampered the Sovietization of these areas.[18] Local populations often viewed these party members as beneficiaries of the old order as well as the new one.

Non-Russians joined the Communist Party, but their percentage in regional party organizations varied widely from one area to another. In 1922, for example, the Crimean Tatars constituted 2.5 per cent of the Crimean Party organization, while Armenians comprised 89.5 per cent of the Communist Party of Armenia.[19] Those who identified themselves as Ukrainians made up only 23.6 per cent of their own regional party.[20] In light of the connection between these social and national divisions, how would communist power root the revolution in the non-Russian areas? How would it establish a productive relationship between the Russians and non-Russians?

Between March 1919 and June 1923, the Russian Communist Party introduced a set of responses to the structural and political problems confronting the non-Russian areas. By developing cultural institutions operating in the native languages and by industrializing the non-Russian areas, the party hoped to bridge the vast gap between the Russian and Russified city and the non-Russian countryside. In time, the party would also augment its ranks by enrolling more non-Russians into the party and soviet organs. The central party, in short, aspired to reduce, if not eliminate, the inequalities produced by four centuries of tsarism. Equalization would incubate the political integration of the diverse peoples of the newly formed USSR. These Soviet policies represented a complete reversal of those Ukrainians had experienced under the last tsars.

Of all of the territories the Bolsheviks won between 1917 and 1921, the Ukrainian provinces – in terms of their geopolitical location, size, and enormous agricultural and industrial potential – represented the greatest prize. But this victory came at a great cost. In order to neutralize the Ukrainian nationalism generated by the war, revolutions, Civil War, and chaos, the Bolshevik Party initiated policies to placate Ukrainian national feelings, but limit their true political content. These policies developed slowly, largely in response to the shifting political fortunes and misfortunes the Bolsheviks experienced as they consolidated power. The creation of the Ukrainian Soviet Socialist Republic, the Communist Party of Ukraine, and the indigenization (or nativization) policy represented three of their most important innovations. They haphazardly designed the first two institutions during the civil and national wars of 1918–21; they inaugurated the third in the 1920s.

Establishing Ukrainization

Despite the formal Soviet recognition of the extensive linguistic autonomy of the non-Russian nationalities in the early 1920s, the exact position of the Ukrainian language in the Ukrainian SSR remained uncertain. During the era of war communism, most Bolshevik government and party officials in the Ukraine refused to recognize the cultural aspirations of the Ukrainian people. In 1919 Christian Rakovsky, the Romanian-born chairman of the Ukrainian Council of People's Commissars, asserted that

Ukrainian should not become the language of administration in the Ukraine because it represented the interests of the Ukrainian-speaking peasants, not the Russian-speaking workers.[21] In accordance with Marxist theory, the workers represented a higher and more complex stage of social development than the peasants.

Even as late as 1923, Dmitrii Lebed, the second secretary of the Central Committee of the Communist Party of Ukraine, actively promoted the "Theory of the Struggle of the Two Cultures." Recognizing the sharp differences between the urban and rural areas in the Ukrainian SSR, this theory favoured the Russified, proletarian urban areas over the largely Ukrainian rural areas. Lebed in effect described Russian culture in Ukraine as urban, advanced, and revolutionary and the Ukrainian culture as rural, backward, and counter-revolutionary. He asserted that to introduce the Ukrainian language "in the party and working class under the present political, economic, and cultural relations between the cities and villages means to adopt the lower culture of the village in preference to the higher culture of the city."[22]

Many prominent communists, Ukrainians and non-Ukrainians alike, opposed this interpretation. Prior to their merger with the Communist Party of Ukraine in March 1920, the Borotbist Party, the former left wing of the Ukrainian Party of Social Revolutionaries, proposed the idea of encouraging the development of Ukrainian culture.[23] Mykola Skrypnyk, the influential Bolshevik commissar of justice, adopted the idea in 1922. Mikhail Frunze, the prominent Soviet military officer and hero of the Civil War, formally initiated the Ukrainization drive at the Seventh Congress of the CP(b)U, held in Kharkiv on 7–10 April 1923. Here, he denounced the legacy of Russian imperialism and praised the decision to encourage speaking Ukrainian, respecting Ukrainian culture, and drawing as many Ukrainians as possible into the party ranks.

On 25 April 1923, the Russian Communist Party issued a resolution at its Twelfth Congress emphasizing that party activists would conduct all propaganda and agitation in the native languages of the non-Russian nationalities.[24] This marked the start of a concerted effort by the central party to introduce preferential policies favouring the non-Russians, especially the Ukrainians.

This April resolution followed the decisions of the Allied Council of Ambassadors to award Galicia to Poland on 14 March 1923 and of Moscow's Communist International (Comintern) to actively exploit the political crisis in Germany with the German Communist Party (KPD).[25] Both groups jointly planned an insurrection in Hamburg, then cancelled it at the last minute, on 21 October, as local units initiated armed actions against the police. This revolution's failure, the last major pro-communist uprising in Europe after the Russian Revolution, caused the Soviet political leadership to abandon all hope for an immediate worldwide revolution. They now re-emphasized the New Economic Policy and moderate nationalities policies in order to stabilize and rebuild the USSR after a decade of war, revolution, Civil War, famine, and utter chaos.

On 16 July 1923, Vlas Chubar, a Ukrainian, became the chairman of the Council of People's Commissars, replacing Rakovsky, who became Soviet ambassador to Great Britain. Eleven days later, the Ukrainian Council of People's Commissars issued a decree on the Ukrainization of elementary schools and cultural institutions. This document emphasized the necessity of making the language of instruction at these institutions conform to the nationality of its students and urged the publication of more textbooks in Ukrainian and in other languages.

The Soviet Ukrainian government issued one of its most decisive decrees in regard to Ukrainization on 1 August 1923:

The Worker-Peasant Government of Ukraine declares it to be essential to centre the attention of the state on the extension of the knowledge of the Ukrainian language. The equality, recognized until now, of the two most widely used languages in Ukraine – Ukrainian and Russian – is not sufficient. As a result of the very weak development of Ukrainian schools and Ukrainian culture in general, the shortage of required school books and equipment, the lack of suitably trained personnel, experience has proven that the Russian language has, in fact, become the dominant one.

In order to destroy this inequality, the Worker-Peasant Government hereby adopts a number of practical measures which, while affirming the equality of languages of all nationalities on Ukrainian territory, will guarantee a place for the Ukrainian language corresponding to the numerical superiority of the Ukrainian people on the territory of the Ukrainian SSR.[26]

The decree obliged all officials dealing with the public to learn Ukrainian. It also demanded that the language of all official documents and correspondence gradually change from Russian to Ukrainian, although Russian and other non-Ukrainian languages could be used locally. Subsequent resolutions and decrees ordered all state institutions, newspapers, and state-owned trade and industrial organizations to adopt Ukrainian instead of Russian as their working language. These measures created a policy giving preference to Ukrainians entering the party, government, and other important organizations. Not only did this policy seek to overcome the separation between the rural Ukrainian and the urban Russian worlds, but by introducing Ukrainian into the urban public sphere, it undermined the status of the pre-revolutionary "bourgeoisie" living in the cities. As envisioned by its promoters, Ukrainization would not introduce bilingualism, but overturn "the existing language hierarchy whereby Ukrainian would supplant Russian as the 'first' and primary language of public discourse."[27]

Whereas the August 1923 decree did not define the equality of Ukrainian and Russian within the framework of a Ukrainian demographic majority, a follow-up decree in April 1925 set the ambitious goal of establishing Ukrainian linguistic hegemony within the republic. Russian would remain Ukraine's link with the political capital in Moscow and therefore would continue to be a mandatory subject in all Ukrainian schools. But "under no circumstances," accord to the Ukrainian Central Committee's resolution of 19 April 1927, "may this be a cover for attempts to create for Russian culture the dominant position it held in Ukraine under tsardom."[28] According to the April 1925 edict, Ukrainian would become the primary language in the public sphere, especially in the areas where the majority of Ukrainians lived. [29] But this policy was easier decreed than implemented.

During the period from 1923 to 1932, the Soviet government endorsed the policy of Ukrainization for several reasons. First, the government sought to neutralize emergent Ukrainian nationalism by publicly condemning tsarist oppression of the non-Russians and by encouraging the development of Ukrainian culture. Second, Ukrainization would help to legitimize Soviet rule by differentiating its nationalities policy from its tsarist predecessor and "by debunking engrained prejudices against Ukrainian culture."[30] Third, the policy provided a convenient means of mobilizing and preparing the population for the impending modernization of the USSR.[31] Since it was much easier to educate the new cadres in their native language, the party emphasized the Ukrainian language in the student's primary, secondary, and technical education. Fourth, Ukrainization had foreign policy implications: the Soviet solution of the national question would demonstrate the superiority of the Soviet system, not only to the seven million Ukrainians living outside the boundaries of the USSR, but also to the restive Western colonies in Asia.[32] The national stage of Soviet policy would precede the communist stage.

This policy played a major role not just as a language transformer, but also as "an instrument of political and social management within the non-Russian areas."[33] In light of its importance, the Soviet authorities sought to regulate language choice and how it would be employed in the public sphere of the non-Russian areas.

Despite the party's public support for this policy, it provoked unusually strong resistance among Russians and the Russian-speaking urban population, which received mixed signals from the authorities.[34] According to George Y. Shevelov, a prominent linguist who lived through this era,

Torn from its only real potential social basis, imposed by a non-Ukrainian party and state machine, deprived of sincerity and spontaneity, consistently counter-balanced by anti-Ukrainian measures, Ukrainization appeared to the average Russian or pro-Russian city dweller as a kind of a comedy, occasionally having some dramatic overtones but still above all a comedy. He learned in what circumstances and to what degree he had to reckon with this official façade, and he learned that it was wise not to transgress boundaries. He knew that, by law, those officials who did not have a command of Ukrainian were to be fired: he also knew that whereas a messenger, a typist, or a secretary was occasionally dismissed on these grounds, the high functionaries ... were in practice excused from Ukrainization. He knew that whereas signboards were scheduled to be redone in Ukrainian, behind the façade the old Russian bureaucratic machine continued to exist.[35]

Even some Ukrainian speakers became uneasy with Ukrainization. Victor Kravchenko, a student at the Kharkiv Technical Institute in 1930–1, asserted that

in theory we Ukrainians in the student body should have been pleased. In practice, we were as distressed by the innovation as the non-Ukrainian minority. Even those who, like myself, had spoken Ukrainian from childhood, were not accustomed to its use as a medium of study. Several of our best professors were utterly demoralized by the linguistic switch-over. Worst of all, our local tongue simply had not caught up with modern knowledge; its vocabulary was unsuited to the purposes of electrotechnics, chemistry, aerodynamics, physics, and most other sciences ...

What should have been a free right was converted, in its application, into an oppressive duty. The use of our language was not merely allowed, it was made obligatory. Hundreds of men and women who could not master it were dismissed from government posts. It became almost counter-revolutionary to speak anything but Ukrainian in public. Children from Russian-speaking homes were tortured and set back in their studies by what was for them a foreign language.[36]

Yet, despite Kravchenko's implication that Ukrainian became the primary language in the public sphere of Kharkiv, Soviet Ukraine's capital, it did not dominate most of the urban centres in southern or eastern Ukraine. Many Russified rural areas in this region also viewed Ukrainization as unnecessary.[37] As Ukrainization represented a soft-line policy, not a hard-line one, the Communist Party and the Soviet government did not provide any mechanisms for the total enforcement of the Ukrainization decrees. Nevertheless, the party understood its potential to change the power relationships in the non-Russian areas.[38]

By 1927, the total number of individuals fired for not learning Ukrainian "certainly exceeded five hundred and may have been as high as one thousand."[39] But this figure was quite small considering the enormous amount of passive resistance the Russian-speaking party and working class generated in the urban areas.[40] The Russian-speaking bureaucrats, most of the long-term Russian and Jewish urban residents, most of the working class, and most of the Russian-speaking intelligentsia (especially engineers and technical workers and instructors in the institutions of higher education) opposed the introduction of a Ukrainian-speaking public sphere.[41] Even some of the higher-ranking members of the CP(b)U, especially in the eastern and industrial areas, decried "forced Ukrainization." Implementing this policy in the towns and cities sharpened the divisions between advocates of pro-Ukrainization and anti-Ukrainization and among Ukrainians, Russians, and Jews. In regard to Ukrainization, it was easier to admit and promote Ukrainians in the party, working class, and trade unions than to transform the Russian-speaking public sphere into a Ukrainian-speaking one.[42]

Ukrainizing the Ukrainian SSR

Even into the 1920s, as Ukrainians retained their majority of the population of the Ukrainian SSR, they did not dominate the larger cities and urban areas. In 1926, almost all of them lived in the rural areas and maintained their peasant culture.[43] In this context, Ukrainians possessed an extremely low percentage (11 per cent) of their total population living in the cities, ranking behind Jews (77.4 per cent urban), Russians (50 per cent), and Poles (20.7 per cent).[44] Russians remained far more influential than the statistics indicate. Russians and the Russian-speaking population dominated the new Soviet Ukrainian Republic. Their concentration in the cities and industrial regions and the assimilation of numerous Ukrainians and Jews into Russian culture contributed to their dominance within non-agricultural occupations, especially within the expanding governmental apparatus and party.

In order to institutionalize the Ukrainian language in public, the Communist Party of Ukraine concentrated on using Ukrainian to raise the level of literacy and education in the republic. Of the entire population of the Ukrainian SSR in 1926, over 6,923,165 individuals were literate in Ukrainian and over 7,075,126 in Russian.[45] These statistics demonstrate the dominance of the Russian language in Ukraine and the difficulty of introducing Ukrainian into the public sphere.

The party and government sought to expand the "market of literates" by initiating a massive literacy campaign in Ukrainian. But the "struggle against illiteracy" floundered in the 1920s. By 1927 approximately five million individuals in Ukraine between the ages of ten and thirty-five still remained illiterate.[46] The number of literates increased during the 1920s, but at a slower pace than the Commissariat of Education anticipated. Despite the advances made by the Ukrainian language, the Russian language remained powerful in Ukraine.

Under the direction of Grigory Grinko (1920–2), Volodymyr Zatonsky (1922–5), Oleksandr Shumsky (1925–7), and Mykola Skrypnyk (1927–33), the Commissariat of Education became the main coordinating body for Ukrainization. On 27 July 1923, the Ukrainian Council of People's Commissars decreed the use of the Ukrainian language in all elementary schools within the next two academic years and introduced it as the language of instruction in all professional schools and political-educational institutions. Soviet Ukrainian leaders commissioned the Commissariat of Education to identify all teachers who did not speak Ukrainian and teach them the language, while educating new cadres of teachers who could provide instruction in Ukrainian. The decree also ordered an increase in the production of Ukrainian textbooks. The schools of the non-Ukrainian minorities would provide instruction in their native languages, but would also require either Russian or Ukrainian as a second language.[47] Throughout the 1920s, schools needed not only highly qualified Ukrainian-language teachers, but regular teachers as well. The teachers themselves did not welcome Ukrainization in a uniform manner. Some equated the Ukrainian language with provincialism and viewed it as "a distorted form of Russian"; others considered Ukrainization as one of the most progressive aspects of Sovietization.[48]

By 1923, if the statistics are accurate, 76 per cent of primary schools conducted lessons in Ukrainian, and by 1925, when the Soviet Ukrainian government decreed compulsory fourth-grade education for all children, 77.8 per cent.[49] During the 1932–3 school year, 88.5 per cent of all primary-school students received instruction in Ukrainian.[50] Despite this progress, the Ukrainian Politburo expressed dissatisfaction with the pace of Ukrainization, claiming that the policy neither satisfied the needs of the economy nor corresponded to the growth of the cultural needs of the workers and peasants.[51] The drive to increase Ukrainian-language schools in Kiev and in other cities constituted a part of a larger campaign to promote Ukrainian as a modern, urban language, equal to Russian.[52] But even in cities with an ever-increasing Ukrainian population, children of recent migrants from the countryside often attended Russian-language schools.[53]

The majority of Ukrainian-language schools were located in the countryside and remained inferior academically, while Russian-language schools existed primarily in urban areas and offered better instruction. One urban school contained more students than several rural schools combined.[54] In any case, oftentimes the authorities and teachers used a language "that bore little resemblance to the Ukrainian the population recognized and employed."[55]

Overall, the quality of Ukrainian-language schools lagged far behind Russian-language schools in the 1920s and 1930s. The number of institutions of higher education with Ukrainian as the language of instruction also increased, from 19.5 per cent in 1923 to 69 per cent in 1929.[56] During the 1928–9 academic year, 56 per cent of the students at these institutions identified themselves as Ukrainians.[57] But here, too, the standing of this Ukrainian-language instruction remains largely unexplored.

Ukrainization, in short, sought to eliminate national discrimination against Ukrainians and other groups and to reverse the Russification of the past without alienating non-Ukrainian groups, especially the Russians. The Soviet government established an extensive Ukrainian-language educational system, subsidized the publication and mass circulation of Ukrainian-language newspapers, journals, and books, expanded the Ukrainian-language theatre, and founded the Ukrainian-language radio and opera. Instruction in adult literacy schools took place almost entirely in Ukrainian. By 1931, the Soviet Ukrainian government published 80 per cent of all books and 90 per cent of all newspapers in Ukrainian.[58] Most importantly, the Soviet effort transformed a predominantly illiterate population into a literate and educated one, despite the overall quality of instruction. According to official statistics that may not reflect reality, only 44 per cent of the population in Ukraine could read in 1926. Thirteen years later, this percentage allegedly doubled to 88.2.[59] Even if an exaggerated claim, most nineteenth-century Ukrainophiles would have enthusiastically approved.

Ukrainization and the Power Elite

Although party leaders pursued the promotion of the Ukrainian language in the public sphere vigorously, this policy failed to make significant progress in government, industry, and higher education. After 1925, the authorities demanded that government employees interact with the public in Ukrainian and employ the language in their workplaces. But language examinations revealed that members of the party and even the Communist Youth League (Komsomol) did not achieve a sufficient level of fluency in Ukrainian to pass the tests. Passive resistance remained a major obstacle. All-Union economic institutions, especially those in Ukraine's eastern industrial regions, refused to Ukrainize themselves and primarily hired Russian-speaking specialists.[60]

The dominance of Russian-language speakers within the urban-based Communist Party of Ukraine, the Komsomol, trade unions, and government – the very agencies that would push for and implement the Ukrainization program – may help explain Ukrainization's mixed record. In 1922, Ukrainians constituted 22.3 per cent of the membership of the CP(b)U, but only 11.3 per cent professed Ukrainian as their primary language.[61] Approximately five years later, on 10 January 1927, Ukrainians constituted 51.9 per cent of the membership and candidate-membership of its party, but only 30.7 per cent identified Ukrainian as their primary language.[62] Although the number of self-identified Ukrainians more than doubled and became the majority of the party in this five-year period, the number of Ukrainians claiming Ukrainian as their native language never exceeded one-third of the party.

Although the Communist Party of Ukraine grew dramatically in the 1920s and 1930s, it remained a small, elite institution, unrepresentative of the Ukrainian people. Although the largest political organization in Ukraine, the party attracted only a small percentage of the total population. The CP(b)U grew from 37,968 members at the end of 1920 to 636,914 members and candidate-members in May 1940. In 1920 only 19 per cent of its members identified themselves as Ukrainians; in 1940, 63.1 per cent did. Between July 1926 and January 1927, Ukrainians achieved a majority in the CP(b)U.[63] But inasmuch as the Communist Party represented a hierarchical, not a democratic, institution, a majority within the party did not necessarily translate into majority rule.

Although they increased in number, Ukrainians also remained underrepresented in the Communist Youth League (Komsomol) and in the trade unions. The number of Ukrainians in the Youth League increased from 59 per cent in 1925 to 72 per cent in 1933.[64] In 1930, 56 per cent of the trade union members described themselves as Ukrainians, but only 43.3 per cent declared Ukrainian as their native language.[65] In 1930, 58.6 per cent of the government's bureaucracy recognized themselves as Ukrainians.[66] As in other cases, the number of Ukrainians claiming Ukrainian as their native language would be much smaller. Thus, native-speaking Ukrainians in the

1923–33 period never dominated the centres of power in the Ukrainian SSR. The native-speaking group would most likely constitute the core that demanded implementation of the Ukrainization program within the party and the government, but it possessed a weak base of support.

Urban Growth and National Change

Many peasants could not conceive of themselves as Ukrainians before 1914. The First World War, the revolutions, and the subsequent civil and national wars aroused their national consciousness. After the final Bolshevik victory, the Soviet government then helped channel this new national consciousness. By establishing adult literacy centres, introducing a compulsory elementary school system, and subsidizing higher education in the Ukrainian language, Ukrainization codified the Ukrainian national culture in the 1920s, undermined the traditional, pre-literate peasant culture, and created an environment capable of nurturing a modern, literate, and urban Ukrainian national culture.

The 1926 Soviet census revealed that 80.1 per cent of the people in the Ukrainian Republic identified themselves as Ukrainians, 9.2 per cent as Russians, and 5.4 per cent as Jews.[67] Ukrainians comprised a majority in each of the six regions of the republic (see map 6). The regions with the highest percentage of Ukrainians were – not surprisingly – the agricultural ones: Polissia, the Left Bank, and the Right Bank, as well as the Dnieper Industrial Region. The areas with the lowest Ukrainian population were the newly industrialized ones: the Steppe and the Donbass (see map 6 and table 6.1). Ukrainians constituted the overwhelming majority of the urban populations in Polissia and the Left Bank, a plurality in the Right Bank and the Dnieper Industrial Region, but a minority in the other two regions.[68]

The Ukrainian peasants who migrated to the cities before the early 1920s gradually absorbed the Russian urban ethos and soon came to identify themselves as Russians. But as the cities and towns grew rapidly in the late 1920s, a product of the overall Soviet industrialization effort, the large number of migrating Ukrainians threatened to reverse this process of acculturation and assimilation.

Between 1920 and 1933, the urban population nearly doubled – from 3,916,300 to 7,158,700.[69] According to the unofficial census of 1937, the urban population of Ukraine amounted to 10,021,767; according to the official census of 1939, the towns and cities contained 11,190,370 men, women, and children. If in 1926, the urban population of the Ukrainian

SSR constituted 18.5 per cent of the total, by 1939 36 per cent of those living in Ukraine resided in urban centres.[70] In the two decades before the outbreak of the Second World War, Ukraine's urban growth and level of urbanization outpaced that of the Soviet Union as a whole.

The highest degree of urbanization occurred in regions with highly developed industrial centres.[71] Following the pattern set in the late nineteenth century, the urban centres of the Donbass, the Dnieper Industrial Region, and the Steppe (regions outside the historic Ukrainian core area) grew at a faster pace than did cities in Polissia, the Right Bank, and the Left Bank, the regions which comprised the core.

From 1920 to 1934 the number of cities within the Ukrainian SSR with more than 100,000 inhabitants grew and their share of the entire urban population increased. In 1926 there were six such cities: Kiev, Odessa, Kharkiv, Dniepropetrovsk, Stalino (today's Donetsk), and Mykolaiv. They constituted 33.5 per cent of the entire urban population of Ukraine. By January 1934 there were eleven cities with a population of over 100,000, comprising approximately 40.8 per cent of the total urban population. Most importantly, the cities – breaking with the previous pattern – now contained more residents who identified themselves as Ukrainians.

In the 1920s the number and percentage of Ukrainians in the republic's cities grew – from 32.2 per cent of the total urban population in 1920 to 47.2 per cent in 1926.[72] The percentage of urbanized Ukrainians in 1926 varied inversely with the size of the town or city, reaching 69.4 per cent of the population of towns under 20,000, but only 33 per cent in cities over 100,000. Given the social factors at work, this pattern is not unexpected.

This pyramid subsequently became more elastic. It began to expand in the 1920s and early 1930s as the number of Ukrainian migrants came to outnumber other migrants. The most dramatic increase in the percentage of Ukrainians took place in the Donbass, the Steppe, and in the Dnieper Industrial Region, where the percentage of Ukrainian growth far surpassed that of the overall population.[73] Such dramatic increases in the numbers of Ukrainians among urban dwellers unquestionably led to the Ukrainization of the cities.

Although 47.2 per cent of the total urban population identified themselves as Ukrainians in 1926, Russian culture dominated the cities and towns. Ukrainians constituted a plurality of the population in Kiev (41.2 per cent), Kharkiv (38.4), and Dniepropetrovsk (36.0), while Russians constituted a majority in Stalino (56.2), and a plurality in Odessa (38.7) and Mykolaiv (44.5). As these statistics demonstrate, Kiev, the centre of the Right Bank and the Ukrainian core, remained the Ukrainian bulwark, however fragile.[74]

As the cities and towns grew in the years following 1926, so did the number of Ukrainians in them. As the Soviet government increased investment in urban industrial centres and built new factories, it also attacked the Ukrainian traditional way of life by introducing forced collectivization (see chapter 6). One migrant described the differences between the life of a worker and a peasant in the late 1920s and why the latter would choose the urban life:

> The worker received wages, i.e., something permanent and steady, even if they were low. But the collective farmers worked the same (amount of hours) or even longer hours and did not receive any steady income. During the first years of industrialization the workers were better off. They received potatoes and bread and other food in larger quantities. This was done especially so as to draw more people into industry.[75]

The most likely candidates for migration included the poor, those who possessed no land or at best small plots (with no draft animals), those of working age (between 16 and 59), and those accused of being "kulaks" (those with large plots of land who hired labour). These migrants realized that their socio-economic future did not lie in the countryside, but in the expanding urban industrial centres.

On the eve of the industrialization period, well over half the population of the Ukraine was of working age, and of these a significant number were moved by their poverty to opt for city life.[76] Thus, land hunger, the lack of draft animals, the abundant labour supply in the countryside, and finally, forced collectivization shifted the previous migration patterns. These factors contributed to the increase in the number of people in the urban labour force, especially in the period between 1928 and 1932. Now, as a result of the pull of the cities and the push of the countryside, more Ukrainian peasants entered the Russified cities. Some urban centres, such as Kiev, became more important than others.

In the nineteenth century, Kiev, the most important urban area in the Ukrainian historic core area, did not serve as Ukraine's "primate city," defined as the region's most populous and most socially and economically developed metropolis.[77] Although it possessed an ancient and important historical legacy, its population (248,000 in 1897) and socio-economic development did not surpass Odessa's (404,000); Kharkov and Ekaterinoslav remained close competitors. As towns and cities started to grow in the 1920s after the war and the national and civil wars, Kiev took the lead. According to the 1926 Soviet census, Kiev possessed 514,000 residents, Odessa 421,000, and Kharkiv 417,000.[78] With industrialization and the

Kremlin's decision to transfer Ukraine's capital from Kharkiv to Kiev in 1934, Kiev solidified its top spot.[79]

In the 1920s, all of Ukraine's towns and cities experienced an unprecedented growth spurt. At first, a significant number of those drawn to the cities were actually returning: they were workers who had abandoned the cities in the early 1920s after the collapse of the early Soviet economy. However, as the number of migrants grew, those who had no urban industrial experience began to dominate the rural-to-urban migration.[80]

Ukrainian migrants played a significant role in this migratory process. By 1933, perhaps even by 1931, Ukrainians constituted over half of the urban population of the Ukrainian Republic, especially in some of the major cities. This suggests that the immigration from the RSFSR and other Soviet republics slowed and that the radical urban growth that occurred in Ukraine after 1926 must have happened at the expense of its countryside, which was overwhelmingly Ukrainian.[81]

Soviet industrialization ignited a radical change in Soviet Ukraine's social composition. In the 1920s, the Ukrainian Republic, long identified with its countryside and peasants, started its long march towards a modern, more urban era. Willingly or unwillingly, those who identified themselves as Ukrainians also entered this new non-rural environment.

Conclusion

Ukrainization was an ambitious attempt to divorce culture from politics. If the non-Russians could employ their languages in the public sphere, educate their children in their native languages, and believe that the world's first proletarian state respected their dignity, then they would satisfy their national-cultural aspirations and would not seek to establish independent states. This idea owed much to Otto Bauer and Karl Renner, the founders of Austro-Marxism and the concept of national-personal autonomy, men who inspired Stalin's attack on them in his first major theoretical work, *Marxism and the National Question* (1913). Now Stalin sought to implement aspects of their ideas.

In 1921, Stalin – the Communist Party's "expert" on nationalities – predicted that cities in non-Russian republics would eventually reflect the national composition of their surrounding countrysides:

It is clear that the Ukrainian nationality exists and that the development of its culture is a communist obligation. One should not go against history. It is clear that if the Russians dominated the cities of the Ukraine until now, then in time these cities will inevitably be Ukrainianized. Forty years ago Riga was a German city, but inasmuch as cities grew at the expense of the countryside, Riga is now completely a Latvian city. Fifty years ago all Hungarian cities had a German character. Now they are all Magyarized. The same will happen in Belarus, where non-Belarusans predominate.[82]

Less than a decade later, in the late 1920s, the large-scale migrations into the cities of the Ukraine changed not only their size but their national composition as well. As a result of the rapid pace of both industrialization and collectivization, a large mass of Ukrainian peasantry began to migrate to the cities, and, by 1931, Ukrainians constituted a majority of the urban population. During Stalin's first five-year plan the movement of Ukrainian peasants to the cities occurred in numbers so large that, for the initial few years, they could not be assimilated to the dominant Russian urban culture or to the new rhythms of factory life, at least not at the start. Concomitantly, the prestige of the Ukrainian national group rose, however temporarily, as the number of city dwellers who claimed Ukrainian as their nationality far outstripped the total number of new urban residents. This meant that many of those who in the 1920 or 1923 censuses had identified themselves as "Russians" re-identified themselves as "Ukrainians" in the 1926 census. This switching of identities demonstrates the fluidity of national identification over a turbulent but short period of time.

As the cities acquired more Ukrainian inhabitants, Ukrainization and the increased urbanization of Ukrainians signalled a potential cultural de-Russification of the cities and of the major industrial areas. While the Soviet authorities anticipated that more Ukrainians would migrate into the cities – although not at the speed with which they did so – they did not count on the unintended political consequences which rapid urban growth engendered. Now a different pool, Ukrainian, not Russian, supplied the institutions of political power – the trade unions, the party, and the bureaucracy, which drew their recruits primarily from the cities.

This rapid rural to urban migration produced a radical cultural and national transformation of the cities. The subsequent social dislocation accelerated the development and the institutionalization of a new and assertive Ukrainian national consciousness, which appeared national in form, socialist in content, and urban in residence. Although difficult to measure, Ukrainization and industrialization produced an unintended political consequence for the All-Union Communist Party – the Ukrainian national communists. This small, but influential group within the newly "Ukrainized" party had viewed the use of nationalist symbolism as a "tactical expedient to drum up support for a politically isolated leadership" in the past.[83] Now, completely enveloped in their republic's environment, these Ukrainian political leaders started to emphasize Soviet Ukrainian priorities, not Soviet ones.

These Ukrainian national communists (such as Mykola Khvylovy, Alexander Shumsky, Mykhailo Volobuev, and even Mykola Skrypnyk) began to take their role as defenders of the Ukrainian cultural and historical heritage very seriously.[84] They sought to take advantage of the urban growth and to press for greater control of the cultural, political, and economic organs within their own republic and within the context of proletarian internationalism. Stalin, who feared any split in the party along national lines, now had to choose between order and legitimacy.[85] Not surprisingly, he embraced order.

6

Hypercentralization, Industrialization, and the Grain Front, 1927–1934

In a speech delivered before an audience of industrial managers on 4 February 1931, Joseph Stalin condemned Russia's chronic underdevelopment. He asserted that

> one feature of the history of old Russia was the continual beatings she suffered because of her backwardness. She was beaten by the Mongol khans. She was beaten by the Turkish beys. She was beaten by the Swedish feudal lords. She was beaten by the Polish and Lithuanian gentry. She was beaten by the British and French capitalists. She was beaten by the Japanese barons. All beat her – because of her backwardness, because of her military backwardness, cultural backwardness, political backwardness, industrial backwardness, agricultural backwardness. They beat her because to do so was profitable and could be done with impunity ... Such is the law of exploiters – to beat the backward and the weak. It is a jungle law of capitalism ... That is why we must no longer lag behind.
>
> ... Do you want our socialist fatherland to be beaten and to lose its independence? If you do not want this, you must put an end to its backwardness in the shortest possible time and develop a genuine Bolshevik tempo in building up its socialist economy. There is no other way. That is why Lenin said on the eve of the October Revolution: "Either we perish, or overtake and outstrip the advanced capitalist countries."
>
> We are fifty or a hundred years behind the advanced countries. We must make good this distance in ten years. Either we do it, or we shall go under.[1]

Stalin's remarks on the Russian/Soviet past expressed the frustrations of all who recognized that in the competitive world of nations, states, empires, and ideological struggles, economic underdevelopment also represented an unwanted reality of economic poverty, political inferiority, military impotency, and an unequal relationship with the developed world, a dysfunctional dependency. Economic and social privation created weakness and constant humiliation. Backwardness, as the party leader suggested, would lead to the extinction of nations, states, and political systems.

Delivered in the third year of the Soviet Union's first five-year economic plan (1928–32), Stalin's speech responded to the uncertainties of the international situation at the end of the 1920s and early 1930s, highlighting the reasons for the Soviet ambition to modernize its economy and society at an accelerated pace. With the country surrounded by hostile capitalist powers, national security concerns trumped all others.[2] At this point in time, the USSR continued to acquire aspects of a "garrison state," a state in which "specialists on violence" become "the most powerful group in society" and in which the authorities define all social changes in terms of "military potential" and national security.[3] This "garrisonization" emerged during the civil and national wars of 1918–21 and spread throughout the Soviet Union to unprecedented levels during the first five-year plan.

Stalin's emphasis on "socialism in one country" and his public conflation of Russia (not the multinational Soviet Union) with the "socialist fatherland" championed a new ideological interpretation – Soviet patriotism – which emphasized that "national differences within the Soviet Union were secondary to the shared history and loyalty that united all Soviet citizens."[4] Despite its self-proclaimed internationalist orientation, the party started to favour Russian interests at the expense of the non-Russian population of the Soviet Union. This speech, moreover, implied a retreat from *korenizatsiia* and from Ukrainization.[5] Within ten years after the start of the New Economic Policy and a moderate Soviet nationalities policy, Stalin and the Communist Party steered the Soviet Union into new, uncharted waters.

Between NEP and Industrialization

The New Economic Policy did not satisfy the many firebrands in the All-Union Communist Party who reluctantly accepted this program as a short-term strategy in the early 1920s. Recognizing the USSR's overall economic inferiority and its dependency on imports from capitalist countries, these radicals claimed that economic restoration to pre-war (1913) levels by 1926 did not go far enough. Despite this recovery, the gap in industrial productivity between the Soviet Union and the world's major industrial powers "remained as great or even greater than it had been before 1914."[6] In light of their ideological predispositions and the British,

French, American, Polish, and Japanese interventions during the Civil War, they perceived the hostile capitalist world constantly on the verge of invading the first socialist state.

By highlighting Soviet vulnerabilities, the artificially induced "war scare" of 1926–7 built on the political panics of the early 1920s and justified the need for a rapid industrialization drive. Although the great fear of 1926–7 emerged from a set of real crises the USSR experienced in those two years, Soviet paranoia and Stalin's opportunism stoked the flames.

Shortly after Moscow's leaders assessed the state of its military preparedness in 1923–4 and acknowledged its weaknesses (a poorly equipped army, an obsolete military technology, and the complete lack of an adequate mobilization plan for war), the USSR experienced a large number of international setbacks and diplomatic embarrassments.[7] In May 1926, Józef Piłsudski – the Soviet arch-enemy – staged a military coup and remained Poland's strongman for another nine years. In the first half of 1927, a large number of Soviet spies were arrested in Europe and Turkey and several important OGPU officers defected to Western capitals. In April 1927, as the Chinese Nationalist leader Chiang Kai-Shek sought to consolidate his power over the Chinese Nationalist Revolution, he massacred thirty to forty thousand of his former allies, the Chinese communists and their supporters. Soviet efforts to influence the Chinese government collapsed. Anglo-Soviet tensions in China and the USSR's modest intervention in the British general strike of 3–12 May 1926 strengthened the anti-Soviet faction within the ruling British Conservative Party, which severed diplomatic relations with Moscow on 26 May 1927 and cancelled the Anglo-Soviet Trade Agreement of 1921. In early June, a young anti-Bolshevik Russian émigré assassinated the Soviet ambassador to Poland. In July, the Berlin police arrested 700 members of the German Communist Party.

Why did all of these reversals happen so quickly and over a short period of time? Various factions within the All-Union Communist Party and the OGPU proposed a vast conspiracy led by Great Britain with its allies, France and Poland (which allegedly supported underground nationalist groups in Georgia and Ukraine), to launch a second war against the USSR. According to this convenient explanation, the world's first proletarian state was in danger of attack by hostile capitalist powers. As a prophylactic measure, the OGPU launched a wave of arrests and a series of summary executions of its class enemies, including twenty noblemen. By the peak of the official media's coverage of this war threat in late May and early June, many Soviet citizens embraced this interpretation and started to hoard food and basic staples.[8]

Although Stalin and his allies initially minimalized the danger of foreign intervention in the winter of 1926–7, he started to exaggerate the Soviet Union's "dire straits" by the summer of 1927 in order to mobilize support for his own policies. Now he insisted that the outbreak of a new imperialist war against the USSR was not a vague danger, but a "real and actual threat."[9] In this dangerous political climate, he accused his internal enemies of trying to split the party. By October 1927, Stalin's allies expelled Leon Trotsky and Grigory Zinoviev from the party's Central Committee and, over the next month, from the party. In January 1928, the Politburo banished Trotsky and his family to Alma-Ata, and one year later deported them from the USSR.[10]

Due to the war scare, rapid industrialization became the new mantra and the communist state's first priority. In light of the Soviet government's repudiation of the tsarist debt in January 1918 and its international reputation as a credit-unworthy state, only the sale of exportable agricultural harvests and valuable artwork could finance the purchase of new machinery from abroad, introduce new technologies, and fund the industrialization effort. This political choice required that the government gain control of all of its economic resources and institute central planning. In order to establish this administrative-command economy, the authorities radically modified the division of economic responsibilities between Moscow and the republics originally negotiated in the early 1920s. This new state-sponsored intervention radically enlarged the Soviet bureaucracy at the central, republican, and local levels and expanded its functions.[11] With industrialization, the state now penetrated all of society's layers, including the countryside, and blurred the boundaries between itself and society at large.

At the Fourteenth Party Congress in December 1925, delegates approved resolutions committing the party to transform the USSR into a self-sufficient industrial power. The Fifteenth Party Conference in October–November 1926 reaffirmed the necessity of the Soviet industrialization drive, but did not create a set schedule or clear goals. Only in December 1927, at the Fifteenth Party Congress, did the party launch a highly ambitious and accelerated industrialization campaign to catch up with the Western capitalist states.

To finance this vast modernization project and to feed the military and the new and expanding urban labour force, party leaders sought to gain direct control over agricultural production in all of the Soviet republics and to exploit the USSR's natural resources more efficiently. Centrally coordinated economic plans defined this dual-pronged "revolution from above." The Soviet government ratified the first five-year plan in April–May 1929, which lasted until the end of 1932, when officials proclaimed with hyperbolic fanfare that it had met the plan's challenging goals fourteen months early. The second five-year plan (1933–7) expanded upon the first, although it promised more modest industrial targets. The outbreak of the conflict with Nazi Germany in 1941 interrupted the third, scheduled for 1938–42. Between 1928 and 1940, as a consequence of these new investments and new construction projects, Ukraine's total industrial output allegedly surged by 340 per cent.[12]

The five-year plans, especially the first, infused enormous sums into the industrial sector, not the consumer goods sector. The Soviet state increased expenditures in Ukrainian industry from 438 million rubles in 1929 to 1.2 billion in 1932.[13] In this period, nearly one-fourth of the nearly 1,500 industrial plants built in the USSR were located in Ukraine. The gigantic Dneprostroi/Dniprohes hydroelectric dam on the Dnieper, Europe's largest, symbolized the entire Soviet industrialization effort.[14]

Central planners placed most capital investments in Ukraine in the traditional industrial areas of the Donbas and the lower Dnieper region, not the densely populated and agriculturally oriented Right Bank, which they believed would serve "as a potential theater of war in the event of a conflict with Poland or Germany."[15] In light of the economic commissars' preference for industry over agriculture, Soviet authorities reinforced the split between Ukraine's eastern and southern industrial areas and its western and central agricultural regions.

With the rapid expansion of Soviet Ukraine's industrial infrastructure, the new factories, mines, and industrial centres needed millions of new workers in order to operate at full capacity. The new urban opportunities, collectivization, and the escalating violence in the countryside pushed millions to migrate to the cities. Between 1926 and 1939, the Ukrainian Republic's urban population exploded from 5.4 to 11.2 million, and by 1939 the percentage of self-identified Ukrainians rose to 58 per cent of the total urban population. At the same time, the percentage of self-identified Ukrainians among the republic's industrial workers increased from 52 to 66 per cent.[16]

Despite these radical socio-economic developments within the Ukrainian SSR, this republic's importance in the overall Soviet industrialization effort declined during the second and third five-year plans.[17] Already in the 1920s, Moscow extracted a considerable share of economic and human resources from Ukraine.[18] In the 1930s, central planners shifted capital and labour from Ukraine to construction sites in the Urals, the Kuznets Basin, and the Volga region, areas far from the contentious Polish-Ukrainian frontiers. The Ukrainian SSR's share of the total capital investments in the

USSR fell from 18.3 per cent in 1933 to 13.5 per cent in 1939, as Soviet authorities sought to develop Siberia's industrial infrastructure. Despite this downtrend, Ukraine remained an important Soviet industrial centre.[19]

The first five-year plan consolidated the Soviet government's centralization of power and limited the sovereignty of the Ukrainian SSR and the other republics. In 1929 the central authorities subordinated the Ukrainian Commissariat of Agriculture to the newly established USSR Commissariat of Agriculture. In 1932, the Soviet government abolished the Supreme Council of the National Economy of the USSR (*Vesenkha*) and of the Ukrainian SSR, replacing it with the All-Union Commissariat of Heavy Industry.

Whereas the Soviet Ukrainian government controlled – directly or indirectly – 81.2 per cent of its industry in 1927, five years later it supervised only 37.5 per cent of all industries located on its territory.[20] The central ministries in Moscow now managed most of the Ukrainian economy, de facto as well as de jure.

"Extraordinary Measures" and the Famine of 1928–1929

Party leaders fervently believed that rapid industrialization necessitated the political and economic integration of the countryside and the acquisition of even larger amounts of exportable grain. According to Viacheslav Molotov, Stalin's long-term deputy, "To survive, the state needed grain. Otherwise, it would crack up – it would be unable to maintain the army, the schools, construction, the elements most vital to the state."[21] In a contentious international political climate, the acquisition of more grain for export demanded the creation of highly extractive economic institutions, designed to wrest "incomes and wealth from one subset of society to benefit a different subset."[22]

By introducing large, centrally managed farms and by standardizing agricultural production, Stalinist modernizers hoped to bring order to the hinterland and ensure a steady collection of grain for the cities and for industrialization by controlling the peasants.[23] But to take complete charge of the rural areas in the Ukrainian SSR and in such regions as the Ukrainian-speaking Kuban in southern Russia would not be easy. In these areas, most peasants possessed small plots and a substantial number engaged in individual, subsistence farming.[24] Collective memories of Cossack self-rule, the national-liberation movements against the Poles, the violent struggles against the Bolshevik regime in 1917–21, and the overall predominance of hereditary (not communal) household land tenure reinforced their individualism and their differences with their Russian neighbours.[25] The overwhelming majority of peasants in these areas, as in most of the USSR, considered collectivization as a form of socio-economic bondage, a "second serfdom."[26] But unlike Russian peasants, these Ukrainian-speaking men and women – largely due to the war, revolutionary, and post-revolutionary periods – could mobilize along national as well as social lines to oppose the new order.

With these limitations, how would the Soviet state acquire more grain? Financial manipulations and heavy taxes had failed to secure surplus cereals from the countryside in the 1920s. The Soviet state raised the price of industrial goods it sold to the peasants while lowering the amount it paid for agricultural goods. The disparities between the high prices for wheat and rye the peasants received in the open market and the low prices they collected from the state only increased in this decade.[27] In response, the peasants reduced their sales to the state and planted less. From their economic perspective, they had no incentive to grow crops beyond their own immediate needs and acted accordingly. Behaving as they did during the Great War and in the immediate post-revolutionary period, the peasants threatened the government's efforts to acquire enough grain to feed its growing urban population and to bankroll its industrialization. Just as the Soviet party-state launched its daring economic drive and as Soviet peasants decreased their production of exportable crops, the world agricultural market recovered from the First World War.

This international conflict delivered a severe blow to European farming production as peasants in both military alliances "put down their plough and took up the sword," losing their horses to military requisitioning and their fields to artillery fire.[28] As the Great War pushed up wheat prices, the United States, Canada, Argentina, and Australia increased their acreage and made their yields more efficient, surpassing Europe's pre-war output.

When the war ended, these overseas producers hoped to retain their new lucrative markets, even though European agricultural cultivation returned to pre-war levels by 1925.[29] This combined European and non-European production flooded the international market and led to a precipitous drop in worldwide wheat prices.[30] In the 1920s and 1930s good harvests outnumbered bad harvests and wheat prices continued to plunge.

If tsarist Russia supplied 25 per cent of the world wheat market in 1913, the USSR furnished only 12 per cent in 1926.[31] Inasmuch as the new revolutionary government did not expect to receive any large international loans, Soviet planners chose to stay the course and increase exports to acquire hard currency. From their perspective, this remained the only option to finance their bold industrialization project.

In order to amass more grain to sell abroad, the party leadership launched a campaign to squeeze, then expropriate, the landholdings of the kulaks, those peasants they considered better off, those who produced the bulk of the exportable grain. In order to do so, the party leaders popularized the notion of class divisions in the countryside. According to this artificial construction of rural reality, the peasantry contained three groups: the poor peasants (the supporters of the working class), the middle peasants (their allies), and the kulaks (their class enemy).[32] The authorities claimed that the kulaks (*kurkuls* in Ukrainian), those who possessed more than nine desiatins (twenty-four acres) of land and who employed at least one worker, constituted 2 to 5 per cent of the population in the grain-producing and grain-consuming regions of the USSR. These kulaks allegedly produced enormous amounts of surplus grain.[33] Most importantly, the party claimed that kulaks exploited the poor and middle peasants and organized peasant resistance to Soviet power.

This cartoonish Marxist interpretation of the countryside exaggerated class divisions and neglected the prevalence of peasant solidarity against outsiders. In reality, many of those hiring labour included disabled war veterans, widows, and families with a number of small children. (The average urban worker, moreover, earned twice as much as those peasants whom Soviet statisticians classified as "wealthy.")[34]

Inasmuch as the authorities needed to create a convenient group of "enemies" to subdue the entire peasant mass, the party launched an offensive against the alleged kulaks, seeking to limit them politically and economically.[35]

The Soviet state in 1926 already levied a heavy tax burden on them. In 1927, the government forced "kulaks" to sell up to 35 per cent of their produce to the state at low prices and deprived them of the right to vote. But additional pressures on this group did not produce the anticipated results – more grain. Instead, these men and women responded to these policies by planting less. In light of poor harvests and bad weather, state procurements of grain sharply declined in 1927 and 1928, forcing the Soviet Ukrainian government to introduce ration cards in Odessa in March 1928, in Mykolaiv in June, and in the major industrial okrugs by September. By 1929, approximately 10 per cent of Ukraine's total population received this welfare benefit.[36] Not all urban residents received ration cards, but the overwhelming majority who lived in the towns and cities did. Moscow and Leningrad started to ration bread in the winter of 1928–9, as did other towns and cities throughout the USSR in the spring and summer of 1929. Shortly afterwards, the authorities limited the sale of sugar, tea, and meat in the urban centres.[37]

As the state procurements of grain and other dietary essentials declined, the subsequent food shortages in the cities – the main bastion of Bolshevik support – shocked the Soviet leadership, especially Stalin. Ignoring proposals to raise the price of grain the Soviet state paid the peasants, he sent his trusted lieutenants throughout the USSR to find more grain and to oversee the timely delivery of grain shipments. As the leader of a successful urban-oriented Marxist political party, Stalin did not feel any love for the peasants, "the dark masses," who – in his opinion and that of his colleagues – possessed a counter-revolutionary and nationalist view of the world and acted as the "natural saboteurs of Soviet power."[38] The exclusion of peasants from the rationing system and the introduction of mass grain requisitions vividly expressed the Soviet government's declaration of war on the peasants.[39] This internal war would not only revolutionize the relationship between all peasants and the Soviet regime, but also redesign the very foundations of Ukrainian society and identity.

Molotov, Stalin's plenipotentiary, arrived in Ukraine on 28 December 1927 and stayed to 6 January 1928. He issued orders to local party and Soviet bodies to increase the amount of grain delivered to state coffers.[40] By employing brutal repressions (arrests, fines, and severe court sentences) against the kulaks and other peasants, Molotov claimed to have raised the amount of grain procured in Ukraine.[41]

He convened a meeting of party activists in Kharkiv and told them that "Ukraine must hand over its grain immediately, without delay."[42] In discussing his actions in Melitopil, where the overwhelming majority of peasants worked their own individual farmsteads, Molotov remembered decades later:

> We took away the grain. We paid them in cash, but of course at miserably low prices. They gained nothing. I told them that for the present peasants had to give us grain on loan. Then I went to the countryside, to the Greek and Ukrainian settlements. I applied utmost pressure to extort the grain. All kinds of rather harsh methods of persuasion had to be applied. We started with the kulak.[43]

After Molotov returned to Moscow, he described his activities to Stalin, who responded with delight, asserting that "I could cover you with kisses in gratitude for your action down there."[44] Inspired by his deputy's ruthlessness, Stalin refined his methods. Between 18 January and 4 February 1928, he visited the agricultural regions in Siberia and the Urals and introduced "extraordinary measures" reminiscent of the crop confiscations under war communism in 1918–20. During his inspection tour, he demanded that party officials seize kulak grain without payment, justifying their actions under Article 107 of the Russian Criminal Code, which prohibited "speculation." Under Stalin's guidance in Siberia, the arbitrary seizure of grain from kulaks as well as from middle peasants and even poor peasants became the standard operating procedure. The authorities now "could choose to regard the mere possession of grain stocks as illegal hoarding with a speculative purpose and therefore, a fit subject for confiscation without payment."[45]

The Soviet state, in short, claimed possession of all grain stocks, including grain reserves and seed grain the peasants kept for the next sowing period. These interventions, in effect, nationalized grain production and its distribution, nullified the limited economic liberties the peasants enjoyed under the New Economic Policy, and foreshadowed a new, more brutal era.

These arbitrary measures which Stalin mastered became known as the "Urals-Siberian" method. Although his colleagues on the Politburo forced him to cut short these wide-scale intercessions after April 1928, he reintroduced them several months later. With the defeat of the pro-NEP faction within the Politburo in the spring of 1929, this institution endorsed this method throughout the USSR. In 1929, the grain requisitioning of kulak surpluses almost seamlessly evolved into the mass collectivization of the majority of all peasants.[46]

Despite the poor harvests and the irregular weather patterns the USSR and the Ukrainian SSR experienced in the summer and fall of 1927, the USSR's primary economic office – the State Planning Committee (Gosplan) – raised Ukraine's grain consignment plan for the following year.[47] In creating the agricultural goals for Ukraine in 1928–9 and beyond, Gosplan exaggerated Ukraine's agricultural potential and underestimated its actual problems. With Stalin's prodding, economic planners constructed radically optimistic plans for agricultural production for the USSR and for the Ukrainian SSR, in particular.[48] In preparing this course of action, they rejected the Soviet Ukrainian government's proposals for a greater diversification of agriculture and did not include any leeway for poor weather patterns, which occurred frequently.[49]

The harvests of 1928–9 did not meet expectations. Despite the crop failure of 1928–9, Soviet authorities demanded that Gosplan's grain consignments be fulfilled. In 1928, the Ukrainian SSR provided the USSR with 40 per cent of its total grain procurements.[50] The Stalinist faction within the party's leadership reintroduced "extraordinary measures" to Ukraine and continued to extract the maximum amount of grain from the peasantry by coercive means, claiming that Ukraine should not only feed itself, but help sustain the rest of the USSR.[51]

Although the Soviet authorities cut back on the export of wheat and rye to Europe and provided Ukraine with some grain, which may have saved tens of thousands of lives, it was not enough to stave off starvation. The Soviet Ukrainian government established the State Commission for Aid to Victims of Crop Failure in the summer of 1928 to provide relief, but it reached "fewer than twenty percent" of the population in the crop-failure regions.[52] Inasmuch as the Soviet authorities in Moscow "never intended to feed all of those who needed food," relief agencies tried to limit aid "to the poorest peasants and nursing mothers and babies."[53] This relief priority would exclude the overwhelming majority of those opposed to the government's policies in the countryside and include those who potentially would join the collective farms.

Despite the massive grain shortfall throughout the USSR, Soviet authorities still believed that they had to continue to ship agricultural products abroad to acquire hard currency to fund the industrialization drive. In light of the scarcity of exportable grain, they sold more non-grain agricultural products abroad, such as meat, fowl, butter, eggs, and sugar, which they extracted from the countryside.[54] The expropriation of grain and common non-grain products the peasants consumed on a regular basis created a rural environment conducive to famine.

This catastrophe hit Ukraine in late 1928 and early 1929 for the first time since 1921–3 and 1924–5 as heavy frosts and erratic temperatures destroyed a third of the entire winter grain crop.[55] The Soviet government did not intend to create a famine in 1928–9, but in conformity with its rosy grain projections and its minimalization of the true extent of the crop failures, it provided very limited aid to help the starving. The USSR's commitment to "industrialization above all" and its extractive policies in the countryside ignited the 1928–9 famine and prepared the way for even deadlier famines in the near future. This grain crisis affected millions of peasants in Ukraine, especially the poorer ones and those in the southern steppe okrugs. This famine led to a reduction in seeded areas and to a serious drop in the overall number of horses, cattle, and domestic animals.

During this famine, the Ukrainian SSR experienced a direct loss of approximately twenty-three thousand men, women, and children and an indirect loss of approximately eighty thousand.[56] Although much smaller in scope and number of victims than the famine of 1932 or the Holodomor of 1933, the famine of 1928–9 prepared the way for the next two by reactivating opposition to the forced grain requisitions and by politicizing the peasants. These consequences – not surprisingly – generated brutal Soviet countermeasures.

In Ukraine, the OGPU registered 150 mass protests against the rural authorities from 1 April to 1 October 1928, and 538 alleged "terrorist acts" in 1927–8 and 1,266 in 1928–9.[57] These crimes included the killing, attempted killing, or wounding of representatives of the Soviet order and arson of socialist property or agricultural institutions. Although special OGPU and police units suppressed many of these protests, the growing resistance convinced Soviet leaders of the need to adopt extreme measures as quickly as possible.[58]

Although most peasants did not directly challenge the authorities, the state's grain requisitions radicalized the peasants, as OGPU agents noted in their internal reports. The peasants concluded that the Soviet government's illegal and arbitrary confiscations, not the "evil" kulaks (as the Soviet media proclaimed), brought on the famine, which embittered them against the state. With the introduction of the Urals-Siberian method during the beginning of the grain procurement plan in Ukraine in early 1928, many in the intelligentsia and the peasantry assessed the crisis in the countryside through a national, not class, prism.

Even Lazar Kaganovich, the leader of the Communist Party of Ukraine, recognized that the convulsions in the countryside strengthened anti-Soviet and national feelings, if not nationalism. Speaking at the plenum of the Central Committee of the CP(b)U in March 1928, he noted that peasants asked provocative questions, such as "Where did they take the grain harvested in Ukraine?" "Why is our grain-growing republic starving now?" and "Who is guilty of the ongoing robbery of the Ukrainian village and the rapid impoverishment of the towns?" Some, according to Kaganovich, concluded that "it would be better if Ukraine separated from Russia. We would live better – but now (we) give bread to Russia and Russia sells it abroad. So it turns out that Ukraine is like a milch cow."[59] Although it is difficult to ascertain how many Ukrainian peasants embraced these views, these negative attitudes most likely grew as collectivization and grain requisitioning absorbed more farms.

As the food situation deteriorated, national discontent surfaced not only in the villages, but also in the towns. "The government ships bread abroad, but we are starving" became a common refrain.[60] According to prominent party leaders in this Soviet Republic, Ukrainian separatism, stimulated by Petliura's followers and by Poland, re-emerged as a very serious threat to the Soviet order, but to what extent still remains unclear.[61]

The agricultural crisis produced, at least in these comments, a fusion of national and social strands in opposition to the Soviet state. It also aggravated anti-Russian and anti-Semitic feelings among a number of Ukrainian peasants, perhaps because of the public prominence of Jews in the All-Union Communist Party and the CP(b)U, the OGPU/NKVD, and among leading party activists collectivizing the countryside.[62] In the absence of professional polling, it is difficult to quantify these attitudes. Nevertheless, collectivization must have inflamed national as well as social tensions in the countryside.

All in all, several factors contributed to the famine of 1928–9 and to the starvation of thousands. The droughts and abrupt climactic changes caused a genuine decline in the availability of grain, but the state-sponsored acquisitions continued, even if the total aggregate collected decreased. The Soviet government acquired the grain by coercive means and determined the amount exported and the amount sent to the cities and to grain-starved regions. This was a political decision, not an agricultural or climactic one. Once the agricultural pie shrank, the leaders of the Soviet party-state could have assessed their priorities and redistributed its grain resources in a more equitable manner to feed its population. But this choice did not appear on the political menu. Industrialization became the alpha and omega of the Soviet system long before Stalin gained control of its commanding heights.

The grain crisis, the Communist Party's reaction, and the peasant response to the governmental intrusion into their economic sphere represented a warning shot. With the introduction of extraordinary measures and compulsory grain requisitions in 1928 and 1929, the Soviet authorities discovered the strengths and weaknesses of the peasant's opposition to the government's intervention and to the future mass collectivization drive. The peasants, in turn, quickly realized that the moderate New Economic Policy had ended. Both sides calculated their risks and rewards and concluded that control of the countryside was essentially a zero-sum game. A greater and more brutal conflagration would soon engulf the farmlands.

De-kulakization, Collectivization, and the Famine, 1929–1932

At the end of December 1929, shortly after Stalin removed Nikolai Bukharin, his heretofore closest ally and the head of the moderate pro-peasant faction in the Politburo, he announced a change in policy. The party would no longer just restrict the "exploiting tendencies" of the kulaks, but "liquidate" them "as a class."[63] Once the authorities removed kulaks and their families from the countryside (a process called "de-kulakization"), the subsequent amalgamation of individual peasant hold-ings into collective farms would produce an overall agricultural output surpassing that of the kulaks. On 30 January 1930, the All-Union Party's Central Committee secretly issued a decree dispossessing the wealthiest peasants and deporting them.[64] Rapidly executed between November 1929 and February 1930, the de-kulakization playbook repeated many of the methods the Bolsheviks had adopted against the Don Cossacks in early 1919, when they proclaimed the need "to neutralize the Cossacks through the merciless extirpation of its elite."[65]

By manipulating the social tensions between the better-off and the poor-est peasants in the villages, the Soviet state isolated the kulaks, branded them as implacable "class enemies," and encouraged their neighbours to divide their lands and take their personal property. Many criminal elements joined the redistribution brigades and the young activists the regime sent to the countryside. Together, these two groups engaged in lawless behaviour, punishing kulaks, not building a new order in the countryside. In some areas, they "drove the dekulakized naked into the streets, beat them, orga-nized drinking bouts in their houses, shot over their heads, forced them to dig their own graves, undressed women and searched them, stole valuables, money etc.," effectively terrorizing not just the kulaks, but the entire rural community.[66] Peasants who may have sympathized with the kulaks did not dare to reveal themselves to their neighbours. By dividing the villages, de-kulakization, in effect, removed the most powerful potential opponents to Bolshevik power from the villages. In place of the old traditional order, the Soviet elite built its own web of institutions in the countryside, populating them with activists from the anti-kulak brigades.[67]

The first wave of de-kulakization in Ukraine started in the first half of 1930.[68] In 1930–1, the Soviet government deported 63,720 kulak house-holds – over 300,000 men, women, and children – from that republic to the Arctic North, the Urals, Siberia, Yakutia, and the Far East.[69] According to one eyewitness, members of these families were

> packed off into the terrible cold – infants, pregnant women piled in cattle cars on top of one another, and right there women gave birth (would there be a worse indignity?), then they were thrown out of the cars like dogs and put in churches and dirty, cold sheds, lice-ridden, freezing, and hungry, and here they are, thousands of them, left to the mercy of fate, like dogs no one wants to notice.[70]

Even if at this point Soviet decision makers did not know their actions would lead to famine and mass starvation, they were assuredly aware of the inhumane suffering they were inflicting on these people. They would soon extend this barbarity against "class enemies" to all peasants. In preparation for this all-out assault, party leaders taught their agents that "peasants who opposed collectivization were agents of the class enemy and that the wrath of the proletariat should be meted out to them."[71] By 1930, if not before, most peasants in the USSR's grain-producing regions recognized the party's hostility towards them.

According to the 1926 Soviet census, the overwhelming majority of Ukraine's twenty-nine million men and women (81 per cent) lived in the countryside and engaged in agricultural pursuits.[72] Nearly 90 per cent of the rural population and rural households identified themselves as Ukrainians, although they were not evenly distributed in all of Ukraine's regions (see map 6 and table 6.1).[73] The highest percentage (over 90 per cent) of Ukrainians lived in the Right Bank, Left Bank, and the Dnieper Industrial Region.[74] The Right and Left Banks also represented the two most densely populated areas of Ukraine, itself the most densely populated republic of the USSR.[75]

In the spring of 1929, the Ukrainian SSR possessed 5.2 million peasant households and 25.4 million peasants, well over 19 per cent of the total Soviet peasant population.[76] Farming the steppe's rich black soil, those peasants who identified themselves as Ukrainians (approximately 22.2 million men, women, and children) represented the largest group of non-Russian peasants, second only to the Russian peasants, within the USSR. The authorities believed that Ukrainian peasants possessed the largest private grain holdings in the USSR and regarded them "more prosperous than Russian peasants and therefore more suspect politically."[77] Moscow also did not trust the former Kuban Cossacks, largely descendants of the Ukrainian or Zaprorizhian Cossacks, who lived in the North Caucasus and who constituted a privileged class.[78]

After the party's agents removed the "kulaks" from the countryside, they "encouraged" the other peasants to join collective farms. But the overwhelming majority of peasants in Ukraine did not welcome the prospect of collectivization. They possessed a tradition of individual farming, however difficult to maintain in the Soviet Union's most overpopulated agricultural region, and few of them wanted to abandon their small, individual plots and voluntarily enter larger government-sponsored collective farms or state farms. Only the poorest, approximately 3 per cent of the

Table 6.1 Ukrainians and the Rural Population of the Ukrainian SSR, 1926

Region	Rural population	Ukrainian population	Percentage
Polissia	2,523,790	2,172,148	86.0
Right Bank	6,711,626	6,221,329	93.0
Left Bank	5,440,965	5,003,793	92.0
Donbass	1,174,381	875,482	75.0
Dnieper Ind. Region	1,923,944	1,753,408	91.0
Steppe	4,492,872	3,316,630	74.0
Moldavian ASSR	493,053	248,193	50.5
TOTAL	22,267,578	19,342,790	86.0

Source: *Statystyka Ukrainy*, no. 96 (1927), xvi–xix, table 3.

Note: Regions and okrugs:

Polissia:	Volyn, Hlukhiv, Konotip, Korosten, Chernihiv
Right Bank:	Berdychiv, Bilotserkiv, Vinnytsia, Uman, Kamianets, Kiev, Mohyliv, Proskuriv, Tulchyn, Shevchenkivsk, Shepetiv
Left Bank:	Kremenchuk, Kupiansk, Luben, Nizhyn, Ozium, Poltava, Prylutsk, Romen, Sumy, Kharkiv
Donbass:	Artemivsk, Luhansk, Stalino
Dnieper Industrial Region:	Dniepropetrovsk, Zaporizhzhia, Kryvorizhzhia
Steppe:	Zinoviev, Mariupil, Melitopil, Mykolaiv (Nikolaev), Odessa, Pershomaisk, Starobil'sk, Kherson, Moldavian ASSR

rural households, joined the new agricultural units in the early 1920s, when peasants could freely choose to accept or reject this new system. As the government pressed this "voluntary" collectivization campaign in 1927 and 1928, less than 6 per cent of the five million peasant households in the Soviet Ukrainian Republic belonged to these collective farms.[79] Officials introduced a set of unrealistic goals, ignoring peasant aspirations to work for themselves on their own private plots.

The countryside became the epicentre of a great struggle to create a new social order under Soviet auspices. According to Lev Kopelev, one of hundreds of thousands of young men and women the party activated to collectivize the Ukrainian rural areas, this epic confrontation encompassed more than an effort to extract grain. It also represented a merciless fight "for the souls of (the) peasants who were mired in political backwardness, in ignorance, who succumbed to enemy agitation, who did not understand the great truth of communism."[80] Peasant economic and political "backwardness," in other words, hampered the emergence of "socialism in one country" and the worldwide revolution. Communists had to uproot the peasant fetish for a private plot of land.

In the Communist Party's view of the world, peasants were too simple to see the radiant future that collectivization and industrialization would bring. The party, not the peasants, had to determine the goals and schedule the pace. The All-Union Communist Party's Central Committee approved the start of mass collectivization on 17 November 1929. On 4 February 1930, Stanislav Kosior, the head of the CP(b)U, declared that the entire Ukrainian countryside should be collectivized by the fall of 1930. By 1 March 1930, 62.8 per cent of all peasant households in Soviet Ukraine allegedly joined some sort of rudimentary collective farm.[81]

But these statistics represented a fantasy world, not reality. The party increased its demands on the peasants, but could not persuade them to deliver. The state's repeated requisitions and claims for the tax arrears mobilized the peasants who overcame their internal divisions and united against the regime's agents.[82] The peasants resisted the authorities passively as well as actively, non-violently as well as violently.

In 1930, approximately 13,754 peasant disturbances (ten times the number recorded the previous year) with 2.5 million participants broke out across the USSR. They flared up in Ukraine, and the Central Black Earth region (which included Tambov province), the North Caucasus, the Middle Volga, the Moscow Region, Western Siberia, and the Tatar Republic within the USSR. Of these regions, the Ukrainian SSR emerged as the one with the most active resistance, with 4,098 demonstrations (29.7 per cent of the total throughout the USSR) and well over one million peasant participants (38.7 per cent of the total).[83] The peasants, according to OGPU reports, demanded an end to involuntary requisitions; the return of collectivized and requisitioned goods and deported families; the disbanding of the Communist Youth League (the Komsomol), which most peasants considered an organization of informants and provocateurs; respect for religious feelings and practices; free elections to the village soviets; and the reintroduction of trade in the countryside.[84] The peasants wanted to maintain their economic and civic autonomy; the Soviet political leaders aspired to crush peasant liberties and completely subordinate them to their urban mission.

In Ukraine, as well as in other non-Russian regions, the OGPU recorded nationalist slogans and rumours concerning the return of Petliura, who had been assassinated in Paris by a Soviet agent on 25 May 1926, "ostensibly in retaliation for pogroms perpetrated by some of his troops, but more likely because of the potential for a renewed alliance between the Polish state and an anti-Soviet and pro-independence Ukrainian national movement."[85]

Stalin and his allies recognized that the countryside and its peasants remained the primary social base for the supporters of Ukrainian nationalism. However uncertain the reality behind this conclusion in the late 1920s and early 1930s, Stalin – who had consistently linked the peasant question with the national question – imagined it true. And if he visualized this reality, it existed. His ominous conclusion demanded the appropriate prophylactic measures. But before the final assault, he launched a tactical retreat.

Acknowledging the peasant opposition to collectivization, Stalin changed his approach, if only temporarily. On 2 March 1930, he published an article criticizing the fanaticism of party workers in the countryside, ordering them to slow the pace of collectivization and allow some peasants to leave the collectives.[86] Because the article only carried Stalin's signature, he "presented himself to the villagers as the reincarnation of the 'good tsars' of bygone days."[87] This article – dubbed the "Dizzy from Success" pronouncement – overturned what the party had already accomplished in the countryside. Despite expectations that most peasants would remain, approximately 65 per cent of all households in Ukraine left the collective farms within six months after Stalin's article appeared.[88] But they enjoyed only a temporary respite from collectivization.

Despite Stalin's illusive change of direction, the Soviet state made a number of significant gains in the countryside, especially in denuding it of the peasant elite (the kulaks) and in creating a beachhead for collectivization. After all, 35 per cent of those collectivized remained in the collective farms, a far higher percentage than in 1928. If 300,000 peasant households belonged to collective farms in 1928, approximately 1.1 million remained by the late summer of 1930, long after Stalin's conciliatory article.[89]

As the countryside calmed down, in July 1930 Moscow's Politburo issued a secret decree restarting the collectivization drive that fall. In December 1930 the Central Committee approved a plan expanding the collective farm network, allowing the authorities to confiscate seed grain from those who did not join these new units.[90] The government employed fines, threats, physical abuse, confiscation, exile, and even executions to persuade peasants to join the new farms. Those who did not experienced "the constant threat of being classified as kulaks and therefore subjected to crippling taxation, which undoubtedly led many middle peasants to conclude that it would be unwise to remain outside the collective farms."[91] Fear, not persuasion, convinced most.

Perceiving the end of their traditional way of life, some peasants crossed the border into Poland. Others set fire to their property and crops, killed their animals, destroyed machinery, assaulted party activists, and participated in sporadic revolts and uprisings. In 1930, the OGPU recorded almost one million acts of individual resistance in Ukraine.[92] That same year the Ukrainian GPU noted that the villages most engaged in opposing collectivization "were often the same ones that had distinguished themselves in the rural disturbances of 1905 or produced an abnormally high proportion of socialist cadres before 1917."[93] Engaging in uncoordinated acts of utter desperation, peasants slaughtered their animals en masse rather than surrender them to the collective farms. Between 1928 and 1932 the number of cattle in Soviet Ukraine fell from 8.6 million to 4.8 million and the number of pigs declined from 7 million to 2 million.[94] The Ukrainian countryside clearly possessed a deep-rooted culture of defying the central authorities, whether tsarist or Soviet.

In response to the widespread opposition to collectivization, the Soviet authorities applied enough coercion and violence to win control of the countryside. By October 1931, 68 per cent of the households in Ukraine – and 87 per cent in the fertile steppe region – joined these new farms.[95] In face of a massive invasion from the cities, most peasants signed up.

If on 1 January 1930 the Ukrainian SSR possessed approximately twenty-five million rural inhabitants engaged in agricultural pursuits, only 20,904 belonged to the Communist Party of Ukraine, which embraced a total of 250,681 members and candidate-members.[96] Many in the rural party leadership had served in the Red Army during the Civil War.[97] Between 1929 and 1932, the rural party grew to 42,000 members. To bolster these small numbers, the party leadership sent another 70,000 heavily armed party members, upping the total to 112,000 in 1932. The party leaders could also press into service nearly 500,000 Komsomol members, thousands of industrial workers and urban party officials who arrived in the villages for shorter or longer periods, and uncounted numbers from OGPU military units.[98] Most of the Komsomol activists remained "lukewarm" supporters of Ukrainization, distrusted the peasantry, and enthusiastically toed the party line, especially in regard to collectivization.[99] (The authorities rarely employed the Red Army, which drew its rank and file from the peasantry; these recruits sympathized with the plight of their rural compatriots.)[100] It is unclear how many "outsiders" the party sent to subdue the countryside, but hundreds of thousands had to have been involved. The polarization of the countryside and the constant search for scapegoats for collectivization's failures led to unprecedented violence, which easily surpassed that of the 1918–21 period.[101]

As the agricultural sector failed to acquire more exportable grain, party leaders introduced even more brutal measures to induce the outcome they desired. In light of Ukraine's successful fulfilment of the agricultural quota in 1930 after a bountiful harvest, central planners increased the allotment in 1931. If the authorities set a goal of 265 million poods of grain for 1927–8, they imposed an impossible target of 510 million poods for 1931–2.[102] Due to unfavourable weather conditions and extensive crop failure, the harvests of 1931 and 1932 produced less than the above-average results of 1930.[103] The party's decision to raise these quotas at this point did not represent a rational economic judgment, but a political one. In 1931–2, in the grain-producing areas, such as Ukraine and the North Caucasus, the state confiscated about half of the harvest.[104] By 1931 the Soviet state's collections of cereals in the largest wheat-growing regions of Ukraine and the northern Caucasus constituted 45–6 per cent of the entire Soviet harvest, stripping the peasants of their food supplies.[105] Many collective farmers met their assigned goals by being forced to surrender their seed grain.[106] Without seed grain, the peasants had nothing left to plant for the next season or to feed themselves. In Ukraine, the Soviet political leadership expanded the brutal grain collections campaign (implemented throughout the USSR) into a total war against the peasants.

Even after the Soviet government employed violent measures against them, the peasants still resisted, but now in a passive manner. They worked "as little and as poorly as possible," stealing, hiding, or destroying the crops they grew.[107] In many respects, they acted as civilian versions of the good soldier Švejk. Thousands of local officials purged in 1932–3 "often concealed or at least tolerated" these peasant slowdowns.[108] These responses to collectivization only enraged the central authorities, who failed to secure the quantity of grain they imagined the countryside should deliver.

Despite appeals by Skrypnyk and others in the Soviet Ukrainian political leadership, Stalin refused to lower the assigned allotments for grain collections.[109] To do so, his lieutenants claimed, threatened the entire industrialization program. By the end of 1931, another famine broke out in the Ukrainian countryside and in the first half of 1932 spread across the republic, subsiding only with the spring harvest.[110] But due to abnormal weather patterns, the rapid commandeering of livestock, and the subsequent peasant slaughter of millions of horses, the fall 1932 harvest produced even less than the poor harvest of 1931, which was lower than the 1930 harvest.[111] Although the authorities lowered Ukraine's grain levy three times, they did little to reduce the highly unrealistic allocations to the point where they would prevent mass starvation.[112]

In her diary entry of 5 April 1932, Oleksandra Radchenko, a rural schoolteacher from central Ukraine, wrote:

Famine, artificially created famine is taking on a nightmarish character. No one can understand why they are pumping out grain to the last kernel, and now having seen the results of such pumping out, they nevertheless continue to demand grain for sowing and sowing material in general. And when the indignant peasant exclaims that all his grain was taken for the grain procurement, he receives a question in reply: "Why did you give everything; you should have realized that you would have to sow with something?" and endless negotiations begin. And the children go hungry, worn out, emaciated, tormented by tapeworms, so they eat only sugar beets – and those will run out soon – and the harvest is still four months away. What will become of us?[113]

Millions starved and many passed away. In 1932, Ukraine experienced 250,000 excess deaths and 67,100 indirect losses, primarily in the countryside.[114] More men, women, and children died during the famine of 1932 than in 1928.

From Famine to the Holodomor, 1932–1933

Many of the party secretaries responsible for implementing the grain collection plans in Ukraine cautiously warned Moscow of its impossible quotas. They understood that the mass protests and demonstrations they encountered represented only a small tip of the iceberg of mass discontent and anger in the countryside.[115] Ukrainian party officials warned Stalin that the harvest of 1932 would produce less than in 1931 and that the famine would intensify in the fall. In their letters to Stalin and Molotov, dated 10 June 1932, high-ranking Ukrainian party leaders Hryhory Petrovsky and Vlas Chubar asked for 1.5 million to 2 million poods of grain to supply the starving Ukrainian countryside.[116]

Although the 1932 harvest did produce less than the poor harvest of 1931, Stalin did not relent.[117] By the early summer of 1932, he resolved that "only a policy of uncompromising harshness would enable the grain collections to succeed."[118] On 15 June, he asserted, "Ukraine has been given more than it should get. There is no reason to give it more grain – and there is nowhere to take it from."[119] Although he admitted the existence of "impoverishment and famine" in a number of fertile Ukrainian districts, he did not view it as an emergency.[120] Three days later, in a letter to Lazar Kaganovich and Molotov, he demanded that "we should add an extra 4–5 percent to the plan in order to cover inevitable errors in the records and fulfill the plan at any cost."[121]

In late June 1932, Stalin and Molotov sent a telegram to the Communist Party of Ukraine and to the Soviet Ukrainian government, stressing the necessity to complete the assigned grain deliveries by all means necessary.[122] At the Third All-Ukrainian Conference of the Communist Party of Ukraine (6–9 July 1932), Molotov and Kaganovich, Stalin's primary troubleshooters, forced members of the reluctant CP(b)U Politburo to agree to fulfil the centrally assigned agricultural plan without any compromises or delays.[123] As Stalin and his closest allies well understood at this point in time, the extreme grain requisitions would spark not just an accidental famine, but an intentional one, the Holodomor.[124]

In response to peasant resistance, Stalin insisted on the promulgation of the "Decree on the Protection of State Property" in early August. This law authorized an individual's execution and confiscation of all personal possessions if he stole property, even a few specks of grain, from a collective farm or cooperative.[125] The Politburo radically modified this decree, insisting that individuals (not kulaks) who engaged in such criminal acts should receive a sentence of only ten years imprisonment. Only those who had been kulaks or who "systematically" stole grain, sugar beet, or animals would be shot.[126]

Despite the ruthless measures the authorities embraced in the late summer, the grain collections did not meet expectations. In early August, Stalin complained about the state of grain accumulation in Ukraine. In September, the republic nearly met the monthly goal imposed by Moscow, but in October and November its peasants faltered. Of all of the major grain-growing areas of the Soviet Union (which included Ukraine, the North Caucasus, the Lower Volga Region, and the Central Volga Region), the Ukrainian SSR produced less than 40 per cent of its assigned quota, the lowest of the four.[127] In the eyes of Stalin and his closest comrades, Ukraine – the USSR's breadbasket – had just become a "slacker republic." In his eyes, not only did the republic not deliver, it *refused* to deliver. In an addendum to a special OGPU report on the anti-collective farm movement in Belarus, Kazakhstan, and Ukraine, written in the late summer of 1932, the authors asserted that "Ukraine stands in first place when it comes to mass anti-Soviet incidents."[128] Stalin, who followed the progress of collectivization closely, most likely read this dispatch. If not, he independently drew the same conclusions. Moscow's central organs had to break Ukraine's resistance and compel its communist party to complete its duties.

Constantly pressured by the All-Union Communist Party, the Central Committee of the CP(b)U and the Soviet Ukrainian government issued a decree on 18 November 1932 punishing independent households as well as collective farms that "maliciously wrecked the grain procurement plan," which included most of the peasants.[129] These men and women now had to return the meagre grain the government had advanced them. Two days later, those who could not meet the grain quotas had to surrender their livestock, their last hope against starvation.[130] These "fines in kind" often exceeded the household's or collective's assigned target; these brutal sanctions, in effect, stripped the household or the collective farm bare.

On 28 November 1932, Soviet authorities expanded the use of "blacklists." They emerged as early as the fall 1929 grain campaign, but became widespread in Ukraine in August 1932, reaching a peak that October and November.[131] By late 1932, the authorities placed well over half of all populated areas in Ukraine, including collective farms, rural soviets, and raions, on these lists.[132] This vicious punishment, as well as the subsequent removal of all edible goods from the villages, represented a disproportionate response to the drop in grain deliveries to the Soviet state – a death sentence. These areas soon became "zones of death."[133]

On 14 December 1932, Stalin and Molotov signed a secret directive which demanded that party cadres "fully complete the grain and sunflower seed procurement plan by the end of January 1933."[134] Both men then ordered all collective farms to deliver all grain, including reserves for seeding and nourishment, leaving nothing for the peasants. To meet this goal, the party intensified repressive measures and increased the number of arrests and deportations. In the final paragraph, the edict granted Stanislav Kosior and Vlas Chubar, the primary party leaders in Soviet Ukraine, the right "to suspend the delivery of goods to especially backward districts until they fulfill the grain procurement plan."[135] These "goods" included food, nails, tools, salt, and gas, the very materials needed to deliver grain into state hands.[136]

Armed Soviet detachments then confiscated harvested grain, seed, and grain reserves, and suspended food deliveries to the recalcitrant villages. Hunger, starvation, and mass death followed. Young Soviet activists, especially those who had some sort of connection with the peasant world, may have experienced pangs of conscience, and feelings of sympathy, pity, and shame, but a "rationalistic fanaticism" justified their heartless methods against the peasants.[137] According to Lev Kopelev, one of these activists, "We were realizing historical necessity. We were performing our new revolutionary duty. We were obtaining grain for the socialist fatherland ... We believed, despite what we ourselves had seen, learned, experienced."[138] For him and for the hundreds of thousands of true believers, the ends justified the means.

Whatever misgivings some party activists may have experienced, they successfully stripped the rural areas of grain and all edible goods. These procurements triggered a famine, which spread across the Ukrainian countryside between November 1932 and June 1933, reaching a peak

in March–April.[139] Deaths rose at a horrendous rate. To stop the migration
of starving peasants to the cities, in December 1932 the Central Executive
Committee of the USSR introduced the internal passport system in the
cities and the mandatory registration of individuals in their places of residence. In addition, it prohibited collective farmers from seeking employment in factories and mines unless these industries drafted them in the
proper bureaucratic manner. The peasants did not receive passports and
experienced discrimination and brutal treatment whenever they entered
the cities in search of food.[140]

Residents of urban areas fared better. The authorities "passportized"
Moscow, Leningrad, Kharkiv, Kiev, Odessa, Minsk, all of the major urban
centres situated within one hundred kilometres of the western border, and
the most important industrial cities by the spring of 1933. In the process
of doing so, they expelled thousands, if not tens of thousands, of vagrants,
"unreliable elements," and people with "a suspicious past" from these cities. With the introduction of internal passports and residence permits,
these coveted entitlements provided some food security for the legal inhabitants of the larger cities.[141]

The Soviet Union's major metropolises, Moscow and Leningrad, received better and more provisions than other cities.[142] Due to the rationing
system in place, their residents may have experienced hunger, but not mass
starvation or famine. But those who lived in Ukraine's cities often witnessed large numbers of bodies of food-deprived peasants "who had somehow bypassed the roadblocks, only to then die in the streets of Kharkiv
and Kiev."[143]

The onslaught of another famine in the fall of 1932 did not impede the
party's final offensive against the peasants. In the early morning of
20 December, Kaganovich forced the Ukrainian Politburo to raise the ap-
portionment for grain requisitions. Nine days later, this political body declared that seed stock reserves also had to be seized in order to fulfil the
new plan.[144] This left nothing for the peasants.

Despite these brutal measures, the December 1932 collections in
Ukraine did not meet the party's goals. Instead of 1,207,000 tons, the authorities collected only 650,000 tons.[145] Stalin felt betrayed. In his view, the
party, which developed makeshift compromises with the grain-producing
regions in lowering the plan's designated targets before August 1932, received little in return. Ukraine could not even meet the reduced standards.
Enough of compromises! The agricultural as well as the industrial plan
had to be fulfilled. Requisition everything!

On 22–3 January 1933, the central Politburo, the Communist Party, and the Soviet government issued directives prohibiting the massive outflow of peasants from Ukraine into other regions or entry into Ukraine of peasants from the North Caucasus. They also ordered the arrest of all those who left Ukraine for the Moscow region, the Central Black Earth Region, Belarus, or the Lower and Middle Volga Regions, which possessed more food. The Politburo also suspended the sale of railway tickets to peasants who did not obtain the proper documents from their local governments (soviets) giving them the right to depart.[146] Approximately 220,000 people were arrested; 190,000 were sent back to their villages to starve.[147] These edicts, in effect, sealed the border between Soviet Ukraine and the rest of the USSR for the peasants. Not only were the peasants segregated from the urban population, they were also quarantined from the city limits and from access to food. They began to die by the millions.[148] According to one survivor:

Driven by hunger, people ate everything and anything: even food that had already rotted – potatoes, beets, and other root vegetables that pigs normally refused to eat. They even ate weeds, the leaves and bark of trees, insects, frogs, and snails. Nor did they shy away from eating the meat of diseased horses and cattle. Often that meat was already decaying and those who ate it died of food poisoning.[149]

As the famine intensified, food dominated people's thoughts and actions. The amount of time and energy "spent in food-seeking activities increase[d] while the time and energy devoted to activities unrelated to hunger decrease[d]."[150] As physiological starvation set in, people became depressed and apathetic.[151] With physical enfeeblement, the survival instinct weakened.[152] The writer Vasily Grossman, a native of Berdichev, graphically described the transition from life to death:

In the beginning, it (hunger) burns and torments you – it tears at your guts, at your soul. And so you try to escape your home. People dig for worms, they gather grass – and yes, they even try to fight their way through to Kiev. Whatever they do, they've got to get out, they've got to get away. And then the day comes when the starving man crawls back into his home. That means hunger has won. This one has given up the struggle; he lies down on his bed and stays there. And once hunger has won, you can't get the man up again, try as you might. Not just because he doesn't have the strength, but because it's all the same to him; he no longer wants to go on living. He just lies there quietly. All he wants is to be left alone. He doesn't want to eat, he can't stop peeing, he has the runs. All he wants is to sleep, to be left in peace. If you just lie there quietly, it means you're near the end.[153]

Millions passed away, transforming the countryside into a silent waste-land. The children died first, followed by the old and then the middle-aged.[154] Far more men died than women, and far more individual peasants (*edinolichniki*), those who did not belong to collective farms, than members of such farms. According to one Western journalist,

> If in many districts ten percent of the collective farmers died, the percentage of mortality among the individual peasants was sometimes as high as twenty-five. Of course, not all who died passed through the typical stages of death from outright hunger, abnormal swellings under the eyes and of the stomach, followed in the last stages by swollen legs and cracking bones. The majority died of slight colds which they could not withstand in their weakened condition; of typhus, the familiar accompaniment of famine; of "exhaustion," to use the familiar euphemistic word in death reports.[155]

The inhabitants of thousands of villages perished in the stillness of their homes and fields, often alone. Only the empty, crumbling peasant struc-tures commemorated the once-bustling village life before mass starvation and death by hunger.

Despite these horrific losses, the Stalinist leadership continued to sell grain to Europe. If the USSR exported less than one million centners of grain in 1928, it traded 13 million in 1929, 48.3 million in 1930, 51.8 million in 1931, and 18.1 million in 1932. Even in the worst year of the famine, in 1933, Soviet authorities shipped almost ten million centners to Western Europe.[156]

Under normal circumstances, Ukraine and the North Caucasus pro-vided half of the USSR's total marketable grain.[157] In 1930 and 1931, the majority of grain (70 per cent) exported from the USSR came from the Ukrainian SSR and the North Caucasus; the rest came from the Lower Volga and the Central Black Earth Region.[158]

Even with the decline in harvests and the decline in grain exports, Stalin did not reallocate the grain the USSR gathered to alleviate the famine. According to Roy Medvedev, "only half of the grain that was exported in 1932–1933 would have been sufficient to save all the southern regions from famine."[159] According to another scholar, the grain exports in 1932–3 were enough "to feed more than five million people for one year."[160] According to a third scholar, "Had Moscow stopped all grain exports and released all strategic grain reserves, the available 2.6 million tons of grain, under optimal conditions of distribution, might have saved up to 7.8 million lives, which was the approximate number of actual deaths of the 1932–1933 famine."[161] But the Kremlin continued to export and did not accept any foreign aid. In 1933, mass death from starvation "could have been averted but was not because the Stalinist regime did not, as yet, wish to end the famine, because it served their geopolitical ends."[162]

Despite a poor harvest, the collapse of the food distribution network, a raging famine engulfing tens of millions of lives, and depressed wheat prices on world markets, grain exports remained the Soviet state's first priority. The ruthless logic of radical collectivization and industrialization induced Stalin and his inner circle to pursue a demographic catastrophe. For party leaders and economic planners, the quality of peasant life in the overpopulated grain-producing areas always remained far less important than the USSR's overall national defence and urban food security. Outside of producing for the urban workers, the military, and industrialization, the peasants remained irrelevant to the scientifically grounded Marxist vision of history. In the Stalinist working-class-centred interpretation of the world, peasants were expendable; defiant Ukrainian peasants, especially those who opposed the Soviet order in 1917–20 (and now collectivization), even more so.

Urban residents also suffered, although certainly not to the degree that the peasants did.[163] In addition to less bread, those living in the cities acquired smaller amounts of meat, dairy products, and fish. Workers in Moscow and Leningrad, "comparatively well provisioned in comparison to other towns, went hungry. Stores did not even have enough food to honor ration cards ... and prices in the free peasant markets skyrocketed."[164] In the cities of Ukraine in the early 1930s, industrial workers received 800 grams of bread as their daily norm, manual workers 600 grams, and office employees 400.[165]

By the summer of 1933, peasants in Ukraine learned their lesson, as Kosior put it, and surrendered. The only way to survive was "to work for the Soviet state."[166] In the last months of 1933, the agricultural situation changed for the better. Collective farmers in the Ukrainian SSR and the North Caucasus harvested more grain than in the previous two years.[167] The urban centres now received more bread, flour, and foodstuffs. Repression abated. But in this period, epidemic diseases, including typhus, spread throughout Ukraine.[168] The All-Union Central Council of Unions, moreover, continued to receive reports from local union and party officials about malnourished workers in the cities.[169]

This total war against the peasants in Ukraine ended in the second half of 1933. Food conditions improved by late 1933 and early 1934, but those who survived the famine in the countryside understood that their plight differed radically from that of those who lived in the towns and cities. By law, economic status, and political position, the peasants remained unequal to their urban cousins until the 1970s and beyond.

In the late 1920s and early 1930s, the Soviet government and the Communist Party embraced a series of decisions to gain total control over the countryside and to ruthlessly exterminate anyone who opposed them. To obtain credits for imports of capital equipment leaders repeatedly proclaimed the need to increase wheat exports. The bumper crop of 1930 helped expand exports from 100,000 metric tons in 1929 to 2.3 million. By 1931, these sales doubled to 5.2 million metric tons, but due to worldwide surpluses the Soviets received less than they anticipated for these crops.[170]

By the fall of 1932 the Soviet regime experienced a major crisis. The decline in the export of grain from 1931 to 1932 (from 5.18 to 1.81 million metric tons) as the world price of grain fell created a crisis in the balance of Soviet payments,

> forcing the state to suspend payments to foreign specialists and workers, many of whom then left. Their departure, in turn, compounded problems in the newly built factories, which still needed parts, machinery, and the advice of those very same foreign experts. Essential raw materials could also not be imported in the required quantities, and many industrial complexes producing tractors, armaments, vehicles, and other machinery had to stop production for weeks at a time, imperiling the Soviet industrialization campaign ... the German bills of exchange, used in 1931 to re-launch industrialization after the 1930 crisis, were coming due, cities teemed with former peasants deeply inimical to the regime, and there was mounting discontent in the workers' ranks. Moscow feared what would happen if another cut in food rations was announced ... Documents began surreptitiously circulating in Party circles attacking Stalin and his policies. Then, on November 7th, following the celebration of the October Revolution's fifteenth anniversary, Stalin's second wife, Nadezhda Alliluyeva, committed suicide.[171]

Driven to accumulate capital for industrial development through the sale of wheat, Soviet leaders desperately sought to acquire more grain and sell it on international markets, depressing prices. In doing so, they ignored the economic realities of supply and demand, undermining the Soviet state's ability to earn more capital by withholding grain and waiting for world prices to rise. Although Stalin and his colleagues responded to the Soviet agricultural crisis by selling less wheat abroad, they did not lower the grain-requisitioning quotas to the point of preventing millions of their own peasants from starving to death.

Population Losses, 1926–1939

Although the Soviet authorities introduced collectivization throughout the USSR, the famines of 1930–4 primarily struck Ukraine (especially its Kiev and Kharkiv oblasts) (see map 7), the northern Caucasus, the middle Volga region, and Kazakhstan, quickly surpassing the famine of 1921–2.[172] As the Russian Empire's and the Soviet Union's long-term breadbasket, Ukraine suffered disproportionate population losses during the collectivization drive, implemented more rapidly and more violently in this republic than in any other Soviet region save Kazakhstan.[173] The politically induced famine constituted one of the twentieth century's greatest demographic catastrophes among the people of Ukraine, producing an even greater impact than that of the First World War. Famine took several million lives and helped undermine the numerical and proportional strength of the Ukrainians within the republic as well as within the USSR.

Serious estimates of the number of deaths in Ukraine in 1932 and 1933 vary from two million to seven million.[174] The most skilful analyses, those by a joint team of French and Ukrainian demographers and those by Oleh Wolowyna and his Ukrainian colleagues, provide more precise figures. The French-Ukrainian team estimated between four million and five million deaths, and the Wolowyna team 4.5 million for 1932 and 1933, representing approximately 15.3 per cent of the total population of the Ukrainian SSR.[175]

According to the most recent research conducted by Wolowyna and his colleagues, between 1932 and 1934 Ukraine lost 3.9 million people in direct losses (excess deaths) and 600,000 in indirect losses (lost births).[176] The total losses in the rural areas equalled 19 per cent of the total 1933 rural population; the corresponding relative total losses in the urban areas approximated 5 per cent of the total 1933 urban population.[177] The largest number, 90 per cent of the total, died in 1933.[178] Possibly 80 per cent of the four million or more Ukrainians who died during the Holodomor "did so in the compressed period of time between March and May 1933."[179] Between 1922 and 1941 more men, women, and children died in the countryside than in the cities, and males suffered higher direct losses than females, both in absolute and relative terms.[180] Excess deaths for children under ten years of age comprised about 25 per cent of all deaths in 1933, both in urban and rural populations.[181]

In conjunction with these losses, changes in Soviet policies towards the non-Russians and the purges of the Soviet Ukrainian political and cultural elites in the 1930s reinforced and accelerated the mass shift from a Ukrainian identity to Soviet and Russian ones, especially in the rapidly expanding urban centres. The Italian consul in Kharkiv, Sergio Gradenigo, predicted in a report to his government that the

> current disaster will bring about a preponderantly Russian colonization of Ukraine. It will transform its ethnographic character. In a future time, perhaps very soon, one will no longer be able to speak of a Ukraine, or of a Ukrainian people, and thus not even of a Ukrainian problem, because Ukraine will become a *de facto* Russian region.[182]

Although Gradenigo's prognosis did not unfold in this manner, Ukraine's demographic catastrophe played a serious and indelible role in the making of Stalinist, post-Stalinist, and post-Soviet Ukraine, especially its political crises after 1991. The population of the Soviet Union expanded by fifteen million between 1926 and 1937 (from 147 million to 162 million), but all Soviet republics or national groups did not grow at the same rate.[183] The overwhelming majority of republics, including the RSFSR, enjoyed an upsurge. Others, such as Ukraine, garnered only a modest accrual from 29 million in 1926 to 30.1 million in 1937, an average annual increase of 100,000.[184] Kazakhstan, however, experienced the most dramatic population loss, from 6.5 million in 1926 to 4.8 million eleven years later.[185]

Rapid collectivization, mass industrialization, the adoption of pro-Russocentric policies, the famines, and the purges upset the demographic balance between Ukrainians and Russians in the USSR (see table 6.2) and within the Ukrainian SSR. Between 1932 and 1933, the number of those who identified themselves as Ukrainians within the USSR declined by approximately 20 to 30 per cent.[186]

Between 1926 and 1937, the population of the USSR shifted radically in favour of the Russians, who increased their proportion of the total Soviet population from 53 to 58 per cent, while the Ukrainians dropped from 21 to 16 per cent.[187] In the RSFSR itself, the self-identified Ukrainian population declined from 7.9 million in 1926 to 3.1 million in 1937.[188] (In 1937, 549,859 self-identified Ukrainians lived in Kazakhstan, which formed part of the RSFSR until 1936, when it became a full union republic.)[189] The changes in the administrative borders within the Soviet Union and the dismantlement of all Ukrainization programs outside the Ukrainian SSR with the 14 December

Table 6.2 Number of Russians and Ukrainians within the USSR, 1926–1939

Year	Russians	Per cent Russian	Ukrainians	Per cent Ukrainian	Total Soviet population
1926	77.8 million	53.0	31.2 million	21.3	146.6 million
1937	93.9 million	58.0	26.4 million	16.3	162.0 million
1939	99.6 million	58.3	28.1 million	16.2	170.6 million

Source: The statistics come from: (1926): Kommunisticheskaia Akademiia, Komissiia po izucheniiu natsional'nogo voprosa, *Natsional'naia politika VKP(b) v tsifrakh* (Moscow: Izd. Kommunisticheskoi Akademii, 1930), 36, 38; (1937): Akademiia nauk SSSR, *Vsesoiuznaia perepis naseleniia 1937 g. Kratkie itogi* (Moscow: Institut istorii SSSR AN SSSR, 1991), 83; and Rossiiskii Gosudarstennyi arkhiv ekonomiki (RGAE), f. 1562, op. 329, d. 145, l. 8; and (1939): RGAE, f. 1562, op. 329, d. 4537, l. 62; in *Vsesoiuznaia perepis' naseleniia 1939 goda/Vsesoiuznai perepis' naseleniia 1937 goda* (Woodbridge, CT: Research Publications (Primary Source Media); Moscow: Federal Archival Service of Russia, 2000), reel 2; and Rossiiskaia Akademiia nauk and Upravlenie statistiki naseleniia Goskomstata, *Vsesoiuznaia perepis' naseleniia 1939 goda: Osnovnye itogi* (Moscow: Nauka, 1992), 57.

1932 Stalin-Molotov decree, may explain the "decline" of nearly half of the self-identified Ukrainian population in Russia from 1926 to 1937.

Although the overall number of residents of Soviet Ukraine increased in this period, its self-identified Ukrainian component shrank from 23.2 million in 1926 to 22.2 million in 1937, then advanced slightly from 1937 to 1939 (23.7 million), if the results of the 1939 census are to be believed. The Ukrainian percentage of the republic's population ebbed away from 80 in 1926 to 78.2 in 1937 to 76.5 by 1939.[190] Parallel to this trend, the rural community plummeted from 23.6 million (in 1926) to 20.1 million (1937), while the population of the urban communities rose from 5.2 to 10 million.[191] But the radical decrease in the number of those self-identified Ukrainians living in the countryside did not necessarily represent an exodus to the cities or assimilation into the Russian culture.

In contrast to the Ukrainians within the Ukrainian SSR, the republic's Russian population increased not only in number, but also in percentage of the total population. The number of Russians surged from 2.7 million (1926) to 3.2 million (1937) to 4.1 million (1939), from 9 per cent of the republic's total population to 13.5 per cent.[192] This represented nearly a 50 per cent increase. Although 100,000 fewer people identified themselves as Jews in 1937 than in 1926, they remained the third most populous national group in Ukraine, still constituting 5 per cent of the total population.

Ukraine's Holodomor of 1932–3 caused this extreme demographic distortion. Marriage and birth rates plunged dramatically and the mortality rate skyrocketed. The people of Ukraine, especially those in the countryside, suffered a monstrous number of excess deaths and lost births.

Kazakhstan also experienced a ruthless collectivization drive, which focused on extensive grain and livestock procurements, not the forced settlement of the republic's nomadic and semi-nomadic peoples. Famine broke out shortly after the Soviet authorities seized most of the Kazakh herds, in part "to replenish the stocks of Kazakhstan's Russian and Ukrainian regions already devastated by collectivization."[193] Recognizing this state effort as an act attacking their way of life, the nomads and pastoralists resisted passively and actively.[194] Almost 1.5 million Kazakh men, women, and children died between 1930 and 1934 and hundreds of thousands fled the republic.[195] Between 33 and 38 per cent of the Kazakh population and 8 to 9 per cent of the Slavic/European population passed away.[196] The proportion of Kazakhs within the USSR fell from 2.6 per cent of the total population in 1926 to 1.7 in 1937, mirroring the overall Ukrainian decline within the Soviet population.[197] Although the Kazakhs lost fewer in absolute numbers than the Ukrainians during the famine, they experienced the deaths of a greater percentage of their total population.[198] There were also several hundred thousand victims in the North Caucasus (including many Ukrainians living there) and, on a smaller scale, in the Volga region.[199]

Conclusion

At the end of the 1920s and the beginning of the 1930s, the USSR and the Ukrainian SSR experienced drought, fluctuations in temperatures, severe crop infestation, and fungal disease, which severely damaged the grain harvests.[200] But the subsequent famines of 1928–9 and 1931–4 did not primarily develop as a consequence of unpreventable natural disasters, deficient harvests, poor weather conditions, the chaos of collectivization, or the isolated overzealousness of those who collectivized the farms, as some scholars have argued.[201] These factors, of course, played a role in the starvation of millions. But, for the most part, political decisions drove the implementation of collectivization, the mania for grain, and the subsequent outbreak and spread of famines.

Stalin's radically optimistic plans for industrialization and collectivization did not recognize the complexity of agricultural production or the human factor. The economic plans the Communist Party embraced left very little room for natural disasters or unfavourable weather patterns. Party leaders irrationally assumed that with the new collective farm system each harvest would top the previous one in terms of quality and quantity.[202]

Assumptions based on ideological fervour did not produce the anticipated results. The party did not seriously prepare the groundwork necessary for collectivization. The manufacture of tractors, the cornerstone of the mechanization of agriculture, did not keep pace with the demands of collectivized agriculture or the peasantry's mass killing of horses, the primary source of energy in the countryside. In the spring of 1933, the total number of work horses through the USSR numbered two million less than in 1932, but tractors and other machinery supplied only 30 per cent of the energy resources employed in collective farms.[203]

In addition to this serious problem, the Soviet government did not extensively construct new storage facilities or add more rolling stock to transport grain to distant cities. Some collection points could not manage the large influx of requisitioned grain, expropriated at great cost, which spoiled in the rain or sun.[204] At the end of 1930, for example, approximately two million tons of unshipped grain rotted at these locations.[205]

The Soviet authorities also did not emphasize mundane matters, such as weeding or crop rotation, which they believed would needlessly divert the agricultural labour force from activities which would increase crop yields over the short term.[206] Hyper-industrialization's demands trumped the need to balance short-term, medium-term, and long-term considerations in the agricultural sphere. To overtake the advanced capitalist countries in a decade, as Stalin demanded, necessitated economic short cuts.

Documents discovered and published in the twenty-first century, especially those from the secret police archives, clearly demonstrate that the collectivization campaign represented something more than the party's mismanagement.[207] Most importantly, the Bolsheviks possessed an ideological view of agriculture and a blind faith in collectivization, which propelled their political decisions, overshadowed their incompetency as agricultural administrators, and allowed them to ignore the possibility of natural disasters or the unintended consequences of their policies. According to the Bolshevik view of the world, collective farms were more productive than individual farms and would provide the means to control the unruly countryside. These new farms would increase the size and the quality of the harvests, feed the expanding urban populations and the enlarged military forces, and provide the hard currency necessary to fund industrialization. No fact or disaster would ever overturn this a priori assumption or challenge this Bolshevik vision of reality.

If mass collectivization appeared as the only means to industrialize the USSR, the party did not need to tolerate dissenting views. By early 1929, Stalin's faction in the Politburo isolated Bukharin's pro-peasant group and removed them in November. In 1930 and 1931 the authorities created an institutional framework to deliver "optimistic assessments of the harvest."[208] The OGPU arrested professional statisticians who objected to irrational economic targets and replaced them with men who produced upbeat statistics and predictions.[209] Failure to achieve the anticipated harvests in 1928, 1931, and 1932 did not undermine their iron-clad Marxist faith in the necessity of creating and maintaining the collective farm system or acquiring massive amounts of grain by coercive means.

Most importantly, the authorities did not provide the peasants with incentives to produce. Before the start of collectivization in 1929, the Soviet government paid low prices for their wheat and rye; after collectivization, most collective farmers received small returns for their "labour days," the highly arbitrary measure of how peasants as members of the collective farms would be paid, in cash or kind.[210] Under the new order, the peasants could not find the motivation to cooperate with the countryside's new commissars.

Following the pattern set by the First World War and refined by the second, the Communist Party introduced large, military-like operations in the countryside to attain ambitious political objectives. It raised the scale of mass violence to unprecedented levels in order to subdue the peasants. By blockading the countryside and extracting its natural resources, the party and its agents gave no quarter. They demolished the complex web of rural relationships and local traditions which had existed for generations, and suppressed all armed and unarmed resistance to the new order. In response to any suspected or actual resistance to the state's grain acquisitions, they annihilated entire communities, deliberately killing, arresting, or deporting hundreds of thousands of peasants. Employing unrestricted means to achieve these ends, the party and its agents targeted non-combatants and disregarded the onset of famine and its starving millions. They demanded the unconditional surrender of their peasants.

A never-ending barrage of unremitting propaganda accompanied the party's advance into the countryside, constantly challenging the reality on the ground and in the field. Following the biases of the Bolshevik Civil War generation, each newspaper account, radio broadcast, and mass agitation and propaganda meeting vilified and dehumanized the opponents of collectivization and requisitioning, justifying their arrests, deportations, imprisonment, and executions. A stark black-and-white view of the world prevailed. "He who is not with us is against us" and "He who does not deliver the assigned grain quota (for any reason) shall not eat" became one of the prevailing slogans of the day.

Stalin and the Soviet political leadership set the famines of 1928–9 and the early 1930s into motion. Although they did not plan the famines, they purposefully facilitated them by imposing impossible requisition allocations and taking grain, seed, and grain reserves from the peasants and by extracting everything edible from the villages in the Ukrainian SSR, forcing people to die from the subsequent malnutrition, diseases, hunger, and starvation.[211] Stalin's total war against the peasants in Ukraine triggered the last major European famines in peacetime.[212] When the famines broke out, the authorities did little to stop them. Instead, they took advantage of the opportunity to punish "disobedient" Ukrainians, those who opposed their rule from late 1917 and who resisted collectivization. They recognized that these "disobedient" and "potentially disobedient" Ukrainians numbered in the millions, if not tens of millions.

Despite Stalin's flexibility concerning the implementation of grain allocations in Georgia in 1931, he insisted that the assigned quotas in Ukraine remain in place and that the Soviet state not provide this grain-producing republic with any food supplies to relieve the mass starvation. He differentiated between the Georgian and the Ukrainian situations. Georgian comrades, he wrote to Kaganovich, "do not understand that the Ukrainian methods of grain procurement, which are necessary and expedient in grain-surplus districts, are unsuitable and damaging in grain-deficit districts, which have no industrial proletariat whatsoever to boot."[213] According to Stalin, the party should apply more violence in the grain-surplus (not the grain-deficit) regions to meet their goals. His private statements emphasized the primacy of gaining total power first and foremost, not overcoming the USSR's economic backwardness by rational means.

Stalin continued to press the issue of grain requisitions in late 1932, even after mass starvation broke out in Ukraine and after warnings from Ukrainian officials. The party leader sent his emissaries, Molotov and Kaganovich, to impel the Communist Party of Ukraine to extract more from the peasants.

The party's development of the collective farm system, the party's command-and-control centres in the alien countryside, made these mass grain removals possible. In April 1933, a party official in a Dniepropetrovsk Oblast, wrote to Stalin and Molotov that "our levers of pressure on the village are immeasurably stronger than last year."[214] Mendel Khataevich, the first secretary of the Dniepropetrovsk oblast party committee, expressed this assessment in blunter terms. In a private conversation he allegedly claimed that a "ruthless struggle" between the Soviet regime and the peasantry over control of the 1933 harvest was "a struggle to the death. This year was a test of our strength and their [peasant] endurance. It took a famine to show them who is master here. It has cost millions of lives, but the collective farm system is here to stay. We've won the war."[215] This total war to subdue the Soviet Union's primary granary included a decimating attack on the Ukrainian intelligentsia and on the republic's Communist Party itself. The newly established Stalinist state embraced the "highest level of extremism" and crushed all potential and imagined opponents, attaining an unprecedented supremacy over the countryside and over the non-Russian republics.[216]

In short, the singled-minded implementation of de-kulakization and mass collectivization generated an enormous amount of violence – and a drastic drop in productivity. The Soviet state, moreover, persecuted, exiled, executed, and starved the peasants in Ukraine for political as well as economic reasons. In doing so, the Stalinist regime did not acquire more effective farm workers or more grain after the collectivization drive ended. The famine, in short, represented the "absolute triumph of politics over economics" and the political "emasculation" of the countryside and Ukrainian culture and traditions.[217] The party remained obsessed with the goal of subjugating the countryside and its peasants, even after mass famine broke out.

From the perspective of Moscow's commissars, the Ukrainian countryside possessed one of the most fertile areas and the highest rural population density in the USSR, as well as the most insubordinate peasants. Of all of the USSR's grain producers, the Ukrainians engaged in the most relentless opposition to collectivization. The authorities would not mourn the disappearance of several million of these peasants. Already in the 1920s, long before the collectivization drive, the Soviet press identified significant numbers of the Ukrainian peasants as followers of Petliura and as ardent Ukrainian national-chauvinists, staunch enemies of the Soviet state.

Even with the famine, the authorities took firm actions to ensure that the collectivization plans remained on the proper express track.[218] They viewed any setbacks from the prism of their class-driven and "Russia/USSR first" ideology. The number of alleged counter-revolutionary, foreign-sponsored, and hostile groups in the countryside multiplied and conveniently justified Stalin's claim that as the USSR moved closer towards socialism, the class struggle would only intensify.[219] In late November 1932, Stalin asserted that anti-Soviet individuals and groups had infiltrated the collective and state farms and that a large number of rural communists with non-Marxist attitudes actively disrupted the Kremlin's grain collections goals.[220] With their removal, the Stalinists completed the assigned mission.[221]

By the end of December 1932, Stalin's OGPU emissary to Ukraine, Vsevolod Balitsky, "substantiated" the party leader's charges. Balitsky and his organization discovered a vast network of nearly one thousand groups of counter-revolutionaries, spies, and wreckers, who took advantage of Soviet policies, such as Ukrainization, in order to sabotage the grain collections and to overthrow the Soviet regime in Ukraine. Members of the national-chauvinist Ukrainian intelligentsia and "traitors with party cards" belonged to these organizations. These Ukrainian nationalists in alliance with Pilsudski, according to Balitsky, had purposely triggered the famines. In the first three weeks of the month, Balitsky's men arrested over twelve thousand men and women.[222]

Although the security chief's accusations had no truth in them, his fabrications had consequences. They confirmed Stalin's suspicions of the Ukrainian peasants, the Ukrainian creative intelligentsia, and Ukrainian communists, raising the issue of their loyalty to the Soviet state.

Stalin then accused the Ukrainian nationalist groups Balitsky uncovered of planning uprisings "to separate Ukraine from the USSR and re-establish capitalism."[223] Following Stalin's logic, Kosior declared in mid-February 1933 that some local party officials employed "kulak arithmetic" in order "to deceive the Soviet state by presenting false data on yields, sown area, and gross production."[224] If senior party officials first blamed the rural communists, Stalin and his inner circle soon denounced the leadership of the Communist Party of Ukraine, which – according to Postyshev – had "facilitated the anti-Soviet activity of Petliura-ite and kulak elements."[225] As Kosior reported on 15 March 1933, "the unsatisfactory course of sowing in many areas" demonstrated "that the famine still [had not] taught reason to many collective farmers," confirming that the Soviet state had employed hunger to teach the peasant a lesson.[226] Even in his 17 March 1933 request for a grain loan and additional rations for starving children, V.I. Cherniavsky, the first party secretary in the Vinnytsia Oblast, conceded that some famine victims were "irresponsible slackers" and that "counter-revolutionary kulak agitation counts on creating a *famine psychosis* in the villages."[227] Ultimately, Stalin and his inner circle blamed the leaders of the CP(b)U and the victims of the state-sponsored famine for their own starvation. Despite the Kremlin's best attempts, the Ukrainian SSR had become a "slacker republic" and had to be severely disciplined with extensive grain confiscations and expanded blacklists.

Between the end of 1932 and the summer of 1933, according to Andrea Graziosi, "famine in the USSR killed in half the time, approximately seven times as many people as the Great Terror of 1937–1938."[228] The brutal August 1932 injunction on socialist property and the subsequent decrees of 18 November 1932, 14–15 December 1932, and 22 January 1933 best expressed Stalin's total war against the Ukrainian peasants and against Ukrainians and Ukrainian culture at its height. Like previous conflicts, this war bred mass arrests, mass deportations, and mass starvation. But Stalin raised the scale and intensity of violence in this war to unprecedented levels and spawned a ruthless environment conducive to genocide, however improvised.[229]

According to the Stalinist world view, Ukraine's Communist Party had allowed the grain operations to fail and had tolerated the existence of a vast insurgent underground in contact with foreign powers (especially Poland) ready to spark an uprising, embrace foreign intervention, and restore capitalism.[230] Many of its party members had cast aside their class vigilance, misunderstood the efforts of the remnants of the old shattered classes to reinvigorate their lost cause, and underestimated the unbreakable link between the national and peasant questions.[231] They had to pay.

Inasmuch as Stalinists sought to raise the USSR's geopolitical status in the world, the suffering and starvation of millions remained irrelevant. The satisfaction of the needs of the proletarian state, as Molotov argued, came before all other priorities, including individual needs.[232] The introduction of coercive political and economic institutions convinced the Soviet leadership that the USSR would overcome its economic backwardness and rejoin the ranks of the world's leading industrial powers, securing its political future as the world's first socialist state.

The Communist Party, a primarily urban political institution, had finally gained control over the wayward countryside two decades after the revolution. Not only did collectivization transform twenty-five million individual peasant households into 250,000 collective farms, it integrated the isolated Russian and non-Russian countrysides into the overall Soviet economy and political system.[233] Although some of the authorities may have believed that collectivization would increase crop yields and raise the living standards throughout the USSR, they were more interested in dominating the countryside and acquiring a slow, but steady supply of grain to the urban centres and for export. The Communist Party now emerged as the party of "victors." In pressing the issue of rapid collectivization and mass grain requisitions in the face of enormous resistance inside and outside the party, Stalin became the undisputed "victor of victors."

7

Hypercentralization and the Political/ Cultural Fronts, 1929–1941

We are out to make a revolution on the international scale, and therefore, if circumstances demand, we shall pay no heed to the interests of individual nationalities but shall sweep everything from our path.

Joseph Stalin, 8 December 1917[1]

Cadres decide everything!

Joseph Stalin, 4 May 1935[2]

By the end of the 1920s and early 1930s, Stalin and his allies marginalized his rivals within the All-Union Communist Party and acquired unprecedented power within the USSR. Now the Stalinists could begin to remake the Soviet present into the socialist future without the political and economic compromises of the 1920s. In order to implement their vision of an internationally strong, internally classless society, they had embraced the radical agendas of collectivization and industrialization, which sparked resistance in the countryside and chaos on the factory floor. These "revolutions from above" sharpened class conflicts and required, in their view, the cleansing of Soviet society of its alleged "bourgeois" past and of all groups and institutions outside the party's direct control. By constantly highlighting the outbreak of class war within the USSR and the inevitability of foreign interventions, the authorities introduced ruthless measures against all of their perceived enemies: the kulaks, the clergy, private traders and small-scale manufacturers, members of the old (non-communist) intelligentsia, defeated political parties, communist opposition groups, and "foreign agents" in the party's ranks.

Official sponsorship of the Cultural Revolution, as Sheila Fitzpatrick defined this period of militant radicalism, lasted from the early summer of

1928 to June 1931, from the Shakhty trial of "bourgeois engineers" to Stalin's conciliatory statement in regard to the old technical intelligentsia.[3] The central communist authorities launched the Cultural Revolution with the Shakhty trial and the subsequent show trials of the "Industrial Party" (1930) and the Mensheviks (1931) in order to mobilize the masses in support of the sacrifices necessary to implement the plan's ambitious goals and to justify subsequent hardships and failures by blaming all enemies, foreign and domestic.[4] The Cultural Revolution represented not just a "revolution from above," but also a "revolution from below."

The party's hysterical attacks on non-communist engineers and specialists attracted many young people, primarily those who lived in the cities. Many of these enthusiasts had been too young to fight on behalf of the Bolshevik cause during the Civil War. They matured during the period of the New Economic Policy and experienced rampant underemployment, if not unemployment. When they asked themselves what they had gained from the Bolshevik Revolution, they found little. To compensate for their perceived inferior social status, they directed their venom against all non-communists and non-proletarians, and even at times against party bureaucrats.[5] They embraced the party's "populist" war against the remnants of the old order with great enthusiasm and pressed the authorities to strike harder and faster against all class enemies. They interpreted the Cultural Revolution, with its uncompromising class war against the "bourgeoisie," as "a replay of the October Revolution and the Civil War."[6] These men and women wholeheartedly threw themselves into implementing the communist cause in the countryside and in the towns and cities.

In addition to its ideological fervour, the Cultural Revolution also provided its young adherents with an important incentive, the possibility to rise above one's humble station in life. The first five-year plan provided new avenues for mass social mobility "as peasants moved into the industrial labor force, unskilled workers became skilled, and skilled workers were promoted into white-collar or managerial positions, or accepted into institutions of higher education."[7] With its condemnation of "bourgeois specialists," the party introduced an ambitious preferential policy promoting workers (*vydvizhenie*) into the ranks of the technical intelligentsia in order to replace these arbitrarily designated "wreckers" and "saboteurs." In the late 1920s and 1930s, hundreds of thousands of those who claimed the status of "workers" took advantage of this policy and gained a rudimentary technical schooling, if not a watered-down engineering education.[8] For them, entry into the party now became easier. As these new cadres acquired promotions, privileges, and power, they identified themselves completely with the regime and emerged as its "new class," the main supporters of the Soviet system until its collapse in the late 1980s.[9]

In the course of the Cultural Revolution, the All-Union Communist Party radically expanded the ranks of its supporters. After launching vicious public attacks against the professional "establishment" in the Russian Federation, the Soviet authorities integrated its members to the new order without massive purges.[10] Most importantly, the new and enlarged cultural, political, and technical elites throughout the USSR owed their existence to the preferential policies the party introduced. Although Stalin may have called off the Cultural Revolution in 1931, militant radicalism and attacks on the non-communist intelligentsia did not end in the non-Russian republics. Instead, they intensified. In Ukraine, the security organs identified, then introduced repressive measures against those Ukrainians who publicly supported Ukrainization (or more generally their own national identity). In addition to the peasantry, the Soviet authorities unleashed waves of state terror against the Ukrainian intelligentsia, the Ukrainian national communists, and refugees from Poland's Ukrainian-speaking lands.[11]

Political Repressions

The first two five-year plans, the Cultural Revolution, the famines and Holodomor, and the purges of the Communist Party of Ukraine seriously undermined the capacity of Soviet Ukrainian civil society – already weakened by war, revolution, and the post-revolutionary civil and national wars – to resist amalgamation into the Stalinist order.[12] During the NEP era, Stalinists and the secret police carefully observed the activities of peasant and Ukrainian organizations, which often conformed to their stereotypes of "counter-revolutionary" behaviour. In 1927, Soviet authorities began to restrict the cooperative movement in the countryside. In 1928, they arrested Metropolitan Vasyl Lypkivsky, all of the bishops, and many of the priests of the Ukrainian Autocephalous Orthodox Church, which had emerged during the revolutionary period and which served the authorities as a counterweight to the more powerful Russian Orthodox Church. By 1931, the Soviet authorities dismantled this independent church with its Ukrainian liturgy.[13]

Between the end of de-kulakization in July 1929 and the start of the mass collectivization drive in early 1930, the authorities arrested a large number of members of the All-Ukrainian Academy of Sciences (VUAN). Before, during, and after the trial of the Union for the Liberation of Ukraine (SVU, *Soiuz vyzvolennia Ukrainy*) in the spring of 1930, the security services incarcerated nearly thirty thousand members of the non-communist intelligentsia.[14]

In a January 1930 letter to the Ukrainian Politburo, Stalin demanded a prompt trial of the members of the SVU. He provided a script of how the proceedings should unfold. The accused would "be charged with preparing an insurrection aimed at exposing Soviet Ukraine to foreign invasion, of committing acts of terrorism, and with scheming to poison senior communist leaders, with doctors to be implicated in this supposed plot."[15] Stalin also insisted that the mass media cover this trial, and not just in Soviet Ukraine.

The Communist Party of Ukraine followed orders. Providing fabricated evidence, the security services charged these writers, scientists, scholars, journalists, actors, community activists, and Galician Ukrainian émigrés with engaging in "counter-revolutionary activity" and with abetting foreign interventionists.[16] Between 19 March and 9 April 1930 the prosecutors at this public trial (the first of those in the non-Russian republics modelled on the Shakhty trial of 1928) accused forty-five men and women of belonging to a counter-revolutionary organization, the Union for the Liberation of Ukraine or its youth wing, the Union of Ukrainian Youth (SUM, or *Spilka ukrains'koi molodi*). Most of those arrested consisted of older Ukrainian intellectuals and leaders of former anti-Soviet political parties, such as the Socialist-Federalists, the Social Democrats, and the Socialist Revolutionaries, those who played an important role during the era of the Central Rada and the Directory.

The SVU trial played a central role in determining the scope of Ukrainization's future implementation after 1930. The Communist Party never trusted those in the dock, members of the pre-war Ukrainian intelligentsia, most of whom actively supported the post-1917 Ukrainian nationalist governments and who played a critical role in the implementation of Ukrainization.[17]

According to the official accusations, the SVU and SUM established branches throughout Ukraine and conspired in planning an insurrection which would restore "a bourgeois-democratic and independent Ukraine." Most of these men and women experienced physical or psychological torture during their imprisonment and most "confessed" to their crimes.[18] The authorities sentenced all of the defendants to long terms in the Solovetsky Islands and in Siberia. They also ordered Mykhailo Hrushevsky, the head of the Central Rada, who returned to Soviet Ukraine in 1924 and who played a leading role in the All-Ukrainian Academy of Sciences in the 1920s, to move to Moscow in March 1931.[19]

The GPU allegedly uncovered three more major counter-revolutionary organizations between 1931 and 1934: the UNTs (*Ukrains'kyi Natsional'nyi Tsentr*, Ukrainian National Center), UVO (*Ukrains'ka viis'kova orhanizatsiia*, the Ukrainian Military Organization), and OUN (*Ob'iednannia Ukrains'kykh natsionalistiv*, Association of Ukrainian Nationalists; not to be confused with the Organization of Ukrainian Nationalists described in chapter 4). Thousands more were arrested, but did not receive a public trial. The Soviet government's spotlight on these "counter-revolutionary" groups, especially the UVO and OUN, highlighted how these groups had perfidiously (in the Soviet view) allied themselves with Polish and Western interventionists.

Following the direct orders of the Kremlin, the GPU organized mass arrests and trials "to prevent the crystallization of a political opposition in Ukraine" during the crisis brought about by the start of collectivization and massive peasant resistance to it. These large-scale "prophylactic measures" targeted those who had espoused Ukrainization and Ukrainian culture in the 1920s.[20] The party leadership feared that the Ukrainian intelligentsia and the peasantry might unite, just as they had during the revolutionary spring of 1917.

In addition to condemnations of former anti-Bolshevik leaders, Stalinists also censured prominent Ukrainian national communists and reassigned them to other parts of the USSR in the second half of the decade. By 1929, the Communist Party had removed or marginalized Mykola Khvylovy, Mykhailo Volobuev, and Alexander Shumsky, prominent Ukrainian national communists.[21] During the de-kulakization and collectivization campaigns, which coincided with the Cultural Revolution, central party leaders launched a new wave of attacks on the Communist Party of Ukraine and on Ukrainian nationalism, which they identified with the kulaks and with foreign interventionists. In 1929, the Ukrainian party organization initiated a purge of "rightists" (alleged followers of Nikolai Bukharin and Alexei Rykov, promoters of moderate agricultural policies within Moscow's Politburo) and expelled twenty-four thousand members.[22]

As the famines swept through the countryside from late 1928 to the early 1930s, Stalin's political machine tightened its grip. Upset by the Ukrainian party leadership's protests against high grain quotas and by the failure to fulfil these orders, the central party accused the CP(b)U of tolerating a Ukrainian nationalist deviation in its ranks on 14 December 1932.[23]

Moscow's Central Committee demanded that the Communist Party of Ukraine and the Soviet Ukrainian government "eliminate Ukrainization's mechanical implementation" and "ensure systematic party management and supervision over Ukrainization."[24] Although Moscow's Politburo never officially abolished Ukrainization within Ukraine, it de-emphasized this policy and rarely made public reference to it in positive terms after 1932.[25]

In this decree, the party's support for the Ukrainian language outside of Ukraine also ended. Stalin and Molotov issued another secret decree on 15 December 1932, demanding that local party organs, governmental bodies, and the press in the North Caucasus, in the Kuban, "switch" from Ukrainian to Russian and introduce Russian as the language of instruction in the schools by the start of the next academic year.[26] The Russian Federation, which opened Ukrainian-language schools and developed a Ukrainian language press for its large Ukrainian minority in the 1920s, closed them down in the spring of 1933.[27] Ukrainization, which operated on two tracks (publicly supported by Moscow, but privately undermined by its security organs), came to an end. Overall, this decree attacked Ukrainization and identified all who opposed the breakneck speed of collectivization and industrialization as Ukrainian "counter-revolutionary elements."[28]

In order to ensure the Ukrainian party's reliability, the central party assigned Pavel Postyshev to the post of second secretary of the CP(b)U and the first secretary of the Kharkiv party provincial committee in January 1933. Vsevolod Balitsky, the new chief of the Ukraine's OGPU and subsequent "guillotine of Ukraine," followed him from Moscow one month later.[29] Both Postyshev and Balitsky had served in Ukraine in the 1920s and had bitterly antagonized Mykola Skrypnyk, the CP(b)U's powerful patron of Ukrainization.[30] Now they returned as Stalin's plenipotentiaries, outranking Skrypnyk, eager to vanquish him.

The two men arrived in Kharkiv just as Adolf Hitler became Germany's new chancellor on 30 January and crushed the powerful Social Democratic and Communist parties. In light of Hitler's rapid consolidation of power, radical territorial demands, and strident anti-communism, a new international conflict appeared on the horizon. Since Stalin understood that Ukraine would play centre stage in this war, the central party had to secure and "to purify" this critical republic as quickly as possible.

Postyshev, Stalin's enforcer, produced results. In February 1933 he pressed the CP(b)U's Central Committee to admit its responsibility for the chaos in the Ukrainian countryside and for the failure to meet grain targets in 1931 and 1932. He also organized a mass purge of the ranks of the CP(b)U (which possessed 520,000 members on 1 June 1932) and called upon the OGPU to strike a "merciless blow" upon all enemies. In 1933, the CP(b)U expelled 100,000 of its members; many of them were arrested shortly afterwards.[31] By January 1934, Postyshev replaced 60 per cent of the district executive committee and village soviet chairs and 50 per cent of all district party secretaries.[32]

On 1 March 1933, Skrypnyk – the CP(b)U's primary advocate of Ukrainization – lost his position as commissar of education and became the head of Ukraine's State Planning Commission, a precarious position at the beginning of the second five-year plan and the Holodomor. In the spring and early summer, his colleagues in the Politburo constantly attacked him, accusing him of promoting "compulsory Ukrainization" and of misusing Marxist theory in presenting his interpretations of the national question in the USSR.[33] Following the 13 May 1933 suicide of Khvylovy, a staunch defender of Ukraine's culture independent of Russia's, Skrypnyk killed himself on 7 July 1933. After his death, more purges took place.

On 22 November 1933, the combined plenum of the CP(b)U's Central Committee and the Central Control Commission passed a resolution declaring that local (Ukrainian) nationalism had emerged as the most dangerous threat to the communist cause in Ukraine, the only such resolution passed in a non-Russian republic.[34] This decision overturned the long-standing interpretation that of the two "national deviations," Great Power chauvinism and local nationalism, the first represented the greatest risk to the long-term stability of the USSR. To justify this ideological U-turn, Stalin's loyalists purposefully blurred Ukrainian nationalism and Ukrainization to smear those they perceived as their political enemies, even at the height of the Kremlin's public support for Ukrainization. Lazar Kaganovich, who headed the CP(b)U from 1925 to 1928 and who promoted Ukrainization with far less enthusiasm than Skrypnyk, often claimed that "every Ukrainian is potentially a nationalist."[35] By the late 1930s, such accusations defied any semblance of reality. A.I. Uspenskii, the chief of Ukraine's secret police and a self-identified Russian, asserted that "75–80 percent of Ukrainians are bourgeois nationalists."[36] Even Nikolai Yezhov, the NKVD's leader before Beria, declared in March 1938 that entire anti-Soviet Ukrainian nationalist divisions freely operated in the underground in Ukraine![37] False accusations based on ideological predispositions intentionally ignored reality.

Anti-Ukrainization within Ukrainization

In Ukraine, the Great Terror of 1936–8, according to Lev Kopelev, "began with the year 1933," long before Kirov's murder.[38] But preparations to unleash this terror started even earlier, shortly after the introduction of the New Economic Policy in 1921.[39]

Despite its victory over the anti-Bolshevik forces that year, the central party (as well as the CP[b]U) remained suspicious of most of the members of the Soviet creative intelligentsia in general and the advocates of Ukrainization, in particular.[40] Already in late November 1922, the Moscow headquarters of the GPU prepared an extensive report on the anti-Soviet attitudes of the Russian intelligentsia in 1921 and 1922.[41] In a secret circular issued by the Moscow headquarters of the GPU on 23 November 1923 to all provincial (*gubernia*) heads throughout the USSR, the GPU's leaders set up a system to observe and record the political feelings and activities of the intelligentsia in the universities, publishing houses, independent creative organizations, and cooperatives. Local agencies of the GPU would create files on all university professors and student activists, noting their previous political activities and their current views of the Soviet government and the Communist Party.[42]

At the end of March 1926, the Ukrainian GPU issued a secret circular, "About Ukrainian Society," reaffirming that the organization should keep track of the Ukrainian intelligentsia's attitudes and opinions concerning domestic and international matters.[43] Shortly afterwards, the Central Committee of the Communist Party of Ukraine approved the GPU's recommendations, which targeted members of the All-Ukrainian Academy of Sciences and Mykhailo Hrushevsky, its president. After claiming that dangerous "right-wing" (anti-communist) groups spread throughout Ukraine, the GPU put into place an extensive system for observing its citizens and probing their political pulse.[44] The party's central organs took Kaganovich's witticism ("every Ukrainian is potentially a nationalist") very seriously.

Several weeks after the Ukrainian GPU's recommendations, Stalin met with Alexander Shumsky, the Ukrainian commissar of education and a strong advocate of Ukrainization. In his description of this private discussion in a letter to Lazar Kaganovich (then the head of the Communist Party of Ukraine) the central party's leader claimed that Shumsky believed that Ukrainization was progressing "far too slowly, that it is looked upon as an imposed obligation, and is being carried out reluctantly and haltingly," and needed more support from party and trade union leaders.[45] Shumsky, according to Stalin, asserted that Ukrainization had to be "carried out first of all within the ranks of the party and among the proletariat," where it encountered much resistance.[46] The Ukrainian commissar criticized Kaganovich's methods and advocated changing the top party and Soviet leaders in the Ukrainian SSR.

In response to Shumsky's assessment of Ukrainization, Stalin agreed that a broad movement favouring Ukrainian culture and the use of Ukrainian in the public sphere had attracted large numbers, but warned that many communists did not "realize the meaning and the importance of the movement and are therefore taking no steps to gain control of it."[47] Most importantly, he insisted that Shumsky committed two serious ideological errors in his criticisms of Ukrainization's implementation. His first, Stalin declared, confused "Ukrainization of the apparatus of our party and other bodies with Ukrainization of the proletariat."[48] Stalin agreed that the apparatus of the party and the Soviet Ukrainian government should be Ukrainianized. But he misleadingly asserted that Shumsky advocated the need "to *compel* the mass of the Russian workers to give up the Russian language and Russian culture and accept the Ukrainian culture and language as their own."[49] Stalin claimed that the forcible Ukrainization of the proletariat from above would be a "utopian and harmful policy, one capable of stirring up anti-Ukrainian chauvinism among the non-Ukrainian sections of the proletariat."[50]

Shumsky, according to Stalin, also failed to recognize the "seamy side" of Ukrainization. Oftentimes, non-communist intellectuals, those who "sought to alienate Ukrainian culture and public life from the general Soviet culture and political life," led the pro-Ukrainization movement. A number of Ukrainian communists, such as Mykola Khvylovy, a prominent writer who advocated Ukraine's distancing from Russia's cultural influences, uncritically absorbed these anti-Soviet views. From the Kremlin's standpoint, these ideas became "an increasingly real danger in Ukraine," presumably because Ukraine's cultural detachment from Russia represented a potential political divorce.[51] (Here, Stalin revealed his unspoken assumption that Russians and the Russian-speaking population supported Soviet power far more than the USSR's non-Russian population.)

Shumsky's ideological errors, in Stalin's view, were interconnected. Shumsky presumed that leading Ukrainian-speaking cadres could easily replace Russian or Russian-speaking ones, but he did not understand the "question of tempo," that this transition was a lengthy, spontaneous, and natural process.[52] Stalin implied that although Ukrainians would eventually constitute the majority of the Ukrainian party and government leaders in the near future, the indigenous communist cadres were not yet qualified for higher positions. Maintaining a steady pace of Ukrainization without stirring up anti-Ukrainian chauvinism among the non-Ukrainians within the working class or allowing the Ukrainization movement to fall into hands of "hostile elements" remained the most important challenge. How could the party establish and maintain the proper tempo? By controlling not only Ukrainization's rhythms, Stalin implied, but Ukrainization itself.

Stalin's concerns, communicated to Kaganovich, may have spurred the Ukrainian party leader to intensify the surveillance of the Ukrainian intelligentsia. In September 1926, four months after Piłsudski's coup in Poland, Ukraine's GPU issued another memorandum, a short overview of the "separatist tendencies" among Ukrainian "counter-revolutionaries," those men who led the Ukrainian National Republic. In the early 1920s, many of them – impressed by the Soviet introduction of Ukrainization – returned from exile and received amnesties from the Soviet government. Most of those who returned engaged in cultural work, primarily in the field of education, and joined the ranks of the Ukrainian Autocephalous Orthodox Church and the All-Ukrainian Academy of Sciences.

This report claimed that these men and women may have publicly recognized the Soviet Ukrainian government but sought to undermine it from within by seeking to create an anti-Soviet "cultural front." Many of these former exiles retained a chauvinistic ideology, professing that Ukraine remained Russia's economically exploited colony, even after the Bolshevik Revolution. According to this memo, many of these émigrés asserted that all government positions should be in the hands of "true Ukrainians" and sought to re-establish ties with the kulaks and their other former supporters in the countryside. Most ominously, the report highlighted the "fact" that a group of students from the Ukrainian-speaking Kuban region aspired to create a powerful, separatist organization of peasants (the Ukrainian Peasant Union) in Ukraine and in the Russian Federation's Kuban, Crimea, the western Don, and the southern parts of the Kursk and Voronezh areas.[53] All in all, the GPU concluded, Ukrainization provided anti-Soviet émigrés with the fig leaf to subvert the Soviet regime in Ukraine. Their possible reconnection with the Ukrainian peasantry and Ukraine's ultimate secession from the USSR remained the GPU's worst-case scenario.

What needed to be done? The September memorandum repeated many of the conclusions from the March circular on the need to watch the émigrés, their relationship with the countryside, and with Ukrainian society as a whole.[54] The GPU organized this widespread surveillance program shortly afterwards.[55]

As implementation of the first five-year plan unleashed massive tensions, fears, and conflicts throughout the USSR, Stalin started to deliver mixed messages concerning Ukrainization. In a long and rambling discussion with a group of Ukrainian writers at the Kremlin on 12 February 1929, he discussed the importance of the national question and the party's active sponsorship of the national cultures of "backward peoples" within the broader framework of industrialization and Soviet national security. He expressed his support for *korenizatsiia*, but not full support. He asserted:

> We must strive to ensure that a worker and peasant coming to a factory or plant or to an agricultural enterprise is literate, having at the very least, a fourth-grade education ... In what language can this be achieved? In Russian?

Or in the native language? If we want to raise the broad masses of people to the highest level of culture ... we must give maximum development to the native language of each nationality, since only in the native language can we achieve this.[56]

Without employing national cultures in raising the masses to the higher level of culture, "we will not be able to make our industry or agriculture suitable for defense."[57]

But Stalin tempered his support for Ukrainization with references to the Russian push-back against Ukrainization. When asked by a writer about the possibility of a transfer of the majority Ukrainian-speaking areas within Russia's Kursk and Voronezh provinces and the Kuban region to the Ukrainian SSR, Stalin replied that "it makes no serious difference, of course, where one district or another of Ukraine or the RSFSR belongs." But this issue and other matters, he asserted, evoked "strong resistance from some Russians." As a consequence, "this question must be dealt with in a careful manner, not getting too far ahead of ourselves so as not to cause a negative reaction among this or that part of the population."[58] By the late 1920s, Stalin recognized that the Russians constituted the most important component of the USSR's diverse population and concluded that the party should appease them.[59]

More ominously, Stalin defended the anti-Bolshevik Mikhail Bulgakov's play, *The Days of the Turbins*, which was then being performed in one of Moscow's theatres. The play depicted the revolutionary period in Ukraine in late 1918 and January 1919, when the peasants rebelled against Hetman Skoropadsky under the banners of the Ukrainian nationalist Symon Petliura and when the Bolsheviks recaptured Kiev.[60]

Oleksa Tesniak, a writer from Kiev, asserted that when he watched the play, "the thing that struck me most was that Bolshevism defeats those people [Russian Whites and Ukrainian nationalists] not because it is Bolshevism, but because it is creating a 'unified, great, and indivisible Russia' [a slogan of the anti-Bolshevik movement]. This is the message which strikes everyone who sees the play, and we would be better off without this kind of victory of Bolshevism." Another writer backed him up by asserting, "It's become almost a tradition of the Russian theater to show Ukrainians as some kind of fools or bandits."[61]

All of the Ukrainian poets, novelists, and critics at this meeting wanted the Kremlin to ban the play. But Stalin claimed that, despite its disdain for Ukrainians and the Ukrainian language, Bulgakov's work provided "more pluses than minuses," inasmuch as it portrayed "the invincible might of communism."[62] He justified his response by pointing out the ease "to cancel this thing or that thing or another thing. But you must understand that there is such a thing as an audience and it wants to see [plays]."[63] Explicitly, Stalin asserted that satisfying the tastes of the audience represented an important factor in Soviet cultural policy. Implicitly, he hinted that the preferences of the *Russian* audiences should drive Soviet cultural policy.

At the meeting, an unknown writer pointed out that the Twelfth Party Congress in 1923 defined two sets of national deviations confronting the Soviet regime: great-power (Russian) chauvinism and local (non-Russian) chauvinism. Although Ukrainians have assimilated this "perfectly well," he claimed, the leading organs, "even in Moscow," have not properly understood these ideological aberrations.[64] In the 1920s in Ukraine, local deviationists, such as Shumsky, had been condemned and their specific ideological mistakes exposed thoroughly, but this was not the case with Russian deviationists.[65]

When some of the writers agreed and named a number of prominent party leaders who spread anti-Ukrainian views, Stalin dismissed these men as insignificant. He claimed that only a small number of minor and wayward officials embraced the ideological error of "great power chauvinism." Stalin's responses to *The Day of the Turbins* and to this question demonstrated his reluctance to implement full Ukrainization, which might upset the sensitivities of the Russian public in Ukraine (as well as in the RSFSR).[66]

For the Ukrainian intelligentsia, full Ukrainization represented full decolonization, a complete break with the tsarist past. For many leading Russians and Russified communists in Ukraine, Ukrainization threatened to de-Russify the cities and undermine their status and power. Many of them possessed a sense of political entitlement. Russia had ruled this area for several hundred years. As leaders of the world's first revolutionary, working-class, anti-imperial, and "affirmative-action" state, they viewed themselves as superior to the local Ukrainian population and would not accept marginality in the near future. For these men, as for Bulgakov, urban centres represented the foundation of progress, culture, and civilization; "barbarian Ukraine" started "where the city ended."[67] Stalin shared their apprehensions and sought to mobilize them for his own purposes.

In response to his justifications for the need to respect the sensitivities of the Russians, one unknown writer quipped: "It's hard to catch a great-power chauvinist by the tail."[68] Stalin then abruptly brought the long meeting to an end.

In dealing with the national question, the party had to confront national deviations, efforts to adapt "the internationalist policy of the working class to the nationalistic policy of the bourgeoisie," which would "undermine the Soviet system and to restore capitalism."[69] In the 1920s the Communist Party of the Soviet Union acknowledged the existence of two national deviations, great-power nationalism and local nationalism. Of these two, party leaders singled out Russian great-power chauvinism as the greatest danger.

By late 1932, the central party reversed its heretofore public approval of Ukrainization (as the above-mentioned decrees of 14–15 December 1932 show). Its critics claimed that this preferential policy represented a Trojan horse for Ukrainian nationalism, which would lead to separatism. In early March 1933, the Ukrainian Politburo sent Stalin a draft of a resolution assessing Ukrainization. Stalin corrected it and expressed his own concerns:

> We fought and undermined the bases of Great Russian chauvinism in order to establish national equality. But in view of the fact that this struggle was frequently waged by nationalistic elements, not always in a Bolshevik manner, not always in the name of internationalism, quite often Great Russian nationalism was supplanted by Ukrainian-Galician nationalism and instead of national equality there emerged another inequality, Ukrainian chauvinism and Ukrainian centrism, not internationalism but nationalism.[70]

Stalin's interpretation represented a new approach in assessing Soviet nationality policy and its implementation in Ukraine. In a November 1933 speech that Stalin heavily edited, Stanislav Kosior, the first secretary of the Communist Party of Ukraine, asserted that "Great Russian chauvinism is still the main danger throughout the Soviet Union and the entire VKP(b). However, this in no way negates the fact that in certain republics of the USSR, particularly in Ukraine, the main danger at the present time is Ukrainian nationalism, which is allied with the imperialistic interventionists."[71] In late January 1934, at the Seventeenth Party Congress, Stalin asserted that in Ukraine until "only very recently, the deviation towards Ukrainian nationalism did not represent the chief danger, but when the fight against it ceased and it was allowed to grow to such an extent that it linked up with the interventionists, this deviation became the chief danger."[72] His view now became the new party line. Ukrainization, as implemented by Shumsky and Skrypnyk, had to be crushed.

Ukrainization Reconfigured

If in 1923 party leaders in Kharkiv envisioned the Ukrainization policy as an effort to win over the peasants to the Soviet cause by moderating the national divisions between Ukraine's rural and urban areas (a policy easier proclaimed than implemented), they launched a more ambitious phase in 1925, concentrating on the Russified cities.[73] But by 1933, the Kremlin's party leaders felt that the compromises on the national question hammered out in the early 1920s no longer addressed the new political realities. With forced collectivization, the "small" famine of 1928–9, the removal of the kulaks in 1930–1, the "minor" famine of 1932, ignited by the heavy-handed grain collection, and the "major" famine of 1933 (the Holodomor), which killed millions, the party gained unprecedented control over the country-side and over the wayward Ukrainian peasantry. Political overtures to the peasants and to Ukrainian society were no longer necessary. The All-Union Communist Party had finally won the civil and national wars of 1918–21.

Despite this victory, Ukrainization still remained in place, although in a revised and subdued form. After denouncing "bourgeois nationalists" and their agents, headed by Skrypnyk, for perverting this policy, Stalin's men advocated a "Bolshevik Ukrainization." This revised version adhered to the ubiquitous slogan, "national in form, socialist in content." Most im-portantly, the complete design and implementation of Soviet nationality policy in this republic came under Moscow's watchful eyes without the regional party's mediation. After several published discussions delineating the differences between "Ukrainization" and "Bolshevik Ukrainization," the authorities de-emphasized this policy and rarely mentioned it in pub-lic. Although party leaders may have tried to reopen the issue of the use of Ukrainian in public in the Stalino, Dniepropetrovsk, and Odessa oblasts in 1935, very little came of it.[74] Although S.V. Kosior, the first secretary of the CP(b)U, claimed at its Thirteenth Party Congress (27 May–3 June 1937) that Ukrainization still remained a vital party policy and that governmen-tal workers "should know the language of the Ukrainian people," his in-terpretation did not represent the views of all of the delegates.[75] When many members of this congress condemned the "insufficient Ukrainization" of the party, the soviets, and particularly the trade unions and Komsomol organizations, they meant the inclusion of more Ukrainians (and not nec-essarily Ukrainian speakers) into the leading institutions, not the need to expand the Ukrainian language or culture in the public sphere.[76]

In order to limit the number of potential advocates of a Skrypnyk-oriented Ukrainization, Postyshev dismantled the Commissariat of Edu-cation and the Institute of Linguistics within the Ukrainian Academy of Sciences and started to purge the party (by 1933–4 the majority of Ukrain-ization's most prominent supporters within the creative intelligentsia had already experienced arrest). Over the long run, Postyshev did far more than just cripple the expansion of the Ukrainian language into the cities or reconfigure Ukrainization. By wielding their revolutionary swords, he and Balitsky decimated Ukrainization's supporters within the Communist Party and among Ukrainian intellectuals and members of Ukraine's civil society. Throughout the 1930s uncounted thousands more were arrested on false charges and forced to confess membership in various nonexistent underground subversive organizations.[77] Those who did not conform to the party's new interpretation (or were perceived to conform reluctantly) were annihilated. Decades into the future, the cultural sophistication of these purged men and women could not be easily replicated or civil society easily reconstructed, even after Ukraine's independence in 1991.[78] The famines, the Holodomor, and the purges represented, in effect, the process of a mass "negative selection" in Ukrainian society.[79]

By the late 1930s, Soviet authorities shifted the uneasy equilibrium between the Ukrainian and Russian languages in the Russian direction. More than two thousand officials within the Commissariat of Education, Ukrainization's command centre, lost their positions. Many subsequently experienced arrest and imprisonment, if not execution. The party suspended publication of Ukrainian dictionaries (new editions started to incorporate Russian terms) and abolished the 1928 standardization of Ukrainian orthography, which Skrypnyk hammered out.[80] Ukrainian as the language of instruction in the primary and secondary schools, in any case, fell from 88.5 per cent in 1932–3 to 78.2 per cent in 1938–9, primarily in the cities, not the countryside, which experienced inferior Ukrainian-language schools to the end of the Soviet period. The percentage of Ukrainian students in higher educational institutions declined from 66.7 per cent in 1930–1 to 54.2 per cent in 1937–8.[81] In the 1930s, the share of Ukrainian-language book titles and newspapers shrank from 79 to 42 per cent and from 89 per cent to 69 per cent, respectively.[82]

Despite the purges of Skrypnyk's Commissariat of Education and the decline in Ukrainian language use in schools, the media, and the public sphere, Ukrainization remained in place, even if not fully actualized. Between 1933 and September 1937, Skrypnyk's successors amended this policy's alleged "mechanical implementation." The redesigned version no longer challenged the Russian language's long-standing hegemony in Ukraine's urban public sphere.[83]

With renewed attacks on "Ukrainian nationalism" and "bourgeois nationalists" in late 1937, the party watered down even this weakened adaptation.[84] On 13 March 1938 the Soviet government issued a secret decree designating the Russian language and literature as required subjects of study in all non-Russian schools throughout the USSR, starting with the new school year in September.[85] The Ukrainian SSR followed suit. Its Politburo formulated two important decrees concerning this matter in April 1938.

The first abolished the small number of schools with languages of instruction in German, Polish, Czech, Greek, and Swedish, integrating their pupils into Ukrainian- or Russian-language schools. The Ukrainian SSR's multilingual educational network now became a bilingual one. The second decree reinforced the Russian language in the Ukrainian-language schools by increasing the number of hours devoted to it during the school week and by stipulating that children should start studying the language earlier (in the second grade in all elementary schools and in the third grade in all middle and incomplete middle schools).[86] Although these laws did not transform Ukrainian-language schools into Russian-language schools, they helped marginalize them.[87]

Yes, all Russian schools in the republic were still required to teach the Ukrainian language "for a specified number of hours per week to each of their students." Yes, a certain number of officials and governmental agencies (such as the Commissariats of Health, Social Welfare, and Education but not the military or the NKVD) employed Ukrainian in the public sphere. But these measures did not necessary "encourage" the public use of Ukrainian, as some Western analysts claim.[88]

In many cases, the existence of Ukrainian-language schools helped inculcate the idea that Ukrainian language and culture remained inferior to the Russian. In the 1920s the quality of Ukrainian-language schools in the cities and the countryside rarely surpassed that of the Russian-language schools. (The attraction of Russified cities, the shortage of highly trained Ukrainian-language teachers, constant educational underfunding, and bureaucratic obstruction handicapped these schools.) In the 1930s, the Soviet Ukrainian government often purged the ranks of the Ukrainian-language teachers, accusing them of "Ukrainian nationalism." In 1938, the party increased the number of hours pupils studied the Russian language and literature, ultimately reducing the time allotted for Ukrainian language and literature. The quality of this Ukrainian-language instruction and the extent to which it differed from Russian-language instruction in Ukrainian- and Russian-language schools must have varied enormously from area to area and from region to region, based on how local officials, teachers, parents, and communities interpreted Kiev's orders to teach Ukrainian.[89] How they identified themselves nationally as well as socially also helped determine their responses to this bilingual, dual-tiered schooling.

But all in all, according to one of the studies produced by Harvard University's Project on the Soviet Social System in the early 1950s, the Soviet leadership ruthlessly "suppress(ed) all spontaneous expressions of Ukrainian culture and national feeling."[90] As a precautionary measure, they closely monitored individuals and groups they did not trust, such the Ukrainian intelligentsia, who usually spoke Russian as fluently as Ukrainian. In practice, the Kremlin and its agents viewed the intelligentsia's public use of Ukrainian as a defiance of the regime and as evidence of national pride.[91]

Between 1933 and 1941, the Soviet Union sent a mixed message to its Ukrainian population in Central, Southern, and Eastern Ukraine. The Ukrainian language would remain in place, but it would remain inferior to Russian, which would dominate the public sphere, the media, the military and the security services, and most of the republic's commissariats. Only mastery of Russian (not Ukrainian) would unlock the opportunities for social mobility and career advancement. Even if an individual spoke Ukrainian, he or she would prefer not to draw attention to it, much less politicize it. Members of the better-educated younger generation, unlike the pre-revolutionary Ukrainian intelligentsia or the supporters of Ukrainization, "ceased to identify themselves vigorously as Ukrainians" and became more receptive to the new Stalinist order.[92] With the introduction of these policies, the Russian culture and language became even more prevalent in the urban setting in the 1930s than in the 1920s, even after the migration of millions of Ukrainians into the cities.[93]

Non-Ukrainian Minorities

Ukraine's largest minorities, such as the Jews, Poles, Germans, Romanians, Greeks, and others also suffered as a result of the radical shift in Soviet nationalities policy in the early 1930s. Preoccupied with the possibility of war with Germany, Poland, and Japan, Moscow's leaders were suspicious of the political loyalties of diasporic peoples, such as the Germans, Poles, Koreans, and Iranians – those who lived within the Soviet state's borders but who retained the culture, if not the language, of their homelands outside the USSR's borders.[94] Soviet authorities ended their indigenization programs and arrested the leading intellectuals and party officials belonging to these groups. They disbanded the Jewish section of the All-Union Communist Party in 1930, arrested the leaders of the Jewish Autonomous Republic in Birobidzhan, reduced the number of Jewish cultural organizations and secondary and vocational schools, and shut down a large number of Yiddish and Hebrew publications. Soviet leaders also targeted German peasants in southern Ukraine and Polish peasants on the Soviet-Polish border areas during collectivization and the famine and even after.[95]

In the 1920s the Soviet authorities sought to delineate the national identities of the population of the Right Bank. Bureaucrats implementing *korenizatsiia* programs in this region – a multi-ethnic borderland where Ukrainians, Jews, Poles, and Germans lived together for centuries – found it difficult to introduce national categories. If masses of peasants spoke Ukrainian, but practised Roman Catholicism, should they be counted as Ukrainians or Poles? In 1925, the Ukrainian NKVD decided that these peasants with hybrid identities belonged to the Polish nation. This decision led to an increase in the number of Poles in Ukraine from 90,300 in 1923 to 369,612 in 1926.[96]

With *korenizatsiia*'s reconfiguration by the beginning of the 1930s, the same security forces which expanded the membership of these groups now sought to destroy them. The political leadership prompted the arrest of 10,800 Soviet citizens of Polish or German nationality in 1934 in Soviet Ukraine and the resettlement of approximately 41,650 Poles, Germans, and kulaks from the western to the eastern areas of Ukraine in early 1935.[97]

Outside of Ukrainians, the NKVD specifically targeted Poles (the largest concentration of the Soviet Union's 600,000 Poles lived in Ukraine), even after Piłsudski's death in May 1935. In the summer of 1936, for example, the authorities deported 69,283 people, mostly Soviet Poles, from Ukraine to Kazakhstan.[98] On 11 August 1937, Yezhov ordered the total elimination of the Polish Military Organization, a group of imagined spies who worked on behalf of the Polish intelligence agencies.[99] Of the 1.3 million people sentenced during the Great Purges, one-third were apprehended in the operations against specific national groups, and nearly half of this total were arrested during the "Polish operation."[100] Of the 55,928 people arrested in Soviet Ukraine during the Polish operation, 47,327 were shot.[101] From this point onward, it appeared as if the Soviet Union would treat all Poles as enemies of the state. National identities or cultural connections, not a person's place in the socio-economic order or his political views, now determined an individual's innocence or guilt.

In 1938 and 1939, Stalin's men dissolved most of the twenty-one non-Ukrainian national districts created in the Ukrainian SSR in the early 1920s, disbanded the German-, Polish-, Czech-, Swedish-, Greek-, and other-language schools, and reorganized them into schools with programs of instruction in Ukrainian or Russian.[102] The Ukrainian Politburo ordered that the Cyrillic script replace the Latin script in the orthography of the Moldovan language.[103] Only the Russian national districts and Russian-language schools remained untouched.

After Kirov's Murder

With the murder of Sergei Kirov, the Leningrad Communist Party boss and popular Politburo member, on 1 December 1934, the NKVD unleashed a new wave of terror throughout the USSR. In 1935 and 1936, Soviet security agencies arrested more spies, Trotskyists, Zinovievites, and former members of non-Bolshevik political parties in the Ukrainian SSR than in any other region of the Soviet Union.[104]

Between October 1936 and November 1938, during the so-called "Great Terror," the NKVD arrested more than 1,575,000 people and executed 681,692 for counter-revolutionary crimes throughout the USSR.[105] In Ukraine in 1937 and 1938, this dreaded organization arrested 267,579 men and women and executed 122,237 of them. Victims included former party leaders and hundreds of the members of the republic's elite, people with non-Bolshevik political affiliations, industrial managers and engineers, intellectuals, clergy, and national minorities, such as the Poles and Germans, who suffered disproportionately as potential "enemy spies."[106] Alleged "kulaks" and "Ukrainian nationalists" also endured extensive repressions.[107]

In addition to real and perceived political opponents, Stalin attempted to annihilate people from formerly privileged classes, such as the nobles; immigrants from foreign countries; fugitives and de-kulakized peasants; marginal people, such as the poor and unemployed; priests and their families; and people who associated with foreigners.[108] The mass terror operations of 1937–8 re-emphasized the need to crush "kulak elements," religious believers, and the "Trotskyist agents of the German-Japanese counter-intelligence services."[109] All in all, the NKVD shot nearly seventy-one thousand inhabitants of Soviet Ukraine during this kulak operation, nearly one-fifth of all executed in the USSR as a whole. Of these seventy-one thousand, over half were accused of Ukrainian nationalism.[110] Most did not experience ordinary trials. Instead, the NKVD tried and sentenced many of them with its three-member "Special Sections."

The Postyshev era ended in mid-March 1937, when the authorities abruptly reassigned the Ukrainian party's second secretary to Kuibyshev, where he continued his struggle against "wreckers," "Trotskyists," and other well-entrenched "counter-revolutionaries." One year later, he was recalled to Moscow, where he was arrested, then disappeared. Balitsky shared his fate.

Delegates to the Thirteenth Congress of the Communist Party of Ukraine (held ten weeks after Postyshev's transfer) may have imagined that they had avoided the tidal waves of purges which engulfed the USSR. But shortly after this meeting ended, the authorities arrested the Red

Army's entire high command, including top army commanders in Ukraine, and shot them. The NKVD also detained many members of the CP(b)U and the Soviet Ukrainian government.[111]

Beginning on 9 July, Moscow's *Pravda* published a number of attacks on the All-Ukrainian Radio Committee and on cadre problems in Vinnytsia, in the Komsomol, and in Ukraine's regional communist party newspapers. All of these attacks directly or indirectly blamed the Ukrainian party's newly elected Central Committee for its lack of vigilance.[112] The Ukrainian Central Committee's public response to these charges in *Pravda* failed to stop the onslaught.[113]

In August, the central Politburo sent a special commission, consisting of Viacheslav Molotov, Nikolai Yezhov, and Nikita Khrushchev to Kiev. They called a plenary session of the CP(b)U Central Committee and expressed no confidence in it or in the Soviet Ukrainian government, headed by Panas Liubchenko. Newspapers soon accused Liubchenko of being a member of an anti-Soviet bourgeois-nationalist organization of former Borotbists. (He had been a Borotbist before joining the Communist Party of Ukraine in 1919.)[114]

Shortly afterwards, Liubchenko committed suicide. The Kremlin then recalled Stanislav Kosior, the head of the Communist Party of Ukraine, to Moscow, and arrested his closest advisers. Stalin's loyalists liquidated the overwhelming majority of the leaders of the CP(b)U, including sixty of sixty-two members and candidate members of the party's newly elected Central Committee, and most of the leading governmental officials.[115] The Central Committee could not hold meetings because it lacked the required quorum.[116]

A small group of emissaries from Moscow, men who held no publicly defined posts, made all of the political decisions in Ukraine.[117] M.I. Bondarenko, who had served under Postyshev in the Kharkiv party organization, became the chair of the People's Commissars on 1 September 1937, but only for another four to five months.[118]

In late 1937, a new updated post-Postyshev order started to emerge when Stalin appointed Nikita Khrushchev as the acting first secretary of the CP(b)U. Stalin's viceroy arrived in Kiev on 27 January 1938, and on 22 February Damian Korotchenko became the new chair of the Council of People's Commissars of the Soviet Ukrainian government. In June, the election of a new Central Committee at the Fourteenth Party Congress (13–18 June 1938) of the CP(b)U ended this year-long period of political uncertainty. This new Central Committee immediately chose Khrushchev as its permanent first secretary.

Taking his responsibilities seriously, the new party chief claimed that Ukraine's difficulties during collectivization were organized "on the orders of Piłsudski and the German fascists" and vowed that the Ukrainian party must "mercilessly smash spies and traitors. And we shall smash them and finish them off."[119] Although Khrushchev did not discuss *korenizatsiia* or Ukrainization in any detail at this congress, he reaffirmed the new political reality that "we Bolsheviks develop the national culture of each people, but we develop each 'national in form and socialist in content.'"[120] Socialist content, as defined by Stalin's inner circle, now became more important than national form.

Born in Russia's Kursk province in 1894, Khrushchev and his family moved to the Donbass mines in 1908.[121] Nikita Sergeevich had started his party career in the Ukrainian Republic in the early 1920s and became a prominent member of the Moscow regional party apparatus, reaching the position of its first secretary in 1935. Now he returned to Ukraine to head its devastated party, which barely survived several sets of radical purges. Its membership dropped from 433,500 in 1934 to 285,800 in 1938.[122] Because most of the major Ukrainian party leaders had been arrested before his arrival, Khrushchev brought his own group of assistants, men he could trust, and with them reconstructed the Ukrainian party from the ground up. In 1938, Ukraine's new party leader assigned a young Leonid Brezhnev to head a department of the Dnieprodzerzhinsk Provincial Committee and then promoted him to secretary of that committee.[123]

Even after Stalin dismissed Yezhov as the head of the NKVD in December 1938, the security services continued to take large numbers of men and women into custody.[124] Between 1938 and 1940, the Ukrainian NKVD apprehended another 165,565 men and women on various political charges.[125]

Seventeen years after the start of the revolutionary period, the Communist Party decisively conquered the Ukrainian agricultural areas. After securing the collective farm system in 1933, the authorities moved the capital of Soviet Ukraine from Kharkiv to Kiev in 1934. Mass collectivization, extensive grain requisitions, famines, the Holodomor, and the purges completely overturned the uneasy political balance established by the NEP and by Ukrainization in the early 1920s. The proportion of those who identified themselves a Ukrainians in the CP(b)U fell from 60 per cent to 57 per cent between 1933 and 1937, before rising to 63 per cent in 1940.[126] But this quantitative increase of Ukrainians did not represent the predominance of Ukrainian speakers within the party's ranks or the emergence of "home rule" for Ukrainians within the USSR. By employing mass violence, the Communist Party transformed the second most important Soviet republic into a Stalinist satrapy.

Mastering State Violence

In light of their perceived insecurity inside and outside of the USSR's borders, Soviet party leaders would not tolerate any opposition, even if passive in form. Most of the party's senior leadership had experienced the barbaric events of the First World War, revolution, and the subsequent civil and national wars. These men assimilated the culture of violence to such a degree that political compromises could no longer assuage them. "All or nothing" became their standard response to any crisis, and they would employ the coercive power of the institutions they controlled against all "counter-revolutionaries" and "class enemies." The communists would confront their opponents, engage in mass violence, introduce heavy-handed administrative measures, and institutionalize dictatorial rule, needlessly splitting Soviet society.[127]

As Sheila Fitzpatrick and David Joravsky pointed out decades ago, the Communist Party leaders acquired a garrison mentality, dividing the world into friends and foes.[128] The Civil War emerged as their most formative experience, far more than the "Marxist-Leninist ideology, Lenin's natural authoritarianism, or the conspiratorial traditions of the pre-revolutionary party."[129] This horrific ordeal, a byproduct of the Russian Revolution (itself a spinoff of the First World War), taught them to embrace violence, coercion, intolerance of dissent, rule by administrative decree, and a centralization of power.

For Stalin's men, the application of state violence not only represented a response to "class enemies," but embodied "a tool for fashioning an idealized image of a better, purer society."[130] They believed that hostile capitalist states encircled the USSR and envisioned an industrialized economy as the first socialist state's best defence against attack. Industrialization meant collectivization. Once the Communist Party encountered resistance in the countryside, the party needed not only "to secure obedience and order," but "explicitly 'to cleanse' the population of pernicious threats, to secure its full health and recovery," even if peasants stopped resisting.[131]

Stalin shared the impatience of this Civil War generation, caught in the netherworld between revolution and the implementation of the revolution's ultimate goals. According to Roman Werfel, one of communist Poland's leading party ideologists in the 1940s and 1950s, Stalin "represented the calvary charge line of thought: a generation that had grown up with the Civil War and charged ahead with sheer force. Unlike the Old Bolsheviks, it was not used to drudgery, to work that was long-term with no immediate, striking effects."[132] For Stalin as for this generation, the era of the New Economic Policy did not produce the adrenaline flow or the metaphorical "comradeship of the trenches" that they had experienced in the past. NEP, after all, represented a detour from their ultimate political goals. Many of those directly engaged in collectivization and grain requisitioning, such as Vsevolod Balitsky in Soviet Ukraine and Efim Evdokimov in the North Caucasus, had served in the same regions during the Civil War and had engaged in grain procurement campaigns during war communism.[133] This time they would accomplish their mission.

Industrialization became the first and only priority and coerced grain collections the only means to this end. In this black-and-white world, the party designated anyone who advocated lowering procurement quotas as a saboteur, an enemy of collectivization, industrialization, the socialist homeland, and the entire communist project.

The collectivization drive vilified the Soviet state's primary enemies, the kulaks and the bourgeois nationalists. Not only did the Bolsheviks smear these groups, they also assessed whether they were "redeemable (and subject to detention and correction) or incorrigible (and hence subject to elimination)."[134] But the Communist Party never defined the term "kulak" precisely.[135] Nor did it define the "bourgeois nationalists." Both became popular and very flexible pejorative terms hurled at all real and imagined enemies. During the collectivization drive, Stalin and his party conflated both terms, and Ukrainian peasants paid a tragic price.

The mass violence and total dehumanization of the enemy built on the horrors of the First World War, the revolution, and the subsequent civil and national wars and became closely intertwined during the party's struggle to collectivize. The party had to identify their opponents, then delegitimize, demonize, isolate, and exterminate these groups, neutralizing their passive supporters. The party's fears and insecurities intensified during collectivization and the famines, especially since many of its members (including Stalin himself) identified the prerogatives of "socialism in one country" with Russia itself. Most importantly, Fitzpatrick pointed out that

the Bolsheviks entered the Civil War perceiving themselves as internationalists and unaware that they had any significant Russian identity. In the course of the Civil War, they saw the failure of international revolution, found themselves adopting quasi-imperialist policies, became defenders of the Russian

heartland against foreign invaders and, in the Polish campaign in the summer
of 1920, observed not only that Polish workers rallied to Piłsudski, but that
Russians of all classes rallied to the Bolsheviks when it was a question of
fighting Poles. These experiences surely had great significance for the future
evolution of the Bolshevik Party and the Soviet regime.[136]

In their long and bloody struggle to gain power between 1917 and 1921,
the Bolsheviks learned first-hand how national identities could prevail
over class identities. Despite their misgivings, they also realized that they
needed to craft policies which outwardly championed both sets of identities, although not with equal emphasis.

During the industrialization campaign, this conflation of state violence
and quasi-Russian identity within the ranks of the Communist Party undermined the Soviet state's support for national diversity within its borders. Industrialization presupposed the total subordination of the peasants,
the vast majority of the USSR's population, to the state. In order to enter
the Marxist promised land, the party – much like the generals of the First
World War, frustrated by the failures of static trench warfare – demanded
only one more savage push.

The collectivization drive of 1929–33 and the purges of the 1930s occurred
throughout the USSR, but they acquired a specifically anti-Ukrainian orientation when applied in the Ukrainian Republic and in the Ukrainian-
speaking areas of Russia.[137] Inasmuch as the Ukrainian SSR constituted the
USSR's most important non-Russian republic, its primary grain exporter, a
region with extensive natural resources, and a rising industrial manufacturer,
the Soviet leadership understood that it had to secure Ukraine internally as
well as externally from threats from neighbouring Poland and a resurgent
Germany. Party leaders exaggerated their anxieties concerning the fulfilment
of grain procurement quotas and interpreted all of their problems through
the prism of internal and external threats to Soviet national security, especially popular resistance to Soviet power in the Ukrainian countryside.[138]

After the introduction of the collective farm system throughout the
Ukrainian SSR, the assessed grain quotas constantly rose and the state's
agents gained control of most of the grain within Ukraine's borders, but
not necessarily the anticipated amount. The authorities in the field, much
less the centre, did not necessarily understand that their unrealistic demands on the countryside created political, socio-economic, and logistical
bottlenecks which reduced the total amounts of grain they would gather
there. Coming from urban environments and wedded to their Marxist ideology, they misunderstood the nature of the crisis in the world grain

markets and most assumed that the peasants were responsible for their own problems – and should suffer the consequences.

The republic's extensive peasant opposition to collectivization reminded the Soviet leadership of the civil and national wars of 1918–21 and convinced them that the party had to introduce extraordinary measures to break the peasants, who in Stalin's mind waged a "war by starvation" against Soviet power.[139] In his view, the peasants were the aggressors and the workers, urban residents, and the Red Army the victims.[140]

This interpretation prompted the outbreak of famine, which in conjunction with the overall ideological purification of Ukrainian society in the 1930s, led to genocide. Inasmuch as the Bolsheviks believed in the class struggle and judged famines from the standpoint of this historical process, they would employ the food supplies they controlled as an instrument of that struggle.[141] Even if the food or emergency seed loans Stalin and the Politburo approved for starving regions reached these areas, it did not necessarily mean that the local cadres would or should deliver them to the majority of peasants. The Bolsheviks, after all, did not consider all famine victims to have a moral right to state provisions. Because the government controlled access to grain within the borders of the USSR, its agents would not feed "counter-revolutionaries." This was a political decision. For Stalin and his acolytes, the famine disposed of class enemies "more efficiently than deportation," "increased the grain balance by reducing the rural over-population" (especially in Ukraine, the USSR's most densely populated republic), and augmented "the disciplining/punishing/socializing/(re)educating of the rural population."[142] Hunger and mass starvation, they imagined, purged the countryside's counter-revolutionaries and expedited the Ukrainian peasantry's political re-education. With the famine, Stalin increased grain requisitions and intentionally provoked the Holodomor. This was a political decision, not an economic one.

Not only did the authorities seek to subordinate the peasants to the state, they also wanted to subject the Ukrainian members of the Soviet body politic, whom they considered problematic, if not disloyal, to their procrustean bed of ideological conformity. By the late 1920s and early 1930s Stalin could not even trust most of the senior party leaders in Ukraine. In an 11 August 1932 memo to Kaganovich, he criticized the republic's political leaders (who had started to defend Soviet Ukrainian prerogatives) and formulated plans to replace them, claiming that counter-revolutionaries and Piłsudski's agents had heavily infiltrated the 500,000-member Communist Party of Ukraine. Without the introduction of "extraordinary measures" and without Ukraine's transformation "as quickly as possible into a real fortress of the

USSR, into a genuinely exemplary republic ... we may lose Ukraine," he asserted.[143] Ukrainization's implementation in Ukraine and Russia (especially in the North Caucasus) had reinvigorated large anti-Soviet groups, and they had to be crushed, he concluded.[144]

In light of such ruthless logic, which blamed the victims, collectivization in the grain-producing areas led to famine, which congealed into an improvised genocide, which encompassed not just the peasants, the reservoir of the nation, but also the Communist Party of Ukraine, the intelligentsia, and the Ukrainian Orthodox Autocephalous Church. These leading groups (the "brain" and the "soul" of the nation, as Raphael Lemkin described them) set and defined the boundaries between the Ukrainians on the one hand and the Poles, Russians, and the Soviet regime on the other.[145] Stalin and his men took advantage of the collectivization and grain-requisition crisis to subdue Ukrainian peasants and to destroy the Ukrainian elites.

The Soviet Union's Communist Party did little to alleviate the famine of 1932–3, in sharp contrast to the tragedy of 1921–2, when the Soviet government authorized Western relief agencies to help combat the disaster. Despite warnings from local officials, party leaders increased the quotas for grain in 1933, requisitioned all available reserves, and forced the starvation of millions. The party's fusion of the extreme ruthlessness unleashed during collectivization, the dismantling of Ukrainization, and the launch of vociferous attacks on "Ukrainian nationalism" produced a toxic environment conducive to genocide, defined as the effort to destroy any national group in whole or in part.[146]

In this radicalized political climate, the Stalinist regime conflated social and national/ethnic categories. Stalin's men verbally and physically assaulted anyone in a leadership position who proudly identified himself or herself as a Ukrainian, and blurred the overall Ukrainian identity with peasants, "kulaks," and "Ukrainian bourgeois nationalists," the sworn enemies of the communist order. They blended class enemies and national enemies into a stew of counter-revolutionaries and refused to nuance the differences between the two. Taken together, collectivization, the Holodomor, anti-Ukrainization, and the purges represented a devastating set of attacks on all things Ukrainian, seriously undermining this national group demographically, politically, and psychologically over the long run.

Stalin, the party's most important expert on the national question, understood that the peasantry "constitutes the main army of the national movement, that there is no powerful national movement without the peasant army, nor can there be." This assertion bolstered his 30 March 1925 claim that the "the peasant question is the basis, the quintessence, of the national question," and not just in Yugoslavia.[147] In Stalin's mind, the peasant and national questions were linked, especially in a geopolitically important region such as Ukraine.[148] If peasants and prominent Ukrainian cultural and political leaders opposed Kremlin orders to denude the countryside of grain, they revealed themselves as disloyal Soviet citizens. Stalin set the tone: Annihilate these enemies. Show no mercy. Party activists in the field, intoxicated by the prospect of building the brave new world that Soviet founders envisioned, enthusiastically expanded on it.

Stalin took advantage of the collectivization and grain-requisition crises and escalated them (especially after early August 1932 and then again in mid-November, shortly after his wife's suicide) in order to subdue the Ukrainian peasants and the elites. When he and the party inaugurated dekulakization and mass collectivization he most likely did not intend to starve millions, but in stoking chaos in the countryside, disrupting the rhythms of peasant life, and introducing large-scale grain requisitions, he generated the subsequent famines, which provoked peasant resistance, which often turned violent. Since the Soviet state possessed a monopoly of the tools of coercion, it won control of the countryside. In confronting the peasants, the Communist Party risked losing its ability to feed the cities and satisfy its urban supporters. It was a reckless gamble, which Stalin won.

In this all-or-nothing struggle, there would be no compromise. As Stalin defined the situation, he and the party sought to build a better future for all Soviet citizens, including the peasants. Inasmuch as the "dark masses" refused to accept Stalin's goodwill, he became enraged and struck out against them. To punish them, he employed the easiest means at his disposal, grain requisitioning to the point of starvation. Stalin understood that the grain requisitions undertaken in 1921–2, 1928–9, and 1932 led to famine and that raising the quotas after August 1932 would do the same. In addition to destroying the independent peasantry and bringing the countryside under central control, he also emasculated the Ukrainian cultural, political, and religious elites. By focusing on the peasantry and the elites, these two policies became an improvised genocide.

Although everyone regardless of their national background suffered collectivization and the grain requisition campaigns in the countryside, Stalin and the senior party leadership were aware that of the four main grain-growing regions in the USSR, the Ukrainian SSR possessed the highest number and percentage of peasants (nearly 90 per cent of the peasants identified themselves as Ukrainians in 1926) who could be mobilized along national lines against the Soviet state. The peasant question, according to Stalin, also represented a national question. In line with this thinking, the

Stalinist regime targeted the peasants in the fertile grain-growing Ukrainian SSR not just because they were peasants, but because they also were Ukrainian peasants.[149]

Conclusion

The Holodomor of 1932–3 and the mass purges of the Ukrainian intelligentsia and the CP(b)U in the 1930s represented more than just a demographic catastrophe for Ukrainians. It also symbolized the destruction of a Ukrainian peasant-centred cultural ecosystem and the integration of its survivors into a new, uncharted, Soviet world. The state's total assault against the peasants shattered the fragile relationships in the countryside, the traditional base of the Ukrainian language and peasant culture. The subsequent mass starvation "decimated the village, wiped out so many bearers of Ukrainian language and traditional culture, produced a generation of orphans who did not remember their elders, issued forth a stream of refugees to the industrial centers who wished to forget the horror they had endured in the villages, and in many cases had no relatives left there."[150] These post-famine consequences, in turn, facilitated and accelerated the processes of Russification in the Ukrainian cities.

Having painfully learned lessons from the Civil War, the party did not want to help strengthen the nationalisms of the non-Russians any further. Its introduction of moderate nationality policies in the early 1920s sought to tolerate the non-Russian identities and cultures by divorcing them from any political aspirations. By the early 1930s the party leadership accepted the idea that it could legitimize an urban-based revolution in a multinational agricultural society by promoting non-Russian cultures, but it could not do so and economically transform that society at the same time. To engage in both projects would cause major social disorders and encourage forces which might challenge the state's unity and the party's political monopoly. The party's Holodomor, the abandonment of *korenizatsiia*, and the purges of the non-Russian cadres followed this conclusion. In place of *korenizatsiia*, a multinational form of legitimacy, the party now turned to a new set of political relationships which emphasized Russian primacy.[151]

The party highlighted a single Soviet identity, with Russian culture as its primary modern component. Stalin's insistence on Russian culture as the only key to modernization promoted stratification and ultimately Russification. In the 1920s non-Russians could perceive themselves as modern; by the 1930s the Soviet mass media identified modernization solely with Russia and with those who spoke Russian. In the early 1920s, the Soviet political leadership, grasping that "national" did not necessarily equal "nationalist," subsidized the blossoming of non-Russian national cultures. But in the harsh political climate of the 1930s, "national" increasingly corresponded with "national-ist."[152] The Soviet state then responded to all "national" and "nationalist" manifestations with unprecedented ruthlessness.

With collectivization and industrialization, Stalin did not completely nullify the 1918–23 arrangements between the Russian centre and the non-Russian periphery. Instead, he left a contradictory legacy for his succes-sors. Even though he purged the indigenous elites and intelligentsia in the non-Russian regions, the multinational structure of the USSR remained, although more so in name only (it now operated on more hyper-centralized, not federal, lines). Although the party leader dissolved or rearranged many Ukrainian institutions, he did not abandon the commitment to national homelands or the party's national-territorial divisions (both became more symbolic than real). Instead, he replaced the more assertive elites (and their potential supporters) with his own compliant ones. Stalin, in effect, forged a unitary state divided against itself.[153]

After 1933, the Soviet government and Communist Party limited the idea of a Ukrainian imagined community. By narrowing the social func-tions of "Ukrainian" in public life, blurring the differences between Ukrainians and Russians, and marginalizing Ukrainian culture, Soviet in-stitutions (even those that survived Stalin's purges) reduced the options Ukrainians could use to define their own national identity and narrowed the already slender psychological distance between the Ukrainians and Russians. As millions of Ukrainians became urbanized after 1933, an in-creasing proportion of them became Russified.[154]

The Ukrainian SSR started to recover demographically from the famines and the Holodomor after the end of the Great Terror in 1938, its popula-tion replenished to a large degree by the Soviet conquest and incorporation of majority Ukrainian-speaking territories in Poland and Romania in 1939 and 1940. But the German invasion of 1941 and the long, bloody German, Hungarian, and Romanian occupation skewed the demographic rela-tionship between Russians and Ukrainians within the USSR and within Ukraine even further, to the disadvantage of the Ukrainians.

PART THREE

The Third Total War
and Its Consequences

8

The Second World War:
The Killing Fields

The default posture of human beings is fear.

Marilynne Robinson[1]

O'BRIEN: "How does one man assert his power over another, Winston?"
WINSTON: "By making him suffer."
O'BRIEN: "Exactly. By making him suffer. Obedience is not enough. Unless he is suffering, how can you be sure that he is obeying your will and not his own? Power is in inflicting pain and humiliation. Power is in tearing human minds to pieces and putting them together in new shapes of your own choosing ... If you want to see a picture of the future, imagine a boot stamping on a human face – forever."

George Orwell, *1984*[2]

The Second World War ignited a monstrous, all-encompassing inferno, a conflagration without end or mercy. Its boundless atrocities and colossal human losses (especially the extermination of the Jews and Romani), deportations, evacuations, and forced labour recruitment altered the political and demographic foundations of East Central Europe and the USSR, especially within the latter's populous, western-most borderlands. This brutal contest helped divide the Poles, Lithuanians, Ukrainians, and Belarusans into modern nations and language communities with their own states.[3] But between 1938 and 1945, the war's historical conjunctures did not favour Ukraine's independence.

Nazi Germany played an important role in these developments even before the Third Reich and the Soviet Union negotiated the Molotov-Ribbentrop pact in late August 1939. With the Munich Agreement, signed by representatives of Germany, Italy, France, and Great Britain on 22 September 1938, Germany acquired the Sudetenland, Czechoslovakia's industrial heartland. Taking advantage of the weakness of the central Czechoslovak government, the Slovaks established their own autonomous government on 6 October. The central government then granted more administrative autonomy to the Ukrainians of Transcarpathia on 11 October. With this act, Transcarpathia became Carpatho-Ukraine (*Karpats'ka Ukraina*). Recognizing Czechoslovakia's impending collapse, Poland and Hungary demanded a common border with each other and the transfer of Carpatho-Ukraine to Hungary, which had administered this area up to 1918. On 2 November 1938, German and Italian diplomats agreed with Hungary's territorial claims and ceded this region's capital, Uzhhorod, and two other important cities (Mukachevo and Berehovo) to Hungary, which gained 1,586 square kilometres (612 square miles) and 181,609 people. Both Hungary and Poland sought to undermine the new Ukrainian autonomous government by engaging in border incursions with small special forces units.[4]

Czechoslovakia's partial dismemberment did not inspire its national minorities to back the post-Munich government. Supporters of a united Czechoslovakia attempted to shore up their support by granting more autonomy to Slovakia and Carpatho-Ukraine, but Slovakia declared its independence on 14 March 1939, as did Carpatho-Ukraine. The new Ukrainian state elected the Rev. August Voloshyn as president and adopted the symbols (the blue-yellow flag, the Trident of St Volodymyr, and the national anthem) of the Ukrainian National Republic of 1917–20.

At the end of 1938, the autonomous government of Carpatho-Ukraine created a paramilitary arm, the Carpathian Sich (*Karpats'ka Sich*), which attracted young activists from Galicia's Organization of Ukrainian Nationalists (OUN). According to one prominent Carpatho-Ukrainian, the newcomers began to introduce "uncompromising new revolutionary methods, which did not always conform to our ... political interests or, at times, to our state needs either."[5] Members of the OUN viewed little Carpatho-Ukraine as the nucleus of a united Ukrainian state, "from Poprad and the Tatra Mountains to the Caspian Sea and the Caucasus Mountains."[6] While leaders of the Carpatho-Ukrainian autonomous government would agree, they understood that the resolution of Europe's "Ukrainian problem" depended on the goodwill of the Great Powers, not Carpatho-Ukraine's "frail resources."[7] In light of its short history, this small statelet would not play the role of Ukraine's Prussia or Piedmont-Sardinia in the twentieth century.

The Hungarian army invaded shortly after Carpatho-Ukraine's declaration of independence and occupied it by mid-April. Despite strong resistance, Transcarpathia/Carpatho-Ukraine became a part of Hungary and remained so until 1945.[8] At the same time that Slovakia and Transcarpathia broke away from Czechoslovakia, Hitler violated the promises he made at Munich and annexed the Czech lands of Bohemia and Moravia into the Third Reich. Betrayed by Hitler's actions, Great Britain and France promised to defend Poland if Germany attacked. Seeking to avoid a two-front war, Hitler initiated secret talks with the USSR, which culminated in the signing of the Molotov-Ribbentrop Non-Aggression Pact on 23 August 1939.

This agreement represented a political alliance, not just an agreement concerning neutrality in case of an attack by a third party. By targeting Poland ("the bastard of Versailles," as Molotov crudely put it), the largest country in the region, Hitler and Stalin upended the treaties ending the First World War and planned to reconfigure East Central Europe. Germany attacked Poland on 1 September 1939, followed by the USSR's invasion on 17 September. By the end of that critical month, the two revisionist powers conquered Poland.

With the new Soviet-German Treaty of Friendship signed on 28 September 1939, the Soviets withdrew from their previously assigned area of central Poland behind the Bug (Buh) River in exchange for Germany's recognition of Soviet interests in Lithuania. The German zone encompassed 188,551 square kilometres (72,800 square miles) of Polish territory, inhabited by 20 million Poles. The Soviet zone embraced 201,294 square kilometres (77,720 square miles), populated by 13.5 million citizens of Poland. Hitler then annexed the Free City of Danzig, the Polish provinces of Poznań, Pomorze, and Łódź, and Polish Upper Silesia to the Third Reich.[9]

In addition to Poland, the non-aggression pact's secret protocols assigned large parts of East Central Europe to the USSR, which forced Romania to surrender the Ukrainian-speaking parts of Bessarabia and Bukovina in June 1940. Soviet authorities then incorporated the central part of Bessarabia into Ukraine's Moldovan ASSR. After transferring 4,921 square kilometres (1,900 square miles) of this autonomous republic to the Ukrainian SSR, the Kremlin created a separate Moldovan Soviet Socialist Republic on 2 August 1940 with a total area of 33,701 square kilometres (13,012 square miles).[10] That summer the world's first socialist state also occupied and annexed Estonia, Latvia, and Lithuania, and started to introduce the radical changes which would transform the political and social landscape of this entire region. The USSR clearly emerged as the primary beneficiary of the Molotov-Ribbentrop Non-Aggression Pact. But only for twenty-one months.

On 22 June 1941 Germany violated all of its agreements and launched a broad-based attack on its ally, sweeping deeply into the USSR by the end of the year. German forces quickly gained control of much of the western portions of the Soviet Union, including the newly expanded Soviet

Ukraine. The ruthless effort to dominate the Ukrainian SSR and its human and natural resources produced one of the major killing fields of the war. Most importantly, almost all of the survivors of the war "had witnessed the brutalization of friends, family members, and neighbors" and experienced long-term grief and traumatization, however difficult to measure.[11] The extensive physical destruction, enormous demographic losses, and vast psychological dislocations helped set the stage for Ukraine's post-war contradictions.

Soviet Occupation of Galicia and Volhynia

On 1 September 1939, Germany attacked Poland from the west; on 17 September, the USSR invaded Poland from the east. The Red Army claimed that Soviet power would liberate the non-Polish minorities from Polish intolerance and the peasants from their oppressive masters.[12] Most importantly, the Soviets sought to impose a "revolution from abroad" by dissolving eastern Poland's political and socio-economic organizations and by remaking the region in the image and likeness of the USSR.[13] Independent Poland disappeared by the end of September, experiencing its fourth partition in two centuries. The Germans annexed Poland's western regions into the Third Reich and created a rump state, the General Government (Generalgouvernement), from the remaining territories.

From September 1939 to the outbreak of the Soviet-German war in June 1941, the communist authorities incorporated Poland's majority Ukrainian- and Belarusan-speaking territories into the USSR and sought to introduce the Stalinist social system into these areas as quickly as possible. The annexed region also included a large number of Poles and Jews who fled Nazi-occupied Poland.[14]

In the chaos and uncertainty during the first few days after the outbreak of the German-Polish War, law and order collapsed as the Polish authorities withdrew, became paralysed, or fled. In light of the political vacuum and the palpable tensions between the Poles and Ukrainians, many young men sought seized weapons in order to defend themselves and their communities. In some cases, Ukrainians sought to settle scores with the Poles. At the same time, some Poles acquired guns from the Polish army. In the confusing atmosphere before Poland's final defeat at the end of September, these soldiers and deserters sought to defend themselves from the Ukrainians, if not to avenge their loss to the Germans. They did not think that the Ukrainians would remain loyal to the defeated Polish state, and acted accordingly.

The Soviets recognized these malevolent social dynamics in Galicia and Volhynia, even before their invasion of Poland on 17 September 1939. In order to crush any potential resistance, the Soviet authorities implemented a pacification model first developed during the Civil War and in the 1930s.[15] Nevertheless, they made a number of accommodations to the local population. In the chaos of the first few days just before and after the Soviet arrival, Ukrainian nationalists and communist groups in Eastern Galicia and Western Volhynia may have killed several thousand Poles.[16] The underground communist forces may have received tacit approval from the new authorities to "square accounts" with their long-standing enemies. But it is highly unlikely that the new Soviet commissars entering Volhynia and Galicia wanted to encourage Ukrainian nationalists to arm themselves and kill Poles. Those guns, after all, would help the nationalists seize power and could be used against the new Soviet regime.

After establishing the first semblance of order, the new rulers introduced policies designed to win the political allegiance of the majority of eastern Poland's Ukrainians and Belarusans.[17] In Eastern Galicia, Volhynia, Bukovina, and Bessarabia, the new regime deposed the old Polish and Romanian elites, introduced Ukrainian as the official language, and converted the Polish- and Romanian-language school systems and bureaucracies into Ukrainian-speaking institutions.

All adults in the newly designated "Western Ukraine" and "Western Belarus" voted on 22 October 1939 for delegates to assemblies that would request incorporation into the USSR.[18] Soviet authorities predetermined the turnout for the elections (at 99.2 per cent, regardless of the actual number of voters who would appear) and the results.[19] With the implementation of these careful preparations, the newly elected assemblies in Western Ukraine and Western Belarus "enthusiastically" voted to join the USSR. The Ukrainian SSR acquired approximately 8.8 million new citizens; the Belarusan SSR approximately 4.6 million.[20]

But even before the region's formal entry into the USSR on 1–2 November 1939, the new authorities integrated this area into the Soviet state's political and social framework.[21] Under the direction of Nikita Khrushchev, Ukraine's party chief, the new Soviet government abolished Polish Roman Catholic monasteries and nationalized the predominantly Jewish retail trades and industries. Jewish artisans and members of the liberal professions now became state employees. The new overseers dissolved all political and civic organizations, including Ukrainian private schools, publishing houses, and the non-communist mass media, and arrested the men and women who headed them.[22] The Communist Party emerged as the only

legal political party. The USSR's dissolution of Poland's pluralistic political system and its organized civil society paved the way for the OUN and
the ideology of integral nationalism to capture the imagination, if not the
loyalty, of many Ukrainians during the war and in the first post-war
years.[23] The Sovietization and Ukrainization processes in Eastern Galicia
and Western Volhynia also radicalized the Poles.

On 29 November 1939, the USSR Supreme Soviet issued a decree granting Soviet citizenship to all who lived in Poland's eastern borderlands
(*kresy*). It included all citizens of Poland who resided in these areas on the
night of 1–2 November and those who had entered the new Soviet zone on
the basis of the 16 November citizen-exchange agreement with Germany.[24]
Most importantly, the new authorities issued internal passports to its new
citizens, counting and categorizing them in terms of national identity and
social class.

Only the Jewish refugees from German-occupied Poland had the choice
whether to accept or reject Soviet citizenship and return to the German-
occupied areas of Poland. According to the September Soviet-Nazi
Boundary and Friendship Treaty, individuals in the Soviet zone could apply to move to the German one. When the German commission arrived in
late 1939–early 1940, "tens of thousands of recent refugees, mostly Jews,
queued up for days to put their names on lists of volunteers to leave the
area of Soviet occupation."[25] The NKVD did not break up this spontaneous anti-Soviet demonstration, but gained access to the lists of applicants.
The successful applicants did not understand what horrible fate awaited
them in the German zone; the unsuccessful applicants did not recognize
that they had signed their own arrest warrants in the Soviet zone.

Although the local population may have welcomed the Red Army "with
smaller or larger ... visible friendly crowds" and constructed triumphal
arches and put up red banners, the locals did not express a uniform response.[26] Many Jews may have greeted the liberators with enthusiasm,
perceiving that only a strong central authority could protect them from
Germany and from the surrounding populations.[27] Although many of the
older people, Orthodox Jews, and the well-off may have had apprehensions about the Soviets, many of the younger Jews did not.[28] In light of the
discrimination they experienced and occasional violence directed against
them, many of the Jews native to Eastern Galicia imagined Soviet rule as a
vast improvement over the Polish administration.[29]

Of the two million Polish Jews in German-occupied Poland, 250,000
fled eastward and made their way to what became the densely populated
Soviet zone.[30] In many areas, these refugees "seemed to double or even

triple the local prewar Jewish population."[31] By the end of 1939, approximately 300,000 to 400,000 refugees (including Poland's Jewish citizens) arrived from German-occupied Poland.[32]

Under Soviet rule, the status of the Jewish population improved dramatically. In many areas, the first Soviet institutions introduced after September 17 included a very high proportion of local Jews. But as the Soviets "consolidated their rule and appointed Soviet personnel to the most significant positions, local Jews were relegated to inferior posts, or removed altogether."[33]

In contrast, the status of the Polish population in the newly proclaimed Western Ukraine instantaneously changed from that of the privileged national minority to one discriminated against. Shocked by this turn of events, many if not most Poles imagined that the Ukrainians had betrayed Poland and stabbed it in the back. Still despondent over the sudden collapse of Poland, many Poles hoped that the Soviets would play a positive role in restraining the Ukrainians from acting against them, at least in the urban areas.[34] For the Poles, the new Soviet authorities played a dual, almost a Dr Jekyll and Mr Hyde, role as the creators of a new law and order – their protectors, as well as their partitioners and oppressors.

At the outbreak of the war on 1 September 1939 Vasyl Mudry, the head of UNDO, declared the loyalty of Ukrainians to the Polish state and the necessity to defend it with arms.[35] But his declaration, a noble effort to defend Ukrainians from future charges of disloyalty to Poland, did not reflect the feelings of the majority of his constituents, who welcomed Poland's demise. But they were uncertain about the future, as was the Polish government, which pre-emptively arrested approximately seven thousand Ukrainian cultural and political leaders in the first two days of the war.[36]

Some Ukrainians, especially the poorest and most ignorant peasants in isolated villages expected a vast improvement under the Soviet regime.[37] But most hesitated to embrace the "liberators." Despite the introduction of pro-Ukrainian policies by the new Soviet authorities, the majority of the Ukrainian population adopted a "wait and see" attitude. Many remembered the Russian occupations of 1914–15 and 1916–17, the Holodomor, and the anti-Ukrainian hysteria in Soviet Ukraine in the 1930s. Most of the estimated eight thousand to twenty thousand members of the OUN, half of them under the age of twenty-one, went underground and survived the occupation far better than their moderate and liberal Ukrainian political opponents.[38] Some OUN cells loyal to the Bandera faction started to conduct assaults on the new Soviet authorities, highlighting their differences with the Melnyk faction.[39]

Even before the Soviet takeover, the OUN split apart. Colonel Andrii Melnyk succeeded the OUN's founder, Evhen Konovalets, whom Soviet agents assassinated in Rotterdam in 1938. But the followers of Stepan Bandera, head of the OUN's Western Ukrainian Territorial Executive Committee (which included Eastern Galicia and Western Volhynia), refused to recognize Melnyk's leadership. Generational and ideological divisions fuelled the power struggle between these two groups. Melnyk supporters (OUN-M), concentrated in the exiled leadership of the OUN, matured during the reign of Austria-Hungary, fought in the First World War, lived in Western Europe (the Polish government wanted their heads), and possessed a more restrained outlook than Bandera's younger, fanatical supporters (OUN-B), who were determined to attain an independent Ukrainian state immediately, without any compromise, and regardless of cost. Much "more radical than mainstream Ukrainian society and more impatient than the OUN leadership in Vienna," they embraced terrorism as the only tool in their arsenal against the Polish state.[40] By 1940, the disagreements between the two rival factions became irreconcilable. Both, however, viewed the Poles and the Russians as their primary enemies and the Jews with great suspicion.

Despite the efforts of the new Soviet regime to "Ukrainize" Eastern Galicia, Western Volhynia, Bessarabia, and Bukovina by replacing Polish and Romanian officials with Ukrainians, it quickly antagonized the nationally conscious Ukrainian intelligentsia and simultaneously alienated the peasantry. The communist government promised to redistribute the lands expropriated from Polish landlords, but instead, the authorities introduced collectivization, which the peasants bitterly opposed. By June 1941, just before the German invasion, Soviet officials enticed only 12.8 per cent of all peasant households to join the collective farms.[41]

More ominously, the peoples of Eastern Galicia experienced four waves of deportations between 1939 and 1941 (9–10 February 1940; 9–10 April 1940; the last week of June 1940; and May–June 1941), not just "voluntary" departures to work in the Donbass.[42] In this period, the Soviets banished most of the former Polish elite, a large number of Polish settlers who had moved into Western Ukraine between 1919 and 1939 as well as active or retired Polish military officers, arrested large numbers of Jewish refugees, local businessmen, and "speculators," and began to detain Ukrainian nationalists. The first wave concentrated on Poles, the second on the Jews, the last one on Ukrainians. All in all, in 1940–1 the Soviets sent between 315,000 and 325,000 men, women, and children to special settlements and nearly 100,000 to the Gulag from Poland's former eastern regions.[43] Poles represented 57–63.5 per cent of those deported; Jews 21–4 per cent; and Ukrainians 8–10.5 per cent.[44] According to one Western scholar, the NKVD made more arrests "in the former eastern Poland than in the rest of the Soviet Union in 1939–41."[45]

The NKVD removed nearly thirty-three thousand Ukrainians, far less than the number of Poles or Jews.[46] Had Hitler not invaded in June 1941, more Ukrainians would have been arrested or deported. Having experienced previous Russian occupations, many understood that they would follow the Poles and the Jews.

In 1939, the Red Army captured almost 200,000 Polish soldiers and officers. In the spring of 1940, on Stalin's orders, the NKVD executed without trial 21,857 Polish officers as well as an indeterminate number of Ukrainians, Belarusans, and Jews at the Katyn Forest and other locations.[47] In late June 1941, just as the Germans marched into Galicia, the panic-stricken Soviets shipped thousands of people from all national groups, primarily specialists and draft-age males, eastward. At the outbreak of the conflict, the NKVD held nearly 150,000 prisoners (not all of them political) in their cells.[48] During this evacuation, NKVD troops in Western Ukraine moved all political and most criminal prisoners with very few exceptions eastwards, killed them, or both.[49] They executed between ten thousand and forty thousand prisoners in Galicia and Western Volhynia in only eight days, often leaving putrefying and unburied bodies in public view.[50] Ukrainians, especially active nationalists, constituted two-thirds of those massacred; Poles about one-quarter; and Jews and others the rest.[51]

Senior NKVD officers knew that these "enemies of the people" could not be reformed and that they would one day oppose the Soviet regime. In their view, these political prisoners should not be transferred into rear areas; they should be eliminated once and for all. After the Germans entered Lviv, many families searched prisons for arrested relatives and friends. But their pursuit proved in vain. Instead of prisoners, they found corpses. "There were heaps of bodies everywhere, many unidentified, many mutilated. Bricked-up cellars full of corpses in the Brygidki and Zamarstynów prisons were not even opened for fear of epidemics."[52] A Ukrainian-American newspaper provided a more graphic account:

In prisons, churches and public buildings heaps of dead civilians were found when the Reds evacuated Western Ukraine before the Nazi advance. Many of them were evidently executed by bombs, for their bodies were mangled and torn. Others showed signs of tortures. Some of the priests, for example, had crosses cut out on their bodies. Corpses of soldiers bore medals nailed into them. Even bodies of women and children bore signs of mutilation.[53]

The prisoners in at least another twenty-five prisons in Western Ukraine and Lithuania experienced summary execution. Political prisoners were targeted first; criminals were not spared.

The extensive brutality of this 1941 prison massacre, the fact that the victims were "discovered within the space of a little more than a week in a single relentless wave," and the extensive publicity surrounding the killings poisoned relations not only between Western Ukrainians and the Soviet government, but also between the Ukrainians, on the one hand, and Poles and Jews, on the other.[54] In Lviv, the Germans initiated and the local OUN-B militias helped actualize one of the first major outbursts of violence against Jews in the Ukrainian-speaking territories during the war.[55] This pogrom occurred between 30 June and 2 July 1941 and attracted large crowds of Ukrainians and Poles outraged by the prison executions. Mass grief fuelled the irrational notion that the Jews were collectively guilty for all the crimes the communists had perpetrated against the local population. Seeking to avenge the grisly deaths of their friends, relatives, and fellow compatriots, members of the hastily assembled crowd mercilessly beat, robbed, humiliated, and sometimes killed their Jewish neighbours, whom they stereotyped as "Judeo-Bolsheviks" or as communist agents. The Germans then organized mass executions. In the first few days of July 1941, between two thousand and seven thousand Jews disappeared during the pogroms and executions, and another thirteen thousand to thirty-five thousand throughout Western Ukraine.[56] In their fury, neighbours slaughtered neighbours or condoned their massacre.

According to the Polish Government-in-Exile in London, approximately 1.5 million Poles, Ukrainians, and others experienced some form of political repression (such as arrest, imprisonment, forcible evacuations, or execution) in the Soviet-occupied areas of the former Polish state.[57] This represented nearly 11 per cent of the total population of the eastern *kresy*. Much like the Russian occupations of Galicia during the First World War, the Soviet "liberation" of 1939–41 quickly embittered the Ukrainian, Polish, Jewish, and Romanian communities against the Soviets and against each other. With the promotion of local Jews, an oppressed minority in Poland, into the new Soviet region's bureaucracy, this "liberation" popularized the stereotype of Jews as "Bolshevik agents" (despite Soviet nationalization of the trades and industries dominated by the local Jewish population). The arrival of 250,000 Jews and approximately 50,000 to 150,000 Poles from German-occupied Poland coincided with the appearance of the Red Army to the most densely populated area in the former Poland. The migration of so many strangers to Eastern Galicia with unclear loyalties in a very short period of time strained the availability of goods and services, especially food. The migrants and the subsequent shortages generated great uncertainty, if not fear. These apprehensions stoked anti-Semitic, anti-Polish, and anti-Ukrainian attitudes. The Soviet interlude exacerbated the already tense pre-war existence among the Ukrainians, Poles, and Jews, and prepared the region for the radicalization of inter-ethnic attitudes and behaviour under German occupation.

German Invasion

Adolf Hitler never intended to adhere to the ten-year Molotov-Ribbentrop pact. In his view of the world, Nazi Germany and the Soviet Union represented two highly antagonistic ideological and racial systems, which inevitably would erupt into a "war of annihilation." German propagandists defined the Soviet Union as a fusion of Jewish and communist interests (a "Judeo-Bolshevist state") and the future struggle as a conflict to liberate its citizens "from the burden of communism [and] from the damned Jews."[58] In conformity with this stark assessment, the Nazis would not follow the rules of war in these eastern battlefields.[59] Hitler wanted to destroy Poland and the USSR as states; liquidate their ruling classes; starve at least thirty million Slavs (Russians, Poles, Ukrainians and Belarusans) to death and kill millions more; open up vast territories in the east to German colonization by expelling the Jews from Nazi-occupied Europe, then exterminate them.[60]

In June 1941, German troops easily sliced through the new Soviet defence perimeters and reached the suburbs of Moscow and Leningrad by the end of the year. By November 1941, the entire territory of the Ukrainian SSR – with the exception of Voroshilovhrad (today's Luhansk) and the northeastern part of the Donbass – fell under German control. By July 1942, the Crimean peninsula (which belonged to the RSFSR, not Soviet Ukraine) also succumbed. The Ukrainian SSR constituted the largest and most populous Soviet administrative unit the Germans occupied on the entire eastern front.

The German conquest quickly destroyed the local population's hopes for political change.[61] Despite the OUN-B's pre-war cooperation with German military intelligence (Abwehr) and the Wehrmacht, the Germans did not honour this organization's pre-emptive declaration of Ukrainian independence in Lviv on 30 June 1941. OUN-B's willingness to cooperate with Germany did not please the Nazis. Ernst Kundt, the undersecretary of state in the General Government, called a meeting on 3 July in Cracow with the four top leaders of the newly proclaimed Ukrainian government and asserted that although the Ukrainians might regard themselves as allies of the Germans, they were not. The Nazis were the "conquerors" of Soviet territories and the Ukrainians were their subordinates. Only the Führer could decide whether or in what form a Ukrainian state and government would emerge.[62] Officials from the General Government arrested the OUN-B leadership within the next two weeks and sent them to concentration camps.

On 16 July 1941 Hitler made his decision. He did not recognize an independent or sovereign Ukraine. Germany had acquired Podlachia from Poland in late 1939. He then divided the Ukrainian-speaking territories under his control into three areas: the General Government, Reichskommissariat (RK) Ukraine, and the German Military Zone. Galicia became the fifth district of the General Government; Volhynia, Central, Southern, and parts of Eastern Ukraine became RK Ukraine. He allowed Romania, his ally, to rule Bukovina and Transnistria, a part of southwestern Ukraine that included Odessa (not to be confused with the breakaway region in present-day Moldova). He continued to favour Hungary's 1939 annexation of Carpatho-Ukraine (see map 8). Hitler asserted that he would not permit Ukrainians to have a puppet government, or the right to bear arms.[63]

Between September 1941 (shortly after the German conquest of Kiev) and 1943, the new administration in the east outlawed the OUN-B and killed or jailed 80 per cent of its leaders.[64] The Germans tolerated the OUN-M until the winter of 1941–2, when they closed down the various cultural and economic organizations that appeared after the June invasion on the territories of what became Reichskommissariat Ukraine.[65]

The OUN-B and OUN-M differed in their views of Germany and the Germans. The young OUN-B cadres embraced a highly romantic, radical devotion to the Ukrainian nation and aspired to create an independent state immediately. Opposed to compromises, they would do anything to get it, with or without Germany. As true believers, they asserted that "whoever is not with us is against us."

After the German arrests and executions of OUN-B leaders and members in the fall of 1941, the survivors had to regroup and rethink their overall strategy and tactics while on the run. By the spring of 1942, they re-established many of their underground networks. But inasmuch as the OUN-B lacked the organizational capacity, the personnel, or resources, it could not radically change events on the ground. Far weaker than the

German army, the Red Army, or the Home Army (see below), the OUN-B reacted to events far more than they steered them, primarily because they did not possess any external sponsors or allies in their quest to create an independent state.

According to the OUN-B, the Poles, the Germans, the Soviets, and the Jews who supported the Poles or the Soviets constituted Ukraine's greatest enemies.[66] Inasmuch as these groups made up the overwhelming majority of Ukraine's neighbours and internal minorities, this did not leave much room for manoeuvre except on a temporary case-by-case basis.

In contrast, members of the OUN-M were older, pragmatic realists, committed to a policy of cooperation with Germany, even after the occupational authorities unleashed waves of atrocities against the locals.[67] According to the OUN-M and OUN-B views of the world, only Germany could overturn the political order in East Central Europe and facilitate the creation of an independent Ukraine.

But the Germans invaded the USSR to subordinate the peoples of the Soviet Union to the Nazi new world order, not liberate them from communism. In stark contrast to the German policy regarding the Russian Empire in the First World War, the Nazis "did not seek to foster independence movements in any part of the territory taken from the USSR."[68] Instead, they only wanted to exploit the Soviet people and to extract their natural resources. Despite peasant expectations that the Germans would dismantle the collective farms, the cornerstone of the Soviet order, the new rulers did not. Even before the German invasion of the USSR, Hitler imagined that Ukraine would become "a common food-supply base" for the Axis powers, the "only source of calories for Germany and its West European empire, which together and separately were net importers of food."[69] Ukraine would serve as Germany's major geopolitical asset in East Central Europe and as its primary breadbasket. Without Ukrainian grain, Germany could not win the war or establish a secure eastern empire.

German Frustrations

Despite their initial triumph, the Nazi leadership, German military commanders, and their front-line troops experienced enormous frustration with the eastern front.[70] Hitler and his inner circle predicted that the entire Soviet political system would collapse by the winter of 1941.[71] The "shock and awe" tactics of the blitzbrieg, those that inflicted the final deathblows to Poland in 1939 and Norway and France in 1940, failed in the Soviet territories.

Stalin did not surrender. Instead, the Soviet authorities resisted as best they could, withdrawing, and initiating a "scorched earth" policy, destroying factories, railways, buildings, dams, and even unharvested fields. They also evacuated over one thousand factories and 3.5 million people (mostly party and state officials, skilled industrial workers, members of the Ukrainian intelligentsia, and their families) to the RSFSR and Central Asia.[72] Although the majority of the Red Army troops did not seriously challenge the German forces, small groups fought stubbornly, inflicting far more casualties than the Germans suffered heretofore on the western front.[73] The German high command and the front-line troops did not anticipate these high losses.

Although the Germans quickly conquered the vast, flat expanses of the European USSR, they could not secure or live off the land. Constantly experiencing exhaustion, malnourishment, disease, high casualties, and a high level of personal insecurity, the troops internalized the Nazi racial ideology and turned the conflict into a war of total hatred and annihilation.[74] The Nazis considered the peoples of East Central Europe *Untermenschen* (subhumans) and trained their troops to think this way:

> The subhuman, this apparently fully equal creation of nature, when seen from the biological viewpoint, with hands, feet, and a sort of a brain, with eyes and a mouth. Nevertheless, it is quite a different, a dreadful creature, is only an imitation of man with man-resembling features, but is inferior to any animal as regards intellect and soul. In its interior, this being is a cruel chaos of wild, unrestricted passions, with a nameless will to destruction, with a most primitive lust, and of unmasked depravity. Not everything is alike that has a human face.[75]

The invaders first targeted the Jews, the Gypsies (the Romani), and communists. By mid-summer 1941 Hitler ordered his troops to immediately execute all communist members of the Soviet state apparatus, as well as the entire Jewish population.

Four operational SS groups, known as *Einsatzgruppen*, followed German troops into the Soviet Union and sought to fulfil this mission. Einsatzgruppe C operated in Ukraine near Kiev and Kharkiv. Einsatzgruppe D worked in Bessarabia and southern Ukraine. In addition to the three thousand members of these Einsatzgruppen, a number of Waffen SS brigades and dozens of German Order Police battalions helped hunt down and annihilate the Jewish population in the German- and Romanian-occupied territories of the USSR. Most importantly, the German military gave the SS Einsatzgruppen a free hand to operate in areas under its administration and assisted in liquidating the Jews.[76]

After July 1941, auxiliary police units (*Schutzmannschaften*), recruited from local inhabitants and subordinated to the SS, reinforced these German forces. At the end of July 1941 SS Chief Heinrich Himmler issued an order establishing these indigenous police formations. In the course of 1942, the number of *Schutzmannschaften* (*Schuma* for short) on the entire eastern front increased from 33,000 to 300,000.[77] One scholar asserts that most of the Schuma in RK Ukraine were Ukrainians, but its ranks also included Russians and members of other nationalities.[78] According to another estimate, approximately 100,000 Ukrainians served in the auxiliary police or the fire brigades during the war.[79]

Several days after the German occupation of Kiev on 19 September 1941, a series of explosions set by the NKVD rocked Khreshchatyk (the city's major avenue), destroyed buildings headquartering the new authorities, and shattered a number of churches and monasteries. According to the prevailing logic employed by the German authorities, "if the NKVD was guilty, the Jews must be blamed."[80] On 29–30 September, the Germans and their allies gathered the city's surviving Jewish population and executed 33,771 of them at Babyn Yar (Babi Yar) over the course of thirty-six hours.[81] Although most of Kiev's Jews had fled before the Germans arrived, tens of thousands had remained. This catastrophe became the "largest single massacre in the history of the Holocaust" to that date.[82] Other horrendous pogroms and executions of Jews took place in Berdychiv, Vinnytsia, Mariupil, Odessa, Dniepropetrovs'k, Kerch, and Kharkiv, often with the participation of the local population, obsessed with anti-Semitic feelings and a blind adherence to the prevailing stereotypes of the Jews as Soviet agents. With the complete breakdown of law and order, the murders of the Jews may have represented "an act of transferred aggression and punishment by proxy. The hated Bolsheviks disappeared from the scene. The Jews, who were perceived to be Soviet collaborators, were then, helpless, fair game, for the enraged Ukrainian mob(s)."[83] Others may have joined in these pogroms in order to acquire tangible economic benefits (such as apartments, food, clothing, and money) at the expense of the victims.

From 22 June 1941 to the end of the winter of 1941–2, these German units, local Ukrainian nationalist militias, and *Schutzmänner* executed the majority of the Jewish population in Eastern Ukraine, Bessarabia, Bukovina, the Crimea, and Transnistria. From the spring of 1942 until the end of the winter of 1942–3, they massacred the majority of Jews in Eastern Galicia and Western Volhynia-Podillia. With the German retreat from Ukraine in the spring of 1943 to the summer of 1944, they murdered all of the Jews still remaining in the ghettos or labour camps or sent them to

Table 8.1 Estimated Number of Jewish Victims and Survivors of the Holocaust in
Ukraine, 1941–1944

Region	No. of Jews under German occupation	No. of victims	No. of survivors
Eastern Ukraine	680,000–710,000	667,000–693,000	13,000–17,000
Bessarabia/ N. Bukovina	227,000–232,000	176,000–179,000	51,000–53,000
Western Volhynia	220,000–240,000	217,000–235,000	3,000–5,000
Eastern Galicia	575,000–600,000	570,000–590,000	7,000–10,000
Total	1,702,000–1,782,000	1,630,000–1,697,000	74,000–85,000

Source: Yitzhak Arad, *The Holocaust in the Soviet Union* (Lincoln: University of
Nebraska Press, 2009), 518–25.

concentration camps in Germany.[84] According to one estimate, between
thirty and forty thousand Ukrainians took part in the Nazi-organized extermination of the Jews.[85]

Of the approximately 2.6 million Jews killed on the territory of the
Soviet Union, the overwhelming majority died in the Ukrainian SSR.[86] By
mid-1941, according to reliable estimates, nearly 1.7 to 1.8 million Jews
lived in the Ukrainian SSR under German occupation, which included the
territories which constituted the original Ukrainian SSR and those annexed in 1939–40.[87] Of these nearly 1.8 million Jews, only approximately
eighty-five thousand survived the Holocaust (see table 8.1).[88]

In comparison with the survivors of other Jewish communities in Nazi-
subjugated Europe, the number and percentage of Soviet Jews who survived the German occupation was the lowest.[89] Of all the conquered
territories of the Soviet Union, only in the region of Transnistria and the
city of Chernivtsi did the Jews who still lived in ghettos and labour camps
outlast the war. The Soviet army's swift advance into this area in March
and April 1944 and the Romanian administration's rapid overturn of its
annihilatory policies made this possible.[90]

Although the Jews and Romani occupied the centre stage in Nazi plans
for extermination, Hitler and his associates also considered Russians and
Ukrainians racially inferior. Reinhard Heydrich, one of the heads of the
Third Reich's Main Security Office, claimed that the "Ukrainians were all
communist in outlook and exceptionally backward in their standard of
living." This group, according to a memo from the Reich Ministry for the
Occupied Eastern Territories, would happily accept "bread and cucum-
bers for their diets."[91]

Members of the Nazi elite did not consistently differentiate between the
Ukrainians and the Russians. They applied the term "Russian" to anyone

who resided in the Soviet Union at the beginning of the war, "along with residents of the districts of Galicia and Bialystock, and thus included Ukrainians."[92] When they distinguished between the two groups, some asserted that the former occupied a higher racial status than the latter.[93] Others claimed that the Ukrainians, especially those living in the countryside, possessed more immunities against the disease of "Judeo-Bolshevism" than the Russians. Following this line of thought, Hitler allowed the release of several hundred thousand Soviet Ukrainian prisoners of war between September and November 1941. Ukrainians comprised 270,095 of the 280,108 Soviet POWs the German military discharged in this period.[94]

Although Hitler hated the Slavs, especially the eastern Slavs, he imagined that the blond, blue-eyed Ukrainians he encountered during his 1942 trip to Reichskommissariat Ukraine "might be the peasant descendants of Germanic tribes which had never migrated." He suggested that Ukrainian women with these physical features conscripted for work in the Reich should be "Germanized after a period of probation."[95]

Ukrainians, in effect, retained a position at the top of the East Slavic hierarchy, at least in the views of certain Nazi leaders. But as subhumans (*Untermenschen*), they occupied a different, inferior, and almost unbridgeable universe from the German one. Although the Nazis targeted Jews, intellectuals, nationalists, and anyone suspected of pro-Soviet sympathies, they did not consider Ukrainians deserving of group destruction.[96] Nazi ideology considered these Slavs expendable, only worthy of exploitation, starvation, and cruelty. Ukrainians experienced persecution, of course, but were not singled out for persecution as were other groups. Only in Reichskommissariat Ukraine under Koch's leadership did the fine line between random persecution and targeted persecution shift often and erratically for Ukrainians.

In light of its racist mindset and acquisition of vast and populous territories, the German high command introduced a brutal set of policies to prevent any resistance, highlighted by the vicious abuse of five million Soviet prisoners of war their military forces captured. In the first six months of the German-Soviet war, the German army took many more POWs than their generals anticipated.

Inasmuch as the German army did not consider their Soviet prisoners of war fellow human beings, its operational plans did not take into account the need to feed, shelter, or provide medical care for the millions they captured. The Germans marched their captives over long distances or transported them by train without protection from the elements. Along the way, they shot stragglers, the wounded, and the exhausted. In the POW camps, they did not register their prisoners by name or provide them with humane treatment. The overcrowded camps did not possess adequate housing or proper sanitary conditions, including toilets. The camps more often than not consisted of open fields, surrounded by barbed-wire fences and watchtowers. Oftentimes the prisoners did not receive any meals on a regular basis (if so, they received less than they needed to survive) and ate whatever (grass, bark, and pine needles) they could find. As prisoners starved, cannibalism spread in the camps.[97]

Not only did the Germans refuse to spend valuable resources to provide for their detainees, but they did not allow the local populations to give them food and water. Camp guards, moreover, shot civilians who tried to help them. Millions died of starvation and disease, the highest number and the highest percentage of the Allied prisoners of war.[98] Germany captured a total of 3.9 million POWs (including an estimated 1.3 million Ukrainians) during the first eight months after its invasion of the USSR. By February 1942 only 1.1 million remained alive.[99]

The German-Soviet war destroyed the communist political order throughout the new and old Soviet Ukrainian territories. By September 1941, Nazi Germany divided the Ukrainian territories in East Central Europe into five areas. The first, the Romanian region (called Transnistria) in Southern Ukraine, included southern Bessarabia, northern Bukovina, and parts of the Odessa, Vinnytsia, and Mykolaiv oblasts. The second, the General Government (with Cracow as its capital), now gained Eastern Galicia (renamed District Galicia) and the territories that once belonged to Poland not incorporated into Germany. The third, Reichskommissariat Ukraine, included Volhynia and Polissia, most of Righ-Bank Ukraine, and part of Poltava Oblast, but excluded the former oblasts of Chernihiv, Sumy, and Kharkiv, and the Donbass, which remained under German military administration (the fourth region). The city of Rivne in Western Volhynia served as Reichskommissariat Ukraine's capital.[100] With Hitler's blessings, Hungary retained its control over Transcarpathia (the fifth area) from April 1939 to October 1944. The division of the Ukrainian SSR into these five domains privileged and unprivileged different sets of people in each administrative region.

German and Romanian Occupation

As the largest and most populous of the four administrative units dividing up the Ukrainian territories, Reichskommissariat Ukraine possessed approximately fifteen to seventeen million people living in a 340,000-square-kilometre area. To extract the most agricultural products, raw materials, and slave labour from this area, Hitler appointed Erich Koch as the head of RK Ukraine. In seeking to implement Hitler's ideologically charged policies, Koch ordered his subordinates never to meet directly with the people they ruled. He also allegedly asserted, "If I find a Ukrainian who is worthy of sitting at the same table with, I must have him shot."[101] Koch, a hardliner, always demanded the harshest possible treatment of RK Ukraine's population. "No German soldier will ever die for that nigger people," he proclaimed, referring to Ukrainians.[102] In a speech to Nazi party officials in Kiev in March 1943, he asserted that "we are a master race that must remember that the lowliest German worker is racially and biologically a thousand times more valuable than the population here."[103]

Despite the merciless methods employed to gather Ukraine's natural resources, the Germans fell short of their assigned goals. Even with grain surpluses in 1942 and 1943, agricultural deliveries to Germany "turned out much smaller than [they] had budgeted for, while [their] attempts to revive the Donbass, Krivyi Rih, and other industrial areas, became a complete failure; the Germans actually sent coal to the Ukraine from Germany."[104] Not only did the extractors experience a shortage of skilled and unskilled labour in those areas with an abundance of natural resources, they also encountered the local population's passive resistance to the entire German colonial project. As these plans miscarried and the Germans started to lose the war on the eastern front, they abandoned all restraint and ignited a killing spree, reminiscent of Belgian King Leopold's crimes against humanity in the Congo at the beginning of the twentieth century.[105]

Within the General Government's jurisdiction, Ukrainians did not experience the viciousness their compatriots experienced in Reichskommissariat (RK) Ukraine. Although the Germans in this administrative zone still considered Ukrainians as *Untermenschen*, they raised their status above that of the Poles and Jews, and sought to use them as a counterweight to the Poles. In Eastern Galicia, "the antagonism between the Poles and Germans was less pronounced than in central Poland." Some Polish peasants actually gained from the German reprivatization of land, which had been collectivized by the Soviets. The occupational authorities permitted a modest Polish cooperative system, a network of social support, and a modest Polish school system, closely supervised by the Germans.[106]

Although both the Poles and Ukrainians suffered from the harsh wartime conditions (especially the scarcity of food, the spread of infectious diseases, forced requisitioning, the *Ostarbeiter* program, the expropriation of housing), the Ukrainians enjoyed a preferential status in the public, national, and cultural spheres. They now staffed and headed the local government, local judicial offices, and auxiliary police. The German authorities actively discriminated against and brutally repressed the Poles, especially their intelligentsia, and started to round up Polish Jews, placing them into makeshift ghettos and then exterminating them. With the introduction of food rationing, the Germans restricted the foodstuffs the Poles could consume; Jews received even lower rations and starved to death in their ghettos and labour camps.[107]

Under the leadership of the geographer Volodymyr Kubijovič, the Ukrainian Central Committee in Cracow (the only officially recognized Ukrainian organization in the General Government or in Reichskommissariat Ukraine) served not only as a social welfare agency, but also as the centre of the Ukrainian community. Despite various restrictions, this committee expanded the number of Ukrainian-language schools from 2,510 in 1939 to over 4,000 in 1942, enlarged the cooperative movement in the countryside, and sought to expand its political and administrative powers on behalf of Ukrainians.[108] Although it could not play a significant role in helping Ukrainians in Reichskommissariat Ukraine, the Ukrainian Central Committee did play a major role in the creation of the SS-Waffen Division Galicia in 1943.

Even before the German loss at Stalingrad, the Waffen-SS, the official designation for combat units of the SS, started to create military detachments of non-Germans who did not meet SS racial standards. Separated into special national formations, these SS field formations spent the entire war under the tactical command of the army and "may be considered a *defacto* branch of the Wehrmacht," not the SS.[109]

Three months after Stalingrad, on 28 April 1943, German occupation authorities in Galicia, in cooperation with the Ukrainian Central Committee and the tacit approval of the Greek Catholic Church, issued a call for Ukrainian volunteers for a new "Galician" SS division, which would recognize the distinctiveness of Galicia, but not necessarily support Ukrainian national aspirations.[110] Members of this new military formation would "fight Bolshevism" and participate in the struggle "for faith and fatherland, for family and native soil" and "for a fair new order of the victorious young Europe," a well-understood reference to the Nazi-led struggle against the communist cause.[111] Many Ukrainians in Galicia realized that the tide had turned against the Germans and that Soviet troops would inevitably arrive at their doorstep. Very few wanted a return to the oppressive and anti-Ukrainian environment of 1939–41. To check this onslaught, many young men enlisted, including an unknown number of those who served as auxiliary policemen.

The response exceeded all expectations. Nearly 100,000 Ukrainians volunteered; fewer than 30,000 were accepted.[112] Although Ukrainians constituted its rank and file (Poles and Jews need not apply), the overwhelming majority of its officers and non-commissioned officers consisted of Germans, many who entertained negative racial stereotypes of Ukrainians.[113] Apart from politically conscious Ukrainians who hoped that their military service would help defend Galicia from the future Soviet onslaught and that their unit could become the nucleus of a national army under the right political circumstances, men who hoped to escape duty in construction battalions or labour service in Germany also joined. The authorities also assigned a small number of political prisoners to the division. Peasants who eked out a living from their small plots of land (which always needed to be tended) and who experienced extensive German requisitions were less enthused about enlisting.[114]

The Polish underground, communists, and members of the OUN-B (who called the Galician Division "a German colonial unit") opposed the division's formation.[115] Even Erich Koch, the head of Reichskommissariat Ukraine, openly questioned the division's reliability before it completed its training.[116] For Koch, the ideological consideration that Ukrainians were and always would be *Untermenschen* overshadowed the pragmatic necessity to compromise in order to win the war.

In May 1944, the division completed its training in Germany. Redesignated as the 14th Waffen-Grenadierdivision der SS (galiz. Nr. 1), its 15,290 men were sent to the eastern front, to the Brody-Tarnów pocket in Galicia. After several days of heavy fighting in July, only three thousand broke out of their encirclement by Soviet troops and survived.[117] The Germans reconstituted the division at Neuhammer and sent it to Slovakia to quell the communist-inspired Slovak Uprising.

On 12 March 1945, when the Soviet army almost reached Berlin, the German minister for the Occupied Eastern Territories, Alfred Rosenberg, recognized the Ukrainian National Committee as the sole representative body of the Ukrainian people. He promised that all Ukrainians serving in various formations of the German army would now constitute a Ukrainian National Army, which would renew the fight for Ukrainian statehood.[118] The Galicia Division would become the First Division of the Ukrainian National Army. Another regiment, formed around Berlin, would become the nucleus of the UNA's Second Division.

Those encased in bombarded bunkers for days at a time in Berlin obviously did not realize the reality of the situation at hand. Nazi racial policies had brought the brutalities of the war to Berlin. Recognition of Ukrainian national aspirations during the Third Reich's last hours would not save it. Transferred to Slovenia from Slovakia, the Galicia Division marched towards Austria, where most of its men surrendered to the British.[119]

Romania, an ally of Germany's during the Second World War, received Hitler's blessings to administer the territory of Transnistria on 30 August 1941. Located between the Dniester and the Bug/Buh Rivers, this 40,000-square-kilometre area contained 2.25 million people. Tiraspol served as its first capital, Odessa as its second. Governed by G. Alecsianu (1941–4), the Romanian authorities sought to exploit the territory economically and favoured the small Romanian minority. They banned all Ukrainian cultural activities. In 1941–3, the Romanian government deported over 101,000 Jews from Bessarabia and Bukovina and over 23,000 Gypsies (Roma) from Romania to Transnistria, where most died. Soviet military forces regained Transnistria in March 1944.[120]

Different Responses

Ukrainians, Russians, ethnic Germans native to Ukraine, Jews, and Poles occupied different positions within the Nazi racial hierarchy and responded differently to German rule. Not unlike the experiences of the Poles and the Polish Jews in Nazi-occupied Poland, the various national groups in Ukraine confronted "different fates in the same war."[121] Pressed by the urge to survive the most violent war in human history, members of each group also reacted in various ways. Throughout the Nazi occupation, pre-war mental attitudes continued to exert a tremendous influence. In reaction to the discrimination, arrests, and deportations their communities suffered in the Soviet period, young male ethnic Germans, even traditionally pacifist Mennonites, openly sympathized with Nazism and volunteered for administrative, military, and police work.[122]

The Ukrainian reaction to the German invasion varied. Ukrainians from the countryside, those middle-aged, and from the recently annexed Western Ukrainian territories embraced the Germans more than urban and young Ukrainians from Eastern Ukraine – at least initially.[123] Having lived in complete isolation from the outside world and distrusting the Soviet propaganda claims made about the Nazi regime, rural Ukrainians misunderstood Hitler's true intentions. As many anticipated that the Germans would liberate them from communism, they spontaneously recreated the pre-revolutionary Ukrainian national and religious life in some areas shortly after the Soviet withdrawal, but before the arrival of the Germans. Many Ukrainians took over the civil and district administrations in some areas and created voluntary associations, schools, churches, theatres, sports organizations, and newspapers and publishing companies.

Organizations that engaged in political activities, such as the OUN-M-led Ukrainian National Rada soon came to the notice of the Germans, who arrested its leaders. By 1942, the Germans removed Ukrainians from the local administration in Reichskommissariat Ukraine and replaced them with Russians, Poles, and ethnic Germans. Unlike the Ukrainians in the General Government, Ukrainians in RK Ukraine did not possess any representative organizations or the possibility of participating even in local government organs.

Many (not all) peasants in Soviet Ukraine initially greeted the Germans with bread and salt, a traditional form of greeting. They imagined the Germans as liberators, so they shared their food with them and tended to the wounded. Their memories of the Holodomor, the Soviet "scorched earth" policy (which adversely affected those left behind after the Soviet retreat), and the mass execution of political prisoners by the Soviets framed their responses to the Germans. The overwhelming majority of peasants wanted a period of decompression, stability, and depoliticization.

To the relief of many, the German occupational authorities did allow the expression of religion. According to one scholar, "40 percent of the churches closed after 1917 were reopened during the German occupation, and by its end, 5,633 Orthodox, 2,326 Uniate, 500 Ukrainian Autocephalous and 652 Roman Catholic churches operated in the entire territory of Ukraine."[124] With the opening of churches, mass baptisms took place.[125]

In October 1941, peasant leaders re-established the All-Ukrainian Cooperative Union, which existed until 1928–9, and recreated other economic institutions serving the countryside.[126] Most peasants hoped for an end to collectivization, but the Germans did not dismantle the collective farms. Like the Soviet leadership before them, the new overseers believed that collectivized agriculture produced more than private agriculture.[127] Desperate for food, the new rulers raised the 1941 Soviet quotas of obligatory agricultural deliveries, and in some regions even doubled them.[128]

The Germans, moreover, did not reciprocate the goodwill they received. Instead, they started to treat peasants as slaves and persecuted them. Many members of the SS and the German army constantly demeaned them in public and engaged in widespread arbitrary violence against them.[129] They harshly abused peasants for any perceived signs of disrespect, introduced curfews, flogged those who failed to meet or surpass work norms, and severely punished even those who carried pocket knives. In response to partisan activity, the occupational authorities introduced collective responsibility on a mass scale (public hangings, mass executions of hostages, and the burning of entire villages). By mid-1942, "most peasants feared for their lives in the presence of a German."[130]

In contrast, young urban Russians and Ukrainians, born in the 1920s and early 1930s, retained a "strong faith in Soviet communism and rarely lost it under the Nazis."[131] Having lived their entire lives under the Soviet system, they believed in communism, but not necessarily in Stalin. Even the Holodomor of 1932–3 did not disillusion them. This should not be surprising. The Soviet authorities killed or exiled the overwhelming majority of the actual or potential opponents of the Soviet system in the 1930s; these young men and women matured as beneficiaries of the Soviet system.[132] By conforming to the Stalinist order, they received good educations and jobs, establishing stable (if not always predictable) careers for themselves. As urban residents, they had access to rationed food (not much by Western standards, but far superior to what those living in the countryside received in the 1930s). Yes, they believed in Soviet communism, but their choice – inasmuch as they possessed any choice – to work in the Stalinist system predisposed them to support the regime wholeheartedly. They, in short, possessed incentives to adapt politically.

As a consequence, urban residents – the better educated and the beneficiaries of the system – expressed greater scepticism of the Germans than the peasants. And the Germans did not disappoint them. The authorities humiliated the residents of the cities, dividing them into "For Germans only" and "non-German" sectors. Buildings used by both the Germans and the local population possessed separate entrances for each group. The authorities even designated stores and latrines "For Germans only."[133]

Because Nazi ideology condemned the cities as centres of political contamination and the German army and air force did not level them as Hitler intended, "starvation of the inhabitants became the default option."[134] The Germans refused to supply the larger cities, especially Kiev, with the necessary food and fuel for heating purposes. Malnutrition, exposure, disease, and mass starvation rapidly followed (Dovzhenko's father died during the enforced starvation of Kiev). The population of Kiev, for example, dropped from 850,000 in June 1941 to 400,000 in October 1941 to 50,000 in November 1943, when the Soviet army liberated the city. During the German occupation, 70–80,000 residents of Kharkiv died of famine.[135]

Germany's eastern worker (*Ostarbeiter*) program also alienated the people. Because the Nazi leadership did not completely transform its economy into a total war economy until 1943, Germany experienced major labour shortages during the first few years of the war. In order to overcome these deficits, its rulers imported prisoners of war and foreign workers from Nazi-occupied Europe to the Reich. By the fall of 1941, the entire German economy had become "heavily and irreversibly dependent on foreign labor."[136] The Germans – despite serious misgivings – then started to recruit Soviet civilians in November 1941. Hundreds of thousands volunteered in the spring of 1942. Most imagined that their lives would improve dramatically within the borders of the Reich.

Instead, they encountered the opposite. Transported to Germany without food, water, or the proper sanitary facilities, they worked long hours and received poor rations, low wages, inadequate housing (oftentimes behind barbed wire), meagre clothing, and insufficient medical care. Like their compatriots in Ukraine, the migrant workers experienced constant indignities, insults, and mistreatment in Germany. The Nazis claimed that eastern workers represented subhumans. They introduced the death penalty for those Ukrainians caught in sexual relationships with Germans. Until 1944, the authorities forced them to wear a distinctive badge, a rectangle with the letters OST (East) in white on a blue background, stitched over the left breast of the worker and visible at all times on every article of clothing.[137]

By the end of 1944, foreign workers – nearly 7.6 million in all – accounted for 20 per cent of Germany's entire labour force. Nearly 1.9 million prisoners of war and 5.7 million civilian workers comprised this group. These outsiders constituted almost 50 per cent of all those employed in German agriculture and in the munitions factories and approximately one-third of the workers in the metal, chemical, construction, and mining industries. They encompassed nearly 250,000 Belgians, 590,000 Italians, 1.3 million French men and women, 1.7 million Poles, and 2.8 million Soviet citizens. The overwhelming majority of the latter, nearly 2.2 million, came from Ukraine; of those, 200,000 to 400,000 from its western areas.[138] Females, with an average age of twenty, composed more than half of the Polish and Soviet civilian workers.[139]

After the Allies introduced round-the-clock bombing of Germany's major industrial centres in 1944, the eastern worker's miserable living conditions worsened. Housed in barracks close to the mines and factories where they worked, they did not receive access to adequate air-raid shelters.[140] Many lost their lives during the last two years of the war.

Rumours about horrible working conditions for easterners reached Ukraine in the summer of 1942 and caused the volunteer pool to dry up. Desperately needing more workers, the Nazi authorities mandated a two-year labour service in Germany for all men and women in Ukraine between the ages of eighteen and twenty.[141] The Germans also introduced brutal recruitment expeditions, surrounding central squares in towns and cities, arbitrarily selecting large numbers of men and women, and immediately transporting them to Germany. Not surprisingly, these actions infuriated the population.

Although the authorities started to treat the eastern workers in Germany better in 1943, these changes came too late. For most of these workers, life in Germany constituted a long, unending nightmare. The ruthless labour recruitment drives in Ukraine, the twentieth-century equivalent of past nomadic slave-hunting expeditions in the steppe, continued unabated.

Nazi racial policies, the German treatment of Soviet POWs, wide-scale arbitrary violence, starvation of the cities, and involuntary labour recruitment divorced many of the Ukrainians from the Germans they may have enthusiastically greeted months before. The Ukrainian population now responded with passive and later with active resistance.[142] All opposition to the Germans, including helping partisans or hiding Jews, provoked brutal reprisals, which decimated entire families and neighbourhoods. Despite these dangers, this spontaneous growth of popular resistance assumed one of three forms: the organized communist movement; the Ukrainian nationalist movement; and a clearly anti-German, but politically unaffiliated movement. The first two movements eliminated the third.

Following Stalin's first major radio address after the outbreak of the war on 3 July 1941, the Communist Party started to organize Soviet partisans and an underground network behind enemy lines. Until mid-1943 the partisans (which grew into a force of approximately 250,000) operated primarily in Belarus, on the extreme northern border of Soviet Ukraine, and in the northern parts of the occupied RSFSR. Central and Southern Ukraine's distance from the front, its unsuitable steppe terrain, and the absence of large numbers of Red Army men cut off by the rapid German advance accounted for the weak partisan movement there. Approximately 80 per cent of the partisans in these northern areas identified themselves as Belarusans or Russians.[143] Until mid-1943, the partisans did not present a Ukrainian face.[144] A communist underground, composed of clandestine CP(b)U and the Komsomol cells, also emerged – primarily in the cities.

The communist partisan movement relied on manpower from parachuted detachments of specially trained and well-armed men, sent into Ukraine from behind the Soviet lines. One of the most famous Soviet partisans, Sydir Kovpak, a Ukrainian from Poltava, led a regiment of 3,500 and embarked on two long-range raids in 1942–4 in northern and western Ukraine. He fought against both the Germans and Ukrainian nationalist units before the Germans pulverized his forces in 1944.[145]

Although these "irregular warriors" did not play a critical role in the Soviet victory over Germany, they "physically controll[ed] the lives and destinies of a small group of civilians" in some areas and harassed the Germans. But, most importantly, they sought to restore, if not expand upon, the pre-1941 Soviet borders. In doing so, these partisans projected Soviet power beyond the territories controlled by the Red Army, frequently "reminding the population of the continual presence and watchful eye of the Soviet regime."[146] Soviet guerrilla activities behind the front lines frightened many people under German occupation and inspired them to hide their anti-Soviet attitudes in public.[147] These underground fighters also intentionally provoked German reprisals against the local populations.[148]

In response to these Soviet partisans, various local Ukrainian self-defence units emerged in Western Volhynia and Polissia, areas conducive for guerilla warfare. Taras Bulba-Borovets (who worked with OUN-M) organized armed Ukrainian groups in these areas in the spring of 1942. He sought to defend the local population from the Germans and from Soviet partisans who had begun to infiltrate Ukraine and who provoked brutal German reprisals. By mid-1943 members of the Bandera wing of the OUN absorbed Bulba-Borovets's group, the Ukrainian Insurgent Army (UPA). Despite OUN-B's initial hesitations about confronting the Germans (the Soviets remained their primary enemy), this group escalated their attacks on the occupiers who requisitioned grain from local peasants and who collected slave labourers. By the fall of 1943, the UPA emerged as one of the strongest anti-German resistance movements outside of Soviet borders. Only Tito's Partisans in Yugoslavia, the Polish Home Army, the French Resistance, and Soviet partisans attracted more fighters.[149]

The year 1943 emerged as a turning point on the eastern front and in the battle for Ukraine. After its victory at Stalingrad in February, the Soviet army captured Kharkiv on 23 August and Kiev on 6 November. By the end of April 1944, all of heretofore German-occupied eastern and central Ukraine fell. The Soviet army then conquered Lviv on 27 July and Transcarpathia on 10 October. Despite the inevitability of Soviet victory, not all acquiesced to a return of Soviet rule.

In a very short span of time, the political realities of East Central Europe changed, then changed again. In the 1930s, the Soviets, the Germans, and the Ukrainian nationalists aspired to remake the political map of Europe, but for different reasons. The Soviets and the Nazis wanted to overturn the Treaty of Versailles, enhance the power and the territories of their own already-existing states, and create their own new orders in their spheres of influence. In contrast, the OUN wanted to establish an independent

Ukrainian state near the heart of Europe, a project the Soviets and the Poles (who represented a status quo power) vehemently opposed.

In light of the European balance of power in the 1930s and 1940s, Ukrainian nationalists viewed the Germans as their only potential strategic partner against the USSR and Poland. Nevertheless, they did not blindly follow a pro-German orientation. Ukrainian revolutionary nationalism remained their primary commitment. In light of their ideological fervour, OUN-B members resembled the Bolsheviks in many respects. In light of their limited options, they felt they had to play the pro-German card, whatever the outcome. Encouraged by their contacts with the German military intelligence, which viewed the OUN favourably, they downplayed the hostility of the Nazi leaders, who did not recognize Ukrainians as colleagues or as equals, much less humans. For members of the OUN-B, it made perfect sense, strategically and tactically, to ally themselves with Germany, which opposed Poland as well as the USSR, and which helped set up the secessionist puppet states of Croatia and Slovakia.

The Polish Factor

Just as the Ukrainian nationalists assessed the state of the world from their own perspective, so did the Polish Government-in-Exile and the Polish Home Army. These Ukrainian and Polish frames of reference remained irreconcilable.

After the German invasion of the USSR in June 1941, the governments of the United Kingdom and the USSR established an anti-German military alliance on 12 July. Poland, Great Britain's closest ally, followed suit. On 30 July 1941 General Władysław Sikorski, the prime minister of the Polish Government-in-Exile, and Ivan Maisky, the Soviet ambassador to Great Britain, reopened full diplomatic relations between Poland and the USSR. In this treaty, the USSR annulled all of its 1939 agreements with Nazi Germany, but it did not explicitly recognize the pre-war Polish-Soviet borders, which the 1921 Treaty of Riga hammered out.[150] Two weeks later, the two governments signed a military alliance treaty, creating a forty-thousand-man Polish army on Soviet soil.

Due primarily to the USSR's refusal to recognize the precise coordinates of Poland's eastern borders after the war, the Polish Government-in-Exile and the USSR became wary allies against Nazi Germany. Both the Soviets as well as the British promised to help the Polish Government-in-Exile's extensive anti-German underground network in Poland, but it "received as little practical support" from the Soviets as it did from the Western Allies.[151]

Shortly after the Polish army surrendered in September 1939, Sikorski established the Union for Armed Struggle (ZWZ) as occupied Poland's military resistance movement, one of the largest in Nazi-subjugated Europe. In February 1942, in response to Nazi terror, he reorganized the ZWZ into the Home Army (*Armia Krajewa*, or AK), which united various independent detachments operating in the German- and Soviet occupied zones and attracted approximately 400,000 men and women. The British hoped to use the Polish Home Army to destroy German lines supplying front-line troops in Soviet territory in order to divert men and supplies from France, the future site of a massive joint Allied invasion.

Led by Piłsudski's acolytes, the AK cautiously accepted the authority of the more broadly based (but fragile) London exile government, composed of representatives of the pre-war political parties opposed to Piłsudski's policies. The London government developed Poland's overall strategy and negotiated with its allies; the AK fought in the streets and fields 1,450 kilometres (900 miles) away. The Polish Government-in-Exile did not directly control all of the Home Army's day-to-day operations. Despite the political and logistical strains between them, both groups proclaimed the necessity to restore Poland to its pre–September 1939 borders. But in the course of the war, the AK – which courageously fought in the disputed territories – watched helplessly as the British and Soviet governments forced the Polish Government-in-Exile to abandon this strategic goal.

Even before Sikorski's death in an airline crash in Gibraltar on 4 July 1943, the uneasy relationship between his government and the USSR collapsed. On 13 April the German mass media announced that their troops had discovered mass graves of Polish officers near the Katyn Forest in former Eastern Poland and claimed that the Soviets had executed them prior to the outbreak of the German-Soviet War on 22 June 1941. The Soviets vociferously denied this accusation, insisting that the Germans committed the crime months after their invasion. The Polish Government-in-Exile, which had always suspected Soviet complicity in the disappearance of twenty-two thousand Polish officers the Red Army captured in September–October 1939, asked the International Red Cross to investigate. Angered that the Poles had publicly questioned the integrity of the Soviet Union's anti-fascist credentials, Stalin broke off relations with the Government-in-Exile and openly cultivated Polish pro-Soviet groups within the USSR in order to form Poland's first post-war government.[152]

In response to the uncertainties concerning Poland's eastern frontiers, the Polish government-in exile and the leadership of the Home Army launched operations to gain as much ground as possible before the Soviet advance into the *kresy*. Committed to its pre-1939 borders and hoping to re-establish ties with the Soviet government, which fervently opposed the OUN and UPA, the Poles did not seriously seek to find any accommodation with these two Ukrainian organizations. Any compromise reached would have challenged Poland's claims to its territorial integrity. Polish policies, not Ukrainian polonophobia, remained the main obstacle to any Polish-Ukrainian agreement. Polish inflexibility on this issue only intensified Ukrainian hatred of the Poles to unprecedented levels.

After the Soviet army crossed the Bug (Buh) River on 22 July 1944 and entered the territory Moscow would designate as the post-war Polish state, the Soviet government created the Polish Committee of National Liberation (PKWN) in Lublin. Partially in response to this political shockwave, on 1 August the AK launched the Warsaw Uprising, which sought to seize the capital from the Germans, just before the arrival of Soviet troops. Shortly after the Germans brutally crushed the largest urban insurrection of the Second World War in early October, Winston Churchill forced Stanisław Mikołajczyk, Sikorski's successor as prime minister, to accept the creation of the Soviet-sponsored Lublin government and Poland's new truncated borders. The Soviet Union recognized the Lublin government as Poland's provisional government on 31 December 1944. At Potsdam, the first Allied summit after the war in Europe ended, the British and US governments acknowledged the PKWN's successor, the Provisional Government of National Unity (TRJN), on 30 June 1945 as Poland's legitimate post-war government. Ostensibly a coalition government, which included Mikołajczyk and other representatives of the London-based Polish Government-in-Exile, the TRJN soon emerged as a communist-led government.[153]

Willing to sacrifice tens of millions of soldiers and civilians and taking advantage of all the opportunities that came his way, Stalin in the course of the war beat back the Germans, reacquired the pre–22 June 1941 Soviet borderlands in the West, occupied Poland, marginalized the Polish Government-in-Exile, neutered the Home Army, and installed a new pro-Soviet government in a smaller Poland. Unable to control events on the ground, the London government and the Home Army watched apprehensively as the Soviets swept away the authority of the Polish Underground State and installed their own administration. Inasmuch as the Soviets possessed the largest land army in Eurasia and the acquiescence of Churchill and Roosevelt, there was very little that these two Polish organizations could do to stem the Soviet tide, save to gain control of as much territory as possible.

In an age of nationalism, most viewed states with large territories as powerful nations. Much like the Poles, Ukrainian nationalists sought to gain possession of the maximum amount of the land they claimed and to fend off the Soviets.[154] Much like the Poles, they failed.

Chełm/Kholm and the Volhynian Massacres

Shortly after the 1941 German invasion, the Poles and Ukrainians in Poland's former eastern territories became involved in one of the most ferocious conflicts of the war. These merciless clashes built on the hostilities generated in interwar Poland and in the first few weeks of the German-Polish War. Sparked by the introduction of radical German occupational policies in the Chełm/Kholm (Kholmshchyna) and Podlachia regions in 1942–3, these anti-Ukrainian and anti-Polish violent outbursts soon engulfed neighbouring Western Volhynia and then Eastern Galicia.

This mass communal violence built on the enormous demographic, religious, and political transformations of the late nineteenth and twentieth centuries, which aroused the residents of this mixed Polish-Ukrainian territory on the frontiers between Poland and the Soviet Union. Located west of the Bug (Buh) River, the Kholm Region bordered on the Polish Lublin region to the west, Volhynia to the east, Podlachia to the north, and Galicia to the south. In the nineteenth century, this region belonged to the Russian Empire. In 1875 the tsarist authorities brutally converted its predominantly Greek Catholic, Ukrainian-speaking population to the Orthodox faith. Shortly after 1905, when Tsar Nicholas II issued a decree on religious tolerance (which still outlawed the Greek Catholics), almost one-third of the 450,000 "new Orthodox" believers converted to Roman Catholicism. These religious transformations reinforced the process by which the Ukrainian-speaking population acculturated (then assimilated) themselves to the Polish language and culture.

By 1914, nearly one-half of the total residents (841,800) of the newly created tsarist gubernia of Kholm identified themselves as Ukrainians, nearly one-quarter as Poles, and 15 per cent as Jews. As the German-Russian front moved eastward after the outbreak of the war, the Russian authorities evacuated the overwhelming majority of its Ukrainian-speakers to the interior of their empire. Not all returned after the two Treaties of Brest-Litovsk, which settled the First World War on the eastern front, or the 1921 Treaty of Riga, which concluded the Polish-Soviet War of 1920.

The Treaty of Riga assigned Eastern Galicia, Western Volhynia, Podlachia, and the Kholm Region to Poland. The Ukrainians now constituted less than one-half of the Kholm Region's total population. Taking advantage of this situation, the new Polish government actively sponsored efforts to transform the Ukrainian minority into loyal Poles and to convert the Orthodox faithful to the newly created "Roman Catholic Church of the Eastern Rite." Hoping to Polonize the entire Ukrainian population, the authorities demolished, desecrated, or converted half of the total number of Orthodox churches to Roman Catholic ones in this area in 1937–8.

Shortly after the German invasion of Poland in 1939, the victors occupied all of the Kholm Region and Podlachia, which became a part of the General Government's Lublin district. As in Galicia, the German occupational authorities allowed the creation of the Ukrainian Central Committee and Ukrainian-language schools. They also tolerated the emergence of the Ukrainian Autocephalous Orthodox Church, modelled on the church the Soviets destroyed in Soviet Ukraine in the early 1930s.[155] Although they considered all Slavs *Untermenschen*, the Germans favoured the Ukrainians over the Poles, which infuriated the latter. The limited empowerment of the Ukrainians came with the disempowerment of the Poles. By raising the political status of the Ukrainians over that of the Poles, the Germans amplified the fears, resentments, and hatreds between these two groups.[156]

In the spring of 1942, escaped Soviet prisoners of war, Soviet partisans, and pro-Soviet Polish units arrived in the Kholm Region and began to attack Ukrainian "collaborators" in the local administration, the Ukrainian intelligentsia, and the Germans. While these irregulars justified their actions as anti-German ones, the local Ukrainian population interpreted them as anti-Ukrainian in nature, especially when the Germans indiscriminately retaliated by burning down entire Polish and Ukrainian villages.[157] In late November 1942, the Germans launched General Plan Ost, an ambitious plan to Germanize the Polish lands and those beyond by expelling the native populations and replacing them with German colonists. During the construction of settler colonies near the city of Zamość (a part of the Kholm Region) between November 1942 and February 1943, the Germans evicted over 110,000 Polish and Ukrainian peasants from nearly 300 villages and hamlets encircling the city.[158] Once the Germans deported the Poles in the area, they brought in a small number of German and Dutch settlers, creating a ring of villages surrounding these colonies to protect them from the hostile Polish population. Despite protests from the Ukrainian Central Committee, the authorities also moved many Ukrainians into the vacated Polish villages, creating in effect a Ukrainian shield for the Aryan colonists.

This game of musical chairs produced rivers of blood. Those forcibly evicted from their small plots of land encountered not only physical and psychological displacement, but also increased competition for scarce food and shelter, and the possibility of death in an unfamiliar environment.

During the German anti-Polish operations, a large number of Poles fled to the forests, where they supplied the Peasant Battalions (*Bataliony Chłopskie*), the Home Army, and the Soviet partisans with new recruits. Many of these refugees dealt with their humiliations by striking back at their neighbours who acquired their property or that of their compatriots. The Polish underground forces sided with their fellow countrymen and started to target the German colonists and the Ukrainian minority, burning down their villages and at times murdering some, if not all, of their inhabitants. The Germans retaliated by indiscriminately executing those they suspected of aiding the Polish and Soviet partisans, Ukrainians as well as Poles.

In creating colonies and in displacing and mingling the local populations in the nationally mixed areas, the Germans, in effect, provoked the Poles, who then attacked the Germans and Ukrainians. By killing a small number of German settlers, the Home Army prompted the Germans to introduce brutal countermeasures against the Ukrainians.[159] All in all, the Poles and the Germans killed nearly four thousand Ukrainian civilians in this region.[160]

In response to this carnage, at least ten thousand Ukrainians from the Kholm Region fled to neighbouring Volhynia and spread stories of Polish atrocities. The fate of the Ukrainians in the Kholm Region, "canaries in the Polish coal mine," terrified the Ukrainians in Volhynia and aroused them against the local Poles, a recipe for disaster.[161] As the demographic and political realities in Volhynia differed radically from those in the Kholm Region, the subsequent Polish-Ukrainian conflict in Volhynia became even bloodier. First of all, the Ukrainians constituted the overwhelming majority of the population (they represented a plurality or the minority in the Kholm Region). Second, Volhynia (unlike Galicia, Podlachia, or the Kholm Region) belonged to Reichskommissariat Ukraine, a territory even more conducive to inter-communal violence than the General Government. Although the Koch regime raised the status of the Ukrainians and lowered that of the Poles, it sought to have these two *Untermenschen* check, if not act against, each other.[162]

The Polish Home Army and the Soviet partisans also operated in German-occupied Volhynia. As the Germans' control weakened, the Home Army decided to reassert the Polish Government-in-Exile's authority over this area and protect its communities. But in light of the small number of Poles scattered across a sea of Ukrainians, pursuing both of these goals at the same time led to an impasse. To proclaim a return to the pre-1939 Polish borders only enraged the Ukrainians and endangered the Polish population. At the same time, OUN-B's goal to wrest this area from the Poles and to create an independent Ukraine only inflamed the Poles.

Since September 1939, the Poles had seen their state destroyed and their national minorities win limited support from the Germans, their hated enemies. In turn, the Ukrainians – who had experienced a dramatic decline in population in the Kholm Region, had encountered extensive discrimination during the period of the Second Polish Republic, and who suffered violence in the Kholm Region – decided to stand their ground in Volhynia. Both the Polish as well as Ukrainian nationalists interpreted their reality in similar terms. Most members of each group felt that they had to not only defend their own physical existence, but also ensure their own national essence as Poles and Ukrainians. To fail meant to lose not just one's family or neighbours, but also one's homeland, a powerful internalized symbol of one's imagined community, linking the past, present, and future.

In late 1942 and early 1943, Poles and Ukrainians began frequent exchanges of gunfire. The first major mass killings of Poles by Ukrainians broke out in April 1943, marking the start of a major OUN-B ethnic cleansing campaign to rid the area of its large Polish population.[163] Who gave the order to spark this conflagration: the entire leadership of the OUN-B Western Ukrainian Territorial Executive Committee? Some faction of it? The OUN-B regional commander? Others?[164] Even decades after the start of this conflict, the identity of those who issued these commands remains unclear, but once the slaughter started, it could not stop.

Although OUN-B leaders designated Russia as enemy number one and recognized that this distant enemy was fast approaching and that its methods were far more brutal than those the Poles employed in the 1930s, they had to deal with the threat at hand.[165] In Volhynia and Galicia, the Poles lived in villages and communities adjacent to Ukrainian ones or in mixed Polish-Ukrainian villages. Many Poles, now official allies of the USSR, cooperated with Soviet partisans against the local Ukrainian population, oftentimes provoking the Germans to annihilate Ukrainian villages.

Most importantly, the OUN-B challenged the Polish Government-in-Exile and the Home Army, which fought to restore the Polish Republic within its pre–1 September 1939 frontiers. Poles claimed Western Volhynia (and the Kholm Region and Eastern Galicia) as part of Poland's patrimony; Ukrainians insisted that these territories belonged to the Ukrainian homeland. Both sides claimed that Western Volhynia represented their native soil and *only* their native soil. To make a long story short, the Poles – the minority of the population – wanted to stay in Volhynia (and control it), while the Ukrainians, the majority of the population, wanted the Poles to cede control or to leave. Both sides would not compromise on this fundamental issue and decided to settle their differences by means of violence.

The Germans stirred this cauldron of brutality in the Polish-Ukrainian borderlands, stoking it to unprecedented levels. Once the Germans arrived in Volhynia in the summer of 1941, they established a local police force (*Schutzmannschaft*) and staffed it with Ukrainians.[166] At first, the new regime relied on volunteers. But with the appearance of Soviet partisans in the Polish-Ukrainian-Belarusan borderlands in 1942, the Germans radically expanded the size of its membership. Since Soviet Ukraine constituted the largest single administrative region in the German-conquered east, most of its new *Schutzmänner* came from there. In order to fill its ranks, they had to procure young men. By the end of 1942, far more police recruits were coerced into service than volunteered.[167]

Each recruit, whether coerced or not, possessed a different reason for joining and remaining in the ranks of the *Schutzmannschaft*. Some men may have wanted to avenge the deaths or deportations of family members or friends from the Soviet era. Others may have enlisted for nationalistic reasons, infiltrating the German police in order to acquire weapons and some training. But most enrolled for more mundane reasons. In serving the German authorities, they avoided forced labour conscription to Germany and received food, regular pay, and protection, a modicum of security in uncertain times.[168] In addition to those who sought to survive and provide for their families, the local police also attracted the ambitious, the unsavoury, and even criminals.[169]

If the statistics for one district in Belarus are representative of all *Schutzmänner*, approximately 90 per cent of the Ukrainian policemen would have been thirty-five years old or younger, men of prime military age.[170] Since most able-bodied men of military age under occupation raised German suspicions, young men had to choose one of three options to secure their physical future, however precarious: (1) paid service in the police force; (2) forced labour in Germany; or (3) enrolment in Ukrainian or Soviet units in the forests. Of these unpalatable opportunities, many settled on police service, which "may have seemed the more attractive of the possible alternatives."[171] Most the conscripted policemen had no overall loyalty to the Germans or an ideological predisposition to fascism.[172] As most young men sought to make the best of their limited options, they should not be condemned for joining the police. But they should be judged and condemned for any and all heinous actions committed after donning German uniforms, especially the mass killing of unarmed Jewish, Polish, and Ukrainian civilians.

Once Soviet partisans began to penetrate Volhynia in the fall of 1942, the German authorities assigned some of the conscripted local policemen to assist SS and military units in punitive missions against suspected Soviet partisan supporters, in addition to special "actions" against ex-communist activists, Jews, Soviet ex-prisoners, and members of the Polish intelligentsia.[173] The Germans introduced draconian measures against the civilian population suspected of helping Soviet partisans. Often arbitrarily implemented, the severe reprisals against possible partisan sympathizers hit "the patriotic Ukrainian peasantry as frequently as they did communist sympathizers." Increasingly, some policemen (not all) became reluctant to suppress their fellow Ukrainians or to round up young men and women for the *Ostarbeiter* program.[174]

But they were stuck, enmeshed in a set of arrangements beyond their immediate control. They could not disobey their superiors. But at the same time, some could not participate in the mass killings of their compatriots or – in some cases – their neighbours. By the fall of 1942, they could not voluntarily leave the ranks of the *Schutzmannschaft*. If they did, the Germans would shoot them for desertion. Even if the Germans allowed them to return to their former lives, the Soviet partisans would not necessarily forgive them for working for the Germans.

Then, in response to a call by the OUN-B leadership in March 1943, approximately six thousand Ukrainian policemen abandoned the Germans with their weapons and headed for the forests.[175] Many joined the OUN-B– led Ukrainian Insurgent Army (UPA) and now fought against three foes – the Germans, the Poles, and the Soviets. Others fell in with the Soviet partisans (in the 1920s and 1930s the Communist Party of Western Ukraine attracted a large number of sympathizers in Volhynia); others went home.

In retaliation, the Germans killed the families of Ukrainian police officers who deserted and destroyed the villages of those who fled with their arms. Using newly recruited Polish policemen to replace the Ukrainians, the Germans promptly carried out these reprisals. "Many who joined the UPA from the German police instantly lost their homes and families," according to Timothy Snyder, "and found a new reason to hate the Poles."[176]

By the summer of 1943, the OUN and UPA used the local Polish alliance with the Germans as a justification for cleansing Western Volhynia of the Polish population. That summer the UPA gained control of the Volhynian countryside from the Germans and began to murder and expel its 200,000–300,000 Polish inhabitants and the remaining Jews.[177] Volhynia suffered mass murder, mutilation of bodies, and the burning of entire villages along with their residents. The overwhelming majority of the victims were unarmed Polish civilians. Polish policemen, self-defence forces, and the Home Army struck back, also indiscriminately killing Ukrainian men, women, and children. Both sides engaged in asymmetrical violence. "An eye for an eye and a tooth for a tooth" quickly escalated to "Several eyes for an eye, and several sets of teeth for a tooth." More so in Western Volhynia than in the Chełm/Kholm Region or Galicia, the horrors Jewish, Polish, and Ukrainian civilians suffered rivalled the brutalities German peasants endured during the Thirty Years War.[178]

Scholars in Poland, Ukraine, the United States, and Europe estimate that in 1943 and 1944 the members of the OUN-B and UPA killed between 25,000 to 70,000 Poles in Western Volhynia, and then another 20,000 to 70,000 in Eastern Galicia. In the same period, the Home Army and other Polish underground units killed 2,000 to 20,000 Ukrainians in Western Volhynia and another 1,000 to 4,000 in Galicia. In both nationally mixed regions, between 50,000 to 100,000 Poles and 8,000 to 20,000 Ukrainians died by violent means.[179] The German authorities did little to stop these ethnic cleansings, and oftentimes provoked them.

As the turbulent waves of emotions produced in this Polish-Ukrainian conflict generated wildly different ways the survivors remembered these events (the Rashomon effect), the range of these estimates is very broad and must be treated with considerable caution. Scholars will need to conduct more research before they can narrow their appraisals of the Polish and Ukrainian civilian casualties to statistics that can be cited with reasonable confidence in order to build a consensus on the overall number of Polish and Ukrainian victims. It is tempting to split the difference between the high and low estimates or to use the highest number of civilian victims to rationalize claims of ethnic cleansing or genocide. The truth of the matter is more complex and difficult to delineate precisely.

In light of the number of Polish and Ukrainian victims in relation to the overall number of Poles and Ukrainians living in the Kholm Region, Western Volhynia, and Eastern Galicia, this Polish-Ukrainian War represented a broad and ferocious ethno-national conflict, an effort by both the OUN-B/UPA and the Home Army to expel the other's compatriots, with one side winning and the other losing, and with both sides engaging in atrocities against civilians. The communal violence in the Kholm Region, Western Volhynia, and Eastern Galicia parallels the violence of the Algerians against the French colonialists, of Irish nationalists against the British, of Jewish nationalists against the British and Palestinians, and Palestinian nationalists against Israelis. In each case, radical nationalists attacked and killed members of other nations who held political power or controlled contested territory. Their methods were criminal and oftentimes abominable, but the years of pent-up fears, private resentments, and public humiliations fuelled the spontaneous rage.[180] Despite the efforts of the Ukrainian Central Committee, the Ukrainian Catholic bishops, and the leaders of the Ukrainian community, peace could not be restored.

Regrettably, in light of the high stakes involved (post-war Polish control of the *kresy* vs local Ukrainian control of the Kholm Region, Western Volhynia, and Eastern Galicia), it was impossible to reconcile these two diametrically opposed goals without the application of mass violence. Because of the savagery involved, both sides could frame this conflict as a struggle between good and evil. Although the OUN-B and UPA killed more Poles than the Home Army killed Ukrainians, both groups were responsible for the violence that broke out in this area. In this war, no group was blameless or absolved from responsibility in killing civilians. Each group contained victims as well as perpetrators, and oftentimes victims became victimizers and victimizers became victims. Although there were many casualties from different political, ethnic, national, or religious persuasions, there were far fewer innocents.

Despite the wide range within these above-mentioned statistics, they possess two common denominators. First of all, in any given region where the Poles or Ukrainians were a minority of the population, its civilian population suffered more than its enemies. Second, in light of the panic this mass violence provoked in the Polish and Ukrainian communities, it produced more violence in terms of scope and intensity.

Atrocities, exaggerations, widespread unverified rumours, and hysteria on both sides mark the Polish-Ukrainian armed struggle of 1942–4. In response to the anti-Ukrainian actions taken in the Kholm Region, refugees fled to Volhynia. Their accounts of the horrors they experienced provoked extensive and brutal anti-Polish massacres in Volhynia. Thousands of Poles then fled Volhynia for Galicia, where they activated the Polish underground to prepare punitive measures against the Ukrainian population. [181] The OUN and UPA struck back. Even after the war in Europe ended, the Polish-Ukrainian conflict continued in a new theatre of operations in southeastern Poland (Zakerzonnia), which contained a large Ukrainian minority. Once set into motion, this epidemic of mass violence could not be easily quarantined or totally eliminated.

Far more so than the first Polish-Ukrainian War of 1918–19, or the Polish-Ukrainian violence in interwar Poland, this second Polish-Ukrainian War, like the Croatian-Serbian War in German-occupied Yugoslavia in 1941 to 1944, destabilized entire societies and poisoned the relationships between neighbours. At the Ukrainian-Polish borderlands, the war accelerated the destruction of the local elites. In addition to the 200,000 Jews massacred in this region, at least 100,000 Polish and Ukrainian non-combatants died during this struggle. It embittered and permanently divorced Ukrainians and Poles from each other, decimated the Jewish population, and solidified the Ukrainian identity among the survivors in this region, but only for a short period of time.[182] Many of the Ukrainian survivors would eventually be deported or killed after the war. The demographic Ukrainization of these borderlands after the war came at the expense of the Jewish and Polish populations living there.

Manipulation of the Ukrainian Identity

With the creation of the Soviet internal passport system in the early 1930s, every citizen at the age of sixteen living in urban areas declared his or her national identity based on that of his or her parents. In the case of "mixed" parentage, children could choose either one of their parents' identities. Once entered into the Soviet system, changes in the passport's "nationality" category could not take place.[183]

For most Soviet citizens, the documentation of national identities did not produce any adverse consequences in the 1930s. Many did not take this registration seriously. But when the German-Soviet War broke out, these passports produced life and death consequences. These documents divided the Soviet citizens into those the Nazis wanted to exterminate immediately (such as the Jews, who possessed their own separate nationality category) and those who remained merely expendable.

Millions of Soviet citizens may have possessed a Ukrainian "nationality" in their passports but did not necessarily imagine themselves as members of a community separate from the Russian-speaking Soviet public. Many of these men and women may have conflated all of the Eastern Slavs into a category *"nashi"* (our people), which included all East Slavs, but excluded Poles, Jews, and ethnic Germans. Millions of peasants (who did not gain access to passports until 1974) may have primarily identified themselves with their village or locality, not their ascribed identity. This should not be surprising. Ukrainization lasted only for a short period of time, and those who promoted it, usually the most nationally conscious, experienced arrest, imprisonment, execution, or exile. Despite its suppression, Ukrainization did raise the level of Ukrainian national consciousness, although it is difficult to ascertain by how much or for how long.[184]

As the supreme arbiter of national hierarchies in RK Ukraine, Koch gave preferential treatment to the Ukrainian language and culture over the Russian. This forced Ukrainization alienated the Russian speakers in the cities, who for the most part imagined Ukrainian as inferior to Russian and led many of them to identify the Ukrainian language and culture with the barbarism of the Nazi order. But Koch's Ukrainization did not reflect the Ukrainization of the 1920s. Although the Germans allowed drama theatres and choir concerts in Ukrainian, they prohibited public recitations of Taras Shevchenko's poems in the Reichskommissariat, considering them inflammatory. The Ministry for the Occupied Eastern Territories, moreover, did not think that Ukrainians needed to learn German or attain an education beyond the fourth grade.[185] Nazi racial ideologists clearly viewed Ukrainians as inferior beings and did not seek to raise their national consciousness, if only to oppose the communist regime they passionately wanted to crush.

When members of the several-thousand-strong OUN expeditionary groups arrived in Soviet Ukraine in June 1941, just ahead or behind the invading German troops, they knew almost nothing about the day-to-day life of the local population and were shocked to encounter very little of the national consciousness they had experienced in Eastern Galicia.[186] Although Ukrainians in the east spoke Ukrainian, they responded unenthusiastically to the integral nationalism Galician Ukrainians aggressively promoted.[187] Having survived the brutalities of collectivization, the famines, and the purges, they rejected the OUN's adherence to authoritarianism and one-party rule. Central and Eastern Ukrainians, moreover, asked penetrating questions about the content of the social and political programs the OUN would introduce after the collapse of Soviet rule, questions that the newcomers could answer only in vague terms.[188] In light of Ukraine's experiences during the First World War, revolution, Civil War, collectivization, industrialization, famine, and the purges, this reaction remained unsurprising. In Reichskommissariat Ukraine, the nationally conscious elite (as well as those who launched the Ukrainian Revolution of 1917–20 and Ukrainization in the 1920s) had been decimated long before the arrival of the Germans.

As a consequence of the above-mentioned spontaneous meetings between the Galicians and their eastern compatriots and the German losses at Stalingrad and Kursk, the leadership of the OUN-B began to reconsider its political program. At the Third Extraordinary Grand Assembly on 21–5 August 1943, at the height of the Polish-Ukrainian conflict in Volhynia, the OUN-B condemned "fascist national-socialist programs and political concepts" as well as "Russian-Bolshevik communism" and proposed a system of free peoples and independent states "[as] the single best solution to the problem of world order." The organization's new social and economic program emphasized a mixed economy, worker participation in management, free movement of labour, and free trade unions. The OUN-B claimed that it would introduce civil liberties, including freedom of the press and speech, even respecting the rights of national minorities.[189]

Although these changes overturned the OUN-B's earlier policy, represented by the slogan "Ukraine for Ukrainians," the organization still viewed itself as the spearhead of the Ukrainian national liberation movement. As a group representing a people without a state, its members were totally committed to the creation of an independent Ukrainian state ex nihilo from all the territories with Ukrainian-speaking majorities in East Central Europe. (In light of their ideological predispositions, its members did not recognize the Ukrainian SSR as an independent or as a Ukrainian state, certainly not as a political entity representing the interests of the Ukrainian majority.) In the course of the Second World War, the OUN-B's political ideology changed from a highly authoritarian one, influenced by the prevailing European fascist ethos that sought to overturn the Treaty of Versailles, to one more moderate and somewhat more liberal, if not social-democratic.[190] But the creation of a Ukrainian state remained the OUN-B's primary goal; only the form of this future state's government changed. The brutal armed struggle would continue until then.

The OUN-B defined itself as a national liberation movement. As such, it was similar in structure, ideology, and ethos to other twentieth-century national liberation movements, not unlike Vietnam's Viet Minh, Algeria's National Liberation Front, Ireland's Sinn Féin and the Irish Republican Army, the Jewish Irgun and Stern Gang, or the Palestine Liberation Organization.[191] All of these organizations fought to create independent states and all employed violence, oftentimes in immoral, senseless, or counterproductive ways against civilians.

Members of the OUN-B lived in an environment of illegality and conspiratorial activity. They were young and fanatical believers in the Ukrainian cause. They remained hostile to all real and perceived enemies, whether the occupying powers, competing national movements, other nations, or potential traitors in their own midst. They embraced violence and often terrorism. Their enemies responded in kind. And most of these perceived enemies (with the exception of the Jews) enjoyed access to larger armies and more guns.

Because the OUN-B was completely dedicated to constructing an independent Ukrainian state from the territories claimed and/or occupied by Poland, the USSR, Romania, Czechoslovakia, and Hungary, the political elites and masses in these states formed after the First World War regarded the Ukrainian nationalist movement (and the OUN-B in particular) as an existential threat that needed eradication.[192] For them, the making of an independent Ukraine meant the unmaking of their own states. By raising the flag of the dispossessed and exploited Ukrainians, the OUN-B threatened the stability and the territorial integrity of all of these East Central European states.

Under these circumstances, the OUN-B could not and would not introduce, let alone implement, the new August 1943 program during a bitter struggle against the largest army on the Eurasian continent and against the Poles in Western Volhynia. Inspired by the complex response the OUN expeditionary groups received in 1941 Soviet Ukraine, this new policy came too late to attract the local population in Central and Eastern Ukraine to the Ukrainian nationalist cause.[193] In any case, by mid-1943 the geopolitical situation in East Central Europe favoured the Red Army. The OUN-B and UPA leadership would find it difficult to introduce these changes in the heat of war.

Soviet victories at Stalingrad and Kursk reinforced the idea that the USSR would soon defeat Nazi Germany. In preparation for this victory, the Communist Party's propaganda machine promoted a dual identity among its non-Russian citizens. By combining the overall Soviet identity and a regional and/or republican identity, the ruling elite hoped to neutralize the anti-Soviet resistance movements in the Soviet western borderlands. In highlighting Soviet Ukrainian patriotism, which emphasized the independence and sovereignty of the Ukrainian SSR within the Soviet family of nations, the authorities implied fundamental changes in the status of the republic and its citizens after the war.[194]

On 1 February 1944, the Supreme Soviet of the USSR allowed the republics of the USSR to create republican military formations and to enjoy relations with foreign countries as well as to create ministries of defence and foreign affairs. The writer Alexander Korniichuk became Soviet Ukraine's foreign minister, and Kovpak the first defence minister. Although Soviet Ukraine never formed independent military formations, it did become a founding member of the United Nations in 1945, remaining a member even before its formal independence in December 1991.

In terms of these identities, the Soviet one preceded the other national identities, with the exception of the Russian, which remained the "more equal" one. As these Ukrainian territories re-entered the USSR, the Soviet state regained control of the Ukrainian cultural elite's ability to represent their own Ukrainian identity and reality. While the Soviet state possessed a monopoly of violence, it could not always dictate its political vision of Ukraine from the top down. Often, as Serhy Yekelchyk recently pointed out, it had to negotiate with the Ukrainian cultural elite over the parameters of the Ukrainian identity.[195] But these accommodations did not include parties of equals.

Collectivization, the Holodomor, and the Soviet terror of the 1930s destroyed the old social fabric and helped reduce an individual's solidarity with others, not only across national communities, but also within one's own group.[196] The German occupation and its brutal reprisals for helping partisans and Jews raised this wide-scale anomie to an unprecedented level. The war produced even more trauma. Each cataclysm built upon the previous one and each expanded the levels of social alienation. Neighbours not only divorced themselves from neighbours, but they may have also experienced a profound social distance within themselves.

The multinational, multicultural, multilingual, and multiconfessional communities across Ukraine, as in most of East Central Europe, lived together, but apart. With rare exceptions, members of each nation constituted a single society centred on itself and did not belong to a commonwealth of different communities. They may have lived next to each other physically, but they did not necessarily interact with each other psychologically. Without regular personal interactions between and among members of these various groups, it was difficult to establish trust, the expectation "that arises within a community of regular, honest, and cooperative behavior, based on commonly shared norms" with other communities.[197] Trust is a necessary ingredient in all social relations, especially in multinational states. Without this mutual dependability, suspicions fester, especially during times of crisis and radical change. Political and economic downturns encourage people in one group to highlight their differences with other groups and to reinforce their suspicions that members of other communities conspire to work against their interests. In the small town of Berezhany (Brzeżany) in Eastern Galicia, for example, Ukrainians, Poles, and Jews did not fraternize with each other before the war, "so that when bad times arrived, there was no one to turn to."[198]

This pattern of social relationships among these groups prevailed throughout Eastern Galicia, Western Volhynia, and even Central Ukraine. Although many Ukrainians possessed negative feelings towards Poles and Jews, it is no less true that many of the latter also had hostile feelings towards Ukrainians. Each national community in Ukraine emphasized ethnic stereotypes in defining their neighbours. In other words, each group could or would not empathize with the others, and when catastrophe stuck, as it often did even before the war, the response was "That's not my problem" (*Tse ne moia sprava*).

In reaction to the various social cataclysms and subsequent traumas they encountered, people built psychological barriers between their own group and other groups, even if they experienced similar traumas. Over time, these invisible ramparts became long, deep, and high Chinese walls, dividing groups by language, religion, and class. Keeping the strangers and "Barbarians" away from one's physical and psychological perimeter became a priority. In the course of the war, solidarity with fellow human beings, especially those outside one's group, quickly evaporated.

Anomie

Reichskommissariat Ukraine built on the Soviet heritage of mistrust and enforced passivity which undermined solidarity with others. The promising social experiments of the 1920s, the New Economic Policy and Ukrainization, started to build a civil society in the first fifteen years of Soviet power, but Stalin's collectivization, industrialization, famine, and massive purges shut down this process. The politics of national categorization in the 1920s and the Stalinist politics of suspicion, denunciation, and a constant search for real and suspected enemies in the 1930s prepared the way for the Nazis. In the Ukrainian-speaking territories of East Central Europe, the official Polish and Romanian policies discriminating against Ukrainians and the subsequent repressions in the 1920s and 1930s, and the oppressive Soviet occupation, extensive deportations, mass arrests, and executions between 1939 and 1941 made cooperation with the Germans – for many – preferable to submission to the Soviets, Poles, or Romanians. As the largest national group in Europe without an independent state, many Ukrainians felt frustrated by the post-war and post-Versailles world and acted upon their resentments.

Between 1918 and 1939, many Ukrainians living in Galicia, Volhynia, and Bukovina embraced integral nationalism and its ultimate goal – the establishment of an independent Ukrainian state. Proponents of this highly authoritarian ideology claimed that this end justified all means used to realize it; many – although not necessarily the majority – approved this interpretation. In his criticism of this immorality, Metropolitan Andrei Sheptytsky called this belief "a politics without God," the attitude that "politics frees a person from the obligation of Divine Law and justifies crime."[199] But depending on the circumstances, true believers of integral nationalism were not necessarily more likely to absorb this moral breakdown and accommodate the occupiers than the non-believers.[200]

In their assessment of the recent past, nationalist ideologists claimed that Ukrainians failed to establish their own independent state in 1917–20 for two reasons. First of all, the Ukrainians – led by moderate socialist and liberal parties, which negotiated various compromises – did not possess the necessary will to create an independent state. Second, the Ukrainian nationalist governments which emerged during the revolutionary period did not – or could not – establish an effective army to vanquish their internal and external enemies. Despite the great hopes and expectations generated by the fall of the tsarist government, a new political order based on respect, dignity, justice, and equal rights did not emerge. Might still defined right.

All integral nationalists understood subconsciously – if not consciously – that in a world of competitive powers the Ukrainians needed a powerful ally, not a domineering protector along the lines of imperial Germany, which intervened in the internal affairs of the Ukrainian National Republic and quickly undermined its credibility with the peasants. These integral nationalists were revolutionaries who wanted to overturn the status quo in East Central Europe and to carve out an independent Ukrainian state from the territories claimed by Poland, Hungary, Romania, and the USSR. They aspired to turn their dreams into reality by means of their own political will and with their own forces; hence, their interest in military formations (the Carpathian Sich, Nachtigall, Rolland, the UPA, the Galicia Division, and the infiltration of the *Schutzmänner*). The acquisition of military training and arms, in whatever way possible, became their primary priority. They recognized that in light of European geopolitical realities, they needed extensive external help to do so. The Great Powers appeared far more hostile to new entrant states on the European continent than they did decades earlier. Inasmuch as Poland and the USSR, the two most powerful countries in East Central Europe, opposed this goal, the enemies of their enemies (such as Germany) now became their only potential allies.

The OUN-B always insisted that no contradictions existed between their proclamations of the necessity of possessing "our own forces ("*nashi syly*") and their willingness to accommodate themselves with Germany, but the reality was always murkier than they hoped. As revolutionaries who thought in geopolitical terms, Ukrainian nationalists assessed their goals within the framework of their geographic neighbourhood. Had the United States or the United Kingdom been closer or had the Allies viewed Poland or the USSR as their primary enemy, the OUN would have sided with them.[201] Geography may not be destiny, but it certainly helps limit one's political options.

The OUN-B hoped to cooperate closely with Germany but did not blindly follow the Germans. They sought to rely on their own assessment of their own interests and with their own forces. When the Third Reich turned against the OUN in mid-summer 1941, the OUN-B went into the underground and introduced limited defensive measures against them. After Stalingrad, the OUN-B sought to rekindle the German-Ukrainian nationalist pre-war relationship, primarily because – even in retreat – Germany remained the strongest revisionist power in Europe. Pragmatic, not ideological, considerations drove the Ukrainian nationalists.

This attempt to establish a pragmatic relationship with the Germans did not necessarily imply "collaboration with the enemy," if one defines collaboration, as does Jan Gross, as "an uneven partnership in which one party operates under duress or even worse, betrays the interests of its own group."[202] Defined in this manner, collaboration is the very opposite of resistance. Stefan Korbonski, one of the Home Army's primary leaders in Warsaw, described how the Polish underground authorities set guidelines for the behaviour of all Poles under German occupation. At its very core, the basic instructions that the Home Army formulated demanded that the Polish population resist the occupying power at all times, either by passive or active means.[203]

Despite the best intentions of those resisting Nazi or communist occupation, very few could consistently apply this moral clarity during the war and occupation in the ethnically mixed Polish-Ukrainian borderlands, if anywhere at all. In face of a large insubordinate Ukrainian population in the *kresy*, what was the best possible way to deal with them? The Polish Home Army and Polish self-defence units cooperated officially and unofficially with Soviet partisans, the Red Army, the Hungarian army, and the German authorities, at times simultaneously, against the OUN, UPA, and the local Ukrainian population. According to one OUN report written about the Polish underground in Volhynia in May 1942, the author wrote: "Everyone works against the Ukrainians. For the Poles, we are their greatest enemies, even greater than the Germans."[204] The Poles might have responded in the same way and with the same tone in regard to the Ukrainians.

In wartime, all belligerents believed that the expediency of victory always trumped moral principles. Like other guerilla units fighting in Volhynia and East Galicia, OUN and UPA units also engaged in authorized and unauthorized efforts to coordinate their operations with the Germans against the Poles.[205] This did not necessarily denote collaboration.

But collaboration or resistance did not constitute the only possible responses to foreign occupation. Other possible responses included passivity, withdrawal and/or neutrality, passive resistance, passive cooperation, alliance seeking, or merely the wish to survive, oftentimes a contingent mix of these reactions. Not everyone could consistently or consciously resist over a long, brutal occupation. Most people do not and did not engage in heroics; most sought to do the best they could under trying and dangerous circumstances. In the wild East, anyone who stood out could be arbitrarily detained or shot.

In the course of the war, the relationship between the OUN-B and the Germans (depending, of course, on whether the Germans in question were diehard Nazis like Erich Koch or more reasonable senior army and military intelligence officers) fluctuated. This was an uneven relationship, one that could easily change and unexpectedly decimate the leadership of the OUN and a significant number of its members. Locked into the framework of their Nazi racial ideology, the Germans could not and would not help create puppet states, such as Slovakia or Croatia, on the eastern front, which would have temporarily satisfied the Ukrainian nationalists.

The overwhelming majority of Ukrainians most likely did not interpret this informal relationship with the Germans as collaboration. Having lived in interwar Poland or Romania, they did not see themselves as full-fledged citizens of Poland or Romania, nor were they treated as such. Once the Germans or Soviets rolled in, they did not believe that they had any obligations of loyalty to the states they despised and which despised them. Individuals and groups made choices based on their perceptions of the contrast between Soviet and German occupational policies in their localities, the strength of Ukrainian national identity and nationalism before the war, accumulated social strains, and the situation on the eastern (and western) fronts.[206]

In order to overcome Ukraine's statelessness, the OUN-B aspired to become allies of Germany as part of their long-term strategic calculations. In light of this organization's overall weaknesses, cooperation with the Germans promised "higher payoffs than fighting" them.[207] Just as Ukrainian nationalists hoped against hope that the German political leadership would help them in their struggle against the USSR, the Polish Government-in-Exile wished to become the USSR's equal ally against Nazi Germany. Poles and Ukrainians assessed their political environments and took calculated risks allying themselves with one of the Great Powers or the other.

Most of the relationships between the Ukrainians and the Germans in Ukraine was not driven by ideological motivations. Most stemmed from individual and group efforts to respond to the traumatizations of the past and present, an effort to survive the most brutal war in human history. Whether at the official political level (OUN-B–German relations), at the elite level (the Greek Catholic Church and the German occupational authorities), or at the popular level (Ukrainian Schutzschaften), most Ukrainians had to deal with the Germans, whether they wanted to or not.

The Nazi occupation created the environment in which certain types of criminal behaviour flourished, and also special conditions for Ukrainians. The Nazi elite imagined that "the Ukrainians (and the Baltic nationalities) were particularly anti-Bolshevik and therefore anti-Semitic, and moreover, sufficiently primitive to perform whatever dirty work was required." In addition to persuasion, Nazis used coercion to encourage Ukrainians to assume the role of perpetrators.[208]

The police auxiliary units are a case in point. The Germans recruited approximately one million men from among the terrorized and starving population in the areas they controlled on the eastern front to reinforce their army and local police.[209] Many joined to get food and a small salary, to survive. The Germans selected many of the Soviet Ukrainian POWs Hitler released in 1941 to serve as concentration and death camp guards and assigned the local Ukrainian police to participate in Jewish ghetto clearings and mass executions. The men who worked these "actions" committed heinous and unforgivable crimes against a defenceless civilian population. Even if they possessed some empathy with fellow human beings at the beginning of the war, these feelings quickly disappeared. Prolonged subjugation and the routinization of mass killings numbed their senses and intoxicated the powerless men with the thrill of invincibility, the "sensation of trampling on an enemy who is helpless."[210] Ideological or political considerations did not enter into the picture. These men served in these functions because they had little choice in the matter. As released POWs, they already wore the mark of Cain. Thus, according to Snyder, "some of the survivors of one German killing policy became accomplices in another, as a war to destroy the Soviet Union became a war to murder the Jews."[211] With Soviet victory, they became the walking dead.

Through no fault of their own, they had surrendered to the Germans and experienced release when most of their Soviet compatriots did not. This permanently branded them. Having few outlets to survive, they served the Germans, who manipulated them. The Nazis "used persuasion and force to facilitate recruitment. They took advantage, too, of the Ukrainians' opposition to and brutalization by Soviet rule." In doing so, the Germans aspired to reduce the overall social inhibitions against mass murder. The June 1941 Soviet massacres of political prisoners not only "desensitized the local population to the extermination of the Jews, but also reduced taboos inhibiting participation in the extermination process."[212] Officially sponsored anti-Semitic ideologies, personal animosities against the Jews, and Soviet and Nazi brutalizations undermined the social restraints of the past and led many to dehumanize others as they had been dehumanized. In the ferocious struggle to create an independent Ukrainian state, the OUB-B and the UPA killed large numbers of unarmed Jewish and Polish civilians and morally compromised their legacy.

The choices that people made during this turbulent time are far more complex than the narratives that neatly divide those who collaborated from those who did not suggest. Very few of those living under the conditions of Soviet or German occupation could maintain an uncompromised moral clarity.

Conclusion

The experiences of death and suffering unleashed by the Second World War on the eastern front produced a far more extensive, "much deeper and more intensely personal," impact than the first total war fought on Ukrainian soil – and perhaps even the Holodomor.[213] Despite the enormous variation in the scope and intensity of the violence directed against members of specific groups, every survivor suffered and endured an unbearable sense of loss and immeasurable trauma.

In Ukraine (as in all German-occupied territories) the Jews and Romani experienced near total annihilation. Both the Soviets as well as the Nazis exterminated anyone who stood out of the crowd, including large numbers of Ukrainian intellectuals and nationalists. Ukrainian nationalist groups avenged their enemies within their own camp, not to mention Poles, Jews, and members of the Soviet army and security forces. The Soviets did the same. Even before the Red Army reoccupied Ukraine in 1943–4, Soviet partisans and intelligence agents recorded the behaviour and loyalties of the people under German rule. After the arrival of the Soviet army, the new administration eliminated the nationalists and those who worked in the German occupational administration, and purified the Soviet body politic.

Although Soviet authorities deported ethnic Germans and the Poles in successive waves between 1935 and 1941, they discovered new, potentially disloyal national minorities in the course of the war. In 1944 they expelled the entire population of Crimean Tatars (approximately 189,000) to Kazakhstan and Central Asia, as well as a large number of Armenians (9,621), Bulgarians (13,422), and Greeks (15,040) from the Russian Federation's Crimea.[214] In response to the ruthless guerilla war conducted by the OUN-UPA in Western Ukraine, Soviet security forces removed approximately 200,000 to 300,000 people between 1946 and 1950.[215]

Earlier – during the war – rumours spread that Soviet authorities would deport all Ukrainians living in Nazi-occupied territory. But these claims concerning Secret Order No. 0078/42, signed by Marshal Georgi Zhukov and Beria, on 22 June 1942, remain unsubstantiated.[216] Although Nikita Khrushchev asserted in his "Secret Speech" at the Twentieth Party Congress in February 1956 that "there were too many Ukrainians, and there was nowhere to deport them to, but otherwise they would have been deported," the accuracy of this statement remains unverified.[217] Despite the document's problematic nature, it highlights the Soviet leadership's anxiety about the overall loyalty of Ukrainians to the Soviet state.

Despite its ambivalence, Stalin's circle did not ignore Ukrainian participation in the war, as it did with the Jews.[218] Despite large-scale opposition against the Soviet regime, many more Ukrainians fought for the Soviets than against them. In 1941–5, 3.2 million Ukrainians enlisted in the Red Army, including 750,000 from the western regions (not necessarily voluntarily). Twice as many Ukrainians from Galicia, Volhynia, Bukovina, and Bessarabia served in the Red Army as contributed to anti-Soviet resistance in 1944–50.[219] Of the 115,000 pro-Soviet partisans who fought in the Ukrainian SSR in the later stages of the war, approximately 57 per cent identified themselves as Ukrainians.[220] In light of this mass (and in many cases enthusiastic) involvement in the Great Fatherland War, Ukrainians soon became an integral part of the new Soviet legitimizing myth of the war.[221] Soviet authorities "made a real effort to include Ukrainians rhetorically and physically in the war effort and in the partisan movement the Ukrainian partisans symbolically and physically contributed to the construction of a 'Soviet Ukraine' which enabled the inclusion of Ukrainians as Soviet patriots."[222] In the midst of the greatest crisis the Soviet Union ever confronted, the Soviet leadership sought to orient its Ukrainian population in a politically acceptable direction and demonized the Ukrainian nationalists.

In ferreting out their actual and potential enemies, the Stalinist leadership also recognized that the vast majority of those who survived the German, Hungarian, and Romanian occupations did not cooperate with or join the Soviet partisan movement until late in the war. Most passively accepted German rule. In assessing the fragility of Soviet power in the western borderlands during the war, Stalin's inner circle introduced a fundamentalist ideological course in the post-war period. In order to redirect the population's understanding of their place in Soviet society, perceptions contaminated by the German occupation and by hopes for a better post-war world, the Soviet leadership had to reconfigure its borders and to purify its new and old citizens.

9

Stalin's Ukraine, 1945–1954

War is not a chess game, but a vast social phenomenon with an infinitely greater and ever-expanding number of variables, some of which elude analysis.

David Galula[1]

The Second World War killed tens of millions, devastated the world economy, forcibly moved millions across continents, and reconfigured Europe's borders and national homelands, especially in East Central Europe. With the destruction of Germany, the Soviet Union created a new regional order in Europe based on the principles of Marxism-Leninism and on Russian national interests. Forged in the first few years after 1945, Soviet control of East Central Europe lasted until the revolutions of 1989. Even with the disintegration of the Marxist multinational federations of the Soviet Union, Yugoslavia, Czechoslovakia, and Serbia into smaller units after 1989, most of the boundaries the Allies established in the immediate post-war period remained until early 2014, when Russia's President Vladimir Putin started to challenge the international post-war order.[2]

The war's horrendous death toll, post-war border changes, and population transfers created a newer, more stable Europe, solidified by Cold War divisions. Its political architects imagined that the newly created equilibrium on the continent would reinforce their own political and social systems. "This war is not as in the past," Stalin lectured Milovan Djilas, a prominent Yugoslav communist, in 1945. "Whoever occupies a territory also imposes his own social system ... It cannot be otherwise."[3] Territorial acquisition and border rectifications would enhance Soviet security; the expansion of this shield would guarantee the survival of this new political and social order not only in East Central Europe, but also in the Soviet heartland.

War Losses

The war's extensive mass atrocities triggered the construction of new frontiers. Of the nearly forty million deaths in Europe, approximately 70 per cent occurred on the eastern front, where the Germans waged an extremely brutal war.[4] Almost twenty-seven million Soviet citizens (including men, women, and children) died during this conflict. This estimate includes "servicemen and partisans who were killed in action or died of wounds, ordinary civilians who died of hunger or disease or were killed during air raids, artillery shelling and punitive actions, and prisoners of war and underground fighters who were tortured and shot in concentration camps."[5] Of these twenty-seven million, the armed forces of the USSR suffered a loss of 8.7 million men and women between 1941 and 1945. But the civilians represented the overwhelming majority of the Soviet war dead, over 18.3 million, according to this conservative account.[6] Most of the civilians, as chapter 8 demonstrates, did not die as an accidental by-product of the war. The Nazis planned to annihilate the Jewish and Romani populations, and as Heinrich Himmler, the head of the dreaded SS, asserted, they arranged to bring the civilian population in the East "to a minimum."[7] In addition to these losses, the Germans forcibly drafted nearly five million Soviet men and women to work as slave labourers in Germany.[8] Twenty-five million became homeless.[9]

The most brutal areas of the Soviet-German conflict in the East took place in Poland, Ukraine, and Belarus. Civilian losses in Poland reached at least 18 per cent of its pre-war population, and in Belarus around 25 per cent.[10] By the end of the war, half of Belarus's population experienced death, expulsion, deportation, or evacuation, the highest of any European country.[11] The territory of the Ukrainian SSR constituted about half of the area of the Soviet Union under German occupation and experienced the destruction of 40 per cent of its natural wealth.[12] If Belarus lost a higher percentage of its civilian population than any other European state or Soviet republic, Ukraine lost the highest absolute number.[13]

According to the best available analysis, the Ukrainian SSR experienced a total of 13.8 million human losses, including a net out-migration of 2.3 million, a deficit in births of 4.1 million, and a loss of 7.4 million due to exceptional mortality, including the murder of approximately 1.7 to 1.8 million Jews. The Soviet occupation of Western Ukraine, the German-Soviet War, the German occupation, and Soviet repressions during the war produced these catastrophic results.[14]

Although Ukraine lost approximately 15 per cent of its total population, demographers – according to Barbara Anderson and Brian Silver – cannot estimate the direct losses individual Soviet national groups experienced during the chaos of war.[15] Soviet authorities did not provide a breakdown by nationality of Soviet casualties during or after the war. They identified the war's victims as "Soviet" citizens. Because of the republic's geographic position at the western borders of the USSR, Ukrainians (who comprised nearly 76 per cent of the republic's population in 1939) must have suffered disproportionately more casualties within their own republic than any other national group, with the exception of the Jews in Ukraine and the Belarusans in Belarus. Despite Stalin's post-war claims, in fact, more Jewish (above all), Belarusan, and Ukrainian civilians more likely had been killed on Nazi-occupied Soviet territory than Russians.[16]

In addition to deaths of millions of civilians and military personnel from Ukraine between 1939 and 1945, this republic also experienced waves of deportations, evacuations, and forced labour conscriptions, which removed millions from its soil. Not all of the deportees, evacuees, or conscripts survived the war, and, of those who did, not all returned home.[17] Migrants from other republics replaced them. The war and population transfers, as Anderson and Silver pointed out, resulted in a disproportionate change in the sex ratios of many non-Russian nationalities in the western republics and "appears to have accentuated and accelerated the process of Russification" in the post-war period.[18]

The absence of large numbers of males forced the Soviet state to attract as many as possible from outside Ukraine, especially in administrative positions. With the enormous losses the Soviet Union experienced, the government and party concentrated on replacing men in the urban centres, not the countryside, which in turn drove the changes in the national composition of the Ukrainian SSR over the long term. Many of those who administered Ukraine before the war and who were evacuated in the summer of 1941 returned. The majority of newcomers and evacuees must have identified themselves as Russians. This expedient solution would bring more Russians into Ukrainian cities in the post-war period and reinforce the number of Russian speakers in them.

The brutal war produced radical demographic changes. While the number and percentage of those who identified themselves as Ukrainians increased slightly between the 1939 and 1959 censuses, the number and percentage of Russians increased dramatically. In 1939, Russians constituted 13 per cent of the population of Ukraine (or 4,175,300). In 1959, as the first post-war census recorded, they comprised 17 per cent (or 7,090,810). Ukraine's Jews suffered the most extensive losses during the war and some migration to Poland after the war. They experienced a sharp decline in their percentage of the total population between the two censuses, from 5 per cent of the republic's population (1,532,776) in 1939 to 2 per cent in 1959 (840,311). In light of the war's extermination of the Jewish population in Ukraine, the overwhelming majority of Ukraine's Jews in 1959 must have arrived after the war ended or returned after their evacuation. The Polish population increased only slightly, from 357,710 in 1939 (before the war) to 363,297 in 1959. (These censuses did not take into account the Soviet Union's acquisition of a large number of Poles in 1939 and their repatriation to Poland in 1945–6.) The 392,458-strong German population in 1939 did not appear as a national category in the 1959 census.[19]

Besides the devastation unleashed by the war, the population of the Ukrainian SSR experienced other demographic convulsions between the Soviet censuses of 1939 and 1959. Border changes and coerced population exchanges within the Ukrainian SSR, between Ukraine and Poland, and between Ukraine and the rest of the USSR also helped transform the national composition of the Ukrainian SSR in the post-war period. In April 1944, after the Red Army retook the Crimea, Stalin deported the entire Crimean Tatar population, most of them to Uzbekistan.[20] The NKVD also removed the majority of Armenians, Bulgarians, and Greeks from the peninsula. Following in the footsteps of the deportations of the German and Polish populations in the 1930s, these wartime expulsions targeted national groups the authorities considered disloyal to the Soviet state. But the post-war population transfers overshadowed the ones conducted before and during the war.

Borders and Population Changes

With the victory over Germany in 1945, the Allied leadership reconstructed the borders of Germany and the countries of East Central Europe, boundaries which their predecessors had established between 1919 and 1921 at the Treaty of Versailles and at the Treaty of Riga. By redefining the new frontiers, the Allied leaders sparked large-scale and coercive migrations between contiguous countries, solidified the post-war contours of Central and Eastern Europe, and reconfigured the national compositions of these countries. Between 1943 and 1948, nearly thirty million Europeans were forced the leave their homes permanently.[21]

In negotiating the occupation and reconstruction of post-war Germany at Potsdam in the summer of 1945, Joseph Stalin, Harry S. Truman, and Winston Churchill (replaced by Clement Attlee after Churchill lost the 2 July election) formally endorsed the expulsion of the Germans from East Central Europe, where they had lived for the past millennium. Within a short period, the newly established communist and coalition governments in Poland, Czechoslovakia, Romania, Yugoslavia, and Hungary, with the help of the USSR, forcibly deported at least twelve million and as many as fourteen million Germans to occupied Germany.[22] Despite Potsdam's official promise that the transfer of populations would take place in an "orderly and humane manner," between 500,000 and 1.5 million Germans died during these merciless treks.[23] Even the victorious Allies embraced the idea of collective guilt.

As the predominant military and political force in East Central Europe after the war, the USSR transformed its map. Poland, which sided with the Allies and emerged as one of the war's winners, came out "22 percent smaller than it had been before the war, while Germany, which lost the war, was 18 percent smaller."[24] The Soviets moved the borders of Poland 200 to 300 hundred kilometres west to the Oder-Niesse Rivers. Poland incorporated the eastern areas of Germany and permanently lost its own eastern territories to Soviet Belarus, Soviet Ukraine, and Soviet Lithuania, almost half (47 per cent) of its pre-war territory.[25] Soviet authorities then forced approximately 2.15 million Poles and 150,000 Jews to leave the territories annexed by the Soviet Union and relocate to Poland.[26] The new Polish government moved the displaced Poles and Jews to the western areas the Germans evacuated. At the same time, approximately two million Poles – forced labourers, POWs, and previous emigrants – returned from the West. Most migrated to Poland's newly acquired western lands.[27] Because Poland had lost its eastern borderlands, "the west was all the most precious."[28]

At the same time that Poland acquired a new Polish population, those who did not identify themselves as Poles were expelled. By 1946, Polish authorities forced approximately 482,000 Ukrainians to leave Poland for Soviet Ukraine.[29] Two-thirds settled in the newly annexed Ukrainian territories and one-third in southern and eastern Ukraine.[30]

The majority of Ukrainians who lived in Poland lived on the frontier areas between Poland and the Soviet Union. These territories included Podlachia, the Lemko Region, and the Sian Region, collectively known as Zakerzonnia, the Transcurzon Lands (the area behind the Curzon Line, a proposed armistice line between Poland and Soviet Russia during their

1919–20 war); it became – with some slight modifications – the Soviet-Polish border after the Second World War.

On the eve of the Second World War, these areas contained a large Ukrainian population (500,000 identified themselves as Ukrainians, with 200,000 who belonged to the Roman Catholic faith, but spoke Ukrainian). The USSR did not annex this territory after the war, but facilitated a large-scale population exchange of Zakerzonnia's Ukrainian population. Despite the Soviet-Polish (TWJK) "voluntary" population transfer agreement of September 1944, most of the Ukrainians in Zakerzonnia did not want to move to the Ukrainian SSR.[31] But the Polish and Soviet governments wanted to uproot them en masse.

A weak OUN-B/UPA force in the area decided to stay and to help defend the Ukrainian population. For the OUN-B and UPA, they understood that if their compatriots left, it would be difficult to claim or defend this territory. If the Ukrainians disappeared, OUN and UPA would not be able, as Mao Ze Dong eloquently put it, to "move amongst the people as fish swim in the sea." In the long run, the armed resistance would not survive. Not surprisingly, the OUN/UPA viewed all Ukrainians who voluntarily registered with the Poles to transfer to Ukraine as traitors and dealt with them by means of violence or threats of violence.[32]

Once the Soviet and Polish security forces forcibly evacuated the local population, OUN/UPA units burned down abandoned Ukrainian villages (so that Poles transferring from Eastern Galicia and Volhynia could not get access to them) and came into conflict with the communist military units. In early 1947, they killed the Polish deputy defence minister, Karol Świerczewski.

Beyond defending the Ukrainian population in Zakerzonnia, OUN-B and UPA did not make any claims to Polish-majority areas in the newly reconstructed Poland. They recognized that these territories belonged to Poland and that the majority Ukrainian-speaking territories, such as Zakerzonnia, should belong to Ukraine. Unfortunately for the Ukrainians and the Poles, nationally mixed areas (such as Chełm/Kholm, Zakerzonnia, Wołyń/Volhynia, and East Galicia) always provoked irreconcilable conflicts over which group should rule the region in question. The new post-war Polish-Soviet border split the first two areas from the second two and both governments sought to homogenize the remaining populations.

The process of creating a nationally pure Poland culminated in the spring and summer of 1947 with the Soviet-sponsored military operation, Operation Vistula (*Akcja Wisla*) against the Ukrainian population of southeast Poland, an area which harboured extensive UPA resistance.[33]

During the largest post–Second World War military operation in Poland, the Soviet Union supervised the brutal transfer of the remaining 140,600 Ukrainians in Poland's southeast to the newly acquired Polish western territories[34] (see map 9). Poland's new elite justified its internal war against the Ukrainians by assuming the latter group's "collective guilt."

As a consequence of these border changes, population transfers, and the Nazi extermination of the Jews, Poland became a nationally homogeneous state. According to demographic analyses of Poland's first post-war census in December 1950, Poles and Roman Catholics constituted 97 per cent of the population, a far higher percentage than in 1931.[35] Although most Poles distrusted their new pro-Soviet government, they approved of these population transfers and the addition of the "recovered territories" in the west, helping entrench communist rule in East Central Europe.[36]

Ukraine also experienced extensive border changes. Soviet authorities had already incorporated Eastern Galicia and Volhynia from Poland and Bukovina and Bessarabia from Romania into the Ukrainian SSR before the end of the war and Transcarpathia from Czechoslovakia in 1945. (Only small numbers of Ukrainians remained in these countries after these boundary rectifications.) With the conclusion of the Second World War, Stalin and his colleagues united the majority of Ukrainians living in East Central Europe into a single Soviet republic, a highly popular move among those Ukrainians living in territories under Soviet control since 1920, but not necessarily among those annexed after 1939.[37]

These border changes, however, did not transform the Ukrainian SSR into a nationally homogeneous entity.[38] After 1945 Ukraine remained nationally diverse, but regionally homogeneous. In the post-war period, it contained four different sets of territories. The western Ukrainian territories, those areas the Soviet Union acquired from Poland, Czechoslovakia, and Romania in 1939–45, became more Ukrainian demographically.[39] In the central, agricultural regions under Soviet control since 1920, the percentage of those who identified themselves as Ukrainians also increased in the 1939–59 period.[40] Yet, the industrial eastern and southern regions under Soviet control since 1920 became more Russian (with the exception of Zaporizhzhia and Mykolaiv/Nikolaev and the city of Kiev)[41] (see map 10). As the authorities reconstructed one of the major industrial heartlands of the USSR after the war, they transferred many Russian and Russified cadres to Ukraine's eastern and southern regions.

The war's casualties and the post-war population transfers established different clusters of "tipping points," that critical mass needed to maintain the Ukrainian language and culture or to abandon it.[42] These demographic changes and the introduction of new institutional arrangements provided a limited social and political menu of options. The masses could make choices after 1945, but only from the list the Soviet authorities provided them.

The Second World War brought immense population changes to Ukraine. With the expansion of the Ukrainian SSR to the west, Kiev now occupied a critical geopolitical position in the centre of Ukraine. As a consequence of its location and post-war reconstruction, Kiev's population grew, surging ahead of Kharkiv, Donetsk, and Odessa. Not only did Kiev enhance its position as Ukraine's "primate city" in the post-war period, it also attracted a majority Ukrainian population by 1959, increasing it in subsequent censuses.[43]

Soviet Post-War Policies

The war's end raised an important, if unspoken, set of questions. How would the Soviet post-war political leadership govern a large, multinational state and economically reconstruct it? How would it integrate the Western Ukrainian and Western Belarusian territories annexed from Poland, Romania, and Czechoslovakia, not to mention Estonia, Latvia, and Lithuania, into the USSR? How would it fuse the various pre-war institutions and political cultures in these areas into a coherent, workable Soviet whole? In what ways would the party maintain ideological purity and focus after the most devastating war in human history? These questions would prove difficult to answer.

For most Soviet citizens, the end of the "Great Fatherland War" inspired hope for the future. Many assumed that the authorities would reward their horrible sacrifices of the 1930s and 1940s, especially the brutalities of collectivization, the famine, and the war. Many looked forward to a less repressive and ideologically driven post-war regime.[44] But Andrei Zhdanov, the head of the Communist Party's ideology section, sought to redirect this anticipation. He led the party's post-war assault on all alleged deviations from socialist realism in the arts, literature, and cinema. Zhdanov and his successors sought to strengthen Soviet "civic emotions" (which included love and gratitude to Stalin and to the Soviet state for their "gift" of life and well-being) and public rituals (which involved Stalinist celebrations, political education, demonstrations of patriotism and hatred of the enemy in the workplace and in the streets, and electoral campaigns and election day itself). These party leaders believed that the public's expression of these emotions and constant participation in these communal rituals served as an indicator of a person's level of integration into the Soviet political system (not necessarily a true reflection of his or her beliefs). Although Soviet citizens found a number of subtle ways to undermine these processes of integration, their public accommodation to them helped shape the post-war Soviet and non-Russian national identities.[45]

Shortly after the war, the authorities also raised everything Soviet and/or Russian above everything non-Soviet or non-Russian. Everything "progressive" in the world originated in Russia. These exaggerated claims reflected the ruling elite's apprehension about the potential attraction of foreign, especially Western, ideas and living standards to the millions of Soviet citizens, especially *Ostarbeiters*, POWs, and soldiers, who had encountered them in Europe. According to the Moscow writer Konstantin Simonov, "The contrast between the standard of living in Europe and among us, a contrast which millions of military people encountered, was an emotional and psychological shock."[46] Even in relatively poor countries of East Central Europe, such as Romania and Poland, the ordinary person lived better than most in the Soviet Union. Zhdanov and his colleagues had to neutralize the psychological impact of these mass experiences before they undermined the Soviet political order. The end of the war would not bring an ideological demobilization or a permanent reconciliation with the United States and Great Britain. In the international realm, the class struggle would continue under new conditions and with new alliances. In the domestic realm, the class struggle reappeared in the newly annexed Soviet territories in the west.

Fighting the UPA

Although the Red Army recaptured the Ukrainian-speaking regions of the western borderlands in 1944, the communist control of these areas extended only to the cities, railroad lines, and strategic military bases. Only after the final victory over Germany in May 1945 did the Soviet government send larger Red Army detachments to fight the Ukrainian Insurgent Army (UPA). But because these military units included many Ukrainians in its ranks, special Interior Ministry (NKVD) troops quickly replaced them. By August 1946, the anti-guerrilla units in Western Ukraine included thirty-four thousand NKVD troops, augmented by the same number of local militia, and a few thousand district policemen. Although the military rarely participated in counter-insurgent operations, the authorities stationed several Red Army divisions in Western Ukraine, just in case.[47]

The Bandera faction of the Organization of Ukrainian Nationalists (OUN-B), a deeply rooted underground network enjoying popular support, organized the largest anti-Soviet resistance movement in East Central Europe. (The Polish Home Army disbanded on 19 January 1945, after the Red Army cleared Poland of most German military forces.) At the peak of its strength in 1944, OUN-B's Ukrainian Insurgent Army attracted between twenty-five thousand and forty-thousand guerrillas and a much larger group of active supporters who procured supplies, collected intelligence, distributed propaganda, and provided medical services, numbering perhaps 400,000 men and women in all.[48]

It is difficult to characterize the typical Ukrainian insurgent, but from the limited records that the UPA commanders created, which survived the conflict, and which were discovered in the archives after 1991, one can establish a provisional profile of the men and women (predominantly men) who entered the ranks of the Ukrainian guerilla movement in Volhynia in 1943–4.[49] Of the ten thousand guerillas in UPA-North, in the "Bohun" military district, records concerning 1,445 men and women survive. Of these, the overwhelming majority (1,133) came from Volhynia; the rest from outside the region. As a territorially based guerilla movement, UPA units often remained close to the areas its rank and file lived in.

Who joined UPA in Volhynia between July 1943 and January 1944? The overwhelming majority (98.3 per cent) of the 1,445 men and women identified themselves as Ukrainians. Over 90 per cent were born in the rural areas or small towns, and a greater part (75 per cent) completed a fourth-grade education or less (the educational opportunities in Volhynia for Ukrainians in the 1930s and 1940s were limited). Before joining the UPA, nearly all of its members engaged in agricultural pursuits and most (70 per cent) were young, between the ages of eighteen and twenty-eight. Three-fourths were unmarried and, if married, without children. The majority never experienced life in uniform.[50]

Most had enlisted in the UPA after the Soviet victories at Stalingrad and Kursk, during the Polish-Ukrainian conflagration in Volhynia in 1943–4. All opposed the return of the pre-war Polish regime as well as the Soviets. Although the overwhelming majority came from families with small, subsistence landholdings, they opposed the collective farm system. They had much to lose when the Soviets would return and reinstitute collectivization, introduced in this region between 1939 and 1941. Significantly, a majority (57.9 per cent) did not possess any previous military experience before joining UPA, which suggested that they did not have any formal relationships with the German occupiers. Of the 42.1 per cent who had served in the military, the majority (59.4 per cent) had worn Polish Army or Red Army uniforms. Of those who acquired training with arms, only 25 per cent had served in the German police, the Wehrmacht, the SD, or German fire brigades; the rest (the older ones) fought in the tsarist army or the army of the Ukrainian National Republic.[51]

The UPA's rank and file attracted new recruits for a wide variety of reasons. Many joined to defend their homes, small plots of land, and families from the Poles and Soviets, who engaged in an informal (if not formal) alliance after July 1941, at least in this region. Not all who joined this anti-Soviet effort shared the OUN-B leadership's view of the world; many Soviet draft evaders and deserters from German units joined the guerillas out of desperation. The fear of arrest and deportation also stoked anti-communist feelings. Many had openly expressed their hostility towards the Soviet regime during the German occupation or worked with the Germans in one capacity or another and had no alternative. If they did not leave during the German retreat, they now had to hide and/or to fight to preserve themselves.

Once young Ukrainian peasants joined UPA, they entered the world of the damned. Unless they surrendered to the Soviets and cooperated fully with them, there was no going back. They could not return to their villages or resume their lives as peasants. Only a total victory would assure their ultimate physical survival. "Victory or Death" became their mantra after mid-1943.

Although small OUN-B and UPA units reached Stalino, Sumy, and other parts of Eastern Ukraine, the Ukrainian resistance concentrated its activities in Galicia and Volhynia, its home base. OUN-B and UPA established contacts with nationally conscious Ukrainians in central, northern, and southern Ukraine during the German occupation and sought to raise the local population's political awareness.[52] Most Ukrainians in Eastern Ukraine, even if they possessed a highly developed national consciousness, recognized that once the Germans lost Stalingrad the struggle for an independent Ukraine became a hopeless cause.

The German atrocities in Reichskommissariat Ukraine and the victorious return of the Red Army outweighed memories of the Holodomor, the purges, and the deportations of the 1930s. In the people's prioritization of memories, the most recent horrors of the German occupation took precedence over those of the Soviet past. The Soviet state, moreover, would never recognize the trauma of the Holodomor. But it constantly condemned Nazi evils and commemorated Soviet victory over the fascists on a regular basis, reinforcing the differences between the memories of those who experienced the Romanian occupation in Transnistria and the German rule over the Galician District and those who survived the war in Reichskommissariat Ukraine or in the German Military District to the east. Although all of these men, women, and children had encountered similar losses and traumas during the conflict, the Soviet regime authorized only one public memory of the war and consigned the other one to the private sphere, hoping it would die out with the older generation.

Since most UPA members came from Galicia and from a peasant background, they thrived on the terrain most hospitable to them, areas which the Soviet military and NKVD did not control completely. The steppes did not work; the forests, mountains, and swamps of Western Ukraine did. Unlike the Ukrainians from Eastern, Southern, or Central Ukraine (who survived Erich Koch's Reichskommissariat Ukraine), Galician Ukrainians, who experienced a more lenient German occupation (in relative terms) in the General Government, developed a different set of memories and came to a different set of conclusions about the return of the Soviets. Ukrainians who survived life in the General Government remembered the Russian occupations during the First World War, the famine of 1932–3 in Eastern Ukraine, and the Soviet repressions and efforts to introduce collectivization in the newly annexed areas in 1939–41. Despite efforts by the Soviet regime to institutionalize a common memory of the "Great Fatherland War," the memories of these negative Russian and Soviet experiences took precedence over the memories of the humiliations and indignities they may have experienced under German occupation.

Inasmuch as the OUN-B and UPA could not outfight the Soviet army, they initiated hit-and-run actions. In the first few years after the war, they planned to remain in place until the international correlation of forces changed in their favour. The leadership as well as a significant majority of the OUN-UPA rank and file expected the outbreak of another world war. In their view of the world, the anti-Nazi British-American-Soviet alliance represented a temporary marriage of convenience. Once the war ended, each state would reassert its pre-war interests, which would lead to an armed conflict between the British and the Americans, on the one hand, and the USSR, on the other. The Western Allies would push back the Soviets and then the Ukrainian nationalists, army ready, would re-establish an independent Ukrainian state. This strategic logic on the part of the OUN-UPA leadership inspired their recruits, much in the same way that fervent communists believed in the inevitability of Soviet victory even in the darkest days of the war. Each group believed that the forces of history were on their side. Many members of the OUN and UPA fervently believed that they had to confront the Soviet regime only for a short period of time until the outbreak of a new war between the USSR and the Western powers. Although a completely logical assessment of the conflicting tensions within the anti-German alliance, they could not know how the war exhausted these democracies and that their wary voters would not support an effort to overturn the Soviet domination of East Central Europe shortly after the surrender of the Germans and the Japanese. The illusion of Western intervention nourished OUN's and UPA's true believers until the late 1940s.

Although UPA's leaders came from the urban middle and lower middle classes, the rank and file came from the countryside. Most of the peasants who voluntarily or involuntarily joined the guerrillas came from families with two to five hectares, households which opposed collectivization.[53] As members of a traditional agrarian society, they wanted to protect their modest households, fixed landholdings, and unmovable crops from the Soviets and "to be left alone."[54]

The fear of the reintroduction of collectivization fuelled anti-communist sentiments more than any other anticipated Soviet action.[55] The Soviet commitment to collectivize agriculture challenged local farming traditions. These peasants, less educated, more conservative, and more religious than urban residents, possessed small landholdings, their primary livelihood.[56] They had struggled against adverse economic conditions and against wealthy Polish landowners for nearly a century after Austria's emperor emancipated them in 1848. They would not give up easily. Many of the peasants in the UPA ranks supported the Greek Catholic Church and opposed its forcible merger with the Russian Orthodox Church in 1946 (see below).

Ukrainian peasants supported the armed nationalist cause as long as they believed the guerrillas would protect them from the Soviets. But the UPA could not win against the largest army in Eurasia. Between 1944 and 1946, these guerrillas killed over 16,000, mostly civilians, no comparison to the huge losses (114,200 killed and 130,715 arrested) they suffered in the same period.[57] These losses (which included a large number of innocent bystanders and draft evaders) shocked the local population, making UPA's active and passive supporters realize that they could not defeat the Soviets without external intervention, which – despite the West's increasing Cold War rhetoric – would not be forthcoming.

With a mixture of limited agrarian reform and massive repressions, the Soviet government undermined the alliance between the nationalists and the peasants and the peasant solidarity in the countryside. With the start of collectivization in 1948–9, the UPA may have regained some of its earlier popularity, but guerrilla attacks on collective farms and the destruction of communal property deprived the peasants of their livelihoods and turned them against the insurgents.[58] This scorched-earth policy became counterproductive.

The longer the Soviets stayed in the western regions, the more time they invested in implementing their counter-insurgency doctrine, honed during the Civil War and in the 1930s. Its major components included the repression of "class enemies," agrarian reform, deportations, occasional amnesties of guerrilla fighters, and the creation of pro-Soviet volunteer militias. These efforts produced results.[59]

Between 1944 and 1952 Soviet military and security forces killed over 153,000 alleged OUN/UPA operatives, arrested over 134,000, and exiled over 203,000 of their family members from Western Ukraine.[60] Of the insurgents killed in this period, two-thirds died between February 1944 and 31 December 1945. During this lopsided conflict, Soviet forces allegedly lost less than 10 per cent of the insurgent casualties.[61]

To stop the local Ukrainian population from supporting the UPA, the NKVD started to deport entire villages to Siberia, as well as all relatives of the insurgents in the spring of 1944. Most were sent to hard-labour camps in Siberia to work in tree-felling operations (essentially a death sentence for anyone sentenced to a ten- or twenty-five year incarceration). In addition to the expulsion of families of suspected OUN/UPA members between 1944 and 1952, the Soviet authorities also removed alleged kulaks, Jehovah's Witnesses, and former members of the Polish Home Army.[62] During this period, the new ruling elite resettled many Western Ukrainian peasants and young people to Eastern Ukraine's steppe region and the Donbass, and many Ukrainians from Eastern Ukraine to Western Ukraine. Many voluntarily resettled Ukrainians from Poland's Zakerzonnia also ended up in Western Ukraine. In addition to these population transfers, the NKVD engaged in mass trials and executions of suspected OUN/UPA members.

In the midst of these repressions, the Soviet Ukrainian government declared seven amnesties between 12 February 1944 and 30 December 1949. The government hoped to peel away their ideologically less-committed enemies (such as the above-mentioned draft evaders and deserters) from the true believers.[63] In many respects, these efforts succeeded. From February 1944 to July 1946, for example, 114,809 fugitives surrendered, the majority claiming to have avoided mobilization into the Red Army.[64] In response to these amnesties, "the OUN killed hundreds of former insurgents, their relatives, and the guerrillas who were merely suspected of intending to desert."[65] The underground sought to prevent the local population from cooperating with the Soviet government by "publicly killing those who collaborate[d], intimidating others who might seek to work with the government."[66] As in most guerrilla wars, those who swore to protect the local population now had to kill some of its members to preserve the very existence of its own organization. Without the organization, they reasoned, there would be no armed resistance to the Soviets. This merciless conflict would not conform to any ethical standards. In less than a decade after the Soviet return to Western Ukraine, the government's repressions, reforms, amnesties, and constant pro-government propaganda attracted "the passive part of the population and intimidate[d] rebel supporters into neutrality."[67] The ruthless Soviet application of force and incentives in the context of nearly ten years of Soviet/German/Soviet occupations exhausted the local population's passive endorsement of the guerrillas.

Without Western intervention, members of Ukrainian society, including the peasants, concluded that armed resistance represented a lost cause. They understood that the Soviets had more troops, were better armed, and that – in light of the Russian occupations of 1914–17, the Holodomor, the Soviet occupation of 1939–41, and the prison massacres of 1941 – they were more powerful and more effective than the Poles and could be more lethal than the Germans. They then reluctantly withdrew their passive and active support of the OUN and UPA.

Recognizing that the political dynamics favouring them had changed, the UPA leaders ceased guerrilla operations at the end of 1949. They could no longer implement their "exhaustion strategy of sapping the energy, resources, and support" of the Soviet government.[68] On 5 March 1950, Soviet security forces discovered UPA commander-in-chief Roman Shukhevych's hiding place by means of an elaborate NKVD counter-intelligence operation. Operatives surrounded the house, but Shukhevych recognized the entrapment, started shooting, then committed suicide.[69] Although armed resistance in Western Ukraine continued until 1953–4, it slowly petered out.[70]

Although the Communist Party operated within a rigid ideological framework that limited its options, its anti-guerrilla campaign in the newly annexed territories embraced flexible and innovative methods. Its successful covert operations, skilful intelligence-gathering operations, ruthless interrogations, and well-timed amnesties produced results.[71] "Operation Motria," for example, represented an astonishingly successful *Mission Impossible*–type counter-intelligence mission against a high-ranking female OUN official in Bukovina.

As the result of an NKVD operation in rural Chernivtsi Oblast in late December 1944, the security forces captured two prominent OUN officials in Bukovina: Artemiziia Hryhorievna Halytska (code name: "Motria"), a member of the OUN since 1937, and Myroslav Ivanovych Haiduk. Motria did not wish to be taken alive and attempted to commit suicide by shooting herself in the head. She survived and the NKVD took her to a hospital in Chernivtsi, where she again attempted to kill herself. Although physically weak, she steadfastly refused to participate in any interrogations.

In order to make her reveal the names of her many subordinates, the NKVD counter-intelligence unit launched an audacious plan. Posing as members of the OUN-B, they raided the hospital and took her to an underground location, where, representing themselves as representatives of the central OUN leadership, they thoroughly debriefed Motria about the contacts between the OUN in Bukovina and the central OUN leadership, information which Haiduk provided. As a result of this grand NKVD deception, the seriously wounded OUN leader revealed the names of hundreds of members of the underground. As a result, the Soviet security forces arrested 123 of them.[72]

Inasmuch as the Soviet regime had few enthusiastic supporters in the western borderlands in the first post-war years, its agents employed cunning, deception, amnesties, and mass violence, often simultaneously, to subdue the local population. The Soviets as well as the insurgents pressed the local population to take sides in public. When forced to choose between government violence and guerrilla violence, the peasants increasingly sided with the stronger opponent, the Soviet state, so as to break the vicious cycle of violence and chaos.

If the potential benefits of opposing the Soviets in the early post-Soviet period outweighed the costs, by the late 1940s the costs of opposing the Soviets exceeded the potential benefits, which depended on the outbreak of a new conflagration and a successful Anglo-American invasion of the USSR. By the late 1940s, after employing these elementary rational calculations, the peasants concluded that they had to save themselves and their families by giving up the struggle against Soviet rule and submitting to the collective farm system.

Collectivization

Having largely won the counter-insurgency struggle against the UPA by the late 1940s, the Soviet government introduced the mass collectivization of agriculture at the end of 1948.[73] Modelled on the Soviet Union's collectivization campaign of the 1930s, the post-1948 drive sought to master the countryside completely without providing an interlude of economic moderation, as did the New Economic Policy of the 1920s.

Transcarpathia, the most isolated of the newly acquired Ukrainian territories, became the first to complete its collectivization drive by the spring of 1949.[74] Due to the party's weakness in the countryside and to the obstruction of the nationalist underground, it took another two years for the overwhelming majority of peasant households in Bukovina and Galicia to join collective farms. By early 1951, Soviet authorities claimed that 95.1 per cent of all households in the countryside belonged to these new rural organizations. In light of the extensive armed resistance by the UPA and the overall passive resistance by the Ukrainian population, the Soviets employed widespread violence to consolidate their control of the countryside.[75] As in Volhynia, both sides engaged in violence. Not surprisingly, the stronger force won.

Abolishing the Ukrainian Greek Catholic Church

In the course of the war, the status of the Russian Orthodox Church (ROC) within the USSR changed "from a probationary servant to junior partner of the state."[76] The ROC sought, with the government's help, to expand its authority at the expense of its religious rivals. The government also strove to eliminate its real, potential, and imagined adversaries. This confluence of interests in regard to the Ukrainian Greek Catholic Church would help define the relationship between the world's first atheistic state and the Russian Orthodox Church until the end of the Soviet era, if not beyond. In the course of the war, Soviet political authorities and the ROC forcibly dissolved the Ukrainian Autocephalous Orthodox Church (which resurrected itself during the German occupation in Eastern Ukraine after its 1930 suppression by the Soviet government). The more powerful Ukrainian Greek Catholic Church in Western Ukraine provided a bigger challenge.

In addition to the 4.3 million Greek Catholics who lived in those areas the USSR formally annexed in November 1939, 2 million Roman Catholics, 1.5 million Orthodox Christians, and 800,000 Jews also resided there.[77] With the decimation of the Jewish population during the war and the involuntary repatriation of the Poles and surviving Jews after the war, the Soviet authorities perceived the Ukrainian Greek Catholic Church as the greatest threat to their totalitarian aspirations.

Like all Catholic institutions in Nazi-occupied Europe, the Greek Catholic Church had to manoeuvre deftly between its moral demands and institutional imperatives in a fluid and oftentimes chaotic political environment.

The overwhelming majority of its faithful lived in Galicia, a part of the General Government. The German authorities favoured the Greek Catholic Church over the Polish Roman Catholic Church, which they actively persecuted. In this brutal and morally corrosive environment, Metropolitan Andrii Sheptytsky, the most respected Ukrainian in Galicia, had to negotiate among German demands, moral claims, and short-term and long-term Greek Catholic and Ukrainian interests. Inevitably (and conveniently), the Soviets interpreted his and his Church's cooperation under occupation with the Germans as collaboration.[78]

As early as the first Soviet occupation of Galicia in 1939–41, Stalin's emissaries covertly started the process of converting the Ukrainian Greek Catholic Church to Orthodoxy but did not officially tip their hand. During the Soviet reoccupation of Galicia and the occupation of Transcarpathia in 1944, the state security and party apparatus assembled the materials necessary to "prove" that the Greek Catholic Church had "collaborated" with the Nazi occupation authorities and their "allies," the OUN and the UPA.[79] In the first months after the return of Soviet power, the Ukrainian Greek Catholic Church did not experience persecution, primarily because of the Communist Party's concentration on winning the war and its efforts to initiate a diplomatic relationship with the Vatican, which increasingly expressed anti-Soviet positions.[80] In this period, the Communist Party of Ukraine urged the Church to help undermine UPA resistance and persuade the insurgents to accept the three amnesties the Soviet government offered in 1944–5.

Only after the death of Metropolitan Andrei Sheptytsky on 1 November 1944 did the Soviet government and ROC's Patriarch Alexius begin to pressure the Greek Catholic bishops and priests to break with Rome and to join the Russian Orthodox Church.[81] Joseph Slipy, Sheptytsky's successor, and his colleagues unanimously rejected this demand. In April and May 1945, the NKVD detained Slipy, five other bishops, and several prominent priests who refused to convert.

Shortly after the arrest of the church hierarchy, Alexius and the NKVD stage-managed the creation of an "initiative" group for Greek Catholic–Russian Orthodox reconciliation. Headed by the Reverend Dr Havril Kostelnyk, the pastor of St George's Greek Catholic Cathedral in Lviv, this group advocated a merger with the Russian Orthodox Church. By August 1945, 255 of the 1,997 Uniate priests had joined the initiative group; by March 1946 this number reached nearly 1,400, mostly due to government pressure, coercion, or blackmail.[82] The authorities continued to take into custody priests who refused to convert, accusing them of participation in the OUN/UPA resistance and collaboration with the Germans. Between 1945 and 1950, 344 Uniate priests were sentenced, typically to ten years' imprisonment, and several died during the pre-trial investigations. The police detained them in the context of the conversion campaign. For the authorities, their refusal to convert trumped any alleged anti-Soviet activities.[83]

With the symbolic support of the majority of the church's priests, Kostelnyk's initiative group organized a synod in March 1946, formally abandoning the Ukrainian religious institution's ties with Rome (which had existed since 1596), and officially returned "to the Holy Orthodox faith of our forefathers."[84] During this process, all of the imprisoned Greek Catholic bishops refused to accept this "reunion."

The OUN also denounced the synod's decision. Although the OUN leaders did not enjoy close ties to the church, they defended it in the immediate post-war period.[85] In July 1946 they threatened to execute those converted priests who would not repudiate their decisions and killed dozens. On 20 September 1948, the OUN assassinated Kostelnyk.[86]

In response to this ecclesiastical and secular resistance, Alexius established his own Orthodox hierarchy in Western Ukraine. He and the Soviet authorities applied their coercive measures in other areas and achieved comparable results. Similar religious mergers took place in Carpatho-Ukraine and in the Prešov/Priashiv region of Czechoslovakia. Many of the faithful boycotted the ROC, and priests secretly continued to conduct Catholic services. The Greek Catholic Church remained active in the underground until its re-legalization under Mikhail Gorbachev in 1989.

The Greek Catholic Church possessed strong roots in the local population and their allegiance to Rome. Stalin understood that these Christian believers would be difficult to integrate into the new Soviet order. Unlike the Ukrainians nurtured in an Orthodox environment, those raised in the Greek Catholic Church possessed a very significant internal component in differentiating themselves from the Russians. This psychological marker could easily be activated against the Soviet state. In the party leader's analysis of the problem, the bitter struggle with Ukrainian nationalism necessitated the abolition of the Greek Catholic Church in Western Ukraine.[87] Whereas the tsarist authorities failed to do so in 1914–15, Stalin did not.

Rebuilding the CP(b)U

In addition to fighting the UPA, collectivizing agriculture, and dissolving the Greek Catholic Church, the communist authorities also rebuilt and reassessed the Communist Party of Ukraine. The CP(b)U, possessing 637,000 members (63 per cent Ukrainian) in 1940, suffered enormous losses during the war.[88] With military demobilizations and party cadre transfers, the party's total membership reached nearly half of its pre-war level (320,000) by January 1946.[89] That year, 90 per cent of the party's current members entered its ranks within the last six years. Inasmuch as Soviet propagandists identified the defence of the socialist fatherland with Great Russian patriotism during the war, party recruitment in this period attracted more Russians than Ukrainians.[90] Nevertheless, by 1950, 59 per cent of the Communist Party of Ukraine's total membership identified themselves at Ukrainians.[91] In the course of the war, the CP(b)U emerged as an entirely new and untested party in need of a thorough re-evaluation.

In Stalin's Kremlin toast during the 25 May 1945 official victory celebrations over Nazi Germany, he honoured the Russian people, "the outstanding nation in the USSR," and started a post-war campaign to associate Ukrainian nationalists with the hated German occupation. As in the 1930s, the authorities employed the pejorative term "Ukrainian nationalist" very loosely, even attacking public expressions of the very Soviet Ukrainian patriotism they had promoted earlier.

In July 1946, the Soviet Central Committee blamed the CP(b)U's Central Committee for failing "to devote the proper attention to the selection and ideological-political education of cadres in the fields of science, literature, and art."[92] Many of the men and women in these important positions expressed a "hostile bourgeois-nationalist ideology" and attempted to reintroduce Ukrainian nationalist concepts, including Hrushevsky's interpretation of the history of the East Slavs. In response, the Ukrainian Central Committee promised to rectify all "errors and shortcomings" and condemned over one hundred Ukrainian intellectuals.[93] These attacks intensified in 1951 and continued into the first half of 1953. Unlike the 1930s, however, mass arrest and terror did not follow. Perhaps this lull represented a respite before Stalin unleashed a new wave of purges on the heels of a public trial exposing the "saboteurs" who were posing as doctors.

The CPSU's Central Committee directed this crusade not only against Ukrainians, but also against other national groups, especially the Jews. In September 1948, the central party unleashed a furious wave of denunciations against Zionism, the state of Israel (founded on 14 May 1948), and Soviet "unpatriotic" Jews throughout the USSR. This so-called "anti-cosmopolitan" campaign of 1948–9 promoted public expressions of xenophobia, anti-Semitism, and strident Russian nationalism. Stalinist condemnations of "disloyal" Jews reached fever pitch with the so-called

Doctor's Plot in early 1953. The authorities accused nine prominent Soviet physicians (six of whom were Jews), who ministered to the Soviet elite, of "heinously" undermining the health of their patients and preparing to kill them. *Pravda*, the Communist Party's daily newspaper, claimed that the "doctor-poisoners" worked for the American and British intelligence services. Luckily for them and for the entire Jewish community, which expected deportation from the Soviet Union's largest cities, Stalin died on 5 March 1953, just before their show trial was scheduled to start.[94]

In contrast to the 1920s and 1930s, when Jews were over-represented in the Communist Party of the Soviet Union and the Communist Party of Ukraine, in the post-war period all Soviet institutions limited their entry into the party, the universities, and specialized schools. The post-war CPU increasingly became a party containing only Russians and Ukrainians.

Population Transfers and Education in Western Ukraine

With the war's end, primary and secondary schooling emerged as one of the Soviet state's first priorities in the newly annexed western provinces.[95] During the 1944–5 academic year, 1,018,290 students attended primary and secondary schools in these provinces, four hundred thousand less than the number during the 1940–1 school year.[96] According to the Ministry of Education of the Ukrainian SSR, the mass transfer of Polish students to Poland, the absence of enough teachers, and the harmful activities of "the Ukrainian-German nationalists" contributed to the decline of student enrolment.

In establishing the Soviet model of education in Western Ukraine, the political authorities vetted the local teachers and found them wanting. They discovered two-thirds of all the teachers "unqualified" and demanded they attend "ideological" retraining classes. Between 1945 and 1951, Kiev sent almost 35,400 teachers to Western Ukraine from Eastern Ukraine. By 1947, teachers from Western Ukraine comprised only 54 per cent of the total number of teachers in this region. Nevertheless, 93 per cent of elementary and secondary school students received instruction in Ukrainian.[97]

In monitoring the teachers and the curriculum, the Soviet state would use the educational system as a tool to create a new Soviet man, *homo Sovieticus*. From Moscow's perspective, the older generation was ideologically contaminated before and during the war. Children, especially the younger ones, represented a blank slate. By taking youngsters out of the home for several hours, then providing after-school activities for them, the Soviet state would have the prime opportunity to inculcate its values to a new generation and transform the problematic Western Ukrainian society over the long run.[98] "Those who own the youth," after all, "own the future."[99]

Concomitantly with these ideological declarations, the authorities dramatically expanded Russian-language education in Western Ukraine for Ukrainians and for the burgeoning Russian population. Prior to 1939, very few Russians lived in this region.[100] Now, according to the census of 1959, the number of Russians was 246,000, or about 6 per cent of the total population of Western Ukraine.[101] Not only did the Russians and Russified Ukrainians from Eastern and Central Ukraine constitute a good number of post-war administrators and leading communist cadres in this region, they also comprised most of the recently arrived skilled workers and technicians. By 1947, the authorities created 249 Russian-language schools (out of 7,430 public schools) in Western Ukraine.[102]

Soviet authorities created twenty-two institutions of higher education in Western Ukraine. At first most provided instruction in Ukrainian. But under the leadership of Leonid Melnikov, the head of the Communist Party of Ukraine (1949–53), most of these institutions converted to Russian, even though the majority of students came from Ukrainian-speaking homes in Western Ukraine. Only the teachers' colleges and agricultural institutes offered Ukrainian-language instruction.[103]

Stalin's Death and After

Stalin's death on 5 March 1953 shocked most Soviet citizens. After thirty years of his rule, many people closely identified him with the Soviet state and the Communist Party, not just because of his officially generated "cult of personality." The majority throughout the USSR, including most Ukrainians, sincerely considered the passing of "our great leader and teacher, our real father and friend" a sorrowful occasion.[104] Not only Stalinist zealots, but also many that he repressed, such as Alexander Solzhenitsyn (a political prisoner at the time), expressed great loss over his passing, if only for show.[105]

If Stalin's death produced uncertainty for the people, it provoked an even greater crisis for the political elite. The Soviet leaders feared that the multinational state spanning eleven time zones Stalin had helped create would collapse. In their first speeches and in the mass media, members of the Communist Party of the Soviet Union's Presidium demanded "unity" and the need to strengthen the friendship of peoples of the USSR.[106] Editorials and articles published in the Ukrainian SSR echoed this overarching theme, still praising Stalin's role in the development of Soviet nationalities policy.[107]

Of all of Stalin's potential successors, Lavrenty Beria – the long-time head of the NKVD – understood the necessity to liberalize the relationship between Moscow and the non-Russian republics. Possessing fewer allies in the Central Committee than either Georgi Malenkov or Nikita Khrushchev, his primary competitors, he had to acquire more in order to protect himself and to jockey for total power. He concentrated his efforts on Ukraine, especially Western Ukraine.

At the Nineteenth CPSU Congress in early October 1952, five months before Stalin's death, Beria emphasized the centrality of the nationalities issue and the need for the Soviet regime to recognize the equality of the non-Russians with the Russians.[108] He highlighted the problems in many recently acquired western borderlands, especially in Western Ukraine, where Russians and Ukrainians from Central and Eastern Ukraine administered the Western Ukrainian population and alienated them. Beria sought to win over the Ukrainian political and cultural elites to his moderate policies, undermining Khrushchev's authority over his former clients. Beria realized that in an age of worldwide decolonization, Soviet nationality policies had to respect the national diversity of the USSR and to offer its national groups, especially those on the western borderlands, carrots as well as sticks. Beria also understood that the Ukrainians would – and should – play an important role in the administration of the USSR.

Weeks after Stalin's death, Beria prepared a highly critical report to the party's Central Committee on the situation in Western Ukraine, advocating an end to the post-war policies promoting Russification. He called for the promotion of self-identified Ukrainians into the political and governmental leadership and the increased use of Ukrainian in the public sphere. His statement helped remove L.G. Melnikov, a Russian and the head of the Communist Party of Ukraine, and replace him with Oleksii Kyrychenko, the CPU's second secretary, the first Ukrainian head of this regional party in its thirty years of existence.

In the spring of 1953, Beria took an even bolder action in extending national rights in Western Ukraine. He transferred the leader of the Greek Catholic Church, Metropolitan Joseph Slipy, who was serving an eight-year sentence in a Mordovian prison camp, to Moscow. His emissaries initiated secret negotiations with Slipy concerning the possible normalization of Soviet relations with the Vatican and the legalization of the Greek Catholic Church in Western Ukraine.[109] Beria's moves on this issue sought to reverse the Stalinist policy of forcibly incorporating the Ukrainian Greek Catholic Church into the Russian Orthodox Church in 1946, a policy Khrushchev implemented when he headed the CPU.[110] The powerful interior minister understood how seriously this policy had alienated the Greek Catholic Ukrainian population of Western Ukraine from the Soviet regime. He imagined that overturning this policy might win him some support from the Western Ukrainian population and might smooth their integration into the Soviet system. After Beria's arrest in June 1953, the authorities ended the talks and sent Slipy back to prison.[111]

As Beria's moderate policies in East Germany rapidly unravelled in June 1953, Khrushchev used the East German crisis to mobilize opposition to Beria within the Presidium. Once Khrushchev rallied his colleagues against Beria and arrested him on 26 June 1953, the party's first secretary continued Beria's policies. The three hundredth anniversary celebrations of the Treaty of Pereiaslav and the "gift" of the Crimea to the Ukrainian SSR raised Ukrainians and the republic to a new, unprecedented level within the Soviet hierarchy.

At the deliberations of the emergency plenum of the Central Committee of the CPSU on 2–4 July 1953, party leaders accused Beria of many far-fetched crimes, such as being a long-term foreign intelligence agent. But of all of his "counter-revolutionary activities," Beria's efforts "to undermine the friendship of the peoples of the USSR, the very foundation of the multi-national socialist state and the most important condition for all the successes of the fraternal Soviet republics" received constant and repeated condemnation.[112] Khrushchev and his colleagues in the Presidium besmirched Beria's initiatives towards the non-Russians because they recognized he could possibly win their support and outmanoeuvre Stalin's old guard. Beria, after all, emerged as the first post-Stalinist leader to propose policies recognizing the dignity and equality of the non-Russians. After Beria's arrest, the party's leadership adopted most of Beria's proposed reforms concerning the non-Russian republics without crediting him.

At the July plenum in Moscow, Z.T. Serdiuk, the first secretary of the Lviv Oblast Committee of the CPU, first mentioned the Treaty of Pereiaslav, which Hetman Bohdan Khmelnytsky's Cossack Host signed with Tsar Aleksei Mikhailovich in January–April 1654.[113] In the midst of a major uprising against the Poles, this treaty transferred the allegiance of the Cossacks from the Polish-Lithuanian Commonwealth to Muscovy. "We are standing on the eve of a historic event," Serdiuk asserted, "the three hundredth anniversary of the union of two peoples – Russian and Ukrainian. Russians and Ukrainians hand-in-hand fought for centuries against our enemies, and here Beria wanted to sow strife."[114] At the plenum, no one else commented on Serdiuk's observation. Nevertheless, the CPSU soon embraced this forthcoming anniversary in order to reassert the "friendship of peoples" within the USSR and to propagate a new, rebranded, and more inclusive nationalities policy.

Reports in the Soviet Ukrainian press about this holiday appeared shortly after Serdiuk's speech. According to the evolving paradigm encompassing this anniversary, the history of Ukraine was intimately intertwined with
that of Russia. "Only thanks to the help of the great Russian people the
workers of Ukraine overthrew the landlords and the capitalists, and established a Soviet government. Only with the great friendship of all Soviet
peoples did Soviet Ukraine blossom and reunite all Ukrainian lands in a
single state."[115] The treaty now became a teleological model not only for the
progressive and mutually enriching history of Russian and Ukrainian relations from Kiev Rus to the period of acquisition and incorporation to the
present, but also for the relationship between the Russians and all the non-
Russians. According to organizers of this celebration, Pereiaslav represented a permanent "reunion" of the Russian and Ukrainian peoples, not a
"union" or a temporary military alliance.

On 12 January 1954, newspapers throughout the USSR published the
full joint CPSU-Soviet government decree concerning the anniversary.
This decree placed the Ukrainians at centre stage within the Soviet pantheon of nations, codifying a new hierarchy within the old paradigm of the
"friendship of peoples." It presented the history of Ukraine, from Rus to
the present, in broad, sweeping strokes. Each historical event conformed
to the overarching theme, the ever-evolving friendship between the
Russian and Ukrainian populations, "two great kindred Slavic peoples."[116]
These quotes highlight the idea that Ukraine possessed a long history with
Russia and that these ties were, are, and will be permanent and inviolable.

Not only were celebrations scheduled throughout the USSR, but also in
the new People's Democracies established by the Soviet Union in East
Central Europe after the war.[117] *Radians'ka Ukraina* announced that even
Poland would celebrate the Treaty of Pereiaslav, an agreement which
helped undermine the Polish-Lithuanian Commonwealth in the seventeenth century and which led to Poland's partitions in the eighteenth.[118]

To highlight the importance of the treaty, the Presidium of the Supreme
Soviet of the USSR approved the transfer of the Crimean Oblast from the
RSFSR to the Ukrainian SSR on 19 February 1954. This peninsula, comprising an area of 27,000 square kilometres (10,425 square miles), adjoined
Ukraine, but always belonged to the RSFSR. Now, in light of its location
and close economic ties with Ukraine, this oblast would come under the
authority of Kiev. M.P. Tarasov, the chair of the Presidium of the RSFSR
Supreme Soviet, claimed that on the occasion of the tricentennial celebrations this transfer "will help further strengthen the fraternal ties between
the Ukrainian and Russian peoples and conforms to the over-all interests of
the Soviet state."[119] Kyrychenko, the first secretary of the Communist

Party of Ukraine and Khrushchev's protégé, asserted that with the incorporation of the Ukrainian-speaking lands of East Central Europe into the Ukrainian SSR in the first half of the twentieth century, Soviet Ukraine emerged as one of Europe's largest states. "Territorially, Ukraine is larger than France, almost twice as large as Italy and considerably richer than either of these countries ... The sovereign Ukrainian Soviet state has emerged in the international arena," Kyrychenko reminded his audience.[120]

Beyond the grandiloquent speeches, the facts remained. Moscow decided to transfer the Crimea to the Ukrainian SSR; Kiev formally endorsed it. Khrushchev played the central role in "conceiving the idea and timing its implementation."[121] Although Khrushchev at this point in time did not completely control the CPSU, his colleagues agreed to allow him to take the lead in concentrating public attention in the direction of the Ukrainian SSR and the Ukrainians.[122] In doing so, Khrushchev re-established his control over the Ukrainian party and provided his clients in that republic with the proper rewards.

Khrushchev, most likely, would not have initiated these pro-Ukrainian policies on his own. Beria provoked Khrushchev, who quickly came to understand the importance of the Ukrainian political elite in the context of the post-Stalinist succession struggle. Khrushchev outmanoeuvred Beria in the first half of 1953 and Malenkov by 1955. Although Beria did not initiate the process of de-Stalinization single-handedly (most of his colleagues in the Presidium agreed that some changes were necessary after Stalin's death, but they disagreed over which ones), he led the charge to provide the local non-Russian elites with more autonomy.

Building on Beria's criticisms of the violations of Soviet nationalities policies, the extensive anniversary celebrations represented a serious attempt to reintegrate the Ukrainians into the Soviet framework. Surpassing all other celebrations of the incorporations of non-Russian groups into the Russian Empire or into the USSR, the Ukrainians would be somewhat more equal than the other peoples of the USSR, but less equal than the Russians. The Ukrainian SSR would serve as the USSR's "second Soviet republic." Ukrainians – in effect – became the junior partners of the Russians in administering the USSR.[123] To highlight this new relationship, the Communist Party leadership transferred the Russian Federation's Crimean Oblast to the Ukrainian SSR, the largest territorial shift from one republic to another in the history of the USSR.

At this point in time, the Crimea was no prize. The peninsula still bore the scars of war with a shattered infrastructure and an unreconstructed economy. Its 1959 population was 50 per cent lower than its 1939 population. In light of the war's casualties, war evacuations (the Germans), and

Soviet deportations (the Crimean Tatars, Bulgarians, Greeks, and Armenians), Crimea lost its rich, multicultural composition and became a predominantly Russian-speaking, unicultural one.[124] If the Ukrainian SSR acquired nearly nine million Ukrainian speakers from Poland, Romania, and Czechoslovakia between 1939 and 1945, it also received nearly 700,000 more Russian speakers with its 1954 Crimean gift. Even Stalin might have approved.[125] Despite the absorption of large numbers of Ukrainians into the Ukrainian SSR in late 1939, the percentage of Ukrainians remained the same in both the 1939 and 1959 censuses – between 76 and 77 per cent of the total population. The war swept away most of Soviet Ukraine's new citizens.

By early 1954, the territory of the Ukrainian SSR reached the peak of its expansion and would emerge in this form after the 1 December 1991 referendum on independence. Lenin, Stalin, and Stalin's successors built on the vision first dreamed in the nineteenth century and on the Ukrainian national movement's achievements in 1917–20. Finally unified in 1954, this land mass possessed a population divided by regions with different cultural, linguistic, national, and religious ways of interpreting the world. The Soviet state sought to integrate these divergent orientations into a single, centralized ideology allied with Moscow, not to create nationally homogeneous non-Russian republics.

Conclusion

Although Stalin fought all real or perceived manifestations of "Ukrainian nationalism," he persuaded Franklin Roosevelt and Winston Churchill to accept the Ukrainian SSR and Belarusian SSR as founding members of the United Nations. Despite the fact that the Ukrainian SSR did not possess true sovereignty and did not play a role independent of the USSR, it became an internationally recognized political entity.

The Soviet Ukrainian Republic's participation in this international organization reprised the paradoxes generated by its establishment in 1918 and its entry into the USSR. The Soviet Union remained a unitary state with a federal facade. But this political entity, a symbol of the apparent institutionalized equality among Soviet nations, took on a life of its own, especially with the post-war increase in the levels of urbanization and educational standards throughout the USSR. These socio-economic developments coincided with the worldwide decolonization process, as Europe's African and Asian overseas colonies, most with populations smaller than Ukraine's, started to gain their independence. China, long castrated by the Western powers, became a united and truly sovereign state under the auspices of the Chinese Communist Party. In the post-war period, Soviet

Ukrainian diplomats at the UN, alongside their colleagues from the USSR and Soviet Belarus, vociferously defended (despite the obvious ironies involved) the right of national self-determination and decolonization.[126]

Soviet Ukraine's joining the USSR as a "sovereign" republic in 1922 and the United Nations in 1945 raised the question of the meaning and the implementation of the term.[127] In the context of the Soviet Union, what did Ukraine's national sovereignty represent? To what extent did "socialist sovereignty" and the international concepts of sovereignty and national self-determination (especially in the era of mass decolonization) converge and diverge? After Stalin's successors wound down his reign of terror, this question begged a thoroughgoing response.

Conclusion

In mental life nothing which had once been formed can perish – that everything is somehow preserved and that in suitable circumstances ... it can once more be brought to light ... on condition that the organ of the mind has remained intact and that its tissues have not been damaged by trauma or inflammation.

Sigmund Freud[1]

Each of the total wars and revolutions in the first half of the twentieth century generated enormous and unprecedented human losses, igniting large-scale political crises within empires, countries, and regions across the world. These states of emergency, Peter Gourevitch emphasized in a different context, "pry open the political scene, throwing traditional relationships into flux. Groups, institutions, and individuals are torn loose from their moorings, their assumptions, their loyalties, 'cognitive road maps.' Circumstances become less certain, and solutions less obvious. Crises thus render politics more plastic."[2] In this political freefall and subsequent social chaos, new openings, opportunities, and possibilities emerged, if only for a short period, forcing people to reassess their identities and their political relationships. Each of these massive social conflagrations weakened or completely shattered civil society's capacity to resist the encroachment of various authoritarian regimes, their introduction of rigid political categorizations based on national, state, and social identities, and their sweeping social engineering projects, launched to "improve the human condition."[3] The total wars in East Central Europe, more so than the ones in the West, triggered new borders as well as a radical set of psychological readjustments and social realignments.[4]

The total wars and revolutions of the twentieth century represented the "critical junctures" in the development of modern Ukraine.[5] Between 1914

and 1954 the Ukrainians and non-Ukrainians living there endured an un-
paralleled and almost uninterrupted cycle of constant mobilizations and
demobilizations, divisions into separate and oftentimes antagonistic national groups, and mass violence. Each of these major turning points produced widespread psychological unmoorings, as people lost their sense of
place in the world. The First World War, the subsequent revolutions and
Civil War, and the famine of 1921–2 initiated the first of four great psychological traumas during the past century. Industrialization, de-kulakization,
collectivization, the famines of 1928–33, and the purges ushered in the second. The Second World War, the Holocaust, and the famine of 1946–7,
which generated millions of deaths, deportations, and voluntary and involuntary population transfers and migrations, inaugurated the third. The
collapse of the USSR, Ukraine's independence, and its uneven adaptation
to the standards of the international political economy precipitated the
fourth mass behavioural disorientation.

As empires collapsed and fell in 1917 and 1918, the new states emerging
throughout East Central Europe and the Russian Empire not only redrew
their borders, but also challenged the loyalties of the men and women who
lived within them. New states introduced new policies which favoured
some of their citizens and discriminated against others. This process of
political breakdown, social disorder, and political reassembly forced the
peoples of Ukraine to examine the fundamental nature of their land, its
borders, and who constituted their compatriots. Although Ukraine represented a homeland for Ukrainians, it also served as a homeland for many
non-Ukrainians, making the process of Ukrainian nation building and
state building difficult and contentious. This conflict over which groups
and which ideology had the right to define Ukraine raised the brutal level
of violence this region endured to unprecedented heights. In the first half
of the twentieth century, mass violence diffused new ideas, options, and
alternatives, and acted as the primary agent of change in East Central
Europe. Over the long run, the unintended consequences emerging from
one crisis often helped to ignite the next.[6] Each catastrophe enhanced
Ukraine's role as a geopolitical pivot and as a cleft state.

Geopolitical Pivot

In an age of long, total wars, Austria-Hungary, Russia, Poland, Romania,
Germany, and the USSR struggled to control Ukraine's land and, most
importantly, its natural resources, especially its bountiful grain supply.
Each grain-consuming state in Europe wanted to secure a food base to

provide the necessary calories to its population, its military and civilians alike. Foodstuffs became a significant factor in this new type of conflict – just as important as oil, if not more so.

With the start of the First World War, the Triple Entente and the Triple Alliance possessed both grain-producing and grain-consuming territories. In the Allied camp, the British and the French were grain importers; the United States – an economically self-sufficient country – supplied them during the war. Germany, the most populous grain-consuming state in Central and Western Europe, also desperately needed grain, but did not a possess a friendly source.

Although the Austro-Hungarian and Russian empires included large grain-producing regions which fed enormous armies, geographic and political circumstances transformed those regions from assets into liabilities. In the case of Austria-Hungary, Hungary remained the Dual Monarchy's major agricultural zone. As antagonisms between Hungary and Austria intensified during the war, Hungarian officials obstructed efforts to feed the Austro-Hungarian armies and diverted their grain to nourish their own towns and cities. Britain's naval blockade prevented Austria from acquiring more grain from overseas and Austrian cities began to starve long before those in Germany or Russia.

The Romanov Empire also experienced problems with its food supply, but not at first. Once the Ottoman Empire declared war on Russia in November 1914 and closed the Bosporus and the Dardanelles, Russia could no longer import Allied supplies or export grain to Europe. Nevertheless, Russia experienced a lopsided and unsustainable economic boom during the war, radically expanding its urban labour force by at least one million by January 1917.[7] By employing the railways, the authorities could initially feed their troops and urban populations far better than any of the war's belligerents, even without the proper storage facilities. But in the course of the long conflict, the railway system also experienced serious problems. The mismanagement of train routes and timetables, not just the deterioration of the rolling stock, caused enormous bottlenecks.[8]

In the course of the war, the southern grain-producing zones of the empire, such as the Ukrainian provinces and Turkestan, could no longer adequately feed the northern grain-consuming industrial zones, such as Petrograd and Moscow. In response to the drop in their standard of living, peasants reduced sowing grain for the market. In light of the rapid increase in the population of the urban centres, the demand for food in the cities outstripped available supplies, and inflation skyrocketed. Starvation in the cities and hunger among front-line troops undermined the war effort, and helped ignite the revolutions of 1917, which heralded the German, Austro-Hungarian, and Ottoman victory over the Russian Empire. In and of itself, the food crisis did not make the Russian Empire collapse. Instead, the food crisis highlighted the autocracy's political failures, "with the war serving to radicalize and extend existing political fissures."[9] Tsarist Russia could not satisfy the economic and, most importantly, the political demands of modern war.[10]

The war and the severe economic downturn delegitimized the Romanov dynasty, replacing it with a Provisional Government. The new regime's continuation of an unpopular war in the face of pressing social demands radicalized millions. Many of these angry and frustrated men and women then embraced what they earlier may have considered extremist solutions, such as nationalism or Bolshevism. Shortly after the Bolsheviks took power in November 1917, Lenin insisted that his political party end the war with the Central Powers in order to save Soviet Russia from certain collapse. The second Treaty of Brest-Litovsk (signed on 3 March 1918) accomplished this mission, but at a very high price. Although the final agreement brought the Great War to an end on the eastern front, the powerful German army also created a new world order in the east. The treaty tore Finland, the Baltic provinces, Poland, Ukraine, and Transcaucasia from Soviet Russia: 3.37 million square kilometres (1.3 million square miles) of territory with a total population of sixty-two million.[11] With the stroke of a few pens, the new Soviet revolutionary state lost 34 per cent of its population, 32 per cent of its agricultural land, 85 per cent of its beet-sugar regions, 54 per cent of its industrial infrastructure, and 89 per cent of its coal mines, much of it concentrated in the new Ukrainian National Republic.[12] Not only did Germany gain control of East Central Europe from the Arctic Ocean to the Black Sea, it also acquired access to new and vast resources of petroleum and wheat after negotiating separate agreements with Romania and Ukraine. In planning to feed their own burgeoning urban populations and military forces, Germany and Austria-Hungary hoped to win the war against the British, French, and Americans on the western front.

Within the context of total war, Germany's, Russia's, and Austria's "food problems" became internationalized and Ukraine's agricultural output, beet-sugar production, industry, and coal mines took centre stage in the conflict between Russia and the Central Powers. The brutal efforts to control this area and to acquire Ukraine's harvests drove the aggrieved peasants to rebel against their subordinate status, resist outside intervention, and reconsider their identities and political loyalties. In the revolutionary period, the Ukrainian national movement promised them "home rule," "national self-determination," and more land.

In competing with the Ukrainian nationalists, the Communist Party established a new political organization, the Ukrainian Soviet Socialist Republic, within the same boundaries as the Ukrainian National Republic and even created a separate, semi-autonomous communist party for the region. Although the Central Rada first delineated the borders of Ukraine and gained partial international recognition at the two Treaties of Brest-Litovsk, Soviet Ukraine consolidated these lines of demarcation, institutionalized them, and included the Donbass and other industrial centres within them. For the first time in its modern history, the region's agricultural and industrial areas belonged to a single administrative unit, congruent with the territory where the majority of Ukrainians lived. Many Russians, Jews, Germans, and Poles also resided there.

The communists created Soviet Ukraine, but would not have done so had the Ukrainian movement and the Rada failed to mobilize the population in the turmoil generated after the tsarist regime fell. Bolshevik leaders did not intend their Soviet state-building project to nurture separatism. After their mission to ignite a world revolution failed, they sought to establish "socialism in one country" within a multinational political entity. By recognizing the national diversity within the USSR, the new authorities believed that they could best propagate their revolutionary message at home and abroad.

In the course of its seventy-five years in power, the Communist Party of the Soviet Union conducted both "nation-building" as well as "nation-destroying" operations on its Russian and non-Russian populations.[13] These all-encompassing experiments reflected the Communist Party's profoundly transformative mission, to move the diverse peoples of the Soviet Union through all of the stages on the Marxist timeline of historical development to the final communist stage.[14] In light of the Soviet Union's economic backwardness, the party designed enormous and radical economic and social schemes necessary to accelerate the process. These ambitious plans would provoke opposition, but the party would crush them. The forces of "history," after all, favoured the communist interpretation of the past, present, and future.

The USSR sought to overcome the social inequality and the economic backwardness of its past in order to triumph over the Western capitalist powers and to create this brave new world. The new revolutionary state inaugurated ambitious modernization projects, provided health care to the masses (which resulted in lower birth and death rates), improved the role of women, abolished religious institutions and created a secular order, transformed its agricultural economy into an industrial one at an enormous human cost, and dramatically expanded its urban populations. Within a short period of time, the Soviet authorities turned a highly illiterate society into a highly literate and well-educated one. While 51 per cent of all Soviet men and women nine years old and older attained literacy by 1926, 81 per cent did so by 1939, if these statistics are accurate.[15] By 1970, the majority of the Soviet population, including those in the Ukrainian SSR, lived in cities and urban centres.[16]

Despite the Bolshevik commitment to the ideology of proletarian internationalism, both Lenin and Stalin understood that national identities would not immediately disappear, not even under socialism. The Great War and the worldwide revolutions and civil wars that followed in its wake demonstrated that a rising tide of nationalism, not class war, had swept the world.

In responding to this challenge, Bolshevik leaders sought to construct a new type of state. As it emerged in the early 1920s, the USSR comprised a set of overlapping national-territorial and economic-administrative units, connected by the party, a network of union-wide institutions, and five-year economic plans.[17] Although the new political entity appeared as an empire containing many nations, its political leadership defined it in anti-imperial terms. The Communist Party of the Soviet Union, which possessed a permanent monopoly on power, served as the state's administrative coordinator, ideological watchdog, and political enforcer.

In addition to setting up the national-territorial structure of the new state, the Bolsheviks promoted a limited national consciousness of its non-Russian populations and established for them many of the institutional foundations of the nation-state, such as precise territories, standardized languages, and national elites and cultures.[18] As long as these "forms" of nationhood would not conflict with the goals of a unitary central state, this strategy (which Terry Martin dubbed "The Affirmative Action Empire") sought to disarm nationalism.[19] Communist Party leaders, in effect, wanted to depoliticize national identities within the USSR, identities which the Great War, the revolutions of 1917, and Civil War mobilized and politicized.[20] Although the non-Russian republics would not possess any more autonomy than any administrative unit in the RSFSR, the Soviet state recognized and even celebrated each republic's non-Russian nationhood. As Richard Pipes first predicted in 1954, this structure would produce unforeseen circumstances.[21]

The Bolsheviks wished to do more than to depoliticize national identities. They sought to prepare the Soviet Union for the communist stage of history by promoting a policy which Francine Hirsch called "state-sponsored evolutionism." This strategy possessed several short-term goals:

to overcome the tsarist imperial legacy of the past, to "assist" the potential victims of Soviet economic modernization, and to differentiate the Soviet state from the "imperialistic empires" it ideologically opposed. To propel the entire population of nearly 150 million "through the Marxist timeline of historical development, to transform feudal era clans and tribes into nationalities, and nationalities into socialist-era nations – which, at some point in the future would merge together under communism" – comprised its long-term mission.[22] Soviet leaders imagined that they would implement this policy by means of persuasion. If logical arguments and negotiations would not work, violence and terror would follow.

This state-sponsored evolutionism possessed two interactive stages. In the first, the authorities would introduce a highly diverse multi-ethnic population to the categories of nations and nationalities. Simultaneously, in the second, they would assimilate those nationally categorized groups into the Soviet framework.[23]

Due to the ideological challenge of Nazi racial theories and to the potential threat of Japanese and German encirclement, this dual-integration process accelerated in the 1930s.[24] In light of the centrifugal orientations in the non-Russian republics, the Soviet state then gave primacy to the Russians and intermingled the ideology of proletarian internationalism with Russian state interests.[25] In response to Japan's and Germany's resurgence in the 1930s, the Soviet state persecuted "diaspora" nationalities, such as the Germans and the Poles, and hardened official attitudes towards the Ukrainian SSR and its political elite.[26] Here, the Soviet authorities limited the national content of this homeland, which bordered the hostile West.

In constructing the USSR, the Communist Party imagined that it could control both the form and the content of national identities within the first socialist state. But by the 1930s, these national forms and contents also changed. Although the national-territorial divisions of the USSR remained, the Soviet state de-emphasized the role of the Ukrainian language and culture, and completely remoulded the Soviet Ukrainian political and cultural elites. The Holodomor, the purges, the Second World War, and the post-war population exchanges played an important role in pruning the Ukrainian body politic of those who emphasized dividing the world into "us" and "them" along national, not class, lines.[27] In assessing the state of Ukrainian national attitudes at the end of the 1930s, Sylvia Gilliam concluded that in Eastern Ukraine the regime promoted a "cultural pride devoid of aspirations of national independence."[28] In light of the mass arrests and executions of the Ukrainian political and cultural elites, this result is not surprising. The brutality of the Second World War reinforced these trends. Until Mikhail Gorbachev's selection as the party's secretary general in 1985, the Soviet post-war political order sustained and even expanded this effort to create neutered national identities.

National identity, much like nationalism, is a "state of mind" which can be activated and deactivated internally depending on the situation, the political environment, the contacts with others, and the opportunities and incentives available.[29] The form and content of national identity are closely intertwined. But national consciousness can emerge even without its forms (officially recognized territories, languages, elites, and cultures), although with great difficulty.[30]

The Soviet Ukrainian Republic became a quasi-sovereign state within the Soviet Union and one of its founding member-states. Although the central authorities curbed this limited sovereignty by the end of the 1920s and early 1930s, the Soviet Ukrainian state remained a "subversive institution" (as Valerie Bunce phrased it) throughout its seven decades of existence, due primarily to its organization as a multinational republic and as the homeland for all Ukrainians.[31] Ukrainization and the radical industrialization program reconfigured the Russian-, Polish-, German-, and Yiddish-speaking towns and cities of Ukraine into Ukrainian- and Russian-speaking ones. These policies created an urban, Ukrainian, and educated elite, a far larger and more assertive ruling group than any in the past in this region. A small number of its most prominent members advocated their own version of national communism and home rule. By the late 1920s, Stalin vociferously objected to their vision of the Ukrainian SSR within the USSR and to their defence of the peasantry.

Collectivization, the Holodomor, and the purges also reinforced Ukraine's geopolitical importance as a republic bordering the contentious Polish frontier and as the Soviet Union's primary granary. In order to transform the USSR into a garrison state to ward off potential German, Polish, and Japanese attack, the Soviet state had to import Western technology and arms and invest in heavy industry, but did not possess access to long-term foreign credits.

To compensate for this financial deficiency, the USSR had to expand its sale of grain on world markets. But as the overproduction of grain sank world grain prices during the 1920s and the Great Depression, the Soviet political leadership decided to squeeze more grain from the peasantry, launching a war against the kulaks, then against all who worked the fields. By herding the peasants into collective farms and setting procurement goals for future harvests, the party hoped to create larger harvests more efficiently and to extract more from the countryside. But the peasants, even in fertile Ukraine, could not meet these highly arbitrary targets set by bureaucrats in Moscow, Kharkiv, or Kiev. Forced collectivization, high grain procurements, and brutal Soviet punitive actions led to famine and the death of over four million men, women, and children.

Whereas the USSR justified its efforts to subjugate the countryside in the context of a worldwide class struggle, Nazi leaders openly boasted that Ukraine would serve as Germany's primary food colony. Hitler asserted in 1939 that "I need Ukraine, so that no one is able to starve us again, like in the last war."[32] He and his subordinates hoped that Ukraine "would produce enough food not only to feed the army, but to supplement the food supply within the Reich."[33] To prevent German starvation, the Nazis planned to deprive the non-German populations of East Central Europe and the USSR of food. They targeted those "useless eaters" who lived in the cities. Nazi Germany's food crisis accelerated the implementation of the Final Solution against the Jews and the deliberate starvation of the Soviet and Polish urban populations.[34]

With Germany's successful invasion and occupation of Ukraine in 1941, Nazi political and military leadership did not take into account Germany's and Austria's frustrating interventions in Ukraine in 1918.[35] Nazi ideology, which celebrated Germans as "the superior race," foreclosed the option of dealing with the local Ukrainian population on the basis of respect. The occupational regime did not dismantle the hated collective farms Stalin erected, but continued to extract grain from them for their own purposes. The military, officers as well as rank-and-file soldiers, internalized Nazi racial theories and humiliated and abused the local population, needlessly alienating them. The *Ostarbeiter* program estranged them even more. Not surprisingly, in light of such behaviour, the Germany army in Reichskommissariat Ukraine could not secure sufficient quantities of food to cover its own needs, much less feed Germany.[36]

In the era of total war, Ukraine's geographic location and its natural resources, especially foodstuffs, enhanced its role as a critical geopolitical pivot. Without Ukraine's grain, no European state which did not possess the resources to feed its own armies over a long period could win control of East Central Europe or aspire to world power.

Divided State

The total wars and revolutions of the twentieth century also reinforced Ukraine's national divisions. By mobilizing millions of heretofore politically uninvolved Ukrainian speakers in the First World War, Russia and

Austria inadvertently converted their peasant conscripts into political actors and introduced their soldiers and civilian populations to a new total war mentality. Each of the subsequent wars and revolutions built on this psychological foundation and mobilized national and social identities.

The total wars (in their traditional state vs state and internal war incarnations) not only generated enormous human losses and border changes, but also mobilized national identities. If most residents of the Ukrainian provinces entered the twentieth century with multiple identities, most at century's end embraced a single exclusive one. The First World War and revolutions ignited this process. States introduced procedures to assess their citizens, categorizing them and dividing them into friends and foes.[37] Their political establishments and security organs did not tolerate national, cultural, or religious connections to outside powers, and during the world's conflagrations, they demonized their internal and external enemies, dehumanized them, abused them, and exterminated them.

The First World War, the revolution, the civil and national wars, and foreign occupations devastated the population in the Ukrainian-speaking territories of the Russian and Austro-Hungarian empires. In the late 1920s and 1930s, the mass violence unleashed by collectivization, mass deportations, the Holodomor, and the purges decimated the Ukrainian population of Ukraine and the USSR, and to a lesser extent the German and Polish populations.

In the course of the Second World War the Germans killed by bullets, bombs, gas, or starvation 6.5 to 7.4 million men, women, and children (most of whom identified themselves as Ukrainians), including nearly 1.7 million Jews.[38] The Soviets removed hundreds of thousands from the Crimea and from the newly annexed territories of Eastern Poland and Romania. On the shifting frontiers between the German and Soviet armies, in Volhynia, the OUN/UPA and the Polish Home Army fought a very brutal war which did not spare the Polish, Jewish, and Ukrainian populations.

The war's political and demographic shifts set the stage for a new postwar environment. Ukraine remained nationally diverse, but regionally homogeneous, divided into five different sets of territories. Each group established different clusters of "tipping points," that critical mass needed to maintain the Ukrainian language and culture, abandon it, or modify it. The differences between Western Ukraine/Central Ukraine and Eastern Ukraine/Southern Ukraine grew stronger even before the USSR Supreme Soviet's transfer of the Crimea (with its predominantly Russian population) from the RSFSR to Ukraine in 1954. Southern Ukraine, a highly nationally mixed region since the eighteenth century, lost large numbers of

its national minorities in the 1930s and during the war. With its incorporation into the Ukrainian SSR in 1954, the Crimea acquired an inherently
Russian identity that outlasted the demise of the Soviet Union.[39]

Even after their incorporation into the USSR, Bukovina, Galicia, and
Transcarpathia retained a "unity in negation." These Ukrainian-speaking
territories did not experience long-term Russian rule; they had developed
within the framework of the evolving Habsburg constitutional order (although Transcarpathian Ukrainian and Rusyn speakers did not enjoy the
same political environment as did the first two crownlands).[40] Under the
Habsburg umbrella, these economically impoverished territories produced a vibrant and pluralistic civil society.

Acquired by Romania, Poland, and Czechoslovakia, these three
Ukrainian-speaking territories remained divorced from the Soviet political sphere, which between the wars endured "some of the most radical
socio-economic changes known to history, and in the 1930s it experienced
systematic, extensive terror that threatened to eradicate Ukrainian national culture completely."[41] The Ukrainians from these territories possessed
highly differentiated levels of national consciousness and different intensi-
ties of feelings of religious cultural superiority or inferiority regarding the
Russians and Poles.[42] This Western Ukrainian legacy remained for decades
afterwards, undermining Soviet efforts to integrate these territories politically as well as psychologically.[43]

In the first half of the twentieth century, Ukraine symbolized one of
Europe's most volatile social laboratories, a borderland which suffered
human slaughter on a ruthless and unprecedented scale.[44] The political and
social experiments performed here transformed the peasant, rural, and illiterate way of life to a highly urban and educated one in less than a century. Within this timeframe, Ukraine – a multicultural region with a
majority Ukrainian-speaking population – became primarily a bicultural
(Ukrainian/Russian) state with a majority of its population identifying
themselves as Ukrainians, although not necessarily Ukrainian speakers in
their personal and professional lives.

The brutality of the Second World War solidified these trends, and the
Soviet post-war political order sustained and even expanded this effort to
create neutered national identities. In the post-war era, new socio-economic
currents and party policies simultaneously promoted greater integration
and greater fragmentation throughout the USSR and the Ukrainian SSR.[45]

Most importantly, how the citizens of Ukraine perceive their own past,
current status, and future of their political community will determine the
expansion or contraction of the Ukrainian nation. The incentives for

individuals to identify themselves as Ukrainians in an increasingly globalized and alienating world remain in flux, as they did in the past and as they will in the future. Mass perceptions of group worth, economic backwardness, feelings of equality with (or inferiority to) the Russians, and standards of personal and national dignity fluctuate and remain difficult to measure and map in a fluid social environment; they remain "incessantly open to interpretation and renegotiation."[46] As in the past, unforeseen crises may produce unexpected responses.

Mass violence, a dynamic interplay of negotiations of the meaning of its indigenous national identities, contradictory state policies, and the ever-shifting international political order made and remade Ukraine in the first half of the twentieth century. Wars, revolutions, radical social dislocations, and tensions between the elites and the masses as well as tensions within these groups in this period helped pave the painful road to modernity. These events and trends reinforced Ukraine's role as a pivotal cleft state, its rifts long institutionalized within the framework of the Soviet Ukrainian state. At the start of the twenty-first century, many in Western Ukraine perceived that their future lay with the European Union and the West; many in the eastern provinces envisaged closer ties with Russia. But this cleftness is not necessarily a permanent feature of Ukraine's political anatomy. Russia's invasion of the Crimea in late February 2014 and its subsequent annexation of this peninsula have radically changed the political dynamics between Russians and Ukrainians in Ukraine and between the citizens of Ukraine and Russia.

As this narrative illustrates, past trends do not necessarily predict future outcomes. Although the assertion that tomorrow is uncertain "is obvious," according to James C. Scott, "so is the capacity of human actors to influence this contingency and help shape the future."[47] The past and present provide a foundation for the future, but more often than not, these tectonic plates shift unexpectedly and reshape the political environment in unanticipated ways, especially when cataclysmic events and new ideas arouse the masses. As independent Ukraine's political and cultural elites struggle to acclimate themselves to the demands of a ruthless international political and economic order, the Ukrainian project – the wager to reinforce the psychological boundaries between Ukrainians and Russians, to join pan-European institutions as an equal partner, and to acquire direct access to the larger world – still remains a work in progress.[48] The 2014 Euromaidan Revolution and the current Russian war against Ukraine may have accelerated these processes.

Archival Abbreviations

RGAE   Rossiiskii gosudarstvennyi arkhiv ekonomiki (Russian State Archive of the Economy), Moscow, the former TsGANKh (Tsentral'nyi gosudarstvennyi arkhiv narodnogo khoziaistva SSSR), the Central State Archive of the National Economy of the USSR (1961–June 1992).

RGASPI   Rossiiskii gosudarstvennyi arkhiv sotsial'no-politicheskoi istorii (Russian State Archive of Socio-Political History), Moscow, the former RTsKhIDNI (the Russian Center for the Preservation and Study of Records of Modern History.

TsDAHOU   Tsentral'nyi Derzhavnyi arkhiv hromads'kykh ob'iednan' Ukrainy (the Central State Archive of Civic Organizations of Ukraine), Kiev.

TsGANKh   See RGAE.

TsGAOR USSR   Tsentral'nyi gosudarstvennyi arkhiv Oktiabr'skoi revoliutsii Ukrainskoi SSR (the Central State Archive of the October Revolution of the Ukrainian SSR), Kiev, now: Tsentral'nyi Derzhavnyi arkhiv vyshchykh orhaniv vlady ta upravlinnia Ukrainy (Central State Archive of the Leading Organs of Government and Administration of Ukraine [TsDAVOVUU]).

VPN 1939 goda/ 1937 goda   *Vsesoiuznaia perepis' naseleniia 1939 goda/Vsesoiuznaia perepis' naseleniia 1937 goda* [All-Union Census of 1939 and All-Union Census of 1937] (Woodbridge, CT: Research Publications [Primary Source Media]; and Moscow: Federal Archival Service of Russia, 2000) (microfilm at the Library of Congress, Washington, DC).

Notes

Introduction

1 Martin Malia, *History's Locomotives: Revolutions and the Making of the Modern World* (New Haven, CT: Yale University Press, 2006), 5. Timothy Snyder's *Bloodlands: Europe between Hitler and Stalin* (New York: Basic Books, 2010) generally follows Malia's model of ever-spiralling violence, but the author starts his argument with the 1920s in the USSR, not Europe in 1914.

2 Quincy Wright, *A Study of War*, 2nd ed. (Chicago: University of Chicago Press, 1965), 303–11.

3 Richard Overy, "Total War II: The Second World War," in *The Oxford History of Modern War*, ed. Charles Townshend, new updated ed. (New York: Oxford University Press, 2005), 139.

4 General Erich Ludendorff, the German First Quartermaster General in 1918, coined the term "total war." See his *Der totale Krieg* (Munich: Ludendorffs Verlag s.m.b.h., 1935). A.S. Rappoport's translation, *The Nation at War* (London: Hutchinson, 1936), mistranslates "totalitarian" for the German word "totale" (total). For short review of total war, see Jeremy Black, *The Age of Total War, 1860–1945* (Lanham, MD, and Boulder, CO: Rowman and Littlefield, 2010).

5 Michael Mann, "The Role of Nationalism in the Two World Wars," in *Nationalism and War*, ed. John A. Hall and Siniša Malešević (New York: Cambridge University Press, 2013), 173.

6 R.J. Rummel, *Death by Government* (New Brunswick, NJ: Transaction, 1994); Martin C.J. Bootsma and Neil M. Ferguson, "The Effect of Public Health Measures on the 1918 Influenza Pandemic in U.S. Cities," *Proceedings of the National Academy of Sciences of the United States of America* 104,

no. 18 (1 May 2007): 7588; Geoff Eley, "Remapping the Nation: War, Revolutionary Upheaval and State Formation in Eastern Europe, 1914–1923," in *Ukrainian-Jewish Relations in Historical Perspective*, ed. Peter J. Potichnyj and Howard Aster (Edmonton, AB: Canadian Institute of Ukrainian Studies, 1988), 218.

7 Gordon Wright, *The Ordeal of Total War, 1939–1945* (New York and London: Harper and Row, 1968), 264. In the Second World War, "the civilian casualties exceeded the military." Gerhard L. Weinberg, *A World at Arms: A Global History of World War II* (New York: Cambridge University Press, 1994), 894. Alexander B. Downs, *Targeting Civilians in War* (Ithaca, NY: Cornell University Press, 2008), 1:259, claims that the two world wars killed approximately forty-three to fifty-four million non-combatants, comprising between 50 to 62 per cent of all war-related deaths. Zbigniew Brzezinski, *Out of Control: Global Turmoil on the Eve of the Twenty-First Century* (New York: Charles Scribner's Sons, 1993), 9, provides a total number of forty-eight million civilian deaths in both world wars.

8 C.R. Nordstrom, "War: Anthropological Aspects," in *International Encyclopedia of the Social and Behavioral Sciences*, ed. Neil J. Smelser and Paul B. Baltes (Amsterdam-Paris-New York: Elsevier, 2001), 24:16,352–3.

9 Eric Hobsbawm, *Age of Extremities: The Short Twentieth Century, 1914–1991* (New York: Vintage, 1994), 51; cited in Ian Kershaw, "War and Political Violence in Twentieth-Century Europe," *Contemporary European History* 14, no. 1 (2005): 109.

10 Hans Speier, "The Effect of War on the Social Order," *Annals of the American Academy Political and Social Science* 216 (1941): 88; and Hans Speier, "Class Structure and 'Total War,'" *American Sociological Review* 4, no. 3 (1939): 371.

11 Harry Eckstein, "Introduction: Toward a Theoretical Study of Internal War," in *Internal War: Problems and Approaches*, ed. H. Eckstein (New York: Free Press, 1964), 3; and idem, "On the Etiology of Internal Wars," *History and Theory* 4, no. 2 (1965): 133.

12 Black, *The Age of Total War*, 9.

13 Arthur Marwick, "Introduction," in *Total War and Social Change*, ed. A. Marwick (New York: St Martin's Press, 1988), xiv; A. Marwick, *War and Social Change in the Twentieth Century: A Comparative Study of Britain, France, and Germany* (London: Macmillan, 1974), 13; and A. Marwick, *British Society since 1945* (London: Allen Lane, 1982), 19–20.

14 Andriy Zayarnyuk, "A Revolution's History, A Historians' War," *Ab Imperio*, no. 1 (2015): 470.

15 Michael Zantovsky, *Havel: A Life* (New York: Grove Press, 2014), 317, in describing the actions of Czech and Slovak dissidents after the end of the Prague Spring and before the Velvet Revolution of 1989.

16 These ideas came from Charles Tilly, "Reflections on the History of European State-Making," in his *The Formation of National States in Western Europe* (Princeton, NJ: Princeton University Press, 1975), 75; C. Tilly, *Coercion, Capital, and European States, AD 990–1990* (Cambridge, MA: Basil Blackwell, 1990), 20–8; C. Tilly, "War in History," *Sociological Forum* 7, no. 1 (1992): 187–95; Simon Philpott, "Call and Response: Violence and the Making of Modern Nations," *Political Theory* 33, no. 3 (2005): 432–6; and Mark Von Hagen, "'U viinakh tvoriat'sia natsii': natsiotvorennia v Ukraini pid chas Pershoi svitovoi viiny," *Ukraina: Protsesy natsiotvorennia*, ed. Andreas Kappeler (Kyiv: K.I.S., 2011), 271–84; Andreas Wimmer, *Waves of War: Nationalism, State Formation, and Ethnic Exclusion in the Modern World* (New York: Cambridge University Press, 2013); and *Nationalism and War*, ed. John A. Hall and Siniša Malešević (New York: Cambridge University Press, 2013) .

17 Central Intelligence Agency, *The World Fact Book*, https://www.cia.gov/library/publications/the-world-factbook/html (accessed 31 July 2015).

18 Jacques Vallin, France Meslé, Serguei Adamets, and Serhii Pyrozhkov, "A New Estimate of Ukrainian Population Losses during the Crises of the 1930s and 1940s," *Population Studies* 56, no. 3 (2002): 249–64; Ella Libanova, Natalia Levchuk, Emelian Rudnyts'kyi, Natalia Runhach, Svetlana Poniakina, and Pavel Shevchuk, "Smernost naseleniia Ukrainy v trudoaktivnom vozraste," *Demoskop Weekly*, 31 March–13 April 2008, http://demoscope.ru/weekly/2008/0327/tema01.php (accessed 28 March 2012); "Naibil'she poterpily lisostepovi raiony Kyivshchyny i Kharkivshchyny, iaki ne vidihravaly providnoi roli u khlibozativliakh," *Uriadovyi kur'ier*, 22 November 2013, 6–7.

19 Zbigniew Brzezinski, *The Grand Chessboard: American Primacy and Its Geostrategic Imperatives* (New York: Basic Books, 1997), 40, 41.

20 Ibid., 41.

21 Ibid.

22 Zbigniew Brzezinski, "Ukraine's Critical Role in the Post-Soviet Space," *Ukraine in the World: Studies in the International Relations and Security Structure of a Newly Independent State*, ed. Lubomyr A. Hajda (Cambridge, MA: Harvard Ukrainian Research Institute, 1998), 4–5.

23 Samuel P. Huntington, *The Clash of Civilizations and the Making of World Order* (New York: Simon and Shuster, 1996), 137–8. Also see Ivan

Katchanovski, *Cleft Countries: Regional Political Divisions and Cultures in Post-Soviet Ukraine and Moldova* (Stuttgart-Hannover: ibidem-Verlag, 2006).

24 Huntington, *Clash of Civilizations*, 137.

25 Ibid., 138.

26 Ibid., 165.

27 "We make up selves from a tool kit of options made available by our culture and society. We do make choices, but we do not determine the options among which we choose." K. Anthony Appiah, "Identity, Authenticity, Survival," in *Multiculturalism: Examining the Politics of Recognition*, ed. Charles Taylor et al. (Princeton, NJ: Princeton University Press, 1994), 155. These ideas follow those of Karl Marx, who wrote in 1852: "Men make their own history, but they do not make it just as they please; they do not make it under circumstances directly found, given and transmitted from the past. The tradition of all dead generations weighs like a nightmare on the brains of the living. And just when they seem engaged in revolutionising themselves and things, in creating something entirely new, precisely in such epochs of revolutionary crisis they anxiously conjure up the spirits of the past to their services and borrow from them names, battle slogans and costumes in order to present the new scene of world history in this time-honored disguise and this borrowed language." Karl Marx, "The Eighteenth Brumaire of Louis Bonoparte," in *The Marx-Engels Reader*, ed. Robert C. Tucker (New York: W.W. Norton, 1973), 437. A slightly different translation appeared in Karl Marx, *The Eighteenth Brumaire of Louis Bonoparte*, ed. C.P. Dutt (New York: International Publishers, 1969), 15.

28 See William H. McNeill, *Europe's Steppe Frontier, 1500–1800* (Chicago: University of Chicago Press, 1964).

29 See Willard Sunderland, *Taming the Wild Field: Colonization and Empire on the Russian Steppe* (Ithaca, NY: Cornell University Press, 2006).

30 Omeljan Pritsak, *The Origin of Rus'* (Cambridge, MA: Harvard Ukrainian Research Institute, 1981); Serhii Plokhy, *The Origins of the Slavic Nations: Premodern Identities in Russia, Ukraine, and Belarus* (New York: Cambridge University Press, 2006); Ihor Ševčenko, *Ukraine between East and West: Essays on Cultural History to the Early Eighteenth Century*, 2nd rev. ed. (Edmonton, AB: Canadian Institute of Ukrainian Studies, 2009); Natalia M. Iakovenko, *Paralel'nyi svit: Doslidzhennia z istorii uiavlen' ta idei v Ukraini XVI–XVII st.* (Kyiv: Krytyka, 2002); Borys A. Gudziak, *Crisis and Reform: The Kyivan Metropolitanate, the Patriarch of Constantinople, and the Genesis of the Union of Brest* (Cambridge, MA: Harvard Ukrainian Research Institute, 2001); Serhii Plokhy, *The Cossacks and Religion in Early Modern Ukraine* (New York: Oxford University Press, 2001); Frank E. Sysyn, *Between Poland and Ukraine: The Dilemma of Adam Kysil, 1600–1653* (Cambridge, MA:

Harvard Ukrainian Research Institute, 1985); Zenon E. Kohut, *Russian Centralism and Ukrainian Autonomy: Imperial Absorption of the Hetmanate, 1760s–1830s* (Cambridge, MA: Harvard Ukrainian Research Institute, 1988); Zenon E. Kohut, *Making Ukraine: Studies on Political Culture, Historical Narrative, and Identity* (Toronto: Canadian Institute for Ukrainian Studies Press, 2011); Timothy Snyder, *The Reconstruction of Nations: Poland, Ukraine, Lithuania, Belarus, 1569–1999* (New Haven, CT: Yale University Press, 2003); Jan Kozik, *The Ukrainian National Movement in Galicia, 1815–1849*, ed. Lawrence D. Orton (Edmonton, AB: Canadian Institute of Ukrainian Studies, 1986); John-Paul Himka, *Religion and Nationality in Western Ukraine: The Greek Catholic Church and the Ruthenian National Movement in Galicia, 1867–1900* (Montreal: McGill-Queen's University Press, 1999); Ann Sirka, *The Nationality Question in Austrian Education: The Case of Ukrainians in Galicia, 1867–1914* (Frankfurt and Bern: Peter D. Lang, 1980); Serhy Yekelchyk, *Ukrainofily: Svit ukrains'kykh patriotiv druhoi polovyny XIX stolittia* (Kyiv: K.I.S., 2010); Yaroslav Hrytsak, *Narys istorii Ukrainy: Formuvannia modernoi natsii XIX–XX stolittia* (Kyiv: Vyd-vo "Heneza," 1996); Serhy Yekelchyk, *Ukraine: Birth of a Modern Nation* (New York: Oxford University Press, 2007); Orest Subtelny, *Ukraine: A History*, 4th ed. (Toronto: University of Toronto Press, 2009); and Paul Robert Magocsi, *A History of Ukraine: The Land and Its Peoples*, 2nd rev. and expanded ed. (Toronto: University of Toronto Press, 2009).

31 Ševčenko, *Ukraine between East and West*, 187–96.

32 Kohut, *Making Ukraine*, 1–57.

33 Subtelny, *Ukraine: A History*; Magocsi, *A History of Ukraine: The Land and Its Peoples*; Yekelchyk, *Ukraine: Birth of a Modern Nation*; Andrew Wilson, *The Ukrainians: Unexpected Nation* (New Haven, CT: Yale University Press, 2000); and Andrew Wilson, *Ukrainian Nationalism in the 1990s: A Minority Faith* (Cambridge and New York: Cambridge University Press, 1997).

34 Snyder, *Bloodlands*.

35 Norman Naimark, *Stalin's Genocides* (Princeton, NJ: Princeton University Press, 2010), and Terry Martin, *The Affirmative Action Empire: Nations and Nationalism in the Soviet Union, 1923–1939* (Ithaca, NY: Cornell University Press, 2001).

Chapter 1

1 Milan Kundera, *Les testament trahis* (Paris: Gallimard, 1993), 25; cited in Uriel Abulof, "'Small Peoples': The Existential Uncertainty of Ethnonational Communities," *International Studies Quarterly* 53, no. 1 (2009), 227.

2 Oleksandr Dovzhenko, "Zapysni knyzhky," in O. Dovzhenko, *Tvory v p"iaty tomakh* (Kyiv: Dnipro, 1966), 5:106–7; cited in Ivan Koszeliwec, *Oleksander Dovzhenko: Sproba tvorchoi biohrafii* (Munich: Suchasnist, 1980), 32–4; and Alexander Dovzhenko, *The Poet as Filmmaker: Selected Writings*, ed. and trans. Marco Carynnyk (Cambridge, MA: MIT Press, 1973), 198–9.

3 Serhyi Chornyi, *Natsional'nyi sklad naselennia Ukrainy v XX storichchi: Dovidnyk* (Kyiv: Kartohrafiia, 2001), 48.

4 For the Russian Empire in 1897, see *Demoscope Weekly*, no. 647–648 (15–30 June 2015), http://demoscope.ru/weekly/ssp/rus_lan_97_uezd_eng.php?reg=0 (accessed 1 August 2015), and for the Austro-Hungarian Empire in 1910, Peter F. Sugar, "The Nature of the Non-Germanic Societies under Habsburg Rule," *Slavic Review* 22, no. 1 (1963): 9.

5 Donald Treadgold, *The Great Siberian Migration: Government and Peasant in Resettlement from Emancipation to the First World War* (Princeton, NJ: Princeton University Press, 1957); and Vsevolod Naulko, "Foreward," in *Ukrainians in the Eastern Diaspora: An Atlas*, comp. Vsevolod Naulko, Ihor Vynnychenko, and Rostyslav Sossa (Kyiv/Edmonton/Toronto: Mapa Ltd. and the Canadian Institute of Ukrainian Studies Press, 1993), 2.

6 See Ewa T. Morawska, *For Bread with Butter: The Life-Stories of East Central Europeans in Johnstown, Pennsylvania, 1890–1940* (New York and Cambridge: Cambridge University Press, 1985).

7 Vsevolod Naulko, *Khto i vidkoly zhyve v Ukraini* (Kiev: Holovna spetsial'na redaktsiia lit-ry movamy nats. menshyn Ukrainy, 1998), 12.

8 See David Saunders, "What Makes a Nation a Nation? Ukrainians since 1600," *Ethnic Groups* 10, vol. 1 (1993):101–24.

9 John A. Armstrong, *Nations before Nationalism* (Chapel Hill: University of North Carolina Press, 1982), 5; cited in ibid., 119.

10 See John-Paul Himka, *Galician Villagers and the Ukrainian National Movement in the Nineteenth Century* (New York: St Martin's Press, 1988).

11 Charles Taylor, "The Politics of Recognition," in *Multiculturalism: Examining the Politics of Recognition*, ed. Charles Taylor et al. (Princeton, NJ: Princeton University Press, 1994), 31.

12 Ibid., 31–2.

13 Charles Tilly, "Political Identities in Changing Polities," *Social Research* 70, no. 2 (2003): 608.

14 Alfred J. Rieber, "Struggle over the Borderlands," in *The Legacy of History in Russia and the New States of Eurasia*, ed. S. Frederick Starr (Armonk, NY, and London: M.E. Sharpe, 1994), 62. On the Normanist–Anti-Normanist debate, see Omeljan Pritsak, *The Origin of Rus'* (Cambridge, MA: Harvard Ukrainian Research Institute, 1981), 1:3–8; on the disagreements between the

Slavophiles and the Westernizers, see Andrzej Walicki, *The Slavophile Controversy: History of a Conservative Utopia in Nineteenth-Century Russian Thought* (Oxford, UK: Clarendon Press, and New York: Oxford University Press, 1975), and A. Walicki, *A History of Russian Thought from the Enlightenment to Marxism* (Stanford, CA: Stanford University Press, 1979).

15 See Rogers M. Smith, *Stories of Peoplehood: The Politics and Morals of Political Membership* (Cambridge, UK, and New York: Cambridge University Press, 2003). For the autobiographies of prominent members of the Ukrainian national movement, such as Taras Shevchenko, Panteleimon Kulish, Mykola (Nikolai) Kostomarov, Mykhailo Drahomanov, Volodymyr Antonovych, Oleksandr Barvins'kyi, Sofia Rusova, Konstantyn Mykhal'chuk, Oleksandr Potebnia, Ivan Nechui-Levyts'kyi, Halyna Zhurba, Ivan Franko, Bohdan Lepkyi, and Stepan Smal'-Stots'kyi, see *Sami pro sebe: Avtobiohrafii vydatnykh ukraintsiv XIX-ho stolittia*, ed. Iurii Luts'kyi (George Luckyj) (New York: Ukrainian Academy of Arts and Sciences in the US, 1989). Also see Mykhailo Hrushevs'kyi, "Spomyny," *Kyiv*, nos. 8–12 (1988) and nos. 8–11 (1989). For a selection of their important writings in English, see *Fashioning Modern Ukraine: Selected Writings of Mykola Kostomarov, Volodymyr Antonovych, and Mykhailo Drahomanov*, ed. Serhiy Bilenky (Edmonton, AB: Canadian Institute of Ukrainian Studies, 2014).

16 Tilly, "Political Identities," 613–14.

17 Joseph Rothschild, "Observations on Political Legitimacy in Contemporary Europe," *Political Science Quarterly* 92, no. 3 (1977): 496.

18 Jack P. Greene, "Paine, America, and the 'Modernization' of Political Consciousness," *Political Science Quarterly* 93, no. 1 (1978): 91.

19 Tilly, "Political Identities," 609.

20 Ukrainian speakers constituted 47.4 per cent of the Kuban Oblast's total population, and less in the other neighbouring majority Russian-speaking provinces: Stavropol (36.6 per cent), Voronezh (36.2), the Don Cossack Oblast (28), Grodno (22.6), Kursk (22.3), and Bessarabia (19.6). See N.A. Troinitskii, ed., *Pervaia vseobshchaia perepis' naseleniia Rossiiskoi Imperii 1897 g.* (Saint Petersburg: Izd. Tsentral'nogo statisticheskago komiteta Ministerstva vnutrennikh del, 1899–1905), table 13, vols. 3, 9, 11, 12, 45, and 47.

21 Ibid., vols. 8, 13, 16, 32, 33, 41, 46, 47, and 48.

22 Orlando Figes, *A People's Tragedy: The Russian Revolution, 1891–1924* (New York: Penguin, 1996), 80.

23 The information in these two paragraphs on the Pale of Settlement comes from H.R., "Pale of Settlement," *Jewish Encyclopedia (1906)*, http://www.jewishencyclopedia.com/articles/11862-pale-of-settlement (accessed 27 July 2012); B.D. Brutskus, compiler, *Statistika evreiskago naselenia*.

Raspredielenie po territorii, demograficheskie i kul'turnye priznaki evreikago naselenia po dannym perepisi 1897 g. (SPB: Tip. „Sever," 1909), table 2; John Klier, "Pale of Settlement," *The YIVO Encyclopedia of Jews in Eastern Europe*, http://www.yivoenclopedia.org/article.aspx/Pale_of_Settlement (accessed 27 July 2012); Peter Potichnyj, "Pale of Settlement," *Encyclopedia of Ukraine* (1985), 3:755–6; and Henry Abramson, "Ukraine," *YIVO Encyclopedia of Jews in Eastern Europe*, http://www.yivoencyclopedia.org/article.aspx/Ukraine (accessed 4 August 2012). For S. An-Ski's ethnographic study of the Pale in the first decade of the twentieth century, see Nathaniel Deutsch, *The Jewish Dark Continent: Life and Death in the Russian Pale of Settlement* (Cambridge, MA: Harvard University Press, 2011). For An-Ski's record of his efforts to provide relief for Jews caught between the warring armies of Russia, Germany, and Austria during the Great War, see S. Ansky, *The Enemy at His Pleasure: A Journey through the Jewish Pale of Settlement during World War I*, ed. and trans. Joachim Neugroschel (New York: Metropolitan Books, 2002).

24 Ivan L. Rudnytsky, "The Ukrainians in Galicia under Austrian Rule." *Nation-Building and the Politics of Nationalism: Essays on Austrian Galicia*, ed. Andrei S. Markovits and Frank E. Sysyn (Cambridge, MA: Harvard Ukrainian Research Institute, 1982), 23. These seven Hungarian counties included Spish (Hungarian: Szepes), Sarysh (H: Sáros), Zemplyn (H: Zémplen), Uzh (H: Ung), Ugocha (H: Ugocsa), Maramorosh (H: Máramaros), and Bereg.

25 In Galicia, the Polish speakers constituted 58.6 per cent of the total population, and the German speakers 1.1 per cent. In Bukovina, Romanian speakers constituted 34.4 per cent and German speakers 21.4 per cent of the total population. Robert A. Kann, *The Multi-National Empire: Nationalism and National Reform in the Habsburg Monarchy, 1848–1918* (New York: Octagon Books, 1964), 2:302. Large numbers of Magyar speakers (413,485), Slovaks (365,240), and Germans (40,535) also lived in Transcarpathia. S. Tomashivs'kyi, "Etnohrafichna karta Uhors'koi Rusi," *Stat'i po slavianovedeniiu* (Saint Petersburg: Rossiiskaia Akademiia nauk, 1910), 3:254–5.

26 Kann, *The Multi-National Empire*, 2:299–300; and Tomashivs'kyi, "Etnohrafichna," 254–5.

27 Chornyi, *National'nyi sklad*, 48.

28 Robert Edelman, *Proletarian Peasants: The Revolution of 1905 in Russia's Southwest* (Ithaca, NY, and London: Cornell University Press, 1987), 39–40.

29 Omeljan Pritsak and John S. Reshetar Jr suggest a five-stage model, which includes the Novhorod-Siversk, Kharkiv, Kiev, Geneva, and Galician stages. See their "Ukraine and the Dialectics of Nation-Building," *Slavic Review* 23, no. 2 (1963): 5–36.

30 Miroslav Hroch, *Social Preconditions of National Revival in Europe: A Comparative Analysis of the Social Composition of Patriotic Groups among the Smaller European Nations* (Cambridge: Cambridge University Press, 1985), 22–3. Hroch defined these three stages as Phase A, B, and C. Roman Szporluk renamed these phases as the academic, cultural, and political stages of all national movements. See Roman Szporluk, *Ukraine: A Brief History* (Detroit: Ukrainian Festival Committee, 1979), 41–54.
31 On this iron distinction, see Pritsak and Reshetar, "Ukraine and the Dialectics of Nation-Building."
32 See George S.N. Luckyj, *Between Gogol and Ševčenko: Polarity in the Literary Ukraine, 1798–1847* (Munich: W. Fink, 1971), and Edyta M. Bojanowska, *Nikolai Gogol: Between Ukrainian and Russian Nationalism* (Cambridge, MA: Harvard University Press, 2007).
33 J.-P. Himka and B. Krawchenko, "Intelligentsia," in *Encyclopedia of Ukraine*, ed. Volodymyr Kubijovyč (Toronto: University of Toronto Press, 1984), 2:337.
34 Ibid., 337–8; and Stephen Velychenko, "Local Officialdom and National Movements in Imperial Russia: Administrative Shortcomings and Under-Government," in *Ethnic and National Issues in Russian and East European History: Selected Papers from the Fifth World Congress of Central and East European Studies, Warsaw, 1995*, ed. John Morrison (New York: St Martin's Press, 2000), 80. Of the 127,000 people the census counted as having occupations involving intellectual labour, less than a third identified themselves as Ukrainians. For example, only 16 per cent of the lawyers, less than a quarter of the teachers, and only 10 per cent of the writers and artists in Ukraine claimed Ukrainian nationality. Himka and Krawchenko, "Intelligentsia," 337–8.
35 Elena Borisënok, *Fenomenon Sovetskoi ukrainizatsii 1920–1930-e gody* (Moscow: Evropa, 2006), 33.
36 For excellent explorations of the development of these processes in the nineteenth century, see Serhiy Bilenky, *Romantic Nationalism in Eastern Europe: Russian, Polish, and Ukrainian Political Imaginations* (Stanford, CA: Stanford University Press, 2012); and Faith Hillis, *Children of Rus': Right Bank Ukraine and the Invention of a Russian Nation* (Ithaca, NY: Cornell University Press, 2013). Also see Aleksei I. Miller, *"Ukrainskii vopros" v politike vlastei i russkom obshchestvennom mnenii (vtoraia polovina XIX v.)* (Saint Petersburg: Aleteiia, 2000), which is better read in the original, not the English translation: *The Ukrainian Question: The Russian Empire and Nationalism in the Nineteenth Century* (Budapest and New York: Central European University, 2003).
37 This paragraph is inspired by Milan Kundera, "The Czech Wager," *New York Review of Books*, 22 January 1981, 21.

38 Vasyl Markus, "Kharkiv University," in *Encyclopedia of Ukraine*, 2:458, 459.

39 Paul Robert Magocsi, "The Ukrainian National Revival: A New Analytical Framework," *Canadian Review of Studies in Nationalism* 16, nos. 1–2 (1989): 51.

40 George G. Grabowicz, *The Poet as Mythmaker: A Study of Symbolic Meaning in Taras Ševčenko* (Cambridge, MA: Harvard Ukrainian Research Institute, 1982), 1; cited in Matthew D. Pauly, *Breaking the Tongue: Language, Education, and Power in Soviet Ukraine, 1923–1934* (Toronto: University of Toronto Press, 2014), 63.

41 See Thomas M. Prymak, *Mykhailo Hrushevsky: The Politics of National Culture* (Toronto: University of Toronto Press, 1987), and Serhii Plokhy, *Unmaking Imperial Russia: Mykhailo Hrushevsky and the Writing of Ukrainian History* (Toronto: University of Toronto Press, 2005). The Canadian Institute of Ukrainian Studies (Edmonton, Alberta) is in the process of publishing all ten volumes of Hrushevshky's magnum opus, *Istoriia Ukrainy-Rusi*, into English.

42 On recent examples of dignity playing a critical role in radical social change, see Leon Aron, "Everything You Think You Know about the Collapse of the Soviet Union Is Wrong," *Foreign Policy* (July/August 2011), and Leon Aron, *Roads to the Temple: Memory, Truth, Ideals, and Ideas in the Making of the Russian Revolution, 1987–1991* (New Haven, CT: Yale University Press, 2012).

43 Rieber, "Struggle over the Borderlands," 68.

44 These ideas come from Rogers Brubaker, *Nationalism Reframed: Nationhood and the National Question in the New Europe* (New York: Cambridge University Press, 1996), 4–5.

45 Marc Raeff, "Patterns of Russian Imperial Policy toward the Nationalities," in *Soviet Nationality Policies*, ed. Edward Allworth (New York: Columbia University Press, 1971), 26.

46 Ibid., 30.

47 See Zenon E. Kohut, *Russian Centralism and Ukrainian Autonomy: Imperial Absorption of the Hetmanate, 1760s–1830s* (Cambridge, MA: Harvard Ukrainian Research Institute, 1988).

48 Raeff, "Patterns of Russian Imperial Policy," 31–2.

49 Ibid., 32.

50 Edward C. Thaden, "Introduction," in *Russification in the Baltic Provinces and Finland, 1855–1914*, ed. Edward C. Thaden (Princeton, NJ: Princeton University Press, 1981), 9.

51 David Saunders, "Russia's Nationality Policy: The Case of Ukraine (1847–1941)," in *Synopsis: A Collection of Essays in Honour of Zenon E. Kohut*, ed.

Serhii Plokhy and Frank E. Sysyn (Edmonton, AB: Canadian Institute of Ukrainian Studies Press, 2005), 406.

52 See Fedir Savčenko, *The Suppression of the Ukrainian Activities in 1876* (Munich: W. Fink, 1970).

53 Imperatorskaia Akademiia nauk, *Ob otmene stesnenii malorusskago pechatnogo slova* (St Petersburg: Imperatorskaia Akademiia nauk, 1910).

54 Oleksandr Lotots'kyi, *Storinky munyloho* (Warsaw: Ukrains'kyi naukovyi institute, 1933), 2:224.

55 By the end of the nineteenth century, many tsarist officials recognized that the Ukrainian-speaking populations of the Habsburg and Romanov empires were related, but considered the Greek Catholics religious renegades. In their view of the world, the Ukrainian-speaking population left the Orthodox Church in 1596 under Polish pressure and began to consider themselves separate from the Russians only then.

56 Theodore R. Weeks, "National Minorities in the Russian Empire, 1897–1917," in *Russia under the Last Tsar: Opposition and Subversion, 1894–1917*, ed. Anna Geifman (Malden, MA: Blackwell, 1999), 118, 119.

57 Ibid., 118.

58 Bohdan Krawchenko, *Social Change and National Consciousness in Twentieth Century Ukraine* (New York: St Martin's Press, 1985), 31.

59 Saunders, "Russia's Nationality Policy," 408.

60 Geroid Tanquary Robinson, *Rural Russia under the Old Regime: A History of the Landlord-Peasant World and a Prologue to the Peasant Revolution of 1917* (New York: Macmillan, 1967), 120.

61 Robert Edelman, *Proletarian Peasants: The Revolution of 1905 in Russia's Southwest* (Ithaca, NY: Cornell University Press, 1987), 63–5. Also see H.R. Weinstein, "Land Hunger and Nationalism in the Ukraine, 1905–1917," *Journal of Economic History* 2, no. 1 (1942): 24–35.

62 Ibid., 100.

63 P.P. Telichuk, *Ekonomichni osnovy ahrarnoi revoliutsii na Ukraini* (Kiev, 1971), 39, 15; Lewis Siegelbaum, "The Odessa Grain Trade: A Case Study in Urban Growth and Development in Tsarist Russia," *Journal of European Economic History* 9 (Spring 1980): 113–51; cited in Edelman, *Proletarian Peasants*, 39–40.

64 Edelman, *Proletarian Peasants*, 41–3.

65 Frank Lorimer, *Population of the Soviet Union: History and Prospects* (Geneva: League of Nations, 1946), 13, 67.

66 Olga Andriewsky, "The Making of the Generation of 1917: Towards a Collective Biography," in Plokhy and Sysyn, *Synopsis*, 22.

67 Saunders, "Russia's Nationality Policy," 409.

68 David Saunders, "Russia, the Balkans, and Ukraine," in *Russia and the Wider World in Historical Perspective: Essays for Paul Dukes*, ed. Cathryn Brennan and Murray Frame (New York: St Martin's Press, 2000), 101.

69 Ronald Wardbaugh, *Languages in Competition: Dominance, Diversity, and Decline* (New York: Oxford University Press, 1987), 19.

70 The phrase comes from Thomas W. Laqueur, "Toward a Cultural Ecology of Literacy in England, 1600–1850," in *Literacy in Historical Perspective*, ed. Daniel P. Resnick (Washington, DC: Library of Congress, 1983), 55.

71 Ivan L. Rudnytsky, *Essays in Modern Ukrainian History* (Edmonton, AB: Canadian Institute of Ukrainian Studies, 1987), 377.

72 Benedict Anderson, *Imagined Communities: Reflections on the Origins and Spread of Nationalism* (London and New York: Verso, 1991).

73 Jan Kozik, *The Ukrainian National Movement in Galicia, 1815–1849* (Edmonton, AB: Canadian Institute of Ukrainian Studies, 1986), 251.

74 Ann Sirka, *The Nationality Question in Austrian Education: The Case of Ukrainians in Galicia, 1867–1914* (Frankfurt am Main: Lang, 1980), 168.

75 Document 174, *Kul'turne zhyttia v Ukraini: Zakhidni zemli: Dokumenty i materialy*, ed. Iurii Slyvka et al. (Kyiv: Naukova dumka, 1995), vol. 1 (1939–1953): 378.

76 Sirka, *The Nationality Question*, 19.

77 Sugar, "The Nature of the Non-Germanic Societies," 17.

78 "Bukovina," in *Encyclopedia of Ukraine*, 1:317; Himka and Krawchenko, "Intelligentsia," 338.

79 Sugar, "The Nature of the Non-Germanic Societies," 16–17; Himka and Krawchenko, "Intelligentsia," 338.

80 "Properly understood, civil society ... encompass[es] all the organizations and associations that exist outside of the state (including political parties) and the market. It includes the gamut of organizations that political scientists traditionally label interest groups – not just advocacy NGOs, but also labor unions, professional associations (such as those of doctors and lawyers), chambers of commerce, ethnic associations, and others. It also incorporates the many other associations that exist for purposes other than advancing specific or political agendas, such as religious organizations, student groups, cultural organizations (from choral societies to bird-watching clubs), sports clubs, and informal community groups." Thomas Carothers, *Critical Mission: Essays on Democracy Promotion* (Washington, DC: Carnegie Endowment for International Peace, 2004), 100.

81 Sirka, *The Nationality Question*, 5.

82 Ibid., 5.

83 Quoted in Arthur J. May, *The Habsburg Monarchy, 1867–1914* (New York: W.W. Norton, 1968), 43. Article 19 of the Austrian constitution, published on 31 December 1867, recognized the equality of all national groups in Austria and the right of each nationality to preserve its language. This constitution also contained an extensive bill of rights. Hans Kohn, *The Habsburg Empire, 1804–1918* (Princeton, NJ: D. van Nostrand, 1961), 47. But, according to Robert A. Kann, Article 19 did not recognize Yiddish as a national language. As a consequence, a "large majority of Jews ... registered as Poles" in the Galician censuses and "after 1900 they registered in ever-increasing numbers as Ruthenians." In Bukovina, they registered uniformly as Germans, and, after 1910, as a separate part of the German national group. Kann, *The Multi-National Empire*, 2:299–300.

84 These characteristics come from Robert Dahl's "Democracy," *International Encyclopedia of Social and Behavioral Sciences*, as interpreted by Bernard Crick, *Democracy: A Very Short Introduction* (New York: Oxford University Press, 2002), 107–8.

85 John-Paul Himka, *Galician Villagers and the Ukrainian National Movement in the Nineteenth Century* (London: Macmillan, 1988).

86 Henryk Sienkiewicz, a Polish journalist and historical novelist, published *With Fire and Sword* (*Ogniem i mieczem*) in 1884. It quickly became a widely read Polish classic. In its depictions of the brutalities of the Khmelnytsky Uprising, it popularized stereotypes of the uncivilized Cossacks and the civilized Poles. This book, more any other, negatively defined "the Ukrainian Other" to Poles in Austria-Hungary, then later in post-1918 Poland. This novel also antagonized the Ukrainians, creating an unbridgeable gulf between the Ukrainians and Poles. See Henryk Sienkiewicz, *With Fire and Sword*, trans. W.S. Kuniczak (New York: Collier Books, Macmillan, 1993). He won the Nobel Prize for Literature in 1905.

87 *Nationbuilding and the Politics of Nationalism: Essays on Austrian Galicia*, ed. Andrei Markovits and Frank E. Sysyn (Cambridge, MA: Harvard Ukrainian Research Institute, 1982).

88 Roman Szporluk, "The Making of Modern Ukraine: The Western Dimension," *Harvard Ukrainian Studies* 25, nos. 1–2 (2001): 65.

89 Interestingly, under the leadership of Dr Julian Romanchuk, the Ukrainian National Democrats called for a national Jewish curia and for equal rights for Jews as a nationality within the Austro-Hungarian Empire. Lila P. Everett, "The Rise of Jewish National Politics in Galicia," in Markovits and Sysyn, *Nationbuilding and the Politics of Nationalism*, 162.

90 W.A. Jenks, *The Austrian Electoral Reform of 1907* (New York: Columbia University Press, 1950).

91 Sirka, *The Nationality Question*, 14.
92 Ibid., 14–15, 149; Everett, "The Rise of Jewish National Politics in Galicia," 173 (quote).
93 Orest Subtelny, *Ukraine: A History*, 3rd ed. (Toronto: University of Toronto Press, 2000), 307.
94 Iulian Bachynsky, *Ukraina irredenta*, 3rd ed. (Berlin: Vyd. Ukrains'koi molodi, 1924), 95, 97.
95 Andriewsky, "The Making of the Generation of 1917," in Plokhy and Sysyn, *Synopsis*, 20, 21, 22, 24.
96 Mykola Mikhnovsky, *Samostiina Ukraina*, introduction by Iurii Kollard (Na chuzhyni: Vyd-vo "Ukrains'kii patriot," 1948), 25, 28–9, 29.
97 Ibid., 30.
98 The number of cooperative organizations, primarily consumer cooperatives and credit unions, grew from 450 in 1900 to 6,510 in 1914. By the early 1920s, approximately 20,000 cooperatives and 270 credit unions enrolled nearly six million members. *Historical Dictionary of Ukraine*, 2nd ed., ed. Ivan Katchanovski, Zenon E. Kohut, Bohdan Y. Nebesio, and Myroslav Yurkevych (Lanham, MD: Scarecrow Press, 2013), 93, 94. Also see Alexander Dillon, "The Rural Cooperative Movement and the Problems of Modernizing in Tsarist and Post-Tsarist Ukraine (New Russia), 1871–1920" (unpublished PhD dissertation, Department of History, Harvard University, 2003).
99 Andreas Kappeler, "A 'Small People' of Twenty-five Million: The Ukrainians circa 1900," *Journal of Ukrainian Studies* 18, nos. 1–2 (1993), 85–92.
100 Ibid., 87.
101 Ibid., 88. Socio-linguists define those who easily shift between two or more languages in conversation as "code switchers."
102 Ibid., 86.
103 George Y. Shevelov, *The Ukrainian Language in the First Half of the Twentieth Century, 1900–1941* (Cambridge, MA: Harvard Ukrainian Research Institute, 1989), 18.
104 Ibid., 19.
105 Kappeler, "A 'Small People' of Twenty-five Million," 87.
106 Document 174, *Kul'turne zhyttia v Ukraini: Zakhidni zemli*, 379.

Chapter 2

1 Dominic Lieven, *The End of Tsarist Russia: The March to World War I and Revolution* (New York: Viking, 2015), 1.
2 Sun Tzu, *The Art of War*, edited and with a forward by James Clavell (New York: Delacorte Press, 1983), 13.

3 Fritz Stern, cited by William Anthony Hay, "On the Origins of World War I: When the Lamps Went Out," *Wall Street Journal*, 28 March 2013.

4 Stéphane Audoin-Rouzeau and Annette Becker, *14–18: Understanding the Great War* (New York: Hill and Wang, 2003), 159.

5 Joshua A. Sanborn, *Drafting the Russian Nation: Military Conscription, Total War, and Mass Politics, 1905–1925* (Dekalb: Northern Illinois University Press, 2003), 4, 8 (quote).

6 Audoin-Rouzeau and Becker, *14–18*, 160–2, develop this phrase.

7 Michael Clodfelter, *Warfare and Armed Conflicts: A Statistical Reference to Casualty and Other Figures, 1618–1991* (Jefferson, NC, and London: McFarland, 1991), 2:705–89.

8 Mark von Hagen, *War in a European Borderland: Occupations and Occupation Plans in Galicia and Ukraine, 1914–1918* (Seattle, WA: Donald W. Treadgold Studies on Russia, East Europe, and Central Asia, University of Washington, 2007), 19.

9 Michael Howard, *The First World War: A Very Short Introduction* (New York: Oxford University Press, 2007), 62.

10 Ibid., 51, 61.

11 For the February Revolution, see Marc Ferro, *The Russian Revolution of February 1917* (Englewood Cliffs, NJ: Prentice-Hall, 1972); Tsuyoshi Hasegawa, *The February Revolution, Petrograd, 1917* (Seattle: University of Washington Press, 1981); and E.N. Burdzhalov, *Russia's Second Revolution: The February 1917 Uprising in Petrograd* (Bloomington: Indiana University Press, 1987).

12 For a thorough discussion of the role of Russian nationalism and the radical and nationalizing consequences of the Great War, see Eric Lohr, *Nationalizing the Russian Empire: The Campaign against Enemy Aliens during World War I* (Cambridge, MA: Harvard University Press, 2003).

13 Howard, *The First World War*, 62.

14 Lohr, *Nationalizing the Russian Empire*, 69.

15 Stanislas Kohn and Alexander F. Meyendorff, *The Cost of the War to Russia* (New Haven, CT: Yale University Press, 1932), 17, 13, 19.

16 Ibid., 145–6. Based the census of 1897, Ukrainians constituted 73 per cent of the total population of the nine provinces.

17 Kohn and Meyendorff, *The Cost of the War to Russia*, 181–2.

18 Peter Gatrell, *Russia's First World War: A Social and Economic History* (Harlow, England: Pearson Education, 2005), 72, 73.

19 Ibid., 167.

20 Kohn and Meyendorff, *The Cost of War to Russia*, 138. Stephan G. Prociuk estimated that the total number of Russian military losses, including soldiers

who died from epidemics, diseases, and accidents, amounted to 2.5 million. S.G. Prociuk, "Human Losses in the Ukraine in World War I and II," *Annals of the Ukrainian Academy of Arts and Sciences in the U.S.* 13, nos. 35–6 (1973–7): 30.

21 Prociuk, "Human Losses in the Ukraine," 31–5.

22 Ella Libanova, Natalia Levchuk, Emelian Rudnyts'kyi, Natalia Runhach, Svetlana Poniakina, and Pavel Shevchuk, "Smernost naseleniia Ukrainy v tru-doaktivnom vozraste," *Demoskop Weekly*, 31 March–13 April 2008, http://demoscope.ru/weekly/2008/0327/tema01.php (accessed 28 March 2012). Prociuk, in contrast, estimated that the Romanov and Habsburg Ukrainian-speaking provinces suffered a total human loss of some six million people during the First World War. Prociuk, "Human Losses in the Ukraine," 30.

23 See Mark von Hagen, "The Russian Imperial Army and the Ukrainian National Movement in 1917," *Ukrainian Quarterly* 54, nos. 3–4 (1998): 220–56.

24 Cited in Raymond Smith, "Editor's Note," in Vincent Shandor, *Carpatho-Ukraine in the Twentieth Century: A Political and Legal History* (Cambridge, MA: Harvard Ukrainian Research Institute, 1997), ix–x.

25 Niccolò Machiavelli, *The Prince*, trans., ed., and with an introduction by Daniel Donno (New York: Bantam, 2003), 66.

26 Andriy Zayarnyuk, "A Revolution's History, A Historians' War," *Ab Imperio* no. 1 (2015): 474.

27 Von Hagen, *War in a European Borderland*, 25.

28 Alexander V. Prusin, "The Russian Military and the Jews in Galicia, 1914–1915," *The Military and Society in Russia, 1450–1917*, ed. Eric Lohr and Marshall Poe (Boston, Leiden, and Cologne: Brill, 2002), 536–7.

29 Gatrell, *Russia's First World War*, 29; von Hagen, *War in a European Borderland*, 29; and Lohr, *Nationalizing the Russian Empire*, 17, 142–50.

30 Prusin, "The Russian Military and the Jews," 532.

31 Dmytro Doroshenko, *Moi spomyny pro nedavnie-mynule (1914–1920)*, 2nd ed. (Munich: Ukrains'ke vydavnytstvo, 1969), 27.

32 Ibid., 24.

33 On the Russian administration's attempts to convert Greek Catholic Ruthenians to the Russian Orthodox faith, see A. Iu. Bakhturina, *Politika Rossiiskoi imperii v vostochnoi Galitsii v gody pervoi mirovoi voiny* (Moscow: Assotsiiatsiia issledovatelei rossiiskogo obshchestva XX veka, 2000), 142–83.

34 For an excellent overview of the first Russian occupation of Galicia, see von Hagen, *War in a European Borderland*, chap. 2. Also see Doroshenko, *Moi spomyny*, 24–8.

35 von Hagen, *War in a European Borderland*, 49fn65.

36 Peter Gatrell, *A Whole Empire Walking: Refugees in Russia during World War I* (Bloomington and Indianapolis: Indiana University Press, 1999), 20.

37 Gatrell, *A Whole Empire Walking*, 16.
38 Prusin, "The Russian Military and the Jews," 540.
39 Mark von Hagen, "The Great War and the Mobilization of Ethnicity in the Russian Empire," in *Post-Soviet Political Order: Conflict and Nation-Building*, ed. Barnett R. Rubin and Jack Snyder (London and New York: Routledge, 1998), 35–6.
40 See von Hagen, *War in a European Borderland*, chap. 4; Paul Robert Magocsi, *A History of Ukraine* (Seattle: University of Washington Press, 1996), 466.
41 Von Hagen, *War in a European Borderland*, 77–9.
42 For Doroshenko's memoirs of his governor-generalship, see Doroshenko, *Moi spomyny*, 96–151.
43 Arthur J. May, *The Passing of the Habsburg Monarchy, 1914–1918* (Philadelphia: University of Pennsylvania Press, 1968), 2:557–8.
44 Norman Stone, *The Eastern Front, 1914–1917* (New York: Charles Scribner's Sons, 1975), 282; von Hagen, *War in a European Borderland*, 81–3.
45 Von Hagen, *War in a European Borderland*, 85.
46 Von Hagen, "The Great War and the Mobilization of Ethnicity," 41.
47 Zayarnyuk, "A Revolution's History, A Historians' War," 475.
48 Gatrell, *A Whole Empire Walking*, 3.
49 Ibid., 143.
50 Ibid., 183–4; quote from 169–70.
51 Ibid., 170.
52 Andreas Wimmer, *Waves of War: Nationalism, State Formation, and Ethnic Exclusion in the Modern World* (New York: Cambridge University Press, 2013), 4, 200.
53 Von Hagen, *War in a European Borderland*, 17, 65; and Fritz Fischer, *Germany's Aims in the First World War*, intro. Hajo Holborn and James Joll (New York: Norton, 1967). Von Hagen believes that Germany's policies in the east evolved in an ad hoc manner. See von Hagen, "The Russian Imperial Army and the Ukrainian National Movement in 1917."
54 Gatrell, *A Whole Empire Walking*, 145, 146; Lohr, *Nationalizing the Russian Empire*, chap. 4 and 141.
55 Gatrell, *A Whole Empire Walking*, 24; Lohr, *Nationalizing the Russian Empire*, chap. 5.
56 For an example of the Ukrainian movement's public declaration of loyalty to Russia, see Symon Petliura's "Voina i ukraintsi," *Ukrainskaia zhizn*, July 1914; republished in *Ukrains'ka suspil'no-politychna dumka v 20 stolitti: Dokumenty i materialy*, ed. Taras Hunczak and Roman Solchanyk (Munich: Suchasnist, 1983), 1:207–10 (cited hereafter as *US-PD*).
57 Gatrell, *A Whole Empire Walking*, 168.

58 "Manifest Holovnoi ukrains'koi rady," *US-PD*, 1:212.

59 Zayarnyuk, "A Revolution's History, A Historians' War," 475–6.

60 "Holovna ukrains'ka rada do vseho ukrains'koho narodu," *US-PD*, 1:213.

61 "Dekliaratsiia Zahal'noi ukrains'koi rady," *US-PD*, 1:222–3.

62 "Do vsikh kul'turnykh narodov svita," *US-PD*, 1:226. This vague and highly contested claim included lands larger than today's Ukraine, with its 603,628 square kilometres.

63 Soiuz Vyzvolennia Ukrainy, "Nasha pliatforma," *US-PD*, 1:216, 217. SVU's call for a constitutional monarch most likely reflected this organization's real-politik. (All of the potential international supporters of an independent Ukraine [the Central Powers] possessed monarchical forms of government.) For a superb biography of one of these potential monarchs, Wilhelm von Habsburg, see Timothy Snyder, *The Red Prince: The Secret Lives of a Habsburg Archduke* (New York: Basic Books, 2008). For a recent history of the SVU, see Ivan Pater, *Soiuz vyzvolennia Ukrainy: Problemy derzhavnosti i sobornosti* (Lviv: Natsional'na Akademiia nauk Ukrainy, Institut Ukrainoznavstva im. I. Kryp'iakevycha, 2000).

64 See the protests by the General Ukrainian Rada (*US-PD*, 1:231–2) and the Ukrainian parliamentary caucus (*US-PD*, 1:232–6).

65 May, *The Passing of the Habsburg Monarchy*, 2:680–1.

66 Mark Cornwall, *The Undermining of Austria-Hungary: The Battle for Hearts and Minds* (New York: St Martin's Press, 2000), 19, 20, 23.

67 For a comparative overview of the fall of these empires, see Aviel Roshwald, *Ethnic Nationalism and the Fall of Empires: Central Europe, Russia, and the Middle East, 1914–1923* (London and New York: Routledge, 2002).

68 Sanborn, *Drafting the Russian Nation*, 205; and Lohr, *Nationalizing the Russian Empire*.

69 Cornwall, *The Undermining of Austria-Hungary*, 34, 35.

70 Ibid., 23.

Chapter 3

1 William Butler Yeats, "The Second Coming," *The Collected Poems of W.B. Yeats*, rev., ed. Richard J. Finneran (New York: Macmillan, 1989), 187.

2 This phrase comes from "Economic chaos drove Russia towards Bolshevism, sometimes despite the Bolsheviks." Norman Stone, *The Eastern Front, 1914–1917* (New York: Charles Scribner's Sons, 1975), 284.

3 See Ronald Grigor Suny, "Nationalism and Class in the Russian Revolution: A Comparative Discussion," in *Revolution in Russia: Reassessments of 1917*, ed. Edith Rogovin Frankel, Jonathan Frankel, and Baruch Knei-Paz (New

York: Cambridge University Press, 1991), 219–46; and John-Paul Himka,
"The National and the Social in the Ukrainian Revolution of 1917–1920,"
Archiv fur Sozialgeschichte, no. 34 (1994): 95–110.

4 Orlando Figes, *A People's Tragedy: The Russian Revolution, 1891–1924* (New York: Penguin, 1996), 71.

5 Quoted in *Visnyk Soiuza Vyzvolennia Ukrainy* 4, no. 22 (27 May 1917): 351; and in Henryk Jabłoński, *Polska Autonomiia Narodowa na Ukrainie, 1917–1918* (Warsaw: Nakl. Milosnikow Historii, 1948), 30.

6 M. Hrushevs'kyi, "Iakoi my khochemo avtonomii i federatsii?" in his *Vybrani pratsi* (New York: Nakladom Holovnoi upravy OURDP v SShA, 1960), 148.

7 According to Roman Szporluk, Poltava ranked "tenth in size among Ukrainian cities in the Russian Ukraine alone and twelfth if those under Austria are included." Roman Szporluk, "Kiev as Ukraine's Primate City," in *Harvard Ukrainian Studies* 3–4, part 2 (1979–80): 845.

8 *Statystyka Ukrainy*, no. 124 (1928): 206–7.

9 Pavlo Khrystiuk, *Zamitky i materialy do istorii ukrains'koi revoliutsii, 1917–1920* (Vienna: Druk J.N. Vernay, 1921), 1:134n.

10 Steven L. Guthier, "The Popular Base of Ukrainian Nationalism in 1917," in *Slavic Review* 38, no. 1 (1979): 30–47; and Mykola Kovalevsky, *Pry dzherelakh borot'by* (Innsbruck, 1960).

11 Figes, *A People's Tragedy*, 79.

12 *1917 god na Kievshchine: khronika sobytii*, ed. V. Manilov (Kiev: Gos. Izd-vo Ukrainy, 1928), 72.

13 Quoted in John Reshetar, Jr, *The Ukrainian Revolution, 1917–1921* (Princeton, NJ: Princeton University Press, 1952), 109.

14 For the text of the First Universal, see Khrystiuk, *Zamitky*, 1:72–4; Dmytro Doroshenko, *Istoriia Ukrainy, 1917–1923* (Uzhhorod, 1932; reprint: New York: Bulava, 1954), 1:89–92; Volodymyr Vynnychenko, *Vidrodzhennia natsii* (Vienna, 1920), 1:219–24; and Iakiv Zozulia, *Velyka Ukrains'ka revoliutsiia* (New York: Ukrainian Academy of Arts and Sciences in the U.S., 1967), 65–8.

15 M. Rafes, *Dva goda revoliutsii na Ukraine: evoliutsiia i raskol "Bunda"* (Moscow: Gos. Izd-vo, 1920), 38.

16 For a text of the Second Universal, see Khrystiuk, *Zamitky*, 1:92–3; Vynnychenko, *Vidrodzhennia natsii*, 1:279–82; Doroshenko, *Istoriia*, 1:115–16; Zozulia, *Velyka*, 68–70; *Visti z Ukrains'koi Tsentral'noi Rady*, no. 10 (June 1917): 1.

17 For the text of the Provisional Government's instruction, see Doroshenko, *Istoriia*, 1:128–9; Zozulia, *Velyka*, 77–9; and Richard Pipes, *The Formation of the Soviet Union*, rev. ed. (New York: Atheneum, 1968), 64–5.

18 Zozulia, *Velyka*, 31.

19 Finland proclaimed its independence on 4 December 1917, quickly followed
    by Ukraine (25 January 1918), Lithuania (16 February 1918), Estonia
    (24 February 1918), Transcaucasia (22 April 1918), Poland (11 November
    1918), and Latvia (30 December 1918).

20 "Third Universal of the Ukrainian Central Rada," in *Ukraine, 1917–1921:
    A Study in Revolution*, ed. Taras Hunczak (Cambridge, MA: Harvard
    Ukrainian Research Institute, 1977), 388.

21 For the text of the Third Universal, see Hunczak, *Ukraine, 1917–1921*, 387–
    91; Doroshenko, *Istoriia*, 1:179–81; Vynnychenko, *Vidrodzhennia natsii*,
    2:74–80; Zozulia, *Velyka*, 70–3; Khrystiuk, *Zamitky*, 2:51–3.

22 Mark von Hagen, "The Entangled Eastern Front and the Making of the
    Ukrainian State: A Forgotten Peace, A Forgotten War and Nation-Building,
    1917–1918" (unpublished conference paper), 9, 10; and B. Halaichuk, V.
    Markus, and I. Vytanovych, "Diplomacy," *Encyclopedia of Ukraine*, ed.
    Volodymyr Kubijovyč (Toronto: University of Toronto Press, 1984), 1:673.

23 See Stalin's articles and speeches attacking the Rada in December 1917
    and January 1918 in J.V. Stalin, *Works* (Moscow: Foreign Languages
    Publishing House, 1953), 4:6–22 and 29–30.

24 Henry Abramson, *A Prayer for the Government: Ukrainians and Jews in
    Revolutionary Times, 1917–1920* (Cambridge, MA: Harvard Ukrainian
    Research Institute and the Harvard Center for Jewish Studies, 1999), 65.

25 "Fourth Universal of the Ukrainian Central Rada," in Hunczak, *Ukraine, 1917–
    1921*, 394. For the text of the Fourth Universal, see ibid., 391–5; Doroshenko,
    Istoriia, 1:264–68; Zozulia, *Velyka*, 73–7; Khrystiuk, *Zamitky*, 2:103–6. For the
    text of the law on national-personal autonomy, see Zozulia, *Velyka*, 77–81.
    For an analysis of this law, see George O. Liber, "Ukrainian Nationalism and
    the 1918 Law on National-Personal Autonomy," *Nationalities Papers* 15, no. 1
    (1987): 22–42, and Abramson, *A Prayer for the Government*.

26 *Ukraine: A Concise Encyclopedia*, ed. Volodymyr Kubijovyč (Toronto:
    University of Toronto Press, 1963), 1:745–6.

27 Oliver H. Radkey, *Russia Goes to the Polls: The Election to the All-Russian
    Constitutent Assembly, 1917* (Ithaca, NY: Cornell University Press, 1989),
    20 and table 1, 148–51. Ukrainian political parties also won votes from those
    Ukrainians serving in the western front (85,602), on the southwestern front
    (168,354), and on the Romanian front (186,219). On the northern front, the
    Ukrainian Socialist Revolutionaries allied themselves with Muslim socialists
    on a joint list and attracted 88,956 votes. Ibid., 160.

28 Zozulia, *Velyka*, 45.

29 Manilov, *1917 god*, 415; Doroshenko, *Istoriia*, 1:143.

30 Compare the results of the elections to the Constituent Assembly in Poltava province, where 93 per cent of the population spoke Ukrainian in 1897, and where the Ukrainian parties received approximately 83.3 per cent of the November 1917 vote. See Oliver H. Radkey, *The Election to the Russian Constituent Assembly of 1917* (Cambridge, MA, 1950), 29n, 30. Of the 8,201,163 votes cast in the Ukrainian provinces, 5,557,560 or approximately 67.7 per cent of the voters voted for Ukrainian parties or joint-SR-Ukrainian lists. Calculated from ibid., 79.

31 For an important assessment of how "market-dominant minorities" and "politically-dominant minorities" interact with "indigenous majorities" environments during periods of radical social change, see Amy Chua, *The World on Fire: How Exporting Free Market Democracy Breeds Ethnic Hatred and Global Instability* (New York: Anchor, 2004).

32 I.L. Claude, Jr, *Swords into Plowshares: The Problems and Progress of International Organization* (New York: Random House, 1956), 137–8; quoted in Rupert Emerson, *From Empire to Nation: The Rise of Self-Assertion of Asian and African Peoples* (Boston: Beacon Press, 1962), 331.

33 Vynnychenko, *Vidrodzhennia*, 1:258.

34 Ibid., 1:256. Stephen Velychenko disputes this assertion. He claims that however "supposedly 'underdeveloped' or 'incomplete' Ukrainian society might have been, it did have a pool of educated men and women (approximately 30,000), who could be administrators, and while national leaders did sometimes fail to understand the importance of bureaucracy and bureaucrats and tried to mobilize the resources that were at their disposal ... the main problem with the Ukrainian (nationalist) governments during the revolutionary years was not a shortage of educated men or those with administrative skill, but of competent leaders." Stephen Velychenko, *State Building in Revolutionary Ukraine: A Comparative Study of Governments and Bureaucrats, 1917–1922* (Toronto: University of Toronto Press, 2011), 247.

35 John Channon, "The Peasantry in the Revolutions of 1917," in *Revolution in Russia*, ed. Frankel, Frankel, and Knei-Paz, 109.

36 See Ilia Vytanovych, "Ahrarna polityka ukrains'kykh uriadiv rokiv revoliutsii vyzvol'nykh zmahan' (1917–1920)," *Ukrains'kyi istoryk* 4, nos. 3–4 (1967): 5–69.

37 V.I. Lenin, "The Constituent Assembly Elections and the Dictatorship of the Proletariat," https://www.marxists.org/archive/lenin/works/1919/dec/16.htm (accessed 21 August 2012).

38 Mark von Hagen, "The Russian Imperial Army and the Ukrainian National Movement in 1917," *Ukrainian Quarterly* 54, nos. 3–4 (Fall-Winter 1998): 225, 229.

39 Ibid., 255.

40 Ibid., 222.

41 Ibid., 255.

42 Ibid.

43 "The Treaty of Peace between Ukraine and the Central Powers (Signed at Brest-Litovsk, 9 February 1918)," in John W. Wheeler-Bennett, *Brest-Litovsk: The Forgotten Peace, March 1918* (New York: W.W. Norton, 1971), 393.

44 Arthur J. May, *The Passing of the Hapsburg Monarchy, 1914–1918* (Philadelphia: University of Pennsylvania Press, 1968), 2:509, 619.

45 "The Peace of Brest-Litovsk – The Treaty of Peace between Russia and Germany, Austria-Hungary, Bulgaria, and Turkey (Signed at Brest-Litovsk, 3 March 1918)," in Wheeler-Bennett, *Brest-Litovsk*, 405.

46 May, *The Passing of the Hapsburg Monarchy*, 2:624.

47 I.F. Beckett, "Total War," in *War, Peace and Social Change in Twentieth Century Europe*, ed. C.M. Emsley, A. Marwick, and W. Simpson (Milton Keyes and Philadelphia: Open University Press, 1989), 37.

48 Michael Mann, "The Role of Nationalism in the Two World Wars," *Nationalism and War*, ed. John A. Hall and Siniša Malešević (New York: Cambridge University Press, 2013), 173; Avner Offer, *World War One: An Agrarian Explanation* (New York: Oxford University Press, 1989).

49 See Oleh S. Fedyshyn, *Germany's Drive to the East and the Ukrainian Revolution, 1917–1918* (New Brunswick, NJ: Rutgers University Press, 1971); and Taras Hunczak, "The Ukraine under Hetman Pavlo Skoropadsky," in Hunczak, *Ukraine, 1917–1921*, 61–82; and Mark von Hagen, *War in a European Borderland: Occupations and Occupational Plans in Galicia and Ukraine, 1914–1918* (Seattle: Herbert J. Ellison Center for Russian, East European, and Central Asian Studies, University of Washington, 2007), chap. 5.

50 For a brief overview of the Directory, see Martha Bohachevsky-Chomiak, "The Directory of the Ukrainian National Republic," in Hunczak, *The Ukraine, 1917–1921*, 82–102.

51 Serhy Yekelchyk, *Ukraine: Birth of a Modern Nation* (New York and Oxford: Oxford University Press, 2007), 81.

52 N. Gergel, "Di pogromen in Ukraine in di yorn 1918–1921," in *Shriftn far ekonomik un statistik*, ed. Yaakov (Jakob) Lestschinsky (Berlin: Judisches Wissenshaftliches Institut, Sektion für Wirtschaft und Statistik, 1928), 1:110; cited in Zvi Gitelman, *Jewish Nationality and Soviet Politics: The Jewish Sections of the CPSU, 1917–1930* (Princeton, NJ: Princeton University Press, 1972), 161.

53 Henry Abramson, "Jewish Representation in the Independent Ukrainian Governments of 1917–1920," *Slavic Review* 50 (Fall 1991): 548, cited in Yekelchyk, *Ukraine*, 81.

54 Yekelchyk, *Ukraine*, 81.
55 Elias Tcherikower, *Antisemitizm i pogromy na Ukraine 1917 – 1918 gg.* (Berlin: Ostjudisches Historisches Archiv, 1923), 216–18; Abramson, *A Prayer for the Government*, chap. 4.
56 Figes, *A People's Tragedy*, 679.
57 Abramson, *A Prayer for the Government*, 110. In an earlier study, Zvi Gitelman estimated that "the direct loss of Jewish life easily exceeded 30,000, and together with those who died from wounds or as a result of illnesses contracted during the pogroms the number of Jewish dead probably reached 150,000, or ten percent of the Jewish population." Gitelman, *Jewish Nationality and Soviet Politics*, 162. For a nuanced assessment of the 1919 pogroms in Ukraine, see Abramson, *A Prayer for the Government*, chap. 4. For other important works on the 1917–21 period, see Elias Heifetz, *The Slaughter of the Jews in the Ukraine in 1919* (New York: T. Seltzer, 1921); Arnold D. Margolin, *The Jews of Eastern Europe* (New York: T. Seltzer, 1926), esp. 126–52; *Les pogroms en Ukraine sous les gouvernements ukrainiens, 1917–1920*, ed. Leo Motzkin (Coeuvres-et-Valsery, France: Ressouvenances, 2010 [1927]); N. Gergel, "The Pogroms in the Ukraine in 1918–21," *YIVO Annual of Jewish Social Science* 6 (1951): 237–52; Taras Hunczak, "A Reappraisal of Simon Petliura and Jewish-Ukrainian Relations, 1917–1921," and Zosa Szajkowski, "A Rebuttal," *Jewish Social Studies* 31 (1969): 163–213; Saul S. Friedman, *Pogromchik* (New York: Hart, 1976); H. Abramson, "Historiography on the Jews and the Ukrainian Revolution," *Journal of Ukrainian Studies* 15, no. 2 (1990): 33–45; and Lars Fischer, "The *Pogromshchina* and the Directory: A New Historiographical Synthesis?" *Revolutionary Russia* 16, no. 2 (2003): 47–93.
58 For the evolution of the Bolshevik views on the national question in the Russian Empire, see Richard Pipes, *The Formation of the Soviet Union: Communism and Nationalism, 1917–1923*, rev. ed. (New York: Atheneum 1968), chap. 1; Walker Connor, *The National Question in Marxist-Leninist Theory and Strategy* (Princeton, NJ: Princeton University Press, 1984), chaps 1–2; and Jeremy Smith, *The Bolsheviks and the National Question, 1917–1923* (New York: St Martin's Press, 1999), chap. 2.
59 I. Kulyk, "Kievskaia organizatsiia v fevrale-oktiabre 1917 g.," *Letopis Revoliutsii* 6, no. 1 (1924): 197. See, especially, V.I. Lenin, "Speech on the National Question, (29 April [12 May] 1917)," in V.I. Lenin, *Collected Works* (London: Lawrence and Wishart, 1964), 24:298, 301; and V.I. Lenin, "The Ukraine, (17 [30] June 1917)," in his *Collected Works*, 25:91–2.
60 Quoted in Jurij Borys, *The Sovietization of Ukraine, 1917–1923: The Communist Doctrine and Practice of National Self-Determination*, rev. ed. (Edmonton, AB: Canadian Institute of Ukrainian Studies, 1980), 136.

61 See Stephen Velychenko, *Painting Imperialism and Nationalism Red: The Ukrainian Marxist Critique of Russian Communist Rule in Ukraine, 1918–1925* (Toronto: University of Toronto Press, 2015).

62 Vsesoiuznaia kommunisticheskaia partiia (bol'shevikov), *Sotsial'nyi i natsional'nyi sostav VKP(b): Itogi vsesoiuznoi partiinoi perepisi 1927 g.* (Moscow, 1928), 158; cited in George Y. Shevelov, *The Ukrainian Language in the First Half of the Twentieth Century (1900–1941): Its State and Status* (Cambridge, MA: Harvard Ukrainian Research Institute, 1989), 90.

63 Pipes, *Formation of the Soviet Union*, 130–1.

64 Quote comes from V.I. Lenin, "Manifesto to the Ukrainian People with an Ultimatum to the Ukrainian Rada," in V.I. Lenin, *Collected Works*, 26:361–3.

65 Pipes, *Formation of the Soviet Union*, 123.

66 Geoffrey Swain, *The Origins of the Russian Civil War* (London and New York: Longman, 1996), 97.

67 Pipes, *Formation of the Soviet Union*, 130.

68 *Ukraine: A Concise Encyclopedia*, 1:797.

69 Pipes, *Formation of the Soviet Union*, 131–2.

70 Ibid., 132.

71 See Andrea Graziosi, *The Great Soviet Peasant War: Bolsheviks and Peasants, 1917–1933* (Cambridge, MA: Harvard Ukrainian Research Institute, 1996), and A. Graziosi, *Bol'sheviki i krestiane na Ukraine: 1918–1919 gody: Ocherk o bol'shevizmakh, national-sotsialistizmakh i krestianskikh dvizheniiakh* (Moscow: Airo-XX, 1997).

72 Pipes, *Formation of the Soviet Union*, 134, 146. On the Borotbists, see Iwan Majstrenko, *Borotbism: A Chapter in the History of Ukrainian Communism* (New York: Research Program on the USSR, 1954).

73 Pipes, *Formation of the Soviet Union*, 139, 140, 143.

74 Smith, *The Bolsheviks and the National Question*, 70; Terry Martin, *The Affirmative Action Empire: Nations and Nationalism in the Soviet Union, 1923–1939* (Ithaca, NY: Cornell University Press, 2001), 278–80. The statistics concerning the Ukrainian population of the Kuban come from the 1926 Soviet census.

75 N. Popov, *Narys Istorii Komunistychnoi partii (bil'shovykiv) Ukrainy*, 5th ed. (Kharkiv, 1931), 176.

76 Ibid., 180; Elena Borisënok, *Fenomenon Sovetskoi ukrainizatsii 1920–1930-e gody* (Moscow: Evropa, 2006), 51.

77 Borisënok, *Fenomenon Sovetskoi ukrainizatsii 1920–1930-e gody*, 51.

78 Majstrenko, *Borotbism*, 103.

79 Arthur E. Adams, *Bolsheviks in the Ukraine: The Second Campaign, 1918–1919* (New Haven, CT: Yale University Press, 1963), 31.

80 M. Ravich-Cherkasskii, *Istoriia Kommunisticheskoi partii Ukrainy* (Kharkov, 1923), 123–4.

81 Vladimir Lenin, "Pis'mo k rabochim i krest'ianam Ukrainy po povodu pobedy nad Denikinym," in V.I. Lenin, *Sochineniia* (Moscow, 1950), 30:267–73.

82 *Ukraine: A Concise Encyclopedia*, 1:604.

83 Ibid., 1:804–5.

84 Ibid., 1:805.

85 Pipes, *Formation of the Soviet Union*, 254.

86 Ibid., 263. According to *Ukraine: A Concise Encyclopedia*, 1:807, the Ukrainian SSR "was recognized de jure as a sovereign state by Germany, Austria, Poland, Czechoslovakia, Italy, Turkey, Latvia, Lithuania, and Estonia; de facto by Great Britain, Bulgaria, Romania, and the League of Nations. The Ukrainian SSR had diplomatic relations with at least six foreign countries and was party to several international conventions of the League of Nations."

87 For these developments, see Pipes, *Formation of the Soviet Union*, 263–5 and 269–70; and Smith, *The Bolsheviks and the National Question*, chap. 7.

88 Pipes, *Formation of the Soviet Union*, 270–1.

89 Borisënok, *Fenomenon Sovetskoi ukrainizatsii*, 76.

90 Elmira Brodskaia, quoted in Tanya Richardson, *Kaleidoscopic Odessa: History and Place in Contemporary Ukraine* (Toronto: University of Toronto Press, 2008), 82.

91 Pipes, *Formation of the Soviet Union*, 273; *Ukraine: A Concise Encyclopedia*, 1:808.

92 *Ukraine: A Concise Encyclopedia*, 1:809.

93 Pipes, *Formation of the Soviet Union*, 276.

94 According to Pipes, the Soviet Union "as it emerged in 1923, was a compromise between doctrine and reality: an attempt to reconcile the Bolshevik strivings for absolute unity and centralization of all power in the hands of the party, with the recognition of the empirical fact that nationalism did survive the collapse of the old order. It was viewed as a temporary solution only, as a transitional stage to a completely centralized and supra-national world-wide Soviet state. From the point of view of self-rule the communist government was even less generous to the minorities than its tsarist predecessor had been: it destroyed independent parties, tribal self-rule, religious and cultural institutions. It was a unitary, centralized, totalitarian state such as the tsarist state had never been. On the other hand, by granting the minorities extensive linguistic autonomy and by placing the national-territorial principle as the base of the party's political administration, the Communists gave constitutional recognition to the multinational structure of the Soviet population. In view

of the importance which language and territory have for the development of national consciousness – particularly for people who, like the Russian minorities during the Revolution, have had some experience of self-rule – this purely formal feature of the Soviet constitution may well prove to have been historically one of the most consequential aspects of the formation of the Soviet Union." Ibid., 296–7. The term "subversive institution" comes from Valerie Bunce, *Subversive Institutions: The Design and Destruction of Socialism and the State* (New York and Cambridge: Cambridge University Press, 1999).

95 Geoff Eley, "Remapping the Nation: War, Revolutionary Upheaval and State Formation in Eastern Europe, 1914–1923," in *Ukrainian-Jewish Relations in Historical Perspective*, ed. Peter J. Potichnyj and Howard Aster (Edmonton, AB: Canadian Institute of Ukrainian Studies, 1988), 207.

96 Peter Holquist, *Making War, Forging Revolution: Russia's Continuum of Crisis, 1914–1921* (Cambridge, MA: Harvard University Press, 2002).

97 *Vtoroi s'ezd KP(b)U. Protokoly* (Kharkiv, 1927), 94–5; cited in Borys, *The Sovietization of Ukraine*, 205.

98 The quote comes from *Budivnytstvo Radians'koi Ukrainy: Zbirnyk, No. 1* (Kharkiv: Derzhavne vyd. Ukrainy, s.a.); cited in Shevelov, *The Ukrainian Language in the First Half of the Twentieth Century*, 87.

Chapter 4

1 Charles de Gaulle, "La limitation des armements," *Lettres, notes et carnets, 1905–1918* (Paris: Plon, 1980), 536; cited in Stéphane Audoin-Rouzeau and Annette Becker, *14–18: Understanding the Great War* (New York: Hill and Wang, 2003), 234.

2 The Supreme Ukrainian Council (Holovna Ukrains'ka Rada, or HUR); the Western Ukrainian National Republic (Zakhidna Ukrains'ka Narodna Respublika, or ZUNR).

3 Estimated from Serhii Chornyi, *Natsional'nyi sklad naselennia Ukrainy v XX storichchi* (Kyiv: Kartohrafiia, 2001), 48–9.

4 Alison Fleig Frank, *Oil Empire: Visions of Prosperity in Austrian Galicia* (Cambridge, MA: Harvard University Press, 2005), 207, 263.

5 Vasyl Kuchabsky, *Western Ukraine in Conflict with Poland and Bolshevism, 1918–1923*, trans. Gus Fagan (Toronto and Edmonton: Canadian Institute of Ukrainian Studies, 2009), xv, 69–70.

6 Frank, *Oil Empire*, 228.

7 On the Polish-Ukrainian War of 1918–19, see Maciej Kozłowski, *Między Sanem a Zbruczem: Walki o Lwów i Galicję Wschodnią 1918–1919* (Cracow: Znak, 1990); idem, *Zapomniana wojna. Walki o Lwów i Galicję Wschodnią*

1918–1919 (Bydgoszcz: Instytut Wydawniczy Świadectwo, 1999); Mykola
Lytvyn and Kim Naumenko, *Istoriia ZUNR* (Lviv: Instytut ukrainoznavstva
im. Ivana Kryp'iakevycha Natsional'noi Akakemii Nauk Ukrainy, 1995);
Mykola Lytvyn, *Ukrains'ko-pol's'ka viina 1918–1919 rr.* (Lviv: Instytut ukrai-
noznavstva im. I. Kryp'iakevycha Natsional'noi Akademii Nauk Ukrainy and
Instytut Skhidno-Tsentral'nyi Ievropy, 1998); Oleksandr Pavliuk, "Ukrainian-
Polish Relations in Galicia in 1918–1919," *Journal of Ukrainian Studies* 23,
no. 1 (Summer 1998): 1–23; Michal Klimecki, *Polsko-ukraińska wojna o
Lwów i Galicję Wschodnią 1918–1919* (Warsaw: Oficyjna Wydawnicza
Volumen, 2000); and Rafał Galuba *"Niech nas rozsądzi miecz i krew... ":
Konflikt polsko-ukraiński o Galicję Wschodnią w latach 1918–1919* (Poznan:
Wydawn. Poznańskie, 2004).

8 Frank, *Oil Empire*, 214.
9 Piotr S. Wandycz, *France and Her Eastern Allies, 1919–1925: French-
   Czechoslovak-Polish Relations from the Paris Peace Conference to Locarno*
   (Minneapolis: University of Minnesota Press, 1962), 105–7.
10 Robert Bideleux and Ian Jeffries, *A History of Eastern Europe: Crisis and
   Change*, 2nd ed. (New York: Routledge, 2007), 329.
11 "The First World War had convinced France, like all the other belligerents, of
   the significance of petroleum ... throughout the 1920s, the French took steps
   to ensure that in the event of another European conflict, their supply of petroleum would be secure. The French owned 55 per cent of the Polish oil industry by 1920 and 75 per cent by 1923." Frank, *Oil Empire*, 234.
12 Marc Bloch best characterized this environment shortly after Nazi Germany
   defeated France in June 1940: "We find ourselves in this appalling situation –
   that the fate of France no longer depends upon the French." M. Bloch,
   Strange Defeat: A Statement of Evidence Written in 1940 (New York:
   Octagon, 1968), 174; cited in Mark Mazower, *Hitler's Empire: How the Nazis
   Ruled Europe* (New York: Penguin, 2009), 416.
13 Audoin-Rouzeau and Becker, *14–18*, 235–6; 166 (quote).
14 Joseph Rothschild, *East Central Europe between the Two World Wars*
   (Seattle: University of Washington Press, 1974), 42.
15 The 1921 Ukrainian population in Poland comes from Antony Polonsky,
   The Little Dictators: The History of Eastern Europe since 1918 (London and
   Boston: Routledge and Kegan Paul, 1975), 158 (table 1), and Rothschild, *East
   Central Europe*, 36 (table 1). The population of Finland and the Baltic states
   in the 1920s comes from B.R. Mitchell, *International Historical Statistics:
   Europe, 1750–2000*, 5th ed. (New York: Palgrave Macmillan, 2003), 3, 4, 6.
16 Oscar I. Janowsky, *Nationalities and National Minorities (With Special
   Reference to East Central Europe)* (New York: Macmillan, 1945), 111; and

Piotr Eberhardt, *Ethnic Groups and Population Changes in Twentieth-Century Central-Eastern Europe: History, Data, and Analysis* (Armonk, NY: M.E. Sharpe, 2003), 449.

17 The Polish Minority Treaty of 28 June 1919, the model for all the other minority treaties, appears in C.A. Macartney, *National States and National Minorities* (New York: Russell and Russell, 1968), 510–14.

18 David J. Smith and John Hiden, *Ethnic Diversity and the Nation-State: National Cultural Autonomy Revisited* (New York: Routledge, 2012).

19 Rogers Brubaker, *Nationalism Reframed: Nationhood and the National Question in the New Europe* (New York: Cambridge University Press, 1996), 4–5.

20 Ibid., 57. On Poland, see Antony Polonsky, "The Breakdown of Parliamentary Government," in *The History of Poland since 1863*, ed. R.F. Leslie (Cambridge: Cambridge University Press, 1983), 148. On Romania, see Irina Livezeanu, *Cultural Politics in Greater Romania: Regionalism, Nation Building, and Ethnic Struggle, 1918–1930* (Ithaca, NY: Cornell University Press, 1995), 192–3.

21 John-Paul Himka, "Western Ukraine between the Wars," *Canadian Slavonic Papers* 34, no. 4, 1992): 397, 398.

22 Ibid., 399.

23 Ibid., 400.

24 Frederick C. Barghoorn, *Soviet Russian Nationalism* (New York: Oxford University Press, 1956); Yitzhak M. Brudny, *Reinventing Russia: Russian Nationalism and the Soviet State, 1953–1991* (Cambridge, MA: Harvard University Press, 1998); David Brandenberger, *National Bolshevism: Stalinist Mass Culture and the Formation of the Modern Russian Identity, 1931–1956* (Cambridge, MA: Harvard University Press, 2002); and *Epic Revisionism: Russian History and Literature as Stalinist Propaganda,* ed. Kevin M.F. Platt and David Brandenberger (Madison: University of Wisconsin Press, 2006).

25 Hugh Seton-Watson, *Eastern Europe between the Wars, 1918–1941* (Hamden, CT: Archon Books, (1962), 413; Janowsky, *Nationalities and National Minorities*, 111, provides a figure of 32,372,200 for 1931.

26 I. Korovytsky and M. Trukhan, "Polish Autocephalous Orthodox Church," *Encyclopedia of Ukraine* (Toronto: University of Toronto Press, 1993), 4:99.

27 Margaret MacMillan, *Paris 1919: Six Months that Changed the World* (New York: Random House, 2002), 226–8; and Arno J. Mayer, *Politics and Diplomacy of Peacemaking: Containment and Counter-Revolution at Versailles, 1918–1919* (London: Weidenfeld and Nicolson, 1968). On France's alliances with Czechoslovakia and Poland in the interwar period, see Piotr S. Wandycz, *France and Her Eastern Allies, 1919–1925,* and Piotr S. Wandycz,

The Twilight of French Eastern Alliances, 1926–1936: French-Czechoslovak-Polish Relations from Locarno to the Remilitarization of the Rhineland (Princeton, NJ: Princeton University Press, 1988).

28 Paul Robert Magocsi, *A History of Ukraine: The Land and the Peoples*, 2nd ed. (Toronto: University of Toronto Press, 2010), 626.

29 Polonsky, *The Little Dictators*, 164 (table 11).

30 Between 1921 and 1937, "Poland experienced an increase of seven million people, bringing the total to 34.2 million; this 26 percent growth rate averaged about 454,000 new mouths to feed annually. Nowhere was this problem more evident than in the rural areas, where the population was crowded in on land that was incapable of supporting it. Various estimates of the surplus population in rural regions have ranged from two to eight million persons, of which three-fifths were of an age to work in industry." Edward D. Wynot, Jr, *Polish Politics in Transition: The Camp of National Unity and the Struggle for Power, 1935–1939* (Athens: University of Georgia Press, 1974), 11–12.

31 Polonsky, *The Little Dictators*, 33.

32 Wynot, *Polish Politics in Transition*, 22.

33 Celia S. Heller, *On the Edge of Destruction: Jews of Poland between the Two Wars* (Detroit: Wayne State University Press, 1994, and New York: Columbia University Press, 1977).

34 Laurence Weinbaum, *A Marriage of Convenience: The New Zionist Organization and the Polish Government, 1936–1939* (Boulder, CO: East European Monographs, 1993), 5.

35 Ibid., 6. For how Polish society represented the Jews, see Joanna B. Michlic, *Poland's Threatening Other: The Image of the Jew from 1880 to the Present* (Lincoln: University of Nebraska Press, 2006), chaps 3–4.

36 Heller, *On the Edge of Destruction*, 132.

37 See Joseph Rothschild, *Piłsudski's Coup d'Etat* (New York: Columbia University Press, 1966).

38 Eberhardt, *Ethnic Groups*, 113, 121, 212. The 5.3 million figure comes from Piotr Ebehardt, *Zminy natsional'noi struktury naselennia Ukrainy v XX stolitti* (Warsaw: PAN IFiPZ, 2006), 122. These statistics are highly problematic. Many Ukrainians refused to participate in the official Polish censuses.

39 Mirosława Papierzyńska-Turek, *Sprawa ukraińska w Drugiej Rzeczypospolitej 1922–1926* (Cracow: Wydawnictwo Literackie, 1979), 20; cited in Himka, "Western Ukraine," 394.

40 Eberhardt, *Ethnic Groups*, 210–12. According to Volodymyr Kubijovyč, Ukrainians were the plurality group in many small towns, but certainly not the majority. In Galician towns with five thousand or more inhabitants, they comprised a 50 per cent or more only in Borshchiv, Melnytsia, Skala,

Horodenka, Yavoriv, Pechenizhyn, Kosiv, Sudova Vyshnia, Deliatyn, Hlyniany, Lopatyn, Staryi Sambir, Zabolotiv, Bohorodchany, Synievidsko Vyzhnie, Terebovlia, Budzaniv, Tysmenytsia, Pomoriany, Zaliztsi, Olesko, and Zhydachiv. Volodymyr Kubijovyč, *Etnichni hrupy pivdenno-zakhidn'oi Ukrainy (Halychyny) na 1. 1. 1939* (Wiesbaden: Otto Harrassowitz, 1983). I am grateful to Roman Senkus, who provided me with this information.

41 Timothy Snyder, *The Reconstruction of Nations: Poland, Ukraine, Lithuania, Belarus, 1569–1999* (New Haven, CT: Yale University Press, 2003), 152–3.

42 Polonsky, *The Little Dictators*, 148.

43 Ibid., 200–1.

44 Frank Golczewski, "Civil War in Occupied Territories: The Polish-Ukrainian Conflict during the Interwar Years and the Second World War," in *Territorial Revisionism and the Allies of Germany in the Second World War: Goals, Expectations, Practices*, ed. Marina Cattoruzza, Stefan Dyroff, and Dieter Langewiesche (New York: Berghahn, 2013), 146.

45 Janusz Radziejowski, *The Communist Party of Western Ukraine, 1919–1929* (Edmonton: Canadian Institute of Ukrainian Studies, 1983), 4–7; cited in Frank, *Oil Empire*, 228–9.

46 Jerzy Lukowski and Hubert Zawadzki, *A Concise History of Poland* (New York and Cambridge: Cambridge University Press, 2001), 210.

47 Document 138, *Kul'turne zhyttia v Ukraini: Zakhidni zemli*, ed. Iurii Slyvka et al. (Kyiv: Naukova dumka, 1995), 1:316.

48 Ievhen Iulian Pelens'kyi, "Suchasne ukrains'ke serednie i vysoke shkil'nytstvo v Halychyni i na Volyni," in *Dvadtsiat'piat'littia tovarystva "Uchytel's'ka hromada": Iuvileinyi naukovyi zbirnyk* (Lviv, 1935), 169. I am grateful to Roman Senkus, who provided me with this citation.

49 S. Vytvytsky and S. Baran, "Western Ukraine under Poland," in *Ukraine: A Concise Encyclopedia*, ed. Volodymyr Kubijovyč (Toronto: University of Toronto Press, 1963), 1:847–8.

50 Radziejowski, *The Communist Party of Western Ukraine* 4–7; and Frank, *Oil Empire*, 228–9. For a history of the Union of Ukrainian Women, see Martha Bohachevsky-Chomiak, *Feminists despite Themselves: Women in Ukrainian Community Life, 1884–1939* (Edmonton, AB: Canadian Institute of Ukrainian Studies, University of Alberta, 1988), or Martha Bohachevsky-Chomiak, *Bilym po bilomu: zhinky v hromads'komu zhytti Ukrainy, 1884–1939* (Kyiv: Lybid, 1995); and Myroslava Diadiuk, *Ukrains'kyi zhinochyi rukh u mizhvoiennii Halychyni: Mizh hendernoiu identychnistiu ta natsional'noiu zaanhazovanistiu* (Lviv: Astroliabia, 2011). For a popular history of Plast, see *Al'manakh 100-littia Plastu* (New York, Toronto, and L'viv: Vydannia Holovnoi plastovoi bylavy, 2012).

51 On the soil and this region's poverty, see Jan T. Gross, *Revolution from Abroad: The Soviet Conquest of Poland's Western Ukraine and Western Belorussia* (Princeton, NJ: Princeton University Press, 1988), 227.

52 Magocsi, *A History of Ukraine*, 629. Also see Stella Hryniuk, *Peasants with Promise: Ukrainians in Southeastern Galicia, 1880–1900* (Edmonton, AB: CIUS Press, 1991); and Stella Hryniuk and Jeffrey Picknicki, *The Land They Left Behind* (Winnipeg: Watson and Dwyer, 1995).

53 For a succinct assessment of the impact of the Great Depression on East Central Europe, see Bideleux and Jeffries, *A History of Eastern Europe*, 344–63.

54 "Slightly fewer than 68,000 migrated," according to Orest T. Martynowych's forthcoming volume on the history of Ukrainians in Canada during the interwar years (Canadian Institute of Ukrainian Studies Press, 2016); Wsevolod W. Isajiw and Andrij Makuch, "Ukrainians in Canada," in *Ukraine and Ukrainians throughout the World*, ed. Ann Lencyk Pawliczko (Toronto: University of Toronto Press, 1994), 333, state that sixty-five to seventy thousand migrated; and Frances A. Swyripa, "Ukrainian Canadians (last edited 4 March 2015)," http://www.thecanadianencyclopedia.ca/en/article/ukrainian-canadians (accessed 28 April 2015), asserts that "some 70,000 Ukrainians" immigrated to Canada for political and economic reasons.

55 See Bohdan Budurowycz, *Polish-Soviet Relations, 1933–1939* (New York: Columbia University Press, 1963); Terry Martin, *The Affirmative Action Empire: Nations and Nationalism in the Soviet Union, 1923–1939* (Ithaca, NY: Cornell University Press, 2001); and Kate Brown, *A Biography of No Place: From Ethnic Borderland to Soviet Heartland* (Cambridge, MA: Harvard University Press, 2004).

56 Timothy Snyder, *Sketches from a Secret War: A Polish Artist's Mission to Liberate Soviet Ukraine* (New Haven, CT: Yale University Press, 2005), 29–30, 73; Radziejowski, *Communist Party of Western Ukraine*; and Roman Solchanyk, "The Communist Party of Western Ukraine, 1919–1938" (unpublished PhD dissertation, Department of History, University of Michigan, 1973).

57 Himka, "Western Ukraine," 407.

58 For what the readers of *Dilo*, the oldest (established in 1880) and most popular Ukrainian-language daily in Eastern Galicia, learned about Soviet Ukrainian politics, forced collectivization, the Holodomor, and anti-Ukrainian arrests and purges in the 1920s and 1930s, see the overview of its contents in Iu. H. Shapoval, *"Dilo" (1880–1939 rr.): Postup ukrains'koi suspil'noi dumky* (Lviv: Naukovo-doslidnyi tsentr periodyky L'vivs'koi naukovoi biblioteky im. V. Stefanyka, and Fakul'tet zhurnalistyky L'vivs'koho derzhavnoho universytetu im. Ivana Franka, 1999), 229–339.

59 Snyder, *Reconstruction of Nations*, 150.
60 Himka, "Western Ukraine," 409.
61 John A. Armstrong, *Ukrainian Nationalism*, 2nd ed. (New York: Columbia University Press, 1963); and Alexander J. Motyl, *The Turn to the Right: The Ideological Origins and the Development of Ukrainian Nationalism, 1919–1929* (Boulder, CO: East European Quarterly Monographs, 1980); and Oleksandr Zaitsev, *Ukrains'kyi integral'nyi natsionalizm (1920–1930-ti roky): Narysy intelektual'noi istorii* (Kiev: Krytyka, 2013).
62 See Lucyna Kulińska, *Działność terrorystyczna i sabotażowa nacjonalistycznych organizacji ukraińskich w Polsce w latach 1922–1939* (Cracow: Księgarnia Akademicka, 2009).
63 The quote comes from Orest Subtelny, *Ukraine: A History*, 3rd ed. (Toronto: University of Toronto Press, 2000), 443.
64 For a biography of Dontsov, see Mykhailo Sosnovs'kyi, *Dmytro Dontsov: Politychnyi portret* (New York: Trident International, 1974). For an excellent analysis of the evolution of Dontsov's political ideas and of his uneasy relationship with the OUN, see Myroslav Shkandrij, *Ukrainian Nationalism: Politics, Ideology, and Literature, 1929–1956* (New Haven, CT: Yale University Press, 2015), 79–131.
65 Zaitsev, *Ukrains'kyi integral'nyi natsionalizm*, 308–26 (citation 325).
66 Thomas Perry Thornton, "Terror as a Weapon of Political Agitation," in *Internal War: Problems and Approaches*, ed. Harry Eckstein (New York: Free Press, 1964), 73. For a thorough explanation of this term, see 73–8.
67 The phrase "epidemic of sabotage" comes from Roman Skakun, *"Patsyfikatsiia": Pol's'ki represii 1930 roku v Halychyni* (Lviv: Vydavnytstvo Ukrains'koho katolyts'koho universytetu, 2012), 19. For a list of the 303 "acts of terror" Ukrainian nationalists committed (as recorded by the Polish authorities of the day) in 1922 and 1923 and the 191 they committed in July–November 1930, see Kulińska, *Działność terrorystyczna*, 161–73, 211.
68 On this Pacification Campaign, see Emil Revyuk, *Polish Atrocities in Ukraine* (New York: Svoboda Press, 1931); Andrzej Chojnowski, *Koncepcje polityki narodowościowej rządów polskich w latach 1921–1939* (Wrocław: Zakład Narodowy im. Ossolińskich, 1979); M.N. Shvaguliak, *Patsyfikatsiia: Pol's'ka represyvna aktsiia v Halychyni 1930 r. i ukrains'ka suspil'nist'* (L'viv: Natsional'na Akademiia nauk Ukrainy, Instytut ukrainoznavstva, 1993); and Skakun, *"Patsyfikatsiia."*
69 The estimate of eight to nine thousand OUN members in 1939 comes from: Roman Wysocki, *Organizacja ukraińskich nacjonalistów w Polsce w latach*

1929–1939: Geneza, struktura, program, ideologia (Lublin: Wydawnictwo
Uniwersytetu Marii Curii-Skłodowskiej, 2003), 337; cited in Shkandrij,
Ukrainian Nationalism, 3. Other scholars have claimed a higher membership
of twenty thousand: Bohdan Krawchenko, "Soviet Ukraine under Nazi
Occupation, 1941–1944," in *Ukraine during World War II: History and Its
Aftermath*, ed. Yury Boshyk (Edmonton, AB: Canadian Institute of
Ukrainian Studies, 1986), 19; and Grzegorz Rossolinski-Liebe, "The
'Ukrainian National Revolution' of 1941: Discourse and Practice of a Fascist
Movement," *Kritika* 12, no. 1 (2011): 92.

70 Thomas L. Friedman, "Who Are We?" *New York Times*, 15 November 2014,
citing Abdullah Hamidaddin, an adviser to the Dubai-based Al-Meshar
Studies and Research Center, which tracks Islamist movements and works to
promote a more pluralistic culture.

71 Maria Savchyn Pyskir, *Thousands of Roads: A Memoir of a Young Woman's
Life in the Ukrainian Underground during and after World War II* (Jefferson,
NC: McFarland, 2001), 12–13 (my emphases).

72 Shkandrij, *Ukrainian Nationalism*, 27.

73 According to Skakun, *"Patsyfikatsiia,"* 82–3, the Polish authorities arrested
over 1,700 men and women and sent 909 cases to trial. The courts released
700 of those detained. Twenty trials took place. Of the 212 defendants, 28
were sentenced to a total of nearly 45 years.

74 See Zaitsev, *Ukrains'kyi integral'nyi natsionalizm*, 308–26.

75 Andriy Zayarnyuk, "A Revolution's History, A Historians' War," *Ab
Imperio*, no. 1 (2015): 463.

76 For an analysis of the relationship between the Ukrainian Greek Catholic
Church and the OUN, see Oleksandr Zaitsev, Oleh Behen, and Vasyl'
Stefaniiv, *Natsionalizm i relihiia: Hreko-katolyts'ka Tserkva i ukrains'kyi
national'nyi rukh u Halychyni (1920–1930-ti roky)* (Lviv: Vydavnytstvo
Ukrains'koho katolyts'koho universytetu, 2011).

77 Bohdan Budurowycz, "Sheptyts'kyi and the Ukrainian National Movement
After 1914," in *Morality and Reality: The Life and Times of Andrii Sheptyts'kyi*,
ed. Paul R. Magocsi (Edmonton: Canadian Institute of Ukrainian Studies,
1989), 56–7, and John-Paul Himka, "Christianity and Radical Nationalism:
Metropolitan Andrei Sheptytsky and the Bandera Movement," in *State
Secularism and Lived Religion in Soviet Russia and Ukraine*, ed. Catherine
Wanner (Washington, DC: Woodrow Wilson Center Press and New York:
Oxford University Press, 2012), 93–116 (esp. 93–7).

78 This slight paraphrase comes from David Kilcullen, *The Accidental Guerrilla:
Fighting Small Wars in the Midst of a Big One* (New York: Oxford

University Press, 2009), 253. Kilcullen did not cover conflicts in Ukraine, but in Iraq, Indonesia, Thailand, East Timor, and Pakistan during "the war on terror." Nevertheless, his book is intellectually very provocative.

79 The phrase comes from ibid., 53.

80 See Snyder, *Reconstruction of Nations*, 144–9.

81 Macartney, *National States and National Minorities*, 522; Snyder, *Sketches*, 285fn14.

82 Snyder, *Sketches*, 77; M. Stech, "Henryk Józewski," *Encyclopedia of Ukraine*, 2:395.

83 Snyder, *Sketches*, 137. Between 1919 and 1939, Wołyń received approximately 260,000 Polish colonists, Polesie at least 40,000, and Małopolska Wschodnia at least 70,000. See Bohdan Hud', *Ukrains'ko-pol'ski konflikty novitn'oi doby: Etnosotsial'nyi aspekt* (Kharkiv: Akta, 2011), 339.

84 Snyder, *Reconstruction of Nations*, 149. For a biography of Józewski, see Snyder's *Sketches*. For a thorough overview of the contentious relationship between the Polish state and Ukrainians in the interwar Wołyń, see Cornelia Schenke, *Nationalstaat und Nationale Frage: Polen und die Ukrainer 1921– 1939* (Hamburg-Munich: Dölling und Galitz Verlag, 2004).

85 The quote comes from Wlodzimierz Dąbrowski, "Ekspozytura z Oddz[iał] II," 2 March 1940, reprinted in *Zeszyty Historyczne*, no. 140 (2002): 107; cited in Snyder, *Sketches*, 44. The phrase "self-appointed guardian" comes from Bideleux and Jeffries, who characterized Piłsudski as "the self-appointed custodian of Polish independence." Bideleux and Jeffries, *A History of Eastern Europe*, 313.

86 The Soviet Union became a member of the League of Nations on 18 September 1934 and was expelled from the organization on 14 December 1939 for its invasion of Finland on 30 November 1939. The Winter War ended with the signing of the Moscow Peace Treaty on 13 March 1940.

87 For an outline of the treaty, see M.K. Dziewanowski, *Joseph Piłsudski: A European Federalist, 1918–1922* (Stanford, CA: Hoover Institution Press, 1969), 270–2. For a good account of the cooperation between Poland and Petliura, see Jan Jacek Bruski, *"Petlurowcy": Centrum Państwowe Ukraińskiej Republiki Ludowej na wychodźstwie (1919–1924)* (Cracow: Arcana, 2004).

88 Dziewanowski, *Joseph Piłsudski*, 326.

89 Compare the list of leading Ukrainian Prometheans in Arkadii Zhukovsky, "Promethean Movement," *Encyclopedia of Ukraine* (1993), 5:238, and their biographies in that encyclopedia.

90 The quoted words come from "Tadeusz Hołówko," in *Encyclopedia of Ukraine* (1988), 2:211. For an overview of his assassination, see Kulińska, *Działność terrorystyczna*, 250–4. For a biography of Hołówko, see Iwo

Werschler, *Tadeusz Hołówko: życie i działalność* (Warsaw: Państwowe Wydawnictwo Naukowe, 1984).
91 Snyder, *Sketches*, 109–14.
92 The phrase comes from David D. Kirkpatrick and Mayy El-Sheikh, "Once upon a Revolution: A Story with No End," *New York Times*, 7 February 2014.
93 Seton-Watson, *Eastern Europe between the Wars*, 415; Janowsky, *Nationalities and National Minorities*, 111, provides a figure of 18,024,269 for 1930.
94 Bideleux and Jeffries, *A History of Eastern Europe*, 329.
95 Polonsky, *The Little Dictators*, 164 (table 11).
96 Between 500,000 and 600,000 Ukrainians, according to official sources provided by Macartney, *National States and National Minorities*, 529, 532; and Eberhardt, *Ethnic Groups*, 299; 900,000 Ukrainians (unofficially), according to D. Pruts'kyi, "Ukraintsi v 'Velykii Rumunii,'" *Nova hromada* (Vienna) 1, nos 3–4 (1923): 16; cited in Himka, "Western Ukraine," 394.
97 Polonsky, *The Little Dictators*, 80.
98 Livezeanu, *Cultural Politics in Greater Romania*, 51.
99 "Bessarabia" and "Bukovina," in *Encyclopedia of Ukraine* (1984), 1:213, 317.
100 Himka, "Western Ukraine," 402.
101 Livezeanu, *Cultural Politics in Greater Romania*, 65.
102 Cited in Magocsi, *A History of Ukraine*, 645.
103 Polonsky, *The Little Dictators*, 164 (table 11).
104 Seton-Watson, *Eastern Europe between the Wars*, 414.
105 Macartney, *National States and National Minorities*, 525–7.
106 Jeremy King, *Budweisers into Czechs and Germans: A Local History of Bohemian Politics, 1848–1948* (Princeton, NJ: Princeton University Press, 2002), 164.
107 Ibid., 169.
108 Eberhardt, *Ethnic Groups*, 127.
109 Ibid., 127.
110 Robert Paul Magocsi, *The Shaping of a National Identity: Subcarpathian Rus': 1848–1948* (Cambridge, MA: Harvard University Press, 1978), 354; Macartney, *National States and National Minorities*, 526–7, provides a figure of 375,000 in Carpatho-Ruthenia and 212,000 in Slovakia.
111 On the Czechoslovak censuses and their definition of "Ruski," see Taras Kuzio, "The Rusyn Question in Ukraine: Sorting out Fact from Fiction," *Canadian Review of Studies of Nationalism*, 32 (2005): 7.
112 Quote comes from Magocsi, *Shaping*, 275.

113 Eberhardt, *Ethnic Groups*, 291; Macartney, *National States and National Minorities*, 526.
114 Quoted in Macartney, *National States and National Minorities*, 202.
115 Magosci, *Shaping*, 647.
116 Himka, "Western Ukraine," 402.
117 Magocsi, *Shaping*, 649.
118 See ibid., chaps. 5–11.
119 Ibid., 221.
120 Ibid., 175.
121 Ibid., 274.
122 *Statystyka Ukrainy*, no. 124 (1928): 203; and Macartney, *National States and National Minorities*, 522, 526–7, 530.
123 Rothschild, *East Central Europe between the Wars*, 42; Paul Robert Magocsi, *A History of Ukraine: The Land and Its Peoples*, 2nd ed. (Toronto: University of Toronto Press, 2010), 630; cited in Shkandrij, *Ukrainian Nationalism*, 22.
124 Eberhardt, *Ethnic Groups*, 212, 213, 214.
125 The "orphans" phrase comes from the Kurdish leader Mullah Mustapha Barzani, cited in "The State That Never Was," *The Economist* (US), 24 June 1989, 38–9.

Chapter 5

1 L. Trotsky, *Between Red and White: A Study of Some Fundamental Questions of Revolution, with particular reference to Georgia* (London: Communist Party of Great Britain, 1922), 86; cited in M.K. Dziewanowski, *Joseph Piłsudski: A European Federalist, 1918–1922* (Stanford, CA: Hoover Institution Press, 1969), 202.
2 Joseph Stalin, "Reply to the Discussion on the Political Report of the Central Committee to the Sixteenth Congress of the C.P.S.U. (B)," in his *Works* (Moscow: Foreign Languages Publishing House, 1955), 13:4–5.
3 This estimate of the total number of deaths from direct combat, anti-White and anti-Red repressions, pogroms, conflicts in the non-Russian areas, disease, and famine from late 1917 to March 1921 comes from R.J. Rummel, *Lethal Politics: Soviet Genocide and Mass Murder since 1917* (New Brunswick: Transaction, 1990), 47.
4 Robert Service, *A History of Twentieth Century Russia* (Cambridge, MA: Harvard University Press, 1997), 123.
5 Ibid. The statistics on enrolment in the Communist Party of the Soviet Union come from T.H. Rigby, *Communist Party Membership in the USSR, 1917–1967* (Princeton, NJ: Princeton University Press, 1968), 52.

6 William B. Husband, "The New Economic Policy (NEP) and the Revolutionary Experiment, 1921–1929," in *Russia: A History*, ed. Gregory L. Freeze (New York: Oxford University Press, 1997), 265.
7 Alec Nove, *An Economic History of the USSR, 1917–1991*, new and final ed. (New York: Penguin, 1992), 74.
8 Husband, "New Economic Policy," 265.
9 Timothy Snyder, *Sketches from a Secret War: A Polish Artist's Mission to Liberate Soviet Ukraine* (New Haven, CT: Yale University Press, 2005), 105.
10 Nove, *Economic History of the USSR*, 129.
11 *Kommunisticheskaia partiia Sovetskogo soiuza v rezoliutsiiakh i resheniiakh s"ezdov, konferentsii i plenumov TsK* (Moscow: Izd-vo polit. Lit-ry, 1973), 2:45–6.
12 Kommunisticheskaia Akademiia, *Natsional'naia politika VKP(b) v tsifrakh* (Moscow: Izdatelstvo Kommunisticheskoi akademii, 1930), 36. The Soviet censuses of 1920, 1923, and 1926 present data in a form different from the Russian Imperial Census of 1897. Whereas the earlier census indicated the native language of the respondents, the census takers of the 1920s asked the person to which nationality he belonged, as well as his native language. The Soviet censuses of 1939, 1959, 1970, and 1979 also collected data for both native language and nationality by self identification. Because native language and national self-identification do not necessarily coincide, I will consider as Ukrainians those who identified themselves as "Ukrainian" in the Soviet censuses of the 1920s. For a comparison of the questionnaires in the 1897, 1920, 1923, and 1926 censuses, see N. Ya.Vorob'ev, *Vsesoiuznaia perepis' naseleniia 1926 g.*, 2nd ed. (Moscow: Gos. Statisticheskoe izd-vo, 1957), 83–104; and Ralph Clem, ed., *Research Guide to the Russian and Soviet Censuses* (Ithaca, NY: Cornell University Press, 1986).
13 Rossiskaia Kommunisticheskaia partiia, *Desiatyi s"ezd RKP(b), mart 1921 g.* (Moscow: Partiinoe izd-vo, 1933), 580.
14 T.H. Rigby, *Communist Party Membership in the USSR, 1917–1967* (Princeton, NJ: Princeton University Press, 1968), 367.
15 The Communist Party of Ukraine (CP[b]U) was subordinate to the RKP(b), then to the renamed All-Union Communist Party (VKP[b]) in 1925 and to the renamed Communist Party of the Soviet Union (1952).
16 Rigby, *Communist Party Membership*, 366.
17 See Liliana Riga, *The Bolsheviks and the Russian Empire* (Cambridge, UK, and New York: Cambridge University Press, 2012).
18 See "V natsional'nomu pytanni. Rezoliutsii XII z'izdu RKP(b) vid 25 kvitnia 1923 r.," in *Kul'turne budivnytstvo v Ukrains'kii RSR: Naivazhlyvishi rishennia komunistychnoi partii i radians'koho uriadu: Zbirnyk dokumentiv* (Kiev: Derzhavne vyd-vo politychnoi literatury URSR, 1959), 1:206–7.

19 Rigby, *Communist Party Membership*, 369.
20 On the growth of party organizations in the non-Russian regions of the USSR in the 1920s, see *Sotsial'nyi i natsional'nyi sostav VKP(b): Itogi vseso-iuznoi partiinoi perepisi 1927 goda* (Moscow-Leningrad: Giz, 1928).
21 George S.N. Luckyj, *Literary Politics in the Soviet Ukraine, 1917–1934* (New York: Columbia University Press, 1956), 45.
22 D. Lebed, "Rech na kievskoi konferentsii," *Kommunist* (Kharkiv), 23 March 1923; quoted in N.N. Popov, *Narys istorii Komunistychnoi Partii (bil'shovykiv) Ukrainy* (Kharkiv: Vydavnytstvo Proletarii, 1928), 281; Ie. F. Girchak, *Na dva fronta v bor'be s natsionalizmom*, (Moscow: Gosizdat, 1930), 20–1; and Robert S. Sullivant, *Soviet Politics and the Ukraine, 1917–1957* (New York: Columbia University Press, 1962), 351–2.
23 "Proekt dekreta o sodeistvii razvitiiu kul'tury ukrainskogo naroda," in *K razresheniiu natsional'nogo voprosa*, 2nd rev. ed. (Kiev, 1920), 15–20; quoted in Iwan Majstrenko, *Borotbism: A Chapter in the History of Ukrainian Communism* (New York: Research Program on the USSR, 1954), 271–6.
24 See "V natsional'nomu pytanni," in *Kul'turne budivnytstvo v Ukrains'kii RSR: vazhlyvishi rishennia Komunistychnoi partii i Radians'koho uriadu, 1917–1959: Zbirnyk dokumentov* (Kiev: Derzhavne vydavnytstvo politychnoi literatury URSR, 1959–1960), 1:201–10.
25 Elena Borisënok, *Fenomenon Sovetskoi ukrainizatsii, 1920–1930-e gody* (Moscow: Evropa, 2006), 86–7, 163.
26 "Pro zakhody zabezpechennia rivnopravnosti mov i pro dopomohu rozvytkovi ukrains'koi movy," in *Kul'turne budivnytstvo Ukrains'kii RSR*, 1:242–7; Luckyj, *Literary Politics*, 44; Sullivant, *Soviet Politics*, 109.
27 Matthew D. Pauly, *Breaking the Tongue: Language, Education, and Power in Soviet Ukraine, 1923–1934* (Toronto: University of Toronto Press, 2014), 296.
28 *Kulturne budivnytstvo v Ukrains'kyi RSR*, 1:348; cited in Ivan Dzyuba, *Internationalism or Russification? A Study in the Soviet Nationalities Problem* (New York: Pathfinder Press, 1974), 181.
29 Terry Martin, *The Affirmative Action Empire: Nations and Nationalism in the Soviet Union, 1923–1939* (Ithaca, NY: Cornell University Press, 2001), 88.
30 Pauly, *Breaking the Tongue*, 160.
31 For an excellent analysis of Ukrainization as a modernizing mission, see ibid., 73–5.
32 See Mykola Skrypnyk, "USRR – Piedmont ukrains'kykh trudiashchykh mas," in his *Statti i promovy z natsional'noho pytannia* (Munich: Suchasnist', 1974), 153–9. As of 9 December 1931, there were over 5,917,000 Ukrainians

in Poland, 780,000 in Romania, and 525,000 in Czechoslovakia. *Ukraine: A Concise Encyclopedia*, ed. Volodymyr Kubijovyč (Toronto: University of Toronto Press, 1963), 1:210–11, table 2.

33 Pauly, *Breaking the Tongue*, 5–6.
34 Martin, *Affirmative Action Empire*, 77; Pauly, *Breaking the Tongue*, 315. Also see Elena Borisënok's accounts of Russian chauvinist opposition to the implementation of Ukrainization in her *Fenomenon Sovetskoi ukrainizatsii 1920 – 1930-e gody*, 127–60.
35 George Y. Shevelov, *The Ukrainian Language in the First Half of the Twentieth Century (1900–1941): Its State and Status* (Cambridge, MA: Harvard Ukrainian Research Institute, 1989), 127.
36 Victor Kravchenko, *I Chose Freedom: The Personal and Political Life of a Soviet Official* (Garden City, NY: Garden City Publishing, 1947), 63–4.
37 See Borisënok, *Fenomenon Sovetskoi ukrainizatsii*, 140–2.
38 Pauly, *Breaking the Tongue*, 202.
39 Martin, *Affirmative Action Empire*, 95.
40 Ibid., 75.
41 Borisënok, *Fenomenon Sovetskoi ukrainizatsii*, 137, 158.
42 Martin, *Affirmative Action Empire*, 85.
43 Calculated by the author from *Ukrainia: Statystychnyi shchorichnyk 1929* (Kharkiv: Tsentralne statystychne upravlinnia, 1929), 22, table 4 (abbreviated hereafter as *USS 1929*). Only 11 per cent of the total Ukrainian population lived in the cities, while 87.5 per cent lived in the rural areas.
44 *USS 1929*, 22.
45 Calculated from table 6-A, *USS 1929*, 18–19. Of the three most populous national groups in Ukraine, 6,468,799 Ukrainians were literate in Ukrainian and 4,719,898 in Russian; 1,419,444 Russians were literate in Russian and 213,215 in Ukrainian; while 935,784 Jews were literate in Russian and 241,151 in Ukrainian. See *USS 1929*, 18–19.
46 M. Skrypnyk, *Rekonstruktsiia krainy i perebudova shkoly* (Kharkiv, 1932), 123; quoted in S. Siropolko, *Narodna osvita na Soviet'sii Ukraini* (Warsaw: Ukrains'kyi naukovy instytut, 1934), 157.
47 "Pro zakhody v spravi ukrainizatsii shkil'no-vykhovnykh ustanov," in *Kul'turne budivnystvo*, 1:239–42.
48 Pauly, *Breaking the Tongue*, 274, 307, 275.
49 Martin, *Affirmative Action Empire*, 79, 84.
50 *Ukraine: A Concise Encyclopedia*, 1:811.
51 "Pro stan narodnoi osvity na Ukraini," in *Kul'turne budivnystvo*, 1:340–5. The decree was issued in January 1927.

52 Pauly, *Breaking the Tongue*, 173.

53 Ibid., 407.

54 "Pro pryvedennia zahal'noho navchannia na Ukraini," in *Kul'turne budiv-nystvo*, 1:300–3.

55 Pauly, *Breaking the Tongue*, 173.

56 *Ukraine: A Concise Encyclopedia*, 1:811.

57 Ivan Bakalo, *Natsional'na polityka Lenina* (Munich: Suchasnist', 1974), 111.

58 Paul Robert Magocsi, *A History of Ukraine* (Seattle: University of Washington Press, 1996), 564. Also see Bohdan Krawchenko, *Social Change and National Consciousness in Twentieth Century Ukraine* (New York: St Martin's Press, 1985), chapters 2–3; 46–153.

59 Tsentral'noe statisticheskoe upravlenie pri sovete ministrov SSSR, *Itogi Vsesoiuznoi perepisi naseleniia 1959 goda: Ukrainskaia SSR* (Moscow: Gostatizdat, 1963), 65, table 25. According to Rossiiskaia Akademiia nauk, *Vsesoiuznaia perepis naseleniia 1939 goda: Osnovnye itogi* (Moscow: Nauka, 1992), 45, table 10, the percentage of literates in Ukraine at nine years of age and above reached 90.4 by 17 January 1939.

60 Martin, *Affirmative Action Empire*, 77, 92–4.

61 KP(b)U, *Itogi partperepisi 1922 goda* (Kharkiv, 1922), 1:xii, 116; also cited in Richard Pipes, *The Formation of the Soviet Union*, rev. ed. (New York: Atheneum, 1968), 278.

62 VKP(b), Tsenral'nyi komitet, Statisticheskii otdel, *Vsesoiuznaia partiinaia perepis' 1927 goda, 7-ii vypusk. Narodnost' i rodnoi iazyk chlenov VKP(b) i kandidatov chleny. II. Sostav kommunistov korennoi narodnosti v natsional'nykh respublikakh i oblastiakh SSSR* (Moscow: VKP(b), Tsenral'nyi komitet, Statisticheskii otdel, 1927), 51; cited in Basil Dmytryshyn, "National and Social Composition of the Membership of the Communist Party (Bolshevik) of the Ukraine, 1918–1928," *Journal of Central European Affairs* 17, no. 3 (1957): 257.

63 Vsevolod Holubnychy, "Outline History of the Communist Party of Ukraine," in V. Holubnychy, *Soviet Regional Economics: Selected Works of Vsevolod Holubnychy*, ed. Iwan S. Koropeckyj (Edmonton, AB: Canadian Institute of Ukrainian Studies, 1982), 128–9, table 1.

64 Paul Robert Magocsi, *A History of Ukraine: The Land and Its Peoples*, 2nd ed. (Toronto: University of Toronto Press, 2010), 574.

65 *Natsional'naia politika VKP(b) v tsifrakh*, 177, tables 17 and 19.

66 *Natsional'naia politika VKP(b)*, 230–1, table 33.

67 *Statystyka Ukrainy*, no. 124 (1928): 4.

68 *Statystyka Ukrainy*, no. 124 (1928): 4–9. On the complexity of ascertaining and assigning national identities in the Right Bank, see Kate Brown's

pioneering work, *A Biography of No Place: From Ethnic Borderland to Soviet Heartland* (Cambridge, MA: Harvard University Press, 2004).

69 In the 1923, 1926, and 1931 censuses the term "urban centre" was defined as "all official cities, small towns, and populated points – even though they did not possess an urban or rural soviet – which met the following conditions: (1) more than five hundred people lived there, and (2) more than half of those considered to be 'economically independent' worked in non-agricultural occupations." *Natsional'naia politika VKP(b)*, v. Nevertheless, many "urban centres" which did not meet these criteria were included in the Soviet censuses of the 1920s. Thus, we should view these censuses with caution. Nevertheless, while they are not as accurate and reliable in all instances as one would desire, the data do provide in varying degrees a reasonable approximation to reality upon which general trends can be analysed.

70 TsGANKh SSSR, f. 1562, op. 329, d. 145, l. 94; and Rossiskaia Akademiia nauk, *Vsesoiuznaia perepis naseleniia 1939 goda*, 22.

71 *Suchasna statystyka naselennya Ukrainy* (Kharkiv: Tsentral'ne statystychne upravlinnia USRR, 1929), 2–3, 33–5.

72 *Naselenie Ukrainy po dannym perepisi 1920 goda* (Kharkiv: Tsentral'ne statystychne upravlinnia USRR, 1923); *Naselennia v mistakh Ukrainy za danymy Vsesoyuznoho mis'koho perepysu 15 bereznya 1923 roku* (Kharkiv: Tsentral'ne statystychne upravlinnia USRR, 1925); and *Korotki pidsumky perepysu naselennia Ukrainy 17 hrudnya roku 1926* (Kharkiv: Tsentral'ne statystychne upravlinnia USRR, 1928).

73 *Naselenie Ukrainy po dannym perepisi 1920 goda*, 32–35; and *Mis'ki selyshcha USRR. Zbirnyk stat.-ekonomichnykh vidomostei* (Kharkiv: Tsentral'ne statystychne upravlinnia USRR, 1929), 2–17.

74 *Korotki pidsumky perepysu naselennia Ukrainy*, 4–9.

75 *Harvard University Refugee Interview Project* (Harvard University), box 5, no. 190 AD/AP, 17.

76 *Statystyka Ukrainy*, no. 86 (1925), 1, 4.

77 Mark Jefferson, "The Law of the Primate City," *Geographical Review* 29 (1939): 227. On the application of this law to Ukraine, see Roman Szporluk, "Kiev as the Ukraine's Primate City," *Harvard Ukrainian Studies* 3–4 (1979–80): part 2, 843–9.

78 Szporluk, "Kiev as the Ukraine's Primate City," 847.

79 Ibid., 849.

80 TsGAOR Ukrainian SSR, f. 337, op. 1, d. 5038, l. 92; cited in F.G. Turchenko, "Onovnye izmeneniia v sotsial'no-klassovoi strukture gorodskogo naseleniia Sovetskoi Ukrainy v 1920-e gody" (kandidat diss., Kharkiv State University, 1976), 99.

81 For calculations supporting these assertions, see George Liber, "Urban Growth and Ethnic Change in the Ukrainian SSR 1923–1933," *Soviet Studies* 41, no. 4 (1989): 588–9.

82 *Stenograficheskii otchet X s"ezda Rossiiskoi Kommunisticheskoi Partii 8-16 marta 1921* (Petrograd: Gos. Izd-vo, 1921), 93.

83 Andrew C. Janos, "Ethnicity, Communism, and Political Change in Eastern Europe," *World Politics* 23, no. 3 (1971): 493–521.

84 See James E. Mace, *Communism and the Dilemmas of National Liberation: National Communism in Soviet Ukraine, 1918–1933* (Cambridge, MA: Harvard Ukrainian Research Institute, 1983); Krawchenko, *Social Change and National Consciousness*; and George O. Liber, *Soviet Nationality Policy, Urban Growth, and Identity Change in the Ukrainian SSR, 1923–1934* (Cambridge and New York: Cambridge University Press, 1992), chap. 7; and Martin, *Affirmative Action Empire*, chap. 6.

85 The clause, "who feared a split in the party along national lines," comes from Borisёnok, *Fenomenon Sovetskoi ukrainizatsii*, 74.

Chapter 6

1 Joseph Stalin, "The Tasks of Business Executives: Speech Delivered at the First All-Union Conference of Leading Personnel of Socialist Industry, 4 February 1931," in J.V. Stalin, *Works* (Moscow: Foreign Languages Publishing House, 1955), 13:40–1.

2 On the international situation in this period, see Max Beloff, *The Foreign Policy of Soviet Russia, 1929–1941*, vol. 1 (London and New York: Oxford University Press, 1947); George F. Kennan, *Soviet Foreign Policy, 1917–1941* (Princeton, NJ: Van Nostrand, 1960); Xenia J. Eudin and Robert M. Slusser, eds., *Soviet Foreign Policy, 1928–1934: Documents and Materials* (University Park, PA: Penn State University Press, 1967); Adam B. Ulam, *Expansion and Co-Existence: Soviet Foreign Policy, 1917–1973*, 2nd ed. (New York: Holt, Rinehart and Winston, 1974); and Jonathan Haslam, *Soviet Foreign Policy, 1930–1933: The Impact of the Depression* (New York: St Martin's Press, 1983); Caroline Kennedy-Pipe, *Russia and the World, 1917–1991* (London and New York: Arnold, 1998), chaps. 1–2.

3 Harold D. Lasswell, "The Garrison State," *American Journal of Sociology* 46, no. 4 (1941): 455, 458.

4 James E. Mace, "Famine and Nationalism in Soviet Ukraine," *Problems of Communism*, May-June 1984, 49.

5 Andrea Graziosi, "'The Uses of Hunger': Stalin's Solution of the Peasant and National Questions in Soviet Ukraine, 1932–1933," in *Famines in European*

Economic History: The Last Great European Famines Reconsidered, ed. Declan Curran, Lubomyr Luciuk, and Andrew G. Newby (New York: Routledge, 2014), 10.

6 Jon Jacobson, *When the Soviet Union Entered World Politics* (Berkeley: University of California Press, 1994), 206. In iron, steel, and petroleum production, according to Jacobson, the USSR "had lost ground relative to Europe and the United States, and while the manufacture of automobiles, trucks, and tractors had led the United States in particular into a new period of economic expansion based on the introduction of new technologies and methods of production, Soviet industry depended almost completely on prerevolutionary plants, machinery, and methods. With the USSR cut off from advanced technology and unable to make substantial new investment, and with a comparatively low level of labor skills available, industrial productivity in the USSR remained one-half of what it was in Britain and only one-seventh that of the United States" (206–7).

7 Ibid., 212–13. On the Frunze Commission and the context of its reforms, see Mark von Hagen, *Soldiers in the Proletarian Dictatorship: The Red Army and the Soviet Socialist State, 1917–1930* (Ithaca, NY: Cornell University Press, 1990), chap. 4.

8 Jacobson, *When the Soviet Union Entered World Politics*, 218.

9 J. Stalin, "The Threat of War," *Works* (Moscow: Foreign Languages, 1954), 9:328.

10 Raymond W. Leonard, *Secret Soldiers of the Revolution: Soviet Military Intelligence, 1918–1933* (Westport, CT: Greenwood Press, 2000), 86–8; and Jacobson, *When the Soviet Union Entered World Politics*, chap. 9. On the war scare crisis of 1927 and its precursors, see Alfred G. Meyer, "The War Scare of 1927," *Soviet Union/Union Soviétique* 5 (1978): 1–25; John P. Sontag, "The Soviet War Scare of 1926–27," *Russian Review* 34 (1975): 66–77; Sheila Fitzpatrick, "The Foreign Threat during the First Five Year Plan," *Soviet Union/Union Soviétique* 5 (1978): 26–35; Valeri A. Shishkin, "The External Factor in the Country's Socioeconomic Development," in "The Soviet Union in the 1920s: A Roundtable," *Soviet Studies in History* 28 (1989); L.N. Nezhinskii, "Byla li voennaia ugroza SSSR v kontse 20-kh – nachale 30-kh godov?" *Istoriia SSSR*, no. 6 (1990): 14–30; and James Harris, "Intelligence and the Threat Perception: Defending the Revolution, 1917–1937," in *The Anatomy of Terror: Political Violence Under Stalin*, ed. James Harris (Oxford: Oxford University Press, 2013), 29–43.

11 See Mykola Doroshko, *Nomenklatura: Kerivna verkhivka Radians'koi Ukrainy (1917–1938 rr.)* (Kiev: Nyka-Tsentr, 2008); and Hennadii Yefimenko,

Natsional'no-kul-turna polityka VKP(b) shchodo radians'koi Ukrainy (1932–1938) (Kiev: In-t istorii Ukrainy NAN Ukrainy, 2001).

12 I.S. Koropeckyj, "Industry," in *Encyclopedia of Ukraine*, ed. Volodymyr Kubijovyč (Toronto: University of Toronto Press, 1986), 2:314.

13 V.A. Smolii, ed., *Istoriia Ukrainy: nove bachennia* (Kyiv: Naukova dumka, 1994), 2:220; cited in Serhy Yekelchyk, *Ukraine: Birth of a Modern Nation* (New York: Oxford University Press, 2007), 105.

14 Stanislav Kulchytsky, *Ukraina mizh dvoma viinamy, 1921–1938 rr.* (Kyiv: Vydavnychyi dim Al'ternatyvy, 1999), 222; cited in Yekelchyk, *Ukraine*, 105. On Dniprohes, see Anne D. Rassweiler, *The Generation of Power: The History of Dneprostroi* (New York and Oxford: Oxford University Press, 1988).

15 Yekelchyk, *Ukraine*, 105. On the Soviet fears of an invasion from Poland and Germany, see Terry Martin, *The Affirmative Action Empire: Nations and Nationalism in the Soviet Union, 1923–1939* (Ithaca, NY: Cornell University Press, 2001), 36, 225–8, 265, 301, 322, 328–9, and 352; and Kate Brown, *A Biography of No Place: From Ethnic Borderland to Soviet Heartland* (Cambridge, MA: Harvard University Press, 2004), 90, 97, 98, 107, 121, 122, 158, and 167.

16 Bohdan Krawchenko, *Social Change and National Consciousness in Twentieth-Century Ukraine* (New York: St Martin's Press, 1985), 118–19; Yekelchyk, *Ukraine*, 106.

17 I.S. Koropeckyj, *Location Problems in Soviet Industry before World War II* (Chapel Hill: University of North Carolina Press, 1971).

18 See M. Volobuev, "Do problemy ukrains'koi ekonomiky," *Bil'shovyk Ukrainy*, 30 January 1928 and 15 February 1928. These articles were republished in *Dokumenty ukrains'koho komunizmu* (New York: Proloh, 1962), 132–230.

19 V. Holubnychy, "History of the Ukrainian Soviet Socialist Republic," in *Ukraine: A Concise Encyclopedia*, ed. Volodymyr Kubijovyč (Toronto: University of Toronto Press, 1963), 1:826.

20 Ibid., 818.

21 V.M. Molotov, *Molotov Remembers: Inside Kremlin Politics: Conversations with Felix Chuev*, ed. Albert Resis (Chicago: Ivan Dee, 1993), 241.

22 Daron Acemoglu and James A. Robinson, *Why Nations Fail: The Origins of Power, Prosperity, and Poverty* (New York: Crown, 2012), 76.

23 James C. Scott, *Seeing Like a State: How Certain Schemes to Improve the Human Condition Have Failed* (New Haven, CT: Yale University Press, 1998), 210.

24 In 1925, according to statistics provided by Soviet Ukraine's Central Statistical Administration, nearly two-thirds (68.9 per cent) of peasant households in Ukraine's northern region produced only enough grain to feed their

own households. Even in the south's richer steppe region, 27.3 per cent of all households were subsistence farmers. Cited in Liudmyla Hrynevych, *Khronika kolektyvizatsii ta Holodomoru v Ukraini 1927–1933 rr.* (Kiev: Krytyka; 2012), vol. 1, book 3, 17–18.

25 *The Holodomor Reader: A Sourcebook on the Famine of 1932–1933 in Ukraine*, comp. and ed. Bohdan Klid and Alexander J. Motyl (Edmonton and Toronto: Canadian Institute of Ukrainian Studies Press, 2012), xxxiv.

26 The constraints imposed by Russian serfdom before 1861 differed from those dictated by Soviet collectivization after 1928, but the term "second serfdom" provided the peasants a convenient phrase to characterize their hatred of the new system.

27 R.W. Davies and Stephen G. Wheatcroft, *The Years of Hunger: Soviet Agriculture, 1931–1933* (New York and Houndsmills, UK: Palgrave Macmillan, 2004), 93.

28 Robert O. Paxton, *French Peasant Fascism: Henry Dorgère's Greenshirts and the Crises of French Agriculture, 1929–1939* (New York: Oxford University Press, 1997), chap. 1.

29 Dietmar Rothermund, *The Global Impact of the Great Depression, 1929–1939* (London and New York: Routledge, 1996), 39–40.

30 Paxton, *French Peasant Fascism*, chap. 1.

31 Volodymyr Serhiichuk, "Ukrains'kyi khlibnyi eksport iak odyn z holovnykh chynnykiv Holodomoru-hentsydu v 1932–33 rokakh," in *Ukrains'kyi khlib na eksport: 1932–33*, ed. Volodymyr Serhiichuk (Kyiv: PP Serhiichuk M.I., 2006), 8.

32 Joseph Stalin, "Right Deviation in the C.P.S.U. (B.): Speech Delivered at the Plenum of the Central Committee and the Central Control Commission of the C.P.S.U. (B.) in April 1929," in his *Works* (New York: Foreign Languages Publication, 1954), 12:1–113.

33 Roman Serbyn, "The Ukrainian Famine of 1932–33 and the United Nations Convention on Genocide," in *Famine in Ukraine, 1932–1933: Genocide by Other Means*, ed. Taras Hunczak and Roman Serbyn (New York: Shevchenko Scientific Society in the U.S., 2007), 53–4. According to Holubnychy, 90.6 per cent of these alleged kulaks did not employ more than one worker. Holubnychy, "History of the Ukrainian Soviet Socialist Republic," 815.

34 Yekelchyk, *Ukraine*, 108. For an assessment of the income of the collective farmer, see Davies and Wheatcroft, *Years of Hunger*, 375–99.

35 Andrea Graziosi, "The Great Soviet Peasant War: Bolsheviks and Peasants, 1917–1933," in *Stalinism, Collectivization and the Great Famine*, ed. Andrea Graziosi (Cambridge, MA: Ukrainian Studies Fund, 2009).

36 Hrynevych, *Khronika kolektyvizatsii ta Holodomoru*, vol. 1, book 3, 119.

37 R.W. Davies, *The Socialist Offensive: The Collectivization of Soviet Agriculture, 1929–1930* (Cambridge, MA: Harvard University Press, 1980), 47, 60; R.W. Davies, *The Soviet Economy in Turmoil, 1929–1930* (Cambridge, MA: Harvard University Press, 1989), 72; Alec Nove, *An Economic History of the USSR, 1917–1991*, rev. ed. (New York: Penguin, 1992), 155; *The War against the Peasantry, 1927–1930: The Tragedy of the Soviet Countryside*, ed. Lynne Viola, V. P. Danilov, N.A. Ivnitskii, and Denis Kozlov (New Haven, CT: Yale University Press, 2005), 35–6, 69, 111–12, and 115.

38 N. Osinsky coined the phrase "natural saboteurs" in a letter to Lenin in 1921, shortly after the Bolshevik Party introduced the NEP. Cited in Graziosi, "Great Soviet Peasant War," 33.

39 Ibid., 38.

40 *The War against the Peasantry, 1927–1930*, document 5, 33–4.

41 V.M. Molotov, "Doklad V.M. Molotova v TsK VKP(b) i STO o poezdke na Ukrainu, Ural i v Bashkiriiu po delam khlebozagotovok (25 January 1928)," *Tragediia sovetskoi derevni: kollektivizatsiia i raskulachivanie: dokumenty i materially*, ed. Viktor Danilov, Roberta Manning, Lynne Viola, et al. (Moscow: Rossiiskaia pol. entsiklopediia, 1999), 1:185 (quote), 186.

42 *Molotov Remembers*, 241.

43 Ibid., 242.

44 Ibid.

45 Alec Nove, *An Economic History of the U.S.S.R.* (Baltimore and London: Penguin, 1969), 152.

46 Moshe Lewin, "The Immediate Background of Soviet Collectivization," in *The Making of the Soviet System*, ed. M. Lewin (New York: Pantheon, 1985), 110; cited in *The War against the Peasantry*, 118.

47 Liudmyla Hrynevych, *Holod 1928–1929 rr. u Radian'skii Ukraini* (Kiev: Natsional'na Akademiia Nauk Ukrainy, Instytut istorii Ukrainy, 2013), 24–6.

48 Ibid., 90, 155, 167.

49 Ibid., 27.

50 Mark Tauger, "Crisis or Famine? The Ukrainian State Commission for Aid to Crop-Failure Victims and the Ukrainian Famine of 1928–29," in *Provincial Landscapes: Local Dimensions of Soviet Power, 1917–1953*, ed. Donald J. Raleigh (Pittsburgh: University of Pittsburgh Press, 2001), 170.

51 Hrynevych, *Holod*, 167, 249–50. Even A.I. Rykov, the chairman of the Council of Ministers of the USSR and a member of the pro-peasant Bukharin faction in the central Politburo, emphasized in late September 1928 in Kharkiv that grain collections in Ukraine had to supply the crop-failure okrugs as well as workers and townspeople. *Visti*, 27 September 1928, 2; cited in Tauger, "Crisis or Famine?" 156.

52 Tauger, "Crisis or Famine?" 168.
53 The first quote comes from ibid., 163; the second from ibid., 168.
54 Hrynevych, *Holod 1928–1929 rr.*, 168.
55 Ibid., 90, 333.
56 Ibid., 339.
57 Ibid., 309, 310.
58 Graziosi, "The Great Soviet Peasant War," 40–1.
59 Cited in Liudmyla Hrynevych, "Stalin's Revolution from Above and the Famine of 1933 as Factors in the Politicization of Ukrainian Society," in Klid and Motyl, *Holodomor Reader*, 13.
60 Cited in ibid., 14.
61 Hrynevych, *Holod 1928–1929 rr.*, 314–15, 317.
62 Ibid., 339. See Iurii Shapoval and Vadym Zolotar'ov, "Ievrei v kerivnytstvi orhaniv DPU-NKVD-USRR-URSR u 1920–1930-kh rr.," *Z arkhiviv VUChK/GPU/NKVD/KGB* 17, no. 1 (2010): 53–93, which discusses the complexity of the inclusion and the motivations of the large number of members of the Ukrainian security services with a Jewish background.
63 Stalin, *Works*, 12:474; *Dokumenty svidetel'stvuiut: Iz istorii derevni nakanune i v khode kollektivizatsii 1927–1932*, ed. V.P. Danilov and N.A. Ivnitskii (Moscow: Izd. Politicheskoi literatury, 1991), 295.
64 *Tragediia sovetskoi derevni*, vol. 3, document 47.
65 Cited in Graziosi, "Great Soviet Peasant War," 41. For a history of the Bolshevik struggle against the Don Cossacks, see Peter Holquist, *Making War, Forging Revolution: Russia's Continuum of Crisis, 1914–1921* (Cambridge, MA: Harvard University Press, 2002).
66 Quote comes from Graziosi, "Great Soviet Peasant War," 41.
67 Ibid., 41–2.
68 Serbyn, "Ukrainian Famine of 1932–33," 55.
69 Mace, "Famine and Nationalism," 39; V.N. Zemskov, *Spetsposelentsy v SSSR, 1930–1960* (Moscow: Nauka, 2003), 17; and Lynne Viola, *The Unknown Gulag: The Lost World of Stalin's Special Settlements* (New York: Oxford University Press, 2007), 195.
70 From a letter to M. Kalinin on the deportation of families from Ukraine and Kursk, cited in Aleksander N. Yakovlev, *A Century of Violence in Soviet Russia* (New Haven and London: Yale University Press, 2002), 35.
71 Davies and Wheatcroft, *Years of Hunger*, 22.
72 *Statystyka Ukrainy*, no. 124 (1928), appendix table 1, 203.
73 *Statystyka Ukrainy*, no. 96 (1927), v; *Statystyka Ukrainy*, no. 124 (1928), table 2, 4.
74 *Statystyka Ukrainy*, no. 96 (1927), table 3, xvi–xix.

75 Calculated from *Statystyka Ukrainy*, no. 124 (1928), table 1, 2.

76 Kommunisticheskaia akademiia, Komissiia po izucheniiu natsional'nogo voprosa, *Natsional'naia politika VKP(b) v tsifrakh* (Moscow: Izd. Kommunisticheskoi Akademii, 1930), table 1, 59.

77 On grain reserves, see Hrynevych, *Holod 1928–1929*, 23, 336; for quote, Hiroaki Kuromiya, "The Soviet Famine of 1932–1933 Reconsidered," *Europe-Asia Studies* 60, no. 4 (2008): 667.

78 Ibid.

79 Yekelchyk, *Ukraine*, 107.

80 Lev Kopelev, *I sotvoril sebe kumira* (Ann Arbor, MI: Ardis, 1978), 249; and Lev Kopelev, *The Education of a True Believer* (New York: Harper and Row, 1980), 226. Gary Kern's translation of Kopelev's memoir into English renders the word "nesoznatel'nosti" as "unconscientiousness." In this context, this word is best translated as "political backwardness."

81 Serbyn, "Ukrainian Famine of 1932–1933," 55, 56.

82 Graziosi, "Great Soviet Peasant War," 44.

83 Ibid., 45; Graziosi, "The Uses of Hunger," 7–8.

84 Graziosi, "Great Soviet Peasant War," 46; Graziosi, "The Uses of Hunger," 8.

85 Graziosi, "Great Soviet Peasant War," 46; quote comes from Graziosi, "The Uses of Hunger," 4.

86 *Pravda*, 2 March 1930; I. Stalin, "Golovokruzhenie ot uspekhov," in his *Sochinenniia*, vol. 12 (Moscow, 1952), 12:191–9.

87 Graziosi, "Great Soviet Peasant War," 46.

88 Serbyn, "Ukrainian Famine of 1932–33," 56, 57; S.I. Bilokin et al., eds, *Holod 1932–1933 rokiv v Ukraini: Prychyny ta naslidky* (Kyiv: Naukova dumka, 2003).

89 Calculated from Yekelchyk, *Ukraine*, 107 (for 1928); Serbyn, "Ukrainian Famine," 55–6 (for 1 March 1930), and 56–7 (for 1 October 1930).

90 Timothy Snyder, *Bloodlands: Europe between Hitler and Stalin* (New York: Basic Books, 2010), 32.

91 Davies and Wheatcroft, *Years of Hunger*, 10.

92 Snyder, *Bloodlands*, 30, 29.

93 Graziosi, "Great Soviet Peasant War," 10.

94 V. Holubnychy, "Collectivization," in *Encyclopedia of Ukraine*, 1:539; and Yekelchyk, *Ukraine*, 109.

95 Serbyn, "Ukrainian Famine of 1932–1933," 58.

96 *Natsional'naia politika VKP(b) v tsifrakh*, 144, 148.

97 Hrynevych, *Khronika kolektyvizatsiia*, vol. 1, book 1, 24.

98 Institut Politychnykh doslidzhen', *Komunistychna partiia Ukrainy: z'izdy i konferentsii* (Kiev: Vyd. "Ukraina," 1991), 149 (on the number of Komsomol and party members); Davies and Wheatcroft, *Years of Hunger*, 6 (on the urban visitors to the countryside).

99 Matthew D. Pauly, *Breaking the Tongue: Language, Education, and Power in Soviet Ukraine, 1923–1934* (Toronto: University of Toronto Press, 2014), 30, 233, 256.

100 See Hrynevych, *Khronika kolektyvizatsii*, vol. 1, book 1, 24.

101 Lynne Viola, "The Second Coming: Class Enemies in the Soviet Countryside, 1927–1935," in *Stalinist Terror: New Perspectives*, ed. J. Arch Getty and Roberta Manning (New York: Cambridge University Press, 1993), 69–70.

102 RGASPI, f. 82, op. 2, d. 136, l. 2; d.137, l. 4; cited in Elena Borisënok, *Fenomenon Sovetskoi ukrainizatsii 1920 – 1930-e gody* (Moscow: Evropa, 2006), 210.

103 Davies and Wheatcroft, *Years of Hunger*, 76, 79–80, 101, 103, 105, 126, 136, 225, 231, 443–6, 448–9, 463–4.

104 Graziosi, "Great Soviet Peasant War," 49.

105 Nicholas Werth, "Strategies of Violence in the Stalinist USSR," in *Stalinism and Nazism: History and Memory Compared*, ed. Henry Russo (Lincoln: University of Nebraska Press, 2004), 80; cited in Norman M. Naimark, *Stalin's Genocides* (Princeton, NJ: Princeton University Press, 2010), 71.

106 Snyder, *Bloodlands*, 34.

107 Leone Sircana, the Italian vice-consul in Novorossisk; cited in Graziosi, "Great Soviet Peasant War," 52.

108 Ibid., 50.

109 See *The Stalin-Kaganovich Correspondence, 1931–1936*, ed. R.W. Davies et al. (New Haven, CT: Yale University Press, 2003).

110 Serbyn, "Ukrainian Famine of 1932–1933," 61.

111 Davies and Wheatcroft, *Years of Hunger*, 136.

112 Michael Ellman, "The Role of Leadership Perceptions and of Intent in the Soviet Famine of 1931–1934," *Europe-Asia Studies* 57, no. 6 (2005): 823; Klid and Motyl, *Holodomor Reader*, xxxvi.

113 "Zi shchodennyka vchytel'ky Oleksandry Radchenko," in *Rozsekrechena pam'iat': Holodomor 1932–1933 rokiv v Ukraini v dokumentakh GPU-NKVD*, ed. V. Borysenko, V. Danylenko, S. Kokin, O. Stasiuk, and Iu. Shapoval (Kiev: Stylis, 2007), 546; excerpts in Kild and Motyl, *Holodomor Reader*, 181.

114 See Omelian Rudnytskyi, Nataliia Levchuk, Oleh Wolowyna, Pavlo Shevchuk, and Alla Savchak, "Demography of a Man-Made Human

Catastrophe: The Case of Massive Famine in Ukraine, 1932–1933,"
Canadian Studies in Population 42, nos. 1–2 (2015), 65 (table 6).

115 Davies and Wheatcroft, *Years of Hunger*, 152–4.

116 "Lyst H. Petrovs'koho do V. Molotova ta I. Stalina pro vazhke prodovol'che stanovyshche ta holod v USRR," in *Holodomor 1932–1933 rokiv v Ukraini: Dokumenty i materialy*, ed. Ruslan Pyrih (Kyiv: Vyd. Dim "Kyievo-Mohylians'ka akademiia, 2007), documents 138, 139; also see Chubar's letter in *Komandyry velykoho holodu: poizdky V. Molotova i L. Kaganovycha v Ukraini ta na pivnichnyi Kavkaz, 1932–1933 rr.*, ed. Valerii Vasiliev and Yurii Shapoval (Kiev: Heneza, 2001), 206–15.

117 *Stalin-Kaganovich Correspondence, 1931–1936*, 107; see doc. 51 (25 July 1932).

118 Davies and Wheatcroft, *Years of Hunger*, 162.

119 "Stalin to Kaganovich (15 June 1932)," in *Stalin-Kaganovich Correspondence*, 136.

120 *Stalin-Kaganovich Correspondence*, 12; see doc. 35.

121 "Stalin to Kaganovich and Molotov (for Members of the Politburo)," *Stalin-Kaganovich Correspondence*, 139.

122 "Stalin to Kaganovich (15 June 1932)," *Stalin-Kaganovich Correspondence*, 137.

123 *Stalin-Kaganovich Correspondence*, 156. For an analysis of this party conference, see "III Konferentsiia KP(b)U: Proloh trahedii holodu," in Vasiliev and Shapoval, *Komandyry Velykoho holodu*, 152–64 (in Ukrainian); 165–78 (in Russian).

124 In 1988, the Ukrainian writer Oleksa Musiienko coined the term *Holodomor*, which fused the words *holod* (hunger, famine) with *moryty* (to destroy by starvation) to describe the famine of 1932–3. The concept means an "intentionally set famine."

125 Pyrih, *Holodomor*, documents 192 and 210; H.M. Mikhalychenko and Ie. P. Shatalina, comps., *Kolektivizatsiia i holod na Ukraini, 1929–1933* (Kiev: Naukova Dumka, 1992), document 278; *Tragediia sovetskoi derevne*, 3:477–9.

126 Davies and Wheatcroft, *Years of Hunger*, 168. Of course, the authorities could arbitrarily define a "one-time" theft as "systematic" theft.

127 Ibid., 169–171.

128 *Tragediia sovetskoi derevni* (2001), 420–1; excerpts appear in Klid and Motyl, *Holodomor Reader*, 238.

129 Pyrih, *Holodomor*, document 293, 388–395; Klid and Motyl, *Holodomor Reader*, 35.

130 Snyder, *Bloodlands*, 43.

131 On 1929 and August 1932, see Davis and Wheatcroft, *Years of Hunger*, 169; on late 1932, see Heorhii Papakin, "Blacklists as a Tool of the Soviet Genocide in Ukraine," *Holodomor Studies* 1, no. 1 (2009): 75.

132 Papakin, "Blacklists as a Tool," 67, 74.

133 "Zones of death" comes from Snyder, *Bloodlands*, 43.

134 F.M. Rudych et al., eds, *Holod 1932–1933 rokiv na Ukraini: Ochyma istorykiv, movoiu dokumentiv* (Kiev: Vyd. Politychnoi literatury Ukrainy,
1990), document 121; Pyrih, *Holodomor*, document 354; *Tragediia sovetskoi
derevni*, 3:576–7.

135 Ibid.

136 Papakin, "Blacklists as a Tool," 74.

137 Kopelev, *Education of a True Believer*, 235.

138 Ibid. The last sentence comes from 265.

139 See Alain Blum, *Naitre: Vivre et mourir en URSS: 1917–1991* (Paris: Plon,
1994), 102–3, for the rates of mortality in this period; cited in Graziosi,
"Great Soviet Peasant War," 53.

140 For the brutality against the peasants in the cities, see Sergio Gradenigo's
"Report to the Royal Embassy of Italy and to the Royal Italian Ministry
of Foreign Affairs, 10 July 1933," in U.S. Commission on the Ukraine
Famine, *Report to Congress* (Washington, DC: Government Printing
Office, 1988), appendix 2, 439. For a full collection of Italian diplomatic
reports, including Gradenigo's, dealing with the situation in Ukraine, see
*Lettere da Kharkov: La carestia in Ukraina e nel Caucaso del Nord nei
rerapporti del diplomatici italiani, 1923–1933* (Turin: Einaudi, 1991); and
*Lysty z Kharkova: Holod v Ukrainita ta na Pivnichnomu Kavkazi v povi-
domlenniah italiis'kykh diplomativ 1932–1933 rokiv*, ed. Iurii Shapoval
and Andrea Graziosi (Kharkiv: Folio, 2007).

141 Graziosi, "The Uses of Hunger," 19.

142 According to Graziosi, "In the first quarter of 1933, for example, the
Soviet capital received 165,000 tons of grain, plus 86,000 for its surrounding province. In contrast, the entire Soviet Ukrainian Republic, with a far
larger population, welcomed only 280,000 tons." Graziosi, "The Uses of
Hunger," 19.

143 Ibid.

144 Pyrih, *Holodomor*, document 365, 496–513.

145 Davies and Wheatcroft, *Years of Hunger*, 195.

146 Pyrih, *Holodomor*, documents 440, 442, 443; Rudych, *Holod 1932–1933*,
document 150, 151; Also see *Tragedia sovetskoi derevni*, 3:634–6; and Terry
Martin, *The Affirmative Action Empire: Nations and Nationalism in the
Soviet Union, 1923–1939* (Ithaca, NY, and London: Cornell University
Press, 2001), 306–307.

147 Andrea Graziosi, "The Soviet 1931–1933 Famines and the Ukrainian
Holodomor: Is a New Interpretation Possible, and What Would Its

Consequences Be?" in Andrea Graziosi, *Stalinism, Collectivization and the Great Famine* (Cambridge, MA: Ukrainian Studies Fund, 2009), 78.

148 For a well-written memoir of collectivization and the famine in a village in Cherkasy okruh between 1929 and 1933, see Miron Dolot, *Execution by Hunger: The Hidden Holocaust* (New York: W.W. Norton, 1985).

149 Ibid., 150.

150 Pitirim Sorokin, *Man and Society in Calamity: The Effects of War, Revolution, Famine, Pestilence upon Human Mind, Behavior, Social Organization, and Cultural Life* (New York: E.P. Dutton, 1942), 51.

151 Ibid., 17.

152 Ibid., 59.

153 Vasily Grossman, *Everything Flows*, translated from the Russian by Robert and Elizabeth Chandler with Anna Aslanyan (New York: New York Review Books, 2009), 136.

154 Ibid., 133.

155 William Henry Chamberlin, *Russia's Iron Age* (London: Duckworth, 1935), 85; cited in Klid and Motyl, *Holodomor Reader*, 140.

156 *Narodnoe khoziaistvo SSSR* (Moscow, 1935), 222; cited in Roy Medvedev, *Let History Judge: The Origins and Consequences of Stalinism*, rev. and expanded ed. (New York: Columbia University Press, 1989), 243

157 Robert Conquest, *The Harvest of Sorrow: Soviet Collectivization and the Terror-Famine* (New York and Oxford: Oxford University Press, 1986), 221.

158 Viktor Kondrashin, "Hunger in 1932–1933: A Tragedy of the Peoples of the USSR," *Holodomor Studies* 1, no. 2 (2009): 16–21; Klid and Motyl, *Holodomor Reader*, 51.

159 Medvedev, *Let History Judge*, 243. According to Snyder, Stalin might have saved millions of lives. "He could have suspended food exports for a few months, released grain reserves (three million tons), or just given peasant access to local grain storage areas. Such simple measures, pursued as late as November 1932, could have kept the death toll to hundreds of thousands rather than the millions." Snyder, *Bloodlands*, 41–2. But in light of his ideological predispositions, Stalin did not choose this option.

160 Michael Ellman, "Stalin and the Soviet Famine of 1932–1933 Revisited," *Europe-Asia Studies* 59, no. 4 (2007): 679.

161 Kuromiya, "The Soviet Famine of 1932–1933 Reconsidered," 665.

162 Graziosi, "The Uses of Hunger," 22.

163 Davies and Wheatcroft, *Years of Hunger*, 230.

164 Wendy Z. Goldman, *Terror and Democracy in the Age of Stalin: The Social Dynamics of Repression* (New York: Cambridge University Press, 2007), 20–1.

165 Robert Conquest, *The Great Terror: A Reassessment* (New York and Oxford: Oxford University Press, 1990), 334.

166 Graziosi, "The Uses of Hunger," 23.

167 Davies and Wheatcroft, *Years of Hunger*, 231, 241.

168 Davies, *Stalin-Kaganovich Correspondence*, 187.

169 Goldman, *Terror and Democracy*, 23.

170 Charles P. Kindleberger, *The World in Depression, 1929–1939* (Berkeley, CA: University of California Press, 1973), 93. In 1930, for example, the USSR exported 4.76 million tons of grain for 702 million rubles, and in 1931 it shipped 5.1 million tons for 523.3 million rubles. See Serhiichuk, *Ukrains'kyi khlib na eksport: 1932–33*, 9.

171 Graziosi, "The Uses of Hunger," 15. The statistics in the first lines of the paragraph come from *Narodnoe khoziaistvo SSSR* (Moscow, 1935), 222; cited in Medvedev, *Let History Judge*, 243.

172 Roy Medvedev, *On Stalin and Stalinism* (New York and Oxford: Oxford University Press, 1979), 75; Medvedev, *Let History Judge*, 240.

173 Yekelchyk, *Ukraine*, 110, 108. Also see Sarah I. Cameron, "The Hungry Steppe: Soviet Kazakhstan and the Kazakh Famine, 1921–1934" (PhD dissertation, Department of History, Yale University, 2010).

174 Statistics on the number of victims of the famine in Ukraine in 1932–3 vary greatly. Pitirim Sorokin claimed that "two to three millions perished in the Russian famine of 1933–1934." Sorokin, *Man and Society in Calamity*, 91. Robert Conquest estimated a loss of five million in Ukraine and two million in Russia, of whom, he estimated, probably one million were Ukrainians in the North Caucasus. He also suggested one million Kazakh losses in 1932. Conquest, *The Harvest of Sorrow*, 306. James E. Mace asserted that a five to seven million loss was "a conservative figure." James Mace "The Famine of 1933: A Survey of Sources," in *Famine in Ukraine, 1932–33*, ed. Roman Serbyn and Bohdan Krawchenko (Edmonton, AB: Canadian Institute of Ukrainian Studies, 1986), 50. Although he did not provide absolute figures for Ukraine, Stephen Wheatcroft estimated the loss of four to five million throughout the USSR. S. Wheatcroft, "More Light on the Scale of Repression and Excessive Mortality in the Soviet Union in the 1930s," in *Stalinist Terror: New Perspectives*, ed. J. Arch Getty and Roberta Manning (New York: Cambridge University Press, 1993), 280. Alec Nove viewed Conquest's statistics as essentially correct, but "somewhat too high for Ukraine, but somewhat too low for Kazakhstan." A. Nove, "Victims of Stalinism: How Many?" in Getty and Manning, *Stalinist Terror*, 266, 274. According to Stanislav Kulchytsky, the leading economic historian of twentieth-century Ukraine, between 3 and 3.5 million people in the republic

died of starvation and malnutrition-related diseases. He estimated that the total demographic losses, including a reduction in the number of children born, totalled between 4.5 and 4.8 million people. S. Kulchytsky, "Teror holodom iak instrument kolektyvizatsii," in *Holodomor 1932–1933 rr. v Ukraini: prychyny i naslidky* (Kyiv: Instytut istorii Ukrainy NANU, 1995), 34; cited in Yekelchyk, *Ukraine*, 112. According to Timothy Snyder, approximately 3.3 million died by starvation and hunger-related disease in Soviet Ukraine in 1932–3. "Of these people, some three million would have been Ukrainians, and the rest Russians, Poles, Germans, Jews, and others. Among the million or so dead in the Soviet Russian Republic were probably at least two hundred thousand Ukrainians, since the famine struck heavily in regions where Ukrainians lived. Perhaps as many as a hundred thousand more Ukrainians were among the 1.3 million people who died in the earlier famine in Kazakhstan. All in all, no fewer than 3.3 million Soviet citizens died in Soviet Ukraine of starvation and hunger-related diseases; and about the same number of Ukrainians by nationality died in the Soviet Union as a whole." Snyder, *Bloodlands*, 53.

175 Jacques Vallin, France Mesle, Serguei Adamets, and Serhii Pyrozhkov, "A New Estimate of Ukrainian Population Losses during the Crises of the 1930s and 1940s," *Population Studies* 56, no. 3 (2002): 249–64; Oleh Wolowyna, "The Famine-Genocide of 1932–33: Estimation of Losses and Demographic Impact" (paper presented to the UNC Conference on the Famine-Genocide in Ukraine, 1932–33, 12 September 2008, Chapel Hill, NC); Rudnytskyi, Levchuk, Wolowyna, Shevchuk, and Savchak, "Demography of a Man-Made Human Catastrophe," 69.

176 Rudnytskyi et al., "Demography of a Man-Made Human Catastrophe," 69. The five authors calculate "excess deaths" (or "direct losses") by estimating all of the deaths which occurred during the famine period, then subtracting the "normal" deaths expected to have occurred had there been no famine. They define "indirect losses" as "the difference between the expected births had there been no famine and actual births" (64).

177 Ibid., 69.

178 In 1933, "the number of deaths reached a value approximately seven times the number of births, that is, there were seven times more deaths than births. In 1933 the life expectancy at birth was 11 years for males and 15 years for females, while in 1942 – the deadliest year of World War Two in Ukraine, life expectancy at birth for males was 18 years and 26 years for females. In other words, in spite of the fact that more persons died in Ukraine in 1942 than in 1933, the impact of the Holodomor (death by starvation) was significantly larger. Close to half of all deaths due to the Holodomor were for

persons under 25 years of age, and in 1933 more than 40 percent of all births died within one year." Wolowyna, "The Famine-Genocide," 11; and Rudnytskyi et al., "Demography of a Man-Made Human Catastrophe," 65.

179 Graziosi, "The Uses of Hunger," 20. According to Rudnytskyi et al., "Demography of a Man-Made Human Catastrophe," 70, the majority of excess deaths occurred in a six-month period, between March and August 1933, with a 77.5 per cent increase in the urban areas and 90.0 per cent in the rural areas.

180 Rudnytskyi et al., "Demography of a Man-Made Human Catastrophe," 65, 66.

181 Ibid., 66.

182 Gradenigo, "Report," 427.

183 Rossiiski Gosudarstennyi arkhiv ekonomiki (RGAE), fond 1562, op. 329, d. 145, l. 8, in *Vsesoiuznaia perepis' naseleniia 1939 goda/Vsesoiuznai perepis' naseleniia 1937 goda* (Woodbridge, CT: Research Publications (Primary Source Media); and Moscow: Federal Archival Service of Russia, 2000, reel 2 (cited hereafter as *VPN 1939 goda/1937 goda*).

184 RGAE, f. 1562, op. 329, d. 199, l. 3, in ibid.; *Statystyka Ukrainy*, no. 124 (1928), xiii.

185 *Natsional'naia politika VKP(b) v tsifrakh*, 45; Akademiia Nauk SSSR, *Vsesoiuznaia perepis' naseleniia 1937 g. Korotki itogi* (Moscow: Institut istorii SSSR AN SSSR, 1991), 28. Kazakhstan's dramatic population loss in this period included (1) large numbers of Kazakhs who fled the republic during collectivization, contributing to the republic's overall population loss, and (2) large numbers of people who resettled in the republic during 1926–37, including special settlers, free agricultural colonists, and labourers with KarLag, thus boosting the republic's overall population numbers. The numbers for Kazakhstan's losses are difficult to measure. See "Introduction," Cameron, "The Hungry Steppe," 1–24.

186 Graziosi, "The Soviet 1931–1933 Famines," 80.

187 The statistics come from: (1926): *Natsional'naia politika VKP(b) v tsifrakh*, 36; (1937): *Vsesoiuznaia perepis naseleniia 1937 g.*, 83; and RGAE, f. 1562, op. 329, d. 145, l. 8; and (1939): RGAE, f. 1562, op. 329, d. 4537, l. 62, in *VPN 1939 goda/1937 goda,* reel 2; and Rossiiskaia Akademiia nauk and Upravlenie statistiki naseleniia Goskomstata, *Vsesoiuznaia perepis' naseleniia 1939 goda: Osnovnye itogi* (Moscow: Nauka, 1992), 57.

188 For 1926: *Natsional'naia politika VKP(b) v tsifrakh*, table 5, 44; for 1937: RGAE, f. 1562, op. 329, d. 145, l. 2, in *VPN 1939 goda/1937 goda,* reel 2.

189 *Vsesoiuznaia perepis' naseleniia 1937 g.*, 96.

190 *Statystyka Ukrainy*, no. 124 (1928), xiii; RGAE, f. 1562, op. 329, d. 145, l. 1; RGAE, f. 1562, op. 329, d. 4535, l. 72, in *VPN 1939 goda/1937 goda,* reel 2; *Vsesoiuznaia perepisaseleniia 1939 goda,* 68.

191 *Statystyka Ukrainy*, no. 124 (1928), xiii; RGAE, f. 1562, op. 329, d. 199, ll. 3, 96–7, in *VPN 1939 goda/1937 goda*, reel 2.

192 *Statystyka Ukrainy*, no. 124 (1928), xiii; RGAE, f. 1562, op. 329, d. 145, l. 1; and RGAE, f. 1562, op. 329, d. 4535, l. 72, in *VPN 1939 goda/1937 goda*, reel 2; *Vsesoiuznaia perepis' naseleniia 1939 goda*, 68.

193 Graziosi, "The Uses of Hunger," 11.

194 See Cameron, "The Hungry Steppe."

195 In 1930–4, Kazakhstan suffered the loss of 1,258,200 in excess deaths and 227,900 in lost births. Rudnytskyi et al., "Demography of a Man-Made Human Catastrophe," tables 8.5 and 8.6. The Kazakhs started dying as early as the fall of 1930, with most perishing in the winter of 1931–2. Of the 1.5 million who passed away, approximately 1.3 million were Kazakh men, women, and children; the authorities identified the remaining 200,000 as members of other national groups. See Cameron, "The Hungry Steppe."

196 Graziosi, "Uses of Hunger," 20.

197 TsGANKh SSSR, fond 1562, op. 329, d.145, l. 15, in *VPN 1939 goda/1937 goda*, reel 2.

198 Martha Brill Olcott made this point in 1981. See her "The Collectivization Drive in Kazakhstan," *The Russian Review* 40, no. 2 (1981): 136. According to RGAE, f. 1562, op. 336, d. 221, l. 13, in *VPN 1939 goda/1937 goda*, reel 9, the number of Ukrainians living in the USSR in 1939 (28,070,404) constituted 90 per cent of their 1926 population; the number of Kazakhs living in the USSR in 1939 (3,098,764) comprised 78.1 per cent of their 1926 population. The Moldovans also lost a substantial number in this period. Their 1939 population constituted 93 per cent of their 1926 population. Of the largest Soviet national groups (those with a population over 250,000), only the Kazakhs, Ukrainians, and Moldovans possessed a smaller population in 1939 than in 1926.

199 Graziosi, "Uses of Hunger," 20.

200 Davies and Wheatcroft, *Years of Hunger*, 68, 119, 120, 123 (weather), 69 (insect infestation), and 132 (fungal disease).

201 See Lynne Viola, *Peasant Rebels under Stalin* (New York: Oxford University Press, 1996), 209; Mark B. Tauger, *Natural Disaster and Human Actions in the Soviet Famine of 1931–1933* (Pittsburgh, PA: Center for Russian and East European Studies, University Center for International Studies, University of Pittsburgh, 2001); and Davies and Wheatcroft, *Years of Hunger*, especially 400–41, who make this argument.

202 On the planned harvests of 1929 to 1932, see Davies and Wheatcroft, *Years of Hunger*, 123.

203 Ibid., 235, 355.

204 Ibid., 263.
205 Graziosi, "Great Soviet Peasant War," 48.
206 On crop rotation, see Davies and Wheatcroft, *Years of Hunger*, 56, 57, 110, 231–2, 234, 268; on weeding, see 67, 68, 124, 128, 240, 272, 466.
207 Pyrih, *Holodomor 1932–1933*; *Rozsekrechena pam'iat'*; and Klid and Motyl, *Holodomor Reader*.
208 Davies and Wheatcroft, *Years of Hunger*, 69.
209 Ibid., 69–70.
210 Ibid., 93, 117.
211 Also see Naimark, *Stalin's Genocides*, 134–5.
212 Graziosi, "Great Soviet Peasant War," 56.
213 "Stalin to Kaganovich (no later than 11 August 1931)," in *Stalin-Kaganovich Correspondence*, 54.
214 Cited in Davies and Wheatcroft, *Years of Hunger*, 237.
215 Quoted in Victor Kravchenko, *I Chose Freedom: The Personal and Political Life of a Soviet Official* (New York: Charles Scribner's Sons, 1946), 130; also cited in Conquest, *Harvest of Sorrow*, 261.
216 The term "highest level of extremism" comes from Medvedev, *On Stalin and Stalinism*, 196.
217 "Absolute triumph," in Grossman, *Everything Flows*, 154; "political emasculation," in Scott, *Seeing Like a State*, 202–3.
218 Davies and Wheatcroft, *Years of Hunger*, 210.
219 Stalin, "Right Deviation in the C.P.S.U.(B.)," 1–113.
220 Davies and Wheatcroft, *Years of Hunger*, 187.
221 Andrea Graziosi called this "negative selection." Graziosi, "The Uses of Hunger," 17.
222 Cited in Klid and Motyl, *Holodomor Reader*, 249.
223 Cited in ibid., 250.
224 Davies and Wheatcroft, *Years of Hunger*, 155 (Kosior quote); and *Sobranie zakonov*, 1932, Article 521 (17 December); cited in Davies and Wheatcroft, *Years of Hunger*, 244 (Soviet law quote). Kosior's speech appeared in *Pravda*, 15 February 1933.
225 *Pravda*, 6 February 1933; cited in Davies and Wheatcroft, *Years of Hunger*, 209.
226 Pyrih, *Holodomor 1932–1933*, 771.
227 Quoted in Davies and Wheatcroft, *Years of Hunger*, 215 (my emphasis).
228 Andrea Graziosi, "The Soviet 1931–1933 Famines," 65.
229 Raphael Lemkin, who persuaded the United Nations to adopt the 1948 Convention on Genocide, asserted that the famine represented "a case of genocide, of the destruction, not of individuals only, but of a culture and

a nation." R. Lemkin, "Soviet Genocide in Ukraine," Raphael Lemkin Papers, 2L-273, reel 3, Manuscripts and Archives Division, New York Public Library, Astor, Lenox and Tilden Foundations, published in *Holodomor Studies* 1, no. 1 (2009): 3–8.

230 See Document No. 47 in *Rozsekrechena pam"iat*, 511–16; excerpts appeared in Klid and Motyl, *Holodomor Reader*, 256.
231 "Vyshe znamia proletarskogo internatsionalizma!," *Pravda*, 10 March 1933, 1; excerpts in Klid and Motyl, *Holodomor Reader*, 259.
232 In late November 1932, Molotov wrote: "A Bolshevik who has thought out and checked the scale and the situation as a whole, must place the satisfaction of the needs of the proletarian state over and above all other priorities." Cited in Davies and Wheatcroft, *Years of Hunger*, 150.
233 Ibid., 435.

Chapter 7

1 *Delo Naroda*, no. 227 (8 December 1917); cited in Oliver Radkey, *Sickle under the Hammer: The Russian Socialist Revolutionaries in the Early Months of Soviet Rule* (New York: Columbia University Press, 1963), 310.
2 I. Stalin, "Rech na vypuske akademikov Krasnoi Armii" (4 May 1935), in I.V. Stalin, *Sochineniia*, ed. Robert H. McNeal (Stanford, CA: Hoover Institution Press, 1967), 1 (14): 61; cited in Sheila Fitzpatrick, "Stalin and the Making of a New Elite, 1928–1939," *Slavic Review* 38, no. 3 (1979): 377.
3 Sheila Fitzpatrick, "Cultural Revolution as Class War," in *Cultural Revolution in Russia, 1926–1931*, ed. Sheila Fitzpatrick (Bloomington: Indiana University Press, 1978), 10–11.
4 For analyses of the trials of the Shakhty engineers and of the Industrial Party, see Kendall E. Bailes, *Technology and Society under Lenin and Stalin: Origins of the Soviet Technical Intelligentsia, 1917–1941* (Princeton, NJ: Princeton University Press, 1978), chaps. 3–4.
5 Fitzpatrick, "Cultural Revolution as Class War," 18.
6 Ibid., 25.
7 Sheila Fitzpatrick, "Introduction," in *Cultural Revolution in Russia, 1926–1931*, 3.
8 Not all who claimed the status of "workers" were actually workers.
9 Fitzpatrick, "Stalin and the Making of a New Elite"; and Sheila Fitzpatrick, *Education and Social Mobility in the Soviet Union, 1921–1934* (Cambridge, UK, and New York: Cambridge University Press, 1979). Milovan Djilas coined the phrase "the new class," but Fitzpatrick uses it in a slightly different way than Djilas does. See Milovan Djilas, *The New Class: An Analysis*

of the Communist System (New York: Praeger, 1957). For an excellent description of the lifestyles of the upper ranks of this new elite, see Vera Dunham, *In Stalin's Time: Middle Class Values in Soviet Fiction* (Cambridge, UK, and New York: Cambridge University Press, 1976).

10 According to Fitzpatrick, the "old [Russian] intelligentsia as a whole had not been subject to mass arrest, like priests, or mass deportations, like peasants. Its members (except for a relatively small number of engineers working as convict specialists) were not sent out of the capitals to the new construction sites or to the countryside to teach in rural schools." Fitzpatrick, "Cultural Revolution as Class War," 37.

11 Terry Martin, *The Affirmative Action Empire: Nations and Nationalism in the Soviet Union, 1923–1939* (Ithaca, NY: Cornell University Press, 2001), 345.

12 James C. Scott, *Seeing Like a State: How Certain Schemes to Improve the Human Condition Have Failed* (New Haven, CT: Yale University Press, 1998), 89.

13 George Y. Shevelov, *The Ukrainian Language in the First Half of the Twentieth Century (1900–1941): Its State and Status* (Cambridge, MA: Harvard Ukrainian Research Institute, 1989), 126.

14 *Ukrains'ka kontrrevoliutsiia sama pro svoiu robotu: za stenohramoiu sudu nad "SVU,"* 4 vols. (Kharkiv: Derzh. Vyd-vo Ukrainy, 1930); and Volodymyr Prystaiko and Iurii Shapoval, *Sprava "spilky vyzvolennia Ukrainy": Nevidomi dokumenty i fakty* (Kiev: INTEL, 1995).

15 Andrea Graziosi, "The Uses of Hunger: Stalin's Solution of the Peasant and National Questions in Soviet Ukraine, 1932–1933," in *Famines in European Economic History: The Last Great European Famines Reconsidered*, ed. Declan Curran, Lubomyr Luciuk, and Andrew Newby (New York: Routledge, 2014), 6.

16 Approximately fifty thousand Galician Ukrainians remained in Eastern Ukraine after the First World War or emigrated to Soviet Ukraine in the 1920s. Olga Bertelsen and Myroslav Shkandrij, "The Secret Police and the Campaign against Galicians in Soviet Ukraine, 1929–1934," *Nationalities Papers* 42, no. 1 (2014): 38. The Soviet political leadership viewed Western Ukrainians as a group "with a strong sense of national identity and internal unity. Whatever their culture, even if they were prepared to work within a proletarian or Soviet state; they were therefore categorized as 'nationalists' and potential separatists" (39).

17 Matthew D. Pauly, *Breaking the Tongue: Language, Education, and Power in Soviet Ukraine, 1923–1934* (Toronto: University of Toronto Press, 2014), 33, 303, 380, 381.

18 For a thorough analysis of these waves of arrests and of those arrested, see Myroslav Shkandrij and Olga Bertelsen, "The Soviet Regime's National Operations in Ukraine, 1929–1934," *Canadian Slavonic Papers* 55, nos. 3–4 (2013): 417–47.

19 See R. Ia. Pyrih, *Zhyttia Mykhaila Hrushevs'koho: ostannie desiatylittia (1924–1934)* (Kiev: Instytut ukrains'koi arkheohrafii AN Ukrainy, 1993); and V. Prystaiko and Iu. Shapoval, *Mykhailo Hrushevs'kyi i HPU – NKVD: Trahichne desiatylittia: 1924–1934* (Kiev: Vydavnytstvo "Ukraina," 1996).

20 Shkandrij and Bertelsen, "The Soviet Regime's National Operations," 420.

21 James E. Mace, *Communism and the Dilemmas of National Liberation: National Communism in Soviet Ukraine, 1918–1933* (Cambridge, MA: Harvard Ukrainian Research Institute, 1983), and George O. Liber, *Soviet Nationality Policy, Urban Growth, and Identity Change in the Ukrainian SSR, 1923–1934* (Cambridge, UK: Cambridge University Press, 1992), chap. 7.

22 Serhy Yekelchyk, *Ukraine: Birth of a Modern Nation* (New York: Oxford University Press, 2007), 103.

23 *Tragediia sovetskoi derevni: kollektivizatsiia i raskulachivanie: dokumenty i materially*, ed. Viktor Danilov, Roberta Manning, Lynne Viola et al. (Moscow: Rossiiskaia pol. entsiklopediia, 1999), 3:576–7.

24 *Holodomor 1932–1933 rokiv v Ukraini: Dokumenty i materialy*, ed. Ruslan Pyrih (Kyiv: Vyd. Dim "Kyievo-Mohylians'ka akademiia, 2007), document 354; *Holod 1932–1933 rokiv na Ukraini: Ochyma istorykiv, movoiu doku-mentiv*, ed. F.M. Rudych et al. (Kiev: Vyd. Politychnoi literatury Ukrainy, 1990), document 121; and *Komandyry velykoho holodu: poizdky V. Molotova i L. Kaganovycha v Ukraini ta na pivnichnyi Kavkaz, 1932–1933 rr.*, ed. Valerii Vasiliev and Yurii Shapoval (Kiev: Heneza, 2001), document 58.

25 Yekelchyk, *Ukraine*, 113.

26 Pyrih, *Holodomor 1932–1933*, document 357; Vasiliev and Shapoval, *Komandyry velykoho holodu*, document 59.

27 Martin, *Affirmative Action Empire*, chaps. 7 and 10. On Ukrainization outside the Ukrainian SSR, see Hennadii Yefimenko, *Natsional'no-kul'turna polityka VKP(b) shchodo Radians'koi Ukrainy (1932–1938 rr.)* (Kiev: Natsional'na Akademiia nauk Ukrainy, Institut istorii Ukrainy, 2001), 113–40.

28 Pyrih, *Holodomor 1932–1933*, document 357; Vasiliev and Shapoval, *Komandyry velykoho holodu*, document 59.

29 Mykola Skrypnyk, Balitsky's future victim, made this assertion. Iurii Shapoval, Volodymyr Prystaiko, and Vadym Zolotar'ov, *ChK-HPU-NKVD v Ukraini: Osoby, fakty, dokumenty* (Kiev: Abris, 1997), 73.

30 Postyshev started to work as a member of the Kiev province party committee in 1923, then became a secretary of the CP(b)U's Central Committee in 1925.

As a member of the Ukrainian Politburo and Organizational Bureau (1926–30), he served as the secretary of the Kharkiv district and city party committees, where he actively purged Trotskyists and Ukrainian national-communists and participated in the industrialization and collectivization campaigns. From January 1930 to January 1933, he became one of the secretaries of the Central Committee of the All-Union Communist Party in Moscow. Balitsky served in the leadership of the Ukrainian Cheka in 1918–22, then became the first head of the GPU in Ukraine from September 1923 to the end of July 1931. On Postyshev: Keenan Hohol and Bohdan Krawchenko, "Pavel Postyshev," *Encyclopedia of Ukraine*, vol. 4 (1993); on Balitsky: Shkandrij and Bertelsen, "The Soviet Regime's National Operations," 419. Also see Iurii Shapoval and Vadym Zolotar'ov, *Vsevolod Balitskii: osoba, chas, otochennia* (Kiev: Stylos, 2002), and Volodymyr Lozyts'kyi, *Politbiuro TsK Kompartii Ukrainy, 1918–1991: Istoriia, osoby, stosunky* (Kiev: Heneza, 2005), 246 (Postyshev) and 148 (Balitsky).

31 Yekelchyk, *Ukraine*, 114; Yefimenko, *Natsional'no-kul'turna polityka VKP(b)*, 52–112; E. Borisënok, *Fenomenon Sovetskoi ukrainizatsii 1920–1930-e gody* (Moscow: Evropa, 2006), 225.

32 Valerii Vasiliev, "The Great Terror in the Ukraine, 1936–38," in *Stalin's Terror Revisited*, ed. Melanie Ilič (New York: Palgrave Macmillan, 2006), 142.

33 For Skrypnyk's views, see Mykola Skrypnyk, *Statti i promovy z natsional'noho pytannia* (Munich: Suchasnist, 1974), and Mykola Skrypnyk, *Vybrani tvory* (Kyiv: Vyd. "Ukraina," 1990). For analyses of the evolution of his political assessments, see James E. Mace, *Communism and the Dilemmas of National Liberation: National Communism in Soviet Ukraine, 1918–1933* (Cambridge, MA: Harvard Ukrainian Research Institute, 1983); George O. Liber, *Soviet Nationality Policy, Urban Growth, and Identity Change in the Ukrainian SSR, 1923–1934* (Cambridge and New York: Cambridge University Press, 1992), chap. 7; and V.F. Soldatenko, *Nezlamnyi: zhyttia i smert' Mykoly Skrypnyka* (Kiev: Knyha pamiatu Ukrainy, 2002).

34 See Stanislav Kosior's 22 November 1933 speech delivered at the CP(b)U's Central Committee and Central Control Commission, *Izvestiia*, 2 December 1933; Hennadii Yefimenko, "The Soviet Nationalities Policy Change of 1933, or Why 'Ukrainian Nationalism' Became the Main Threat to Stalin in Ukraine," *Holodomor Studies* 1, no. 1 (2009): 27.

35 N.S. Khrushchev, *Khrushchev Remembers* (Boston: Little, Brown, 1970), 172; cited in Hiroaki Kuromiya, *The Voices of the Dead: Stalin's Great Terror in the 1930s* (New Haven and London: Yale University Press, 2007), 15.

36 Quoted from Oleksander Loshytskyi, "Laboratoria: Novi dokumenty i svidchennia pro masovi represii 1937–1938 rokiv na Vinnychchyni," *Z arkhiviv*

VUChK-HPU-NKVD-KHB, nos. 1–2 (1998): 215; cited in Kuromiya, *Voices*, 15.

37 Quoted from Loshytskyi, "Laboratoria," 215; cited in Kuromiya, *Voices*, 15.

38 Lev Kopelev, *The Education of a True Believer* (New York: Harper and Row, 1980), 277.

39 See V.G. Makarov and V.S. Khristoforov, "Predislovie," in *Vysylka vmesto rasstrela: Deportatsiia intelligentsia v dokumentakh VChK-GPU*, ed. V.G. Makarov and V.S. Khristoforov (Moscow: Russkii put', 2005), 5–48.

40 For the political outlook of the Russian non-Bolshevik intellectuals in the revolutionary period, see Jane Burbank, *Intelligentsia and Revolution: Russian Views of Bolshevism, 1917–1922* (New York: Oxford Univesity Press, 1986).

41 See documents 84 and 86 in Makarov and Khristoforov, "Predislovie," 131–8; 139–64. They are based on reports written by the GPU's informants and active agents, as well as general observations.

42 Vasyl Danylenko, "Politychnyi kontrol' dukhovnoho zhyttia v Ukraini 1920-kh rokiv," in his *Ukrains'ka intelihentsiia i vlada: Zvernennia Sekretnoho viddilu DPU USRR 1927–1929 rr.* (Kiev: Tempora, 2012), 20–1.

43 *Tsirkuliarnoe pis'mo Gosudarsvennogo politicheskogo upravleniia (Sekretnyi otdel) ob ukrainskom separatizme* (Kharkov, 4 September 1926), appended in full at the end of an article by Yuri Shapoval, "'On Ukrainian Separatism': A GPU Circular of 1926," *Harvard Ukrainian Studies* 18, nos. 3–4 (1994): 301.

44 V.A. Hrechenko and O.N. Iarmysh, *Ukraina u dobu "rann'oho" totalitarizmu (20-ti roku XX st.)* (Kharkiv: Vyd. NUVS, 2001), 114; cited in Danylenko, *Ukrains'ka intelihentsiia*, 25.

45 J.V. Stalin, "To Comrade Kaganovich and Other Members of the Political Bureau of the Central Committee, Ukrainian C.P.(B.)," in J.V. Stalin, *Works* (Moscow: Foreign Languages Publishing House, 1954), 8:157.

46 Ibid., 158.

47 Ibid., 159.

48 Ibid.

49 Ibid.

50 Ibid., 160.

51 Ibid., 160, 161.

52 Ibid., 162, 160.

53 Agitation on behalf of peasant unions in Ukraine and the Northern Caucasus also appeared in OGPU analyses in December 1927 and January 1928. See *The War against the Peasantry, 1927–1930: The Tragedy of the Soviet Countryside*, ed. Lynn Viola, V.P. Danilov, N.A. Ivnytskii, and Denis Kozlov (New Haven, CT: Yale University Press, 2005), 38–9, 40.

54 *Tsirkuliarnoe pis'mo Gosudarsvennogo politicheskogo upravleniia (Sekretnyi otdel) ob ukrainskom separatizme*, 275–302.
55 See Danylenko, *Ukrains'ka intelihentsiia i vlada*, a collection of 140 GPU weekly reports on the activities and attitudes of the Ukrainian intelligentsia from 1 January 1927 to 31 December 1929.
56 Leonid Maximenkov, "Stalin's Meeting with a Delegation of Ukrainian Writers on 12 February 1929," *Harvard Ukrainian Studies* 16, nos. 3–4 (1992): 403.
57 Ibid., 404.
58 All quotes in this paragraph come from ibid., 410.
59 On 12 December 1930, Stalin wrote a letter to the Soviet Russian writer Demyan Bedny admonishing him for slandering the USSR and its "Russian" working class. He asserted: "The whole world now admits that the centre of the revolutionary movement has shifted from Western Europe to Russia. The revolutionaries of all countries look with hope to the USSR as centre of the liberation struggle of the working people throughout the world and recognize it as their only Motherland. In all countries the revolutionary workers unanimously applaud the Soviet working class, and first and foremost the *Russian* working class, the vanguard of the Soviet workers, as their recognized leader that is carrying out the most revolutionary and active policy ever dreamed of by the proletarians of other countries. The leaders of the revolutionary workers in all countries are eagerly studying the highly instructive history of Russia's working class, its past and the past of Russia, knowing that besides reactionary Russia there existed also revolutionary Russia ... All this fills (cannot but fill!) the hearts of Russian workers with a feeling of revolutionary national pride that can move mountains and perform miracles." J.V. Stalin, "To Comrade Demyan Bedny (Excerpts from a Letter)," in J.V. Stalin, *Works* (Moscow: Foreign Languages Publishing House, 1954), 13:25–6.
60 Mikhail Bulgakov's *The Days of the Turbins (Dni Turbinykh)* became one of the most popular plays ever produced by the Moscow Art Theater. Based in part on the playwright's novel *The White Guard* (which did not appear in print in the USSR until 1966), the play concerned the fate of the Turbins, a Russian family sympathetic to the anti-Bolshevik Whites, as they encounter Hetman Pavlo Skoropadsky, the Imperial German Army, the Reds, and the Ukrainian nationalists in Kiev. In the course of the play, the Turbins and their friends demean Ukrainians, Ukrainian culture, and Skoropadsky's limited Ukrainization. By depicting the Whites as normal human beings, not demons, Bulgakov earned the wrath of critics. But theatregoers wanted to see the play. In March 1929, one month after Ukrainian writers met with Stalin, the Soviet government banned the performance of all of his plays and prohibited the publication of his other works. After Bulgakov appealed to Stalin, the

Soviet government ordered the Moscow Art Theater to revive the play in 1932. All in all, *The Days of the Turbins* had 987 performances between 1926 and 1941; Stalin saw it more than twenty times. Evgeny Dobrenko, "Introduction," in Mikhail Bulgakov, *The White Guard*, trans. Marian Schwartz (New Haven, CT: Yale University Press, 2008), xix; Will Self, "The *White Guard* by Mikhail Bulgakov," *The Guardian*, 19 March 2010.

61 Maximenkov, "Stalin's Meeting with a Delegation of Ukrainian Writers," 420.
62 Ibid., 421.
63 Ibid., 422.
64 Ibid., 424.
65 Ibid., 424–5.
66 Ibid., 425.
67 Dobrenko, "Introduction," xxvi.
68 Maximenkov, "Stalin's Meeting with a Delegation of Ukrainian Writers," 426.
69 Stalin, *Works*, 13:368–9.
70 RGASPI, f. 558, l. 11, d. 1132, fols. 119–20; cited in Hennadiii Yefimenko, "The Kremlin's Nationality Policy in Ukraine after the Holodomor of 1932–1933," in *After the Holodomor: The Enduring Impact of the Great Famine of Ukraine*, ed. Andrea Graziosi, Lubomyr A. Hajda, and Halyna Hryn (Cambridge, MA: Harvard Ukrainian Research Institute, 2013), 77.
71 Stalin's changes to Kosior's theses and his entire speech were published in *Komunist Ukrainy*, no. 4 (2004); cited in Yefimenko, "The Kremlin's Nationality Policy," 81
72 Stalin, *Works*, 13:369.
73 On Ukrainization in 1923, see Pauly, *Breaking the Tongue*, 2.
74 On this attempt, see Yefimenko, "The Kremlin's Nationality Policy," 89–90.
75 Quote from Institute politychnykh doslidzhen', *Komunistychna partiia Ukrainy: z"izdy i konferentsii* (Kiev: Vyd. "Ukraina," 1991), 168.
76 The quote comes from Shevelov, *The Ukrainian Language*, 142–3.
77 Hryhory Kostiuk, *Stalinist Rule in the Ukraine: A Study of the Decade of Mass Terror, 1929–1939* (New York: Praeger, 1960).
78 This statement was inspired by Shevelov, *The Ukrainian Language*, 143, who wrote his survey in the 1980s, before the collapse of the USSR.
79 Andrea Graziosi employed this term in his "The New Soviet Archival Sources: Hypotheses for a Critical Assessment," *Cahiers du Monde Russe* 40, nos. 1–2 (1999): 16; the phrase reappears in his "The Uses of Hunger," 17.
80 Graziosi, "The Uses of Hunger," 24–5.
81 V. Holubnychy, "History of the Ukrainian Soviet Socialist Republic," in *Ukraine: A Concise Encyclopedia*, ed. Volodymyr Kubijovyč (Toronto: University of Toronto Press, 1963), 1:825.

82 Bohdan Krawchenko, *Social Change and National Consciousness in Twentieth-Century Ukraine* (New York: St Martin's Press, 1985), 134–41; cited in Yekelchyk, *Ukraine*, 116.

83 Pauly, *Breaking the Tongue*, 336, 337.

84 Yefimenko, *Natsional'no-kul'turna polityka VKP(b)*, 142.

85 Peter A. Blitstein, "Nation-Building or Russification? Obligatory Russian Instruction in the Soviet Non-Russian Schools, 1938–1953," in *A State of Nations: Empire and Nation-Building in the Age of Lenin and Stalin*, ed. Ronald Grigor Suny and Terry Martin (New York: Oxford University Press, 2001), 253.

86 "Pro reorhanizatsiiu natsional'nykh shkil na Ukraini" (10 April 1938), TsDAHOU, f. 1, op. 6, d. 463, ll. 2–4; and "Pro obov'iazkove navchannia rossiiskoi movy v nerosiiskykh shkolakh Ukrainy" (20 April 1938), TsDAHOU, f. 1, op. 6, d. 478, ll. 115–21.

87 H.H. Yefimenko, *Natsional'na polityka kerivnytstva VKP(b) v Ukraini 1932–1938 gg. (osvita ta nauka)* (Kiev: Instityt istorii Ukrainy, 2000), 26, 34; cited in Pauly, *Breaking the Tongue*, 336. Elena Borisënok disputes that this "new course" represented a policy of Russification. She claims that the policies which emerged in the 1930s represented an intense centralization drive with the goal of creating a new socialist culture, with internationalism at its core. E. Borisënok, *Fenomenon Sovetskoi ukrainizatsii 1920–1930-e gody* (Moscow: Evropa, 2006), 232.

88 See, for example, Sylvia Gilliam, "The Nationality Questionnaire," in *The Nationality Problem in the Soviet Union: The Ukrainian Case*, ed. Sylvia Gilliam, Irving Rostow, and John S. Reshetar (Project on the Soviet Social System [AF No. 33(038)-12909], Russian Research Center, Harvard University, 1954), 11.

89 On 16 May 2006, I spoke with Ivan Dziuba (born in 1931), a prominent Soviet Ukrainian dissident and the second minister of culture (1992–1994) in Ukraine's post-communist government. According to my notes from that day, "When I asked about his life in the Donbass in his youth, he mentioned how he went to a Russian-language school, inasmuch as there were no Ukrainian-language ones in his area. The Russian school had compulsory courses in Ukrainian and, he said, the school authorities took it seriously." That's how he learned Ukrainian in one of the most Russified areas of Ukraine.

90 Gilliam, "The Nationality Questionnaire," 11.

91 Ibid.

92 The citation comes from ibid., 46. She defines the better-educated as those "who had eight or more years (of schooling), including partial technicums; the less educated – those with seven years or less of education" (93).

93   Robert Conquest, *The Great Terror: A Reassessment* (New York and Oxford: Oxford University Press, 1990), 272; Roy Medvedev, *Let History Judge: The Origins and Consequences of Stalinism*, rev. and expanded ed. (New York: Columbia University Press, 1989), 803; and Yekelchyk, *Ukraine*, 114.

94   Norman M. Naimark, *Stalin's Genocides* (Princeton, NJ: Princeton University Press, 2010), 81.

95   Barry McLoughlin, "Mass Operations of the NKVD, 1937–1938: A Survey," in *Stalin's Terror: High Politics and Mass Repression in the Soviet Union*, ed. Barry McLoughlin and Kevin McDermott (New York: Palgrave MacMillan, 2003), 123; and Kate Brown, *A Biography of No Place: From Ethnic Borderland to Soviet Heartland* (Cambridge, MA: Harvard University Press, 2004), 146. For an assessment of the official repression of the Poles, see Nikita Petrov and Arsenii Roginskii, "The 'Polish Operation' of the NKVD, 1937–38," in McLoughlin and McDermott, 53–172.

96   Brown, *A Biography of No Place*, 42–3.

97   Timothy Snyder, *Bloodlands: Europe between Hitler and Stalin* (New York: Basic Books, 2010), 91. Brown, *A Biography of No Place*, 133, provides a smaller number. Also see her chap. 5.

98   Ibid.

99   Snyder, *Bloodlands*, 93.

100 N.V. Petrov and A. Roginskii, "'Pol'skaia operatsiia' NKVD 1937–1938 gg.," in *Represii protiv poliakov*, ed. A.E. Gur'ianov (Moscow, 1997), 28; cited in Brown, *A Biography of No Place*, 155.

101 Snyder, *Bloodlands*, 99.

102 See "Pro reorhanizatsiiu natsional'nykh raioniv ta sil'rad URSR v zvychaini raiony ta silrady," *Protokoly No. 11–19 zasedanii Politbiuro TsK KP(b) Ukrainy* (3 January–25 March 1938), TsDAHOU, f. 1 op. 6, d. 462, ll. 62–5.; and "Pro reorhanizatsiiu natsional'nykkh shkil na Ukraini," *Protokoly No. 20-24 zasedanii Politbiuro TsK KP(b) Ukrainy* (10 April–17 June 1938), TsDAHOU, f. 1 op. 6, d. 463, ll. 2–4.

103 "Pro zaminy latyns'koho shryfta rosiis'kym po Moldavs'kii ARSR (25 March 1938)," TsDAHOU, f. 1, op. 6, d. 462, l. 140.

104 Vasiliev, "The Great Terror in the Ukraine, 1936–38," 142.

105 Wendy Z. Goldman, *Terror and Democracy in the Age of Stalin: The Social Dynamics of Repression* (New York: Cambridge University Press, 2007), 1–2.

106 Ivan Bilas, *Represyvno-karal'na systema v Ukraini, 1917–1953: Suspil'no-politychnyi ta istoryko-pravovyi analiz* (Kyiv: Lybid-Viis'ko Ukrainy, 1994), 1:379; cited in Yekelchyk, *Ukraine*, 115. Kuromiya, *Voices*, 13, provides a figure of 123,421 people sentenced to be shot during these years.

107 Vasiliev, "The Great Terror in the Ukraine, 1936–38," 151.

108 Kuromiya, *Voices*, 258.

109 McLoughlin, "Mass Operations of the NKVD," 120, 121.

110 Snyder, *Bloodlands*, 84, 81.

111 See *Ukraina v dobu "Velykoho teroru": 1936–1938 roky*, ed. Iurii Shapoval and Hiroaki Kuromiya (Kiev: Lybid', 2009).

112 Gr. Pevzner, "Kto rukovodit radioveshchaniem na Ukraine?" *Pravda*, 9 July 1937, 6; E. Fomenko, "Eshche raz ob ukrainskom radioveshchanii," *Pravda*, 15 July 1937, 6; "Ot redaktsii," *Pravda*, 15 July 1937, 6; *Pravda*, 17 July 1937; "Chto eto – neitralitet?, *Pravda*, 20 July 1937, 2; "Navesti bol'shevistskii poriadok v radioveshchanii (lead editorial)," *Pravda*, 22 July 1937, 1; Gr. Pevzner, "Tak bol'sheviki ne podbiraiut kadry (g. Vinnitsia)," *Pravda*, 22 July 1937, 4; A. Vadimov, "Na plenume TsK Komsomola Ukrainy," *Pravda*, 25 July 1937, 2; "Ne ostanovlivat'sia na polputi! (o *Proletarskoi pravde* v Kieve)," *Pravda*, 24 July 1937, 4.

113 See, for example, "O sostoianii radioveshchaniia na Ukraine. Postanovlianie TsK KP(b)U po stat'iam, napechatannym v *Pravde*," *Pravda*, 21 July 1937, 2.

114 Lozyts'kyi, *Politbiuro: TsK Kompartii*, 219.

115 Shevelov, *The Ukrainian Language*, 147–8.

116 William Taubman, *Khrushchev: The Man and His Era* (New York: W.W. Norton, 2003), 116.

117 Shevelov, *The Ukrainian Language*, 149.

118 "M.I. Bondarenko – Predsedatel' Sovnarkoma USSR," *Pravda*, 2 September 1937, 6. For a brief overview of his career, see Lozyts'kyi, *Politbiuro: TsK Kompartii*, 149.

119 First quote taken from Institute politychnykh doslidzhen', *Komunistychna partiia Ukrainy: z"izdy i konferentsii*, 177; second quote from Taubman, *Khrushchev*, 120.

120 Quote from Institute politychnykh doslidzhen', *Komunistychna partiia Ukrainy: z"izdy i konferentsii*, 180.

121 Iurii Shapoval, "The Ukrainian Years," *Nikita Khrushchev*, ed. William Taubman, Sergei Khrushchev, and Abbott Gleason (New Haven, CT: Yale University Press, 2000), 8, 9.

122 I.D. Nazarenko, *Ocherki po istorii Kommunisticheskoi partii Ukrainy* (Kiev: Izd-vo polit. Lit-ry Ukrainy, 1964); cited in Medvedev, *Let History Judge*, 412.

123 Conquest, *The Great Terror*, 224; Medvedev, *Let History Judge*, 195; Yekelchyk, *Ukraine*, 117.

124 Goldman, *Terror and Democracy*, 259.

125 Taubman, *Khrushchev*, 116.

126 N.A. Barsukov, A.P. Shaidullin, and I.N. Iudin, "KPSS – Partiia internatsional'naia," *Voprosy istorii KPSS*, no. 7 (July 1966), 12; cited in T.H. Rigby, *Communist Party Membership in the USSR, 1917–1967* (Princeton, NJ: Princeton University Press, 1968), 371n11.

127 Sheila Fitzpatrick, "The Civil War as a Formative Experience," in *Bolshevik Culture: Experiment and Order in the Russian Revolution*, ed. Abbot Gleason, Peter Kenez, and Richard Stites (Bloomington, IN: Indiana University Press, 1985), 74.

128 See ibid. 57–76; and David Joravsky, "Cultural Revolution and the Fortress Mentality," in Gleason, Kenez, and Stites, *Bolshevik Culture*, 93–113.

129 Fitzpatrick, "The Civil War," 57.

130 Peter Holquist, "State Violence as Technique: The Logic of Violence in Soviet Totalitarianism," in *Landscaping the Human Garden: Twentieth-Century Population Management in a Comparative Framework*, ed. Amir Weiner (Stanford, CA: Stanford, University Press, 2003), 20.

131 Ibid., 27.

132 Taken from an interview with Roman Werfel in Teresa Toranska, *"Them": Stalin's Polish Puppets* (New York: Harper and Row, 1987), 102.

133 Andrea Graziosi, "The Uses of Hunger,"8.

134 Holquist, "State Violence," 42.

135 Moshe Lewin, "Who Was the Soviet Kulak?" *Soviet Studies* 18, no. 2 (1966): 189–212, and his *The Making of the Soviet System: Essays in the Social History of Interwar Russia* (New York: New Press, 1994), 121–41; R.W. Davies and Stephen G. Wheatcroft, *The Years of Hunger: Soviet Agriculture, 1931–1933* (New York: Palgrave Macmillan, 2004), 21–5.

136 Fitzpatrick, "The Civil War," 61. For an early (1919) Ukrainian communist criticism of the connections between Bolshevism and Russian imperialism, see Vasyl Shakhrai and Serhii Mazlakh, *On the Current Situation in Ukraine*, ed. Peter J. Potichnyj (Ann Arbor: University of Michigan Press, 1970). Also see Stephen Velychenko, *Painting Imperialism and Nationalism Red: The Ukrainian Marxist Critique of Russian Communist Rule in Ukraine, 1918–1925* (Toronto: University of Toronto Press, 2015).

137 For an assessment of the seven crucial policies that applied only or mainly in Soviet Ukraine in late 1932 and early 1933, see Snyder, *Bloodlands*, 42–6.

138 "The party's geopolitical calculations," according to Andrea Graziosi, "heavily influenced the indigenization programs in each non-Russian area. Since Moscow concentrated its attention on the security of the USSR's western borderlands and on Ukraine, in particular, its leaders reacted against all internal opposition to collectivization and manifestations of 'Ukrainian nationalism' far more brutally than in the Caucasus, Central Asia, or the Far

North, regions geographically distant from the sources of the threat they perceived." Andrea Graziosi, "The Uses of Hunger," 10.

139 In a letter to Mikhail Sholokhov, dated 6 May 1933, Stalin responded to Sholokhov's complaints about the lawlessness of the collectivization drive in the North Caucasus, and asserted that " the respected peasants of your region (and not only your region) carried out a sitdown strike (sabotage!) and would not have objected to leaving the workers and the Red Army without bread. The fact that this sabotage was quiet and apparently harmless (bloodless) does not alter the fact that the respected peasants waged a silent war against Soviet power. [This is] a war by starvation, dear Comrade Sholokhov … the respected peasants are not as innocent as it might appear from afar." "Sholokhov i Stalin. Perepiska nachala 30-x godov (Stupitel'naia stat'ia Iu. G. Murina)," *Voprosy istorii*, no. 3 (1994): 22.

140 Snyder, *Bloodlands*, 42.

141 Michael Ellman, "The Role of Leadership Perceptions and of Intent in the Soviet Famine of 1931–1934," *Europe-Asia Studies* 57, no. 6 (2005): 832.

142 Ibid., 839fn49.

143 Stalin to Kaganovich, 11 August 1932, *The Stalin-Kaganovich Correspondence, 1931–36*, ed. R.W. Davies, Oleg V. Khlevniuk, E.A. Rees, Liudmila P. Kosheleva, and Larisa A. Rogovaya (New Haven, CT: Yale University Press, 2003), 179–81. According to Stalin, "The most important issue right now is Ukraine. Things in Ukraine have hit rock bottom. Things are bad in regard to the party. There is talk that in two regions of Ukraine (I think it is the Kiev and Dniepropetrovsk regions) about 50 percent district party committees have spoken out against the grain procurement plan, deeming it unrealistic. The situation in the other district party committees, people say, is no better. What does this look like? This is not a party but a parliament, a caricature of a parliament. Instead of leading the districts, Kosior keeps maneuvering between the directives of the CC of the VKP and the demands of the district committees – and now he has maneuvered himself into a total mess. Lenin was right in saying that a person who does not have the courage to swim against the current when necessary cannot be a real Bolshevik leader. Things are bad with the Soviets. Chubar is no leader. Things are bad with the GPU. Redens is not up to leading the fight against the counterrevolution in such a large and distinctive republic as Ukraine.

Unless we begin to straighten out the situation in Ukraine, we may lose Ukraine. Keep in mind that Piłsudski is not daydreaming, and his agents in Ukraine are many times stronger than Redens or Kosior thinks. Keep in mind, too, that the Ukrainian Communist Party (500,000 members, ha-ha) has quite a lot (yes, quite a lot!) of rotten elements, conscious and unconscious Petliura adherents, and, finally, direct agents of Piłsudski. As soon as things get worse, these elements will waste no time opening a front inside (and outside) the party against the party. The worst aspect is that the Ukraine leadership does not see these dangers. Things cannot go on this way." *The Stalin-Kaganovich Correspondence, 1931–36*, 180. Since the USSR and Poland had actually signed a non-aggression pact on 25 July 1932, less than three weeks before this outburst, "Stalin was exploiting a non-existent foreign threat to justify the liquidation of his internal enemies, using this tactic to further consolidate his position, as he had done in the past, more than once, most famously against Trotsky in 1927." Andrea Graziosi, "The Uses of Hunger," 14.

144 Ellman, "The Role of Leadership Perceptions," 833.
145 Raphael Lemkin, "Soviet Genocide in Ukraine," *Holodomor Studies* 1, no. 1 (2009): 4.
146 According to Article 2 of the Convention on the Prevention and Punishment of the Crime of Genocide, adapted by the United Nations General Assembly on 9 December 1948, genocide "means any of the following acts committed with the intent to destroy, in whole or in part, a national, ethnical, racial or religious group, such as: (a) killing members of the group; (b) causing serious bodily or mental harm to members of the group; (c) deliberately inflicting on the group conditions of life calculated to bring about its physical destruction in whole or in part; (d) imposing measures intended to prevent births within the group; and (e) forcibly transferring children of the group to another group." *Blackstone's Statutes: International Human Rights Documents*, ed. P.R. Ghandhi (New York: Oxford University Press, 2004), 19.
147 J.V. Stalin, "Concerning the National Question in Yugoslavia," *Works* (Moscow: Foreign Languages Publishing House, 1954), 7:71–2.
148 Graziosi, "The Uses of Hunger," 18.
149 Ibid., 21.
150 Frank E. Sysyn, "The Famine of 1932–1933 in the Discussion of Russian-Ukrainian Relations," *The Harriman Review* 15, nos. 2–3 (May 2005): 81.
151 David Brandenberger, *National Bolshevism: Stalinist Mass Culture and the Formation of the Modern Russian National Identity, 1931–1956* (Cambridge, MA: Harvard University Press, 2002).
152 Kuromiya, *Voices*, 124.
153 Seweryn Bialer, "Comment – The Impact of Common RSFSR/USSR Institutions," in *Ethnic Russia in the USSR: The Dilemma of Dominance*, ed. Edward Allworth (New York: Praeger, 1980), 198–9.
154 Ivan Dzyuba, *Internationalism or Russification? A Study in the Soviet Nationalities Problem* (New York: Monad Press, 1974).

Chapter 8

1 Cited in Wyatt Mason, "The Revelations of Marilynne Robinson," *New York Times Magazine*, 1 October 2014.
2 George Orwell, *Nineteen Eighty-Four* (New York: Plume, 2003), 276, 277.
3 See Timothy Snyder, *The Reconstruction of Nations: Poland, Ukraine, Lithuania, Belarus, 1565–1999* (New Haven: Yale University Press, 2003).
4 For a history and collection of documents concerning Poland's intervention in Carpatho-Ukraine in the fall of 1938 and spring of 1939, see *Akcja "Łom": Polskie działania dywersyjne na Rusi Zakarpackiej w świetle dokumentów Oddziału II Sztabu Głównego WP*, ed. Paweł Samuś, Kazimierz Badziak, and Giennadij Matwiejew (Warsaw: Adiutor, 1998).
5 Vincent Shandor, *Carpatho-Ukraine in the Twentieth Century: A Political and Legal History* (Cambridge, MA: Harvard Ukrainian Research Institute, 1997), 166.
6 Ibid., 167.
7 Ibid., 168.
8 On the history of Carpatho-Ukraine and the Hungarian invasion, see ibid., chaps. 5–8.
9 V.S. Kozhurin, "O chislennosti naselennia SSSR nakanune Velikoi Otechestvennoi voiny (Neizvestnye dokumenty)," *Voenno-istoricheskii zhurnal*, no. 2 (1991): 23; Halik Kochanski, *The Eagle Unbowed: Poland and the Poles in the Second World War* (Cambridge, MA: Harvard University Press, 2012), 96.
10 Stephen Fischer-Galati, "Moldavia and the Moldavians," in *Handbook of Major Soviet Nationalities*, ed. Zev Katz, Rosemarie Rogers, and Frederic Harned (New York: Free Press, 1975), 415, 418.
11 Wendy Lower, *Nazi Empire-Building and the Holocaust in Ukraine* (Chapel Hill, NC: University of North Carolina Press, 2005), 206, 205. On the traumatization of the war, see Catherine Merridale, *Night of Stone: Death and Memory in Twentieth Century Russia* (New York: Viking, 2000), and Orlando Figes, *The Whisperers: Private Life in Stalin's Russia* (New York: Picador, 2007), chap. 6.
12 Timothy Snyder, *Bloodlands: Europe between Hitler and Stalin* (New York: Free Press, 2010), 128.
13 Kochanski, *Eagle Unbowed*, 120. The term "revolution from abroad" comes from Jan Gross, *Revolution from Abroad: The Soviet Conquest of Poland's Western Ukraine and Western Belorussia* (Princeton, NJ: Princeton University Press, 1988).
14 Gross, *Revolution from Abroad*, 3, 17.

15　Alexander Statiev, *The Soviet Counterinsurgency in the Western Borderlands* (New York and Cambridge: Cambridge University Press, 2010), 34.

16　Gross claims that "thousands of Poles were killed" but does not provide a more detailed number or the circumstances. For a description and analysis of these atrocities, see Gross, *Revolution from Abroad*, 35–41, 50–3. As is always the case in an environment of chaotic hostilities at the confluence of war, long-standing national struggles, and the collapse of states, the precise numbers of victims and the assignation of responsibility are difficult to determine. Ewa Siemaszko estimated that OUN-led violence took the lives of at least 1,036 Poles in Volhynia and 2,242 in Galicia in 1939. Ewa Siemaszko, "Bilans zbrodni," *Biuletyń Instytut Pamięci Narodowej* 7–8, nos. 116–17 (2010): 80–1; cited in John-Paul Himka, "The Lviv Pogrom of 1941: The Germans, Ukrainian Nationalists, and the Carnival Crowd," *Canadian Slavonic Papers* 53, nos. 2–4 (2011): 214n128. Also see Grzegorz Motyka, *Od Rzezi Wołyńskiej do Akcji "Wisła": Konflikt polsko-ukraiński 1943–1947* (Cracow: Wydawnictwo Literackie, 2011), 45–51. Many of those Poles killed by Ukrainian nationalists may have been Polish soldiers or fully armed deserters who sought to avenge their military defeat by the Germans on the local Ukrainian population. Many refused to disarm. See Ivan Patryliak, *"Peremoha abo smert'": Ukrains'kyi vyzvol'nyi rukh u 1939–1960 rr.* (L'viv: Chasopys, 2012), 26–32.

17　Joseph B. Schechtman, *European Population Transfers, 1939–1945* (New York: Oxford University Press, 1946), 371.

18　For a descriptive analysis of how the Soviets organized these elections, see Gross, *Revolution from Abroad*, chap. 2.

19　Kochanski, *Eagle Unbowed*, 123.

20　Kozhurin, "O chislennosti naselennia SSSR," 23.

21　Orest Subtelny, "The Soviet Occupation of Western Ukraine, 1939–1941: An Overview," in *Ukraine during World War Two: History and Its Aftermath*, ed. Yury Boshyk (Edmonton, AB: Canadian Institute of Ukrainian Studies, 1986), 9.

22　Shimon Redlich, *Together and Apart in Brzezany: Poles, Jews, and Ukrainians, 1919–1945* (Bloomington: Indiana University Press, 2002), 81. On how the Soviets took over the Shevchenko Scientific Society and transformed it into a branch of the Academy of Sciences of the Ukrainian SSR, see document 258, *Kul'turne zhyttia v Ukraini: Zakhidni zemli*, ed. Iurii Slyvka et al (Kyiv: Naukova dumka, 1995), 1:588–92.

23　Andriy Zayarnyuk, "A Revolution's History, A Historians' War," *Ab Imperio* 1 (2015): 463.

24　Kochanski, *Eagle Unbowed*, 124.

25 Gross, *Revolution from Abroad*, 150. In late 1939 or early 1940, I.S. Serov, the head of the Ukrainian NKVD, described the following scene to Nikita S. Khrushchev, who recorded it in his memoirs: "There are long lines standing outside the place where people register for permission to return to Polish territory. When I took a closer look, I was shocked to see that most of the people in line were members of the Jewish population. They were bribing the Gestapo agents to let them leave as soon as possible to return to their original homes." N.S. Khrushchev, *Khrushchev Remembers*, with an introduction, commentary, and notes by Edward Crankshaw; trans. and ed. Strobe Talbott (Boston: Little, Brown, 1970), 141.

26 The citation concerning crowds comes from Gross, *Revolution from Abroad*, 20, 29, 42; cited in Statiev, *Soviet Counterinsurgency*, 39.

27 Gross, *Revolution from Abroad*, 33. Gross provided a different interpretation in his *Neighbors: The Destruction of the Jewish Community in Jedwabne, Poland* (Princeton, NJ: Princeton University Press, 2001), and in his "Themes for a Social History of War Experience and Collaboration," and his "A Tangled Web: Confronting Stereotypes Concerning Poles, Germans, Jews, and Communists," in *The Politics of Retribution in Europe: World War II and Its Aftermath*, ed. Istvan Deak, Jan T. Gross, and Tony Judt (Princeton, NJ: Princeton University Press, 2000), 15–35, 74–129.

28 Redlich, *Together and Apart*, 87.

29 Gross, *Revolution from Abroad*, 206.

30 Kochanski, *Eagle Unbowed*, 108, 107.

31 Redlich, *Together and Apart*, 86.

32 Kochanski, *Eagle Unbowed*, 121.

33 Redlich, *Together and Apart*, 80.

34 Gross, *Revolution from Abroad*, 33, 45.

35 Volodymyr Viatrovych, *Druha Pol's'ko-ukrains'ka viina, 1942–1947: Dokumenty* (Kiev: Vydavnychyi dim "Kyievo-Mohylians'ka akademiia," 2011), 46.

36 Patryliak, *"Peremoha abo smert',"* 25.

37 Redlich, *Together and Apart*, 88.

38 See chap. 4, note 65. Also see Maria Savchyn Pyskir, *Thousands of Roads: A Memoir of a Young Woman's Life in the Ukrainian Underground during and after World War II*, trans. Ania Savage (Jefferson, NC: McFarland, 2001).

39 Iu. A. Kyrychuk, "Radians'kyi terror 1939–1941 rr.," *Politychnyi terror i terroryzm v Ukraini, XIX–XX st.: Istorychni narysy* (Kyiv: Naukova dumka, 2002), 576–95; cited in *The Great West Ukrainian Prison Massacre of 1941: A Sourcebook*, ed. Ksenya Kiebuzinski and Alexander J. Motyl (Amsterdam: Amsterdam University Press, 2016), 28–33.

40 Myroslav Shkandrij, *Ukrainian Nationalism: Politics, Ideology, and Literature, 1929–1956* (New Haven, CT: Yale University Press, 2015), 41.

41 Statiev, *Soviet Counterinsurgency*, 42.

42 On the deportations, see Gross, *Revolution from Abroad*, chap. 6.

43 Stanisław Ciesielski, Grzegorz Hryciuk, and Aleksander Srebrakowski, *Masowe deportacje ludności w Związku Radzieckim* (Toruń: Wydawnictwo Adam Marszalek, 2004), 246–7; *Wysiedlenia, wypędzenia i ucieczki 1939–1959: Atlas ziem polskich, Polacy, Żydzi, Niemcy, Ukraińcy*, ed. Witold Syenkiewicz and Grzegorz Hryciuk (Warsaw: Demart, 2008), 37–41, 107–9, 205–7; Albin Głowacki, "Deportowani w latach 1940–1941," in *Polska 1939–1945: Straty osobowe i ofiary represji pod dwiema okupacjami*, ed. Wojciech Materski and Tomasz Szarota (Warsaw: Instytut Pamięci Narodowej, 2009), 243–5.

44 Ciesielski, Hryciuk, and Srebrakowski, *Masowe deportacje ludności w Związku Radzieckim*, 246–7; *Wysiedlenia, wypędzenia i ucieczki 1939–1959*, 37–41; 107–9, 205–7; and Głowacki, "Deportowani w latach 1940–1941," 243–5.

45 Timothy Snyder, *Sketches from a Secret War: A Polish Artist's Mission to Liberate Soviet Ukraine* (New Haven, CT: Yale University Press, 2005), 177.

46 *Wysiedlenia, wypędzenia i ucieczki 1939–1959*, 207.

47 See J.K. Zawodny, *Death in the Forest: The Story of the Katyn Forest Massacre* (Notre Dame, IN: University of Notre Dame Press, 1962). For the recently published documents concerning Katyn, see *Katyn: A Crime without Punishment*, ed. Anna M. Cienciala, Natalia S. Lebedeva, and Wojciech Materski (New Haven, CT, and London: Yale University Press, 2007).

48 Gross, *Revolution from Abroad*, 155, made these estimates. He also provided a compelling argument that the NKVD arrested approximately 500,000 men and women in Western Ukraine and Western Belarus in 1939–41.

49 Gross, *Revolution from Abroad*, 179; Kochanski, *Eagle Unbowed*, 129.

50 Subtelny, "The Soviet Occupation of Western Ukraine," 11, 12; Kiebuzinski and Motyl, *The Great West Ukrainian Prison Massacre*, 8, and especially notes 20–4.

51 Kiebuzinski and Motyl, *The Great West Ukrainian Prison Massacre*, 8, and 13–14; Himka, "The Lviv Pogrom of 1941," 211.

52 Gross, *Revolution from Abroad*, 181.

53 "Many Victims of Soviet Terror in Western Ukraine Identified: More than 14,000 Executed by the Reds," *Ukrainian Weekly*, 2 September 1941.

54 Kiebuzinski and Motyl, *The Great West Ukrainian Prison Massacre*, 14.

55 Raul Hilberg defined pogroms as "short, violent outbursts by a community against its Jewish population," in his *The Destruction of the European Jews* (Chicago: Quadrangle Books, 1961), 203; cited in Himka, "The Lviv Pogrom of 1941," 211–12.

56 Ibid., 221; and Grzegorz Rossolinski-Liebe, "The 'Ukrainian National
     Revolution' of 1941: Discourse and Practice of a Fascist Movement," *Kritika*
     12, no. 1 (Winter 2011): 102. Myroslav Shkandrij provided a more nuanced
     assessment of the OUN's complicity in the anti-Jewish pogrom during the
     first days of the war. See Shkandrij, *Ukrainian Nationalism*, 65–6.
57 Subtelny, "Soviet Occupation," 11. Jan Gross provides a slightly lower figure:
     "Together with POWs and those arrested in the intervals, about 1.25 million
     Polish citizens (of a total of roughly 13.5 million) found themselves in the
     summer of 1941 residing in the labor camps, in prisons, and in forced settle-
     ments all over the Soviet Union." Gross, *Revolution from Abroad*, 146.
     Nevertheless, this, as Gross reminds us, is "a staggering number for a popula-
     tion of 13.5 to 14 million (including refugees from central and western
     Poland)" (155).
58 Yitzhak Arad, *The Holocaust in the Soviet Union* (Lincoln: University of
     Nebraska Press, 2009), 67, 68 (quote from Nazi propaganda pamphlet).
59 Mark Mazower, *Hitler's Empire: How the Nazis Ruled Europe* (New York:
     Penguin, 2008), 139.
60 Snyder, *Bloodlands*, x, 159–60.
61 On Ukrainian attitudes in Western Ukraine between 1939 and 1941, see
     Vladyslav Hrynevych, *Nepryborkane riznoholossia: Druha svitova viina i
     suspil'no-politychni nastroi v Ukraini, 1939 – cherven' 1941 rr.* (Kiev: "Lira,"
     2012).
62 Rossolinski-Liebe, "'Ukrainian National Revolution,'" 104, 105.
63 Shkandrij, *Ukrainian Nationalism*, 59.
64 Ryszard Torzecki, *Polacy i Ukraińcy: Sprawa ukraińska w czasie II Wojny
     Swiatowej na terenie II Rzeczyspopolitej* (Warsaw: Polskie Wydawnictwo
     Nauke, 1993), 247; cited in Shkandrij, *Ukrainian Nationalism*, 60.
65 Myroslav Yurkevych, "Galician Ukrainians in German Military Formations
     and in the German Administration," in Boshyk, *Ukraine during World War
     Two*, 83; cited in Statiev, *Soviet Counterinsurgency*, 56, 60.
66 See Alexander J. Motyl, "The Ukrainian Nationalist Movement and the Jews:
     Theoretical Reflections on Nationalism, Fascism, Rationality, Primordialism,
     and History," *Polin: Studies in Polish Jewry* 26 (2014): 275–95.
67 John A. Armstrong, *Ukrainian Nationalism*, 2nd ed. (New York: Columbia
     University Press, 1963).
68 Norman Davies, *No Simple Victory: World War II in Europe, 1939–1945*
     (New York: Penguin, 2008), 165.
69 Mazower, *Hitler's Empire*, 134; Snyder, *Bloodlands*, 161.
70 These statistics come from John Barber and Mark Harrison, *The Soviet
     Home Front, 1941–1945: A Social and Economic History of the USSR in*

World War II (London: Longman, 1991), 29–30. The surrender of over three million Soviet soldiers in a six-month period represented the largest capture of soldiers in the history of warfare. For an assessment of the frustrations of front-line German soldiers, see Omer Bartov, *The Eastern Front, 1941–1945: German Troops and the Barbarisation of Warfare*, 2nd ed. (New York: Palgrave, 2001).

71 Edward C. Homze, *Foreign Labor in Nazi Germany* (Princeton, NJ: Princeton University Press, 1967), 67.

72 Bohdan Krawchenko, "Soviet Ukraine under Nazi Occupation," in Boshyk, *Ukraine during World War Two*, 16. The Soviet leadership, unfortunately, did not evacuate the Jews. For an analysis of these evacuations, see Rebecca Manley, *To the Tashkent Station: Evacuations and Survival in the Soviet Union at War* (Ithaca, NY: Cornell University Press, 2009).

73 During its campaign in Western Europe in 1940, the German army lost approximately 156,000 men, including 30,000 dead. By December 1941, six months into Operation Barbarossa, it experienced heavier losses on the eastern front: 750,000, including 200,000 dead. Barber and Harrison, *Soviet Home Front*, 28.

74 On the haunting parallels between the German soldiers on the steppe in the First World War and the Second World War, see Vejas Gabriel Liulevicius, *War Land on the Eastern Front: Culture, National Identity, and German Occupation in World War I* (New York: Cambridge University Press, 2000). Also see Theo J. Shulte, *The German Army and Nazi Policies in Occupied Russia* (Oxford and New York: Berg, 1989).

75 From an article about "subhumans," edited by the SS Main Office and prepared primarily for the indoctrination of SS recruits, "Document No. 1805," International Military Tribunal, *Trial of the Major War Criminals* (Nuremberg: Secretariat of the Tribunal, 1946); cited in Ihor Kamenetsky, *Secret Nazi Plans for Eastern Europe: A Study of Lebensraum Policies* (New Haven, CT: College and University Press, 1961), 38–9; and in R.J. Rummel, *Death by Government* (New Brunswick, NJ, and London: Transaction, 1994), 118–19. For the complete article, see Kamenetsky, *Secret Nazi Plans*, appendix 2, 189–92.

76 Yitzhak Arad, "The Destruction of the Jews in German-Occupied Territories of the USSR," in *The Unknown Black Book: The Holocaust in the German-Occupied Soviet Territories*, ed. Joshua Rubenstein and Ilya Altman (Bloomington: Indiana University Press, 2008), xiv–xv.

77 Martin Dean, *Collaboration in the Holocaust: Crimes of the Local Police in Belarus and Ukraine* (New York: St Martin's Press, 2000), 27, 60.

78 Karel C. Berkhoff, *Harvest of Despair: Life and Death in Ukraine under Nazi Rule* (Cambridge, MA: Harvard University Press, 2004), 42.

79 Dieter Pohl, "Ukrainische Hilfskräfte bim Mord an den Juden," in *Die Täter der Shoah: Fanatische Nationalsozialisten oder ganz normale Deutsche?* ed. Gerhard Paul (Göttingen: Wallstein Verlag, 2000), 219; cited in John-Paul Himka, "The Reception of the Holocaust in Postcommunist Ukraine," in *Bringing the Dark Past to Light: The Reception of the Holocaust in Postcommunist Europe*, ed. with intro. by John-Paul Himka and Joanna Beata Michlic (Lincoln: University of Nebraska Press, 2014), 631.
80 Snyder, *Bloodlands*, 201.
81 Snyder, *Bloodlands*, 202, 408. M.I. Koval, "The Nazi Genocide of the Jews and the Ukrainian Population," in *Bitter Legacy: Confronting the Holocaust in the USSR*, ed. Zvi Gitelman (Bloomington: Indiana University Press, 1997), 59n, claims that fifty-two thousand Jews were shot at Babyn Yar from 29 September to 3 October 1941.
82 Wendy Morgan Lower, "From Berlin to Babi Yar: The Nazi War against the Jews, 1941–1944," *Journal of Religion and Society* 9 (2007): 1–14.
83 Redlich, *Together and Apart*, 132.
84 Arad, *The Holocaust*, 125. For an overview of the Holocaust in Ukraine, see chaps. 10, 12–17, 19–22, and 24–5.
85 Pohl, "Ukrainische Hilfskräfte," 219; cited in Shkandrij, *Ukrainian Nationalism*, 67.
86 The statistic, 2.6 million Soviet Jews, comes from Snyder, *Bloodlands*, 221.
87 Arad, *The Holocaust*, 518–25; and Jacques Vallin, France Mesle, Serguei Adamets, and Serhii Pyrozhkov, "A New Estimate of Ukrainian Population Losses during the Crises of the 1930s and 1940s," *Population Studies* 56, no. 3 (2002): 249–64 (citation on 263).
88 Arad, *The Holocaust*, 518–25. According to John-Paul Himka, approximately "2.5 million people whom the invading Germans would have deemed Jews" lived in the territory of present-day Ukraine on the eve of the Second World War. Under a million were evacuated east when the Germans attacked. About 1.5 million Jews were murdered in the Holocaust." Himka, "The Reception of the Holocaust," 628.
89 Arad, *The Holocaust*, 531.
90 Ibid., 345, 346.
91 Ulrich Herbert, *Hitler's Foreign Workers: Enforced Foreign Labor in Germany under the Third Reich* (New York: Cambridge University Press, 1997), 164, 177.
92 Ibid., 165.
93 Richard J. Overy, *Russia's War* (New York: Penguin, 1998), 135. As Lower pointed out, "According to the racial hierarchy of Nazi ideology in which the Germans ranked supreme, Ukrainians fell under the Baltic peoples but above those slated for immediate destruction – the Jews, the Gypsies, and

other 'Asiatics,' followed by Poles and to a lesser extent the Great Russians and Belorussians." Lower, *Nazi Empire-Building*, 27. Also see Bohdan Wytwycky (Vitvitsky), *The Other Holocaust: Many Circles of Hell: A Brief Account of 9–10 Million Persons Who Died with the 6 Million Jews under Nazi Racism* (Washington, DC: Novak Report on the New Ethnicity, 1980).

94 Lower, *Nazi Empire-Building*, 65.

95 Quoted in Herbert, *Hitler's Foreign Workers*, 188.

96 Barber and Harrison, *Soviet Home Front*, 21; Overy, *Russia's War*, 133.

97 Snyder, *Bloodlands*, 176–7.

98 Barber and Harrison, *Soviet Home Front*, 28. "In German prisoner-of-war camps for Red Army soldiers, the death rate over the course of the war was 57.5 percent … In German prisoner-of-war camps for soldiers of the Western Allies, the death rate was less than five percent. As many Soviet prisoners-of-war died *on a single day* in autumn 1941 as the British and American prisoners-of-war in the course of the entire Second World War." Snyder, *Bloodlands*, 181–2 (his emphasis).

99 Homze, *Foreign Labor*, 81; Herbert, *Hitler's Foreign Workers*, 161; and *Krakivski visti*, 11 November 1941, and *Oborona Ukrainy*, 1 August 1942; cited in Krawchenko, "Soviet Ukraine under Nazi Occupation," 16. Of the millions the German captured, they "shot, on a conservative estimate, half a million Soviet prisoners-of-war. By way of starvation or mistreatment during transit, they killed about 2.6 million more. All in all, perhaps 3.1 million Soviet prisoners-of-war were killed." Snyder, *Bloodlands*, 184.

100 Karel C. Berkhoff, *Harvest of Despair: Life and Death in Ukraine under Nazi Rule* (Cambridge, MA: Belknap Press, Harvard University Press, 2004), 37, 39.

101 Quoted in ibid., 37.

102 Quoted in Mazower, *Hitler's Empire*, 458.

103 Quoted in Berkhoff, *Harvest of Despair*, 47.

104 Alexander Werth, *Russia at War, 1941–1945* (New York: Dutton, 1964), 602.

105 See Adam Hochschild, *King Leopold's Ghost: A Story of Greed, Terror, and Heroism in Colonial Africa* (Boston: Houghton Mifflin, 1998).

106 Redlich, *Together and Apart*, 99.

107 Kochanski, *Eagle Unbowed*, 263–4.

108 Jan T. Gross, *Polish Society under German Occupation: The Generalgouvernement, 1939–1944* (Princeton, NJ: Princeton University Press, 1979), 188–9; Berkhoff, *Harvest of Despair*; and Mazower, *Hitler's Empire*, 458–9.

109 George H. Stein, *The Waffen-SS: Hitler's Elite Guard at War, 1939–1945* (Ithaca, NY: Cornell University Press, 1966), xxx, xxxi, and xxxii (quote).

110 Notes from the 12 April 1943 meeting of German administrators concerning the formation of a division from the Ukrainian population of Galica, in Taras Hunczak, *On the Horns of a Dilemma: The Story of the Ukrainian Division* Halychyna (Lanham, MD: University Press of America, 2000), 186.

111 From the appeal by Dr Otto Wachter, governor of Galicia, "To the Conscriptable Youth of Galicia" in Hunczak, *On the Horns of a Dilemma*, 184.

112 Stein, *The Waffen-SS*, 185.

113 Hunczak, *On the Horns of a Dilemma*, 64.

114 Ibid., 31.

115 Ibid., 27–8.

116 Ibid., 55. Koch's racist reaction did not differ very much from Hitler's. During the night of 23–4 March 1945, with Soviet troops less than 160 kilometres (100 miles) from Berlin, Hitler asserted: "One never knows what's floating around. I've just heard, to my surprise, that a Ukrainian SS-Division has suddenly turned up. I knew absolutely nothing about this Ukrainian SS-Division … If it is comprised of (former) Austrian Ruthenians, one can do nothing other than immediately to take away their weapons. The Austrian Ruthenians were pacifists. They were lambs, not wolves. They were miserable even in the Austrian Army. The whole business is a delusion." Stein, *The Waffen-SS*, 194, 195.

117 Hunczak, *On the Horns of a Dilemma*, 86; and Stein, *The Waffen-SS*, 187. On the Battle of Brody, see *Brody: zbirnyk stattei i narysiv*, ed. Oleh Lysiak (Drohobych-Lviv: Vidrodzhennia, 2003).

118 Hunczak, *On the Horns of a Dilemma*, 128–9.

119 Stein, *The Waffen-SS*, 187. After extensive screenings in internment camps in Rimini, the British determined that these men had not engaged in crimes against humanity. See *Commission of Inquiry on War Criminals: Report – Part I: Public* (Ottawa: Canadian Government Publishing Centre, 1986), 251; cited in Hunczak, *On the Horns of a Dilemma*, 163.

120 A. Zhukovsky, "Transnistria," in *Encyclopedia of Ukraine*, ed. Danylo H. Struk (Toronto: University of Toronto Press, 1984), 5:274–5.

121 Snyder, *Bloodlands*, 280.

122 Berkhoff, *Harvest of Despair*, 226–31.

123 Amir Weiner, *Making Sense of War: The Second World War and the Fate of the Bolshevik Revolution* (Princeton, NJ: Princeton University Press, 2001), 308.

124 Statiev, *Soviet Counterinsurgency*, 65.

125 Lev Shankovs'kyi, *Pokhidni hrupy OUN: Prychyny do istorii pokhidnykh hrup OUN na tsentral'nykh i skhidnykh zemliakh Ukrainy v 1941–1943 rr.* (Munich: Vyd. "Ukrains'kyi samostiinyk," 1958), 7.

126 Ibid., 7–8.
127 Berkhoff, *Harvest of Despair*, 41.
128 Alexander Dallin, *German Rule in Russia, 1941–1945: A Study of Occupation Policies*, 2nd, rev., ed. (Boulder, CO: Westview Press, 1981), 114, 375; Krawchenko, "Soviet Ukraine under Nazi Occupation," 27; cited in Statiev, *Soviet Counterinsurgency*, 63.
129 Berkhoff, *Harvest of Despair*, 99.
130 Ibid., 136, 132 (quote on 140); Krawchenko, "Soviet Ukraine under Nazi Occupation," 27.
131 Berkhoff, *Harvest of Despair*, 227.
132 According to Sylvia Gilliam, members of the well-educated younger generation were "consistently less anti-Russian, had less anti-semitism, and [were] also less likely to condemn the nationality policies of the regime ... there is a striking correspondence here between the goals of the regime – cultural pride devoid of national independence aspirations, – and the expressed attitudes of the best educated younger respondent." Sylvia Gilliam, "The Nationality Questionnaire," in *The Nationality Problem in the Soviet Union: The Ukrainian Case*, ed. Sylvia Gilliam, Irving Rostow, and John S. Reshetar (Project on the Soviet Social System [AF No. 33(038)-12909], Russian Research Center, Harvard University, 1954), x.
133 Berkhoff, *Harvest of Despair*, 227–9.
134 Ibid., 104–5.
135 The figures for Kiev in 1941 come from Berkhoff, *Harvest of Despair*, 169; for 1943 from Alexander Dovzhenko, *The Poet as Filmmaker: Selected Writings*, ed. and trans. Marco Carynnyk (Cambridge, MA: MIT Press, 1973), 93; and for Kharkiv from Krawchenko, "Soviet Ukraine under Nazi Occupation," 27.
136 Herbert, *Hitler's Foreign Workers*, 1.
137 Ibid., 165; Homze, *Foreign Labor*, 172–3; Myroslav Yurkevich, "Ostarbeiter," in *Encyclopedia of Ukraine*, ed. Danylo Husar Struk (Toronto: University of Toronto Press, 1986), 3:729.
138 The figure of 200,000 is from Herbert, *Hitler's Foreign Workers*, 197; 400,000 is from Dallin, *German Rule in Russia*, 452; David R. Marples, *Stalinism in Ukraine in the 1940s* (New York: St Martin's Press, 1992), 52; cited in Statiev, *Soviet Counterinsurgency*, 63.
139 Herbert, *Hitler's Foreign Workers*, 1.
140 Ibid., 317.
141 Krawchenko, "Soviet Ukraine under Nazi Occupation," 28.
142 Homze, *Foreign Labor*, 309.

143　Earl Ziemke, "Composition and Morale of the Partisan Movement," in *Soviet Partisans in World War II*, ed. John A. Armstrong (Madison: University of Wisconsin Press, 1964), 150.

144　Armstrong, *Soviet Partisans*, 44.

145　Ibid., 745.

146　Alexander Dallin, Ralph Mavrogordato, and Wilhelm Moll, "Partisan Psychological Warfare and Popular Attitudes," in Armstrong, *Soviet Partisans*, 337.

147　Statiev, *Soviet Counterinsurgency*, 74.

148　Shankovs'kyi, *Pokhidni hrupy OUN*, 47–8; Dallin, Mavrogordato, and Moll, "Partisan Psychological Warfare and Popular Attitudes," 222; Kenneth Slepyan, *Stalin's Guerillas: Soviet Partisans in World War II* (Lawrence: University Press of Kansas, 2006), 74, 157, 160; and Aleksandr Gogun, *Stalinskie kommandos: Ukrainskie partyzanskie formirovaniia 1941–1944* (Moscow: ROSSPEN, 2012), 376–89, 486, 487.

149　Compare Statiev, *Soviet Counterinsurgency*, 81, and Kochanski, *Eagle Unbowed*.

150　See Anna M. Ciencala, "General Sikorski and the Conclusion of the Polish-Soviet Agreement of 30 July 1941: A Reasssessment," *Polish Review* 41, no. 4 (1996): 413, 414.

151　Norman Davies, *God's Playground: A History of Poland* (New York: Columbia University Press, 1982), 2:272.

152　Anita Prazmowska, *Poland: A Modern History* (London: I.B. Tauris, 2010), 141–2.

153　Ibid., 142.

154　Davies, *God's Playground*, 2:522.

155　The information on Kholm and the Kholm Region in this paragraph and in the preceding three paragraphs comes from Volodymyr Kubijovič, "Kholm Gubernia" and "Kholm Region," *Encyclopedia of Ukraine*, 2:480–5.

156　See Roger D. Petersen, *Understanding Ethnic Violence: Fear, Hatred and Resentment in Twentieth Century Eastern Europe* (New York: Cambridge University Press, 2002).

157　Viatrovych, *Druha Pol's'ko-ukrains'ka viina*, 60, 61.

158　Joseph Poprzeczny, *Odilo Globocnik: Hitler's Man in the East* (Jefferson, NC: McFarland, 2004), 182; Patryliak, *"Peremoha abo smert'*," 334; Viatrovych, *Druha Pol's'ko-ukrains'ka viina*, document 11 ("Ohliad sytuatsii na Kholmshchyni na vesni 1943 r."), 163.

159　Patryliak, *"Peremoha abo smert'*," 336.

160　Ibid., 364–7.

161 Patryliak asserted that 5,000 to 6,000 Ukrainians were killed and 20,000 fled the Kholm and neighbouring Hrubyshev Regions between 1942 and mid-1944. Ibid., 364.

162 Document 26 ("Zaiava Orhanizasii ukrains'kykh natsionalistiv [samostiinykiv-derzhavnykiv] z pryvodu podii na Volyni vlitku 1943 roku") (July 1943), Viatrovych, *Druha Pol's'ko-ukrains'ka viina*, 226.

163 Ibid., 77.

164 For a nuanced assessment of the start of this critical event, see Shkandrij, *Ukrainian Nationalism*, 69.

165 Viatrovych, *Druha Pol's'ko-ukrains'ka viina*, 66.

166 "In the ethnically mixed areas of the *kresy*, the Germans generally staffed the police with men who were not Poles." Dean, *Collaboration in the Holocaust*, 65.

167 Ibid., 71.

168 Ibid., 60, 67.

169 Ibid., 61.

170 Ibid., 73.

171 Ibid., 71.

172 Ibid.

173 Ibid., 69; Armstrong, *Soviet Partisans*, 147–8.

174 Armstrong, *Soviet Partisans*, 148.

175 Dean, *Collaboration in the Holocaust*, 145.

176 Snyder, *Reconstruction of Nations*, 173.

177 The precise number of Poles in Volhynia in 1941–5 is unknown. The last Polish census of 1931 recorded 346,640 Poles (or 16.6 per cent of the total population) in this province. Serhii Chornyi, *Natsional'nyi sklad naseleniia Ukrainy v XX storichchi: Dovidnyk* (Kyiv: Kartohrafiia, 2001), 62. From 1931 Volhynia experienced a population growth, but also extensive Soviet deportations and executions during the years 1939–41. After 22 June 1941, Volhynia also experienced German executions and deportations and labour conscriptions to Germany. Iaroslav Dashkevych estimates that in 1943 approximately 220,000 Poles lived in this province. See his article, "Tretii front u mizhnarodnii hri v mynulomu i teper," in *Ukrains'kyi vyzvol'nyi rukh*, ed. V. Viatrovych (Lviv: Ms, 2003), 2:139; cited in Viatrovych, *Druha Pol's'ko-ukrains'ka viina*, 100.

178 Dean, *Collaboration in the Holocaust*, 146, made this analogy.

179 For estimates of the number of Poles killed by Ukrainians and Ukrainians killed by Poles during the Second World War and immediately after, see: Aleksandr Gogun, *Mezhdu Gitlerom i Stalinom: ukrainskie povstantsy*, 2nd ed. (Moscow: ZAO "OLMA Media Group," 2012); Alexander Gogun,

Stalin's Commandos: Ukrainian Partisan Forces on the Eastern Front
(London: I.B. Tauris, 2015); Grzegorz Motyka, *Ukraińska partyzantka*
1942–1960: Działalność Organizacji Ukraińskich Nacjonalistów i
Ukraińskiej Powstańczej Armii (Warsaw: Instytut Studiów Politycznych
PAN: RYTM, 2006); G. Motyka, *Od rzezi wołyńskiej do Akcji "Wisła"*;
G. Motyka, *Antypolska akcja OUN-UPA 1943–1944: Fakty i interpretacje*
(Warsaw: Instytut Pamięci Narodowej, 2002); Marek Jasiak, "Overcoming
Ukrainian Resistance: The Deportation of Ukrainians within Poland in
1947," in *Redrawing Nations: Ethnic Cleansing in East Central Europe,*
1944–1948, ed. Phillip Ther and Ana Siljak (Lanham, MD: Rowman and
Littlefield, 2001), 178–95; Torzecki, *Polacy i Ukraińcy;* Timothy Snyder,
"The Causes of Ukrainian Polish Ethnic Cleansing 1943," *Past and Present*,
no. 179 (2008): 221; Snyder, *The Reconstruction of Nations;* Snyder,
Bloodlands; Grzegorz Hryciuk, *Przemiany narodowościowe i ludnościowe w*
Galicji Wschodniej i na Wołyniu w latach 1931–1948 (Torun: Wydawnictwo
Adam Marszałek, 2005), 279, 315; Per Anders Rudling, "Theory and
Practice: Historical Representation of Wartime Accounts of the Activities of
the OUN-UPA," *East European Jewish Affairs* 36, no. 2 (December 2006):
163–79; Rossolinski-Liebe, "The 'Ukrainian National Revolution' of 1941,"
83–114; Ahonen Pertti, *People on the Move: Forced Population Movements*
in Europe in the Second World War and Its Aftermath (New York: Berg,
2008); Ewa Siemaszko, "Bilans Zbrodni," 77–90; Davies, *God's Playground;*
Lucyna Kulińska, *Dzieci Kresów* (Cracow: Echo, 2009): 467; *Antypolska ak-*
cja nacjonalistów ukrainskich w Malopolsce Wschodniej i na Wołyniu w świa-
tle dokumentów Rady Głównej Oprekuńczej 1943–1944: Zestawienie ofiar,
ed. Lucyna Kulińska and Adam Roliński (Cracow: Fundajca Centrum
Dokumentacji Czynu Niepodleglościowego, 2012); and John-Paul Himka,
"Interventions: Challenging the Myths of Twentieth Century Ukrainian
History," in *The Convolutions of Historical Politics*, ed. Alexei Miller and
Maria Lipmann (Budapest and New York: Central European University
Press, 2012); Patryliak, *"Peremoha abo smert'"*; and Viatrovych, *Druha*
Pol's'ko-ukrains'ka viina.

180 Motyl, "The Ukrainian Nationalist Movement and the Jews," 288.
181 Viatrovych, *Druha Pol's'ko-ukrains'ka viina*, 108.
182 Snyder, *Reconstruction of Nations*, 168–78.
183 For a history of the Soviet passport system, see Marc Garcelon, "Colonizing
the Subject: The Genealogy and Legacy of the Soviet Internal Passport," in
Documenting Individual Identity: The Development of State Practices in the
Modern World, ed. Jane Caplan and John Torpey (Princeton, NJ: Princeton
University Press, 2001), 83–100.

184 See Krawchenko, "Soviet Ukraine under Nazi Occupation." Berkhoff, *Harvest of Despair*, provides a more cautious assessment.

185 Berkhoff, *Harvest of Despair*, 194, 199, 195–6, 200.

186 Rossolinski-Liebe, "'Ukrainian National Revolution,'" 92, claims that 750 to 7,000 OUN-B members joined the expeditionary groups.

187 See Weiner, *Making Sense of War*, chap. 5.

188 Shankovs'kyi, *Pokhidni hrupy OUN*, 185.

189 "Materiialy III nadzvychainoho velykoho zbory Orhanizatsii ukrains'kykh natsionalistiv," in *Ukrains'ka suspil'no – polityczna dumka v 20 stolitti: Dokumenty i materially*, ed. Taras Hunczak and Roman Solchanyk (Munich: Suchasnist, 1983), 3:65–73; and Peter J. Potichnyj and Yevhen Shtendera, *The Political Thought of the Ukrainian Underground* (Edmonton, AB: Canadian Institute of Ukrainian Studies, 1986).

190 According to Alexander J. Motyl, "nationalism can possess liberal and democratic aspirations as it can have fascist and authoritarian aspirations" ("The Ukrainian Nationalist Movement and the Jews," 278). For a documentary overview of the evolution of the views of the OUN-B and of the UPA, see Potichnyj and Shtendera, *Political Thought of the Ukrainian Underground*; and Shkandrij, *Ukrainian Nationalism*.

191 Motyl, "The Ukrainian Nationalist Movement and the Jews," 281.

192 Ibid.

193 On the impact of the experiences of the OUN's expeditionary groups in the 1943 OUN program, see Shankovs'kyi, *Pokhidni hrupy OUN*, 317.

194 Ibid., 15.

195 Serhy Yekelchyk, *Stalin's Empire of Memory: Russian-Ukrainian Relations in the Soviet Historical Imagination* (Toronto: University of Toronto Press, 2004).

196 Armstrong, *Soviet Partisans in World War II*, 4.

197 The passage in quotes comes from Francis Fukuyama, *Trust: The Social Virtues and the Creation of Prosperity* (New York: Free Press, 1995), 26.

198 Interview with Dmytro Bartkiw (London, October 1997), in Redlich, *Together and Apart*, 130.

199 John-Paul Himka, "Ukrainian Collaboration in the Extermination of the Jews during the Second World War: Sorting Out the Long-Term and Conjunctural Factors," in *The Fate of the European Jews, 1939–1945: Continuity or Contingency?* ed. Jonathan Frankel (New York and Oxford: Oxford University Press, 1997), 179.

200 See Eric Hoffer, *The True Believer: Thoughts on the Nature of Mass Movements* (New York: Harper and Row, 1966).

201 These ideas come from Alexander J. Motyl, who reviewed the 2013 and 2014 drafts of this book.

202 Gross, *Polish Society under German Occupation*, 117.
203 Stefan Korbonski, *Fighting Warsaw: The Story of the Polish Underground State, 1939–1945* (London: George Allen and Unwin, 1956), 116, 117–19.
204 Document 5 ("Vytiah iz 'Ohliadu zhyttia na pivnichno-zakhidnykh ukrains'kykh zemliakh (za misiatsi kviten'-traven' 1942 roku"), in Viatrovych, *Druha Pol's'ko ukrains'ka viina*, 127.
205 Ibid., 127.
206 Statiev, *Soviet Counterinsurgency*, 100.
207 Motyl, "The Ukrainian Nationalist Movement and the Jews," 283.
208 Himka, "Ukrainian Collaboration," 173.
209 Snyder, *Bloodlands*, 186.
210 George Orwell, *Nineteen Eighty-Four*, part III, chap. 3.
211 Snyder, *Bloodlands*, 186.
212 Himka, "Ukrainian Collaboration," 184.
213 This partial quote comes from Zayarnyuk, "A Revolution's History," 472. The point about the relative impact of these three total wars on the citizens of Ukraine is mine, not Zayarnyuk's.
214 Aleksander M. Nekrich, *Punished Peoples: The Deportation and Fate of Soviet Minorities at the End of World War Two* (New York: W.W. Norton, 1978); Barber and Harrison, *Soviet Home Front*, 115; Norman M. Naimark, *Fires of Hatred: Ethnic Cleansing in Twentieth Century Europe* (Cambridge, MA: Harvard University Press, 2001), chap. 3. The statistics come from Naimark, *Fires of Hatred*, 102, 103. Snyder, *Bloodlands*, 330–1, asserts that the NKVD deported 180,014 Crimean Tatars.
215 The figure of 203,662 is from Ihor Vynnychenko, *Ukraina 1920–1980-kh: Deportatsii, zaslannia, vyslannia* (Kyiv: Vydavntstvo "Radu," 1994), 82; the figure of 300,000 is from Richard Overy, *Russia's War: A History of the Soviet War Effort* (New York: Penguin, 1998), 311–12.
216 Compare Marius Broekmeyer, *Stalin, the Russians, and Their War* (Madison: University of Wisconsin Press, 2004), 178–9; and N.L. Pobol' and P.M. Polian, comps., *Stalinskie deportatsii 1928–1953 gg.* (Moscow: Mezhdunarodnyi fond "Demokratiia" and "Materik," 2005), 781–2. For the full text of this alleged order deporting Ukrainians, see ibid., 787–8.
217 For the quote from Khrushchev, see Broekmeyer, *Stalin, the Russians, and Their War*, 178–9.
218 Kenneth Slepyan, *Stalin's Guerillas: Soviet Partisans in World War II* (Lawrence: University Press of Kansas, 2006), 216–217. According to Yitzhak Arad, Stalin and his closest comrades downplayed the Soviet Jewish role in the Great Fatherland War and in the Holocaust because Nazi anti-Judeo-Bolshevist propaganda "fell on fertile ground. Many Soviet civilians and soldiers were tainted by anti-Semitism, and many of them

would have been pleased to see the Jews disappear, even if this involved cruelty and murder. To counter this propaganda, the Soviet authorities presented Germany as striving to exterminate the Russians and other Slavic nations, while downplaying the murder of Jews and their singular fate under German occupation. The objective of Soviet propaganda was to increase the Soviet soldiers' motivation to fight the German enemy and increase the war effort among the Soviet people in the rear area." Arad, *The Holocaust*, 543–4. On this point, see Leonard Schapiro, *The Communist Party of the Soviet Union*, 2nd ed. (New York: Random House, 1971), 542–3. Snyder asserts that the Holocaust could never become part of the Soviet history of the war because it raised the issue of the involvement of Soviet citizens with the Germans in the mass murder of the Jews. Snyder claims that "collaboration undermined the myth of a united Soviet population defending the honor of the fatherland by resisting the hated fascist invader." Snyder, *Bloodlands*, 342–3.

219 Statiev, *Soviet Counterinsurgency*, 78.

220 Gogun, *Stalinskie commandos*, 342; and Alexander Gogun, *Stalin's Commandos: Ukrainian Partisan Forces on the Eastern Front* (London: I.B. Tauris, 2015).

221 See Weiner, *Making Sense of War*.

222 Slepyan, *Stalin's Guerillas*, 216–17.

Chapter 9

1 David Galula, *Counterinsurgency Warfare: Theory and Practice* (New York: Praeger, 1964), ix; cited in David Kilcullen, *The Accidental Guerilla: Fighting Small Wars in the Midst of a Big One* (New York: Oxford University Press, 2009), xxi.

2 For overviews of these Allied negotiations, see S.M. Plokhy, *Yalta: The Price of Peace* (New York: Penguin, 2011); Herbert Feis, *Between War and Peace: The Potsdam Conference* (Princeton, NJ: Princeton University Press, 1967); and James L. Gormly, *From Potsdam to the Cold War: Big Three Diplomacy, 1945–1947* (Wilmington, DE: SR Books, 1990).

3 Milovan Djilas, *Conversations with Stalin* (New York: Harcourt, Brace, and World, 1962), 114.

4 Gerhard L. Weinberg, *A World at Arms: A Global History of World War II* (New York: Cambridge University Press, 1994), 1,041; as cited in Mark Kramer, "Introduction," in *Redrawing Nations: Ethnic Cleansing in East Central Europe, 1944–1948*, ed. Phillip Ther and Ana Siljak (Lanham, MD: Rowman and Littlefield, 2001), xii, 5.

5 G.F. Krivosheev et al., *Soviet Casualties and Combat Losses in the Twentieth Century* (London: Greenhill Books, and Mechanicsburg, PA: Stackpole Books, 1997), 83–4. Also see A.A. Sheviakov, "Gitlerovskii genotsid na territoriskh SSSR," *Sotsiologicheskie issledovaniia*, no. 12 (1991), and "Zhertvy sredi mirnogo naseleniia v gody Otechestvennoi voiny," *Sotsiologicheskie issledovanie*, no. 11 (1992).

6 Krivosheev et al., *Soviet Casualties*, 83–5. For political reasons, Soviet leaders have always massaged the actual number of deaths the Soviet Union experienced between 1941 and 1945. In February 1946 Stalin presented a figure of seven million Soviet war losses. In April 1965, Marshal Konev, one of the battlefront commanders in the Great Patriotic War, announced that ten million soldiers and sailors died in the war but did not provide the number of civilians lost. In the 1960s, Nikita Khrushchev asserted "an excess of 20 million," including military and civilian losses. In 1985, Army General M.M. Kozlov claimed that more than twenty million Soviet citizens, "part of them civilians," perished in the war. With Gorbachev's *glasnost*, new studies of the war revised these statistics upward. John Erickson, "Foreward," in ibid., vii.

7 Karel C. Berkhoff, *Harvest of Despair: Life and Death in Ukraine under Nazi Rule* (Cambridge, MA: Harvard University Press, 2004), 46.

8 V.I. Zemskov, "K voprosu o repatriatsii sovetskikh grazhdan 1944–1951 gody," *Istoriia SSSR*, no. 4 (1990): 26.

9 Geoffrey Hosking, *The First Socialist Society: A History of the Soviet Union from Within*, enlarged ed. (Cambridge, MA: Harvard University Press, 1990), 297.

10 Norman Davies, *No Simple Victory: World War II in Europe, 1939–1945* (New York: Penguin, 2006), 356. On losses in Belarus, see *Velikaia Otechestvennaia voina, 1941–1945*, ed. V.A. Zolotarev and G.N. Sevost'ianov (Moscow: Nauka, 1999), 4:267; cited in Alexander Statiev, *The Soviet Counterinsurgency in the Western Borderlands* (New York and Cambridge, UK: Cambridge University Press, 2010), 64.

11 Timothy Snyder, *Bloodlands: Europe between Hitler and Stalin* (New York: Basic Books, 2010), 251.

12 David Marples, *Stalinism in Ukraine in the 1940s* (Edmonton: University of Alberta Press, 1992), 54; Davies, *No Simple Victory*, 301; *Povidomlennia nadzvychainoi derzhavnoi komisii po vstanovlenniu i rozsliduvanniu zlochyniv nimetsko-fashysytskykh zaharbnykiv* (Kiev, 1945), 2; cited in Vsevolod Holubnychy, "Outline History of the Communist Party of Ukraine," in his *Soviet Regional Economics: Selected Works of Vsevolod Holubnychy* (Edmonton, AB: Canadian Institute of Ukrainian Studies Press, 1984), 112.

13 Davies, *No Simple Victory*, 20.

14 Jacques Vallin, France Mesle, Serguei Adamets, and Serhii Pyrozhkov, "A New Estimate of Ukrainian Population Losses during the Crises of the 1930s and 1940s," *Population Studies* 56, no. 3 (2002): 249–64 (citation on 263); and Yitzhak Arad, *The Holocaust in the Soviet Union* (Lincoln: University of Nebraska Press, 518–25 (see table 8.1).

15 Marples, *Stalinism in Ukraine*, 63; Barbara A. Anderson and Brian D. Silver, "Demographic Consequences of World War II on the Non-Russian Nationalities of the USSR," in *The Impact of World War II on the Soviet Union*, ed. Susan J. Linz (Totowa, NJ: Rowman and Allanheld, 1985), 208.

16 Snyder, *Bloodlands*, 342.

17 Although most of the Ukrainian foreign workers in occupied Germany returned to the USSR after the war, approximately 750,000 foreign workers, mostly those from territories claimed by the Soviet Union, refused repatriation to their homelands. Edward C. Homze, *Foreign Labor in Nazi Germany* (Princeton, NJ: Princeton University Press, 1967), 298.

18 Anderson and Silver, "Demographic Consequences," 208.

19 Figures for 1939: TsGANKh, f. 1562, op. 329, d. 4535, l. 72 in *VPN 1939 goda/1937 goda*, reel 5; Rossiiskaia Akademiia nauk and Upravlenie statistiki naseleniia Goskomstata, *Vsesoiuznaia perepis' naseleniia 1939 goda: Osnovnye itogi* (Moscow: Nauka, 1992), 68; for 1959: Soviet Union, Tsentral'noe statisticheskoe upravlenie, *Itogi Vsesoiuznoi perepisi naseleniia 1959 goda: Ukrainskaia SSR* (Moscow: Gosstatizdat, 1963), 168. The Russian population in Western Ukraine in the interwar period was negligible.

20 Snyder, *Bloodlands*, 330–1.

21 Phillip Ther, "A Century of Forced Migration: The Origins and Consequences of 'Ethnic Cleansing,'" in Ther and Siljak, *Redrawing Nations*, 44.

22 Ther and Siljak, *Redrawing Nations*, xii, 5, claim "approximately 12 million" Germans; R.M. Douglas asserts the twelve to fourteen million figure. See R.M. Douglas, *Orderly and Humane: The Expulsion of the Germans after the Second World War* (New Haven, CT, and London: Yale University Press, 2012), 1.

23 Mark Kramer cites a figure of 1.4 million victims: M. Kramer, "Introduction," in Ther and Siljak, *Redrawing Nations*, 27n6. R.M. Douglas presents a mortality range of 500,000 to 1.5 million. As all statistics dealing with war losses, this figure is contested. Douglas, *Orderly and Humane*, 1.

24 Teresa Torańska, *"Them": Stalin's Polish Puppets* (New York: Harper and Row, 1987), 250.

25 Snyder, *Bloodlands*, 326.

26 "By Soviet-Polish agreements of 1944 and 1945, ethnic Poles and Jews (but not other nationalities) who had been citizens before 17 September 1939 and

who resided in the eastern provinces that were now incorporated into the Soviet Union, had the option of moving from the Soviet Union to Poland. Conversely, Ukrainians, Russians, Belarussians, and Lithuanians (but not Jews) had the option of moving to the Soviet Union. More than half a million Ukrainians, Russians, Belarussians, and Lithuanians actually moved from Poland to the Soviet Union under this agreement – probably involuntarily in many cases, since they evidently constituted the great majority of the population eligible for transfer. Two million Poles, or about half those eligible for transfer, made the journey in the opposite direction. In addition, a substantial group of Jews got out of the Soviet Union via the Polish-Soviet exchange though a high proportion of them subsequently left Poland for Palestine and other destinations." Sheila Fitzpatrick, "Postwar Soviet Society: The 'Return to Normalcy,' 1945–1953," in Linz, *The Impact of World War II on the Soviet Union*, 133. Piotr Eberhardt provided the statistics: Piotr Eberhardt, *Ethnic Groups and Population Changes in Twentieth-Century Central-Eastern Europe: History, Data, Analysis* (Armonk, NY: M.E. Sharpe, 2003), 140.

27 Eberhardt, *Ethnic Groups and Population Change*, 140.
28 Snyder, *Bloodlands*, 326.
29 Ther, "A Century of Forced Migration," 56; Ivan Bilas, *Represyvno-karal'na systema v Ukraini 1917–1953* (Kiev: Lybid'-Viis'ko Ukrainy, 1994), 1:229, 230: and Ihor Vynnychenko, *Ukraina 1920–1980-kh: Deportatsii, zaslannia, vyslannia* (Kiev: vyd. "Radu," 1994), 66. Eberhardt, *Ethnic Groups and Population Change*, 140, provides a figure of 481,000 Ukrainians and 34,000 Belarussians. Marek Jasniak, "Overcoming Ukrainian Resistance: The Deportation of Ukrainians within Poland in 1947," in Ther and Siljak, *Redrawing Nations*, 181, lists 80,000 Belarusans. Also see Timothy Snyder's article, "'To Resolve the Ukrainian Problem Once and for All': The Ethnic Cleansing of Ukrainians in Poland, 1943–1947," *Journal of Cold War Studies* 1, no. 2 (1999): 86–120; and Orest Subtelny, "Expulsion, Resettlement, Civil Strife: The Fate of Poland's Ukrainians, 1944–1947," in Ther and Siljak, *Redrawing Nations*, 155–72.
30 Vynnychenko, *Ukraina 1920–1980-kh*, 67.
31 Anatolny Rusnachenko, *Zburenyi narod: Natsional'no-vyzvol'nyi rukh v Ukraini i natsional'ni rukhy opory v Bilorusii, Lytvii, Latvii, Estonii* (Kiev: Pul'sary, 2002), 183.
32 Ibid., 188.
33 On the Ukrainian national movement and the OUN-B/UPA in Zakerzonnia between 1939 and and 1948, see ibid., chap. 3.
34 Kramer, "Introduction," 13.
35 Eberhardt, *Ethnic Groups and Population Change*, 142, 143.

36 Snyder, *Bloodlands*, 325.
37 Amir Weiner, *Making Sense of War: The Second World War and the Fate of the Bolshevik Revolution* (Princeton, NJ: Princeton University Press, 2001), 337–8.
38 According to the 1939 census (taken before the annexation of Ukrainian territories from Poland, Romania, and Czechoslovakia), 23,667,509 individuals (or 76 per cent of the total population of the Ukrainian SSR) identified themselves as Ukrainians. According to the 1959 census, the first since the end of the war, 32,158,493 people (or 77 per cent of the total population) identified themselves as Ukrainians. Source for 1939: TsGANKh, f. 1562, op. 529, d. 4535, l. 72 in *VPN 1939 goda/1937 goda*, reel 5; for 1959: *Itogi Vsesoiuznoi perepisi naseleniia 1959 goda: Ukrainskaia SSR*, 168.
39 In the 1930s, 63.4 per cent of the population of the territories annexed to the Soviet Union from Poland, 61.6 per cent of the population from Czechoslovakia, and 43.4 per cent of the population from Romania identified themselves as Ukrainians (see Eberhardt, *Ethnic Groups and Population Change*, 212, 213, 214). According to the Soviet census of 1959, Ukrainians comprised 91 per cent of the Lviv, Ivano-Frankivsk, and Ternopil oblasts (which constituted Poland's interwar Galicia) and 94 per cent of the Volyn and Rivne oblasts (which comprised Poland's interwar Volhynia); 75 per cent of the Zakarpats'ka Oblast (Czechoslovakia's former Transcarpathia); and 67 per cent of the Chernivtsi Oblast (Romania's interwar Bukovina). See *Itogi Vsesoiuznoi perepisi nadeleniia 1959 goda: Ukrainskaia SSR*, 176–8.
40 Source for 1939: TsGANKh, f. 1562, op. 329, d. 4535, ll. 72–4, *in VPN 1939 goda/1937 goda*, reel 5; for 1959: *Itogi Vsesoiuznoi perepisi naseleniia 1959 goda: Ukrainskaia SSR*, 174–9.
41 Ibid.
42 On tipping points in post-war Ukraine, see my "Imagining Ukraine: Regional Differences and the Emergence of an Integrated State Identity, 1926–1994," *Nations and Nationalism* 4, no. 2 (1998): 187–206.
43 Roman Szporluk, "Kiev as the Ukraine's Primate City," *Harvard Ukrainian Studies* 3–4 (1979–80), part 2: 848–9.
44 See Elena Zubkova, *Russia after the War: Hopes, Illusions, and Disappointments, 1945–1957* (Armonk, NY: M.E. Sharpe, 1998).
45 Serhy Yekelchyk, *Everyday Politics in the Wake of Total War: Kyiv, 1943–1953* (New York: Oxford University Press, 2014).
46 Konstantin Simonov, "Glazami cheloveka moego pokoleniia: razmyshleniia o I. V. Staline," *Znamia*, no. 3 (1988): 48; cited in Zubkova, *Russia after the War*, 18.

47 Statiev, *Soviet Counterinsurgency*, 318n5.
48 Ibid., 106n27.
49 Ivan Patryliak, *"Peremoha abo smert'": Ukrains'kyi vyzvol'nyi rukh u 1939–1960 rr.* (L'viv: Chasopys, 2012), 188.
50 Ibid., 223.
51 Ibid., 208.
52 See Volodymyr Semystyaha, "New Documentary Information about Maksym Bernats'kyi, a Leader of the Ukrainian Underground in Eastern Ukraine during World War II," *Harvard Ukrainian Studies* 18, nos. 3–4 (1994): 303–26. Bernats'kyi was the editor-in-chief of *Nove zhyttia*, a regional Ukrainian-language newspaper in Voroshylovhrad (today's Luhansk), published three times weekly between 18 August 1942 and 31 January 1943, with a circulation of three to twenty thousand copies. Also see Ievhen Stakhiv, *Kriz' tiurmy, pidpillia i kordony: Povist' moho zhyttia* (Kiev: Rada, 1995).
53 Statiev, *Soviet Counterinsurgency*, 100. In 1946, in Lviv Oblast, 58.2 per cent of peasant households possessed less than two hectares of arable land and were regarded as poor; 39.2 per cent held two to five hectares and were identified as middle peasants; and only 2.6 per cent owned more than five hectares and were labelled kulaks (100). According to Statiev, "More of the middle peasants resented rather than supported the new Soviet administration because their social status had dropped relative to their poorer neighbors, and the few benefits they had received from Soviet reforms often were outweighed by higher taxes and the fear of collectivization and deportation. The borderline between kulaks and middle peasants has always been blurred" (153).
54 Kilcullen, *The Accidental Guerilla*, xiv, 75.
55 Statiev, *Soviet Counterinsurgency*, 104.
56 Ibid., 116.
57 Ibid., 110, table 4.4; 125.
58 Ibid., 132.
59 Ibid., 8
60 Vladyslav Hrynevych, "Stalins'ka imperiia v borot'bi z ukrains'kym povstans'kym rukhom," in *"Osobye papki" Stalina i Molotova pro natsional'no-vyzvol'nu borot'bu v Zakhidnii Ukraini u 1944–1948 rr.: zbirnyk dokumentiv*, comp. Iaroslav Dashkevych and Vasyl' Kuk (L'viv: Literaturna agentsiia Piramida, 2010), 43.
61 See *"Osobye papki" Stalina i Molotova*.
62 Vynnychenko, *Ukraina 1920–1980-kh*, 82.
63 Statiev, *Soviet Counterinsurgency*, 199–200.

64 Ibid., 202.
65 Ibid., 204.
66 Kilcullen, *The Accidental Guerilla*, 30.
67 Statiev, *Soviet Counterinsurgency*, 5.
68 Kilcullen, *The Accidental Guerilla*, 52.
69 *Roman Shukhevych u dokumentakh radians'kykh orhaniv derzhavnoi bezpeky* (1940–1950), ed. Volodymyr Serhiichuk (Kiev: PP Serhiichuk M.I., 2007).
70 Statiev, *Soviet Counterinsurgency*, 134.
71 Ibid., 338.
72 Document 64, *"Osobye papki" Stalina i Molotova*, 216–20.
73 Marples, *Stalinism in Ukraine*, 163.
74 Ibid., 114.
75 Ibid., 129.
76 Quote taken from Harvey Fireside, *Icon and Swastika: The Russian Orthodox Church under Nazi and Soviet Control* (Cambridge, MA: Harvard University Press, 1971), 52; cited in Statiev, *Soviet Counterinsurgency*, 270.
77 Statiev, *Soviet Counterinsurgency*, 42.
78 On the complexities of Sheptytsky's moral stance, see John-Paul Himka, "Christianity and Radical Nationalism: Metropolitan Andrei Sheptytsky and the Bandera Movement," in *State Secularism and Lived Religion in Soviet Russia and Ukraine*, ed. Catherine Wanner (Washington, DC: Woodrow Wilson Center Press, and New York: Oxford University Press, 2012), 93–116.
79 The Greek Catholic Church did not collaborate with the Nazis or the Ukrainian nationalists. Metropolitan Sheptytsky opposed both. See Andrii Kravchuk, *Christian Social Ethics in Ukraine: The Legacy of Andrei Sheptytsky* (Toronto: Canadian Institute of Ukrainian Studies Press, 1997); and *Morality and Reality: The Life and Times of Andrei Sheptyts'kyi*, ed. Paul Robert Magocsi (Edmonton, AB: Canadian Institute of Ukrainian Studies, University of Alberta, 1989).
80 Statiev, *Soviet Counterinsurgency*, 265.
81 For documents concerning the pressure on the Ukrainian Greek Catholic Church and its "conversion" to Russian Orthodoxy, see documents 114–18, 120, 121, 124, 128, 129, 131, 139, and 233, in *Kul'turne zhyttia v Ukraini: Zakhidni zemli*, ed. Iurii Slyvka et al. (Kyiv: Naukova dumka, 1995), 1:259–546.
82 Statiev, *Soviet Counterinsurgency*, 267.
83 Bohdan R. Bociurkiw, *The Ukrainian Greek Catholic Church and the Soviet State (1939–1950)* (Edmonton, AB: Canadian Institute of Ukrainian Studies Press, 1996), 245; cited in Statiev, *Soviet Counterinsurgency*, 268.

84 Document no. 246 in *Pravda pro Uniiu. Dokumenty i materialy*, ed. V. Malanchuk et al. (Lviv: Kameniar, 1968), 365; cited in Statiev, *Soviet Counterinsurgency*, 268.

85 See document 121, *Kul'turne zhyttia v Ukraini*, 280–2.

86 Statiev, *Soviet Counterinsurgency*, 268, 269.

87 Bociurkiw, *The Ukrainian Greek Catholic Church*.

88 Vsevolod Holubnychy, "Outline History of the Communist Party of Ukraine," in *Soviet Regional Economics: Selected Works of Vsevolod Holubnychy*, ed. Iwan S. Koropeckyj (Edmonton, AB: Canadian Institute of Ukrainian Studies Press, 1982), table 1, 128–9; T.H. Rigby, *Communist Party Membership in the USSR, 1917–1967* (Princeton, NJ: Princeton University Press, 1968), 371.

89 Rigby, *Communist Party Membership*, 264, 265; Y. Bilinsky and V. Holubnychy, "Communist Party of Ukraine," in *Encyclopedia of Ukraine*, ed. Volodymyr Kubijovič (Toronto: University of Toronto Press, 1984), 1: 551.

90 Rigby, *Communist Party Membership*, 376n. According to the source Rigby cites, 87 per cent of the 1,784,015 members and candidate-members of the CPSU recruited between 1941 and 1944 identified themselves as Russians and only 7 per cent as Ukrainians. V.K. Molochko, "Kommunisticheskaia partiia i massy v period stroitel'stva sotsializma," in *Partiia i massy*, ed. K.I. Suvorov, I.G. Riabtsev, and A.F. Iudenkov (Moscow: Mysl, 1966), 82.

91 Taras Kuzio, *Ukraine: Perestroika to Independence*, 2nd ed. (London: Macmillan, 2000), 44.

92 *Pravda*, 23 August 1946; cited in Holubnychy, "Outline History," 115–17.

93 Ibid.

94 Gennadii Kostyrchenko, *Out of the Red Shadows: Anti-Semitism in Stalin's Russia* (Amherst, NY: Prometheus, 1995); Joshua Rubenstein and Vladimir P. Naumov, eds, *Stalin's Secret Pogrom: The Postwar Inquisition of the Jewish Anti-Fascist Committee* (New Haven, CT: Yale University Press, 2001). The term "heinously" comes from an official source cited in Jonathan Brent and Vladimir P. Naumov, *Stalin's Last Crime: The Plot against Jewish Doctors, 1948–1953* (New York: HarperCollins, 2003), 288.

95 These included the Volyn, Drohobych, Lviv, Rivne, Stanyslaviv, Ternopil', Izmail, and Chernivtsi oblasts.

96 *Kul'turne zhyttia v Ukraini: Zakhidni zemli*, vol. 1, document 107, 243, 242.

97 I. Bakalo, T. Pliushch, and B. Struminsky, "Education," in *Encyclopedia of Ukraine* (Toronto: University of Toronto Press, 1984), 1:802.

98 The OUN issued a short brochure, "Vkazivky bat'kam u vykhovani ditei," in 1950 providing instructions on how parents could neutralize the lessons their children learned in school. See document 284, *Kul'turne zhyttia v Ukraini*, 646–51.

99 A slogan from the German Young Pioneers, founded after 1945. Quoted in
    Anne Applebaum, *Iron Curtain: The Crushing of Eastern Europe, 1944–
    1956* (New York: Doubleday, 2012), 148.
100 On 1 January 1939, the three Polish provinces of Lwów, Stanisławów, and
    Tarnopol, possessed a population of 5,824,100. Ukrainians constituted
    64.4 per cent of the population, Poles 25.0 per cent, Jews 9.8 per cent;
    49,200 (0.8 per cent) belonged to other groups, mainly Germans. Volodymyr
    Kubijovič, *Etnichni hrupy pivdennozakhidnoi Ukrainy (Halychyny) na 1. I.
    1939* (Wiesbaden, Germany: Otto Harrassowitz, 1983), xiv, xxiii.
101 *Itogi Vsesoiuznoi perepisi naselennia 1959 goda: Ukrainskaia SSR*, 188–9.
102 Bakalo, Pliushch, and Struminsky, "Education," in *Encyclopedia of Ukraine*,
    1:802.
103 Ibid.
104 TsDAHOU, 1/24/ 2743, l. 3.
105 Alexander Solzhenitsyn, *The Gulag Archipelago* (New York: Harper and
    Row, 1978), 3:421–2. Surrounded by those who wept, Solzhenitsyn recorded
    his reaction to hearing of Stalin's death: "My face, trained to meet all occa-
    sions, assumed a frown of mournful attention" (421).
106 For a history of the evolution of the "friendship of peoples," see Lowell
    Tillett, *The Great Friendship: Soviet Historians on the Non-Russian
    Nationalities* (Chapel Hill: University of North Carolina Press, 1969).
107 See, for example, "Neporyshna iednist' i druzhba narodiv Radians'koi
    Ukrainy," *Radians'ka Ukraina*, 14 March 1953, 1 (editorial). For Stalin's im-
    portance to Ukrainians, see R. Symonenko, "Stalin-vyzvolytel'
    ukrains'koho narodu," *Radians'ka Ukraina*, 14 March 1953, 2.
108 Charles H. Fairbanks, Jr, "National Cadres as a Force in the Soviet System:
    The Evidence of Beria's Career, 1949–1953," in *Soviet Nationality Policies
    and Practices*, ed. Jeremy R. Azrael (New York: Praeger, 1978), 155.
109 Bohdan R. Bociurkiw, "The Ukrainian Catholic Church in the USSR under
    Gorbachev," *Problems of Communism* (November–December 1990): 3;
    cited in Amy Knight, *Beria: Stalin's First Lieutenant* (Princeton, NJ:
    Princeton University Press, 1993), 189.
110 Bociurkiw, *The Ukrainian Greek Catholic Church*, 3.
111 Knight, *Beria*, 189.
112 "Resolution on the Criminal Anti-Party and Anti-Government Activities of
    Beria of the Plenum of the Central Committee of the CPSU," in *The Beria
    Affair: The Secret Transcripts of the Meeting Signalling the End of Stalinism*,
    ed. S.M. Stickle (New York: Nova Science, 1992), 188.
113 This treaty is very controversial. Various ideological movements have inter-
    preted this treaty in different ways. At the heart of the disagreement is the

issue of whether the treaty was a temporary military alliance or a permanent absorption of Ukraine into the Russian Empire. See M. Iu. Braichevskyi, *Pryiednannia chy vozz'iednannia? Krytychni zauvahy z pryvodu odniiei kontseptsii* (Toronto: Novi dni, 1972); John Basarab, *Pereiaslav 1654: A Historiographical Study* (Edmonton, AB: Canadian Institute of Ukrainian Studies, 1982); and *Pereiaslavs'ka rada 1654: Istoriohrafiia ta doslidzhennia*, ed. Pavlo Sokhan et al. (Kyiv: Smoloskyp, 2003).

114 Z.T. Serdiuk, in *Beria Affair*, 53.

115 O. Khablo, "Mohutnii zasib vykhovannia pobuttia druzhby narodiv: Do 15-richchia kyivs'koho filialu Tsentral'noho muzeiu V. I. Lenina," *Radians'ka Ukraina*, 29 August 1953, 3.

116 "Theses on the 300th Anniversary of the Reunification of Ukraine and Russia (1654–1954)," *Pravda* and *Izvestiia*, 12 January 1954, 2; cited in *The Current Digest of the Soviet Press (CDSP)* 6, no. 51 (1954): 3. Also published in *Radians'ka Ukraina*, 12 January 1954, 3–4.

117 For an account of the planned celebrations in Warsaw, Prague, and Sofia, see "Trudiashchi krain narodnoi demokratii vidznachaiut' 300-richchia vozz'iednannia Ukrainy z Rosiieiu," *Radians'ka Ukraina*, 19 January 1954, 3.

118 "Pidhotovka do sviatkuvannia 300-richchia vozz'iednannia Ukrainy z Rosiieiu," *Radians'ka Ukraina*, 15 January 1954, 4.

119 Cited in "In the Presidium of the USSR Supreme Soviet," *Pravda* and *Izvestiia*, 27 February 1954, 2; cited in *CDSP* 6, no. 9 (1954): 23.

120 A.I. Kirichenko, "On the 300th Anniversary of the Reunification of Ukraine with Russia," *Pravda* and *Izvestiia*, 23 May 1954, 2–4; cited in *CDSP* 6, no. 21 (1954): 17.

121 Gwendolyn Sasse, *The Crimea Question: Identity, Transition, and Conflict* (Cambridge, MA: Harvard Ukrainian Research Institute, 2007), 110, 125.

122 According to Bill Taubman, Khrushchev "was promoted from ordinary Central Committee secretary to First Secretary in September 1953, a move that allowed him to mobilize the party machinery." William Taubman, *Khrushchev: The Man and His Era* (New York: W.W. Norton, 2004), 258. By the end of 1953, "Khrushchev's approval was required for all major decisions. After February 1954, Khrushchev occupied the seat of honor when the Presidium gathered for ceremonial occasions in the Great Kremlin palace. In March 1954, Khrushchev's protégé, Ivan Serov, took charge of the KGB" (264). For the most thorough assessment of the nuances of the Crimean transfer, see Sasse, *The Crimea Question*, chap. 5.

123 Yaroslav Bilinsky coined this phrase in his *The Second Soviet Republic: The Ukraine after World War II* (New Brunswick, NJ: Rutgers University Press, 1964).

124 For the Crimea, compare the censuses of 1939 and 1959: *Vsesoiuznaia perepis' naseleniia 1939 goda*, 67; and *Itogi Vsesoiuznoi perepisi naseleniia 1959 goda: Ukrains'kaia SSR*, 184.

125 Stalin, on 12 February 1929, asserted to an audience of Ukrainian writers that "it makes no difference, of course, where one district or another of Ukraine or the RSFSR belongs." Leonid Maximenkov, "Stalin's Meeting with a Delegation of Ukrainian Writers on 12 February 1929," *Harvard Ukrainian Studies* 16, nos. 3–4 (1992): 403 (see chap. 7).

126 See Konstantyn Sawczuk, *The Ukraine in the United Nations Organization: A Study in Soviet Foreign Policy, 1944–1950* (Boulder, CO: East European Quarterly Press, 1975).

127 See Vernon A. Aspaturian, *The Union Republics in Soviet Diplomacy: A Study of Soviet Federalism in the Service of Soviet Foreign Policy* (Geneva: E. Droz, 1960), chaps. 4–5; and Sawczuk, *The Ukraine in the United Nations Organization*, chap. 8.

Conclusion

1 Sigmund Freud, *Civilization and Its Discontents*, trans. and ed. James Strachey (New York: W.W. Norton, 1961), 16, 18.

2 Peter A. Gourevitch, "Breaking with Orthodoxy: The Politics of Economic Policy Responses to the Depression of the 1930s," *International Organization* 38, no. 1 (1984): 99; cited in Grzegorz Ekiert, *The State against Society: Political Crises and Their Aftermath in East Central Europe* (Princeton, NJ: Princeton University Press, 1996), 305–6.

3 James C. Scott, *Seeing Like a State: How Certain Schemes to Improve the Human Condition Have Failed* (New Haven, CT, and London: Yale University Press, 1998), 89, quote on 88.

4 Mark Roseman, "War and the People: The Social Impact of Total War," in *The Oxford History of Modern War*, ed. Charles Townshend (Oxford, UK, and New York: Oxford University Press, 2005), 299.

5 The term "critical junctures" comes from Ekiert, *The State against Society*, xi.

6 See Timothy Snyder, *Bloodlands: Europe between Hitler and Stalin* (New York: Basic Books, 2010).

7 Norman Stone, *The Eastern Front, 1914–1917* (New York: Charles Scribner's Sons, 1975), 284–5, 286, 288.

8 Ibid., 300, 299.

9 Peter Holquist, *Making War, Forging Revolution: Russia's Continuum of Crisis, 1914–1921* (Cambridge, MA: Harvard University Press, 2002), 45.

10 Stone, *The Eastern Front*, 144.

11 Peter Gatrell, *Russia's First World War: A Social and Economic History* (Harlow, England: Pearson Education, 2005), 229.

12 *Foreign Relations of the United States, 1918: Russia* (Washington, DC: U.S. Government Printing Office, 1919), 1:490; cited in John W. Wheeler-Bennett, *Brest-Litovsk: The Forgotten Peace, March 1918* (New York: W.W. Norton, 1971), 269.

13 See Walker Connor, "Nation-Building or Nation-Destroying?" *World Politics* 24, no. 3 (1972): 319–55; Walker Connor, *Ethnonationalism: The Quest for Understanding* (Princeton, NJ: Princeton University Press, 1994), chap. 2; Robert Conquest, *The Nation Killers: The Soviet Deportation of Nationalities* (London: Macmillan, 1970); Robert Conquest, *Stalin – Breaker of Nations* (New York: Viking, 1991).

14 Francine Hirsch, *Empire of Nations: Ethnographic Knowledge and the Making of the Soviet Union* (Ithaca, NY: Cornell University Press, 2005), 8.

15 The people of Ukraine attained slightly higher percentages: 57.5 per cent in 1926 and 85.3 per cent in 1939. Both sets of statistics come from TsGANKh SSSR, f. 162, op. 329, d. 4535, l. 28.

16 According to the 1970 Soviet census, the first after 1959, 56 per cent of the Soviet population lived in urban areas, as did 55 per cent of the Soviet Ukrainian population. Russia (1923– USSR), Tsentral'noe statisticheskoe up-ravlenie, *Itogi Vsesoiuznoi perepisi naseleniia 1970 goda, tom IV* (Moscow: Statistika, 1973), 20, 27 (USSR); 152, 158 (Ukrainian SSR).

17 Hirsch, *Empire of Nations*, 273.

18 Terry Martin, *The Affirmative Action Empire: Nations and Nationalism in the Soviet Union, 1923–1939* (Ithaca, NY: Cornell University Press, 2001), 1, 9.

19 Ibid., 1, 3.

20 Ibid., 13.

21 Richard Pipes, *The Formation of the Soviet Union: Nationalism and Communism, 1917–1923*, rev. ed. (New York: Atheneum, 1968), 296–7.

22 Hirsch, *Empire of Nations*, 8–9.

23 Ibid., 14.

24 Ibid., 15.

25 Frederick C. Barghoorn, *Soviet Russian Nationalism* (New York: Oxford University Press, 1956); Piotr Wandycz, *Soviet-Polish Relations, 1917–1921* (Cambridge, MA: Harvard University Press, 1969), 287; Yitzhak Brudny, *Reinventing Russia: Russian Nationalism and the Soviet State, 1953–1991* (Cambridge, MA: Harvard University Press, 1998); Martin, *Affirmative Action Empire*, chap. 10; David Brandenberger, *National Bolshevism: Stalinist Mass Culture and the Modern Russian National Identity, 1931–1956* (Cambridge, MA: Harvard University Press, 2002); and *Epic Revisionism:*

Russian History and Literature as Stalinist Propaganda, ed. Kevin M.F. Platt and David Brandenberger (Madison: University of Wisconsin Press, 2006).

26 On the persecution of the Poles and Germans, see Hirsch, *Empire of Nations*, 8; and Martin, *Affirmative Action Empire*, chap. 8.

27 *Landscaping the Human Garden: 20th Century Population Management in a Comparative Framework*, ed. Amir Weiner (Stanford, CA: Stanford University Press, 2003).

28 Sylvia Gilliam, "The Nationality Questionnaire" (unpublished ms. of the Project on the Soviet Social System, Harvard University, 1954), 47.

29 "Nationalism is a state of mind in which the supreme loyalty of the individual is felt to be due the nation-state." Hans Kohn, *Nationalism: Its Meaning and History* (Princeton, NJ: D. Van Nostrand, 1955), 9.

30 Connor, "Nation-Building or Destroying?" 337; Connor, *Ethnonationalism*, 43.

31 Valerie Bunce, *Subversive Institutions: The Design and Destruction of Socialism and the State* (New York: Cambridge University Press, 1999).

32 Quoted in Alex J. Kay, *Exploitation, Resettlement, Mass Murder, Political and Economic Planning for German Occupation Policy in the Soviet Union, 1940–1941* (Oxford: Berghahn, 2006), 39–40; cited in Lizzie Collingham, *The Taste of War: World War II and the Battle for Food* (New York: Penguin, 2012), 37.

33 Collingham, *Taste of War*, 180.

34 Ibid., 183.

35 Ibid., 182.

36 Ibid., 185–6.

37 See Jane Caplan and John Torpey, eds, *Documenting Individual Identity: The Development of State Practices in the Modern World* (Princeton, NJ: Princeton University Press, 2001).

38 Ella Libanova, Natalia Levchuk, Emelian Rudnyts'kyi, Natalia Runhach, Svetlana Poniakina, and Pavel Shevchuk, "Smertnost naseleniia Ukrainy v trudoaktivnom vozraste," *Demoskop Weekly*, March 31–April 13, 2008, http://demoscope.ru/weekly/2008/0327/tema01.php (accessed 28 March 2012); Jacques Vallin, France Mesle, Serguei Adamets, and Serhii Pyrozhkov, "A New Estimate of Ukrainian Population Losses during the Crises of the 1930s and 1940s," *Population Studies* 56, no. 3 (2002): 249–64 (citation on 263); Yitzhak Arad, *The Holocaust in the Soviet Union* (Lincoln: University of Nebraska Press, 518–25 (see table 8.1 in this volume).

39 See Gwendolyn Sasse, *The Crimea Question: Identity, Transition, and Conflict* (Cambridge, MA: Harvard Ukrainian Research Institute, 2007) and Karl D. Qualls, *From Ruins to Reconstruction: Urban Identity in Soviet Sevastopol after World War II* (Ithaca, NY: Cornell University Press, 2009).

40 John-Paul Himka, "Western Ukraine between the Wars," *Canadian Slavonic Papers* 34, no. 4 (1992): 392.

41 Ibid., 393.

42 Marc Raeff, "Patterns of Russian Imperial Policy toward the Nationalities," in *Soviet Nationality Policies*, ed. Edward Allworth (New York: Columbia University Press, 1971), 21–40.

43 See Yaroslav Bilinsky, "The Incorporation of Western Ukraine and Its Impact on Politics and Society in Soviet Ukraine," in *The Influence of East Europe and the Soviet West on the USSR*, ed. Roman Szporluk (New York: Praeger, 1975), 180–228 ; Roman Szporluk, *Russia, Ukraine, and the Breakup of the Soviet Union* (Stanford, CA: Hoover Institution Press, 2000); and William Jay Risch, *The Ukrainian West: Culture and the Fate of Empire in Soviet Lviv* (Cambridge, MA: Harvard University Press, 2011).

44 Thomas Masaryk's dictum that Europe after the First World War had become "a laboratory atop a vast graveyard" inspired this sentence. Cited in Maurice Baumant, *La faillite de la paix, 1918–1939*, 2nd ed. (Paris: Presses universitaires de France, 1946), 8; Erik Goldstein, *Winning the Peace: British Diplomatic Strategy, Peace Planning, and the Paris Peace Conference, 1916–1920* (Oxford, UK: Clarendon Press, 1991), 4; Mark Mazower, *Dark Continent: Europe's Twentieth Century* (New York: A.A. Knopf, 1999); and Volker R. Berghahn, *Europe in the Era of Two World Wars* (Princeton, NJ: Princeton University Press, 2006), 2.

45 David Reynolds, *One World Divisible: A Global History since 1945* (New York: W.W. Norton, 2000), 4 and passim.

46 This phrase comes from Charles Tilly, "Introduction," in *Citizenship, Identity, and Social History*, ed. Charles Tilly (New York: Cambridge University Press, 1996), 12.

47 Scott, *Seeing Like a State*, 344.

48 The components of this "wager" come from Zayarnyuk, "A Revolution's History," 475; and Roman Szporluk, "From an Imperial Periphery to a Sovereign State," *Daedalus* 126, no. 3 (1997): 85–119; republished in his *Russia, Ukraine, and the Breakup of the Soviet Union* (Stanford, CA: Hoover Institution Press, 2000), chap. 15, 361–94.

Index

academic stage (Hroch), 19–20, 27
Academy of Sciences, Russian, 24, 34
administrative-command economy,
134. *See also* central planning
"Affirmative Action Empire," 284
Africa, and Ukraine, 277
agricultural policies: under All-Union
Communist Party, 131–68; under
Russian Communist Party, 112;
under Pavlo Skoropadsky, 68;
Soviet grain acquisitions, 137–8;
violence and drop in productivity,
166. *See also* State Commission for
Aid to Victims of Crop Failure of
the Ukrainian SSR
agriculture: subsistence farming in
Ukraine, 136; world agricultural
market recovery, 137; WWI and
world agricultural market, 137
Alaska, 7
Albania, 84
Alexander II, xv, 22
Alexander III, 22, 23
Alexius, Patriarch of the Russian
Orthodox Church: and Orthodox
hierarchy in Western Ukraine, 269;
efforts to merge the Greek Catholic

Church with the ROC, 268–9;
[Havril] Kostelnyk and Initiative
Group for Greek Catholic and
Russian Orthodox reconciliation,
268; Kostelnyk's synod and the
Greek Catholic Church's "reunion" with the Russian Orthodox
Church (1946), 269; number of
arrests (1945–50) of those who
refused to convert, 269; number
of priests who joined the group,
268–9; opposition by Greek
Catholic hierarchy, 269; OUN
assassination of Kostelnyk (1948),
269; OUN opposition, 269; OUN's
threats to execute converted priests,
269; similar religious "reunions"
in Carpatho-Ukraine and Prešov-
Priashiv region of Czechoslovakia,
269
Algeria: violence against the French,
237; Algerian National-Liberation
Front and OUN-B, 241
All-Russian Congress of Soviets,
Second (October 1917), 56
All-Ukrainian Academy of Sciences
(VUAN), 171, 172; Postyshev's

(1939), 202; German and Italian agreement (1938) to Polish and Hungarian demands, 202; Hungarian invasion (1939), 202; OUN and lack of German support for its independence, 107–8; Poland's and Hungary's demands that Carpatho-Ukraine become a part of Hungary (1938), 202; as Ukraine's Prussia or Piedmont-Sardinia, 202

Caspian Sea, 202

catastrophe, demographic, 159, 160

cattle, decline (1928–32), 149

Caucasus, 33, 49

Caucasus Mountains, 202

censuses: Austro-Hungarian (1900), 28; Austro-Hungarian (1910), 17, 28, 29; Czechoslovak (1921), 104; Czechoslovak (1930), 104; Imperial Russian (1897), 16, 20, 35, 57, 127; Polish (1931), 87; Polish (1950), 257; Romanian (1930), 101; Soviet (1920), 129; Soviet (1923), 129; Soviet (1926), 114, 125–6, 127, 129, 145, 160–2; Soviet (1937), 125, 160–2; Soviet (1939), 125, 126, 277; Soviet (1959), 253–4, 258, 272, 277; Wołyń (1937), 96

Central Asia, 114; deportations of Germans to, 50

Central Asians, underrepresented in Communist Party, 115

Central Black Earth region, peasant resistance to collectivization (1930), 147

Central Executive Committee of the USSR, and internal passport system, 154

central planning, economic, 134

Central Powers, 40, 47, 51, 52, 67, 68; end of war, 81. *See also* Triple Alliance/Quadruple Alliance

Central Rada. *See* Ukrainian Central Rada

Central Ukrainian Council, 50, 51

Cernăuți (Chernivtsi/Czernowitz/ Chernovtsy), 30, 266; Russian conquests during Great War, 45, 47; University of, 29, 102

chaos, post-revolutionary political and social (1918–19), 68, 69, 84

Cheka and one-party state, 112

Chełm/Kholm Province, 84; and arrival of German and Dutch settlers, 232; composition of the population (1914), 231; evacuations during WWI, 231; German evictions of Poles and Ukrainians, 232; German occupational policies (1939–44), 231–2; German tolerance of Ukrainian Autocephalous Orthodox Church (1939–44), 232; Home Army in, 233; Nazi racial hierarchies and Ukrainian empowerment, 232; Polish isolation of region from Galicia, 86; Polish Peasant Battalions in, 233; Polish and Soviet attacks on Ukrainians, 232; Polish-Ukrainian violence, 232; Polish weakening of Ukrainian Greek Catholic and Orthodox churches, 86, 232; polonization of Ukrainian population, 231–2; similarities and differences among Galicia, Kholm Region, Podlachia, and Volhynia, 233; Treaty of Riga (1921), 231; tsarist religious conversions of Ukrainian Greek Catholic population to

of the CPU Central Committee
(1946), 270; arrests of Central
Committee members (1937), 188;
Beria, removal of Melnikov, and
replacement with Kyrychenko,
273; Central Committee and
Molotov-Yezhov-Khrushchev special commission (1937), 188; CPU
Central Committee's condemnation of Ukrainian intellectuals,
270; CPU Central Committee's
condemnation of Ukrainian nationalism (1933), 175; and distrust
of pre-war Ukrainian intelligentsia,
172; founding, 74; Fourteenth
Party Congress (1938), 188; home
rule, 189–190; influence of culture
of violence on party leadership
and membership, 190–1; mass
purges of CP(b)U, destruction of
Ukrainian cultural ecosystem, and
Russification, 196–7; membership,
74, 270; national composition and
number of Ukrainian speakers
within its ranks (1933–40), 189;
non-Ukrainian members, 75; party
leadership and garrison mentality,
190–1; percentage of Ukrainians
(1922), 115; Politburo's dissatisfaction with pace of Ukrainization,
122–3; *Pravda*'s attacks on Central
Committee (1937), 188; rebuild-
ing and reconfiguring after WWII
CPU, 269–70; regional divisions,
75; as regional unit of Russian
Communist Party, 75; reliability of
CPU and Postyshev and Balitsky,
174; Russian Communist Party's
creation of the CPU and recognition of Ukraine's multinational
diversity, 283; Seventh Congress
(1923) and Ukrainization, 117;
Soviet limitations on Jewish entry
into the party, 271; Stalinist accusations against rural communists,
167; Stalin's death, 272–7; Stalin's
mistrust of senior CP(b)U leaders, 193–4; suspicions of Ukrainian
intelligentsia and advocates of
Ukrainzation, 167, 175; Third
All-Ukrainian Conference (1932),
151–2; Thirteenth Party Congress
(1937), 182, 187; Ukrainian national
communists, 129–30, 173
Communist Party of Western
Ukraine, 91–2
Communist Youth League
(Komsomol): and collectivization,
149, 153; and Ukrainization, 149.
See also Kopelev, Lev
Congress Kingdom of Poland, 23
Congress of Soviets of the USSR,
First (December 1922), 78
Congress of Vienna, 23
Constantinople, 8
Constituent Assembly (1917–18):
All-Russian, 59; elections to, 55;
elections in Ukrainian provinces,
63, 67
Constituent Assembly, Ukrainian
(January 1918), elections to, 63
constitution, preparations for a
Ukrainian (1917–18), 60
constitution, Soviet Russian (1919),
112
cooperative movement: in Austria-
Hungary, 31; in Imperial
Russia, 34, 58; in Poland, 91; in
Reichskommissariat Ukraine, 223;
in Soviet Ukraine, 171

advance (1941), 211; German
national and racial constructs of
Russians and Ukrainians, 216–17;
German troop internalization of
Nazi racial ideology and transformation of conflict into war of
annihilation, 214; Hitler's view of
Ukraine as a "food-supply base"
for the Axis powers, 213; invasion
of Poland (1939), 203, 204; invasion of USSR (1941), 203–4; Main
Security Office, 216; Ministry for
the Occupied Eastern Territories,
216; Molotov-Ribbentropf Pact,
201; Moscow leaders and the possibility of war with, 185; Munich
Agreement (1938), 201; and Nazi
racial theories, 108; number,
national composition, and gender
of foreign workers in German
labour force (1944), 225; OUN and
Germany as its only possible strategic partner, 227–8, 245; role in the
division of Belarusans, Lithuanians,
Poles, and Ukrainians into separate
communities, 201; Soviet-German
Boundary and Friendship Treaty
(1939), 206; Soviet-German
Citizen-Exchange Agreement
(1939), 206; Soviet-German Treaty
of Friendship (1939), the division of Poland, and recognition of
Soviet interests in Lithuania, 203;
Sudetenland, 201; targeting of Jews,
Romani, and communists, 214;
Ukrainians at top of the East Slavic
racial hierarchy, 217; Ukrainians
as Untermenschen, 217; views of
the peoples of East Central Europe

as subhumans, 214; violations of
Munich Agreement, 203
Gilliam, Sylvia, 285–6
Gogol, Nikolai (Mykola Hohol), 20
Gorbachev, Mikhail, and Soviet post-
war neutered national identities,
286
Gosplan. *See* State Planning Committee
Gourevitch, Peter, and the consequences of total war, 279
GPU: and one-party state, 112; and
political surveillance reports
of Soviet intelligentsia, 176–8;
Ukrainian GPU report on Ukrainian "counter-revolutionaries"
(1926), 177–8
Gradenigo, Sergio, on the consequences of the Holodomor, 160
grain, and extractive institutions,
136, 140; Austria-Hungary,
Russian Empire, Poland, Romania,
Germany, and USSR and their
struggle to control grain and establish food-base in Ukraine, 280,
286–7; Austrian and German need
(1918) for, 68; Austro-Hungarian
Empire's grain-producing and
grain-consuming regions, 281;
collectivization and forced grain
requisitions, 142, 143, 189; collectivization and world grain
markets, 192–3; crop rotation, 163;
European grain-producing and
grain-consuming states, 280–2;
export of, 26, 136, 141, 142, 143,
149; famine (1928–9), 141–2;
famine (1932–3), 142; famine as
instrument of class struggle, 193,

of Galicia, 30; German preference for Greek Catholic Church over Polish Roman Catholic Church in General Government, 268; German tolerance of religious expression in RK Ukraine during occupation (1941–4), 223; merger with Russian Orthodox Church (1946), 263, 267–9; Kostelnyk and Initiative Group for Greek Catholic and Russian Orthodox reconciliation, 268; Kostelnyk's synod and the Greek Catholic Church's "reunion" with the Russian Orthodox Church (1946), 269; moral demands and institutional imperatives in fluctuating political environment, 267; number of arrests (1945–50) of those who refused to convert, 269; number of Greek Catholic believers in Western Ukraine (1939), 267; number of priests who joined Kostelnyk's group, 268–9; opposition by Greek Catholic hierarchy, 269; opposition by OUN, 269; OUN assassination of Kostelnyk (1948), 269; OUN's threats to execute converted priests, 269; Patriarch Alexius and the Orthodox hierarchy in Western Ukraine, 269; Polish as the church's working language, 30; in Polish-Lithuanian Commonwealth, 18, 263; question of cooperation and collaboration, 268; re-legalization of Greek Catholic Church under Gorbachev (1989), 269; religious "reunions" in Carpatho-Ukraine and Prešov-Priashiv region of Czechoslovakia, 269; repressed by Russian government in Galicia in

WWI, 46, 47; response of Ukrainian Greek Catholic bishops to mass intercommunal violence in Volhynia, 238; role in creating Ukrainian identity, 14, 36; Sheptytysky as intermediary between German occupational authorities and Greek Catholic and Ukrainian interests, 268; Slipy as Sheptytsky's successor, 268; Soviet efforts to initiate post-1945 diplomatic relationship with the Vatican and the conversion process, 268; Stalin's understanding of role of Greek Catholic Church in Ukrainian life, 269; UPA rank and file and the Greek Catholic Church, 263

Greeks: Greek-language schools in Ukraine and shift in Soviet nationalities policy (1930s), 186; Soviet deportations of from the Crimea (1944), 249, 254; in Soviet Ukraine, 185

Grinko, Grigory, xv, 122

Grodno, 13

Gross, Jan, on collaboration, 246

Grossman, Vasily, on the famine of 1932–3, 155–6

Habsburg Monarchy 9, 28. *See also* Austro-Hungarian Empire

Haiduk, Myroslav Ivanovych, 265–6

Halyts'ka, Artemiziia Hryhorievna ("Motria"), 265–6

Hamburg Insurrection (1923), 117–18

harvests, poor, 150–1

Hasidic movement, 17

Haskalah (enlightenment) movement, 17

health care, rural, 25

increase in industrial expenditures for, 135; increase in Ukrainian output, 135; industrial productivity between USSR and other industrial powers, 132; location of new industries, 135; need for new workers, 135; in nineteenth century, 27, 39; percentage increase of Ukrainians among workers (1926–39), 135; and psychological unmoorings, 280; and social mobility and cultural revolution, 170; and Soviet grain acquisition, 137–8; Stalin and, 131; in twentieth century, 111; and underdevelopment (economic), 131–2; and war scare (1926–7), 133, 134
influenza outbreak (winter 1918–19), 3–4
Initiative Group for Greek Catholic and Russian Orthodox reconciliation, 268–9. *See also* Kostelnyk, Havril
Institute of Linguistics, Ukrainian Academy of Sciences, 182
integral nationalism, 92, 244; explanation for failure to establish an independent Ukrainian state in 1917–20, 245; and interest in military formations, 245; and need for a powerful ally, 245; opposed to liberal nationalism, 91; and Organization of Ukrainian Nationalists (OUN), 92; Sheptytsky's criticisms of OUN and integral nationalism, 95, 244
intelligentsia: All-Union Communist Party's distrust of, 172; Balitsky's charges of "anti-Soviet activities," 167; in Bukovina, 29; East European 15, 16; emergence in

Ukrainian-speaking provinces, 20; in Galicia, 29; GPU surveillance of, 176; mass arrests, 171–2; mass purges, 196–7, 285; public use of Ukrainian, 185; Russified Ukrainian, 65; Stalin and, 194; Ukrainian, 15, 20–2, 25, 26, 27
Iran, 6
Iranians, Moscow's suspicions of, 185
Ireland, violence against the British, 237
Israel: Irgun and Stern Gangs and OUN-B, as national liberation movements, 241; Jewish nationalist violence against the British and Palestinians, 237; Palestinian nationalist and Islamist violence against Israelis, 237
Italy, and Munich Agreement (1938), 201; unification (1870), 39
Ivanov, Nikolai, General, 45
Izmail Province, xxi

Japan, possibility of war with, 185
Jewish Autonomous Republic (Birobidzhan), 185
Jews, 13, 14; arrival in Eastern Galicia, 211; in Austro-Hungarian Empire, 18; differentiated Soviet policies toward national groups, 210–11; Einsatzgruppen, and extermination of Jewish population (1941–4), 215; Hitler's plans (1941) to exterminate, 211; within Jewish sections of the All-Union Communist Party, 185; and national-personal autonomy, 59, 62, 63; number of Jewish victims of intercommunal violence in Volhynia, Eastern Galicia, and Kholm Region, 238–9; number

256–7; OUN/UPA hostility toward Ukrainians who voluntarily registered to transfer, 256; between Poland and Ukraine (1944–6), 254; Polish expulsion of Ukrainians (1946) from Zakerzonnia, 255–6; and Polish student transfers, 271; post-WWII population transfer to Western Ukraine from Central, Southern, and Eastern Ukraine, 271–2; between Soviet Ukraine and USSR, 254; teacher transfer from Eastern to Western Ukraine, 271; Ukrainian as language of instruction in Western Ukraine in early post-WWII period, 271, 272; Ukrainian population in Zakerzonnia, 256

Postyshev, Pavel, 167, 187, 188; dismantlement of the Commissariat of Education and Institute of Linguistics, 182; CPU Central Committee's failure to meet grain targets, 174; and "negative selection," 183; purge of CP(b)U, 174–5, 182–3; and Ukrainization, 174

poverty, rural, in Lwów, Stanisławów and Tarnopol, 91

Poznań, German annexation of (1939), 203

preference policies: and enlarged elites, 171; governmental during WWI, 47; of workers in late 1920s, 170–1. *See also* indigenization; Ukrainization

primate city. *See* Kiev

prisoners of war, 44; cannibalism among Soviet POWs, 218; and diffusion of Ukrainian idea in WWI, 51; German mistreatment of Soviet

POWs, 217–18; Hitler's release of Ukrainian POWs, 217; national composition of Soviet POWs, 217; numbers of Soviets captured, 218; post-war political reintegration, 259

Project on the Soviet Social System, Harvard University, 185

proletarian internationalism, 284–5

Promethean League, 97–101; Central Ukrainian participation in, 99; Tadeusz Hołówko and, 100; Józewski's role, 97; Piłsudski's role, 97; Polish alliance with Belarus, Lithuania, and Ukraine against Russia, 97; supporters of Ukrainians, 99–100; Western Ukrainian rejection of, 99

Prosvita, 90

Provisional Government, 41, 47, 55, 57, 59, 62, 65, 69, 72, 111; and Bolsheviks on national question, 71; cooperation with Ukrainian Central Rada, 61; demise of PG, 61; reactions to Ukrainian Central Rada, 59, 60, 61; and Ukrainian autonomy, 60–1

Prussia, as model for Carpatho-Ukraine, 202

Przemyśl, Russian conquests during the Great War, 45

purges: All-Union Communist Party and purge of Ukrainian "rightists," 173; in countryside, 150; of CP(b)U, the destruction of the Ukrainian cultural ecosystem, and Russification, 196–7, 285; Postyshev's purge of CP(b)U, 174–5; as response to national security concerns, 190; and state terror in Ukraine, 171–5, 196–7, 285

"prophylactic measures," 173; state terror against Ukrainization, 171–5

Tesniak, Oleksa, criticisms of Bulgakov's *The Days of the Turbins*, 179

Texas, 7

Third Reich (Nazi Germany). *See* Germany (Third Reich)

Thornton, T.P., on terror, 93

total war: civil society and, 279; collectivization and famines (1928–33) as, 131–68; Communist Party's intolerance of dissenting views, 164–6; Communist Party's supremacy over the countryside and non-Russian republics, 166; and consequences in the twentieth century, 279; in East Central Europe, 279; evolution of, 3; and Peter Gourevitch, 279; against the peasants, 150, 158, 166; and psychological unmoorings, 280; and revolutions as "critical junctures" in the development of modern Ukraine (1914–54), 279–80; Russian Empire's failure to satisfy economic and political demands of total war (1914–18), 282; Stalin's total war against Ukrainian peasants, intelligentsia, and culture, 167–8; against Ukrainian intelligentsia and on the CPU, 166; WWI as, 39–54; WWII as, 202–50

tractors and horses, 163

Transcarpathia, and Carpathian Sich, 202; adoption of national symbols from Ukrainian National Republic (1917–20), 202; autonomous (1938), 104; becomes Carpatho-Ukraine, 202; collectivization in (1948–9),

267; Czechoslovak government's national security concerns about, 105; declaration of independence (1939), 202; diffusion of Ukrainian idea during Great War, 44, 54; Hungarian invasion (1939), 202; Hungarians in, 105; Jews in (1910), 18; literacy increase, 105; Magyarization of 29; national identity, 105; part of Czechoslovakia xx, xxi, 84, 103–6; part of Hungary and Austrian Empire, xx, 14, 28, 29, 36, 44, 57; partial partition by Hungary (1938), 201; Poland and Hungary's demands that Carpatho-Ukraine become part of Hungary (1938), 201; political autonomy, 105; poverty, 105; primary schools, 105; Soviet capture (1944), 227; Subcarpathian Rus, 104; as Ukraine's Prussia or Piedmont-Sardinia, 202

Transcaucasia, and the Second Treaty of Brest Litovsk (1918), 282

Transnistria xx, 218; G. Alecsianu (1941–4), 222; arrival of Soviet military (1944), 222; deportations of Jews and Roma, 222; Einsatzgruppen (1941–2), 215; included territories, 217; location, 222; population, 222; post-war memories of the Romanian occupation of Transnistria, 261–2; under Romanian jurisdiction (1941–4), 212, 222; size, 222; Tiraspol and Odessa as capitals, 222

Transylvania: to Romania (1919–20), 101; Romanian population in, 102

treason: Austrian military suspicions of Czechs, Serbs, Romanians, and Ukrainians, 53, 54; disloyalty and

Ukrainian language: identification of
Ukrainian language with barbarism of the Nazis, 240; Koch's
limited preferential treatment of
Ukrainian language and culture
over the Russian, 239–40; in the
1920s, 116–21; post-1945 clusters of
"tipping points," 257–8; promotion
of Ukrainian language, 125, 182;
Russification after 1945, 253–4;
secret decrees on Russian language
and literature, 184
Ukrainian Military Command, 51
Ukrainian Military Organization
(UVO): in Galicia, 93; Sich
Riflemen and Ukrainian WWI
veterans, 93; in Soviet Ukraine, 173;
terrorist activities, 93
Ukrainian National Army, 221
Ukrainian National Center (UNTs),
173
Ukrainian national communists,
129–30, 173
Ukrainian National Democratic
Alliance (UNDO): conflicts with
OUN, 95; declaration of loyalty
to the Polish state (Sept. 1939),
204, 207; founding, 89; and liberal
nationalism, 91; limited political
influence in Poland, 96; moderation, 95; non-violent manner, 96;
relations with Polish government,
89–90 ; and Ukrainian reaction to
outbreak of WWII, 89
Ukrainian National Rada (OUN-M),
223
Ukrainian National Republic (term),
xvi, 61, 62, 74, 96–7, 98; defeat
by Bolsheviks (1919), 73; exiled
UNR, Petliura, and Ukrainians in

Poland, 100; and First Treaty of
Brest-Litovsk, 67; loss of protection by Austria-Hungary and
Germany (1918), 69; merger with
West Ukrainian National Republic
(1919), 69, 82; and national-personal
autonomy, 63; natural resources,
and the Second Treaty of Brest
Litovsk (1918), 282; and pogroms,
70; and Promethean League,
99–100; recognition by European
powers, 74; and Second Treaty of
Brest-Litovsk, 67, 68
Ukrainian Party of Socialist
Revolutionaries, 58, 63, 73. See also
Borotbists
Ukrainian project: accelerated after
the Euromaidan Revolution (2014),
xxi, 290; as work in progress, 290
Ukrainian Revolution (1917–20),
55–80; consequences for Czechoslovakia, Poland, Romania, and
USSR, 81, 83–4
Ukrainian Scientific Institute
(Warsaw), 99
Ukrainian Social Democrats, 172
Ukrainian Socialist-Federalists, 172
Ukrainian Socialist Revolutionaries,
172
Ukrainian Soviet Socialist Republic
(Ukrainian SSR), 116, 192; ac-
quisition of Ukrainian speakers
and additional Russian speakers
(1939–54), 277; administrative-
territorial structure, xix–xxii, 73,
76, 78; anti-Polish measures in
Western Ukraine (1939–41), 208;
attraction of Ukrainian SSR to
Ukrainians in Wołyń/Volhynia,
96; border changes and forced

population transfers between
Poland and Ukraine (1944–6), 254;
Central Executive Committee of,
78; changes in the demographic
relationship between Russians and
Ukrainians due to WWII, 197; class
conflict in countryside, 138, 146;
collectivization in Eastern Galicia,
Western Volhynia, Bessarabia,
and Bukovina (1939–41), 208;
control over its economy and
industry (1927–32), 136; creation of
Moldovan SSR (1940), 203; creation
of Ukrainian SSR in framework
of UNR's Third Universal, 79;
Curzon Line between Poland and
USSR (1920), 255–6; Curzon Line
as new Polish-Soviet border after
WWII, 55–6; decline in number of
rural residents (1926–37), 159–62;
decline in number of self-identified
Ukrainians (1926–37), 161; decline in self-identified Ukrainian
percentage of Soviet Ukraine's
total population (1926–39), 161;
decrease in number of those who
self-identified themselves as Jews
(1926–37), 161; defining borders,
72, 74; demographic consequences
of the famine of 1932–3, 159, 160,
197; deportations, evacuations, and
forced labour conscriptions (1939–
45), 253; deportations from Eastern
Galicia (1940–1) and their national
composition, 208–9; destruction
of its natural wealth, 252; differentiated Soviet policies toward
national groups in Eastern Galicia,
Western Volhynia, Bessarabia,
and Bukovina (1939–41), 210–11;

economic revival (1921–6) in, 113;
estimates of number of deaths due
to famine of 1932–3, 159; German
brutalization of Ukraine (1941–4),
204; German division of Ukrainian
SSR into five separate administrative units, 218; German invasion (1941), 203–4, 211; German
invasion and local population's
hopes for political change, 211;
German occupation (1941–4), 211;
German population in, 185, 254;
government decrees (secret) on the
Russian language and literature,
184; Greeks in Soviet Ukraine, 185,
249, 254; Hitler's view of Ukraine
as "food-supply base," 213; incorporation of Eastern Galicia and
Western Volhynia into Ukrainian
SSR (1939), 197, 203, 204, 205;
incorporation of Ukrainian-
speaking territories of Bessarabia
and Bukovina into Ukrainian SSR
(1940), 197, 203, 204; incorporation of Transcarpathia (1945) into
Ukrainian SSR, 257; increase in
industrial expenditures in USSR
and Ukrainian SSR, 135; increase
in number of Russians within
republic (1939–59), 253–4; increase
in number of Russians in Ukrainian
SSR (1926–39), 161; increase in
number of Ukrainians in Ukrainian
SSR (1937–9), 161; Jewish losses
(1941–4), 253–4; Jewish population (1926), 215; Jews in Soviet
Ukraine, 185; Kiev as Ukraine's
"primate" city, 256, 258; language
and cultural policy (early 1920s)
in, 116–17; as major grain-growing

448

(1918) in Lemberg/Lviv/Lwów, 81; war casualties (1914–17), 43, 243

Ukrainian-speaking territories in Polish Republic: agricultural economy, 89; geographical distribution in, 89; Ukrainian population (1921–39), 89

Ukrainian-speaking territories in Russian Empire, 16–17, 34–6; Crimea Tatars in (1897), 17; Jews in (1897), 17; Left Bank, 18–19; Lutherans in (1897), 17; Novorossiia, 19; population of (1897), 13, 16; Roman Catholics in (1897), 17; rural population (1897) 18; trust between Ukrainians and non-Ukrainians, 63–4; war casualties (1914–17), 43. *See also* Bessarabia; Chernigov; Don Cossack; Ekaterinoslav; Grodno; Kharkov; Kherson; Kiev; Kuban; Kursk; Podolia; Poltava; Tavrida; Volhynia; Stavropol; Voronezh

Ukrainization, 92, 194, 244; All-Union Communist Party and, 173–4; anti-Ukrainization, 175–81; arrests of supporters among creative intelligentsia, 182; Balitsky's charges of anti-Soviet activities by Ukrainian intelligentsia during Ukrainization and collectivization, 167; Bolshevik Ukrainization as "national in form, socialist in content," 182; compulsory, 175; and creation of urban, Ukrainian, and educated elite, 286; decrees on, 118–19; demographic Ukrainization of Volhynia, 239; differences between self-identified Ukrainians and Ukrainian-speakers and their

support for, 124–5; enforcement of, 121; evolution of, 116–21; as expansion of self-identified Ukrainians, 182; full Ukrainization as full de-colonization, 180; and growth in Communist Party of Ukraine,124; and growth in Communist Youth League, 124; implementation in Ukraine and North Caucasus, 194; and industrialization in towns and cities, 286; Kaganovich, Ukrainization, and Ukrainian nationalism, 175; literacy and education, 122; Koch's limited Ukrainization in 1940s, 239–40; literacy campaign, 122; and New Economic Policy, 189; number of newspapers, journals, and books, 123, 183; opera, radio, and theatre, 123; outside of the Ukrainian SSR after 14 December 1932 decree, 160–1; passive resistance, 124; as peasant-oriented policy (1923), 181–2; policy justification, 119; politics and culture, 138; and power elite, 123–5; preference for Ukrainians, 118–19; problems in government, industry, and higher education, 123; problems in party and Communist Youth League, 124; promotion of Ukrainian language, 118, 119; "prophylactic measures" against, 173; and public sphere, 119–21, 122; reconfigured, 182, 183–4; and reinvigoration of anti-Soviet opposition, 194; resistance against, 120–21; retreat from, 132; Russian push-back against, 179; and secret Soviet government decree on Russian language and literature, 183–4; and Soviet passport system, 239; and state terror against supporters of, 171–5; Shumsky's and Skrypnyk's interpretations overturned by 1934, 181; Shumsky, Stalin, and the pace of, 176–7; Stalin on anti-communists as leaders of Ukrainization movement, 177; Stalin's mixed messages on Ukrainization (1929), 178–81; and SVU trial, 172; as urban-oriented policy (1925), 182; as a variant of Bauer and Renner's idea of national-personal autonomy, 128

Ukrainophile movement, 24, 26, 27, 28–33; in Austria-Hungary, 35, 36, 45; in Russian Empire, 36

Uman, 17

underdevelopment (economic), and the need for industrialization, 131–2

underground, communist (during German occupation, 1941–4), 226

Uniates. *See* Greek Catholics

Union for Armed Struggle (ZWZ), 229

Union for the Liberation of Ukraine (during WWI), 51; (after WWI), mass arrests during trial of, 171–2; in 1929–30, 171–2; Stalin's plans for a speedy trial of, 172

Union of Soviet Socialist Republics (USSR), 9, 107, 132, 245; acquisition of majority of Ukrainian-speaking territories, 84; administrative-territorial structure, xix, 78; annexation of territories from Poland, Romania and Czechoslovakia, 258; aspirations to overturn Treaty of Versailles, 227; Belarusans in, 114; beneficiary of the Molotov-Ribbentropf Pact, 203; changes in

demographic relationship between Russians and Ukrainians due to WWII, 197; collapse of the USSR and psychological unmoorings, 280; consequences of Ukrainian Revolution (1917–21) for, 81, 83–4; constitutions of 1924, 1936, and 1977, 78; creation of Moldovan SSR (1940), 203; and de-emphasis of Ukrainian language and culture, 285; economic revival (1921–6) in, 113; elections in Galicia and Volhynia to approve Soviet incorporation (1939), 205; and evolution of forms and contents of national identities within, 285; evolution as garrison state, 132, 286; expansion of Soviet power into East Central Europe, 251; and expulsion of Germans from East Central Europe, 255; and famine of 1932–3, 156–7; fear of another Polish invasion, 92; Finns in, 114; foreign policy setbacks, 133; formation, 74, 77–8; German invasion of (1941), 203–4; hybrid socialist-Russo-nationalizing state, 86; incorporation of Ukrainian-speaking territories of Poland and Romania into Ukrainian SSR (1939–40), 197, 203, 204, 205; invasion of Poland (1939), 203, 204; Latvians in, 114; literacy rates throughout, 114; as Marxist multinational federation, 251; national composition of newly incorporated territories, 204; national-territorial structure and promotion of a limited national consciousness, 284; non-recognition of Romania's